UNWIN HYMAN

DICTIONARY OF

ECONOMICS

SECOND EDITION

*Christopher Pass, Bryan Lowes,
and Leslie Davies*

This edition published in Great Britain by Unwin
Hyman, a division of HarperCollins Publishers Ltd in
1999 for Bookmart Ltd, Enderby, Leicester.

First published 1998
2nd Edition 1993

© 1988, 1993 C Pass, B Lowes, L davies

ISBN 0 26 1672 134

Diagrams: Gordon Barr, Roy Boyd

A catalogue record for this book is
available from the British Library.

Printed and Bound in Great Britain by
Caledonian International Book Manufacturing Ltd, Glasgow, G64

PREFACE

This dictionary contains material especially suitable for students reading 'foundation' economics courses at polytechnics and universities, and for students preparing for advanced school economics examinations. The dictionary will be useful also to 'A' and degree-level students reading economics as part of broader-based business studies, commerce or social science courses, as well as to students pursuing professional qualifications in the accountancy and banking areas. Finally, it is expected that the dictionary will be of interest to general readers of the economic and financial press.

The dictionary provides a comprehensive coverage of mainstream economic terms, focusing in particular on theoretical concepts and principles and their practical applications. Key economic terms are given special prominence, including, where appropriate, diagrammatic illustration. In addition, the dictionary includes various business and commercial terms which are relevant to an understanding of economic analysis and applications. It is, of course, difficult to draw a precise dividing line between economic and economics-related material and other subject matter. Accordingly, readers are recommended to consult other volumes in this series in particular, the *Collins Dictionary of Business*, should they fail to find a particular entry in this dictionary. In the interests of brevity, we have kept institutional minutiae and description, as well as historical preamble, to a minimum.

To cater for a wide-ranging readership with varying degrees of knowledge requirements, dictionary entries have been structured, where appropriate, so as to provide firstly a basic definition and explanation of a particular concept, leading through cross references to related terms and more advanced refinements of the original concept.

Cross references are denoted both in the text and at the end of entries by reproducing the keywords in SMALL CAPITAL LETTERS.

Acknowledgements

We should like to thank Monica Thorp and Edwin Moore of Collins for their excellent work in preparing the manuscript for publication. Particular thanks are due to Sylvia Ashdown and Sylvia Bentley for their patience and efficiency in typing the manuscript.

Christopher Pass, Bryan Lowes

A

ability-to-pay principle of taxation the principle that TAXATION should be based on the financial standing of the individual. Thus, persons with high income are more readily placed to pay large amounts of tax than people on low incomes. In practice, the ability-to-pay approach has been adopted by most countries as the basis of their taxation systems (see PROGRESSIVE TAXATION). Unlike the BENEFITS-RECEIVED PRINCIPLE OF TAXATION, the ability-to-pay approach is compatible with most governments' desire to redistribute income from higher income earners to low income earners. See REDISTRIBUTION-OF-INCOME PRINCIPLE OF TAXATION.

above-normal profit or **excess profit** a PROFIT greater than that which is just sufficient to ensure that a firm will continue to supply its existing product or service (see NORMAL PROFIT). Short-run (i.e. temporary) above-normal profits resulting from an imbalance of market supply and demand promote an efficient allocation of resources if they encourage new firms to enter the market and increase market supply. By contrast, long-run (i.e. persistent) above-normal profits (MONOPOLY or *supernormal profits*) distort the RESOURCE ALLOCATION process because they reflect the overpricing of a product by monopoly suppliers protected by BARRIERS TO ENTRY. See PERFECT COMPETITION.

above-the-line promotion the promotion of goods and services through media ADVERTISING in the press and on television and radio, as distinct from *below-the-line promotion* such as direct mailing and in-store exhibitions and displays. See SALES PROMOTION.

absenteeism unsanctioned absences from work by employees. The level of absenteeism in a particular firm often reflects working conditions and morale amongst workers in that firm and affects the firm's PRODUCTIVITY. See SUPPLY-SIDE ECONOMICS.

absolute advantage an advantage possessed by a country when, using a given resource input, it is able to produce more output than other countries possessing the same resource input. This is illustrated in Fig. 1 on page 2 with respect to two countries (A and B) and two goods (X and Y). Country A's resource input enables it to produce either 100X or 100Y; the same resource input in Country B enables it to produce either 180X or 120Y. It can be seen that Country B is absolutely more efficient than Country A since it can produce more of both goods. Superficially this suggests that there is no basis for trade between the two countries. However, it is COMPARATIVE ADVANTAGE, not absolute advantage, which determines whether INTERNATIONAL TRADE is beneficial or not, because even if Country B is more efficient at producing both goods it may pay Country B to specialize (see SPECIALIZATION) in producing good X at which it has the greater advantage.

Physical output of X and Y
from a given factor input

Country	Good	
	X	Y
A	100	100
B	180	120

Fig. 1. **Absolute advantage.** The relationship between resource input and output.

absolute concentration measure see CONCENTRATION MEASURES.

ACAS see ADVISORY, CONCILIATION AND ARBITRATION SERVICE.

accelerator the relationship between the amount of net or INDUCED INVESTMENT (gross investment less REPLACEMENT INVESTMENT) and the *rate of change* of NATIONAL INCOME. A rapid rise in income and consumption spending will put pressure on existing capacity and encourage businesses to invest not only to replace existing capital as it wears out but also to invest in *new* plant and equipment to meet the increase in demand.

By way of simple illustration, let us suppose a business meets the existing demand for its product utilizing 10 machines, one of which is replaced each year. If demand increases by 20 per cent, it must invest in two new machines to accommodate that demand, in addition to the one replacement machine.

Investment is thus, in part, a function of changes in the level of income: $I = f(\Delta Y)$. A rise in induced investment, in turn, serves to reinforce the MULTIPLIER effect in increasing national income.

The combined effect of accelerator and multiplier forces working through an *investment cycle* has been offered as an explanation for changes in the level of economic activity associated with the BUSINESS CYCLE. Because the *level* of investment depends upon the *rate of change* of GNP, when GNP is rising rapidly then investment will be at a high level, as producers seek to add to their capacity (time t in Fig. 2). This high level of investment will add to AGGREGATE DEMAND and help to maintain a high level of GNP. However, as the rate of growth of GNP slows down from time t onward, businessmen will no longer need to add as rapidly to capacity, and investment will decline towards replacement investment levels. This lower level of investment will reduce aggregate demand and contribute towards the eventual fall in GNP. Once GNP has persisted at a low level for some time, then machines will gradually wear out and businessmen will need to replace some of these machines if they are to maintain sufficient production capacity to meet even the lower level of aggregate demand experienced. This increase in the level of investment at time t_1 will increase aggregate demand and stimulate the growth of GNP.

Like FIXED INVESTMENT, investment in stock is also to some extent a function of the rate of change of income so that INVENTORY INVESTMENT is subject to similar accelerator effects.

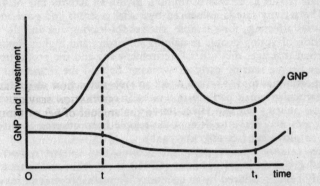

Fig. 2. Accelerator. The graph shows how gross national product and the level of investment vary over time. See entry.

acceptance the process of guaranteeing a loan which takes the form of a BILL OF EXCHANGE which will be repaid even if the original borrower is unable to pay. This is done by a commercial institution which signs, that is 'accepts', the bill drawn up by the borrower in return for a fee. See ACCEPTING HOUSE.

accepting house a MERCHANT BANK or similar organization that underwrites (guarantees to honour) a commercial BILL OF EXCHANGE in return for a fee. See DISCOUNT, REDISCOUNTING, DISCOUNT MARKET.

account period a designated trading period for the buying and selling of FINANCIAL SECURITIES on the STOCK EXCHANGE. On the UK stock market all trading takes place within a series of end-on fortnightly account periods. All purchases and sales agreed during a particular account period must be paid for or settled shortly after the end of the account period.

accounts the financial statements of an individual or organization prepared from a system of recorded financial transactions. Public limited JOINT-STOCK COMPANIES are required to publish their year-end financial statements, which must comprise at least a PROFIT-AND-LOSS ACCOUNT and BALANCE SHEET, to enable SHAREHOLDERS to assess their company's financial performance during the period under review.

acquisition see TAKEOVER.

activity rate or **participation rate** the proportion of a country's total POPULATION which makes up the country's LABOUR FORCE. For example, the UK's total population in 1995 was 58 million and its labour force numbered 28 million, giving an overall activity rate of 48%. Similar activity rate calculations can be done for subsets of the population such as men, women, ethnic groups, etc. For example, in the UK the female population in 1995 was 29 million and the female labour force was 12 million, giving an activity rate of 41%.

The activity rate is influenced by social customs and government policies affecting, for example, the school-leaving age and the proportion of young people remaining in further and higher education beyond that age; the 'official' retirement age and the proportion of older people retiring early or working beyond the retirement age. Opportunities for PART-TIME WORK and job-sharing can also influence in particular female participation rates. In addition, government TAX-ATION policies can also affect activity rates insofar as high marginal tax rates may serve to deter some people from offering themselves for employment (see POVERTY TRAP).

See LABOUR MARKET, DISGUISED (CONCEALED) UNEMPLOYMENT.

actual gross national product (GNP) the level of real output currently being produced by an economy. Actual GNP may or may not be equal to a country's POTENTIAL GROSS NATIONAL PRODUCT. The level of actual GNP is determined by the interaction of AGGREGATE DEMAND and potential GNP. If aggregate demand falls short of potential GNP at any point in time then actual GNP will be equal to aggregate demand, leaving a DEFLATIONARY GAP (output gap) between actual and potential GNP. However, at high levels of aggregate demand (in excess of potential GNP), potential GNP sets a ceiling on actual output, and any excess of aggregate demand over potential GNP shows up as an INFLATIONARY GAP.

Over time the rate of growth of actual GNP will depend upon the rate of growth of aggregate demand, on the one hand, and the growth of potential GNP, on the other.

actuary a statistician who calculates insurance risks and premiums. See RISK AND UNCERTAINTY, INSURANCE COMPANY.

adaptive-expectations (of inflation) the idea that EXPECTATIONS of the future rate of INFLATION are based on the inflationary experience of the recent past. As a result, once under way, inflation feeds upon itself with, for example, trade unions demanding an increase in wages in the current pay round which takes into account the expected future rate of inflation which, in turn, leads to further price rises. See EXPEC-TATIONS–ADJUSTED/AUGMENTED PHILLIPS CURVE, INFLATIONARY–SPIRAL, RATIONAL EXPECTATIONS HYPOTHESIS, ANTICIPATED INFLATION.

'adjustable peg' exchange-rate system a form of FIXED EXCHANGE-

RATE SYSTEM originally operated by the INTERNATIONAL MONETARY FUND, in which the EXCHANGE RATES between currencies are fixed (pegged) at particular values (for example, £1 = $3); but which can be changed to new fixed values should circumstances require it. For example, £1 = $2, the re-pegging of the pound at a lower value in terms of the dollar (DEVALUATION); or £1 = $4, the re-pegging of the pound at a higher value in terms of the dollar (REVALUATION).

adjustment mechanism a means of correcting balance of payments disequilibria. There are three main ways of removing payments deficits or surpluses: (a) external price adjustments; (b) internal price and income adjustments; (c) trade and foreign-exchange restrictions. See BALANCE-OF-PAYMENTS EQUILIBRIUM.

adjustment speed the rate at which MARKETS adjust to changing economic circumstances. Adjustment speeds will tend to vary between different types of market. For example, in the case of the FOREIGN EXCHANGE MARKET, the exchange rate of a currency will tend to adjust rapidly to EXCESS SUPPLY or EXCESS DEMAND for it. A similar rapid response tends to characterize COMMODITY MARKETS and MONEY MARKETS, with commodity prices and INTEREST RATES changing quickly as supply or demand conditions warrant. Product markets (see PRICE SYSTEM) tend to adjust more slowly because the prices of products are usually fixed administratively and are generally changed infrequently in response to major supply or demand changes. Finally, some commodity markets, in particular the LABOUR MARKET, tend to adjust more slowly still because wages tend to be fixed through longer-term collective bargaining arrangements.

See WAGE STICKINESS.

administered price 1. a price for a PRODUCT which is set by an individual producer or group of producers. In PERFECT COMPETITION characterized by many very small producers, the price charged is determined by the interaction of market demand and market supply and the individual producer has no control over this price. By contrast, in an OLIGOPOLY and a MONOPOLY large producers have considerable discretion over the prices they charge and can, for example, use some administrative formula like FULL-COST PRICING to determine the particular price charged. A number of producers may combine to administer the price of a product by operating a CARTEL or price-fixing agreement.

2. a price for a product, or CURRENCY, etc., which is set by the government or an international organization. For example, an individual government or INTERNATIONAL COMMODITY AGREEMENT may fix the prices of agricultural produce or commodities such as tin to support producers' incomes; under an internationally managed FIXED EXCHANGE-RATE SYSTEM member countries establish fixed values for the exchange rates of their currencies.

See PRICE SUPPORT, PRICE CONTROLS.

administrator see INSOLVENCY ACT, 1986.

ad valorem tax a TAX which is levied as a percentage of the price of a unit of output.

See SPECIFIC TAX, VALUE-ADDED TAX.

advances see LOANS.

advertisement a written or visual presentation in the MEDIA of a BRAND of a good or service which is used both to 'inform' prospective buyers of the product's attributes and to 'persuade' them to purchase it in preference to competing brands. Advertisements are usually featured as part of an 'advertising campaign' involving a series of presentations of the brand in the media over a run of weeks, months or even years which is designed to reinforce the 'image' of the brand, thereby expanding sales of the product and establishing BRAND LOYALTY.

See ADVERTISING.

advertising a means of stimulating demand for a product and establishing strong BRAND LOYALTY. Advertising is one of the main forms of PRODUCT DIFFERENTIATION competition, and is used both to inform prospective buyers of a brand's particular attributes and to persuade them that the brand is superior to competitors' offerings.

There are two contrasting views of advertising's effect on MARKET PERFORMANCE. Traditional, 'static' market theory, on the one hand, emphasizes the misallocative effects of advertising. Here advertising is depicted as being solely concerned with brand-switching between competitors within a static overall market demand and serves to increase total supply costs and the price paid by the consumer. This is depicted in Fig. 3a. (See PROFIT MAXIMIZATION).

The alternative view of advertising emphasizes its rôle as one of expanding market demand and ensuring that firms' demand is maintained at levels which enable them to achieve economies of large-scale production (see ECONOMIES OF SCALE). Thus, advertising may be associated with a higher market output and lower prices than allowed for in the static model. This is illustrated in Fig. 3b.

advertising agency a business which specializes in providing marketing services for firms. Agencies usually devise, programme and manage specific ADVERTISING CAMPAIGNS on behalf of clients.

See ADVERTISEMENT, ADVERTISING.

Advertising Standards Authority (ASA) a body which regulates the UK ADVERTISING industry to ensure that ADVERTISEMENTS provide a fair, honest and unambiguous representation of the products they promote.

Advisory, Conciliation and Arbitration Service (ACAS) a body established in the UK in 1975 to provide counselling services with regard to INDUSTRIAL RELATIONS and employment policy matters, in particular that of MEDIATION, CONCILIATION and ARBITRATION in cases of INDUSTRIAL DISPUTE.

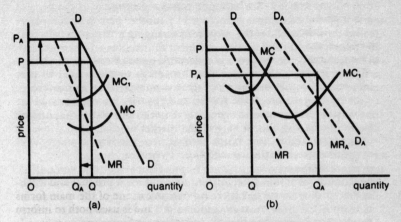

Fig. 3. **Advertising.** (a) The static market effects of advertising on demand (D). The profit maximizing (see PROFIT MAXIMIZATION) price-output combination (PQ) without advertising is shown by the intersection of the marginal revenue curve (MR) and the marginal cost curve (MC). By contrast, the addition of advertising costs serves to shift the marginal cost curve to MC$_1$, so that the PQ combination (shown by the intersection of MR and MC$_1$) now results in higher price (P$_A$) and lower quantity supplied (Q$_A$). (b) The initial profit-maximizing price-output combination (PQ) without advertising is shown by the intersection of the marginal revenue curve (MR) and the marginal cost curve (MC). The effect of advertising is to expand total market demand from DD to D$_A$D$_A$ with a new marginal revenue curve (MR$_A$). This expansion of market demand enables the industry to achieve economies of scale in production which more than offsets the additional advertising cost. Hence, the marginal cost curve in the expended market (MC$_1$) is lower than the original marginal cost curve. The new profit maximizing price-output combination (determined by the intersection at MR$_A$ and MC$_1$) results in a lower price (P$_A$) than before and a larger quantity supplied (Q$_A$).

See BARRIERS TO ENTRY, MONOPOLISTIC COMPETITION, OLIGOPOLY, DISTRIBUTIVE EFFICIENCY.

AFBD see THE ASSOCIATION OF FUTURES BROKERS AND DEALERS.

after-sales service the provision of back-up facilities by a supplier or his agent to a customer after he has purchased the product. After-sales service includes the replacement of faulty products or parts and the repair and maintenance of the product on a regular basis. These services are often provided free of charge for a limited period of time through formal guarantees of product quality and performance, and thereafter, for a modest fee, as a means of securing continuing

7

customer goodwill. After-sales service is thus an important part of competitive strategy. See PRODUCT DIFFERENTIATION.

agent a person or company employed by another person or company (called the principal) for the purpose of arranging CONTRACTS between the principal and third parties. An agent thus acts as an intermediary in bringing together buyers and sellers of a good or service, receiving a flat or sliding-scale commission, brokerage or fee related to the nature and comprehensiveness of the work undertaken and/or value of the transaction involved. Agents and agencies are encountered in one way or another in most economic activities and play an important rôle in the smooth functioning of the market mechanism.

See ESTATE AGENT, INSURANCE BROKER, STOCKBROKER.

aggregate concentration see CONCENTRATION MEASURES.

aggregate demand or **aggregate expenditure** the total amount of expenditure (in nominal terms) on domestic goods and services. In the CIRCULAR FLOW OF NATIONAL INCOME MODEL aggregate demand is made up of CONSUMPTION expenditure (C) (see CONSUMPTION, sense 1), INVESTMENT EXPENDITURE (I), GOVERNMENT EXPENDITURE (G) and net EXPORTS (exports less imports) (E):

$$\text{aggregate demand} = C + I + G + E$$

Some of the components of aggregate demand are relatively stable and change only slowly over time (e.g., consumption expenditure); others are much more volatile and change rapidly, causing fluctuations in the level of economic activity (e.g., investment expenditure).

Aggregate demand interacts with AGGREGATE SUPPLY to determine the EQUILIBRIUM LEVEL OF NATIONAL INCOME. Government seek to regulate the level of aggregate demand in order to maintain FULL EMPLOYMENT, avoid INFLATION, promote ECONOMIC GROWTH and secure BALANCE-OF-PAYMENTS EQUILIBRIUM through the use of FISCAL POLICY and MONETARY POLICY.

See AGGREGATE DEMAND SCHEDULE, ACTUAL GROSS NATIONAL PRODUCTS, DEFLATIONARY GAP, INFLATIONARY GAP, BUSINESS CYCLE, STABILIZATION POLICY, POTENTIAL GROSS NATIONAL PRODUCT.

aggregate demand/aggregate supply approach to national income determination see EQUILIBRIUM LEVEL OF NATIONAL INCOME.

aggregate demand schedule a schedule depicting the total amount of spending on domestic goods and services at various levels of NATIONAL INCOME. It is constructed by adding together the CONSUMPTION, INVESTMENT, GOVERNMENT EXPENDITURE and EXPORTS schedules, as indicated in Fig. 4a.

A given aggregate demand schedule is drawn up on the usual CETERIS PARIBUS conditions. It will shift upwards or downwards if some determining factor changes. See Fig. 4b.

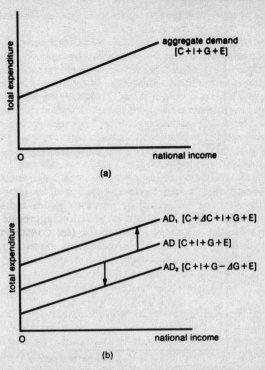

Fig. 4. **Aggregate demand schedule** (a) The graph shows how AGGRE-GATE DEMAND varies with the level of NATIONAL INCOME. (b) Shifts in the schedule due to determining factor changes. For example, if there is an increase in the PROPENSITY TO CONSUME, the consumption schedule will shift upwards serving to shift the aggregate demand schedule upwards from AD to AD_1; a reduction in government spending will shift the schedule downwards from AD to AD_2.

Alternatively, the aggregate demand schedule can be expressed in terms of various levels of real national income demanded at each PRICE LEVEL as shown in Fig. 4c. This alternative schedule is also drawn on the assumption that other influences on spending plans are constant. It will shift rightwards or leftwards if some determining factors change. See Fig. 4d. This version of the aggregate demand schedule parallels at the macro level the demand schedule and DEMAND CURVE for an individual product, though in this case the schedule represents demand for *all* goods and services and deals with the general price level rather than a particular price.

aggregate expenditure see AGGREGATE DEMAND.

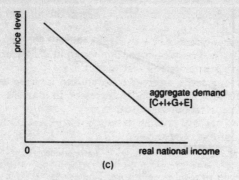

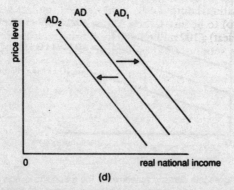

Fig. 4. **Aggregate demand schedule** (c) The graph plots the quantity of real national income demanded against the price level. (d) Shifts in the schedule due to determining factor changes. For example, if there is an increase in the propensity to consume, the aggregate demand schedule will shift rightwards from AD to AD₁; a reduction in government spending will shift the schedule leftwards from AD to AD₂.

aggregate supply the total amount of domestic goods and services supplied by businesses and government, including both consumer products and capital goods. Aggregate supply interacts with AGGREGATE DEMAND to determine the EQUILIBRIUM LEVEL OF NATIONAL INCOME (see AGGREGATE SUPPLY SCHEDULE).

In the short term, aggregate supply will tend to vary with the level of demand for goods and services, though the two need not correspond exactly. For example, businesses could supply more products than are demanded in the short term, the difference showing up as a build-up of unsold STOCKS (unintended INVENTORY INVESTMENT). On the other hand, businesses could supply less products than are demanded in the short term, the difference being met by running down stocks. However, discrepancies between aggregate supply and aggregate demand cannot be very large or persist for long, and generally businesses will only offer to supply output if they expect spending to be sufficient to sell all that output.

Over the long term, aggregate supply can increase as a result of increases in the LABOUR FORCE, increases in CAPITAL STOCK and improvements in labour PRODUCTIVITY.

See ACTUAL GROSS NATIONAL PRODUCT, POTENTIAL GROSS NATIONAL PRODUCT, ECONOMIC GROWTH.

aggregate supply schedule a schedule depicting the total amount of domestic goods and services supplied by businesses and government at various levels of total expenditure. The AGGREGATE SUPPLY schedule is generally drawn as a 45° line because business will offer any particular level of national output only if they expect total spending (AGGREGATE DEMAND) to be just sufficient to sell all of that output. Thus, in Fig. 5a (overleaf) £100 million of expenditure calls forth £100 million of aggregate supply, £200 million of expenditure calls forth £200 million of aggregate supply, and so on. However, this process cannot continue indefinitely, for once an economy's resources are fully employed in supplying products then additional expenditure cannot be met from additional domestic resources because the potential output ceiling of the economy has been reached. Consequently beyond the full-employment level of national product, Y_f, the aggregate supply schedule becomes vertical. See POTENTIAL GROSS NATIONAL PRODUCT, ACTUAL GROSS NATIONAL PRODUCT.

Alternatively, the aggregate supply schedule can be expressed in terms of various levels of real national income supplied at each PRICE LEVEL as shown in Fig. 5b. This version of the aggregate supply schedule parallels at the macro level the supply schedule and SUPPLY CURVE for an individual product, though in this case the schedule represents the supply of *all* goods and services and deals with the general price level rather than a particular product price. Fig. 5c shows a shift of the aggregate supply curve to the right as a result of, for example, increases in the labour force or capital stock and technological advances.

Aggregate supply interacts with aggregate demand to determine the EQUILIBRIUM LEVEL OF NATIONAL INCOME.

aggregated rebate a trade practice whereby DISCOUNTS on purchases are related not to customers' individual orders but to their total purchases over a period of time. Aggregated rebates are used to foster buyer loyalty to the supplier, but it can produce anticompetitive effects because it encourages buyers to place the whole of their orders with the one supplier, to the exclusion of competing suppliers. See COMPETITION POLICY, RESTRICTIVE TRADE PRACTICE.

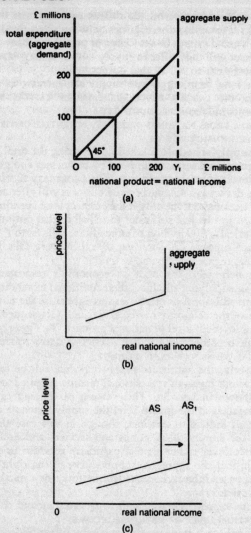

Fig. 5. Aggregate supply schedule. See entry.

agricultural policy a policy concerned both with protecting the economic interests of the agricultural community by subsidizing farm prices and incomes, and with promoting greater efficiency by encouraging farm consolidation and mechanization.

The rationale for supporting agriculture partly reflects the 'special case' nature of the industry itself: agriculture, unlike manufacturing industry, is especially vulnerable to events outside its immediate control. Supply tends to fluctuate erratically from year to year depending upon such vagaries as the weather and the incidence of pestilence and disease (S_1, S_2 and S_3 in Fig. 6a), causing wide changes in farm prices and farm incomes. Over the long term, while the demand for many basic foodstuffs and animal produce has grown only slowly (from

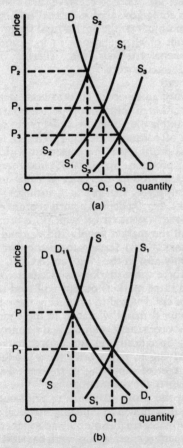

Fig. 6. **Agricultural policy**. (a) The short-term shifts in supply (S) and their effects on price (P) and quantity (Q). (b) Long-term shifts caused by the influence of productivity improvement on supply.

AID

DD to D_1D_1 in Fig. 6b), significant PRODUCTIVITY improvements associated with farm mechanization, chemical fertilizers and pesticides, etc., have tended to increase supply at a faster rate than demand (from SS to S_1S_1 in Fig. 6b), causing farm prices and incomes to fall.

Farming can thus be very much a hit-and-miss affair, and governments concerned with the impact of changes in food supplies and prices (on, for example, the level of farm incomes, the balance of payments and inflation rates), may well feel some imperative to regulate the situation. But there are also social and political factors at work; for example, the desire to preserve rural communities and the fact that, even in some advanced industrial countries (for example, the European Community), the agricultural sector often commands a political vote out of all proportion to its economic weight. See ENGEL'S LAW, COBWEB THEOREM, PRICE SUPPORT, INCOME SUPPORT, COMMON AGRICULTURAL POLICY.

aid see ECONOMIC AID.

allocative efficiency an aspect of MARKET PERFORMANCE that denotes the optimum allocation of scarce resources between end uses, in order to produce that combination of goods and services which best accords with the pattern of consumer demand. This is achieved when all market prices and profit levels are consistent with the real resource costs of supplying products. Specifically, consumer welfare is optimized when for each product the price is equal to the lowest real resource cost of supplying that product, including a NORMAL PROFIT reward to suppliers. Fig. 7a depicts a normal profit equilibrium under conditions of PERFECT COMPETITION with price being determined by the intersection of the market supply and demand curves and with MARKET ENTRY/MARKET EXIT serving to ensure that price (P) is equal to minimum supply cost in the long run (AC).

By contrast, where some markets are characterized by monopoly elements, then in these markets output will tend to be restricted so that less resources are devoted to producing these products than the pattern of consumer demand warrants. In these markets, prices and profit levels are not consistent with the real resource costs of supplying the products. Specifically, in MONOPOLY markets the consumer is exploited by having to pay a price for a product which exceeds the real resource cost of supplying it, this excess showing up as an ABOVE-NORMAL PROFIT for the monopolist.

Fig. 7b depicts the profit maximizing price–output combination for a monopolist, determined by equating marginal cost and marginal revenue. This involves a smaller output and a higher price than would be the case under perfect competition, with BARRIERS TO ENTRY serving to ensure that the output restriction and excess prices persist over the long run. See PARETO OPTIMALITY.

Alternative Investment Market see UNLISTED SECURITIES MARKET.

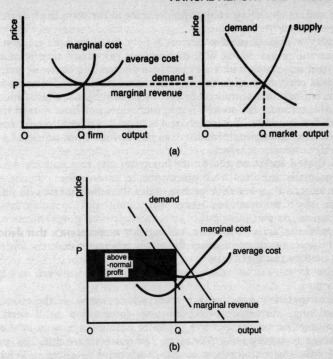

Fig. 7. **Allocative efficiency**. (a) A normal profit equilibrium under conditions of perfect competition. (b) The profit maximizing price-output combination for a monopolist.

amalgamation see MERGER.

annual general meeting (AGM) the yearly meeting of SHARE-HOLDERS which JOINT-STOCK COMPANIES are required by law to convene, in order to allow shareholders to discuss their company's ANNUAL REPORT AND ACCOUNTS, elect DIRECTORS and agree the DIVIDEND payouts suggested by directors. In practice, annual general meetings are usually poorly attended by shareholders and only rarely do directors fail to be re-elected on the strength of PROXY votes cast in favour of the directors.

annual report and accounts a yearly report by the directors of a JOINT-STOCK COMPANY to the SHAREHOLDERS. It includes a copy of the company's BALANCE SHEET and a summary PROFIT-AND-LOSS ACCOUNT, along with other information which directors are required by law to disclose to shareholders. A copy of the annual report and accounts is sent to every shareholder prior to the company's ANNUAL GENERAL MEETING.

annuity a series of equal payments at fixed intervals from an original lump sum INVESTMENT. Where an annuity has a fixed time span it is termed an *annuity certain* and the periodic receipts comprise both a phased repayment of principal (the original lump sum payment) and interest such that at the end of the fixed term there is a zero balance on the account. An *annuity in perpetuity* does not have a fixed time span but continues indefinitely and receipts can therefore only come from interest earned. Annuities can be obtained from pension funds or life insurance schemes.

anticipated inflation the future INFLATION rate in a country which is generally expected by business people, trade union officials and consumers. People's anticipations about the inflation rate will influence their price-setting, wage bargaining and spending/saving decisions. As part of its policy to reduce inflation, governments seek to influence anticipations by 'talking down' prospects of inflation, publishing norm percentages for prices and incomes, etc. Contrast UNANTICIPATED INFLATION.

See EXPECTATIONS, EXPECTATIONS-ADJUSTED/AUGMENTED PHILLIPS CURVE.

anticompetitive practice a practice which may have the effect of restricting, distorting or eliminating competition in a market. Examples of anticompetitive practices include EXCLUSIVE DEALING, REFUSAL TO SUPPLY and TIE-IN SALES. The COMPETITION ACT, 1980 provides for the investigation of anti-competitive practices in Britain. See COMPETITION POLICY.

anti-dumping duty see COUNTERVAILING DUTY.

antimonopoly policy see COMPETITION POLICY.

antitrust policy see COMPETITION POLICY.

application money the amount payable per share on application for a new SHARE ISSUE.

applied economics the application of economic analysis to real world economic situations. Applied economics seeks to employ the predictions emanating from ECONOMIC THEORY in offering advice on the formulation of ECONOMIC POLICY. See ECONOMIC MODELS, HYPOTHESIS, HYPOTHESIS TESTING.

appreciation 1. an increase in the value of a CURRENCY against other currencies under a FLOATING EXCHANGE-RATE SYSTEM. An appreciation of a currency's value makes IMPORTS (in the local currency) cheaper and EXPORTS (in the local currency) more expensive, thereby encouraging additional imports and curbing exports and so assisting in the removal of a BALANCE OF PAYMENTS surplus and the excessive accumulation of INTERNATIONAL RESERVES.

How successful an appreciation is in removing a payments surplus depends on the reactions of export and import volumes to the change in relative prices; that is, the PRICE ELASTICITY OF DEMAND for exports and imports. If these values are low, i.e., demand is inelastic, trade volume will not change very much and the appreciation may in fact make the surplus larger. On the other hand, if export and import demand is elastic then the change in trade volumes will operate to remove the surplus. BALANCE-OF-PAYMENTS EQUILIBRIUM will be restored if the sum of export and import elasticities is greater than unity (the MARSHALL-LERNER CONDITION). See REVALUATION for further points. Compare DEPRECIATION (1). See INTERNAL-EXTERNAL BALANCE MODEL.

2. an increase in the price of an ASSET. Also called *capital appreciation*. Assets held for long periods, such as factory buildings, offices or houses, are most likely to appreciate in value because of the effects of INFLATION and increasing site values, though the value of short term assets like STOCKS can also appreciate. Where assets appreciate then their REPLACEMENT COST will exceed their HISTORIC COST and such assets may need to be revalued periodically to keep their book values in line with their market values. See DEPRECIATION (2), INFLATION ACCOUNTING.

APR the 'annualized percentage rate of INTEREST' charged on a LOAN. The APR rate will depend on the total 'charge for credit' applied by the lender and will be influenced by such factors as the general level of INTEREST RATES, and the nature and duration of the loan.

Where lenders relate total interest charges on INSTALMENT CREDIT loans to the *original* amount borrowed, this can give a misleading impression of the interest rate being charged, for as borrowers make monthly or weekly repayments on the loan they are reducing the amount borrowed and interest charges should be related to the lower *average* amount owed. For example, if someone borrows £1000 for one year with a total credit charge of £200, the 'simple interest' charge on the original loan is 20%. However, if the loan terms provide for monthly repayments of £100, then at the end of the *first* month the borrower would have repaid a proportion of the original £1000 borrowed and by the end of the *second* month would have repaid a further proportion of the original loan, etc. In effect, therefore, the borrower does *not* borrow £1000 for one whole year but much less than this over the year *on average*, as he or she repays part of the outstanding loan. If the total credit charge of £200 were related to this much smaller *average* amount borrowed to show the 'annualized percentage rate', then this credit charge would be nearer 40% than the 20% quoted.

To make clear to the borrower the *actual* charge for credit and the 'true' rate of interest, the CONSUMER CREDIT ACT, 1974 requires lenders to publish both rates to potential borrowers.

a priori, *adj*. known to be true independently of the subject under debate. Economists frequently develop their theoretical models by reasoning, deductively, from certain prior assumptions to general predictions.

For example, operating on the assumption that consumers behave rationally in seeking to maximize their utility from a limited income, economists' reasoning leads them to the prediction that consumers will tend to buy more of those products whose relative price has fallen. See ECONOMIC MAN, CONSUMER EQUILIBRIUM.

arbitrage the buying or selling of PRODUCTS, FINANCIAL SECURITIES or FOREIGN CURRENCIES between two or more MARKETS in order to take profitable advantage of any differences in the prices quoted in these markets. By simultaneously buying in a low-price market and selling in the high-price market a dealer can make a profit from any disparity in prices between them, though in the process of buying and selling the dealer will add to DEMAND in the low-price market and add to SUPPLY in the high-price market and so narrow or eliminate the price disparity.

See SPOT MARKET, FUTURES MARKET, COVERED INTEREST ARBITRAGE.

arbitration a procedure for settling disputes, most notably INDUS-TRIAL DISPUTES in which a neutral third party or arbitrator, after hearing presentations from all sides in dispute, issues an award binding upon each side. Arbitration is mostly used only as a last resort when normal negotiating proceedings have failed to bring about an agreed settlement.

In the UK the ADVISORY, CONCILIATION AND ARBITRATION SERVICE (ACAS) acts in this capacity. See MEDIATION, COLLECTIVE BARGAINING, INDUSTRIAL RELATIONS.

arc elasticity a rough measure of the responsiveness of DEMAND or SUPPLY to changes in PRICE, INCOME, etc. In the case of PRICE ELASTICITY OF DEMAND it is the ratio of the percentage change in quantity demanded (Q) to the percentage change in price (P) over a price range such as P_0P_1 in Fig. 8. Arc elasticity of demand is expressed notationally as:

$$e = \frac{Q_1 - Q_0}{P_1 - P_0} \times \frac{P_1 + P_0}{Q_1 + Q_0}.$$

where P_0 = original price, Q_0 = original quantity, P_1 = new price, Q_1 = new quantity.

Because arc elasticity measures the elasticity of demand (e) over a price range or arc of the demand curve it is only an approximation of demand elasticity at a particular price (POINT ELASTICITY). However, the arc elasticity formula gives a reasonable degree of accuracy in approximating point elasticity when price and/or quantity changes are small. See also ELASTICITY OF DEMAND.

articles of association the legal constitution of a JOINT-STOCK COM-PANY which governs the internal relationship between the company and its members or SHAREHOLDERS. The articles govern the rights and duties of the membership and aspects of administration of the company. They will contain, for instance, the powers of the directors, the conduct of meetings, the dividend and voting rights assigned to separate classes of shareholders, and other miscellaneous rules and regulations. See MEMORANDUM OF ASSOCIATION.

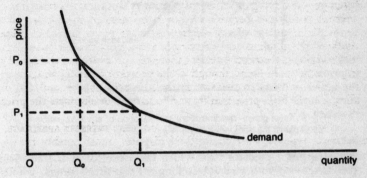

Fig. 8. Arc elasticity. See entry.

ASA see ADVERTISING STANDARDS AUTHORITY.

ask price see BID PRICE.

asset an item or property owned by an individual or a business which has a money value. Assets are of three main types: (a) physical assets such as plant and equipment, land, consumer durables (cars, washing machines, etc); (b) financial assets such as currency, bank deposits, stocks and shares; (c) intangible assets such as BRAND NAMES, KNOW-HOW and GOODWILL.

See INVESTMENT, LIQUIDITY, BALANCE SHEET, LIABILITY.

asset-growth maximization a company objective in the THEORY OF THE FIRM which is used as an alternative to the traditional assumption of PROFIT MAXIMIZATION. Salaried managers of large JOINT-STOCK COMPANIES are assumed to seek to maximize the rate of growth of net assets as a means of increasing their salaries, power, etc, subject to maintaining a minimum share-value, so as to avoid the company being taken over with the possible loss of jobs. In Fig. 9 the rate of growth of assets is shown on the horizontal axis, and the ratio of the market value of company shares to the book value of company net assets (the share-valuation ratio) on the vertical axis. The valuation curve rises at first as increasing asset growth increases share value but beyond growth rate (G) excessive retention of profits to finance growth will reduce dividend payments to shareholders and depress share values. Managers will tend to choose the fastest growth rate (G*) which does not depress the share valuation below the level (V¹) at which the company risks being taken over. See also MANAGERIAL THEORIES OF THE FIRM, FIRM OBJECTIVES, DIVORCE OF OWNERSHIP FROM CONTROL.

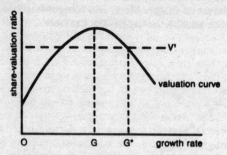

Fig. 9. **Asset-growth maximization**. The variation of share valuation ratio against the company growth rate.

asset-stripper a predator firm which takes control of another firm (see TAKEOVER) with a view to selling off that firm's ASSETS, wholly or in part, for financial gain rather than continuing the firm as an on-going business.

The classical recipe for asset-stripping arises when the realizable market value of the firm's assets are much greater than what it would cost the predator to buy the firm; i.e., where there is a marked discrepancy between the asset-backing per share of the target firm and the price per share required to take the firm over. This discrepancy usually results from a combination of two factors: (a) gross under-valuation of the firm's assets in the BALANCE SHEET, (b) mismanagement or bad luck resulting in low profits or losses, both of which serve to depress the firm's share price.

asset-value theory (of exchange rate determination) an explanation of the volatility of EXCHANGE RATE movements under a FLOATING EXCHANGE-RATE SYSTEM. Whereas the PURCHASING-POWER PARITY THEORY suggests that SPECULATION is consistent with the achievement of BALANCE-OF-PAYMENTS EQUILIBRIUM, the asset-value theory emphasizes that in all probability it will not be. In this theory the exchange rate is an asset price, the relative price at which the stock of money, bills and bonds and other financial assets of a country will be willingly held by foreign and domestic asset holders. An actual alteration in the exchange rate or a change in expectations about future rates can cause asset holders to alter their portfolios. The resultant change in demand for holdings of foreign currency relative to domestic currency assets can at times produce sharp fluctuations in exchange rates. In particular, uncertainty about future market rates and the unwillingness of banks and other large financial participants in the foreign exchange markets to take substantial positions in certain currencies, especially SOFT CURRENCIES, may diminish funds for stabilizing speculation that would in turn diminish or avoid erratic exchange rate movements.

If this should prove the case then financial asset-switching is likely to reinforce and *magnify* exchange-rate movements initiated by current account transactions (i.e., changes in imports and exports), and in consequence may produce exchange rates that are inconsistent with effective overall balance-of-payments equilibrium in the longer run.

associated company a JOINT-STOCK COMPANY in which another company or group has a significant, but not controlling, shareholding (specifically 20% or more of the voting shares but not more than 50%). In such a situation the investing company can exert influence on the commercial and financial policy decisions of the associated company, though in principle the associated company remains independent under its own management, producing its own annual accounts, and is not a subsidiary of the HOLDING COMPANY.

Association of British Insurers see INSURANCE COMPANY.

Association of Futures Brokers and Dealers (AFBD) see THE SECURITIES ASSOCIATION.

Association of Investment Trust Companies see INVESTMENT TRUST COMPANY.

assumptions see ECONOMIC MODEL.

assurance see INSURANCE.

atomistic competition see PERFECT COMPETITION.

auction a method of selling GOODS and SERVICES by competitive bidding. The sale will be made to the highest bidder subject to a reserve price being attained.

audit the legal requirement for a JOINT-STOCK COMPANY to have its BALANCE SHEET and PROFIT-AND-LOSS ACCOUNT (the financial statements) and underlying accounting system and records examined by a qualified auditor, so as to enable an opinion to be formed as to whether such financial statements show a TRUE AND FAIR VIEW and that they comply with the relevant statutes.

See also ENVIRONMENTAL AUDIT, VALUE FOR MONEY AUDIT.

Austrian school a group of late 19th century economists at the University of Vienna who established and developed a particular line of theoretical reasoning. The tradition originated with Professor Carl Menger who argued against the classical theories of value which emphasised PRODUCTION and SUPPLY. Instead, he initiated the 'subjectivist revolution', reasoning that the value of a good was not derived from its cost but from the pleasure, or UTILITY, the CONSUMER can derive from it. This type of reasoning led to the MARGINAL UTILITY theory of value whereby successive increments of a commodity yield DIMINISHING MARGINAL UTILITY.

Friedrich von Wieser developed the tradition further, being credited with introducing the economic concept of OPPORTUNITY COST. Eugen von Böhm-Bawerk helped to develop the theory of INTEREST and CAPITAL, arguing that the price paid for the use of capital is dependent upon consumers' demand for present CONSUMPTION relative to future consumption. Ludwig von Mises and Friedrich von Hayek subsequently continued the tradition established by Carl Menger et al. See also CLASSICAL ECONOMICS.

authorized or **registered** or **nominal share capital** the maximum amount of SHARE CAPITAL which a JOINT-STOCK COMPANY can issue at any time. This amount is disclosed in the BALANCE SHEET and may be altered by SHAREHOLDERS at the company ANNUAL GENERAL MEETING. See also ISSUED SHARE CAPITAL.

automatic (built-in) stabilizers elements in FISCAL POLICY which serve to automatically reduce the impact of fluctuations in economic activity. A fall in NATIONAL INCOME and output reduces government TAXATION receipts and increases its unemployment and social security payments. Lower taxation receipts and higher payments increase the government's BUDGET DEFICIT and restore some of the lost income (see CIRCULAR FLOW OF NATIONAL INCOME MODEL). See FISCAL DRAG.

automatic vending a means of retailing products to consumers via vending machines. Automatic vending has been employed extensively in selling, for instance, food, beverages and cigarettes. The use of vending machines has also become prominent in the banking/building society sector as a means of dispensing cash.

automation the use of mechanical or electrical machines such as robots to undertake frequently repeated production processes to make them self-regulating thus minimizing or eliminating the use of labour in these processes. Automation often involves high initial capital investment but, by reducing labour costs, cuts VARIABLE COST per unit.

See FLEXIBLE MANUFACTURING SYSTEM, PRODUCTIVITY, TECHNOLOGICAL PROGRESSIVENESS, CAPITAL-LABOUR RATIO, MASS PRODUCTION, COMPUTER.

autonomous consumption that part of total CONSUMPTION expenditure which does not vary with changes in NATIONAL INCOME or DISPOSABLE INCOME. In the short term, consumption expenditure consists of INDUCED CONSUMPTION (consumption expenditure which varies directly with income) and autonomous consumption. Autonomous consumption represents some minimum level of consumption expenditure which is necessary to sustain a basic standard of living, and which consumers would therefore need to undertake even at zero income.

See CONSUMPTION SCHEDULE.

autonomous investment that part of real INVESTMENT that is independent of the level of, and changes in, NATIONAL INCOME. Autonomous investment is mainly dependent on competitive factors such as plant modernization by businesses in order to cut costs or to take advantages of a new invention.

See INDUCED INVESTMENT, INVESTMENT SCHEDULE.

average cost (long run) the unit cost (TOTAL COST divided by number of units produced) of producing outputs for plants of *different* sizes. The position of the SHORT-RUN average total cost (ATC) curve depends on its existing size of plant. In the long run a firm can alter the size of its plant. Each plant size corresponds to a different U-shaped short-run ATC curve. As the firm expands its scale of operation it moves from one curve to another. The path along which the firm expands – the LONG-RUN ATC curve – is thus the *envelope curve* of all the possible short-run ATC curves (see Fig. 10a overleaf).

It will be noted that the long-run ATC curve is typically assumed to be a shallow U-shape, with a least-cost point indicated by output level OX. To begin with, average cost falls (reflecting ECONOMIES OF SCALE); eventually, however, the firm may experience DISECONOMIES OF SCALE and average cost begins to rise.

However, empirical studies of companies' long-run average-cost curves suggest that diseconomies of scale are rarely encountered within the typical output ranges over which companies operate, so that most companies' average cost curves are L-shaped as in Fig. 10b. In cases where diseconomies of scale are encountered the MINIMUM EFFICIENT SCALE at which a company will operate corresponds to the minimum point of the long run average cost curve (Fig. 10a). Where diseconomies of scale are not encountered within the typical output range, minimum efficient scale corresponds with the output at which economies of scale are exhausted and constant returns to scale begin (Fig. 10b). Compare AVERAGE COST, (SHORT RUN).

average cost (short run) the unit cost (TOTAL COST divided by number of units produced) of producing particular volumes of output in a plant of a given (fixed) size.

Average total cost (ATC) can be split up into average FIXED COST (AFC) and average VARIABLE COST (AVC). AFC declines continuously as output rises as a given total amount of fixed cost is 'spread' over a greater number of units. For example, with fixed costs of £1,000 per year and annual output of 1,000 units, fixed costs per unit would be £1, but if annual output rose to 2,000 units the fixed cost per unit would fall to 50p (see AFC curve in Fig. 11a on page 25).

Over the whole potential output range within which a firm can produce, AVC falls at first (reflecting increasing RETURNS TO THE VARIABLE FACTOR INPUT output increases faster than costs), but then rises (reflecting DIMINISHING RETURNS to the variable inputs – costs increase faster than output), as shown by the AVC curve in Fig. 11a. Thus the conventional SHORT-RUN ATC curve is U-shaped.

However, over the more restricted output range in which firms

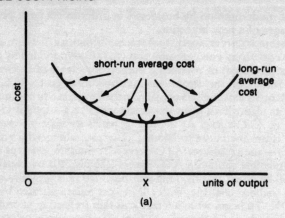

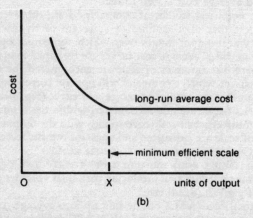

Fig. 10. **Average cost (long run)**. (a) The characteristic U-shape of the long-run average cost curve. (b) The characteristic L-shaped curve that in practice normally results from expansion.

typically operate, constant returns to the variable input are more likely to be experienced, where, as more variable inputs are added to the fixed inputs employed in production, equal increments in output result. In such circumstances AVC will remain constant over the whole output range (as in Fig. 11b) and as a consequence ATC will decline in parallel with AFC. Compare AVERAGE COST (LONG RUN). See LOSS, LOSS MINIMIZATION.

average-cost pricing 1. a pricing method which sets the PRICE of a product by adding a percentage profit mark-up to AVERAGE COST or

24

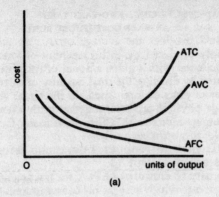

(a)

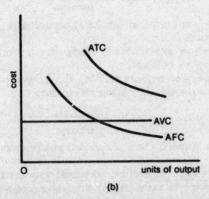

(b)

Fig. 11. **Average cost (short run).** (a) The characteristic curves of average total cost (ATC), average variable cost (AVC), and average fixed cost (AFC), over the whole output range. (b) The characteristic curves of ATC and AFC and constant line of AVC over the restricted output range.

unit total cost. This method is identical in most respects to FULL–COST PRICING; indeed, the terms are often used interchangeably.

2. a pricing principle which argues for setting PRICES equal to the AVERAGE COST of production and distribution, so that prices cover both MARGINAL COSTS and FIXED OVERHEADS costs incurred through past investments. This involves the (sometimes arbitrary) apportionment of fixed (overhead) costs to individual units of output, though it does seek to recover in the price charged all the costs which would have been avoided by not producing the product.

AVERAGE FIXED COST

See MARGINAL-COST PRICING, TWO-PART TARIFF.

average fixed cost see AVERAGE COST (SHORT RUN).

average physical product the average OUTPUT in the SHORT RUN theory of supply produced by each extra unit of VARIABLE FACTOR INPUT (in conjunction with a given amount of FIXED FACTOR INPUT). This is calculated by dividing the total quantity of OUTPUT produced by the number of units of input used. In the SHORT RUN theory of supply, average physical product, together with AVERAGE REVENUE per unit of output, indicates to a firm how many factor inputs to employ in order to maximize profit.

See MARGINAL PHYSICAL PRODUCT, DIMINISHING RETURNS, RETURNS TO THE VARIABLE-FACTOR INPUT.

average propensity to consume (APC) the fraction of a given level of NATIONAL INCOME which is spent on consumption:

$$APC = \frac{consumption}{income}$$

Alternatively, consumption can be expressed as a proportion of DISPOSABLE INCOME.

See CONSUMPTION EXPENDITURE, PROPENSITY TO CONSUME, MARGINAL PROPENSITY TO CONSUME.

average propensity to import (APM) the fraction of a given level of NATIONAL INCOME which is spent on IMPORTS:

$$APM = \frac{imports}{income}$$

Alternatively, imports can be expressed as a proportion of DISPOSABLE INCOME.

See also PROPENSITY TO IMPORT, MARGINAL PROPENSITY TO IMPORT.

average propensity to save (APS) the fraction of a given level of NATIONAL INCOME which is saved (see SAVING):

$$APS = \frac{saving}{income}$$

Alternatively, saving can be expressed as a proportion of DISPOSABLE INCOME.

See also PROPENSITY TO SAVE, MARGINAL PROPENSITY TO SAVE.

average propensity to tax (APT) the fraction of a given level of NATIONAL INCOME which is appropriated by the government in TAXATION:

$$APT = \frac{taxation}{income}$$

See also PROPENSITY TO TAX, MARGINAL PROPENSITY TO TAX, AVERAGE RATE OF TAXATION.

average rate of taxation the total TAX paid by an individual divided by the total income upon which the tax was based. For example, if an individual earned £10,000 in one year upon which that individual had to pay tax of £2,500, the average rate of taxation would be 25%. See STANDARD RATE OF TAXATION, MARGINAL RATE OF TAXATION, PROPENSITY TO TAX, PROPORTIONAL TAXATION, REGRESSIVE TAXATION, PROGRESSIVE TAXATION.

average revenue the total revenue received (price × number of units sold) divided by the number of units. Price and average revenue are in fact equal: i.e., in Fig. 12, the price £10 = average revenue (£10 × 10 ÷ 10) = £10. It follows that the DEMAND CURVE is also the average revenue curve facing the firm.

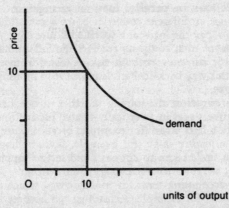

Fig. 12. **Average revenue**. The demand curve or average revenue curve.

average revenue product the total REVENUE obtained from using a given quantity of VARIABLE-FACTOR INPUT to produce and sell output, divided by the number of units of input. The average revenue product of a factor is given by the factor's AVERAGE PHYSICAL PRODUCT multiplied by the AVERAGE REVENUE or PRICE of the product. The average revenue product, together with average cost, indicates to a firm how many factor inputs to employ in order to maximize profit in the SHORT RUN.

See MARGINAL REVENUE PRODUCT.

average total cost see AVERAGE COST (SHORT RUN), AVERAGE COST (LONG RUN).

average variable cost see AVERAGE COST (SHORT RUN), AVERAGE COST (LONG RUN).

B

back door the informal mechanism whereby the Bank of England buys back previously issued TREASURY BILLS in the DISCOUNT MARKET at their ruling market price in order to release money to help the DISCOUNT HOUSES overcome temporary liquidity shortages. This is done as a means of increasing the liquid funds available not only to the discount houses themselves, but also to the COMMERCIAL BANKS at prevailing interest rates to enable them to maintain their lending.
Compare FRONT DOOR.

back-to-back loan or **parallel loan** an arrangement under which two companies in different countries borrow each other's currency and agree to repay the loans at a specified future date. At the expiry date of the loans each company receives the full amount of its loan in its domestic currency without risk of losses from exchange rate changes. In this way back-to-back loans serve to minimize EXCHANGE RATE EXPOSURE.

backward integration the joining together in one firm of two or more successive stages in a vertically-related production/distribution process, with a later stage (for example, bread making) being combined with an earlier stage (for example, flour milling). Backward integration is undertaken to cut costs and secure supplies of inputs. See VERTICAL INTEGRATION, FORWARD INTEGRATION.

bad debt an accounting term for money owed which is unlikely to be paid because, for example, a customer has become insolvent (see INSOLVENCY). Such bad debts are written off against the PROFITS of the trading period as a business cost. See CREDIT CONTROL.

balanced budget a situation where GOVERNMENT EXPENDITURE is equal to TAXATION and other receipts. In practice, most governments run unbalanced budgets as a means of regulating the level of economic activity.
Where the government spends more than it receives in taxation then a BUDGET DEFICIT is incurred. Where the government spends less than it receives in taxation then a BUDGET SURPLUS ensues. See BUDGET, FISCAL POLICY, PUBLIC SECTOR BORROWING REQUIREMENT.

balanced budget multiplier a change in AGGREGATE DEMAND brought about by a change in GOVERNMENT EXPENDITURE which is exactly matched by a change in revenues received from TAXATION and other sources. The change in government expenditure has an immediate effect on aggregate demand and generates income of an equivalent size. By contrast, the change in taxation does not change aggregate demand by an equivalent amount because some of the increased/

reduced DISPOSABLE INCOME will be offset by changes in SAVING. Consequently, an increase in government expenditure and taxation of equal amounts will have a net expansionary effect on aggregate demand and incomes, while a decrease in government expenditure and taxation of equal amounts will have a net contractionary effect. See BUDGET, FISCAL POLICY.

balance of payments a statement of a country's trade and financial transactions with the rest of the world over a particular period of time, usually one year. Fig. 13 shows a standard presentation of balance of payments. The account is divided up into two main parts: (a) current account, and (b) investment and other capital transactions.

Current account	£ million	
Visible balance (Balance of Trade)		
Food, beverages and tobacco	−4,076	
Basic materials	−3,509	
Oil, Lubricants	3,691	
Manufactures	−7,995	
Other items	261	
Invisible balance		−11,628
Service balance	6,142	
Interest, profits and dividends balance	9,572	
Transfers balance-mainly Government		
EC commitments	−6,978	
		8,736
Current balance		−2.892

(a)

Transactions in UK external assets and liabilities (investment and other capital transactions)

UK external assets (increase)	−124,045	
UK external liabilities (increase)	124,491	
Net transactions		446
Overall balance		−2,446

(b)

Fig. 13. **Balance of Payments**. The UK balance of payments for 1995. The balancing item in (b) includes errors and omissions in recording transactions, and leads and lags in currency payments and receipts. Source: *UK Balance of Payments*, CSO (Pink Book), 1996.

The current account shows the country's profit or loss in day-to-day dealings. It is made up under two headings. The 'visible' trade balance (BALANCE OF TRADE) indicates the difference between the value of EXPORTS and IMPORTS of goods (raw materials and fuels, foodstuffs, semi-processed products and finished manufactures). The second group of transactions make up the INVISIBLE BALANCE. These transactions include earnings from and payments for such services as banking, insurance and tourism. It also includes interest and profits on investments and loans, government receipts and spending on defence, overseas administration, etc.

In addition to current account transactions there are also currency flows into and out of the country related to capital items – investment monies spent by companies on new plant and the purchase of assets, borrowing by the government, and interbank dealings in sterling and foreign currency.

The current balance, and the investment and other capital flows, together with the balancing item, result in the *balance for official financing*. This figure shows whether the country has incurred an overall surplus or deficit. If the balance of payments is in surplus the country can add to its INTERNATIONAL RESERVES and, if necessary, repay borrowings; if it is in deficit this has to be covered by running down its international reserves or by borrowing.

A balance-of-payments deficit or surplus can be remedied in a number of ways, including external price adjustments, internal price and income adjustments, and trade and currency restrictions.

See BALANCE-OF-PAYMENTS EQUILIBRIUM.

balance-of-payments disequilibrium see BALANCE-OF-PAYMENTS EQUILIBRIUM.

balance-of-payments equilibrium a situation where, over a run of years, a country spend and invests abroad no more than other countries spend and invest in it. Thus, the country neither adds to its stock of INTERNATIONAL RESERVES, nor sees them reduced.

In an unregulated world it is highly unlikely that external balance will always prevail. Balance of payments deficits and surpluses will occur, but provided they are small, *balance-of-payments disequilibrium* can be readily accommodated. The main thing to avoid is a FUNDAMENTAL DISEQUILIBRIUM – a situation of chronic imbalance.

There are three main ways of restoring balance-of-payments equilibrium, should an imbalance occur:

(a) *external price adjustments*. Alterations in the EXCHANGE RATE between currencies involving (depending upon the particular exchange rate system in operation) the DEVALUATION/DEPRECIATION and REVALUATION/APPRECIATION of the currencies concerned to make exports cheaper/more expensive and imports dearer/less expensive in foreign currency terms. For example, with regard to exports, in

UK domestic price of a product	Exchange rate	Price of the UK product exported to US
£1	£1 = $1.60	$1.60
£1	£1 = $1.40	$1.40

(a)

UK domestic price of a product	Exchange rate	Price of the UK product exported to US
£1	£1 = $1.60	$1.60
75p	£1 = $1.60	$1.20

(b)

Fig. 14. Balance-of-payments equilibrium. (a) Exchange rate adjustment. (b) Internal price adjustment.

Fig. 14a if the pound–dollar exchange rate is devalued from $1.60 to $1.40 then this would allow British exporters to reduce their prices by a similar amount, thus increasing their price competitiveness in the American market.

(b) *internal price and income adjustments.* The use of deflationary and reflationary (see DEFLATION, REFLATION) monetary and fiscal policies to alter the prices of domestically produced goods and services vis-a-vis products supplied by other countries so as to make exports relatively cheaper/dearer and imports more expensive/cheaper in foreign currency terms. For example, again with regard to exports, if it were possible to reduce the domestic price of a British product, as shown in Fig. 14b, given an unchanged exchange rate, this would allow the dollar price of the product in the American market to be reduced, thereby improving its price competitiveness vis-a-vis similar American products. The same policies are used to alter the level of domestic income and spending, including expenditure on imports.

(c) *trade and foreign exchange restrictions.* The use of TARIFFS, QUOTAS, FOREIGN EXCHANGE CONTROLS, etc. to affect the price and availability of goods and services, and of the currencies with which to purchase these products.

Under a FIXED EXCHANGE-RATE SYSTEM, minor payments imbalances are corrected by appropriate domestic adjustments (b), but fundamental disequilibriums require, in addition, a devaluation or revaluation of the currency (a). However, it must be emphasized that a number of favourable conditions must be present to ensure the success of devaluations and revaluations (see DEPRECIATION).

In theory, a FLOATING EXCHANGE-RATE SYSTEM provides an 'automatic' mechanism for removing payments imbalances in their incipiency (that is, before they reached 'fundamental' proportions): a deficit results in an immediate exchange-rate depreciation, and a surplus results in an immediate appreciation of the exchange rate. (see PURCHASING-POWER PARITY THEORY) However, again, a number of favourable conditions must be present to ensure the success of depreciations and appreciations. See also J-CURVE, INTERNAL-EXTERNAL BALANCE MODEL, MARSHALL-LERNER CONDITION, TERMS OF TRADE.

balance of trade a statement of a country's trade in GOODS (visibles) with the rest of the world over a particular period of time. The term 'balance of trade' specifically excludes trade in services (invisibles), and concentrates on the foreign currency earnings and payments associated with trade in finished manufactures, intermediate products, and raw materials which can be seen and recorded by a country's customs authorities as they cross national boundaries.

See BALANCE OF PAYMENTS.

balance sheet an accounting statement of a firm's ASSETS and LIABILITIES on the last day of a trading period. The balance sheet lists the assets which the firm owns and sets against these the balancing obligations or claims of those groups of people who provided the funds to acquire the assets. Assets take the form of FIXED ASSETS and CURRENT ASSETS, while obligations take the form of SHAREHOLDERS' CAPITAL EMPLOYED, long term loans and CURRENT LIABILITIES.

balances with the Bank of England deposits of money by the COMMERCIAL BANKS with the Bank of England. The Bank of England acts as the 'bankers' bank' and commercial banks settle indebtedness between themselves by transferring ownership of these balances. Such balances are included as part of the commercial banks' CASH RESERVES RATIO and RESERVE ASSET RATIO. In addition to the balances held for settling indebtedness, the banks may be required from time to time to make SPECIAL DEPOSITS with the Bank, which has the effect of reducing their reserve assets.

balancing item see BALANCE OF PAYMENTS.

bank a deposit-taking institution which is licensed by the monetary authorities of a country (the Bank of England in the UK) to act as a repository for money deposited by persons, companies and institutions, and which undertakes to repay such deposits either immediately on demand (CURRENT ACCOUNTS, sense 2) or subject to due notice being given (DEPOSIT ACCOUNTS). Banks perform various services for their customers (money transmission, investment advice, etc.) and lend out money deposited with them in the form of loans and overdrafts or use their funds to purchase financial securities, in order to operate at a profit. There are many types of banks, including COMMERCIAL BANKS, MERCHANT BANKS, SAVINGS BANKS and INVEST-

MENT BANKS. In recent years many BUILDING SOCIETIES have also established a limited range of banking facilities.

See BANKING SYSTEM, CENTRAL BANK, FINANCIAL SYSTEM.

bank deposit a sum of money held on deposit with a COMMERCIAL
BANK (or SAVINGS BANK). Bank deposits are of two main types: sight
deposits (CURRENT ACCOUNTS) which are withdrawable on demand;
time deposits (DEPOSIT ACCOUNTS) which are withdrawable subject
usually to some notice being given. Sight deposits represent instant
LIQUIDITY they are used to finance day-to-day transactions and regular payments either in the form of a CURRENCY withdrawal or a
CHEQUE transfer. Time deposits are usually held for longer periods
of time to meet irregular payments and as a form of savings.

Bank deposits constitute an important component of the MONEY
SUPPLY. See BANK DEPOSIT CREATION, MONETARY POLICY.

bank deposit creation or **credit creation** or **money multiplier**
the ability of the COMMERCIAL BANK system to create new bank
deposits and hence increase the MONEY SUPPLY. Commercial banks
accept deposits of CURRENCY from the general public. Some of this
money is retained by the banks to meet day-to-day withdrawals (see
RESERVE-ASSET RATIO). The remainder of the money is used to make
loans or is invested. When a bank on-lends it creates additional
deposits in favour of borrowers. The amount of new deposits the
banking system as a whole can create depends on the magnitude of
the reserve-asset ratio. In the example set out in Fig. 15 (overleaf)
the banks are assumed to operate with a 50% reserve-asset ratio:
Bank 1 receives initial deposits of £100 million from the general
public. It keeps £50 million for liquidity purposes and on-lends £50
million. This £50 million when spent is redeposited with Bank 2;
Bank 2 keeps £25 million as part of its reserve assets and on-lends
£25 million; and so on. Thus, as a result of an initial deposit of £100
million, the banking system has been able to 'create' an additional
£100 million of new deposits.

Since bank deposits constitute a large part of the MONEY SUPPLY,
the ability of the banking system to 'create' credit makes it a prime
target for the application of MONETARY POLICY as a means of regulating
the level of spending in the economy.

Bank for International Settlements (BIS) an international bank
situated in Basle and established in 1930, which originally acted as a
coordinating agency for the central banks of Germany, France, Italy,
Belgium and the UK in settling BALANCE-OF-PAYMENTS imbalances
and for other intercentral bank dealings. Nowadays its membership
comprises all West European central banks together with the US,
Canada and Japan. Although the INTERNATIONAL MONETARY FUND is
the main institution responsible for the conduct of international monetary affairs, and the EUROPEAN MONETARY SYSTEM specifically for

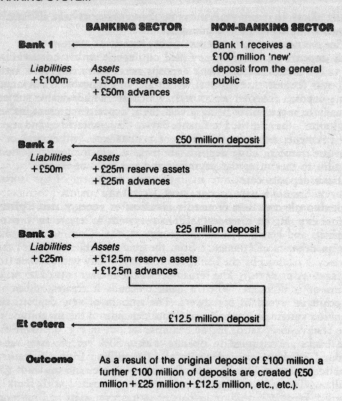

BANKING SECTOR   **NON-BANKING SECTOR**

Bank 1 ⟵——————————— Bank 1 receives a
£100 million 'new'
deposit from the general
public

     Liabilities   *Assets*
      +£100m   +£50m reserve assets
                +£50m advances

Bank 2 ⟵——————— £50 million deposit
     Liabilities   *Assets*
      +£50m   +£25m reserve assets
                +£25m advances

Bank 3 ⟵——————— £25 million deposit
     Liabilities   *Assets*
      +£25m   +£12.5m reserve assets
                +£12.5m advances

Et cetera ⟵——————— £12.5 million deposit

Outcome   As a result of the original deposit of £100 million a
further £100 million of deposits are created (£50
million + £25 million + £12.5 million, etc., etc.).

Fig. 15. **Bank deposit creation.** Deposit creation operated with a 50%
reserve-asset ratio in a multibank system.

EUROPEAN COMMUNITY members, the BIS is still influential in providing a forum for discussion and surveillance of international banking practices.

banking system a network of COMMERCIAL BANKS and other more specialized BANKS (INVESTMENT BANKS, SAVINGS BANKS, MERCHANT BANKS) which accept deposits and savings from the general public, firms and other institutions, and which provide money transmission and other financial services for customers, operate loan and credit facilities for borrowers, and invest in corporate and government securities. The banking system is part of a wider FINANCIAL SYSTEM and exerts a major influence on the functioning of the 'money economy' of a country. Bank deposits occupy a central position in the country's MONEY SUPPLY and hence the banking system is closely regulated by the money authorities.

See CENTRAL BANK, CLEARING HOUSE SYSTEM.

bank loan the advance of a specified sum of money to an individual or business (the borrower) by a COMMERCIAL BANK, SAVINGS BANK, etc. (the lender). A bank loan is a form of CREDIT which is often extended for a specified period of time, usually on fixed-interest terms related to the base INTEREST RATE with the principal being repaid either on a regular instalment basis or in full on the appointed redemption date. Alternatively, a bank loan may take the form of overdraft facilities under which customers can borrow as much money as they require up to a pre-arranged total limit and are charged interest on outstanding balances.

In the case of business borrowers, bank loans are used to finance WORKING CAPITAL requirements and are often renegotiated shortly before expiring to provide the borrower with a 'revolving' line of credit.

Depending upon the nature of the loan and the degree of risk involved, bank loans may be unsecured or secured, the latter requiring the borrower to deposit with the bank COLLATERAL SECURITY (e.g. title deeds to a house) to cover against default on the loan.

bank note the paper CURRENCY issued by a CENTRAL BANK which forms part of a country's MONEY SUPPLY. Bank notes in the main constitute the 'high value' part of the money supply.

See MINT, LEGAL TENDER, FIDUCIARY ISSUE.

Bank of England the CENTRAL BANK of the UK.

bank rate the INTEREST RATE charged by the Bank of England to the DISCOUNT HOUSES when they were short of funds and forced to borrow from the Bank. Bank rate was formerly used in Britain as an instrument of MONETARY POLICY to control the general level of interest rates in the economy. It was replaced in 1972 by the *minimum lending rate* which itself was abolished in 1984 as part of the government's move towards a more flexible approach to interest rates. The present interest rate charged by the central bank (the BILL DISCOUNTING RATE) is not established administratively by the central bank, like its predecessors, but changes directly in response to changes in the supply and demand for short-term funds, as reflected in the INTERBANK CLEARING INTEREST RATE.

bankruptcy see INSOLVENCY.

bank statement a periodic record of an individual's or business's transactions with a BANK (or BUILDING SOCIETY) which itemizes on the one hand cash deposits and cheques paid in, and on the other hand cash withdrawals and cheques drawn and presented against the account.

bar chart or **histogram** a chart that portrays data in pictorial form, and shows the relative size of each category in a total by means of the relative height of its 'bar' or 'block'.

bargaining see BARTER, COLLECTIVE BARGAINING.

barometric forecasts see FORECASTING.

barometric price leader see PRICE LEADER.

barriers to entry an element of MARKET STRUCTURE which refers to obstacles in the way of potential newcomers to a MARKET. These obstacles operate in a number of ways to discourage entry:

(a) lower cost advantages to established firms arising from the possession of substantial market shares and the realization of ECONOMIES OF LARGE SCALE production and distribution.

(b) strong consumer preferences for the products of established firms resulting from PRODUCT DIFFERENTIATION activities.

(c) the control of essential raw materials, technology and market outlets by established firms either through direct ownership or through PATENTS, FRANCHISES and EXCLUSIVE DEALING CONTRACTS.

(d) large capital outlays required by entrants to set up production and to cover losses during the initial entry phase.

The economic significance of barriers to entry lies in their capacity for blocking MARKET ENTRY, thereby allowing established firms to earn ABOVE-NORMAL PROFIT and affecting the RESOURCE ALLOCATION function of markets.

One, or some combination, of the above factors may pose particular problems for a small-scale, GREENFIELD type of entrant. However, they may be of little consequence to a large conglomerate firm possessing ample financial resources, and which chooses to effect entry by MERGER with, or TAKEOVER of, an established producer. Moreover, the basic assumption of much entry theory that established firms invariably possess advantages over potential entrants must also be challenged. In a dynamic market situation, entrants may be in a position to introduce new technology ahead of existing firms, or to develop innovative new products, thereby giving them COMPETITIVE ADVANTAGES over established firms.

See also CONDITION OF ENTRY, LIMIT PRICING, POTENTIAL ENTRANT, OLIGOPOLY, MONOPOLY, FLEXIBLE MANUFACTURING SYSTEM.

barriers to exit an element of MARKET STRUCTURE which refers to obstacles in the way of a firm contemplating leaving a MARKET which serve to keep the firm in the market despite falling sales and profitability. Exit barriers include: whether the firm owns the assets it uses or leases them; whether assets are special-purpose or can be redeployed to other uses; whether assets are resaleable in second-hand markets; the extent of market excess capacity and the extent of shared production and distribution facilities. Barriers to exit determine the ease with which firms can leave declining markets and thus affect both the profitability of firms and the smooth functioning of markets.

See PRODUCT LIFE CYCLE, PRICE SYSTEM, CONTESTABLE MARKET.

barter the EXCHANGE of one economic good or service for another. Barter as an exchange mechanism, however, suffers from a number of serious disadvantages:

(a) for barter to take place there must be a 'coincidence of wants', that is, each party to the barter must be able to offer something which the other wants. For example, an apple-grower wishing to obtain oranges must not only find an orange-grower, but must particularly find an orange-grower wishing to acquire apples. Finding appropriate exchange partners can involve lengthy search activity which reduces the time available for actually producing goods;

(b) Even if the parties meet up, they then have to agree on an appropriate 'rate of exchange', for example, how many apples are to be exchanged for one orange? Haggling over exchange terms is again time-consuming, and where agreement cannot be reached between the two parties each will then have to seek out new exchange partners.

Overall, barter is a very inefficient means of organizing transactions in an economy, and has been largely superseded by the use of MONEY systems in modern economies.

See COUNTERTRADE, BLACK ECONOMY.

base rate the INTEREST RATE which is used by the COMMERCIAL BANKS to calculate rates of interest to be charged on loans and overdrafts to their customers. For example, a large company might be charged, say, an interest rate of base rate plus 2% on a loan, whereas a smaller borrower might be charged, say, base rate plus 4%. Formerly, base rates were linked directly to BANK RATE, but are now determined by the supply and demand for short-term funds as reflected in the INTERBANK CLEARING INTEREST RATE, PRIME RATE.

base year the initial period from which a system of INDEXATION proceeds. For example, the present British Retail Price Index has as the base period 1987 = 100, with the average price of a typical basket of goods in 1987 being taken as the basis for the index. The 1995 index number was 149 for all items in the basket of goods. Convention dictates that the base period always commences from the number 100. See PRICE INDEX.

basing point price system a form of pricing products such as cement which are bulky and expensive to transport which involves charging different prices to customers based in different locations. Customers located near to the supply source (or 'base point') are charged a lower delivery price compared to customers further afield.

See PRICE DISCRIMINATION, DELIVERED PRICE.

batch production the manufacture of a product in small quantities using labour-intensive methods of production (see LABOUR-INTENSIVE FIRM/INDUSTRY). Batch production is typically employed in industries where the product supplied is nonstandardized, with consumers demanding a wide variety of product choice. Batch production industries are usually characterized by low levels of SELLER CONCENTRATION, easy entry conditions and high unit costs of supply. See PRODUCTION, MASS PRODUCTION, CONDITION OF ENTRY, FLEXIBLE MANUFACTURING SYSTEM.

bear a person who expects future prices in a STOCK EXCHANGE or COMMODITY MARKET to fall, and who seeks to make money by selling shares or commodities.

Compare BULL. See SPOT MARKET, FUTURES MARKET, BEAR MARKET.

bear market a situation where the prices of FINANCIAL SECURITIES (stocks, shares, etc.) or COMMODITIES (tin, wheat, etc.) are tending to fall as a result of persistent selling and only limited buying.

See SPECULATOR. Compare BULL MARKET.

bearer bonds FINANCIAL SECURITIES which are not registered under the name of a particular holder but where possession serves as proof of ownership. Such securities are popular in the American financial system, but fairly rare in Britain, where the names of holders of STOCKS and SHARES are recorded in a company's share register.

beggar-my-neighbour policy a course of action which is entered into by a country unilaterally in pursuit of its own self interest in INTERNATIONAL TRADE even though this might adversely affect the position of other countries. For example, country A might decide to impose TARIFFS or EXCHANGE CONTROLS, on imports from other countries in order to protect certain domestic industries. The great danger with this type of policy, however, is that it can be self-defeating; that is, other countries may retaliate by imposing tariffs, etc., of their own on country A's exports with the result that everybody's exports suffer. To avoid confrontation of this kind various international organizations have been established to regulate the conduct of international trade and monetary dealings.

See GENERAL AGREEMENT ON TARIFFS AND TRADE, INTERNATIONAL MONETARY FUND, EXPORT INCENTIVES, IMPORT RESTRICTIONS, DIRTY FLOAT, DUMPING.

behavioural theory of the firm an alternative to the traditional, profit-maximizing THEORY OF THE FIRM which stresses the nature of large companies as complex organizations, beset by problems of goal conflict and communications. The behavioural theory examines the inherent conflict between the goals of individuals and sub-groups within the organization and suggests that organizational objectives grow out of the interaction among these individuals and sub-groups.

Cyert and March, who helped develop the behavioural theory, suggested five major goals which are relevant to companies' sales, output and pricing strategies: (a) production goal; (b) inventory goal; (c) sales goal; (d) market-share goal; (e) profit goal. Each of these goals will be the primary concern of certain managers in the organization and these managers will press their particular goals. The goals become the subject of 'bargaining' among managers and such overall goals as do emerge will be compromises, often stated as satisfactory-level targets (see SATISFICING THEORY). However, this intergroup conflict rarely threatens the organization's survival because ORGANIZATIONAL SLACK provides a pool of emergency resources which permit managers to meet their goals when the economic environment becomes hostile.

In order to achieve rational decision-making it would be necessary to eradicate inconsistencies between goals and resolve conflicts between objectives. Traditional economic theory suggests that rationality can be achieved, painting a picture of 'ECONOMIC MAN' able to specify his objectives and take actions consistent with their achievement. By contrast, the behavioural theory argues that goals are imperfectly rationalized so that new goals are not always consistent with existing policies; and that goals are stated in the form of aspiration-level targets rather than maximizing goals, targets being raised or lowered in the light of experience. Consequently not all objectives will receive attention at the same time and objectives will change with experience.

The behavioural theory also focuses attention on internal communications problems in large organizations, pointing out that decision-making is distributed throughout the firm rather than concentrated at the apex of the organization pyramid. This happens because lower-level managers do not just execute the orders of those at the top; they exercise initiative (a) in detailed planning within broad limits set by a top management, (b) in summarizing information to be passed upwards as a basis for decision-making by their superiors. These communications problems make it difficult for senior managers to impose their objectives upon the organization.

Though the behavioural theory of the firm is somewhat descriptive, lacking the determinism necessary to generate testable predictions, it has offered many useful insights into the objectives of large companies.

See also MANAGERIAL THEORIES OF THE FIRM, PROFIT MAXIMIZATION.

below-the-line promotion SEE ABOVE-THE-LINE PROMOTION.

benefits-received principle of taxation the principle that those who benefit most from government-supplied goods and services should pay the TAXES which finance them. The problem with this proposition, apart from the obvious difficulties of quantifying the benefits received by individuals particularly as regards the provision of items such as national defence, fire service, etc., is that it cannot be reconciled with the wider responsibilities accepted by government in providing social services and welfare benefits, i.e. it would make no sense at all to tax an unemployed man in order to finance his unemployment pay. See ABILITY-TO-PAY PRINCIPLE OF TAXATION, REDISTRIBUTION-OF-INCOME PRINCIPLE OF TAXATION.

Bertrand duopoly see DUOPOLY.

bid 1. an offer by one company to purchase all or the majority of the SHARES of another company as a means of effecting a TAKEOVER. The bid price offered by the predator for the voting shares in the victim company must generally exceed the current market price of those shares, the difference being a premium which the predator must pay for control of the company. However, on occasions the market price of the shares may subsequently rise to exceed the initial bid price where investors either feel that the bid price undervalues the company, or where investors anticipate, for example, the possibility of a second party making a higher bid. The offer price could be paid solely in cash, or in a mix of cash and shares in the acquirer's own company, or solely in terms of the acquirer's shares (called a paper bid). In order to finance a takeover bid, a predator company may raise loans. See TAKEOVER BID (leveraged bid).

2. an indication of willingness to purchase an item which is for sale at the prevailing selling price. This may occur at auction when many purchasers bid for items on sale, the final sale going to the purchaser offering the highest price unless a predetermined reserve price has been set which was not reached. See AUCTION.

bid price the price at which a dealer in a FINANCIAL SECURITY (such as a STOCK or SHARE), FOREIGN CURRENCY or COMMODITY (tin, wheat, etc.) is prepared to buy a security, currency or commodity. Such dealers usually cite two prices to potential customers, the smaller, bid price, and a higher 'offer price' or 'ask price' at which they are prepared to sell a security, etc. The difference between the bid and offer price (referred to as the 'spread') represents the dealer's profit margin on the transaction.

See MARKET MAKER.

big bang see STOCK EXCHANGE.

bilateral flows movements of money between sectors of the economy to match opposite flows of goods and services. For example, income in return for factor inputs supplied, and consumption expenditure in payment for goods and services consumed. Bilateral flows make it possible to ignore flows of goods and services in the economy and to concentrate on money movements in the CIRCULAR FLOW OF NATIONAL INCOME MODEL.

bilateral monopoly a market situation comprising one seller (like MONOPOLY) and one buyer (like MONOPSONY.)

bilateral oligopoly a market situation with a significant degree of seller concentration (like OLIGOPOLY) and a significant degree of buyer concentration (like OLIGOPSONY.) See COUNTERVAILING POWER.

bilateral trade the trade between two countries. Bilateral trade is

a part of INTERNATIONAL TRADE which is multilateral in scope. See
MULTILATERAL TRADE, COUNTERTRADE.

bill 1. a financial instrument such as a BILL OF EXCHANGE and TREASURY
BILL which is issued by a firm or government as a means of borrowing
money.

2. the colloquial term used to describe an INVOICE (a request for
payment for products received).

3. a draft of a particular piece of legislation which forms the basis
of an Act of Parliament, such as the Fair Trading Act 1973.

bill-discounting interest rate the INTEREST RATE at which the CEN-
TRAL BANK is prepared to lend money to the DISCOUNT HOUSES. This
rate is not established administratively by the central bank as it was
formerly under BANK RATE, but changes directly in response to
changes in the supply and demand for short-term funds.

bill of exchange a FINANCIAL SECURITY representing an amount of
CREDIT extended by one business to another for a short period of time
(usually three months). The lender draws up a bill of exchange for
a specified sum of money payable at a given future date and the
borrower signifies his agreement to pay the amount indicated by
signing (accepting) the bill. Most bills are 'discounted' (i.e., bought
from the drawer) by the DISCOUNT MARKET for an amount less than
the face value of the bill (the difference between the two constitutes
the interest charged). Bills are frequently purchased by the COMMER-
CIAL BANKS to be held as part of their RESERVE ASSET RATIO. See DIS-
COUNT, ACCEPTING HOUSE, DISCOUNT HOUSE.

birth rate the number of people born into a POPULATION per thousand
per year. In 1995, for example, the UK birth rate was 13 people per
1000 of the population. The difference between this rate and the DEATH
RATE is used to calculate the rate of growth of the population of a
country over time. The birth rate tends to decline as a country attains
higher levels of economic development. See DEMOGRAPHIC TRANSITION.

black economy NONMARKETED ECONOMIC ACTIVITY which is not
recorded in the NATIONAL INCOME ACCOUNTS, either because such
activity does not pass through the market place or because it is illegal.
Illegality is not the same as nonmarketed activity. Illegal economic
activity may operate quite efficiently in the usual PRICE SYSTEM which
is determined by SUPPLY and DEMAND. Examples may be the purchase
and sale of illegal drugs on the street, or alcohol in the US prohibition
era of the 1920s, or foodstuffs in Britain during the Second World
War when RATIONING was in force. Nonmarketed activity does not
have a price determined by demand and supply. Certain nonmarketed
activity may be undertaken for altruistic reasons, for example, the
services of a housewife on behalf of her family, and the work of
charity volunteers. Other nonmarketed activity is done on a BARTER
basis, for example, where a mechanic services a motor car of an

electrician who in return installs new light fittings in the mechanic's house. Money has not changed hands and the activity is not recorded. Most references to the black economy refer to the illegal situation of people working without declaring their income. See BLACK MARKET.

black knight see TAKEOVER BID.

black market an 'unofficial' market which often arises when the government holds down the price of a product below its equilibrium rate and is then forced to operate a RATIONING system to allocate the available supply between buyers. Given that some buyers are prepared to pay a higher price, some dealers will be tempted to divert supplies away from the 'official' market by creating an under-the-counter secondary market. See BLACK ECONOMY.

board of directors the group responsible to the SHAREHOLDERS for running a JOINT-STOCK COMPANY. Often boards of directors are comprised of full-time salaried company executives (the executive directors) and part-time, nonexecutive directors. The board of directors meets periodically under the company chairman to decide on major policy matters within the company and the appointment of key managers. Directors are elected annually at the company ANNUAL GENERAL MEETING, TWO-TIER BOARD.

bond a FINANCIAL SECURITY issued by businesses and by the government as a means of BORROWING long-term funds. Bonds are typically issued for periods of several years; they are repayable on maturity and bear a fixed NOMINAL (COUPON) INTEREST RATE.

Once a bond has been issued at its nominal value then the market price at which it is sold subsequently will vary in order to keep the EFFECTIVE INTEREST RATE on the bond in line with current prevailing interest rates. For example, a £100 bond with a nominal 5% interest rate paying £5 per year would have to be priced at £50 if current market interest rates were 10%, so that a buyer could earn an effective return of £5/50 = 10% on his investment.

In addition to their rôle as a means of borrowing money, the monetary authorities use government bonds as a means of regulating the MONEY SUPPLY. For example, if the authorities wish to reduce the money supply they can issue bonds to the general public thereby reducing the liquidity of the banking system as customers draw cheques to pay for these bonds.

See also OPEN MARKET OPERATION, BANK DEPOSIT CREATION, PUBLIC SECTOR BORROWING REQUIREMENT, SPECULATIVE DEMAND FOR MONEY, CONSOLS.

bonus scheme a form of INCENTIVE PAY SCHEME whereby an individual's or group's WAGES are based on achievement of individual or group output targets. Bonus schemes often provide for a guaranteed basic wage for employees.

See PAY.

bonus shares SHARES issued to existing SHAREHOLDERS in a JOINT-STOCK COMPANY without further payment on their part. See CAPITALIZATION ISSUE.

boom a phase of the BUSINESS CYCLE characterized by FULL EMPLOYMENT levels of output (ACTUAL GROSS NATIONAL PRODUCT) and some upward pressure on the general PRICE LEVEL (see INFLATIONARY GAP). Boom conditions are dependent on there being a high level of AGGREGATE DEMAND which may come about autonomously or be induced by expansionary FISCAL POLICY and MONETARY POLICY. See DEMAND MANAGEMENT.

borrower a person, firm or institution who obtains a LOAN from a LENDER in order to finance CONSUMPTION or INVESTMENT. Borrowers are frequently required to offer some COLLATERAL SECURITY to lenders, for example, property deeds, which lenders may retain in the event of borrowers failing to repay the loan. See DEBT, DEBTOR, FINANCIAL SYSTEM.

Boston matrix a matrix (developed by the Boston Consulting Group) for analysing product-development policy within a firm and the cash-flow implications of product development. Fig. 16 on page 44 shows the matrix, which is used to identify products which are cash generators and products which are cash users. One axis of the matrix measures market growth rate; because the faster the growth rate for a product the greater will be the capital investment required and cash used. The other axis measures market share; because the larger the market share the greater will be the profit earned and cash generated. The market growth/share matrix encompasses four extreme product types:

(a) star products – those which have a high growth rate (so that they tend to use cash); and a high market share (so that they tend to generate cash). Star products are usually new products in the growth phase of the PRODUCT LIFE CYCLE.

(b) problem child products – those which have a high growth rate (and so tend to use cash); and a low market share (so that they tend to generate little cash). Problem products are frequently a cash drain but they have potential if their market share can be improved.

(c) cash cow products – those which have a low growth rate; and a high market share (so that they tend to generate a lot of cash). Cash cows are usually mature products in the latter phases of the product life cycle.

(d) dog products – those which have a low growth rate; and a low market share which tend to generate cash. Dog products generally have little potential for future development.

It is important for any firm to have a balanced portfolio of mature 'cash cow' products, newer 'stars', etc; and to use the cash generated by cash cows to help the development of problem children if its product development policy is to ensure the firm's long term survival. See PRODUCT PERFORMANCE, DIVERSIFICATION, PRODUCT-MARKET MATRIX.

		Market share	
		High	Low
Market growth rate	High	Star	Problem Child
	Low	Cash Cow	Dog

Fig. 16. **Boston matrix**. The matrix identifies cash generators and cash users.

boycott 1. the withholding of supplies of GOODS from a distributor by a producer or producers in order to force that distributor to resell those goods only on terms specified by the producer. In the past, boycotts were often used as a means of enforcing RESALE PRICE MAINTENANCE.
    2. the prohibition of certain imports or exports, or a complete ban on INTERNATIONAL TRADE with a particular country by other countries.

brand the name, term or symbol given to a product by a supplier in order to distinguish his offering from that of similar products supplied by competitors. Brand names are used as a focal point of PRODUCT DIFFERENTIATION between suppliers.
    In most countries brand names and trade marks are required to be registered with a central authority so as to ensure that they are uniquely applied to a single, specific product. This makes it easier for consumers to identify the product when making a purchase and also protects suppliers against unscrupulous imitators. See INTELLECTUAL PROPERTY RIGHTS, BRAND TRANSFERENCE.

brand loyalty the continuing willingness of consumers to purchase and repurchase the brand of a particular supplier in preference to competitive products. Suppliers cultivate brand loyalty by PRODUCT DIFFERENTIATION strategies aimed at emphasizing real and imaginary differences between competing brands. See ADVERTISING.

brand proliferation an increase in the number of brands of a particular product, each additional brand being very similar to those already available. Brand proliferation occurs mainly in oligopolistic markets (see OLIGOPOLY) where competitive rivalry is centered on PRODUCT DIFFERENTIATION strategies, and is especially deployed as a means of MARKET SEGMENTATION. In the THEORY OF MARKETS, 'excessive' brand proliferation is generally considered to be against consumers' interests because it tends to result in higher prices by increasing total ADVERTIS-ING and sales promotional expenses.

brand switching the decision by consumers to substitute an alternative BRAND for the one they currently consume. Brand switching may be induced by ADVERTISING designed to overcome BRAND LOYALTY to existing brands.

brand transference the use of an existing BRAND name for new or modified products. Brand transference or extension seeks to capitalize on consumers' BRAND LOYALTY towards the firm's established brands to gain rapid consumer acceptance of a new product.

brand value the money value of an established BRAND name. The valuation of a brand reflects the BRAND LOYALTY of consumers towards it, built up by cumulative ADVERTISING.

See TAKEOVER.

break-even the short-run rate of output and sales at which a supplier generates just enough revenue to cover his fixed and variable costs, earning neither a PROFIT nor a LOSS. If the selling price of a product exceeds its unit VARIABLE COST then each unit of product sold will earn a CONTRIBUTION towards FIXED COSTS and profits. Once sufficient units are being sold so that their total contributions cover the supplier's fixed costs then the company breaks even. If less than the break-even sales volume is achieved then total contributions will not meet fixed costs and the supplier will make a loss. If the sales volume achieved exceeds the break even volume, total contributions will cover the fixed costs and leave a surplus which constitutes profit. See Fig. 17 (overleaf).

Bretton Woods System see INTERNATIONAL MONETARY FUND.

bridging loan a form of short-term LOAN used by a borrower as a continuing source of funds to 'bridge' the period until the borrower obtains a medium- or long-term loan to replace it. Bridging loans are used in particular in the housing market to finance the purchase of a new house while arranging long-term MORTGAGE finance and awaiting the proceeds from the sale of any existing property.

British Technology Group a UK organization formed in 1981 by the merger of the National Research and Development Corporation and the National Enterprise Board to promote industrial efficiency and innovation by sponsoring and financing industrial investment and restructuring. See INDUSTRIAL POLICY.

budget (firm) a firm's planned revenues and expenditures for a given future period. Annual or monthly sales, production, cost and capital expenditure budgets provide a means for the firm to plan its future activities, and by collecting actual data about sales, product cost, etc. to compare with budget the firm can control these activities more effectively.

budget (government) a financial statement of the government's

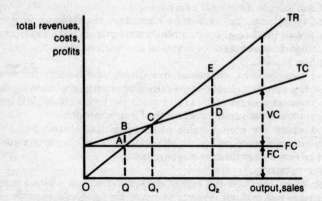

Fig. 17. **Break-even.** A supplier's typical short-run costs and revenues. Fixed costs do not vary with output and so are shown as the horizontal line FC. Total cost comprises both fixed costs and total variable costs and is shown by line TC. Total revenue rises as output and sales are expanded and is depicted by line TR. At low levels of output like Q total costs exceed total revenues and the supplier makes a loss equal to AB. At high levels of output like Q_2 revenues exceed costs and the supplier makes a profit equal to DE. At output Q_1 total revenues exactly match total costs (at C) and the supplier breaks even.

planned revenues and expenditures for the fiscal year. The main sources of current revenues as shown in Fig. 18a are TAXATION, principally income and expenditure taxes, and NATIONAL INSURANCE CONTRIBUTIONS. The main current outgoings of GOVERNMENT EXPENDITURE, are the provision of goods and services (principally wage payments to health, education, police and other public service employees) and TRANSFER PAYMENTS (old-age pensions, etc.).

The budget has two main uses: (a) it forms the basis of the government's longer-term financial planning of its own economic and social commitments; (b) it is an instrument of FISCAL POLICY in regulating the level (and composition) of AGGREGATE DEMAND in the economy. A BUDGET SURPLUS (revenues greater than expenditures) reduces the level of aggregate demand. By contrast, a BUDGET DEFICIT (expenditure greater than revenues) increase aggregate demand. Fig. 18b shows UK budget deficits (and surpluses) over the past decade.

See DEMAND MANAGEMENT, PUBLIC FINANCE.

budget (household) a household's planned income and expenditure for a given time period. The household's expenditure will depend upon its DISPOSABLE INCOME and the THEORY OF CONSUMER BEHAVIOUR

£ million

Current receipts		250,941
Of which:		
Taxes on income	(90,672)	
Taxes on expenditure	(103,444)	
National insurance	(44,251)	
Current expenditure		275,549
Of which:		
Spending on provision of goods and services	(179,679)	
Transfer payments	(83,016)	
Debt interest	(25,363)	
Capital receipts		2,686
Taxes on capital, etc.		
Capital expenditure		14,556
Of which:		
Capital formation	(12,453)	
Overall budget deficit		–36,478

(a)

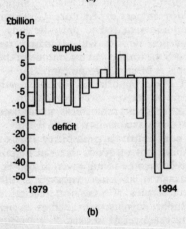

(b)

Fig. 18. **Budget (government)**. (a) The UK budget for 1995 (b) UK budget deficits and surpluses, 1979–94. Source: *UK National Accounts*, 1996.

seeks to show how households, or consumers, allocate their income in spending on various goods and services.

See CONSUMER EQUILIBRIUM.

budget deficit the excess of GOVERNMENT EXPENDITURE over government receipts in any one fiscal year. Government receipts are primarily in the form of TAXATION of individuals and institutions but there are other miscellaneous receipts such as the sale of government holdings in private or public enterprises. The operation of a budget deficit (*deficit financing*) is a tool of FISCAL POLICY to enable government to influence the level of AGGREGATE DEMAND and EMPLOYMENT in the economy. Such a policy was advocated by KEYNES in the 1930s to offset the DEPRESSION which occurred at that time. Opinion prior to this was that the government should operate a BALANCED BUDGET policy, allowing the economy to respond in its own way without government intervention. Keynes argued that government should intervene by deliberately imbalancing its budget in order to inject additional aggregate demand into a depressed economy and vice versa.

Since the second world war most western governments have tended to operate a budget deficit to keep employment high and to promote long-term ECONOMIC GROWTH. This has been financed by increasing the PUBLIC SECTOR BORROWING REQUIREMENT (PSBR) through the issue of TREASURY BILLS and long-term bonds. This is acceptable as long as the economy is growing and the interest payments on such borrowings do not become disproportionate to the overall level of government expenditure. Government borrowing in excess of the amount required to promote long term growth and effect counter-cyclical policies will ultimately result in INFLATION. Consequently both the timing and magnitude of the expenditure over and above receipts is of crucial importance.

BUDGET SURPLUS is the opposite of the above whereby there is an excess of government receipts over expenditure.

See AUTOMATIC (BUILT-IN) STABILIZERS, KEYNESIAN ECONOMICS, BUSINESS CYCLE, DEMAND MANAGEMENT.

budget line or **consumption possibility line** a line showing the alternative combinations of goods that can be purchased by a consumer with a given income facing given prices. See Fig. 19. See also CONSUMER EQUILIBRIUM, REVEALED PREFERENCE THEORY, PRICE EFFECT.

budget surplus a surplus of TAXATION receipts over GOVERNMENT EXPENDITURE. Budget surpluses are used as an instrument of FISCAL POLICY to reduce the level of AGGREGATE DEMAND in the economy. See BUDGET DEFICIT, PUBLIC SECTOR BORROWING REQUIREMENT.

buffer stock a stock of a COMMODITY (copper, wheat, etc.) which is held by a trade body or government as a means of regulating the price of that commodity. An 'official' price for the commodity is established and if the open-market price falls below this because there is excess supply at the fixed price, then the authorities will buy the surplus and add it to the buffer stock in order to force the price back up. By contrast, if the open-market price rises above the fixed price because there is an excess demand at the fixed price, then the authorities will sell some of their buffer stock in order to bring the price

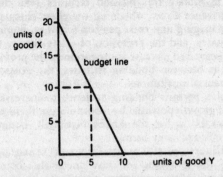

Fig. 19. **Budget line**. If a consumer has an income of £10 and the price of good X is 50 pence and the price of good Y is £1, he can buy 20 units of X or 10 units of Y, or some combination of both, for example 10 units of X and 5 units of Y. The slope of the budget line measures the relative prices of the two goods.

down. Through this mechanism the price of the commodity can be stabilized over time, avoiding erratic, short-term fluctuations in price.

Thus this mechanism attempts to avoid erratic short-term fluctuations in price. However, if the official price is set at too high a level, this will encourage over-supply in the long term and expensively-accumulating stocks; while if the official price is set at too low a level this will discourage supply in the long term and lead to shortages.

See INTERNATIONAL COMMODITY AGREEMENT, PRICE SUPPORT, COMMON AGRICULTURE POLICY.

building society a financial institution which offers a variety of savings accounts to attract deposits, mainly from the general public, and which specializes in the provision of long-term MORTGAGE loans used to purchase property. In recent years, many of the larger UK building societies have moved into the estate agency business. Additionally, they have entered into arrangements with other financial institutions which have enabled them to provide their depositors with limited banking facilities (the use of cheque books and credit cards, for instance) and other financial services, a development which has been given added impetus by the BUILDING SOCIETIES ACT, 1986.

Building society deposits constitute an important source of liquidity in the economy and count as 'broad money' in the specification of the MONEY SUPPLY.

See FINANCIAL SYSTEM.

Building Societies Act, 1986 a UK Act which gave BUILDING SOCIETIES new powers to augment their traditional MORTGAGE business by providing a range of other financial services for their customers. These include money transmission facilities (via cheque books), arranging insurance cover, obtaining travellers cheques and foreign currencies, managing unit trust pension schemes, buying and selling stocks and shares, and the provision of estate agency facilities. The Act has thus served to increase competition in the provision of financial services as between building societies, the COMMERCIAL BANKS and other financial institutions.

The Act also permits building societies to increase their capital resources and growth potential by incorporating themselves as JOINT-STOCK COMPANIES (as has the Abbey National), issuing shares and securing a stock exchange listing.

built-in stabilizers see AUTOMATIC (BUILT-IN) STABILIZERS.

bulk buying the purchase of raw materials, components and finished products in large quantities, thereby enabling a BUYER to take advantage of DISCOUNTS off suppliers' LIST PRICES. A supplier may offer a price discount to encourage the placement of large orders as a means of obtaining extra sales in order to exploit fully the ECONOMIES OF SCALE in production and distribution. In many cases, however, the initiative lies with buyers, with powerful retailing and wholesaling groups exacting favourable price concessions from suppliers by playing one supplier off against another.

See CHAIN STORE, OLIGOPSONY, MONOPSONY.

bull a person who expects future prices in a STOCK EXCHANGE or COMMODITY MARKET to rise and who seeks to make money by buying shares or commodities. Compare BEAR.

See SPOT MARKET, FUTURES MARKET, BULL MARKET.

bullion precious metals such as GOLD, silver, platinum, etc., which are traded commercially in the form of bars and coins for investment purposes, and which are used to produce jewellery and as industrial base metals. Some items of bullion, gold in particular, are held by CENTRAL BANKS and are used as INTERNATIONAL RESERVES to finance balance of payments imbalances.

bullion market a MARKET engaged in the buying and selling of precious metals such as GOLD and silver and gold and silver coins such as 'Krugerrands' and 'Sovereigns'. The London Bullion Market is a leading centre for such transactions.

bull market a situation where the prices of FINANCIAL SECURITIES (stocks, shares, etc.) or COMMODITIES (tin, wheat, etc.) are tending to rise as a result of persistent buying and only limited selling. Compare BEAR MARKET.

See SPECULATOR.

Bundesbank the CENTRAL BANK of Germany.

burden of debt interest charges on DEBT which arise as a result of BORROWING by individuals, firms and governments.

In the case of governments, interest charges on the NATIONAL DEBT are paid for out of TAXATION and other receipts. The term 'burden' would seem to imply that government borrowing is a 'bad' thing in so far as it passes on financial obligations from present (overspending) generations to future generations. However, the fundamental point to emphasize is that the interest paid on the national debt is a TRANSFER PAYMENT and *does not* represent a net reduction in the capacity of the economy to provide goods and services, provided that most of this debt is owed to domestic citizens.

INFLATION has the effect of eroding the real burden of debts which are denominated in NOMINAL VALUES.

See PUBLIC SECTOR BORROWING REQUIREMENT.

burden of dependency the non-economically active POPULATION of a country in relation to the employed and self-employed LABOUR FORCE. Dependants include very young, very old and disabled members of the community, their unpaid carers and the unemployed who must rely on the efforts of the labour force to provide them with goods and services. Countries with a proportionately large dependent population need to levy high taxes upon the labour force to finance the provision of TRANSFER PAYMENTS such as pensions, child benefit and unemployment benefit.

burden of taxation see TAX BURDEN.

business a supplier of goods and services. The term can also denote a FIRM. In economic theory businesses perform two rôles. On the one hand they enter the market place as producers of goods and services bought by HOUSEHOLDS; on the other hand they buy factor inputs from households in order to produce those goods and services. The term 'businesses' is used primarily in macro (national income) analysis, while the term 'firms' is used in micro (supply and demand) analysis.

See also CIRCULAR FLOW OF NATIONAL INCOME MODEL.

business cycle or **trade cycle** fluctuations in the level of economic activity (ACTUAL GROSS NATIONAL PRODUCT) alternating between periods of depression and boom conditions.

The business cycle is characterized by four phases (see Fig. 20): (a) DEPRESSION, a period of rapidly falling AGGREGATE DEMAND accompanied by very low levels of output and heavy UNEMPLOYMENT which eventually reaches the bottom of the trough; (b) RECOVERY, an upturn in aggregate demand accompanied by rising output and a reduction in unemployment; (c) BOOM, aggregate demand reaches and then exceeds sustainable output levels (POTENTIAL GROSS NATIONAL PRODUCT) as the peak of the cycle is reached. Full employment is reached and the emergence of excess demand causes the general price level to increase (see INFLATION); (d) RECESSION, the boom comes to an end, and is followed by recession. Aggregate demand falls, bringing with

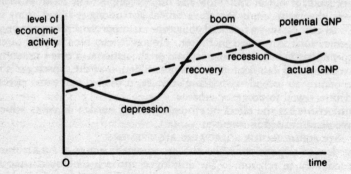

Fig. 20. **Business cycle.** Fluctuations in the level of economic activity.

it, initially, modest falls in output and employment, but then as demand continues to contract, the onset of depression.

What causes the economy to fluctuate in this way? One prominent factor is the volatility of FIXED INVESTMENT and INVENTORY INVESTMENT expenditures (the investment cycle), which are themselves a function of businesses' EXPECTATIONS about future demand. At the top of the cycle income begins to level-off and investment in new supply capacity finally 'catches up' with demand (see ACCELERATOR). This causes a reduction in INDUCED INVESTMENT and, via contracting MULTIPLIER effects, leads to a fall in national income which reduces investment even further. At the bottom of the depression investment may rise exogenously (due, for example, to the introduction of new technologies) or through the revival of REPLACEMENT INVESTMENT. In this case, the increase in investment spending will, via expansionary multiplier effects lead to an increase in national income and a greater volume of induced investment.

See also DEMAND MANAGEMENT, KONDRATIEF CYCLE, SECULAR STAGNATION.

Business Expansion Scheme a UK facility (1981–94) aimed at encouraging small business start-ups by giving ENTREPRENEURS generous tax-relief on their investments. See also INDUSTRIAL POLICY. It was replaced in 1994 by the Enterprise Investment Scheme.

business strategy the formulation of long-term plans and policies by a firm which interlocks its various production and marketing activities in order to achieve its business objectives.

See FIRM OBJECTIVES, COMPETITIVE STRATEGY, HORIZONTAL INTEGRATION, VERTICAL INTEGRATION, DIVERSIFICATION.

buyer a purchaser of a GOOD or SERVICE. A broad distinction can be made between purchasers of items such as raw materials, components, plant and equipment which are used to produce other products (referred to as 'industrial buyers') and purchasers of products for personal consumption (referred to as 'consumers').

In general, industrial buyers (in the main purchasing/procurement officers) are involved in the purchase of 'functional' inputs to the production process, usually in large quantities and often involving the outlay of thousands of pounds. Their particular concern is to obtain input supplies which are of an appropriate quality and possess the technical attributes necessary to ensure that the production process goes ahead smoothly and efficiently. In selling to industrial buyers, personal contacts, the provision of technical advice and back-up services are important.

Buyers of consumer goods, by contrast, typically buy a much wider range of products, mainly in small quantities. Purchases are made to satisfy some 'physical' or 'psychological' need of the consumer. Thus, it is important for suppliers to understand the basis of these needs and to produce and promote BRANDS which satisfy identifiable consumer demands. In this context, ADVERTISING and SALES PROMOTION are important tools for shaping consumers' perceptions of a brand and establishing BRAND LOYALTY.

See PRODUCT DIFFERENTIATION.

buyer concentration an element of MARKET STRUCTURE which refers to the number and size distribution of buyers in a market. In most markets buyers are numerous, each purchasing only a tiny fraction of total supply. In some markets, however, most notably in INTERMEDIATE GOODS industries, a few large buyers purchase a significant proportion of total supply. Such situations are described as OLIGOPSONY, or in the case of a single buyer, MONOPSONY.

Market theory predicts that MARKET PERFORMANCE will differ according to whether there are many buyers in the market, each accounting for only a minute fraction of total purchases, (PERFECT COMPETITION), or only a few buyers, each accounting for a substantial proportion of total purchases (oligopsony), or a single buyer (monopsony).

See COUNTERVAILING POWER, MARKET CONCENTRATION, SELLER CONCENTRATION, BULK BUYING.

buyer's market a SHORT-RUN market situation in which there is EXCESS SUPPLY of goods or services at current prices which forces prices down to the advantage of the buyer. Compare SELLER'S MARKET.

by-product a product which is secondary to the main product emerging from a production process. For example, the refining of crude oil to produce petroleum generates a range of by-products like bitumen, naptha and creosote.

C

called up capital the amount of ISSUED SHARE CAPITAL which share-holders have been called upon to subscribe to date, where a JOINT-STOCK COMPANY issues SHARES with phased payment terms. Called up capital is usually equal to PAID UP CAPITAL except where some shareholders have failed to pay instalments due (CALLS IN ARREARS).

See SHARE ISSUE.

call money or **money-at-call and short notice** CURRENCY (notes and coins) loaned by the COMMERCIAL BANKS to DISCOUNT HOUSES. These can be overnight (24 hour) loans or one-week loans. Call money is included as part of the commercial banks' RESERVE ASSET RATIO.

call option see OPTION.

calls in arrears the difference which arises between CALLED UP CAPITAL and PAID UP CAPITAL where a JOINT-STOCK COMPANY issues SHARES with phased payment terms and shareholders fail to pay an instalment.

See SHARE ISSUE.

Cambridge equation see QUANTITY THEORY OF MONEY.

CAP see COMMON AGRICULTURAL POLICY.

capacity 1. the maximum amount of output that a firm or industry is physically capable of producing given the fullest and most efficient use of its existing plant. In microeconomic theory, the concept of *full capacity* is specifically related to the cost structures of firms and industries. Industry output is maximized (i.e., full capacity is attained) when all firms produce at the minimum point on their long-run average total cost curves (see PERFECT COMPETITION). If firms fail to produce at this point then the result is EXCESS CAPACITY.

2. in macroeconomics, capacity refers to POTENTIAL GNP. The percentage relationship of actual output in the economy to capacity (i.e. potential national income), shows capacity utilization. See also MONOPOLISTIC COMPETITION.

capital the contribution to productive activity made by INVESTMENT in *physical capital* (for example, factories, offices, machinery, tools) and in HUMAN CAPITAL (for example, general education, vocational training). Capital is one of the three main FACTORS OF PRODUCTION, the other two being LABOUR and NATURAL RESOURCES. Physical (and human) capital make a significant contribution towards ECONOMIC GROWTH.

See CAPITAL FORMATION, CAPITAL STOCK, CAPITAL WIDENING, CAPI-

TAL DEEPENING, GROSS FIXED CAPITAL FORMATION, CAPITAL ACCUMULATION.

capital account 1. the section of the NATIONAL INCOME ACCOUNTS which records INVESTMENT expenditure by government on infrastructure such as roads, hospitals and schools; and investment expenditure by the private sector on plant and machinery.

2. the section of the BALANCE OF PAYMENTS accounts which records movements of funds associated with the purchase or sale or long term assets and borrowing or lending by the private sector.

capital accumulation or **capital formation 1.** the process of adding to the net physical CAPITAL STOCK of an economy in an attempt to achieve greater total output. The accumulation of CAPITAL GOODS represents foregone CONSUMPTION which necessitates a reward to capital in the form of INTEREST, greater PROFITS or social benefit derived. The *rate* of accumulation of an economy's physical stock of capital is an important determinant of the rate of growth of an economy and is represented in various PRODUCTION FUNCTIONS and ECONOMIC GROWTH models. A branch of economics, called DEVELOPMENT ECONOMICS, devotes much of its analysis to determining appropriate rates of capital accumulation, type of capital required and types of investment project to maximize 'development' in underdeveloped countries (see DEVELOPING COUNTRY). In developed countries, the INTEREST RATE influences SAVINGS and INVESTMENT (capital accumulation) decisions, to a greater or lesser degree, in the private sector (see KEYNESIAN ECONOMICS) and can therefore be indirectly influenced by government. Government itself invests in the economy's INFRASTRUCTURE. This direct control over capital accumulation, and the indirect control over private investment, puts the onus of achieving the economy's optimal growth path on to the government. The nature of capital accumulation (whether CAPITAL WIDENING or CAPITAL DEEPENING) is also of considerable importance. See also CAPITAL CONSUMPTION, INVENTION, INNOVATION, CAPITAL–OUTPUT RATIO.

2. the process of increasing the internally available CAPITAL of a particular firm by retaining earnings to add to RESERVES.

capital allowances standard allowances, for TAXATION purposes, against expenditure on FIXED ASSETS by a firm in lieu of DEPRECIATION. A business may choose its own rates of depreciation for fixed assets which may differ from the statutory capital allowances. Capital allowances may also be varied by the government as a tool of FISCAL POLICY to encourage or discourage capital INVESTMENT. See CAPITAL GOODS, DEPRECIATION (2).

capital appreciation see APPRECIATION (2).

capital budgeting the planning and control of CAPITAL expenditure within a firm. Capital budgeting involves the search for suitable INVESTMENT opportunities; evaluating particular investment projects;

raising LONG-TERM CAPITAL to finance investments; assessing the COST
OF CAPITAL; applying suitable expenditure controls to ensure that
investment outlays conform with the expenditures authorized; and
ensuring that adequate cash is available when required for
investments.

See INVESTMENT APPRAISAL, DISCOUNTED CASH FLOW, PAYBACK
PERIOD, MARGINAL EFFICIENCY OF CAPITAL/INVESTMENT.

capital consumption the reduction in a country's CAPITAL STOCK
incurred in producing this year's GROSS NATIONAL PRODUCT (GNP). In
order to maintain (or increase) next year's GNP a proportion of new
INVESTMENT must be devoted to replacing worn-out and obsolete
capital stock. Effectively, capital consumption represents the aggregate of firms' DEPRECIATION charges for the year.

capital deepening an increase in the CAPITAL input in the economy
(see ECONOMIC GROWTH) at a *faster* rate than the increase in the LABOUR
input so that proportionally more capital to labour is used to produce
national output. See CAPITAL WIDENING, CAPITAL-LABOUR RATIO, PRO-
DUCTIVITY.

capital employed see SHAREHOLDER'S CAPITAL EMPLOYED, LONG-TERM
CAPITAL EMPLOYED.

capital expenditure see INVESTMENT.

capital formation see CAPITAL ACCUMULATION.

capital gain the surplus realized when an ASSET (house, SHARE, etc.)
is sold at a higher price than was originally paid for it. However
because of INFLATION it is important to distinguish between NOMINAL
VALUES and REAL VALUES. Thus what appears to be a large nominal
gain may, after allowing for the effects of inflation, turn out to be a
very small real gain. Furthermore in an ongoing business, provision
has to be made for the REPLACEMENT COST of assets which can be
much higher than the HISTORIC COST of these assets being sold. See
CAPITAL GAINS TAX, CAPITAL LOSS, REVALUATION PROVISION, APPRECI-
ATION (2).

capital gains tax a TAX on the surplus obtained from the sale of an
ASSET for more than was originally paid for it. Because capital gains
tax is generally levied on the nominal CAPITAL GAIN then in a period
of rapid INFLATION it can seriously over-tax companies whose real
gains (after allowing for the high REPLACEMENT COST of assets) are
considerably smaller than their nominal gains. However, it is possible
to allow for this by taxing only those gains which exceed the rate of
inflation.

capital gearing or **leverage** the proportion of fixed-interest LOAN
CAPITAL TO SHARE CAPITAL employed in financing a company. Where
a company raises most of the funds which it requires by issuing shares
and uses very few fixed interest loans it has a low capital gearing;
where a company raises most of the funds which it needs from fixed

interest loans and few funds from SHAREHOLDERS it is highly geared.

Capital gearing is important to company shareholders because fixed interest charges on loans have the effect of gearing up or down the eventual residual return to shareholders from trading profits. When the trading return on total funds invested exceeds the interest rate on loans, any residual surplus accrues to shareholders, enhancing their return. On the other hand when the average return on total funds invested is less than interest rates, then interest still has to be paid and this has the effect of reducing the residual return to shareholders. Thus, returns to shareholders vary more violently when highgeared.

The extent to which a company can employ fixed-interest capital as a source of long term funds depends to a large extent upon the stability of its profits over time. For example, large retailing companies whose profits tend to vary little from year to year tend to be more highly geared than, say, mining companies whose profit record is more volatile.

capital goods the long-lasting *durable goods* such as machine tools and furnaces which are used as FACTOR INPUTS in the production of other products, as opposed to being sold directly to consumers. See CAPITAL, CONSUMER GOODS, PRODUCER GOODS.

capital inflow a movement of funds into the domestic economy from abroad representing either the purchase of domestic FINANCIAL SECURITIES and physical ASSETS by foreigners, or the borrowing (see BORROWER) of foreign funds by domestic residents.

Capital inflows involve the receipt of money by one country, the host, from one or more foreign countries, the source countries. There are many reasons for the transfer of funds between nations:

(a) foreign direct INVESTMENT by MULTINATIONAL COMPANIES in physical assets such as the establishment of local manufacturing plant.

(b) the purchase of financial securities in the host country which are considered to be attractive PORTFOLIO investments.

(c) host-government borrowing from other governments or international banks to alleviate short-term BALANCE OF PAYMENTS deficits.

(d) SPECULATION about the future EXCHANGE RATE of the host country currency and interest rates, expectation of an appreciation of the currency leading to a capital inflow as speculators hope to make a capital gain after the APPRECIATION of the currency.

By contrast, a CAPITAL OUTFLOW is the payment of money from one country to another for the sort of reasons already outlined. See also FOREIGN INVESTMENT, HOT MONEY.

capital-intensive firm/industry a firm or industry which produces its output of goods or services using proportionately large inputs of CAPITAL equipment and relatively small amounts of LABOUR. The proportions of capital and labour which a firm uses in production depends mainly on the relative prices of labour and capital inputs and their relative productivities. This in turn depends upon the degree of standardization of the product. Where standardized products are sold in large quantities it is possible to employ large-scale capital-intensive production methods which facilitate ECONOMIES OF SCALE. Aluminium smelting, oil refining and steelworks are examples of capital-intensive industries. See MASS PRODUCTION; CAPITAL-LABOUR RATIO.

capitalism see PRIVATE-ENTERPRISE ECONOMY.

capitalization issue or **scrip issue** the issue by a JOINT-STOCK COMPANY of additional SHARES to existing SHAREHOLDERS without any further payment being required. Capitalization issues are usually made where a company has ploughed back profits over several years and so has accumulated substantial RESERVES or has revalued its fixed assets and accumulated capital reserves. If the company wishes to capitalize the reserves it can do so by creating extra shares to match the reserves, and issue them as BONUS SHARES to existing shareholders in proportion to their existing shareholdings. See also RETAINED PROFIT.

capital-labour ratio the proportion of CAPITAL to LABOUR inputs in an economy. If capital inputs in the economy increase over time at the same rate as the labour input then the capital-labour ratio remains unchanged (see CAPITAL WIDENING). If capital inputs increase at a faster rate than the labour input then CAPITAL DEEPENING takes place. The capital-labour ratio is one element in the process of ECONOMIC GROWTH. See CAPITAL-INTENSIVE FIRM/INDUSTRY, LABOUR-INTENSIVE FIRM/INDUSTRY, AUTOMATION.

capital loss the deficit realized when an ASSET (house, SHARE etc) is sold at a lower price than was originally paid for it. Compare CAPITAL GAIN.

capital market the market for long-term company LOAN CAPITAL and SHARE CAPITAL and government BONDS. The capital market together with the MONEY MARKET (which provides short-term funds) are the main sources of external finance to industry and government. The financial institutions involved in the capital market include the CENTRAL BANK, COMMERCIAL BANKS, the saving-investing institutions, (INSURANCE COMPANIES, PENSION FUNDS, UNIT TRUSTS, and INVESTMENT TRUST COMPANIES), ISSUING HOUSES and MERCHANT BANKS.

New share capital is most frequently raised through issuing houses or merchant banks which arrange for the sale of shares on behalf of client companies. Shares can be issued in a variety of ways, including: directly to the general public by way of an 'offer for sale' (or an 'introduction') at a prearranged fixed price; an 'offer for sale by TENDER' where the issue price is determined by averaging out the bid prices offered by prospective purchasers of the share subject to a minimum price bid; a RIGHTS ISSUE of shares to existing shareholders at a fixed price; a placing of the shares at an arranged price with selected investors, often institutional investors. See STOCK EXCHANGE.

capital movements the flows of FOREIGN CURRENCY between countries representing both short-term and long-term INVESTMENT in physical ASSETS and FINANCIAL SECURITIES and BORROWINGS. See CAPITAL INFLOW, CAPITAL OUTFLOW, BALANCE OF PAYMENTS, FOREIGN INVESTMENT.

capital outflow a movement of domestic funds abroad representing either the purchase of foreign FINANCIAL SECURITIES and physical ASSETS by domestic residents, or the BORROWING of domestic funds by foreigners. See CAPITAL INFLOW, BALANCE OF PAYMENTS, FOREIGN INVESTMENT, HOT MONEY.

capital-output ratio a measure of how much additional CAPITAL is required to produce each extra unit of OUTPUT, or put the other way round, the amount of extra output produced by each unit of added capital. The capital-output ratio indicates how 'efficient' new INVESTMENT is in contributing to ECONOMIC GROWTH. Assuming, for example, a 4:1 capital-output ratio each four units of extra investment enables national output to grow by one unit. If the capital-output ratio is 2:1, however, then each two units of extra investment expands national income by one unit. See CAPITAL ACCUMULATION, PRODUCTIVITY.

capital stock the net accumulation of a physical stock of CAPITAL GOODS (buildings, plant, machinery, etc.) by a firm, industry or economy at any one point in time (see POTENTIAL GROSS NATIONAL PRODUCT).

The measurements most frequently used for the value of a country's capital stock are from the NATIONAL INCOME and expenditure statistics. These statistics take private and public expenditure on capital goods and deduct CAPITAL CONSUMPTION (see DEPRECIATION sense 2) to arrive at net accumulation (which may be positive or negative). The more relevant value of capital stock, from the economist's point of view, is the present value of the stream of income such stock can generate. More broadly, the size of a country's capital stock has an important influence on its rate of ECONOMIC GROWTH.

See CAPITAL ACCUMULATION, CAPITAL WIDENING, CAPITAL DEEPENING, DEPRECIATION METHODS, PRODUCTIVITY, CAPITAL-OUTPUT RATIO.

capital transfer tax see WEALTH TAX.

capital widening an increase in the CAPITAL input in the economy (see ECONOMIC GROWTH) at the same rate as the increase in the LABOUR input so that the proportion in which capital and labour are combined to produce national output remains unchanged. See CAPITAL DEEPENING, CAPITAL-LABOUR RATIO, PRODUCTIVITY.

cardinal utility the (subjective) UTILITY or satisfaction that a consumer derives from consuming a product, measured on an *absolute* scale. This implies that the *exact* amount of utility derived from consuming a product can be measured, and early economists suggested that utility could be measured in discrete units referred to as UTILS. However, because it proved impossible to construct an accurate measure of cardinal utility, ORDINAL UTILITY measures replaced the idea of cardinal utility in the theory of CONSUMER EQUILIBRIUM.

See DIMINISHING MARGINAL UTILITY.

cartel a form of COLLUSION between a group of suppliers aimed at suppressing competition between themselves, wholly or in part. Cartels can take a number of forms. For example, suppliers may set up a sole selling agency which buys up their individual output at an agreed price and arranges for the marketing of these products on a coordinated basis. Another variant is where suppliers operate an agreement (see RESTRICTIVE TRADE AGREEMENT) which sets uniform selling prices for their products, thereby suppressing price competition, but with suppliers then competing for market share through PRODUCT DIFFERENTIATION strategies. A more comprehensive version of a cartel is the application not only of common selling prices and joint marketing, but also restrictions on production involving the assignment of specific output quotas to individual suppliers, and coordinated capacity adjustments, either removing over-capacity or extending capacity on a coordinated basis.

Cartels are usually established with the purpose of either exploiting the joint market power of suppliers to extract MONOPOLY profits, or as a means of preventing cut-throat competition from forcing firms to operate at a loss, often resorted to in times of depressed demand (a so-called 'crisis cartel'). In the former case, a central administration agency could determine the price and output of the industry, and the output quotas of each of the separate member firms in such a way as to restrict total industry output and maximize the joint-profits of the group. Price and output will thus tend to approximate those of a profit-maximizing monopolist. See Fig. 21.

A number of factors are crucial to the successful operation of a cartel, in particular the participation of all significant suppliers of the product and their full compliance with the policies of the cartel. Non-participation of some key suppliers and 'cheating' by cartel members, together with the ability of buyers to switch to substitute products, may well serve to undermine a cartel's ability to control prices. In many countries, most notably the US and European Community, cartels concerned with price fixing, market sharing and restrictions on production and capacity are prohibited by law.

See COMPETITION POLICY, ORGANIZATION OF PETROLEUM EXPORTING COUNTRIES (OPEC).

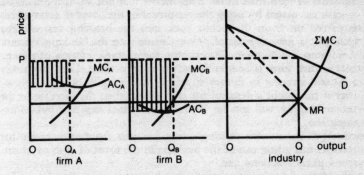

Fig. 21. **Cartel**. D is the industry demand curve, showing the aggregate quantity which the combined group may sell over a range of
possible prices and MR is the industry marginal revenue curve. The
industry marginal cost curve $\sum MC$ is constructed from the marginal
cost curves of the individual firms making up the cartel. For any
given level of industry output the cartel is required to calculate the
allocation of the ouput among member firms on the basis of their
individual marginal costs to obtain the lowest possible aggregate
cost of producing their output.

To maximize industry profit the cartel will set price OP and produce
output OQ. Quotas of Q_A and Q_B are given to firms A and B respectively where a horizontal line drawn from the intersection of MR and
$\sum MC$ (the line of aggregate marginal costs) intersects MC_A and MC_B.

Profit contributed by each firm is computed by multiplying the
number of units produced by the difference between industry price
and the firm's average cost at that level of output.

The aggregate profit is then divided among the member firms in
some agreed manner, not necessarily, it is to be noted, in the same
proportion as actually contributed by each of the individual firms.
Disputes over the sharing of aggregate profit frequently lead to the
break-up of cartels.

Other, looser, forms of cartel like the ORGANIZATION OF PETROLEUM
EXPORTING COUNTRIES, merely jointly determine industry price but not
output quotas.

cash see CURRENCY.

cash and carry a form of wholesaling which requires customers
(predominantly RETAILERS) to pay cash for products bought and to
collect these products themselves from a warehouse.

See DISTRIBUTION CHANNEL.

cash card see COMMERCIAL BANK.

cash discount see DISCOUNT.

cash drain a constraint on the expansion of the MONEY SUPPLY through
BANK DEPOSIT CREATION caused by individuals retaining larger

amounts of cash than usual. This means that not all of the increase in cash calculated by using the reciprocal of the RESERVE ASSET RATIO is passed on from the public back into the banking system. For example, a new deposit of £100 is made into the banking system. Assuming a 10% reserve asset ratio, the average fraction of money held in cash form is one-tenth and the reciprocal 10. Thus ultimately a £1,000 increase in money supply is theoretically possible. However if the public's demand for cash grows then the increase in the money supply will not be 10 times the initial deposit, but something less.

cash flow the money coming into a business from sales and other receipts and going out of the business in the form of cash payments to suppliers, workers, etc.

cash limits a means of controlling public sector spending by setting maximum expenditure totals for government departments or nationalized industries, deliberately making no allowance for inflation.

See GOVERNMENT (PUBLIC) EXPENDITURE.

cash ratio see CASH RESERVE RATIO.

cash reserve ratio the proportion of a COMMERCIAL BANK's total assets which it keeps in the form of *highly* liquid assets to meet day-to-day currency withdrawals by its customers and other financial commitments. The cash reserve ratio comprises TILL MONEY (notes and coins held by the bank) and its operational BALANCES WITH THE BANK OF ENGLAND. The cash reserve ratio is a narrowly defined RESERVE ASSET RATIO which can be used by the monetary authorities to control the MONETARY BASE of the economy.

See BANK DEPOSIT CREATION, MONETARY BASE CONTROL, MONETARY POLICY.

caveat emptor a Latin phrase meaning 'let the buyer beware'. Put simply this means that the supplier has no legal obligation to inform buyers about any defects in his goods or services. The onus is on the buyer to determine for himself that the good or service is satisfactory. Compare CAVEAT VENDOR.

caveat vendor a Latin phrase meaning 'let the seller beware'. In brief this means that the supplier may be legally obliged to inform buyers of any defects in his goods or services. Compare CAVEAT EMPTOR.

census a comprehensive official survey of households or businesses undertaken at regular intervals in order to obtain socio-economic information. In the UK, a *population census* has been carried out every 10 years since 1891 to provide information on demographic trends. This data is useful to the government in the planning of housing, education and welfare services. A *production census* is carried out annually to provide details of industrial production, employment, investment, etc. A *distribution census* provides data about wholesaling and retailing. This information can be used by the government in formulating its economic and industrial policies.

central bank a country's leading BANK which acts as banker to the government and the BANKING SYSTEM and acts as the authority responsible for implementing the government's MONETARY POLICY. Central banks such as the Bank of England in the UK handle the government's financial accounts in conjunction with the TREASURY, taking in receipts from taxation and the sale of government assets, and making disbursements to the various government departments to fund their activities. The central bank acts as the government's broker in its borrowing and lending operations, issuing and dealing in government BONDS and TREASURY BILLS to underpin its year-to-year budgetary position and management of the country's NATIONAL DEBT.

COMMERCIAL BANKS hold accounts with the central bank and, in its rôle as banker to the banking system, the central bank makes it possible for banks to settle their indebtedness with one another by adjusting their accounts as appropriate (see CLEARING HOUSE SYSTEM).

The Bank of England and its satellite, the Royal Mint, are responsible for issuing the country's basic stock of money – LEGAL TENDER consisting of bank notes and coins (see MONEY SUPPLY). The central bank occupies a key rôle in the management of the money supply, influencing the level of bank deposits and credit creation by the financial institutions, particularly commercial banks, as well as the structure of INTEREST RATES in the economy, through buying and selling operations in the market for short- and long-dated financial securities, and acts as LENDER OF LAST RESORT to the banking system. See DISCOUNT MARKET, STOCK EXCHANGE.

The central bank is also responsible for managing the country's EXCHANGE RATE and holding the country's stock of INTERNATIONAL RESERVES to be used in the financing of balance of payments deficits. The Bank of England operates a 'Foreign Exchange Equalization Account' which it uses to intervene in the FOREIGN EXCHANGE MARKET, buying and selling currencies to support the exchange rate at a particular level or to ensure that it falls (depreciates) or rises (appreciates) in an 'orderly' manner.

The main central banks are the Bank of England, Federal Reserve (USA), Banque de France and Deutsche Bundesbank (Germany). These vary in the degree of closeness of their relationship to government, the Bank of England being owned and closely controlled by the government, whereas the Bundesbank operates fairly autonomously. See BANK DEPOSIT CREATION.

centralization the concentration of economic decision-making centrally rather than diffusing such decision-making to many different decision-makers. In a country, this is achieved by the adoption of a CENTRALLY PLANNED ECONOMY where the State undertakes to own, control and direct resources into particular uses. In a firm, centraliz-ation involves top managers retaining authority to make all major decisions and issuing detailed instructions to particular divisions and departments.

See U-FORM ORGANIZATION.

centrally planned economy or **command economy** or **collectiv-ism** a method of organizing the economy to produce goods and services. Under this ECONOMIC SYSTEM economic decision-making is centralized in the hands of the state with collective ownership of the means of production, (except labour). It is the state which decides what goods and services are to be produced in accordance with its centralized NATIONAL PLAN. Resources are allocated between produc-ing units, and final outputs between customers by the use of physical quotas.

The main rationale underlying State ownership of industry is the view that the collective ownership of the means of production 'by the people for the people' is preferable to a situation in which the ownership of the means of production is in the hands of the 'capitalist class' who are able to exploit their élite position to the detriment of the populace at large. State control of industry enables the economy as a whole to be organized in accordance with some central plan, which by interlocking and synchronizing the input-output require-ments of industry is able to secure an efficient allocation of productive resources. Critics of State-owned economic systems argue, however, that in practice they tend to be 'captured and corrupted' by powerful State officials, and that their top-heavy bureaucratic structures result in a highly inefficient organization of production and insensitivity to what customers actually want.

See PRIVATE-ENTERPRISE ECONOMY, MIXED ECONOMY, NATIONALIZ-ATION, COMMUNISM.

Central Statistical Office (CSO) a UK government department responsible for the collection, analysis and publication of national economic statistics such as the NATIONAL INCOME ACCOUNTS and BALANCE-OF-PAYMENTS accounts.

certificate a document signifying ownership of a FINANCIAL SECURITY (STOCK, SHARE, etc.). In the UK such certificates are issued in the name of the person or company recorded in the company's register of SHAREHOLDERS as the owner of these shares, new certificates being issued to buyers when shares are sold. In countries like the USA, where BEARER BONDS are used, stock certificates merely note the number of stocks or shares represented, and do not include the name of the owners, the holder of the certificate being presumed to be the owner.

certificate of deposit a FINANCIAL SECURITY issued by BANKS, BUILD-ING SOCIETIES and other financial institutions as a means of borrowing money for periods ranging from one month to five years. Once issued, certificates of deposit may be bought and sold on the MONEY MARKET and are redeemable on their maturity for their face value plus accrued interest.

certificate of incorporation a certificate issued by the COMPANY REGISTRAR to a new JOINT-STOCK COMPANY whose MEMORANDUM OF ASSOCIATION and ARTICLES OF ASSOCIATION are acceptable to the Registrar. A company starts its legal existence from the date of its incorporation and thereafter is able to enter into contracts, etc. in its own name.

certificate of origin a document used to authenticate the country of origin of internationally traded goods. Most trading countries are prepared to accept certificates of origin issued by government departments of their trade partners or their appointees (CHAMBERS OF COMMERCE in the UK). However, complications as to their precise country of origin often arise in the case of goods which are assembled in one country using components which are in the main imported from others.

See LOCAL CONTENT RULE, EXPORT.

ceteris paribus a Latin term meaning 'other things being equal' which is widely used in economic analysis as an expository technique. It allows us to isolate the relationship between two variables. For example, in demand analysis, the DEMAND CURVE shows the effect of a change in the price of a product on the quantity demanded on the assumption that all of the 'other things' (incomes, tastes, etc.) influencing the demand for that product remain unchanged.

chain store a multibranch retail firm. All types of retailer, ranging from SPECIALIST SHOPS to DEPARTMENT STORES, can be organized to take advantage of the economies of HORIZONTAL INTEGRATION. Unlike single-shop concerns, chain stores are able to maximize their sales potential through geographical spread and maximize their competitive advantage by being able to secure BULK BUYING price concessions from manufacturers and the supply of OWN LABEL BRANDS. See SUPERMARKET, DISCOUNT STORE, COOPERATIVE, DO-IT-YOURSELF STORE, RETAILER, DISTRIBUTION CHANNEL.

Chamberlin, Edward (1899–1967) an American economist who helped develop the theory of MONOPOLISTIC COMPETITION in his book *The Theory of Monopolistic Competition*. Prior to Chamberlin's work economists classified markets into two groups: (a) perfect competition where firm's products are perfect substitutes; (b) monopoly, where a firm's product has no substitutes. Chamberlin argued that in real markets goods are often partial substitutes for other goods, so that even in markets with many sellers the individual firm's demand curve might be downward sloping. He then proceeded to analyse the firm's price and output decisions under such conditions and derive the implications for market supply and price. See also ROBINSON.

Chamber of Commerce an organization which operates primarily to serve the needs of the business community in an industrial city or area. Chambers of Commerce provide a forum for local businessmen and traders to discuss matters of mutual interest and provide a range of services to their members, especially small businesses, including, for example, in the UK, information on business opportunities locally and nationally and, in conjunction with the DEPARTMENT OF TRADE AND INDUSTRY, export advisory services, export market intelligence, etc.

change in demand see DEMAND CURVE (SHIFT IN).

change in supply see SUPPLY CURVE (SHIFT IN).

cheap money a government policy whereby the CENTRAL BANK is authorized to purchase government BONDS on the open market to facilitate an increase in the MONEY SUPPLY (see MONETARY POLICY).

The increase in money supply serves to reduce INTEREST RATES which encourages INVESTMENT because previously unprofitable investments now become profitable due to the reduced cost of borrowing (see MARGINAL EFFICIENCY OF CAPITAL/INVESTMENT).

Cheap money policy, through MONEY SUPPLY/SPENDING LINKAGES, increases AGGREGATE DEMAND. Contrast TIGHT MONEY.

See LIQUIDITY TRAP.

cheque a means of transferring or withdrawing money from a BANK or BUILDING SOCIETY current account. In the former case, the drawer of a cheque creates a written instruction to his bank or building society to transfer funds to some other person's or company's bank or building society account (the 'payee'). In the latter case, money may be withdrawn in cash by a person or company writing out a cheque payable to themselves. Cheques may be 'open', in which case they may be used to draw cash, or 'crossed' with two parallel lines, in which case they cannot be presented for cash but must be paid into the account of the payee.

See COMMERCIAL BANK.

cheque card see COMMERCIAL BANK.

Chicago school a group of economists at Chicago University, most notable of whom is Milton FRIEDMAN, who have adopted and refined the QUANTITY THEORY OF MONEY, arguing the need for governments to control the growth of the MONEY SUPPLY over the long term. Within the broad parameters set by stable money growth the Chicago school stresses the importance of the market system as an allocative mechanism, leaving consumers free to make economic decisions with minimal government interference. See MONETARISM.

Chinese wall the segregation of the stockbroking, jobbing (see MARKET MAKER), fund management, etc., activities of a financial institution in order to protect the interest of its clients. For example, the same institution could be responsible for making a market in a particular financial security, while at the same time offering investment advice to clients to purchase this security, with the danger that the advice given will not be impartial. See CITY CODE.

choice the necessity for CENTRALLY PLANNED ECONOMIES and PRIVATE ENTERPRISE ECONOMIES to have to choose which goods and services to produce and in what quantities, arising from the relative SCARCITY of economic resources (FACTORS OF PRODUCTION) available to produce those goods and services. See ECONOMICS, PREFERENCES.

c.i.f., *abbrev. for* cost-insurance-freight, i.e. charges which are incurred in transporting imports and exports of goods from one country to another. In BALANCE OF PAYMENTS terms c.i.f. charges are added to the basic prices of imports and exports of goods in order to compute the total foreign currency flows involved. See F.O.B.

circular flow of national income model a simplified exposition of money and physical or real flows through the economy which serves as the basis for macroeconomic analysis. In Fig. 22a (overleaf), the solid lines show how, in monetary terms, HOUSEHOLDS purchase goods and services from BUSINESSES using income received from supplying factor inputs to businesses (CONSUMPTION EXPENDITURE). In physical terms (shown by the broken lines), businesses produce goods and services using factor inputs supplied to them by households.

The basic model can be developed to incorporate a number of 'INJECTIONS' to, and 'WITHDRAWALS' from, the income flow. In Fig. 22b, not all of the income received by households is spent – some is saved. SAVINGS is a 'withdrawal' from the income flow. INVESTMENT expenditure 'injects' funds into the income flow. Part of the income accruing to households is taxed by the government and serves to reduce disposable income available for consumption expenditure. TAXATION is a 'withdrawal' from the income flow. GOVERNMENT EXPENDITURE on products and factor inputs 'injects' funds into the income flow. Households spend some of their income on imported goods and services. IMPORTS are a 'withdrawal' from the income flow. On the other hand, some output is sold to overseas customers. EXPORTS represent a demand for domestically produced goods and services and hence constitute an 'injection' into the income flow. See also AGGREGATE DEMAND, EQUILIBRIUM LEVEL OF NATIONAL INCOME MODEL.

City code a regulatory system operated voluntarily by interested parties to the UK STOCK EXCHANGE that lays down 'rules of good conduct' governing the tactics and procedures used in TAKEOVER BIDS and MERGERS. The general purpose of the code is to ensure that all SHAREHOLDERS (both the shareholders of the firm planning the takeover and those of the target firm) are treated equitably, and that

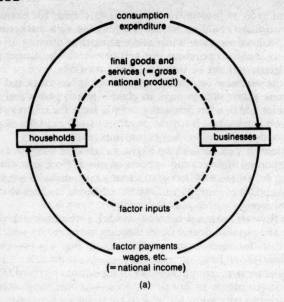

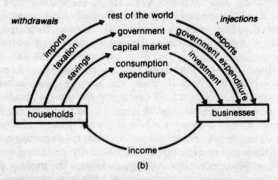

Fig. 22. **Circular flow of national income model.** (a) The basic model of the relationship between money flows and physical flows. (b) A more complex model, incorporating injections to and withdrawals from the income flow.

the parties involved in arranging a takeover bid do not abuse privileged 'insider' information, or misuse such tactics as CONCERT PARTIES, DAWN RAIDS and CHINESE WALLS.

The City code is administered by the *City Panel on Takeovers and Mergers*, which is responsible for formulating rules of practice and for investigating suspected cases of malpractice.

See also INSIDER TRADING.

City (of London) the centre of the UK's FINANCIAL SYSTEM, embracing the MONEY MARKETS (commercial banks, etc.) CAPITAL MARKET (STOCK EXCHANGE), FOREIGN EXCHANGE MARKET, COMMODITY MARKETS and INSURANCE MARKETS. The City of London is also a major international financial centre and earns Britain substantial amounts of foreign exchange on exports of financial services.

City Panel on Takeovers and Mergers see CITY CODE.

classical economics a school of thought or a set of economic ideas based on the writings of SMITH, RICARDO, MILL, etc., which dominated economic thinking until about 1870, when the 'marginalist revolution' occurred.

The classical economists saw the essence of the economic problem as one of producing and distributing the economic wealth created between landowners, labour and capitalists; and were concerned to show how the interplay of separate decisions by workers and capitalists could be harmonized through the market system to generate economic wealth. Their belief in the power of market forces led them to support LAISSEZ-FAIRE and they also supported the idea of FREE TRADE between nations. After about 1870 classical economic ideas receded as the emphasis shifted to what has become known as NEO-CLASSICAL ECONOMIC ANALYSIS, embodying marginalist concepts.

Classical economists denied any possibility of UNEMPLOYMENT caused by deficient AGGREGATE DEMAND, arguing that market forces would operate to keep aggregate demand and POTENTIAL GROSS NATIONAL PRODUCT in balance (SAY'S LAW). Specifically they argued that business recessions would cause interest rates to fall under the pressure of accumulating savings, so encouraging businesses to borrow and invest more; and would cause wage rates to fall under the pressure of rising unemployment, so encouraging businessmen to employ more workers.

See LABOUR THEORY OF VALUE, KEYNES, PRIVATE ENTERPRISE ECONOMY.

clearing bank see COMMERCIAL BANK.

clearing house system a centralized mechanism for settling indebtedness between financial institutions involved in money transmission and dealers in commodities and financial securities. For example, in the case of UK commercial banking, when a customer of bank A draws a cheque in favour of a customer of bank B, and the second customer pays in the cheque to bank B, then bank A is indebted to bank B for the amount of that cheque. There will be many thousands of similar transactions going on day-by-day, creating indebtedness between all banks. The London Clearing House brings together all of these cheques, crosscancels them and determines at the end of each day any net indebtedness between the banks. This net indebtedness is then settled by transferring balances held by the COMMERCIAL BANKS at the CENTRAL BANK (Bank of England).

A similar 'clearing' function is performed in the commodities and financial securities market by, for example, the International Commodities Clearing House and the London Financial Futures Exchange.

See STOCK EXCHANGE, FUTURES MARKET, COMMODITY MARKET.

closed economy an economy that is not influenced by any form of INTERNATIONAL TRADE, that is, there are no EXPORTS or IMPORTS of any kind. By concentrating on a closed economy it is possible to simplify the CIRCULAR FLOW OF NATIONAL INCOME MODEL and focus upon income and expenditure within an economy.

In terms of the circular flow, AGGREGATE DEMAND in a closed economy is represented by:

$$Y = C + I + G \qquad \text{where } Y = \text{national income}$$
$$C = \text{consumption expenditure}$$
$$I = \text{investment expenditure}$$
$$G = \text{government expenditure}$$

By contrast, the OPEN ECONOMY allows for the influence of imports and exports and here aggregate demand is represented in the circular flow as:

$$Y = C + I + G + (X - M) \qquad \text{where } X = \text{exports}$$
$$M = \text{imports}$$

closed shop a requirement that all employees in a given workplace or ORGANIZATION be members of a specified TRADE UNION. Closed shops are often imposed by powerful trade unions as a means of restricting the supply of labour and maintaining high wage rates for members.

See SUPPLY-SIDE ECONOMICS.

club principle a means of allocating the common overhead costs incurred in providing a good or service to each individual consumer. For example, residents may create a club to arrange for the resurfacing of a private road. See COLLECTIVE PRODUCTS, FREE-RIDER.

Cobb-Douglas production function a particular physical relationship between OUTPUT of products and FACTOR INPUTS (LABOUR and CAPITAL) used to produce these outputs. This particular form of the PRODUCTION FUNCTION suggests that where there is effective competition in factor markets the ELASTICITY OF TECHNICAL SUBSTITUTION between labour and capital will be equal to one; that is, labour can be substituted for capital in any given proportions and vice versa, without affecting output.

The Cobb-Douglas production function suggests that the share of labour input and the share of capital input are relative constants in an economy, so that although labour and capital inputs may change in absolute terms, the *relative* share between the two inputs remains constant.

See PRODUCTION POSSIBILITY BOUNDARY, CAPITAL–LABOUR RATIO, PRODUCTION FUNCTION, CAPITAL–INTENSIVE FIRM/INDUSTRY, LABOUR-INTENSIVE FIRM/INDUSTRY, ISOQUANT CURVE, ISOQUANT MAP.

cobweb theorem a theory designed to explain the path followed in moving toward an equilibrium situation when there are lags in the adjustment of either SUPPLY or DEMAND to changes in prices. COMPARATIVE STATIC EQUILIBRIUM ANALYSIS predicts the effect of demand or supply changes by comparing the original equilibrium price and quantity with the new equilibrium which results. The cobweb theorem focuses upon the dynamic process of adjustment in markets by tracing the path of adjustment of prices and output in moving from one equilibrium situation toward another (see DYNAMIC ANALYSIS).

The cobweb theorem is generally used to describe oscillations in prices in agricultural markets where the delay between, for example, planting and harvesting means that supply reacts to prices with a time lag. The simplest case where current quantity demanded responds to current price while current quantity supplied depends upon price in the previous period is depicted in Fig. 23. In the Fig., D_t denotes quantity demanded in the current period, S_t denotes quantity supplied, while price is denoted by P_t, and price in the previous period is denoted by P_{t-1}. If demand were to fall rapidly such that the demand curve shifted left from D_t to D^1_t then comparative static analysis suggest that the market will eventually move from equilibrium point E (with price OP_1 and quantity OQ_1). to equilibrium point E^1 (with price OP_4 and quantity OQ_4). Dynamic analysis suggest that the path followed will be less direct than this.

Starting from the original equilibrium price OP_1, which has prevailed in years $t-1$ and t, farmers will have planned to produce quantity OQ_1. However, after the contraction in demand in year t, supply will exceed demand by QQ_1, and in order to sell all the quantity OQ_1 coming onto the market, price has to fall to OP_2. The lower price OP_2 which prevails in year t will discourage farmers from producing and they will reduce acreage devoted to this crop so that in the next year $t+1$ a much smaller quantity OQ_2 is supplied.

In year $t+1$, and at price OP_2, demand now exceeds supply by the amount $Q_1 Q_2$, and in order to ration the limited supply OQ_2 which is available price will rise to OP_3. This higher price in year $t+1$ will encourage farmers to increase their acreage planted so that in the following year $t+2$, a larger quantity OQ_3 will be supplied which means that in year $t+2$ supply exceeds demand and price will fall below OP₃ which will discourage planting for the following year, and so on. The eventual result of this process of adjustment is that a new equilibrium is achieved at E¹ but only after a series of fluctuating prices in intermediate periods are experienced. See AGRI-CULTURAL POLICY.

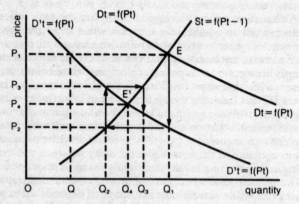

Fig. 23. **Cobweb theorem**. See entry.

coin the metallic CURRENCY which forms part of a country's MONEY SUPPLY. Various metals have been used for coinage purposes. Formerly, gold and silver were commonly used but these have now been replaced in most countries by copper, brass and nickel. Coins in the main constitute the 'low value' part of the money supply.
See MINT, LEGAL TENDER.

collateral security the ASSETS pledged by a BORROWER as security for a LOAN, for example, the title deeds of a house. In the event of the borrower defaulting on the loan the LENDER can claim these assets in lieu of the sum owed. See DEBT, DEBTOR.

collective bargaining the negotiation of PAY, conditions of employment, etc. by representatives of the labour force (usually trade union officials) and management. Collective bargaining agreements are negotiated at a number of different levels ranging from local union branches and a single factory to general unions and an entire industry.

Increasingly, plant- and company-level collective bargaining has dealt with PRODUCTIVITY as well as wages and conditions, with trade unions and the workforce offering to relax RESTRICTIVE LABOUR PRAC-TICES in return for improved wages and conditions. Such relaxations allow the firm to utilize labour more efficiently and flexibly, helping to improve the competitiveness of the firm.

Industry-wide bargaining can have inflationary consequences when trade unions use comparability arguments for wage increases with high percentage wage increases in industries which have experienced large productivity gains being extended on comparability grounds to other industries where the increases are not entirely justified on efficiency grounds. The selective use of comparability arguments for wage increases and pressures to maintain traditional WAGE DIFFEREN-TIALS can lead to COST PUSH INFLATION.

See TRADE UNION, INDUSTRIAL RELATIONS, INDUSTRIAL DISPUTE.

collective products any goods or services that cannot be provided other than on a group basis because the quantity supplied to any one individual cannot be independently varied. It is virtually impossible to get consumers to reveal their preferences regarding collective goods because rational consumers will attempt to become FREE-RIDERS, each understating his demand in the hope of avoiding his share of the cost without affecting the quantity he obtains. Consequently such products cannot be marketed in the conventional way and we cannot use market prices to value them. Many goods and services supplied by government are of a collective nature, for example, national defence and police protection, and here government decides on the amounts of such products to provide and compels individuals to pay for them through taxation. See CLUB PRINCIPLE, SOCIAL PRODUCTS.

collectivism see CENTRALLY PLANNED ECONOMY.

collusion a form of INTERFIRM CONDUCT pattern in which firms arrive at an agreement or 'understanding' covering their market actions. Successful collusion requires the acceptance of a common objective for all firms (for example, JOINT-PROFIT MAXIMIZATION) and the suppression of behaviour inconsistent with the achievement of this goal (for example, price competition). Collusion may be either overt or tacit. Overt collusion usually takes the form of either an express agreement in writing or an express oral agreement arrived at through direct consultation between the firms concerned. Alternatively, collusion may take the form of an 'unspoken understanding' arrived at through firms' repeated experiences with each other's behaviour over time.

The purpose of collusion may be jointly to monopolize the supply of a product in order to extract MONOPOLY profits, or it may be a 'defensive' response to poor trading conditions, seeking to prevent prices from dropping to uneconomic levels. Because, however, of its generally adverse effects on market efficiency (cushioning inefficient, high-cost suppliers), and because it deprives buyers of the benefits of competition (particularly lower prices), collusion is either prohibited outright by COMPETITION POLICY or permitted, as in the UK, to continue only in exceptional circumstances.

See CARTEL, RESTRICTIVE TRADE AGREEMENT, OLIGOPOLY, DUOPOLY, INFORMATION AGREEMENT, RESTRICTIVE PRACTICES COURT.

COLLUSIVE DUOPOLY

collusive duopoly see DUOPOLY.

comecon see COUNCIL FOR MUTUAL ECONOMIC ASSISTANCE.

command economy see CENTRALLY PLANNED ECONOMY.

commercial bank or **clearing bank** a BANK which accepts deposits of money from customers and provides them with a payments transmission service (CHEQUES), together with saving and loan facilities.

Commercial banking in the UK is conducted on the basis of an interlocking 'branch' network system which caters for local and regional needs as well as allowing the major banks such as Barclays and NatWest to cover the national market. Increasingly, the leading banks have globalized their operations to provide traditional banking services to international companies as well as diversifying into a range of related financial services such as the provision of MORTGAGES, INSURANCE and UNIT TRUST investment and SHARE PURCHASE/SALE.

Bank deposits are of two types: (a) sight deposits, or *current account* deposits, which are withdrawable on demand and which are used by depositors to finance day-to-day personal and business transactions as well as to pay regular commitments such as instalment credit repayments. Most banks now pay interest on outstanding current account balances.

(b) time deposits, or *deposit accounts*, which are usually withdrawable subject to some notice being given to the bank and which are held as a form of personal and corporate saving and to finance irregular, 'one-off' payments. Interest is payable on deposit accounts, normally at rates above those paid on current accounts, in order to encourage clients to deposit money for longer periods of time, thereby providing the bank with a more stable financial base.

Customers requiring to draw on their bank deposits may do so in a number of ways: direct cash withdrawals are still popular and have been augmented by the use of *cheque/cash cards* for greater convenience (i.e. cheque/cash cards can be used to draw cash from a dispensing machine outside normal business hours). However, the greater proportion of banking transactions is undertaken by cheque and CREDIT CARD payments and by such facilities as 'standing orders' and 'direct debits'. Payment by cheque is the commonest form of non-cash payment involving the drawer detailing the person or business to receive payment and authorizing his bank to make payment by signing the cheque, with the recipient then depositing the cheque with his own bank. Cheques are 'cleared' through an inter-bank CLEARING HOUSE SYSTEM with customers' accounts being debited and credited as appropriate. Credit cards enable a client of the bank to make a number of individual purchases of goods and services on CREDIT over a particular period of time which are then settled by a single debit to the person's current account or, alternatively, paid off on a loan basis (see below).

Under a standing order arrangement, a depositor instructs his bank to pay from his account a regular fixed sum of money into the account of a person or firm he is indebted to, again involving the respective debiting and crediting of the two accounts concerned. In the case of a direct debit, the customer authorizes the person or firm to whom he is indebted to arrange with his bank for the required regular payment to be transferred from his account.

Commercial banks make *loans* to personal borrowers to finance the purchase of a variety of products, while they are a major source of WORKING CAPITAL finance for businesses covering the purchase of short-term assets such as materials and components and the financing of work-in-progress and the stockholding of final products. Loans may be for a specified amount and may be made available for fixed periods of time at agreed rates of interest, or may take the form of an *overdraft* facility, where the person or firm can borrow as much as they require up to a pre-arranged total amount and is charged interest on outstanding balances.

A commercial bank has the dual objective of being able to meet currency withdrawals on demand and of putting its funds to profitable use. This influences the pattern of its asset holdings; a proportion of its funds are held in a highly liquid form (the RESERVE ASSET RATIO), including TILL MONEY, BALANCES WITH THE BANK OF ENGLAND, CALL MONEY with the DISCOUNT MARKET, BILLS OF EXCHANGE and TREASURY BILLS. These liquid assets enable the bank to meet any immediate cash requirements that its customers might make, thereby preserving public confidence in the bank as a safe repository for deposits. The remainder of the bank's funds are used to earn profits from portfolio investments in public sector securities and fixed-interest corporate securities, together with loans and overdrafts.

BANK DEPOSITS are a key element in the MONEY SUPPLY. See BANK DEPOSIT CREATION, MONETARY POLICY, FINANCIAL SYSTEM.

commission 1. payments to AGENTS for performing services on behalf of a seller or buyer. Commissions are usually based on the value of the product being sold or bought. Examples of commissions include salespersons' commissions, estate agents' fees and insurance brokers' commissions.

2. a body which acts as an 'official' regulatory or administrative authority with respect to a specified activity. For example, the MONOPOLIES AND MERGERS COMMISSION hears cases of monopolies, mergers and anti-competitive practices referred to it by the Office of Fair Trading under UK competition policy. The European Commission is the main body responsible for the day-to-day administration of the affairs of the EUROPEAN COMMUNITY.

commodity 1. see GOODS.

2. raw materials rather than goods in general: for example, tea, coffee, iron ore, aluminium, etc.

commodity broker a dealer in raw materials. See COMMODITY MARKET.

commodity market a market for the buying and selling of agricultural produce and minerals such as coffee and tin. Commodity business is conducted through various international commodity exchanges, some of the more prominent ones being based in London, for example the London Metal Exchange and the London International Financial Futures Exchange.

Commodity markets provide an organizational framework for the establishment of market prices and 'clearing' deals between buyers and sellers (see CLEARING HOUSE SYSTEM). Commodity dealers and brokers act as intermediaries between buyers and sellers wishing to conclude immediate spot transactions (see SPOT MARKET) or to buy or sell forward (see FUTURES MARKET).

Common Agricultural Policy (CAP) the policy of the EUROPEAN COMMUNITY (EC) for assisting the farm sector. The main aims of the CAP are fair living standards for farmers and an improvement in agricultural efficiency (see AGRICULTURAL POLICY).

The CAP is administered by the European Agricultural Guidance and Guarantee Fund, with major policy and operational decisions (e.g., the fixing of annual farm prices) residing in the hands of the Council of Ministers of the EC. The farm sector is assisted in four main ways:

(a) around 70 – 75% of EC farm produce benefits directly from the operation of a PRICE SUPPORT system which maintains EC farm prices at levels in excess of world market prices. The prices of milk, cereals, butter, sugar, pork, beef, veal, certain fruits and vegetables and table wine are fixed annually, and once determined are then maintained at this level by support buying of output which is not bought in the market. MONETARY COMPENSATION AMOUNTS are used to convert the common price for each product into national currencies and to realign prices when the exchange rates of member's currencies change.

(b) Variable TARIFF rates are used to increase import prices to internal price-support levels in the cases of the products referred to above, thus ensuring that EC output is fully competitive. The 25% of EC farm produce which is not subject to direct price-support relies entirely on tariff protection to maintain high domestic prices.

(c) EXPORT SUBSIDIES are used to enable EC farmers to lower their export prices and thus compete successfully in world markets.

(d) Grants are given to facilitate farm modernization and improvements as a means of improving agricultural efficiency.

The CAP is the largest single component of the EC's total budget. In 1995 it accounted for 52% of total EC spending. Over 90% of the CAP's budget in recent years has been spent on price-support and export subsidies.

Although the CAP can claim a number of successes, most notably the attainment of EC self-sufficiency in many food products, critics complain it has many drawbacks: consumers lose out because they are required to pay unnecessarily high prices for food products; resources are misallocated because inefficient, high cost farmers are over protected, and too little of the CAP's resources are devoted to long-term structural reform and modernization of the sector; artificially high prices supported by intervention buying encourages gross overproduction and results in large surpluses ('mountains') of produce which is expensive to stockpile and difficult to sell off; subsidized exports from the EC can depress world farm prices making life even more difficult for the less-developed countries, many of whom (specifically non-LOMÉ AGREEMENT countries) had already been hard hit by the trade diversionary effects of the EC (see TRADE DIVERSION). See INCOME SUPPORT, GENERAL AGREEMENT ON TARIFFS AND TRADE.

common external tariff see CUSTOMS UNION, COMMON MARKET.

common law the body of law built-up over many years as a result of previous court decisions interpreting legislation. These establish legal precedents which then need to be followed consistently in subsequent court cases. Compare STATUTE LAW.

common market a form of TRADE INTEGRATION between a number of countries in which members eliminate all trade barriers (TARIFFS, etc.) amongst themselves on goods and services and establish a uniform set of barriers against trade with the rest of the world, in particular, a common external tariff (see CUSTOMS UNION). In addition, a common market provides for the free movement of labour and capital across national boundaries. The aim of a common market is to secure the benefits of international SPECIALIZATION, thereby improving members' real living standards.

The short and medium-term impact of the formation of a common market is mainly felt through an increase in trade between member countries. TRADE CREATION is typically associated with a reallocation of resources within the market favouring least-cost supply locations and a reduction in prices resulting from the elimination of tariffs and lower production costs. (See GAINS FROM TRADE.)

In addition, a common market can be expected to promote longer-term (dynamic) changes conducive to economic efficiency through:

(a) COMPETITION. The removal of tariffs, etc., can be expected to widen the area of effective competition; high-cost producers are eliminated, while efficient and progressive suppliers are able to exploit new market opportunities.

(b) ECONOMIES OF SCALE. A larger 'home' market enables firms to take advantage of economies of large scale production and distribution, thereby lowering supply costs and enhancing COMPARATIVE ADVANTAGE.

(c) TECHNOLOGICAL PROGRESSIVENESS. Wider market opportunities and exposure to greater competition can be expected to encourage firms to invest and innovate new techniques and products.

(d) INVESTMENT and ECONOMIC GROWTH. Finally, the 'virtuous' circle of rising income per head, growing trade, increased productive efficiency and investment may be expected to combine to produce higher growth rates and real standards of living.

The EUROPEAN COMMUNITY is one example of a common market.

communism a political and economic doctrine which advocates that the state should own all property and organize all the functions of PRODUCTION and EXCHANGE, including LABOUR. Karl MARX succinctly stated his idea of communism as 'from each according to his ability, to each according to his needs'. Communism involves a CENTRALLY PLANNED ECONOMY where strategic decisions concerning production and distribution are taken by government as opposed to being determined by the PRICE SYSTEM as in a market based PRIVATE ENTERPRISE ECONOMY. China still organizes its economy along communist lines, but in recent years Russia and other former Soviet Union countries and various East European countries have moved away from communism to more market-based economies.

community charge see LOCAL TAX.

company see FIRM.

company formation the process of forming a JOINT-STOCK COMPANY, which involves a number of steps: (a) the drawing up of a MEMORANDUM OF ASSOCIATION; (b) the preparation of ARTICLES OF ASSOCIATION; (c) application to the COMPANY REGISTRAR for a CERTIFICATE OF INCORPORATION; (d) issue SHARE CAPITAL; (e) the commencement of trading.

company laws a body of legislation providing for the regulation of JOINT-STOCK COMPANIES. British company law encouraged the development of joint-stock companies by establishing the principle of LIMITED LIABILITY and provides for the protection of SHAREHOLDERS' interests by controlling the formation and financing of companies. The major provisions of UK company law are the 1948, 1976 and 1989 Companies Acts. See ARTICLES OF ASSOCIATION, MEMORANDUM OF ASSOCIATION.

company registrar the officer of a JOINT-STOCK COMPANY who is responsible for maintaining an up-to-date SHARE REGISTER and for issuing new SHARE CERTIFICATES and cancelling old share certificates as shares are bought and sold on the STOCK EXCHANGE.

Many companies, however, have chosen to sub-contract these tasks to specialist institutions, often departments of commercial banks.

The rôle of the company registrar identified above should not be confused with that of the rôle of the government's REGISTRAR OF COMPANIES, who is responsible for supervising *all* joint-stock companies.

comparability an approach to WAGE determination in which levels or increases in wages for a particular group of workers or for an industry are sought or offered through COLLECTIVE BARGAINING which maintains a relationship to those for other occupations or industries. Comparability can lead to COST PUSH INFLATION.

comparative advantage the advantage possessed by a country engaged in INTERNATIONAL TRADE if it can produce a given good at a lower resource input cost than other countries. Also called *comparative cost principle*. This proposition is illustrated in Fig. 24 with respect to two countries (A and B) and two GOODS (X and Y).

The same given resource input in both countries enable them to produce either the quantity of good X or the quantity of good Y indicated in Fig. 24. It can be seen that country B is absolutely more efficient than country A since it can produce more of both goods. However, it is comparative advantage not ABSOLUTE ADVANTAGE which determines whether trade is beneficial or not. Comparative advantage arises because the marginal OPPORTUNITY COSTS of one good in terms of the other differ as between countries (see HECKSCHER-OHLIN FACTOR PROPORTIONS THEORY).

It can be seen that country B has a comparative advantage in the production of good X for it is able to produce it at a lower factor cost than country A; the resource or opportunity cost of producing an additional unit of X is only 2/3 Y in country B, whereas in country A it is 1Y.

Country A has a comparative advantage in the production of good Y for it is able to produce it at lower factor cost than country B; the resource or opportunity cost of producing an additional unit of Y is only 1X, whereas in country B it is 1½X.

Both countries, therefore, stand to increase their economic welfare if they specialize (see SPECIALIZATION) in the production of the good in which they have a comparative advantage (see GAINS FROM TRADE entry for an illustration of this important proposition). The extent to which each will benefit from trade will depend upon the real terms of trade at which they agree to exchange X and Y.

A basic assumption of this presentation is that factor endowments, and hence comparative advantages, are 'fixed'. Dynamically, however, comparative advantage may well change. It may do so in response to a number of influences, including:

(a) the initiation by a country's government of structural programmes leading to resource redeployment. For example, a country which seemingly has a comparative advantage in the supply of primary products such as cotton and wheat may nevertheless abandon or de-emphasize it in favour of a drive towards industrialization and the establishment of comparative advantage in higher value-added manufactured goods;

(b) international capital movements and technology transfer, and relocation of production by MULTINATIONAL COMPANIES. For example, Malaysia developed a comparative advantage in the production of natural rubber only after UK entrepreneurs established and invested in rubber-tree plantations there.

Country	Output of good		Opportunity cost ratio	
	X	Y	X	Y
A	100	100	1 :	1
B	180	120	1 :	$\frac{2}{3}$ (or 1$\frac{1}{2}$:1)

Fig. 24. **Comparative advantage**. The physical output of X and Y from a given factor input, and the opportunity cost of X in terms of Y. The opportunity cost of producing one more unit of X is 1Y in country A, and 2/3Y in country B. The opportunity cost of producing one more unit of Y is 1X in country A, and 1½X in country B.

comparative cost principle see COMPARATIVE ADVANTAGE.

comparative static equilibrium analysis a method of economic analysis which compares the differences between two or more equilibrium states which result from changes in EXOGENEOUS VARIABLES. Consider, for example, the effect of a change in export demand on the EQUILIBRIUM LEVEL OF NATIONAL INCOME as shown in Fig. 25. Assume that foreigners demand more of the country's products. Exports rise and the aggregate demand schedule shifts upwards to a new level (AD$_2$) resulting in the establishment of a new equilibrium level of national income Y$_2$ (at point H). The effect of the increase in exports can then be measured by comparing the original level of national income with that of the new level of national income. See DYNAMIC ANALYSIS, EQUILIBRIUM MARKET PRICE (CHANGES IN).

compensation principle see WELFARE ECONOMICS.

competition 1. a form of MARKET STRUCTURE in which the number of firms supplying the market is used to indicate the type of market it is, e.g. PERFECT COMPETITION (many small competitors), OLIGOPOLY (a few large competitors).

2. a process whereby firms strive against each other to secure customers for their products, i.e., the active rivalry of firms for customers using price variations, PRODUCT DIFFERENTIATION strategies, etc. From a wider public-interest angle, the nature and strength of competition has an important effect on MARKET PERFORMANCE and hence is of particular relevance to the application of COMPETITION POLICY.

See COMPETITION METHODS, MONOPOLISTIC COMPETITION, MONOPOLY.

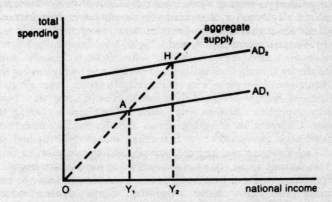

Fig. 25. **Comparative static equilibrium analysis**. The initial level of
national income is Y_1 (at point A) where the AGGREGATE DEMAND SCHED-
ULE (AD$_1$) intersects the AGGREGATE SUPPLY SCHEDULE (AS).

Competition Act 1980 a UK Act which extended UK competition
law by giving the OFFICE OF FAIR TRADING wider powers to deal with
restraints on competition such as EXCLUSIVE DEALING, REFUSAL TO SUP-
PLY, TIE-IN SALES, etc. Previously these practices could only be dealt
with in the context of a full-scale and lengthy monopoly probe,
whereas the Act now allows the OFT to deal with them on a separate
one-off basis.

See COMPETITION POLICY.

competition laws a body of legislation providing for the control of
monopolies, mergers and takeovers, restrictive trade agreements and
anti-competitive practices. UK competition law is contained in a
number of statutes, including the FAIR TRADING ACT, 1973, COMPE-
TITION ACT, 1980, RESTRICTIVE TRADE PRACTICES ACT, 1956, 1968, 1976,
and RESALE PRICES ACT, 1964, 1976. These laws are administered by
the OFFICE OF FAIR TRADING.

In the European Community, competition law is enshrined in
Articles 85 and 86 of the Treaty of Rome and the 1990 Merger Regu-
lation. These laws are administered by the European Commission's
Competition-Directorate.

See COMPETITION POLICY, COMPETITION POLICY (UK), COMPETITION
POLICY (EC).

competition methods an element of MARKET CONDUCT that denotes
the ways in which firms in a MARKET compete against each other.
There are various ways in which firms can compete against each
other:

(a) PRICE. Sellers may attempt to secure buyer support by putting their product on offer at a lower price than that of rivals. They must bear in mind, however, that rivals may simply lower their prices also with the result that all firms finish up with lower profits.

(b) Nonprice competition, including (i) physical-PRODUCT DIFFERENTIATION. Sellers may attempt to differentiate technically similar products by altering their quality and design, and by improving their performance. All these efforts are intended to secure buyer allegiance by causing buyers to regard these products as in some way 'better' than competitive offerings. (ii) *product differentiation via selling techniques*. Competition in selling efforts includes media ADVERTISING, general SALES PROMOTION (free trial offers, money-off coupons), personal sales promotion (representatives), and the creation of distribution outlets. These activities are directed at stimulating demand by emphasizing real and imaginary product attributes relative to competitors. (iii) *New* BRAND *competition*. Given dynamic change (advances in technology, changes in consumer tastes), a firm's existing products stand to become obsolete. A supplier is thus obliged to introduce new brands or redesign existing ones to remain competitive.

(c) *low-cost production* as a means of competition. Though cost-effectiveness is not a direct means of competition, it is an essential way to strengthen the market position of a supplier. The ability to reduce costs opens up the possibility of (unmatched) price cuts, or allows firms to devote greater financial resources to differentiation activity.

See also MONOPOLISTIC COMPETITION, OLIGOPOLY, MARKETING MIX, PRODUCT–CHARACTERISTICS MODEL, PRODUCT LIFE–CYCLE.

competition policy a policy concerned with promoting the efficient use of economic resources and protecting the interests of consumers. The objective of competition policy is to secure an optimal MARKET PERFORMANCE: specifically, least–cost supply, 'fair' prices and profit levels, technological advance and product improvement. Competition policy covers a number of areas, including the monopolization of a market by a single supplier (DOMINANT FIRM), the creation of monopoly positions by MERGERS and TAKEOVERS, COLLUSION between sellers, and ANTICOMPETITIVE PRACTICES.

Competition policy is implemented mainly through the control of MARKET STRUCTURE and MARKET CONDUCT but also, on occasions, through the direct control of market performance itself (by, for example, the stipulation of maximum levels of profit).

There are two basic approaches to the control of market structure and conduct: the nondiscretionary approach and the discretionary approach. The nondiscretionary approach lays down 'acceptable' standards of structure and conduct and prohibits outright any transgression of these standards. Typical ingredients of this latter approach include:

(a) the stipulation of maximum permitted market share limits (say, no more than 20% of the market) in order to limit the degree of SELLER CONCENTRATION and prevent the emergence of a monopoly supplier. Thus, for example, under this ruling any proposed merger or takeover which would take the combined group's market share above the permitted limit would be automatically prohibited.

(b) the outright prohibition of all forms of 'shared monopoly' (RESTRICTIVE TRADE AGREEMENTS, CARTELS) involving price fixing, market sharing, etc.

(c) the outright prohibition of specific practices designed to reduce or eliminate competition, for example, EXCLUSIVE DEALING, REFUSAL TO SUPPLY, etc.

Thus, the nondiscretionary approach attempts to preserve conditions of WORKABLE COMPETITION by a direct attack on the possession and exercise of monopoly power as such.

By contrast, the discretionary approach takes a more pragmatic line, recognizing that often high levels of seller concentration and certain agreements between firms may serve to improve economic efficiency rather than impair it. It is the essence of the discretionary approach that each situation be judged on its own merits rather than be automatically condemned. Thus, under the discretionary approach, mergers, restrictive agreements and specific practices of the kind noted above are evaluated in terms of their possible benefits and detriments. If, on balance, they would appear to be detrimental, then and only then are they prohibited.

The US by and large operates the nondiscretionary approach; the UK has a history of preferring the discretionary approach; while the European Community combines elements of both approaches.

See COMPETITION POLICY (UK), COMPETITION POLICY (EC), PUBLIC INTEREST, WILLIAMSON TRADE-OFF MODEL, OFFICE OF FAIR TRADING, MONOPOLIES AND MERGERS COMMISSION, RESTRICTIVE PRACTICES COURT, HORIZONTAL INTEGRATION, VERTICAL INTEGRATION, DIVERSIFICATION, CONCENTRATION MEASURES.

competition policy (European Community) covers three main areas of application under European Community COMPETITION LAWS:

(a) CARTELS. Articles 85(1) and (2) of the Treaty of Rome prohibit cartel agreements and 'CONCERTED PRACTICES' (i.e. formal and informal collusion) between firms involving price fixing, limitations on production, technical developments and investment, and market sharing whose effect is to restrict competition and trade within the European Community (EC). Certain other agreements (for example, those providing for joint technical research and specialization of production) may be exempted from the general prohibition contained in Articles 85(1) and (2) provided they do not restrict inter-state competition and trade.

(b) MONOPOLIES/DOMINANT FIRMS. Article 86 of the Treaty of Rome prohibits the abuse of a dominant position in the supply of a particular product if this serves to restrict competition and trade within the EC. What constitutes 'abusive' behaviour is similar to the criteria applied in the UK, namely, actions which are unfair or unreasonable towards customers (e.g. PRICE DISCRIMINATION between EC markets), retailers (e.g. REFUSAL TO SUPPLY) and other suppliers (e.g. selective price cuts to eliminate competitors). Firms found guilty by the European Commission of illegal cartelization and the abuse of a dominant position can be fined up to 10% of their annual sales turnover.

(c) MERGERS/TAKEOVERS. The Commission can investigate mergers involving companies with a combined worldwide turnover of over ECU 5 billion (£3.7 bn) if the aggregate EC-wide turnover of the companies concerned is greater than ECU 250 million. Again, the main aim is to prevent mergers likely adversely to affect competition and trade within the EC.

competition policy (UK) covers six main areas of application under UK COMPETITION LAWS:

(a) MONOPOLIES. A monopoly position is defined as a situation where one firm supplies at least one-quarter of a specified good or service (DOMINANT FIRM MONOPOLY), or where two or more firms, supplying collectively at least one-quarter of a specified good or service, pursue policies which restrict competition between them (COMPLEX MONOPOLY). The OFFICE OF FAIR TRADING (OFT) is responsible for referral of selected goods and services monopolies (both private and public sector) to the MONOPOLIES AND MERGERS COMMISSION (MMC) for investigation and report and the implementation (where appropriate) of the MMC's recommendations. Monopoly positions are evaluated by the MMC in terms of whether or not they operate in the 'public interest'.

(b) MERGERS and TAKEOVERS. Mergers and takeovers fall within the ambit of the legislation if they create or intensify a monopoly position (defined by the one-quarter market share rule) or where the value of assets taken over exceeds £70 million. The OFT is responsible, in conjunction with the Secretary of State for Industry, for the referral of selected mergers to the MMC for investigation and report and the implementation (where appropriate) of the MMC's recommendations. Again, the criterion of the 'public interest' is used to assess whether or not a particular merger or takeover is to be allowed to proceed or vetoed.

(c) RESTRICTIVE TRADE AGREEMENTS. Parties to restrictive trade agreements are compulsorily required to register such agreements with the OFT. This applies to (i) all goods and services agreements which contain restrictions (i.e. anti-competitive provisions) relating to prices charged, terms and conditions, qualities and descriptions, processes, areas and persons to be supplied; (ii) INFORMATION AGREEMENTS (goods only) relating to prices and terms and conditions. The OFT is responsible for the referral of agreements to the RESTRICTIVE PRACTICES COURT RPC for investigation and report, and the implementation of the recommendations of the Court. Restrictive agreements are presumed to operate against the 'public interest' and are invariably prohibited unless the parties to them can gain exemption by satisfying the Court that, on balance, they confer net economic benefit.

(d) RESALE PRICE MAINTENANCE (RPM). Manufacturers' stipulation of the resale prices of their products is generally prohibited in the UK, although under the RESALE PRICES ACTS it is possible for a manufacturer to obtain exemption by satisfying the RPC that, on balance, rpm confers net economic benefit. The OFT is responsible for monitoring manufacturers' policies towards retail prices and can take action against 'suspected' cases of manufacturers attempting (illegally) to enforce rpm. Manufacturers can, however, take action against retailers who use their products as LOSS LEADERS.

(e) ANTI-COMPETITIVE PRACTICES. Various trade practices such as EXCLUSIVE DEALING, REFUSAL TO SUPPLY, FULL-LINE FORCING, etc. may be investigated both by the OFT itself and (if necessary) by the MMC, and prohibited if they are found to be unduly restrictive of competition.

(f) CONSUMER PROTECTION. The OFT is also charged with protecting consumers' interests generally, both by taking action against unscrupulous trade practices such as false descriptions of goods and weights and measures, denial of proper rights of guarantee to cover defective goods, etc., and by encouraging groups of suppliers to draw up voluntary codes of 'good' practice.

competitive advantage the possession by a firm of various assets and attributes (low-cost plants, innovative brands, ownership of raw material supplies, etc.) which gives it a competitive edge over rival suppliers. To succeed against competitors in winning customers on a viable (profitable) and sustainable (long-run) basis, a firm must, depending on the nature of the market, be cost-effective and/or able to offer products which customers regard as preferable to the products offered by rival suppliers. The former enables a firm to meet and beat competitors on price, while the latter reflects the firm's ability to establish PRODUCT DIFFERENTIATION advantage over competitors.

See ECONOMIES OF SCALE, EXPERIENCE CURVE, RESEARCH AND DEVELOPMENT.

competitive strategy an aspect of BUSINESS STRATEGY which involves the firm developing policies to meet and beat its competitors in supplying a particular product. This requires the firm to undertake an *internal* appraisal of its resources and capabilities relative to competitors to identify its particular strengths and weaknesses. It also requires the firm to undertake an *external* appraisal of the nature and strength of the various 'forces driving competition' in its chosen markets, namely (a) rivalry amongst existing firms, (b) bargaining power of input suppliers, (c) bargaining power of customers, (d) threat of new entrants and (e) the threat of substitute products. Consideration of the above factors should lead to the formulation of a generic strategy for competitive success based upon either industry-wide cost leadership or PRODUCT DIFFERENTIATION, or a more narrowly focused strategy which aims to build COMPETITIVE ADVANTAGE in a narrower segment of the market.

competitive tender an invitation for private sector firms to submit TENDERS (price bids) for contracts to supply goods or services to the public sector which the public sector have traditionally supplied for themselves. Competitive tendering seeks to introduce competition in the provision of goods or services and thus reduce the costs to government departments, local authorities and health authorities.

See DEREGULATION.

complementary products GOODS or SERVICES whose demands are interrelated (a *joint demand*), so that an increase in the price of one of the goods results in a fall in the demand for the other. For example, if the price of tennis rackets goes up, this results not only in a decrease in the demand for rackets but, because less tennis is now played, a fall also in the demand for tennis balls. See SUBSTITUTE PRODUCTS, CROSS-ELASTICITY OF DEMAND.

complex monopoly a situation defined by UK COMPETITION POLICY as one in which two or more suppliers of a particular product restrict competition between themselves. 'Complex monopoly' in essence refers to an OLIGOPOLY situation where the firms concerned, although pursuing individual (i.e. non-collusive) policies, nonetheless behave in a uniform manner and produce a result which is non-competitive (i.e. similar to COLLUSION). The problem is that it is often difficult to distinguish between competitive and non-competitive situations. For example, if firms charge identical prices, is this reflective of competition (i.e. prices which are brought together *because* of competition) or a deliberate suppression of competition?

compound interest the INTEREST on a LOAN which is based not only on the original amount of the loan but the amount of the loan plus previous accumulated interest. This means that over time interest charges grow exponentially, for example, a £100 loan earning compound interest at 10% per annum would accumulate to £110 at the end of the first year and £121 at the end of the second year, etc., based on the formula:

compound sum = principal $(1 + $ interest rate$)^{\text{number of periods}}$

that is, $121 = 100 (1 + 0.1)^2$. Compare SIMPLE INTEREST.

computer an electronic/electromechanical device which accepts alphabetical and numerical data in a predetermined form, stores and processes this data according to instructions contained in a computer program, and presents the analysed data.

Computers have dramatically improved the productivity of data processing in commerce and business; for example, computer-aided design and computer-aided manufacturing systems have improved the speed and cost with which new components or products can be assigned and subsequently scheduled for production; computer-aided distribution and stock control systems such as ELECTRONIC POINT OF SALE (EPOS) have helped to minimize stockholdings and improved customer services; computers have rapidly taken over the manual tasks of keeping accounting records such as company sales and payroll. Computers have also played a prominent rôle in speeding up the response of commodity and financial markets to changing demand and supply conditions by processing and reporting transactions quickly.

See STOCK EXCHANGE, AUTOMATION, MASS PRODUCTION.

concealed unemployment see DISGUISED UNEMPLOYMENT.

concentration measures the measures of the size distribution of firms engaged in economic activities.

The broadest concentration measure is the *aggregate concentration* measure which looks at the share of total activity in an economy accounted for by the larger firms, for example, the proportion of total industrial output accounted for by the largest 200 firms; or the share of total manufacturing output produced by the 100 largest companies. Various size criteria may be used for this measure, in particular, sales, output, numbers employed and capital employed, each of which can give slightly different results because of differences in capital intensity. Such measures serve to give an overall national view of concentration and how it is changing over time.

Though aggregate concentration measures are useful they are generally too broad for purposes of economic analysis where interest focuses upon markets and performance in these markets. Consequently economists have developed several measures of MARKET concentration which seek to measure SELLER or BUYER CONCENTRATION. The most common of these measures is the CONCENTRATION RATIO, which records the percentage of a market's sales accounted for by a given number of the largest firms in that market. In the UK it has been usual to estimate the concentration ratio for the three or (more recently) five largest firms; whereas in the US the four-firm concentration ratio tends to be employed.

However, the concentration ratio only records seller concentration at one point along the cumulative concentration curve, as Fig. 26a

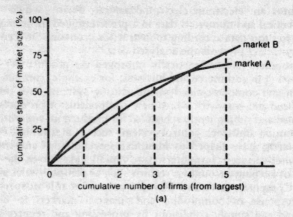

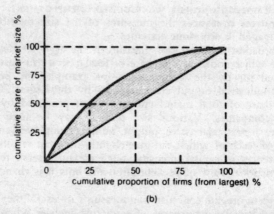

Fig. 26. **Concentration measures.** (a) Cumulative concentration curves, showing the cumulative share of market size accounted for by various (cumulative) *numbers* of firms. (b) The Lorenz curve shows the cumulative share of market size on one axis accounted for by various (cumulative) *percentages* of the number of firms in the market.

indicates. This makes it difficult to compare concentration curves for two different markets, like A and B in the figure, where their concentration curves intersect. For example, using a three-firm concentration ratio, market A is more concentrated while using a five-firm ratio shows market B to be more concentrated. An alternative concentration index called the HERFINDAHL INDEX gets around this problem by taking into account the number and market shares of all firms in the market. The Herfindahl index is calculated by summing the squared market shares of all firms. The index can vary between a value of zero (where there are a large number of equally-sized firms) and one (where there is just one firm).

Concentration measures like the concentration ratio and the Herfindahl index are known as *absolute concentration* measures since they are concerned with the market shares of a given (absolute) number of firms. By contrast, *relative concentration measures* are concerned with inequalities in the share of total firms producing for the market. Such irregularities can be recorded in the form of a Lorenz curve as in Fig. 26b. The diagonal straight line shows what a distribution of complete equality in firm shares would look like, so the extent to which the Lorenz curve deviates from this line gives an indication of relative seller concentration. For example, the diagonal line shows how we might expect 50% of market sales to be accounted for by 50% of the total firms, whilst in fact 50% of market sales are accounted for by the largest 25% of total firms, as the Lorenz curve indicates. The *Gini coefficient* provides a summary measure of the extent to which the Lorenz curve for a particular market deviates from the linear diagonal. It indicates the extent of the bow-shaped area in the Fig. by dividing the shaded area below the Lorenz curve by the area above the line of equality. The value of the Gini coefficient ranges from zero (complete equality) to one (complete inequality).

In practice, most market concentration studies use concentration ratios calculated from data derived from the census of production.

concentration ratio a measure of the degree of SELLER CONCENTRATION in a MARKET. The concentration ratio shows the percentage of market sales accounted for by, for example, the largest four firms or largest eight firms. The concentration ratio is derived from the market concentration curve, which can be plotted on a graph with the horizontal scale showing the number of firms cumulated from the largest size and the vertical scale showing the cumulative percentage of market sales accounted for by particular numbers of firms. See Fig. 27. See CONCENTRATION MEASURES, MARKET STRUCTURE.

concerted practice a situation where rival firms, without being party to a formal CARTEL agreement, nonetheless informally 'coordinate' their behaviour in respect of prices, output levels, etc., thereby eliminating competition between themselves.

See COMPETITION POLICY (EC), COLLUSION.

concert party a group of individuals or firms that acts 'in concert', pooling its various resources in order to effect the TAKEOVER of a company. See TAKEOVER BID, CITY CODE.

conciliation a procedure for settling disputes, most notably INDUS-

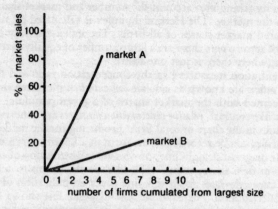

Fig. 27. **Concentration ratio.** Market A is here highly concentrated, with the four largest firms accounting for 80% of market sales, while market B has a relatively low level of concentration.

TRIAL DISPUTES, in which a neutral third party meets with the disputants and endeavours to help them resolve their differences and reach agreement through continued negotiation. In the UK the ADVISORY, CONCILIATION AND ARBITRATION SERVICE acts in this capacity. See MEDIATION, ARBITRATION, INDUSTRIAL RELATIONS, COLLECTIVE BARGAINING.

condition of entry an element of MARKET STRUCTURE which refers to the ease or difficulty new suppliers face in entering a market. Market theory indicates that at one extreme, entry may be entirely 'free', with, as in PERFECT COMPETITION, new suppliers being able to enter the market and compete immediately on equal terms with established firms; at the other extreme, in OLIGOPOLY and MONOPOLY markets, BARRIERS TO ENTRY operate which severely limit the opportunity for new entry. The significance of barriers to entry in market theory is that they allow established firms to secure a long-term profit return in excess of the NORMAL PROFIT equilibrium attained under fully competitive ('free' entry) conditions.

See MARKET ENTRY, POTENTIAL ENTRANT, LIMIT PRICING.

Confederation of British Industry (CBI) a UK organization that represents the collective interests of member companies in dealings with government and TRADE UNIONS.

conglomerate firm see FIRM.

consolidated fund the UK government's account at the Bank of England into which it pays its TAXATION and other receipts, and which it uses to make payments.

consols government BONDS which have an indefinite life rather than a specific maturity date. People acquire consols in order to buy a future nominal annual income without any expectation of repayment of the issue, though they can be bought and sold on the STOCK EXCHANGE. Because they are never redeemed by the government the market value of consols can vary greatly in order to bring their EFFECTIVE INTEREST RATE in line with their NOMINAL INTEREST RATE. For example, a £100 consol with a nominal rate of interest of 5% would yield a return of £5 per year. If current market interest rates were 10%, then the market price of the consol would need to fall to £50 so that a buyer would earn an effective return on it of £5/£50 = 10%.

consortium a temporary grouping of independent firms, organizations and governments, brought together to pool their resources and skills in order to undertake a particular project such as a major construction programme or the building of an aircraft, or to combine their buying power in bulk-buying factor inputs.

conspicuous consumption the CONSUMPTION of goods and services not for the UTILITY derived from their use but for the utility derived from the ostentatious exhibition of such goods and services.

A person may buy and run a Rolls-Royce motor car not just as a vehicle for transportation but because it suggests to the outside world something about the owner. That person may wish to be seen as affluent or a person of taste. This phenomenon (known as the VEBLEN EFFECT) can be viewed as an alternative to the more usual consumption theories where the quantity of a particular good varies inversely with its price (a downward-sloping DEMAND CURVE). A conspicuous consumption good may well have an UPWARD-SLOPING DEMAND CURVE so that the quantity demanded increases with its price.

constant returns 1. (in the SHORT RUN) constant returns to the VARIABLE FACTOR INPUT that occur when additional units of variable input added to a given quantity of FIXED FACTOR INPUT generate equal increments in output. With an unchanged price for variable factor inputs, constant returns will cause the short-run unit variable cost of output to stay the same over an output range. See RETURNS TO THE VARIABLE FACTOR INPUT.

2. (in the LONG RUN) constant returns that occur when successive increases in all factor inputs generate equal increments in output. In cost terms this means the long run unit cost of output remains constant so long as factor input prices stay the same. See MINIMUM EFFICIENT SCALE, ECONOMIES OF SCALE.

consumer the basic consuming/demanding unit of economic theory. In economic theory, a consuming unit can be either an individual purchaser of a good or service, a HOUSEHOLD (a group of individuals who make joint purchasing decisions), or a government.

See BUYER.

consumer credit LOANS made available to buyers of products to assist them in financing purchases. Consumer credit facilities include HIRE PURCHASE, BANK LOANS and CREDIT CARDS.

Consumer Credit Act, 1974 a UK Act which provides for the licensing of persons and businesses engaged in the provision of consumer CREDIT (specifically, moneylenders, pawnbrokers and INSTALMENT CREDIT traders – but not banks which are covered by separate legislation) and the regulation of DEBTOR-CREDITOR contracts. The Act contains important provisions protecting creditors from 'extortionate' rates of interest. The Act is administered by the OFFICE OF FAIR TRADING in conjunction with the DEPARTMENT OF TRADE AND INDUSTRY.

See CONSUMER PROTECTION, APR.

consumer durables CONSUMER GOODS such as houses, cars, televisions which are 'consumed' over relatively long periods of time rather than immediately. Compare CONSUMER NONDURABLES.

consumer equilibrium the point at which the consumer maximizes his TOTAL UTILITY or satisfaction from the spending of a limited (fixed) income. The economic 'problem' of the consumer is that he has only a limited amount of income to spend and therefore cannot buy all the goods and services he would like to have. Faced with this constraint, demand theory assumes that the goal of the consumer is to select that combination of goods, in line with his preferences, which will maximize his total utility or satisfaction. Total utility is maximized when the MARGINAL UTILITY of a penny's worth of good X is exactly equal to the marginal utility of a penny's worth of all of the other goods purchased; or, restated, when the prices of goods are different, the marginal utilities are proportional to their respective prices. For two goods X and Y total utility is maximized when:

$$\frac{\text{marginal utility of X}}{\text{price of X}} = \frac{\text{marginal utility of Y}}{\text{price of Y}}$$

Consumer equilibrium can also be depicted graphically using INDIFFERENCE CURVE analysis. See Fig. 28. See also REVEALED PREFERENCE THEORY, PRICE EFFECT, INCOME EFFECT, SUBSTITUTION EFFECT, ECONOMIC MAN, CONSUMER RATIONALITY, PARETO OPTIMALITY.

consumer goods any products such as washing machines, beer, toys, that are purchased by consumers as opposed to businesses. Compare CAPITAL GOODS, PRODUCER GOODS.

consumerism an organized movement to protect the economic interests of CONSUMERS. The movement developed in response to the growing market power of large companies and the increasing technical complexity of products. It embraces bodies such as the Consumers Association in the UK, which is concerned with product testing and informing consumers through publications such as *Which?*. Con-

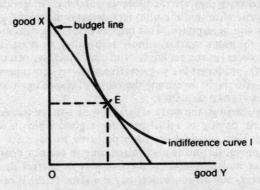

Fig. 28. **Consumer equilibrium**. The optimal combination of Good X and Good Y is at point E when the BUDGET LINE is tangential to indifference curve I. At this point the slope of the budget line (the ratio of prices) is equal to the slope of the indifference curve (the ratio of marginal utilities), so the goods' marginal utilities are proportional to their prices.

sumerism has been officially incorporated into British COMPETITION POLICY since the 1973 FAIR TRADING ACT.

See CONSUMER PROTECTION.

consumer nondurables CONSUMER GOODS which yield up all their satisfaction or UTILITY at the time of consumption. They include such items as beer, steak or cigarettes. Compare CONSUMER DURABLES.

consumer protection measures taken by the government and independent bodies such as the Consumers' Association in the UK to protect consumers against unscrupulous trade practices such as false descriptions of goods, incorrect weights and measures, misleading prices and defective goods.

See TRADE DESCRIPTIONS ACT 1968, WEIGHTS AND MEASURES ACT 1963, CONSUMER CREDIT ACT 1974, PRICE MARKING (BARGAIN OFFERS) ORDER 1979, OFFICE OF FAIR TRADING, COMPETITION POLICY, CONSUMERISM.

consumer rationality or **economic rationality** the assumption, in demand theory, that CONSUMERS attempt to obtain the greatest possible satisfaction from the money resources they have available when making purchases. Because economic theory tends to sum household demands in constructing market DEMAND CURVES, it is not important if a few households do not conform to rational behaviour as long as the majority of consumers or households act rationally.

See ECONOMIC MAN.

consumer sovereignty the power of CONSUMERS to determine what is produced since they are the ultimate purchasers of goods and services. In general terms, if consumers demand more of a good then more of it will be supplied. This implies that PRODUCERS are 'passive agents' in the PRICE SYSTEM, simply responding to what consumers want. However, in certain kinds of market (notably, OLIGOPOLY and MONOPOLY), producers are so powerful vis-à-vis consumers that it is they who effectively determine the range of choice open to the consumer. See REVISED SEQUENCE.

consumers' surplus the extra satisfaction or UTILITY gained by consumers from paying an actual price for a good which is *lower* than that which they would have been prepared to pay. See Fig. 29a. The consumers' surplus is maximized only in PERFECT COMPETITION, where price is determined by the free play of market demand and supply forces, and all consumers pay the same price. Where market price is not determined by demand and supply forces in competitive market conditions, but is instead determined administratively by a profit-maximizing MONOPOLIST, then the resulting restriction in market output and the increase in market price causes a loss of consumer surplus, indicated by the shaded area PP_mXE in Fig. 29b. If a DISCRIMINATING MONOPOLIST were able to charge a separate price to each consumer which reflected the maximum amount that the consumer was prepared to pay, then the monopolist would be able to appropriate all the consumer surplus in the form of sales revenue. Compare PRODUCERS' SURPLUS.

See DIMINISHING MARGINAL UTILITY, DEADWEIGHT LOSS.

consumption the satisfaction obtained by CONSUMERS from the use of goods and services. Certain CONSUMER DURABLE products like washing machines are consumed over a longish period of time, while other products like cakes are consumed immediately after purchase. The DEMAND CURVE for a particular product reflects consumers' satisfactions from consuming it. See WANTS, DEMAND.

consumption expenditure the proportion of NATIONAL INCOME or DISPOSABLE INCOME spent by HOUSEHOLDS on final goods and services. Consumption expenditure is the largest component of AGGREGATE DEMAND and spending in the CIRCULAR FLOW OF NATIONAL INCOME. It is one of the most stable components of aggregate demand, showing little fluctuation from period to period.

See CONSUMPTION SCHEDULE, VEBLEN EFFECT.

consumption function a statement of the general relationship between the dependent variable, CONSUMPTION EXPENDITURE, and the various independent variables which determine consumption such as current DISPOSABLE INCOME and income from previous periods and WEALTH. See CONSUMPTION SCHEDULE, LIFE-CYCLE HYPOTHESIS, PERMANENT-INCOME HYPOTHESIS, WEALTH EFFECT.

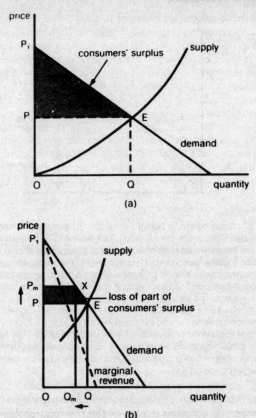

Fig. 29. **Consumers' surplus.** (a) At the EQUILIBRIUM PRICE OP utility from the marginal unit of the good is just equal to its price; all previous units yield an amount of utility which is greater than the amount paid by the consumer, insofar as consumers would have been prepared to pay more for these intramarginal units than the market price. The total consumer surplus is represented by the shaded area PEP₁. (b) The loss of consumers' surplus due to monopoly.

consumption possibility line see BUDGET LINE.

consumption schedule a schedule depicting the relationship between CONSUMPTION EXPENDITURE and the level of NATIONAL INCOME or DISPOSABLE INCOME. Also called *consumption function*. At low levels of disposable income households consume more than their current income (see DISSAVINGS), drawing on past savings, borrowing, or selling assets in order to maintain consumption at some desired mini-

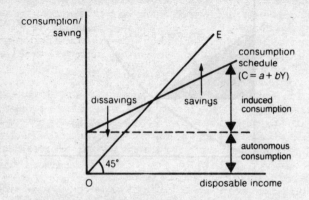

Fig. 30. **Consumption schedule.** A simple consumption schedule which takes the linear form $C = a + bY$, where C is consumption and a is the minimum level of consumption expenditure at zero disposable income (autonomous consumption). Thereafter consumption expenditure increases as income rises (induced consumption), and b is the proportion of each extra £ (pound) of disposable income which is spent. The 45° line OE shows what consumption expenditure would have been had it exactly matched disposable income. The difference between OE and the consumption schedule indicates the extent of dissavings or SAVINGS at various income levels. The slope of the consumption schedule is equal to the MARGINAL PROPENSITY TO CONSUME. See SAVINGS SCHEDULE, LIFE-CYCLE HYPOTHESIS, PERMANENT-INCOME HYPOTHESIS.

mum level (AUTONOMOUS CONSUMPTION). At higher levels of disposable income they consume a part of their current income and save the rest (see SAVINGS). See Fig. 30.

See INDUCED CONSUMPTION.

contestable market a MARKET where new entrants face costs similar to those of established firms and where, on leaving, firms are able to recoup their capital costs, less depreciation. Consequently, it is not possible for established firms to earn ABOVE-NORMAL PROFIT as this will be eroded by the entry of new firms, or, alternatively, the mere threat of such new entry may be sufficient to ensure that established firms set prices which yield them only a NORMAL PROFIT return. Perfectly competitive markets (see PERFECT COMPETITION) are all contestable, but even some oligopolistic markets (see OLIGOPOLY) may be contestable *if* entry and exit are easily affected.

See WORKABLE COMPETITION, CONDITION OF ENTRY, BARRIERS TO ENTRY, BARRIERS TO EXIT.

contract a legally enforceable agreement between two or more parties. A contract involves obligations on the part of the contractors which may be expressed verbally or in writing. For example, one company may enter into an agreement to supply a product to another company at a given future date and on specified terms. Both parties would then be legally bound to honour their agreement to sell and to buy the product.

contract curve see EDGEWORTH BOX.

contribution the difference between a product's SALES REVENUE and its VARIABLE COSTS. If total contributions are just large enough to cover FIXED COSTS then the producer BREAKS-EVEN; if contributions are less than fixed costs the producer makes a LOSS; while if contributions exceed fixed costs then the producer makes a PROFIT. See LOSS MINIMIZATION, MARGINAL COST PRICING.

conventional sequence see REVISED SEQUENCE.

convertibility the extent to which one foreign currency or INTERNATIONAL RESERVE ASSET can be exchanged for some other foreign currency or international reserve asset.

International trade and investment opportunities are maximized when the currencies used to finance them are fully convertible, i.e. free of FOREIGN EXCHANGE CONTROL restrictions.

convertible loans long-term LOANS to a JOINT-STOCK COMPANY which may be converted at the option of the lender into ORDINARY SHARES at a predetermined share price.

conveyance a document which transfers the legal ownership of land and buildings from one person/business to another person/business. See MORTGAGE.

cooperative a form of business FIRM which is owned and run by a group of individuals for their mutual benefit. Examples of cooperatives include:

(a) *worker* or *producer cooperatives* – businesses that are owned and managed by their employees, who share in the net profit of the business.

(b) *wholesale cooperatives* – businesses whose membership comprises a multitude of small independent retailers. The prime objective of such a group is to use its combined BULK BUYING power to obtain discounts and concessions from manufacturers similar to those achieved by larger SUPERMARKET chains.

(c) *retail cooperatives* – businesses that are run in the interest of customers holding membership rights which entitle them, for instance, to receive an annual dividend or refund in proportion to their spending at the cooperative's shops.

See WHOLESALER, RETAILER, DISTRIBUTION CHANNEL.

copyright the ownership of the rights to a publication of a book, manual, newspaper, etc., giving legal entitlement and powers of redress against theft and unauthorized publication or copying. See INTELLECTUAL PROPERTY RIGHT.

Copyright, Designs and Patents Act, 1988 a UK Act which provides for the establishment and protection of the legal ownership rights of persons and businesses in respect of various classes of 'intellectual property', in particular COPYRIGHTS, DESIGN RIGHTS and PATENTS.

The Act is administered in part by the PATENTS OFFICE, with cases of unauthorized copying, patent infringements, etc. being handled by the courts.

corner, *vb*. to buy or attempt to buy up all of the supplies of a particular product on the MARKET, thereby creating a temporary MONOPOLY situation with the aim of exploiting the market.

corporate governance the issue of who governs or controls JOINT-STOCK COMPANIES. With the DIVORCE OF OWNERSHIP FROM CONTROL, salaried professional managers have come to exercise control over large companies, displacing owners and shareholders, though the accumulation of large shareholdings by INSTITUTIONAL INVESTORS has increased their potential for exercising control. Corporate governance may affect the objectives which large joint-stock companies pursue, in particular profit and growth.

See FIRM OBJECTIVES, MANAGERIAL THEORIES OF THE FIRM, MANAGEMENT UTILITY MAXIMIZATION.

corporate sector that part of the ECONOMY concerned with the transactions of BUSINESSES. Businesses receive income from supplying goods and services and influence the workings of the economy through their use of, and payment for, factor inputs and INVESTMENT decisions. The corporate sector, together with the PERSONAL SECTOR and FINANCIAL SECTOR, constitute the PRIVATE SECTOR. The private sector, PUBLIC (GOVERNMENT) SECTOR and FOREIGN SECTOR make up the national economy.

See CIRCULAR FLOW OF NATIONAL INCOME MODEL.

corporation 1. a private enterprise FIRM incorporated in the form of a JOINT-STOCK COMPANY.

2. a publicly-owned business such as a nationalized industry.

corporation tax a DIRECT TAX levied by the government on the PROFITS accruing to businesses. The rate of corporation tax charged is important to a firm insofar as it determines the amount of after-tax profit it has available to pay DIVIDENDS to shareholders or to reinvest in the business.

See TAXATION, FISCAL POLICY, RETAINED PROFIT.

correlation a statistical term that describes the degree of association between two variables. When two variables tend to change together then they are said to be correlated, and the extent to which they are correlated is measured by means of the CORRELATION COEFFICIENT.

correlation coefficient a statistical term (usually denoted by *r*) that measures the strength of the association between two variables.

Where two variables are completely unrelated then their correlation coefficient will be zero; where two variables are perfectly related then their correlation would be one. A high correlation coefficient between two variables merely indicates that the two generally vary together – it does not imply causality in the sense of changes in one variable causing changes in the other.

Where high values of one variable are associated with high values of the other (and vice versa), then they are said to be *positively correlated*. Where high values of one variable are associated with low values of the other (and vice versa), then they are said to be *negatively correlated*. Thus correlation coefficients can range from +1 for perfect positive association to −1 for perfect negative association, with zero representing the case where there is no association between the two.

The correlation coefficient also serves to measure the *goodness of fit* of a regression line (see REGRESSION ANALYSIS) which has been fitted to a set of sample observations by the technique of ordinary least squares. A large positive correlation coefficient will be found when the regression line slopes upward from left to right and fits closely with the observations; a large negative correlation coefficient will be found when the regression line slopes downward from left to right and closely matches the observations. Where the regression equation contains two (or more) independent variables a multiple correlation coefficient can be used to measure how closely the three-dimensional plane, representing the multiple regression equation, fits the set of data points.

corset see SPECIAL DEPOSITS.

cost the payments (both EXPLICIT COSTS and IMPLICIT COSTS) incurred by a firm in producing its output. See TOTAL COST, AVERAGE COST, MARGINAL COST, PRODUCTION COST, SELLING COST.

cost-based pricing pricing methods which determine the PRICE of a product on the basis of its production, distribution and marketing costs.

See AVERAGE-COST PRICING, FULL-COST PRICING, MARGINAL-COST PRICING.

cost-benefit analysis a technique for enumerating and evaluating the total SOCIAL COSTS and total social benefits associated with an economic project. Cost-benefit analysis is generally used by public agencies when evaluating large-scale public INVESTMENT projects such as major new motorways or rail lines, in order to assess the welfare or net social benefits which will accrue to the nation from these projects. This generally involves the sponsoring bodies taking a broader and longer-term view of a project than would a commercial organization concentrating on project profitability alone.

The main principles of cost-benefit are encompassed within four key questions:

(a) which costs and which benefits are to be included. All costs and benefits should be enumerated and ranked according to their remoteness from the main purpose of the project so that more remote costs and benefits might be excluded. This requires careful definition of the project and estimation of project life, and consideration of EXTERNALITIES and SECONDARY BENEFITS.

(b) how these costs and benefits are to be valued. The values placed on costs and benefits should pay attention to likely changes in relative prices but not the general price level, since the general price level prevailing in the initial year should be taken as the base level. Though market prices are normally used to value costs and benefits, difficulties arise when investment projects are so large that they significantly affect prices; where monopoly elements distort relative prices; where taxes artificially inflate the resource costs of inputs; and where significant unemployment of labour or other resources means that labour or other resource prices overstate the social costs of using these inputs which are in excess supply. In such cases SHADOW PRICES may be needed for costs and benefits. In addition, there are particular problems of establishing prices for INTANGIBLE PRODUCTS and COLLECTIVE PRODUCTS.

(c) the interest rate at which costs and benefits are to be discounted. This requires consideration of the extent to which social time preference will dictate a lower DISCOUNT RATE than private time preference because social time preference discounts the future less heavily; and OPPORTUNITY COST considerations which mitigate against using a lower discount rate for public projects for fear that mediocre public projects may displace good private sector projects if the former have an easier criterion to meet.

(d) the relevant constraints. This group includes legal, administrative and budgetary constraints, and constraints on the redistribution of income. Essentially, cost-benefit analysis concentrates on the economic efficiency benefits from a project and providing the benefits exceed the costs recommends acceptance of the project, regardless of who benefits and who bears the costs. However, where the decision-maker feels that the redistribution of income associated with a project is unacceptable, he may reject that project despite its net benefits.

There is always uncertainty surrounding the estimates of future costs and benefits associated with a public investment project, and cost-benefit analysis needs to allow for this uncertainty by testing the sensitivity of the net benefits to changes in such factors as project life and interest rates.

See WELFARE ECONOMICS, COST EFFECTIVENESS, TIME PREFERENCE, ENVIRONMENTAL AUDIT, VALUE FOR MONEY AUDIT, ENVIRONMENTAL IMPACT ASSESSMENT.

cost centre an organizational sub-unit of a firm which is given responsibility for minimizing COSTS but has no control over its product pricing and revenues. Cost centres facilitate management control by helping to ascertain a unit's operating costs.

See PROFIT CENTRE, INVESTMENT CENTRE.

cost effectiveness the achievement of maximum provision of a good or service from *given* quantities of resource inputs. Cost effectiveness is often established as an objective when organizations have a given level of expenditure available to them and are seeking to provide the maximum amount of service, in a situation where service outputs cannot be valued in money terms (e.g., the UK National Health Service). Where it is possible to estimate the money value of outputs as well as the money value of inputs then COST-BENEFIT techniques can be applied.

See VALUE FOR MONEY AUDIT.

cost function a function that depicts the general relationship between the COST of FACTOR INPUTS and the cost of OUTPUT in a firm. In order to determine the cost of producing a particular output it is necessary to know not only the required quantities of the various inputs but also their prices. The cost function can be derived from the PRODUCTION FUNCTION by adding the information about factor prices. It would take the general form:

$$Q_c = f(p1 \; I1, \; p2 \; I2 \; \text{---} \; pn \; In)$$

where Q_c is the cost of producing a particular output Q, and $p1$, $p2$, etc., are the prices of the various factors used, while $I1$, $I2$, etc., are the quantities of factors 1, 2, etc., required. The factor prices $p1$, $p2$ etc., which a firm must pay in order to attract units of these factors will depend upon the interaction of the forces of demand and supply in factor markets.

See EFFICIENCY, ISOCOST LINE, ISOQUANT CURVE.

cost minimization production of a given OUTPUT at minimum cost by combining FACTOR INPUTS with due regard to their relative prices. See COST FUNCTION, ISOQUANT CURVE.

cost of capital the payments made by a firm for the use of long-term capital employed in its business. The average cost of capital to a firm which uses several sources of long-term funds (e.g., LOANS, SHARE CAPITAL (EQUITY), to finance its investments will depend upon the individual cost of each separate source of capital (for example, INTEREST on loans) weighted in accordance with the proportions of each source used. See CAPITAL GEARING, DISCOUNT RATE.

cost of goods sold or **cost of sales** the relevant cost that is compared with sales revenue in order to determine GROSS PROFIT in the PROFIT-AND-LOSS ACCOUNT. Where a trading company has STOCKS of finished goods, the cost of goods sold is not the same as purchases of finished goods. Rather, purchases of goods must be added to stocks at the start of the trading period to determine the goods available for sale, then the stocks left at the end of the trading period must be deducted from this to determine the cost of the goods which have been sold during the period. See STOCK VALUATION.

cost of living the general level of prices of goods and services measured in terms of a PRICE INDEX. To protect peoples' living standards from being eroded by price increases (INFLATION), wage contracts, old age pensions, etc., sometimes contain cost-of-living adjustment provisions which automatically operate to increase wages, pensions, etc., in proportion to price increases. See INDEXATION.

cost-plus pricing a pricing method which sets the PRICE of a product by adding a profit mark-up to AVERAGE COST or unit total cost. This method is similar to that of FULL-COST PRICING insofar as the price of a product is determined by adding a percentage profit mark-up to the product's unit total cost. Indeed, the terms are often used interchangeably. However, cost-plus pricing is used more specifically to refer to an agreed price between a purchaser and the seller, where the price is based on actual costs incurred plus a fixed percentage of actual cost or a fixed amount of profit per unit. Such pricing methods are often used for large capital projects or high technology contracts where the length of time of construction or changing technical specifications lead to a high degree of uncertainty about the final price.

Cost-plus pricing is frequently criticized for failing to give the supplier an incentive to keep costs down.

cost price a PRICE for a product which just covers its production and distribution COSTS with no PROFIT MARGIN added.

cost-push inflation a general increase in PRICES caused by increases in FACTOR INPUT costs. Factor input costs may rise because raw materials and energy costs increase due to world-wide shortages, or the operation of CARTELS (oil for example) and where a country's EXCHANGE RATE falls (see DEPRECIATION (1)); or because WAGE RATES in the economy increase at a faster rate than output per man (PRODUCTIVITY). In the latter case institutional factors such as the use of COMPARABILITY and WAGE DIFFERENTIAL arguments in COLLECTIVE BARGAINING and persistence of RESTRICTIVE LABOUR PRACTICES can serve to push up wages and limit the scope for productivity improvements. Faced with increased input costs producers try to 'pass-on' increased costs by charging higher prices. In order to maintain profit margins, producers would need to pass on the full increased costs in the form of higher prices, but whether they are able to depends upon PRICE ELASTICITY OF DEMAND for their products. See INFLATION, INFLATIONARY SPIRAL, COLLECTIVE BARGAINING.

Council for Mutual Economic Assistance (COMECON) an organization which until recently coordinated the central planning of the Soviet Union and a number of socialist eastern European countries and sought to promote greater trade between them.

council tax see LOCAL TAX.

countercyclical policy see DEMAND MANAGEMENT.

countertrade the direct or indirect exchange of goods for other goods in INTERNATIONAL TRADE. Countertrade is generally resorted to when particular FOREIGN CURRENCIES are in short supply, or when countries apply FOREIGN EXCHANGE CONTROLS.

There are various forms of countertrade, including:

(a) BARTER – the direct exchange of product for product.

(b) compensation deal – where the seller from the exporting country receives part payment in his own currency and the remainder in goods supplied by the buyer.

(c) buyback – where the seller of plant and equipment from the exporting country agrees to accept some of the goods produced by that plant and equipment in the importing country as part payment.

(d) counterpurchase – where the seller from the exporting country receives part payment for the goods in his own currency and the remainder in the local currency of the buyer, the latter then being used to purchase other products in the buyer's country.

See EXPORTING.

countervailing duty a TAX levied on an imported product (see IMPORTS) which raises the price in the domestic market as a means of counteracting 'unfair' trading practices by other countries. Countervailing duties are frequently employed against imported products which are deliberately 'dumped' (see DUMPING) or subsidized by EXPORT INCENTIVES.

See TARIFF, IMPORT DUTY, BEGGAR-MY-NEIGHBOUR POLICY.

countervailing power the ability of large buyers to offset the market power of large suppliers as in BILATERAL OLIGOPOLY. Large buyers usually have the upper hand in a vertical market chain (for example, multiple retailers buying from food manufacturers) because, unless suppliers collude (see COLLUSION), a large buyer is able to play one supplier off against another and obtain favourable discounts on bulk purchases. Provided that competition is strong in final selling markets countervailing power can play an important rôle in checking monopolistic abuse.

GALBRAITH uses the phrase 'countervailing power' in a slightly different way to refer to the growth of trade unions and consumer groups in response to the growth of large firms.

coupon 1. a document that shows proof of legal ownership of a FINANCIAL SECURITY and entitlement to payments thereon. For example, a SHARE certificate or BEARER BOND certificate.

2. a means of promoting the sale of a product by offering coupons to buyers of the product which can be redeemed for cash, gifts or other goods.

coupon interest rate the INTEREST RATE payable on the face value of a BOND. For example, a £100 bond with a 5% coupon rate of interest would generate a nominal return of £5 per year.

See EFFECTIVE INTEREST RATE.

Cournot, Augustin (1801–77) a French economist who explored the problems of price in conditions of competition and monopoly in his book: *The Mathematical Principles of the Theory of Wealth* (1838).

Cournot concentrated attention on the exchange values of products rather than their utilities; and he used mathematics to explore the relationship between the sale price of products and their costs, developing the idea of a MONOPOLY price. Cournot is also known for his work on DUOPOLY, his analysis showing that two firms would react to one another's output changes until they eventually reached a stable output position from which neither would wish to depart.

Cournot duopoly see DUOPOLY.

covenant a specific condition in a legal agreement or CONTRACT. For instance, a formal agreement between a COMMERCIAL BANK and a JOINT-STOCK COMPANY to which it is loaning money might contain a covenant stipulating a limit on dividend distributions from profits.

covered interest arbitrage the borrowing and investing of foreign currencies to take advantage of differences in INTEREST RATES between countries. For example, a company could borrow an amount of one currency (say, the UK pound (£)), convert this into another currency (say, the US dollar ($)) and invest the proceeds in the USA. Concurrently, the company would sell $s for £s in the FUTURES MARKET for delivery at a future specified date. The company would earn a profit on such a transaction if the rate of return on its investment in the USA was greater than the combined expenses of interest payments on the amount of £s borrowed and the costs of concluding the forward exchange contract. Covered interest ARBITRAGE takes advantage of (and in the process tends to eliminate) any temporary discrepancies between relative interest rates in two countries and the forward exchange rate of the two country's currencies.

See INTERNATIONAL FISHER EFFECT.

covering a means of protecting the domestic currency value of the future proceeds of an international trade transaction, usually by buying or selling the proceeds of the transaction in the FUTURES MARKET for foreign currencies.

crawling-peg exchange rate system a form of FIXED EXCHANGE RATE SYSTEM in which the EXCHANGE RATES between currencies are fixed (pegged) at particular values (for example £1 = $2), but which are changed frequently (weekly or monthly) by small amounts to new fixed values to reflect underlying changes in the FOREIGN EXCHANGE

MARKETS. For example, £1 = $1.90 cents, the repegging of the pound at a lower dollar value (DEVALUATION), or £1 = $2.10 cents, the repegging of the pound at a higher dollar value (REVALUATION).

credit a financial facility which enables a person or business to borrow MONEY to purchase (i.e. take immediate possession of) products, raw materials and components, etc. and to pay for them over an extended time period. Credit facilities come in a variety of forms, including BANK LOANS and OVERDRAFTS, INSTALMENT CREDIT, CREDIT CARDS and TRADE CREDIT. Interest charges on credit may be fixed or variable according to the type of facilities offered or, in some cases, 'interest free' as a means of stimulating business.

In many countries CREDIT CONTROLS are used as an instrument of MONETARY POLICY, with the authorities controlling both the availability and terms of credit transactions.

See CONSUMER CREDIT ACT 1974, INTEREST RATE.

credit card a plastic card or token used to finance the purchase of products by gaining point-of-sale CREDIT. Credit cards are issued by commercial banks, hotel chains, and larger retailers.

credit controls 1. the regulation of borrowing from the FINANCIAL SYSTEM as part of MONETARY POLICY. OPEN MARKET OPERATIONS are one general means of limiting the expansion of credit. A more selective form of control is consumer INSTALMENT CREDIT regulation (hire purchase). Under this arrangement the purchase of certain goods is regulated by the authorities stipulating the minimum down-payment and the maximum period of repayment.

2. the control which a firm exercises over its TRADE DEBTORS in order to ensure that customers pay their DEBTS promptly and to minimize the risk of bad debts. The purpose of credit control is to minimize the funds which a firm has to tie up in debtors so improving profitability and LIQUIDITY.

See FACTORING, WORKING CAPITAL.

credit creation see BANK-DEPOSIT CREATION.

creditor a person or business that is owed money by an individual or firm for goods, services or raw materials that they have supplied but for which they have not yet been paid (trade creditors), or because they have made LOANS. Creditors are also termed 'accounts payable'.

See DEBTORS, CREDIT.

credit squeeze any action taken by the monetary authorities to reduce the amount of CREDIT granted by COMMERCIAL BANKS, FINANCE HOUSES, etc. Such action forms part of the government's MONETARY POLICY directed towards reducing AGGREGATE DEMAND by making less credit available and forcing up INTEREST RATES.

creeping inflation small increases in the general level of prices in an economy. See INFLATION, HYPERINFLATION.

cross-elasticity of demand a measure of the degree of responsiveness of the DEMAND for one good to a given change in the PRICE of some other good.

$$\text{cross elasticity of demand} = \frac{\text{\% change in quantity demanded of good A}}{\text{\% change in price of good B}}$$

Products may be regarded by consumers as substitutes for one another in which case a rise in the price of good B (tea, for example) will tend to increase the quantity demanded of good A (coffee, for example). Here the cross-elasticity of demand will be *positive* since as the price of B goes up the quantity demanded of A rises as consumers now buy more A in preference to the more expensive B. Alternatively, products may be regarded by consumers as complements which are jointly demanded in which case a rise in the price of good B (tea, for example) will tend to decrease not only the quantity demanded of good B but also another good A (sugar, for example). Here the cross-elasticity of demand will be *negative* since a rise in the price of B serves to reduce the quantity demanded of A.

The degree of substitutability between products is reflected in the magnitude of the cross-elasticity measure. If a small increase in the price of good B results in a large rise in the quantity demanded of good A (highly cross-elastic), then goods A and B are close substitutes. Likewise, the degree of complementarity of products is reflected in the magnitude of the cross-elasticity measure. If a small increase in the price of good B results in a large fall in the quantity demanded of good A (highly cross-elastic), then goods A and B are close complements.

Cross-elasticities provide a useful indication of the substitutability of products and so help to indicate the boundaries between markets. A group of products with high cross-elasticities of demand constitutes a distinct market whether or not they share common technical characteristics; for example, mechanical and electronic watches are regarded by consumers as close substitutes.

See MARKET.

cross-subsidization the practice by firms of offering internal subsidies to certain products or departments within the firm financed from the profits generated by other products or departments. Cross-subsidization is often used by diversified and vertically integrated firms as a means of financing new product development; DIVERSIFICATION into new areas; or to facilitate price cuts to match intense competition in certain of its markets.

See VERTICAL INTEGRATION, PRICE-SQUEEZE.

crowding-out effect an increase in GOVERNMENT EXPENDITURE that has the effect of reducing the level of private sector spending. Financial crowding-out of the type described in the caption to Fig. 31 would only occur to the extent that the MONEY SUPPLY is fixed, so

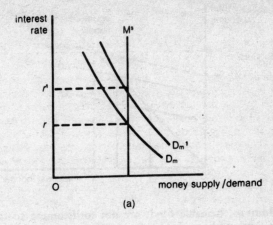

(a)

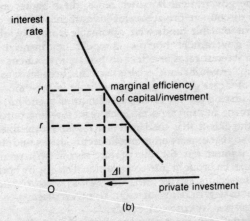

(b)

Fig. 31. 'Crowding out' effect. (a) An increase in government expenditure raises real NATIONAL INCOME and output (see EQUILIBRIUM LEVEL OF NATIONAL INCOME) which in turn increases the demand for money from D_m to $D_m{}^1$, with which to purchase the greater volume of goods and services being produced. (b) This causes the equilibrium RATE OF INTEREST to rise (from r to r^1) which then reduces – 'crowds out' – an amount of private INVESTMENT (Δ). (c) (see p 109) An increase in government expenditure by itself would increase AGGREGATE DEMAND from AD to AD¹, but, allowing for the fall in private investment, the net result is to increase aggregate demand to only AD².

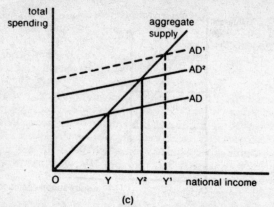

(c)

that additional loanable funds are not forthcoming to finance the government's additional expenditure. If money supply is fixed then increases in the PUBLIC SECTOR BORROWING REQUIREMENT associated with additional government expenditure will tend to increase interest rates as the government borrows more, these higher interest rates serving to discourage private sector investment. On the other hand, if additional loanable funds were obtainable from, say, abroad, then additional government borrowing could be financed with little increase in interest rates or effect on private investment.

The term 'crowding-out' is also used in a broader sense to denote the effect of larger government expenditure in pre-empting national resources, leaving less for private consumption spending, private sector investment and for exports. Such real crowding out would only occur to the extent that total national resources are fixed and fully employed so that expansion in public sector claims on resources contract the amount left for the private sector. Where unemployed resources can be brought into use additional claims by both the public and private sectors can be met. See MONEY–SUPPLY/SPENDING LINKAGES, MARGINAL EFFICIENCY OF CAPITAL/INVESTMENT.

CSO see CENTRAL STATISTICAL OFFICE.

cum-dividend, *adj.* (of a particular SHARE) including the right to receive the DIVIDEND which attaches to the share. If shares are purchased on the STOCK EXCHANGE 'cum. div.', the purchaser would be entitled to the dividend accruing to that share when the dividend is next paid. Compare EX-DIVIDEND.

currency the BANK NOTES and coins issued by the monetary authorities which form part of an economy's MONEY SUPPLY. The term 'currency' is often used interchangeably with the term *cash* in economic analysis and monetary policy.

currency appreciation see APPRECIATION (1).

currency depreciation see DEPRECIATION (1).

currency matching see EXCHANGE RATE EXPOSURE.

currency swap see SWAP.

current account 1. a statement of a country's trade in goods (visibles) and services (invisibles) with the rest of the world over a particular period of time. See BALANCE OF PAYMENTS.

2. an individual's or company's account at a COMMERCIAL BANK or BUILDING SOCIETY into which the customer can deposit cash or cheques and make withdrawals on demand on a day-to-day basis. Current accounts (or sight deposits as they are often called) offer customers immediate liquidity with which to finance their transactions. Most banks and building societies pay INTEREST on current account balances which are in credit.

See BANK DEPOSIT, DEPOSIT ACCOUNT.

current assets ASSETS such as STOCKS, money owed by DEBTORS, and cash, which are held for short-term conversion within a firm as raw materials are bought, made up, sold as finished goods and eventually paid for.

See FIXED ASSETS, WORKING CAPITAL.

current liabilities all obligations to pay out cash at some date in the near future, including amounts which a firm owes to trade CREDITORS and BANK LOANS/overdrafts.

See WORKING CAPITAL.

current yield see YIELD.

Customs and Excise a governmental agency for the collection of INDIRECT TAXES levied in accordance with appropriate rates, rules and regulations. In the UK, Her Majesty's Customs and Excise typically collects revenue from VALUE ADDED TAX and EXCISE DUTY payable on alcoholic drink, tobacco and betting. The agency also enforces the laws regarding the import and export of certain goods, collects IMPORT DUTIES, and seeks to prevent attempts to avoid paying import duties by smuggling. See also INLAND REVENUE.

customs duty a TAX levied on imported products (see IMPORTS). Unlike TARIFFS, customs duties are used primarily as a means of raising revenue for the government rather than as a means of protecting domestic producers from foreign competition. See TAXATION.

customs union a form of TRADE INTEGRATION between a number of countries, in which members eliminate all trade barriers (TARIFFS, etc.) amongst themselves on goods and services, and establish a uniform set of barriers against trade with the rest of the world, in particular a *common external tariff*. The aim of a customs union is to secure the benefits of international SPECIALIZATION, thereby improving members' real living standards. See GAINS FROM TRADE, TRADE CREATION, EUROPEAN COMMUNITY.

cyclical fluctuation the short-term movements, both upwards and downwards in some economic variable around a long-term SECULAR TREND line. See Fig. 32. See DEMAND MANAGEMENT.

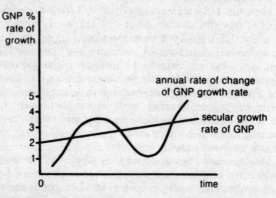

Fig. 32. **Cyclical fluctuation**. The pronounced short-term swings in output growth rates over the course of the BUSINESS CYCLE, around a rising long-term trend growth line for the country's GROSS NATIONAL PRODUCT.

cyclically-adjusted public-sector borrowing requirement see PUBLIC-SECTOR BORROWING REQUIREMENT.

cyclical unemployment the demand-deficient UNEMPLOYMENT that occurs as a result of a fall in the level of AGGREGATE DEMAND and business activity during the RECESSION and DEPRESSION phases of the BUSINESS CYCLE.

cyclical variation see TIME-SERIES ANALYSIS.

D

dawn raid a situation in which a potential TAKEOVER bidder for a company buys a substantial shareholding in the target company at current market prices, often through intermediaries (to disguise the identity of the bidder). This shareholding can then be used as a platform for a full takeover bid for all the shares at a stated offer price. See TAKEOVER BID, CITY CODE.

DE see DEPARTMENT OF EMPLOYMENT.

deadweight loss the reduction in CONSUMERS' SURPLUS and PRODUCERS' SURPLUS which results when the output of a product is restricted to less than the optimum efficient level which would prevail under PERFECT COMPETITION. Fig. 33 shows the demand and supply curves for a product and their interaction establishes the equilibrium market price OP. At this price consumers' surplus is shown as the diagonally shaded area ABP and producers' surplus as the vertically shaded area APO. If output is restricted from OQ to OQ_1 then the price paid by consumers would rise to OP_1 and consumers' surplus would be reduced by the amount ACE; while the price received by producers would fall to OP_2 and producers' surplus would be reduced by the amount ADE.

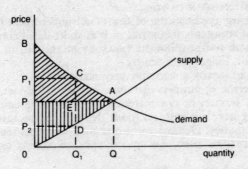

Fig. 33. **Deadweight loss.**

Deadweight loss is particularly likely to occur in markets dominated by MONOPOLY suppliers who restrict output in order to keep prices high.

dear money see TIGHT MONEY.

death rate the number of people in a POPULATION who die per thousand per year. In 1994, for example, the UK death rate was 12 people per 1,000 of the population. The difference between this rate and the BIRTH RATE is used to calculate the rate of growth of the population of a country over time. The death rate tends to decline as a country attains higher levels of economic development. See DEMOGRAPHIC TRANSITION.

debentures a means of financing companies through fixed-interest LOANS secured against company ASSETS.

In some cases the company may offer a specific asset such as a particular machine as security for the loan; in other cases lenders are offered security by means of a general claim against all company assets in the event of default. See LOAN CAPITAL.

debt an amount of money owed by a person, firm or government (the borrower) to a lender. Debts arise when a person, etc. spends more than their current income or when they deliberately plan to borrow money to purchase specific goods, services or ASSETS (houses, financial securities, etc.). Debt contracts provide for the eventual repayment of the sum borrowed and include INTEREST charges for the duration of the loan. An individual's debt can include MORTGAGES, INSTALMENT CREDIT, BANK LOANS and OVERDRAFTS; a firm's debt can include fixed-interest DEBENTURES, LOANS, BILLS OF EXCHANGE and bank loans and overdrafts; a government's debt can take the form of long-term BONDS and short-term TREASURY BILLS (see NATIONAL DEBT).

See also INTERNATIONAL DEBT.

debt capital see LOAN CAPITAL.

debt financing the financing of firms' and governments' deficits by the issue of FINANCIAL SECURITIES such as short-dated company BILLS OF EXCHANGE and government TREASURY BILLS; and, in the case of government, longer-term BONDS.

See PUBLIC SECTOR BORROWING REQUIREMENT.

debtor a person or business that owes money to individuals or firms for goods, services or raw materials that they have bought but for which they have not yet paid (trade debtors), or because they have borrowed money. Debtors are also termed 'accounts receivable'.

See CREDITORS, DEBT, CREDIT CONTROL, WORKING CAPITAL, BAD DEBT.

debt servicing the cost of meeting INTEREST payments and regular contractual repayments of principal on a LOAN along with any administration charges borne by the BORROWER.

decentralization the diffusion of economic decision-making to many different decision-makers rather than concentrating such decision-making centrally. In an economy this is achieved by the adoption of the PRICE SYSTEM which devolves decisions to individual consumers and suppliers. In a firm, decentralization involves delegating authority to make decisions 'down the line' to particular divisions and departments.

See PRIVATE ENTERPRISE ECONOMY, M-FORM ORGANIZATION.

decreasing returns to scale see DISECONOMIES OF SCALE.

decreasing returns to the variable-factor input see DIMINISHING RETURNS.

deficiency payment see INCOME SUPPORT.

deficit see BUDGET DEFICIT, BALANCE OF PAYMENTS.

deficit financing see BUDGET DEFICIT, PUBLIC SECTOR BORROWING REQUIREMENT.

deflation a reduction in the level of NATIONAL INCOME and output, usually accompanied by a fall in the general price level (DIS-INFLATION).

A deflation is often deliberately brought about by the authorities in order to reduce INFLATION and to improve the BALANCE OF PAYMENTS by reducing import demand. Instruments of deflationary policy include fiscal measures (e.g., tax increases) and monetary measures (e.g., high interest rates). See MONETARY POLICY, FISCAL POLICY.

deflationary gap or **output gap** the shortfall in total spending (AGGREGATE DEMAND) at the FULL EMPLOYMENT level of national income (POTENTIAL GNP). Because of a deficiency in spending some of the economy's resources lie idle and ACTUAL GNP is below that of potential GNP. To counteract this deficiency in spending, the authorities can use FISCAL POLICY and MONETARY POLICY to expand aggregate demand. See Fig. 34 (overleaf).

See also DEFLATION, REFLATION, INFLATIONARY GAP.

deindustrialization a sustained fall in the proportion of national output accounted for by the industrial and manufacturing sectors of the economy, a process which is often accompanied by a decline in the number of people employed in industry (compare INDUS-TRIALIZATION).

There is a well-established trend in advanced economies for the industrial sector to grow more slowly than the service sector, as shown in Fig. 35. For the UK the share of industry in GDP fell from 43% in 1960 to 32% in 1994, while the share of services increased from 54% to 66%. Over the same period employment in industry in the UK fell from 11.8 million in 1960 to 4.1 million in 1995.

Changes in sector shares may simply reflect changes in the pattern of final demand for goods and services over time, and as such may be considered a 'natural' development associated with a maturing economy. On the other hand, deindustrialization which stems from supply-side deficiencies (high costs, an over-valued exchange rate, lack of investment and innovation) which put a country at a competitive disadvantage in international trade (see IMPORT PENETRATION) is

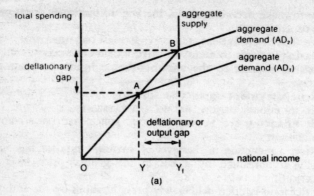

(a)

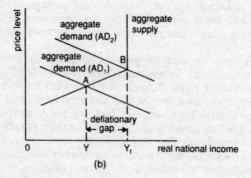

(b)

Fig. 34. **Deflationary gap**. (a) The AGGREGATE SUPPLY SCHEDULE is drawn as a 45° line because businesses will offer any particular level of output only if they expect total spending (aggregate demand) to be just sufficient to sell all of that output. However, once the economy reaches the full employment level of national income (OY$_f$), then actual output cannot expand further and at this level of output the aggregate supply schedule becomes vertical.

(b) Alternatively, aggregate supply can be depicted in terms of the various levels of real national income supplied at each price level. Again, once the economy reaches the full employment level of real national income the aggregate supply schedule becomes vertical.

In both (a) and (b), if aggregate demand is at a low level (AD$_1$) then actual output (OY) will be determined by the intersection of AD$_1$ and the aggregate supply schedule at point A; this output (OY) is less than potential output (OY$_f$), leaving an output gap. An output gap can be removed by the authorities by expanding aggregate demand to the full employment level of aggregate demand (AD$_2$) where actual output (determined by the intersection of AD$_2$ and the aggregate supply schedule at point B) corresponds with potential GNP.

a more serious matter. In this case, deindustrialization often brings with it a fall in national output, rising unemployment and balance of payments difficulties.

The extent of deindustrialization in the UK was even more marked in the early 1980s because of Britain's artificially high exchange rate, bolstered by UK oil exports, which caused Britain to lose overseas markets. See STRUCTURE OF INDUSTRY, STRUCTURAL UNEMPLOYMENT.

	Agriculture		Industry		Manufacturing		Services	
	1960	1994	1960	1994	1960	1994	1960	1994
UK	3	2	43	32	32	22	54	66
US	4	2	38	29	29	17	58	69
Japan	13	2	45	40	34	27	42	58
Germany	6	1	53	38	40	27	41	61

Fig. 35. **Deindustrialization**. The distribution of gross domestic product shows how the industrial sector in advanced economies grows more slowly than the service sector. The figures for industry include those for manufacturing. Source: *World Development Report*, World Bank, 1996.

delivered pricing the charging of a PRICE for a product that includes the cost of transporting the product from the manufacturer to the customer. The delivered prices quoted by a manufacturer might accurately reflect the actual costs of transportation to different areas, or alternatively, discriminatory prices might be used to cross-subsidize areas in order to maximize sales across the country.

See BASING POINT PRICE SYSTEM.

delivery note a document sent by a supplier to a customer at the time when products are supplied that itemizes the physical quantities of product supplied. Thereafter an INVOICE is usually sent to the customer showing the money value of products supplied. Compare STATEMENT OF ACCOUNT.

demand or **effective demand** the WANT, need or desire for a product backed by the money to purchase it. In economic analysis, demand is always based on 'willingness and ability to pay' for a product, not merely want or need for the product. CONSUMERS' total demand for a product is reflected in the DEMAND CURVE. Compare SUPPLY.

demand curve a line showing the relationship between the PRICE of a PRODUCT or FACTOR OF PRODUCTION and the quantity DEMANDED per time period, as in Fig. 36.

Most demand curves slope downwards because (a) as the price of the product falls, consumers will tend to substitute this (now relatively cheaper) product for others in their purchases; (b) as the price of the product falls, this serves to increase their real income allowing

DEMAND CURVE (SHIFT IN)

them to buy more products (see PRICE EFFECT, INCOME EFFECT, SUBSTITUTION EFFECT). However in a small minority of cases products can have an UPWARD-SLOPING DEMAND CURVE.

The slope of the demand curve reflects the degree of responsiveness of quantity demanded to changes in the products price. For example, if a large reduction in price results in only a small increase in quantity demanded (as would be the case where the demand curve has a steep slope) then demand is said to be *price inelastic* (see PRICE-ELASTICITY OF DEMAND).

The demand curve interacts with the SUPPLY CURVE to determine the EQUILIBRIUM MARKET PRICE. See DEMAND FUNCTION, DEMAND CURVE (SHIFTS IN), DIMINISHING MARGINAL UTILITY, MARGINAL REVENUE PRODUCT.

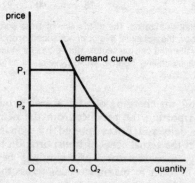

Fig. 36. **Demand curve.** Demand is the total quantity of a good or service which buyers are prepared to purchase at a given price. Demand is always taken to be *effective demand*, backed by the ability to pay, and not just based on want or need. The typical market demand curve slopes downwards from left to right, indicating that as price falls more is demanded (that is, a movement along the existing demand curve). Thus, if price falls from OP_1 to OP_2, the quantity demanded will increase from OQ_1 to OQ_2.

demand curve (shift in) a movement of the DEMAND CURVE from one position to another (either left or right) as a result of some economic change other than price. A given demand curve is always drawn on the CETERIS PARIBUS assumption that all of the other factors affecting demand (income, tastes, etc.) are held constant. If any of these change, however, then this will bring about a shift in the demand curve. For example, if income increases, the demand curve will shift to the right, so that more is now demanded at each price than formerly. See Fig. 37. See also DEMAND FUNCTION, INCOME-ELASTICITY OF DEMAND.

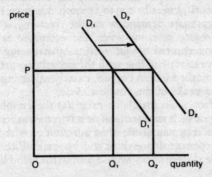

Fig. 37. **Demand curve (shift in).** An increase in income shifts the demand curve D,D, to D_2D_2, increasing the quantity demanded from OQ_1 to OQ_2. The magnitude of this shift depends upon the INCOME ELASTICITY OF DEMAND for the product.

demand deposit see BANK DEPOSIT, COMMERCIAL BANK.

demand elasticity see ELASTICITY OF DEMAND.

demand for a factor input see DERIVED DEMAND.

demand function a form of notation which links the DEPENDENT VARIABLE, quantity demanded (Qd), with various INDEPENDENT VARIABLES which determine quantity demanded such as product price (P), income (Y), prices of substitute products (Ps), advertising (A), etc:

$$Qd = f(P, Y, Ps, A, \text{ etc})$$

Changes in any of these independent variables will affect quantity demanded, and if we wish to investigate the particular effect of any one of these variables upon quantity demanded, then we could (conceptually) hold the influence of the other independent variables constant (CETERIS PARIBUS), whilst we focus upon the particular effects of that independent variable. See DEMAND CURVE, DEMAND CURVE (SHIFTS IN).

demand management or **stabilization policy** the control of the level of AGGREGATE DEMAND in an economy, using FISCAL POLICY and MONETARY POLICY to moderate or eliminate fluctuations in the level of economic activity associated with the BUSINESS CYCLE. The general objective of demand management is to 'fine-tune' aggregate demand so that it is neither deficient relative to POTENTIAL GROSS NATIONAL PRODUCT (thereby avoiding a loss of output and UNEMPLOYMENT) nor overfull (thereby avoiding INFLATION).

An unregulated economy will tend to go through periods of

depression and boom as indicated by the continuous line in Fig. 38. Governments generally try to smooth out such fluctuations by stimulating aggregate demand when the economy is depressed and reducing aggregate demand when the economy is over-heating. Ideally, the government would wish to manage aggregate demand so that it grows exactly in line with the underlying growth of potential GNP, the dashed line in Fig. 38, exactly offsetting the amplitude of troughs and peaks of the business cycle.

However, two main problems exist: (a) the establishment of the correct timing of such an INJECTION or WITHDRAWAL; (b) the establishment of the correct magnitude of an injection or withdrawal into the economy (to counter depressions and booms). With perfect timing and magnitude the economy would follow the trend line of potential GNP.

A number of stages are involved in applying a stabilization policy as shown in the figure. For example, at time period zero the onset of a recession/depression would be reflected in a downturn in economic activity, though delays in the collection of economic statistics means that it is often time period 1 before data becomes available about unemployment rates, etc. Once sufficient data is to hand, the authorities are able to diagnose the nature of the problem (time period 2) and plan appropriate intervention such as tax cuts or increases in government expenditure (time period 3). At time period 4 the agreed measures are then implemented, though it may take some time before these measures have an effect on CONSUMPTION, INVESTMENT, IMPORTS, etc. (see MULTIPLIER). If the timing of these activities is incorrect, then the authorities may find that they have stimulated the economy at a time when it was already beginning to recover from recession/depression, so that their actions have served to exacerbate the original fluctuation (dotted line 1 in Fig. 38). The authorities could also exacerbate the fluctuation (dotted line 1) if they get the magnitudes wrong by injecting too much purchasing power into the economy, creating conditions of excess demand.

If the authorities can get the timing and magnitudes correct, then they should be able to counterbalance the effects of recession/depression and follow the path indicated as dotted line 2 in Fig. 38. Reducing the intensity of the recession in this way requires the authorities to FORECAST accurately the onset of recession some time ahead, perhaps while the economy is still buoyant (time period 6). On the basis of these forecasts the authorities can then plan their intervention to stimulate the economy (time period 7), activate these measures (time period 8), so that these measures begin to take effect and stimulate the economy as economic activity levels fall (time period 9).

Much government action is inaccurate in timing and magnitude due to the institutional and behavioural complexities of the economy. Where the government has not been successful in adequately eradicating such peaks and troughs in the business cycle, it is frequently accused of having stop-go policies (see STOP-GO CYCLE), that is, of making injections into a recovering economy which then 'overheats', and subsequently withdrawing too much at the wrong time, 'braking' too hard.

Demand management represents one facet of government macroeconomic policy, other important considerations being SUPPLY-SIDE policies which affect the rate of growth of potential GNP and EXCHANGE RATE policies which affect the competitiveness of internationally traded goods and services.

See DEFLATIONARY GAP, INFLATIONARY GAP, EQUILIBRIUM LEVEL OF NATIONAL INCOME, AUTOMATIC (BUILT-IN) STABILIZERS, INTERNAL-EXTERNAL BALANCE MODEL, PUBLIC FINANCE, BUDGET.

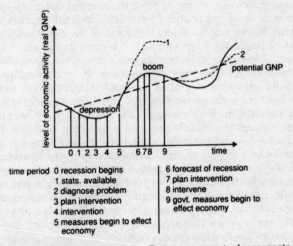

time period 0 recession begins
             1 stats. available
             2 diagnose problem
             3 plan intervention
             4 intervention
             5 measures begin to effect
               economy

             6 forecast of recession
             7 plan intervention
             8 intervene
             9 govt. measures begin to
               effect economy

Fig. 38. **Demand management**. The management of aggregate demand in an economy.

demand-pull inflation a general increase in prices caused by a level of AGGREGATE DEMAND in excess of the supply potential of the economy. At full employment levels of output (POTENTIAL GROSS NATIONAL PRODUCT) excess demand bids up the price of a fixed real output (see INFLATIONARY GAP). According to MONETARISM, excess demand results from too rapid an increase in the MONEY SUPPLY.

See INFLATION, QUANTITY THEORY OF MONEY, COST-PUSH INFLATION.

demand schedule a table listing various prices of a product and the specific quantities demanded at each of these prices. The information provided by a demand schedule can be used to construct a DEMAND CURVE showing the price-quantity demanded relationship in graphical form.

demand theory see THEORY OF DEMAND.

de-merger the break-up of a company, often originally formed through a MERGER, into two (or more) separate companies. This is most easily achieved when the original businesses comprising the merger have continued to be run as separate divisions of the enlarged group. In this case, for example, the A-B company could be split into separate quoted companies, A and B, with the company's existing shareholders being given shares in *both* companies. Thus, unlike a DIVESTMENT (the sale of a division to outside interests) or a MANAGEMENT BUY-OUT (the sale of a division to its existing management), initially at least the companies continue to be owned by their existing shareholders.

A de-merger may occur because the merged company has failed to perform up to expectations because of internal conflicts of management, or may result from a rethink of the company's BUSINESS STRATEGY favouring a concentration on 'core' businesses.

demographic transition a POPULATION cycle which is associated with the ECONOMIC DEVELOPMENT of a country. In underdeveloped countries (i.e., subsistence agrarian economies) BIRTH RATES and DEATH RATES are both high, so there is very little change in the overall size of the population. With economic development (i.e., INDUSTRIALIZATION), INCOME PER HEAD begins to rise and there is a fall in the death rate (through better nutrition, sanitation, medical care, etc.,), which brings about a period of rapid population growth. Provided ECONOMIC GROWTH is consistently greater than the increase in population, income per head continues to expand and eventually serves to reduce the birth rate (small families become the 'norm' in society as people seek to preserve their growing affluence). At this point population growth slows down and may eventually level-off. See Fig. 39. See POPULATION TRAP, DEVELOPING COUNTRY.

Most advanced industrial countries have gone through a demographic transition of the kind described above and are today characterized by both low birth and death rates and slow-growing populations.

demography the study of human POPULATIONS including their total size, population changes over time as determined by changes in BIRTH RATES, DEATH RATES and MIGRATION; the age and sex distribution of populations and their geographical and occupational distributions. Statistical data on populations is compiled from CENSUSES of population, and records of births, deaths, etc. See DEMOGRAPHIC TRANSITION.

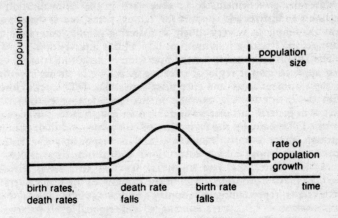

Fig. 39. **Demographic transition.** The levelling-off of the rate of population growth during a country's economic development.

Department of Employment (DE) the UK government department responsible for administering the government's EMPLOYMENT LAWS and policies. The DE seeks to promote the efficient use of labour resources by running local employment offices, which help workers seeking employment to find jobs, and industrial training schemes designed to improve job skills.

Department of Health the UK government department responsible for administering the National Health Service.

Department of Social Security (DSS) the UK government department responsible for administering the government's social security programmes. The DSS pays SOCIAL SECURITY BENEFITS such as state pensions, unemployment and sickness benefit, and collects NATIONAL INSURANCE CONTRIBUTIONS to help finance these payments and services.

Department of the Environment (DOE) the UK government department responsible for monitoring and controlling environmental pollution and for the regulation of local authorities.

Department of Trade and Industry (DTI) the UK government office which is primarily responsible for implementing and administering the government's industrial and trade policies. A particular concern at the DTI is the promotion of greater efficiency through an INDUSTRIAL POLICY programme which includes support for new business start-ups, consultancy services for small firms, research and development, and technology transfer. In the past the DTI has been required by governments to involve itself in the rationalization of declining industries and support for 'failing' firms, but at the present time the emphasis is very much on fostering greater 'enterprise' by business itself with a minimum of direct State intervention.

The DTI is responsible for the operation of REGIONAL POLICY, vetting applications for regional selective assistance by firms investing in 'development areas' and enterprise zones. The DTI works closely with the OFFICE OF FAIR TRADING in matters affecting COMPETITION POLICY in general and merger and takeover investigations in particular; the DTI regulates the formation of companies and their conduct through the COMPANY REGISTRAR, and is responsible for issuing licences to deposit-taking institutions and authorizing dealers in stocks and shares, etc. (see FINANCIAL SERVICES ACT, 1986). Finally, the DTI plays a prominent part in the running of the UK's overseas trade affairs, representing the country's interests at international (GENERAL AGREEMENT ON TARIFFS AND TRADE) and regional levels (EUROPEAN COMMUNITY). The DTI is important in the promotion of exports through the Export Market Information Centre, British Overseas Trade Board, and related back-up facilities and services including the EXPORT CREDIT GUARANTEE DEPARTMENT.

department store a large RETAIL OUTLET. Department stores may be under single-shop ownership, or run as a multiple CHAIN STORE business. Unlike most other retailers who tend to specialize in relatively narrow ranges of products, the essential characteristic of a department store is the great variety of products it stocks: 'everything under one roof'.

See RETAILER, DISTRIBUTION CHANNEL.

dependent variable a variable which is affected by some other variable in a model. For example, the demand for a product (the dependent variable) will be influenced by its price (the INDEPENDENT VARIABLE). It is conventional to place the dependent variable on the left-hand side of an EQUATION.

See DEMAND FUNCTION, SUPPLY FUNCTION.

deposit account or **time account** or **savings account** an individual's or company's account at a COMMERCIAL BANK into which the customer can deposit cash or cheques and from which he or she can draw out money subject to giving notice to the bank. Deposit accounts (unlike CURRENT ACCOUNTS which are used to finance day-to-day transactions) are mainly held as a form of personal and corporate SAVING and used to finance irregular 'one-off' payments. INTEREST is payable on deposit accounts, normally at rates above those paid on current accounts in order to encourage clients to deposit money for longer periods of time. Unlike a current account, cheques cannot generally be drawn against deposit accounts.

See BANK DEPOSIT.

depreciation 1. a fall in the value of a CURRENCY against other currencies under a FLOATING EXCHANGE RATE SYSTEM, as shown in Fig. 40a. A depreciation of a currency's value makes IMPORTS (in the local currency) more expensive and EXPORTS (in the local currency) cheaper, thereby reducing imports and increasing exports, and so assisting in the removal of a BALANCE OF PAYMENTS deficit. For example, as shown in Fig. 40b, if the pound–dollar exchange rate depreciates from £1.60 to £1.40, then this would allow British exporters to reduce their prices by a similar amount, thus increasing their price competitiveness in the American market (though they may choose not to reduce their prices by the full amount of the depreciation in order to boost profitability, or devote more funds to sales promotion, etc.) By the same token, the depreciation serves to raise the sterling price of American products imported into Britain, thereby making them less price-competitive than British products in the home market.

In order for a currency depreciation to 'work' three basic conditions must be satisfied:

(a) how successful the depreciation is depends on the reactions of export and import volumes to the change in relative prices, i.e., the PRICE ELASTICITY OF DEMAND for exports and imports. If these volumes are low, i.e., demand is inelastic, trade volumes will not change much and the depreciation may in fact worsen the situation. On the other hand, if export and import demand is elastic then the change in trade volume will improve the payments position. Balance-of-payments equilibrium will be restored if the sum of export and import elasticities is greater than unity (the MARSHALL-LERNER CONDITION).

(b) on the supply side, resources must be available, and sufficiently mobile, to be switched from other sectors of the economy into industries producing exports and products which will substitute for imports. If the economy is fully employed already, domestic demand will have to be reduced and/or switched by deflationary policies to accommodate the required resource transference.

(c) over the longer term, 'offsetting' domestic price, rises must be contained. A depreciation increases the cost of essential imports of raw materials and foodstuffs which can push up domestic manufacturing costs and the cost of living. This in turn can serve to increase domestic prices and money wages thereby necessitating further depreciations to maintain price competitiveness.

See BALANCE-OF-PAYMENTS EQUILIBRIUM, INTERNAL-EXTERNAL BALANCE MODEL, PRICE ELASTICITY OF SUPPLY. Compare APPRECIATION (1).

2. the fall in the value of an ASSET during the course of its working life. Also called *amortization*. The condition of plant and equipment used in production deteriorates over time and these items will eventu-

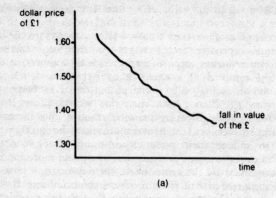

Exchange rate	UK domestic price of a product	Price of the UK product exported to US	US domestic price of a product	Price of the US product imported into UK
£1 = $1.60	£1	$1.60	$1	62p
£1 = $1.40	£1	$1.40	$1	71p

(b)

Fig. 40. **Depreciation**. (a) A depreciation of the pound against the dollar. (b) The effect of depreciation on export and import prices.

ally have to be replaced. Accordingly, a firm is required to make financial provision for the depreciation of its assets.

Depreciation is an accounting means of dividing up the historic cost of a FIXED ASSET over a number of accounting periods which correspond with the asset's estimated life. The depreciation charged against the revenue of successive time periods in the PROFIT-AND-LOSS ACCOUNT serves to spread the original cost of a fixed asset which yields benefits to the firm over several trading periods. In the period-end BALANCE SHEET such an asset would be included at its cost less depreciation deducted to date. This depreciation charge does not attempt to calculate the reducing market value of fixed assets, so that balance sheets do not show realization values.

Depreciation formulas base the depreciation charge on the HISTORIC COST of fixed assets. However, during a period of INFLATION it is likely that the REPLACEMENT COST of an asset is likely to be higher than its original cost. Thus, prudent companies need to make provision for higher replacement costs of fixed assets.

See INFLATION ACCOUNTING, CAPITAL CONSUMPTION, APPRECIATION (2).

depressed area a region of an economy which is characterized by significantly higher rates of UNEMPLOYMENT and lower levels of INCOME PER HEAD compared to the national average. See REGIONAL POLICY.

depression a phase of the BUSINESS CYCLE characterized by a severe decline (*slump*) in the level of economic activity (ACTUAL GROSS NATIONAL PRODUCT). Real output and INVESTMENT are at very low levels and there is a high rate of UNEMPLOYMENT. A depression is caused mainly by a fall in AGGREGATE DEMAND, and can be reversed provided that the authorities evoke expansionary FISCAL POLICY and MONETARY POLICY.

See DEFLATIONARY GAP, DEMAND MANAGEMENT.

deregulation the removal of controls over economic activity which have been imposed by the government or some other regulatory body, for example an industry trade association. Deregulation may be initiated either because the controls are no longer seen as necessary (for example, the ending of PRICE CONTROLS to combat inflation), or because they are overly restrictive, preventing companies from taking advantage of business opportunities; for example, the ending of most FOREIGN EXCHANGE CONTROLS by the UK in 1979 was designed to liberalize overseas physical and portfolio investment.

Deregulation has assumed particular significance in the context of recent initiatives by the UK government to stimulate greater competition by, for example, allowing private companies to compete for business in areas (such as local bus and parcel services) hitherto confined to central government or local authority operators. See COMPETITIVE TENDERING.

Conversely, government initiatives can be seen to have promoted regulation insofar as, for example, the PRIVATIZATION of nationalized industries has in some cases led to greater regulation of their activities via the creation of regulatory agencies (such as Ofgas in the case of the gas industry and Oftel in the case of the telecommunications industry) to ensure that the interests of consumers are protected.

derived demand the DEMAND for a particular FACTOR INPUT or PRODUCT that is dependent on there being a demand for some other product. For example, the demand for labour to produce motor cars is dependent on there being a demand for motor cars in the first place; the demand for teacups is dependent on there being a demand for tea. See MARGINAL REVENUE PRODUCT, FACTOR MARKETS, COMPLEMENTARY PRODUCTS.

deseasonalized data see TIME SERIES ANALYSIS.

design rights the legal ownership by persons or businesses of original designs of the shape or configuration of industrial products. In the UK, the COPYRIGHT, DESIGNS AND PATENTS ACT, 1988 gives protection to the creators of industrial designs against unauthorized copying for a period of ten years after the first marketing of the product.

devaluation an administered reduction in the EXCHANGE RATE of a currency against other currencies under a FIXED EXCHANGE RATE SYSTEM; for example, the lowering of the UK pound (£) against the US dollar ($) from one fixed or 'pegged' level to a lower level, say from £1 = $3 to £1 = $2, as shown in Fig. 41. Devaluations are resorted to by governments to assist in the removal of a BALANCE OF PAYMENTS DEFICIT. The effect of a devaluation is to make IMPORTS (in the local currency) more expensive, thereby reducing import demand, and EXPORTS (in the local currency) cheaper, thereby acting as a stimulus to export demand. Whether or not a devaluation 'works' in achieving balance of payments equilibrium, however, depends on a number of factors, including: the sensitivity of import and export demand to price changes, the availability of resources to expand export volumes and replace imports and, critically over the long term, the control of inflation to ensure that domestic price rises are kept in line with or below other countries' inflation rates. (See DEPRECIATION (1) for further discussion of these matters.) Devaluations can affect the business climate in a number of ways, but in particular provide firms with an opportunity to expand sales and boost profitability. A devaluation increases import prices, making imports less competitive against domestic products, encouraging domestic buyers to switch to locally produced substitutes. Likewise, a fall in export prices is likely to cause overseas customers to increase their demand for the country's exported products in preference to locally produced items and the exports of other overseas producers. If the pound, as in our example above, is devalued by one-third, then this would allow British exporters to reduce their prices by a similar amount, thus increasing their price competitiveness in the American market. Alternatively they may choose not to reduce their prices by the full amount of the devaluation in order to increase unit profit margins and provide additional funds for advertising and sales promotion, etc.

Contrast REVALUATION. See INTERNAL-EXTERNAL BALANCE MODEL.

developed country an economically advanced country whose economy is characterized by a large industrial and service sectors and high levels of INCOME PER HEAD. See STRUCTURE OF INDUSTRY, DEVELOPING COUNTRY, ECONOMIC DEVELOPMENT.

developing country, less developed country, underdeveloped country, emerging country or **Third World country** a country characterized by low levels of GROSS DOMESTIC PRODUCT and INCOME PER HEAD. Such countries are typically dominated by a large PRIMARY SECTOR producing a limited range of agricultural and mineral products in which the majority of the POPULATION exists at or near subsistence levels, producing barely enough for their immediate needs, and thus

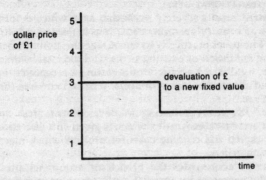

Fig. 41. **Devaluation**. A devaluation of the pound against the dollar.

being unable to release the resources required to support a large urbanized industrial population. The term 'developing' indicates that, as seen by most such countries, the way to improve their economic fortunes is for them to diversify the industrial base of the economy by, in particular, establishing new manufacturing industries and by adopting the PRICE SYSTEM. To facilitate an increase in urban population necessary for INDUSTRIALIZATION, a nation may either IMPORT the necessary commodities from abroad with the FOREIGN EXCHANGE earned from the EXPORT of (predominantly) primary goods, or it can attempt to improve its own agriculture. With appropriate ECONOMIC AID from industrialized countries and the ability and willingness on the part of a developing country, the transition into a NEWLY-INDUSTRIALIZED COUNTRY could be made.

However, certain problems do exist. For instance, increases in real income which are achieved need to be maintained, which means keeping the population number in check. The illiteracy and social customs for large families tend to work against governmental efforts to increase the STANDARD OF LIVING of its citizens. Also, most of the foreign exchange earned by such countries is by exporting, mainly COMMODITIES but increasingly augmented by manufactures as their industrialization programmes progress. In both these areas, however, the developing countries have been up against adverse developments in the world economy, particularly since the oil price increases of 1973 and the advent of recessionary conditions and the spread of PROTECTIONISM.

See ECONOMIC DEVELOPMENT, STRUCTURE OF INDUSTRY, DEMOGRAPHIC TRANSITION, POPULATION TRAP, INTERNATIONAL COMMODITY

AGREEMENTS, UNITED NATIONS CONFERENCE ON TRADE AND DEVELOPMENT, INTERNATIONAL DEBT.

development area a severely DEPRESSED AREA which is formally recognized by a country's REGIONAL POLICY as in need of industrial regeneration. The usual practice is to encourage the establishment of new firms, the expansion of existing firms, and the establishment of new industries by offering a variety of investment incentives: investment grants and allowances, tax write-offs, rent and rate free (or reduced) factories, etc.

In the UK, firms investing in development areas are offered REGIONAL SELECTIVE ASSISTANCE which is given on a discretionary basis to cover capital and training costs for projects which meet specified job-creation criteria.

development economics the branch of economics that seeks to explain the processes by which a DEVELOPING COUNTRY increases in productive capacity, both agricultural and industrial, in order to achieve sustained ECONOMIC GROWTH.

Much work in development economics has focused upon the way in which such growth can be achieved. For instance, the question of whether agriculture ought to be developed in tandem with industry, or whether leading industries should be allowed to move forward independently, so encouraging all other sectors of society. Another controversial question is whether less-developed countries are utilizing the most appropriate technology. Many economists argue for intermediate technology as most appropriate rather than very modern plants initially requiring Western technologists and managers to run them. Socio-cultural factors are also influential in attempting to achieve take-off into sustained economic growth.

See ECONOMIC DEVELOPMENT, INFANT INDUSTRY.

differentiated product see PRODUCT DIFFERENTIATION.

diminishing average returns see DIMINISHING RETURNS.

diminishing marginal rate of substitution see MARGINAL RATE OF SUBSTITUTION.

diminishing marginal returns see DIMINISHING RETURNS.

diminishing marginal utility a principle which states that as an individual consumes a greater quantity of a product in a particular time period, the extra satisfaction (UTILITY) derived from each additional unit will progressively fall as the individual becomes satiated with the product. See Fig. 42.

The principal of diminishing MARGINAL UTILITY can be used to explain why DEMAND CURVES for most products are downward-sloping, since if individuals derive less satisfaction from successive units of the product they will only be prepared to pay a lower price for each unit.

Demand analysis can only be conducted in terms of diminishing

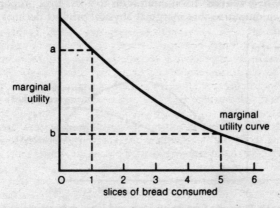

Fig. 42. **Diminishing marginal utility**. To a hungry man the utility of the first slice of bread consumed will be high (O_a) but as his appetite becomes satiated, successive slices of bread yield smaller and smaller amounts of satisfaction; for example, the fifth slice of bread yields only O_b of additional utility.

marginal utility if CARDINAL UTILITY measurement is possible. In practice, it is not possible to measure utility precisely in this way, so that demand curves are now generally constructed from INDIFFERENCE CURVES which are based upon ORDINAL UTILITY.

See CONSUMER EQUILIBRIUM, REVEALED PREFERENCE.

diminishing returns the law in the SHORT RUN theory of supply of diminishing marginal returns or *variable factor proportions* that states that as equal quantities of one VARIABLE FACTOR INPUT are added into the production function (the quantities of all other factor inputs remaining fixed), a point will be reached beyond which the resulting addition to output (that is, the MARGINAL PHYSICAL PRODUCT of the variable input) will begin to decrease as shown in Fig. 43. As the marginal physical product declines, this will eventually cause AVERAGE PHYSICAL PRODUCT to decline as well (*diminishing average returns*).

The marginal physical product changes because additional units of the variable factor input do not add equally readily to units of the fixed factor input. At low level of output, marginal physical product rises with the addition of more variable inputs to the (underworked) fixed input, the extra variable inputs bringing about a more intensive use of the fixed input. Eventually, as output is increased an optimal factor combination is attained at which the variable and fixed inputs are mixed in the most appropriate proportions to maximize marginal physical product. Thereafter, further additions of variable inputs to the (now overworked) fixed input leads to a less than proportionate increase in output so that marginal physical product declines.

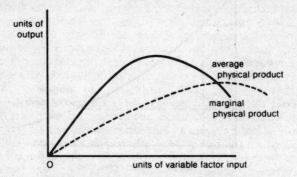

Fig. 43. **Diminishing returns**. The rise and fall of units of output as units of variable factor input are added to the production function.

See RETURNS TO THE VARIABLE FACTOR INPUT.

direct cost the sum of the DIRECT MATERIALS cost and DIRECT LABOUR cost of a product. Direct cost tends to vary proportionately with the level of output.

See VARIABLE COST.

direct debit see COMMERCIAL BANK.

direct investment any expenditure on physical ASSETS such as plant, machinery and stocks. See INVESTMENT.

directive (bank) an instrument of MONETARY POLICY involving the control of bank lending as a means of regulating the MONEY SUPPLY. If, for example, the monetary authorities wish to lower the money supply, they can 'direct' the banks to reduce the total amount of loan finance made available to personal and corporate borrowers. A reduction in bank lending can be expected to lead to a multiple contraction of bank deposits, and, hence, a fall in the money supply. See BANK DEPOSIT CREATION.

direct labour 1. that part of the labour force in a firm which is directly concerned with the manufacture of a good or the provision of a service. Contrast INDIRECT LABOUR.

2. workers employed directly by local or central government to perform tasks rather than contracting out such tasks to private-sector companies. For example, a local authority might employ its own permanent construction workers to repair council houses rather than putting such repair work out to local firms.

See VARIABLE COST, PRIVATIZATION.

direct materials raw materials which are incorporated in a product. Contrast INDIRECT MATERIALS. See VARIABLE COST.

direct tax a TAX levied by the government on the income and wealth received by households and businesses in order to raise revenue and as an instrument of FISCAL POLICY. Examples of a direct tax are INCOME TAX, CORPORATION TAX and WEALTH TAX. Direct taxes are progressive in so far as the amount paid varies according to the income and wealth of the taxpayer. By contrast, INDIRECT TAX is regressive in so far as the same amount is paid by each tax paying consumer regardless of their income. See TAXATION, PROGRESSIVE TAXATION, REGRESSIVE TAXATION.

dirty float the manipulation by the monetary authorities of a country's EXCHANGE RATE under a FLOATING EXCHANGE RATE SYSTEM primarily in order to gain a competitive advantage over trade partners. Thus, the authorities could intervene in the FOREIGN EXCHANGE MARKET to stop the exchange rate from otherwise appreciating (see APPRECIATION 1) in the face of market forces, or, alternatively they could deliberately engineer a DEPRECIATION of the exchange rate. See BEGGAR-MY-NEIGHBOUR POLICY.

discount 1. a deduction from the published LIST PRICE of a good or service allowed by a supplier to a customer. The discount could be offered for prompt payment in cash (*cash discount*) or for bulk purchases (*trade discount*). Trade discounts may be given to enable suppliers to achieve large sales volumes and thus ECONOMIES OF SCALE; or may be used as a competitive stratagem to secure customer loyalty; or may be given under duress to large, powerful buyers. See AGGREGATED REBATE, BULK BUYING.

2. the sale of new STOCKS and SHARES at a reduced price. In the UK this involves the issue of a new share at a price below its nominal value. In other countries where shares have no nominal value it involves the sale of new shares below their current market price.

3. the purchase of a particular company's issued stock or share at a price below the average market price of those of other companies operating in the same field. The price is lower because investors feel less optimistic about that company's prospects.

4. a fall in the prices of all stocks and shares in anticipation of a downturn in the economy.

5. the purchase of a BILL OF EXCHANGE, TREASURY BILL or BOND for less than its nominal value. Bills and bonds are redeemable at a specific future date at their face value. The original purchaser will buy the bill or bond for less than its nominal or face value (at a discount). The discount between the price which he pays and the nominal value of the bill or bond represents interest received on the loan made against the security of the bill or bond. If the owner of the bill or bond then wishes to sell it prior to maturity (rediscount it) then he will have to accept less than its nominal value (though more than he paid for it). The difference between the original price which he paid and the price received will depend largely upon the length of time before maturity. For example, if a bond with a nominal value of £1,000 redeemable in one year's time were bought for £900, then the £100 discount on redemption value represents an interest rate of £100/900 = 11.1% on the loan.

6. the extent to which a foreign currency's market EXCHANGE RATE falls below its 'official' exchange rate under a FIXED EXCHANGE RATE SYSTEM.

discounted cash flow a cash flow associated with economic projects that are adjusted to allow for the timing of the cash flow and the potential interest on the funds involved. Such an allowance for timing is important for most INVESTMENT projects have their main costs or cash outflows in the first year or so, while their revenues or cash inflows are spread over many future years.

For example, with interest rates at 10% a company could invest £100 now and have it accumulate at compound interest of £110 at the end of one year and £121 at the end of two years. So £100 in the hands of the company now is worth the same as £110 in a year's time or £121 in two year's time. Looking at this cash flow the other way round, the company would regard £110 receivable in one year's time or £121 receivable in two year's time as having a present value of £100. Following this principle, it is possible to calculate the present value of the estimated stream of future cash outflows associated with an investment project, and the *present value* of the estimated stream of future cash inflows from the project and compare the two. If the present value of the cash inflows from the project exceeds the present value of outflows when both are discounted at, say 10% then the *net present value* is positive. This suggests that it would be worthwhile for a company to use its own money or borrow money at 10% and undertake the project, for it will earn a return in excess of its financing costs.

Alternatively, it is possible to calculate the percentage internal rate of return which will equate the present value of the stream of cash outflows associated with an investment project with the present value of the stream of cash inflows from the project, so as to give a zero net present value. This calculated internal rate of return can then be compared with a predetermined DISCOUNT RATE which is usually based on market rates of interest. If the calculated internal rate of return (say, 15%) exceeds the discount rate (say, 12%) then the project is worthwhile, otherwise not.

See CAPITAL BUDGETING.

discount house a financial institution (unique to the UK financial system) which specializes in the buying and selling of short-dated commercial BILLS OF EXCHANGE and government TREASURY BILLS in the DISCOUNT MARKET. They make their profit by borrowing money short-term from COMMERCIAL BANKS (CALL MONEY) and lending money for longer periods (up to three months), the small differential in interest rates between their short-term borrowing and longer-term lending constituting their profit.

See TENDER ISSUE.

discount market a market engaged in the buying and selling of short-dated BILLS OF EXCHANGE and TREASURY BILLS. Such transactions are conducted through a number of DISCOUNT HOUSES which use money borrowed primarily from the COMMERCIAL BANKS (usually on a revolving day-to-day basis – CALL MONEY) to purchase bills (i.e. to 'discount' them) which they then hold until maturity or sell to each other ('re-discount') or more commonly on-sell to the commercial banks (see DISCOUNT (5)). When the discount houses find themselves temporarily unable to cover their purchase commitments by borrowing from the commercial banks, it is possible for them to obtain additional funds from the Bank of England in its capacity as the 'LENDER OF LAST RESORT'.

See TENDER ISSUE.

discount rate the INTEREST RATE at which the streams of cash inflows and outflows associated with an INVESTMENT project are to be discounted. For private-sector projects the discount rate is frequently based upon the weighted-average COST OF CAPITAL to the firm, with the interest cost of each form of finance (long term loans, overdrafts, equity, etc.) being weighted by the proportion which each form of finance contributes to total company finances.

The discount rate for public-sector investment projects involves more complex considerations. It can be argued that while individuals have a limited lifespan and so will not look too many years ahead in looking for returns on investment, society continues indefinitely as some individuals die and are replaced by others being born, so that society will tend to look further ahead in looking for returns. This disparity between *private time preference* and *social time preference* means that society will tend to discount the future less heavily than the individual and would favour a lower discount rate. On the other hand, opportunity cost considerations may make it difficult for society to apply a lower, less stringent, discount rate to public sector projects than is applied in the private sector, otherwise inferior projects in the public sector could divert funds away from superior projects in the private sector. The social opportunity cost discount rate may well therefore need to be similar to the private sector rate. Finally, the government borrowing rate is a risk-free interest rate since it entails little risk of default in repaying the loan, while private sector rates entail a risk premium, so that the government borrowing rate may be too low in opportunity-cost terms.

In most public investment appraisals the discount rate applied has tended to follow current prevailing private-sector interest rates.

See INVESTMENT APPRAISAL, DISCOUNTED CASH FLOW, PAYBACK PERIOD, COST-BENEFIT ANALYSIS, TIME PREFERENCE.

discount store a self-service RETAIL OUTLET which tends to specialize in a narrow range of products and which uses aggressive cut-pricing techniques to maximize store sales. Discount stores are usually run as part of a multiple CHAIN STORE business which is able to derive considerable benefits from concentrated BULK BUYING from manufacturers.

See RETAILER, DISTRIBUTION CHANNEL.

discretionary competition policy an approach to the control of MARKET STRUCTURE and MARKET CONDUCT which involves the individual examination of, for example, MERGERS, RESTRICTIVE TRADE AGREEMENTS and practices, etc., in terms of their advantages and disadvantages in order to determine whether or not their economic effects are, on balance, beneficial or harmful. See COMPETITION POLICY, WILLIAMSON TRADE-OFF MODEL, PUBLIC INTEREST.

discriminating monopolist a monopolist (see MONOPOLY) who is sometimes able to increase his profit by dividing his market and charging discriminating prices. Apart from the requirement that the two markets are in some way distinct such that buyers in one market cannot resell to those being asked a higher price in another market, price discrimination is only worthwhile when the PRICE ELASTICITY OF DEMAND in each market is different. See Fig. 44. In principle, if a monopolist was able to charge each consumer the maximum amount that the consumer would be willing to pay for each unit bought, then the monopolist would be able to appropriate all the CONSUMER SURPLUS in the form of sales revenue.

discriminatory tariff a TARIFF that is applied on an imported product at different rates depending upon the country of origin of those IMPORTS. Discriminating tariffs distort the pattern of international trade and are generally prohibited by the GENERAL AGREEMENT ON TARIFFS AND TRADE (GATT) unless practised within a CUSTOMS UNION.

diseconomies of scale the possible increase in long-run unit or AVERAGE COST which may occur as the scale of the firms' output is increased beyond some critical point.

Initially, as output is increased long-run average costs may at first decline, reflecting the presence of ECONOMIES OF SCALE, but after a certain point long-run average costs may start to rise. See Fig. 45.

The most frequently cited sources of such diseconomies are the managerial and administration problems of controlling and coordinating large-scale operations and labour relations problems in large plants. See MINIMUM EFFICIENT SCALE, EXTERNAL DISECONOMIES OF SCALE.

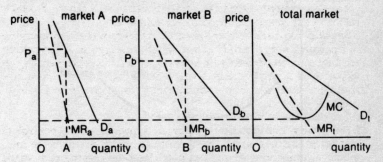

Fig. 44. **Discriminating monopolist.** A price-discriminating model, involving two markets. The demand curve facing the monopolist in market A (D_a) is less elastic than that in market B (D_b). The horizontal addition of D_a and D_b gives D_t, and the horizontal addition of the MARGINAL REVENUE curves MR_a and MR_b gives MR_t. MC is the monopolist's MARGINAL COST curve. The profit maximizing output (see PROFIT MAXIMIZATION) for the monopolist is determined by the intersection of the MC curve for his total output and the aggregated MR_t curve. The broken horizontal line connects the two diagrams at the level where the MR of the monopolist in market A is equal to the MR in market B, and this aggregate MR_t is equal to the MC of the total output. It follows that the profit maximizing output in market A is OA and in market B, OB. At these respective outputs, the discriminating monopolist will charge OP_a in market A and the lower price OP_b in market B.

disequilibrium a situation where a state of EQUILIBRIUM has not been attained, or having been attained, ceases to be maintained. If there is a natural tendency towards equilibrium the system is said to be *stable*. If the reverse is true, the system is said to be *unstable*. See COBWEB THEOREM, DYNAMIC ANALYSIS.

disguised (concealed) unemployment a form of UNEMPLOYMENT in which people able and willing to work do not register as unemployed and seeking work, which results in their absence from the official unemployment figures. Unless there are clear incentives for people to register as unemployed (by, for example, linking registration with entitlement to unemployment payments) then the official unemployment figure may considerably understate the actual level of unemployment.

See POVERTY TRAP.

disinflation a fall in the general price level, frequently accompanied by a reduction in the level of national income (DEFLATION). A disinflation is often deliberately brought about by the authorities in order to combat INFLATION and to eliminate a BALANCE OF PAYMENTS deficit. Instruments

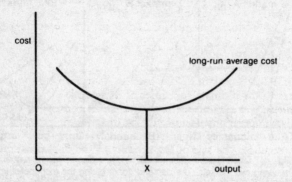

Fig. 45. **Diseconomies of scale**. In the range of output beyond point X, the firm is experiencing diseconomies of scale with costs increasing as output increases.

of disinflationary policy include fiscal measures (e.g., tax increases), monetary measures (e.g., higher interest rates), and prices and income controls. See FISCAL POLICY, MONETARY POLICY, PRICES AND INCOME POLICY, INFLATIONARY GAP, INTERNAL–EXTERNAL BALANCE MODEL.

disintermediation a situation where a FINANCIAL INTERMEDIARY such as a BUILDING SOCIETY is forced to reduce its lending operations because of the withdrawal of deposits from it, and because it is unable to attract new funds. Disintermediation usually occurs (and then only temporarily) when an intermediary (see INTERMEDIATION) fails to adjust its borrowing rates on deposits promptly when interest rates rise, so that its rates are insufficiently competitive vis-a-vis other deposit-taking institutions.

disinvestment 1. a decrease in a country's CAPITAL STOCK that occurs when there is insufficient new INVESTMENT to cover CAPITAL CONSUMPTION/DEPRECIATION (capital lost due to wear and tear).

2. the sale or closure by a firm of part of its business.

See DIVESTMENT.

disposable income the amount of current income available to HOUSEHOLDS after payment of personal INCOME TAXES and NATIONAL INSURANCE CONTRIBUTIONS. Disposable income may be reduced further where households enter into long-term contractual payments such as PENSION contributions and MORTGAGE payments. Disposable income is an important determinant of the level of CONSUMPTION expenditure and SAVING in the economy. See CONSUMPTION SCHEDULE, SAVINGS SCHEDULE.

dissaving the excess of current CONSUMPTION expenditure over current DISPOSABLE INCOME, the difference being met by HOUSEHOLDS drawing on their past SAVING. See SAVINGS SCHEDULE.

distribution the process of storing and moving products to customers, often through intermediaries such as WHOLESALERS and RETAILERS.

See DISTRIBUTION CHANNEL.

distribution census see CENSUS.

distribution channel the route used to distribute a good from the producer to the ultimate consumer of that good.

Functionally, a typical distribution channel consists of three basic interrelated operations: manufacturing (making the product); wholesaling (the holding of large STOCKS and 'breaking-bulk' into retail packs); retailing (the sale of the product to the final consumer) (see WHOLESALER, RETAILER). *Organizationally*, these functions may be undertaken by firms which specialize at a particular stage in the chain or they may be combined together, wholly or partially, and undertaken by the one firm as an integrated operation (see VERTICAL INTEGRATION). The attractions of 'INTERNALIZING' the distribution function include the avoidance of TRANSACTION COSTS involved in dealing through the market, better control and coordination of the movement of products, various advantages over competitors (see FORECLOSURE, PRICE SQUEEZE) and the more effective MARKETING of products.

Thus, depending on the 'traditions' of the trade, the nature of the product and the characteristics of the market being served, and the relative costs and marketing effectiveness of using different channel intermediaries, a number of distributive channel configurations may be identified, as Fig. 46 illustrates. Line 1 shows a conventional channel structure with the products being 'moved' on an arms'-length basis, that is, through independent intermediaries at each separate stage.

Alternatively (line 2) a retailer such as a SUPERMARKET chain may buy in bulk direct from manufacturers and undertake the wholesaling

1. Manufacturing (M) → wholesaling (W) → retailing (R) → buyers

2. M → [WR] → buyers

3. [MW] → R → buyers

4. [MWR] → buyers

→ = independent function
□ = integrated function

Fig. 46. **Distribution channels**.

function itself as an integrated wholesaling-retailing operation; a manufacturer may combine the production and wholesaling functions (line 3), on-selling to independent retailers or, alternatively, combine all three operations (line 4), selling directly to final buyers. Additionally, at some stage in a channel, agents, whose primary function is to generate new business contacts, may be employed.

For many products, distributive arrangements are multidimensional with a variety of modes employed, depending upon which MARKET or MARKET SEGMENTS are being targetted.

distribution costs the COSTS involved in the physical distribution of products. They include packaging and transport costs, warehousing and stockholding costs. See OVERHEADS.

distribution of income see INCOME DISTRIBUTION.

distributive efficiency an aspect of MARKET PERFORMANCE that denotes the EFFICIENCY of a market in distributing its outputs from suppliers to consumers. The costs of distribution include transportation, storage and handling expenses, together with the distributor's profit margins. In addition, suppliers incur SELLING COSTS (ADVERTISING and other PRODUCT DIFFERENTIATION expenditures) in creating and sustaining a demand for their products. Optimal distributive efficiency is achieved when physical distribution costs are minimized and selling costs are maintained at the minimum level to sustain total market demand.

disutility the dissatisfaction or pain that an individual encounters in consuming a product or in working. Compare UTILITY.

diversification or **conglomerate integration** the process whereby a firm expands by supplying a range of different products and as such operates in a number of markets rather than a single market. There may be links between the products based on complementary research, production or marketing functions (e.g., two products which utilize a common technological base – steel razor blades and garden spades – and which are sold through the same outlets – supermarkets), or the products may be entirely unrelated (for example, cigarettes and banking services).

From the firm's point of view the main attractions of diversification are:

(a) the ability to spread risks by offering a number of products in different markets such that poor sales or losses in one market can be offset by good sales and profits achieved in other markets, thus facilitating a good average performance by the firm overall. By contrast, a one-product firm is extremely vulnerable to cyclical fluctuations in sales over a business cycle.

(b) (from a longer-term strategic perspective), the ability to reorientate its activities away from mature and declining markets into new areas of higher growth and profit potential. A one-product firm is especially vulnerable to both product and market obsolescence in a world of increasing technical complexity and change as new products are invented and new consumer demands created (see PRODUCT-MARKET MATRIX; BOSTON MATRIX).

Diversification is especially associated with the expansion of large, oligopolistic firms (see OLIGOPOLY) controlled in the main by professional managers rather than the firms' shareholders (see DIVORCE OF OWNERSHIP FROM CONTROL) who pursue growth and long-run profit maximization objectives rather than the goal of static (short-run) profit maximization as portrayed in the traditional THEORY OF THE FIRM (see MANAGERIAL THEORIES OF THE FIRM).

The growing importance of large diversified firms raises some fundamental issues with regard to resource allocation processes. Specifically, RESOURCE ALLOCATION decisions are determined less by competition in markets and have come to depend more on the planning of activities within firms. Competition for investment funds in the market is replaced by competition for funds between various branches within the company, with retained profits providing the finance and senior head office staff acting as an internal capital market, channelling funds from low profit to high profit areas. Managers rather than markets become the main arbiters in the resource allocation process. Yet this can be compatible with a diversified firm having only a small market share in each of its many markets, and so no measurable market power of the conventional kind.

In terms of its wider impact on resource allocation, diversification may, on the one hand, promote greater efficiency and stimulate competition, thereby improving resource allocation, or, on the other hand, by limiting competition, it may lead to a less efficient use of resources.

Diversification may produce *synergy* (i.e., the 2 + 2 = more than 4 effect). Synergy results from complementary activities or from the carry-over of management capabilities. For example, in the case of a diversified merger, one firm may have a strong production organization, while the other excels in marketing – joining the two renders both firms more effective. Similarly, a high degree of carry-over of management expertise may make it possible to reduce production costs and improve product quality of the combined group.

Diversification can serve to increase the degree of competition by facilitation entry into industries where entry barriers are too high for smaller, more specialized firms without the financial resources of the conglomerate, i.e., the alternative profit sources to withstand initial losses in new markets whilst getting established.

Diversification can, however, produce various anticompetitive effects. For example, diversified firms are in a position to cross-subsidize temporary losses in a particular market with profits earned elsewhere. This allows the diversified firm to practise predatory pricing in the market to drive out competitors or discipline them, so raising prices to monopoly levels in the long run. The same financial power and cross-subsidizing capabilities of the diversified firm can be used to bear the short-run costs of deterring new entrants into one of its markets, thereby raising entry barriers.

Where diversified firms face each other in a number of markets then they may adopt a less competitive stance, each firm avoiding taking competitive action in markets where it is strong, for fear of risking retaliatory action by diversified rivals in other markets where it is weak. Here firms may develop 'spheres of influence', adopting live-and-let-live policies by dominating in certain of their markets and recognizing the domination of rivals in other markets. The result of such behaviour is a lack of vigorous competition with higher prices to the detriment of consumers.

The interdependence of diversified firms as buyers and sellers may also distort competition. Where firm A is both an important supplier to firm B for one product, and an important customer of firm B for another product, they may engage in reciprocal dealing, buying from firms that are good customers rather than alternative suppliers. The practice allows diversified firms to increase their market shares and increase obstacles to new entry.

Thus, diversification may produce, simultaneously, both beneficial or detrimental results. Under UK COMPETITION POLICY a proposed MERGER (TAKEOVER) between two firms supplying unrelated products, involving assets in excess of £70 million can be referred to the MONOPOLIES AND MERGERS COMMISSION to determine whether or not it operates against the public interest. See OFFICE OF FAIR TRADING, VERTICAL INTEGRATION, HORIZONTAL INTEGRATION, TRANSFER PRICING.

divestment the closure or sale by a firm of one or more of its operating units (for example, a production plant) or a whole business division. In the former case, divestment usually occurs in order to rationalize production and/or to concentrate the firm's output in a more modern plant. In contrast, the divestment of a whole business division represents a more fundamental strategic decision on the part of the firm. Divestment in this case may reflect a number of considerations, including a desire to pull out of an unprofitable, loss-making activity; the divestment of 'peripheral' businesses in order to release cash and managerial resources which, in opportunity cost terms, could be more effectively redeployed in the firm's other activities; divestment may reflect a major rethink of a firm's strategic positioning involving a retrenchment back to 'core' businesses. Finally, divestment may be required so as to avoid the opposition of the COMPETITION POLICY authorities, particularly in cases of merger and takeover.

Divestment by one firm, in turn, often presents an opportunity for some other firm to diversify (see DIVERSIFICATION) into new business areas, or for former competitors to increase their market shares.

See RATIONALIZATION, BOSTON MATRIX, DE-MERGER, MANAGEMENT BUY-OUT.

dividend a payment made by a JOINT-STOCK COMPANY to its SHAREHOLDERS for providing SHARE CAPITAL. Dividends are a distribution of the PROFITS of the company.

dividend cover ratio or **times covered ratio** a measure of the extent to which a firm's earnings cover DIVIDEND payments on SHARES, that expresses PROFIT after tax and interest charges as a ratio of total dividend payments. For example, if a firm's profit after tax was £100,000 and its dividend payments were £50,000, then its dividend cover ratio would be 2 : 1.

dividend yield the DIVIDEND paid by a JOINT-STOCK COMPANY for a given accounting period (usually one year) as a proportion of the current market price of its share. For example, if Company X declared a dividend of 50p per ORDINARY SHARE for the twelve month accounting period ended 31st December, and the current market price of one ordinary share in Company X was £10, the dividend yield would be:

$$\frac{\text{Dividend per share}}{\text{Price per share}} = \frac{50\text{p}}{£10} = 5\%$$

division of labour see SPECIALIZATION.

divorce of ownership from control a situation where although a firm is owned by its SHAREHOLDERS it is actually controlled by the firm's management (the board of directors, appointed by the shareholders at the annual general meeting to run the business on their behalf). Because the average size of individual shareholding tends to be small and shareholders are remote from day-to-day decision making, it is the firm's management which effectively determines the policies of the firm. Recognition of the control power exercised by management has led economists to develop theories of the firm which substitute managerial objective for the traditional hypothesis of PROFIT MAXIMIZATION. See MANAGERIAL THEORIES OF THE FIRM.

DOE DEPARTMENT OF THE ENVIRONMENT.

do-it-yourself (DIY) store a RETAIL OUTLET which specializes in the sale of equipment and materials primarily for home improvement purposes. See RETAILER, DISTRIBUTION CHANNEL.

dollar ($) the domestic CURRENCY of the USA. The dollar also performs various international rôles, in particular, as an INTERNATIONAL RESERVE asset, and as the numeraire of the international oil trade. See also EUROCURRENCY MARKET.

Domar economic growth model a theoretical construct which examines the dual rôle of INVESTMENT in both expanding AGGREGATE

DOMAR ECONOMIC GROWTH MODEL

DEMAND and the economy's AGGREGATE SUPPLY capacity (POTENTIAL GROSS NATIONAL PRODUCT) over time.

As one of the components of aggregate demand, investment expenditure has the effect of adding to total demand. According to the Keynesian theory of income determination, income will increase until the saving generated by the additional income offsets the higher level of investment (see EQUILIBRIUM LEVEL OF NATIONAL INCOME). Thus, if we designate the increase in investment as ΔI, income (Y) will increase by the amount:

$$\Delta Y = \frac{\Delta I}{\infty}$$

where ∞ is the MARGINAL PROPENSITY TO SAVE.

This short-term theory of income determination ignores the other effect of investment spending, i.e., that it adds to productive capacity. This capacity-creating effect is negligible in the short term, but ECONOMIC GROWTH has to do with the long term, and in the long term the rôle of investment in adding to productive capacity needs to be considered along with its demand-creating effect.

The question posed by Domar was: 'if investment increases productive capacity and also creates income, at what rate should investment grow in order to make the increase in income equal to that of productive capacity?' To answer this question, Domar set up an equation, one side of which represented the rate of increase of productive capacity, the other the rate of increase of income, and the solution of which gave the required rate of growth.

Let each pound of investment, I, add to productive capacity by the amount £θ per year. For example, if it requires £3,000 of capital to produce £1,000 of output per year, θ will be one-third or 33% per year. The symbol θ represents the CAPITAL–OUTPUT RATIO, which is the relationship between increments of investment and the resulting increments of output. The productive capacity of the economy has therefore increased by $I\theta$, which is the capacity-creating effect of investment and the supply side of our equation.

To utilize this additional capacity, demand must increase by an equal amount. Turning to the demand side of the equation, MULTIPLIER theory tells us that with any given marginal propensity to save, £, an increase in national income is a function not of I but of the increment in investment, ΔI, that is, the absolute annual increase in investment. The corresponding absolute annual increase in income is then:

$$\Delta Y = \Delta I . \frac{I}{\infty}$$

where $1/\pounds$ is the multiplier. To fulfil the condition that income and capacity should increase at the same rate requires that:

$$\frac{\Delta I}{I} = \propto \theta$$

The left-hand side expression is the annual percentage rate of growth of investment which, to maintain an assumed full employment with growing productive capacity, must grow at the annual percentage rate $\pounds\theta$. Income must also grow at the same annual percentage rate.

See SOLOW ECONOMIC GROWTH MODEL, HARROD ECONOMIC GROWTH MODEL.

domestic credit expansion (DCE) a monetary aggregate that is sometimes used by the INTERNATIONAL MONETARY FUND in requiring monetary restraint on the part of a member country with a balance of payments deficit as a condition of access to the Fund's resources. The main elements of DCE are made up primarily of the annual rate of change of the domestic MONEY SUPPLY (defined in a number of possible ways) and annual rate of change of external borrowing by the private and public sectors. Under a FIXED EXCHANGE-RATE SYSTEM excessive monetary expansion either by an increase in the money supply or overseas financing can lead to domestic price levels rising at a faster rate than trade partners, resulting in a balance-of-payments deficit. It follows, therefore, that monetary restraint (or, in the last resort, a currency DEVALUATION) is necessary to restore balance-of-payments equilibrium. Under a FLOATING-EXCHANGE-RATE SYSTEM, tight control of monetary expansion is less urgent, it is argued, because divergences in domestic price levels between countries will be offset by exchange rate movements.

See PURCHASING POWER PARITY THEORY.

dominant firm a firm that accounts for a significant proportion of the supply of a particular good or service. Such a firm exercises a considerable degree of power in determining the supply terms of the product (see PRICE LEADERSHIP) and may be tempted to further its own interests at the expense of consumers. A *monopoly firm* is one that controls the entire supply of a particular product (see MONOPOLY).

Under UK COMPETITION POLICY a dominant firm is defined as a firm which supplies one-quarter or more of a specified good or service. See OFFICE OF FAIR TRADING, MONOPOLIES AND MERGERS COMMISSION.

dominant firm-price leader see PRICE LEADERSHIP.

double coincidence of wants see BARTER.

double taxation the TAXATION OF INCOMES and PROFITS, first in the country where they arise, and again when these incomes and profits are remitted to the income earner's home country. Such double taxation can be a significant deterrent to international labour and capital movements. For this reason many countries have negotiated double taxation agreements which limit taxation liability to the country in which the income is earned.

See UNITARY TAXATION.

Dow-Jones Index see SHARE-PRICE INDEX.

drawing right see INTERNATIONAL MONETARY FUND.

DSS see DEPARTMENT OF SOCIAL SECURITY.

DTI see DEPARTMENT OF TRADE AND INDUSTRY.

dual economy an economy in which capital-intensive and techno-logically-advanced sectors exist in mutual cohabitation with labour-intensive and technologically-primitive sectors. An area of study within DEVELOPMENT ECONOMICS, the problem is whether to achieve ECONOMIC GROWTH through leading technological sectors or to attempt to spread an economy's resources more thinly across all sec-tors to achieve balanced growth. The concept is mainly applied within the context of a DEVELOPING COUNTRY.

See INDUSTRIALIZATION.

dumping the EXPORT of a good at a price below that charged for the good in the domestic market. Dumping may occur as a short-term response to a domestic recession (i.e., surplus output is sold abroad at a cut-price simply to off-load it), or as a longer-term strategic means of penetrating export markets (once a foothold has been gained prices would then be increased to generate profits). Either way, dumping is viewed as 'unfair' trade, and is outlawed by international trade pacts such as the GENERAL AGREEMENT ON TARIFFS AND TRADE. See BEGGAR-MY-NEIGHBOUR POLICY, COUNTERVAILING DUTY.

duopoly a subset of OLIGOPOLY describing a MARKET situation in which there are only two suppliers. There are a number of models of duo-poly markets which fall into two main categories:

(a) nonreactive models that do not allow for any anticipation by one firm of his competitor's reaction to either a price or quantity change. For example, in the *Bertrand duopoly* model, each supplier assumes that his rival will not change price in response to his own initial price cut, and this assumption will encourage him to cut his price in order to increase his sales. Since both firms reason in this way the price will eventually be driven down to the competitive level (i.e., a NORMAL PROFIT equilibrium). In the *Cournot duopoly* model it is quantity not price which is adjusted, with one firm altering its output on the assumption that his rival's output will remain unchanged. Since both firms reason in this way output will eventually be expanded to the point where the firms share the market equally and both secure only normal profits.

(b) reactive models that explicitly assume that the two firms recog-nize that their actions are interdependent and hence will attempt to avoid mutually ruinous forms of rivalry. Also called *collusive duopoly*. Specifically, firms will attempt to maximize their joint profits by establishing agreed prices above the competitive equilibrium price. This can be achieved by informal means such as the acceptance by both duopolists that one of them acts as price leader (see PRICE LEADER-SHIP model) or by means of formal COLLUSION between the two duopolists (see CARTEL).

duopsony a MARKET situation in which there are only two buyers, but many sellers.

Compare DUOPOLY.

durable good a CONSUMER GOOD such as a motor car, and CAPITAL GOOD such as a machine, which is used up over relatively long periods of time rather than immediately.

Contrast NONDURABLE GOOD.

dynamic analysis a method of economic analysis which traces out the path of adjustment from one state of EQUILIBRIUM to another. Consider, for example, the effects of a change of the export demand on the EQUILIBRIUM LEVEL OF NATIONAL INCOME.

See Fig. 47.

See COMPARATIVE STATIC EQUILIBRIUM ANALYSIS, DISEQUILIBRIUM.

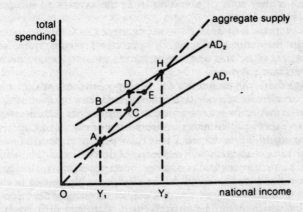

Fig. 47. Dynamic analysis. An increase in export demand raises AGGREGATE DEMAND from AD_1 to AD_2 and results in an increase in the equilibrium level of national income from Y_1 to Y_2. In moving from Y_1 to Y_2, a number of steps are involved. The initial increase in exports raises aggregate demand from A to B and produces an increase in real output from B to C. This extra output creates, via the MULTIPLIER EFFECT, additional income and expands aggregate demand further from C to D. The extra spending in turn produces an increase in real output from D to E. These movements continue until a new equilibrium position is reached at point H.

E

earned income the return accruing to LABOUR for work done. The distinction between earned and unearned INCOME is made by the INLAND REVENUE for ease of assessment and collection of INCOME TAX. Earned income comprises WAGES, SALARIES, FEES, COMMISSION and PROFITS attributable to sole proprietors and partners within partnerships. *Unearned income*, by contrast, is primarily the return accruing to NATURAL RESOURCES and CAPITAL in the form of rental income, DIVIDENDS or INTEREST received. Earned income is generally taxed progressively, commencing with a tax-free income band and progressively increasing the rate of TAXATION in predetermined bands of income as income increases.

The distinction between earned and unearned income is not a valid one in economics as all FACTORS OF PRODUCTION can be said to 'earn' income. Even from the taxation authorities' view the distinction has been controversial, the argument being put forward that unearned income is the result of investing from the SAVINGS of income previously earned.

See INCIDENCE OF TAXATION, PROGRESSIVE TAXATION.

earnings the returns accruing to FACTORS OF PRODUCTION, such as WAGES, SALARIES, FEES and COMMISSIONS, PROFITS, RENTS, DIVIDENDS and INTEREST payments.

earnings drift the propensity for earnings, primarily WAGES and SALARIES, to increase at a rate faster than agreed rates per unit of LABOUR. Many factors contribute towards an earnings drift such as OVERTIME, bonuses, special agreements, restructuring of PIECEWORK agreements and so forth. Areas where a particular skill is in demand will pay higher rates than areas where shortages do not exist. The ability to negotiate such terms and conditions, sometimes informally, between employer and employee, leads to a significant weakening in the case for an incomes policy as a tool of economic management due to the ease by which it can be circumvented. Earnings drift tends to be associated with conditions of full employment where employers are more readily prepared to concede wage increases to retain their labour force.

See INFLATION, PRICES AND INCOMES POLICY.

earnings per share NET PROFIT after tax accruing to the ordinary shareholders in a JOINT-STOCK COMPANY, divided by the number of ORDINARY SHARES.

earnings yield NET PROFIT after tax per ordinary share (EARNINGS PER SHARE) of a JOINT-STOCK COMPANY for a given accounting period, expressed as a percentage of the current market price per share. For example, if profit after tax was £1 per share and the market price per share was £10 then the earnings yield would be 10%. Earnings yield is the mirror image of the PRICE-EARNINGS RATIO.

Earnings yield depends upon DIVIDEND YIELD and DIVIDEND COVER. For example, if dividend yield was 5% and the dividend was covered twice over then the earnings yield would be 5% × 2 or 10%.

EC see EUROPEAN COMMUNITY.

econometrics the discipline within economics that attempts to measure and estimate statistically the relationship between two or more economic variables. For example, economic theory suggests that consumption expenditure is a function of disposable income ($C = f(Y)$) or, more precisely, that consumption expenditure is linked to disposable income through the equation: $C = a + b . Y$. For each level of disposable income, consumption can be measured and a statistical relationship established between the two variables by making numerical estimates of the parameters, a and b in the equation. Because consumption is dependent upon income it is termed the DEPENDENT VARIABLE, whilst disposable income is termed the INDEPENDENT VARIABLE. Econometric models can have many hundreds of measured variables, linked by several hundred estimated equations, not just one, as is the case when models are constructed for macroeconomic FORECASTING purposes.

See REGRESSION ANALYSIS.

economic aid the provision of financial and physical forms of assistance to (mainly) the DEVELOPING COUNTRIES as a means of strengthening their economies. Economic aid is provided both on a bilateral basis by individual governments and private institutions (commercial banks, for example), and on a multilateral basis through the WORLD BANK and other international organizations, for example, the European Community's Overseas Development Fund. Such assistance 'tops-up' the foreign exchange earnings and domestic savings of recipient countries, as well as providing techniques and managerial resources and expertise which would otherwise be unobtainable locally.

See ECONOMIC DEVELOPMENT, INTERNATIONAL DEBT.

economically active population the proportion of a country's POPULATION which is involved in the production and distribution of goods and services, that is, the LABOUR FORCE.

economic cost see OPPORTUNITY COST.

economic development a process of economic transition involving the structural transformation of an economy through INDUSTRIALIZATION and a raising of GROSS NATIONAL PRODUCT and INCOME PER HEAD. Generally speaking DEVELOPING COUNTRIES are characterized by subsistence primary production (mainly agriculture) and low levels of income per head; DEVELOPED COUNTRIES are characterized by large manufacturing and service sectors and high levels of income per head.

Capital INVESTMENT is a significant factor in the transformation process. Investment not only enlarges an economy's capacity to produce goods and service and raise the PRODUCTIVITY of resources, but also, via multiplier effects, increases aggregate demand and national income. An increase in national income raises the level of savings, thereby providing the finance for further capital accumulation. See Fig. 48.

See DEMOGRAPHIC TRANSITION, STRUCTURE OF INDUSTRY, ECONOMIC AID.

| | Income per head | Economic structure | | |
| | | Gross Domestic Product (%) | | |
	US$ dollars	Agriculture	Industry	Services
Developing countries				
Egypt	720	20	21	59
Mozambique	90	33	12	55
Rwanda	80	51	9	40
Ethiopia	100	57	10	33
Developed countries				
UK	18,340	2	32	66
Japan	34,630	2	40	58
US	25,880	2	29	69
Germany	25,580	1	38	61

Fig. 48. **Economic development**. The income per head and economic structure for selected countries, 1994. Source: *World Development Report*, World Bank, 1996.

economic efficiency an aspect of PRODUCTION which seeks to identify for a given level of OUTPUT, that combination of FACTOR INPUTS which minimizes the COST of producing that output. More broadly, economic efficiency is equated with the effectiveness of RESOURCE ALLOCATION in the economy as a whole such that outputs of goods and services fully reflect consumer preferences for these goods and services as well as individual goods and services being produced at minimum cost through appropriate mixes of factor inputs.

See EFFICIENCY, COST FUNCTION.

economic forecasts see FORECASTING.

economic goods see GOODS.

economic growth the growth of the real OUTPUT of an economy over time. Economic growth is usually measured in terms of an increase in real GROSS NATIONAL PRODUCT (GNP) or GROSS DOMESTIC PRODUCT (GDP) over time (see Fig. 49) or an increase in INCOME PER

HEAD over time. The latter measure relates increases in total output to changes in the population. Therefore, if total output rises only a little faster than the increase in population, then there will be only a small improvement in average living standards.

The achievement of a high rate of economy growth is one of the four main objectives of MACROECONOMIC POLICY. The significance of economic growth lies in its contribution to the general prosperity of the community. Growth is desirable because it enables the community to consume more private goods and services, and it also contributes to the provision of a greater quantity of social goods and services (health, education, etc.), thereby improving real living standards. However, rapid economic growth can also contribute to the exhaustion of finite natural resources and exacerbate problems of environmental pollution.

The ability of an economy to produce more goods and services is dependent on a number of factors:

(a) an increase in the stock and quality of its capital goods (CAPITAL ACCUMULATION). See INVESTMENT.

(b) an increase in the quantity and quality of its LABOUR FORCE.

(c) an increase in the quantity and quality of its NATURAL RESOURCES.

(d) an efficient use of these factor inputs so as to maximize their contribution to the expansion of output, through improved PRODUCTIVITY.

(e) The development and introduction of innovative techniques and new products (TECHNOLOGICAL PROGRESSIVENESS).

The latter two factors are especially important where a country's economic position is materially affected by INTERNATIONAL TRADE influences, underlining the importance of competitiveness for countries who are significant exporters and importers (see IMPORT PENETRATION).

Whether or not an economy actually realizes its growth potential is dependent on one further consideration:

(f) the level of AGGREGATE DEMAND. The level of demand needs to be high enough to ensure the full utilization of the increased productive capabilities of the economy.

Governments can stimulate the growth process by increasing current spending in the economy through tax cuts (see FISCAL POLICY), and by increasing the money supply and reducing interest rates (see MONETARY POLICY). Additionally, they can operate on the supply-side of the economy by promoting enterprise initiatives and providing resources for improving productivity and research (see SUPPLY-SIDE ECONOMICS, INDUSTRIAL POLICY).

See PRODUCTION POSSIBILITY BOUNDARY, CAPITAL-LABOUR RATIO, CAPITAL-OUTPUT RATIO, CAPITAL WIDENING, CAPITAL-DEEPENING, POTENTIAL GROSS NATIONAL PRODUCT, DOMAR ECONOMIC GROWTH

MODEL, HARROD ECONOMIC GROWTH MODEL, SOLOW ECONOMIC
GROWTH MODEL, INTERTEMPORAL SUBSTITUTION.

Average annual growth rate of GDP

%

	1965–80	1980–90	1991	1992	1993	1994	1995
Japan	6.4	4.1	4.3	1.1	0.1	0.6	0.5
US	2.7	3.4	−0.7	2.6	3.0	4.1	2.9
Germany	3.3	2.1	1.0	2.1	−1.2	2.9	2.6
UK	2.3	3.1	−2.2	−0.6	1.9	3.8	2.7

Fig. 49. **Economic growth**. The increase in GROSS DOMESTIC PRODUCT
(GDP) in selected countries, 1965–95. Source: *World Development
Report*, World Bank and IMF, 1996.

economic growth models see DOMAR ECONOMIC GROWTH MODEL,
HARROD ECONOMIC GROWTH MODEL, SOLOW ECONOMIC GROWTH
MODEL.

economic man an assumption in economic theory that individuals
act rationally in specifying their objectives and then take decisions
which are consistent with those objectives. Thus, the ENTREPRENEUR
will set a goal of PROFIT MAXIMIZATION and will adjust his output and
price to achieve this goal. Again, the CONSUMER will seek to maximize
his UTILITY or satisfaction and will determine his purchases in the light
of his tastes for products and the relative prices of those products. See
Fig. 50 for an illustration of rational consumer choice. See CONSUMER
RATIONALITY, CONSUMER EQUILIBRIUM, BEHAVIOURAL THEORY OF THE
FIRM.

economic model a construct or model incorporating two or more
variables that: (a) describes the relationship that exists between the
variables; (b) depicts the economic outcome of their relationships;
(c) predicts the effects of changes in the variables on the economic
outcome.

Economic models are used to summarize the essential characteristics of complex economic phenomena in order to simplify them
and render them amenable to analysis. This normally requires the
model-builder to make certain simplifying *assumptions* about human
behaviour. For example, in order to analyse demand, economists
assume that consumers seek to maximize their satisfaction (utility)
and that they will rationally consume more of a product whose price
has fallen, and vice versa.

There are numerous economic models portrayed in this book; for
example, EQUILIBRIUM MARKET PRICE, EQUILIBRIUM MARKET PRICE

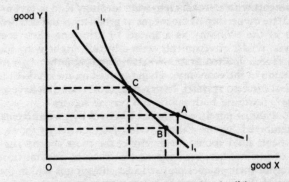

Fig. 50. **Economic man**. The graph demonstrates why, if the assumption of rational consumer behaviour holds, a consumer's INDIFFERENCE CURVES cannot cross. Indifference curves II and I_1I_1 show a consumer's preference between two products, X and Y. Point A on indifference curve II represents a higher level of satisfaction to the consumer than point B on indifference curve I_1I_1 because point A represents more of both products than point B. Yet point C lies on both curves. This suggest that the consumer, having preferred the combination of goods indicated by point A to the combination represented by point B, now regards them as equal at point C. If the consumer is rational, such an inconsistent or intransitive set of preferences would not arise; hence indifference curves do not intersect.

(CHANGES IN), EQUILIBRIUM LEVEL OF NATIONAL INCOME, MULTIPLIER. See also ECONOMETRICS, HYPOTHESIS TESTING, ENDOGENOUS VARIABLE, EXOGENOUS VARIABLE.

economic order quantity see STOCKHOLDING (INVENTORY) COSTS.

economic planning see INDICATIVE PLANNING, CENTRALLY PLANNED ECONOMY, NATIONAL PLAN.

economic policy the strategies and measures adopted by the government to manage the economy as a means of achieving its economic objectives. In general terms, governments are concerned with (at the macro-level) securing full employment (see UNEMPLOYMENT), price stability (see INFLATION), ECONOMIC GROWTH and BALANCE OF PAYMENTS equilibrium, and (at the micro-level) an efficient use of resources. In practice, given the complexities of the economy and its exposure to international influences, the simultaneous achievement of all these objectives is virtually impossible, so that a degree of prioritizing is required. Inevitably, political as well as economic considerations will influence this process.

The priority accorded to different economic objectives will reflect the ideology of the ruling government (which at the extremes could range from democratically elected to non-elected dictatorships). Governments with a broadly left-wing ideology tend to favour widespread State ownership of the means of production and detailed intervention in the economy as a means of achieving their economic objectives; whilst governments with a broadly right-wing ideology tend to favour limited State ownership and minimum government intervention in the economy, relying instead on the market mechanism (see ECONOMIC SYSTEM). In practice, most countries have a MIXED ECONOMY, featuring both public and private sectors.

The pursuit of purely economic objectives by governments needs to be tempered by the various value judgements or views which governments hold about, for example, the most appropriate distribution of income between citizens (see INCOME DISTRIBUTION), and the effects of their policies on particular sub-groups within the community and the desirability of helping some groups at the expense of others. Governments also hold different value judgements with regard to the priority accorded to national defence, law and order, protection of the environment, and many other non-economic issues. All of these so-called 'normative' elements can have an impact on the formulation of economic objectives and policies (see NORMATIVE ECONOMICS).

At the MACROECONOMIC POLICY level, various general measures can be used by governments operating in mixed economies to achieve their objectives, including FISCAL POLICY (the manipulation of tax rates and government expenditure), MONETARY POLICY (the control of the money supply and interest rates), PRICES AND INCOMES POLICIES (controls on costs and prices), and the management of the EXCHANGE RATE to influence the country's external trade and payments position. These policies are augmented at a more specific level by measures designed to encourage industrial investment, research and development and enterprise, and to protect consumers' interests (see INDUSTRIAL POLICY, REGIONAL POLICY, COMPETITION POLICY).

Fiscal and monetary policies, the main measures used by successive governments in the UK since 1945, operate on the level and distribution of spending in the economy. They are thus essentially demand-side measures. In recent years greater emphasis has been given to the need to improve the supply-side of the economy, reflected, in particular, by attempts to inject greater flexibility into the workings of the labour market by breaking down the power of trade union monopolies.

See WELFARE ECONOMICS, SUPPLY-SIDE ECONOMICS, MICROECONOMIC POLICY.

economic rent a money payment made for a FACTOR OF PRODUCTION which is over and above the minimum payment to keep it in its present use. This minimum payment is known as TRANSFER EARNINGS and it represents an OPPORTUNITY COST. Thus, for example, a person might just be willing to work as a lecturer for a minimum of £1000 per month, because he could earn this amount working in his 'next best' job as a taxi driver. If his actual earnings are £1100 per month, then his monthly earnings would comprise transfer earnings of £1000 and economic rent of £100. Economic rent is a *surplus* insofar as its payment is not necessary to ensure a supply of a particular factor of production. Fig. 51 shows the demand for, and supply of, lecturers at the prevailing market wage rate (OW) which is equal to, say, £1100 per month, enough to induce sufficient lecturers (OQ) to offer themselves to work and meet the demand for their services (D). At this wage rate the last (marginal) people offering their services as lecturers will only do so for £1100 per month, since this is the amount they could currently earn elsewhere as, say, driving instructors. However, since all lecturers of a common grade would be paid the same per month, an intra-marginal lecturer (Q_1) would be paid wage rate OW even though he would have been prepared to work as a lecturer for a smaller wage (OW_1). The economic rent of the intra-marginal lecturer is equal to WW_1. *Total* transfer earnings in the figure are equal to the diagonally shaded area *below* the supply curve and economic rent is equal to the vertically shaded area *above* the supply curve.

The economic rent earned by a factor of production depends essentially upon the demand for the products made with that factor and thus the DERIVED DEMAND for that factor. Thus, for example, if the demand for lecturers was to rise from D to D_1 in Fig. 51, then in order to induce more people to enter lecturing and thus increase the supply of lecturers to OQ_2, wage rates would need to rise to OW_2. This would mean that existing lecturers such as Q_1 would now earn a higher wage rate and secure a larger economic rent (W_1W_2). By contrast, if the demand for lecturers falls, then so will their wage rates, with some lecturers transferring to better-paid employments whilst those remaining earn wages much closer to their transfer earnings.

The effect of demand upon transfer earnings and economic rent will depend upon the PRICE ELASTICITY OF SUPPLY of a factor of production. If the supply curve for a factor is comparatively price-elastic, then most of the factor earnings would take the form of transfer earnings and little economic rent would accrue – for example, the market for unskilled labourers. In the extreme case of a horizontal supply curve for a factor of production which is in perfectly price-elastic supply, then all the earnings would be transfer earnings and no economic rent would accrue. By contrast, if the supply curve for a factor is comparatively price-inelastic, then most of the factor earnings would take the form of economic rent – for example, the market for sports champions and pop music entertainers. In the extreme case of a vertical supply curve for a factor of production which is in perfectly price-inelastic supply, then all the earnings would be economic rent.

Some factors of production may be in relatively price-inelastic supply in the short run but more elastic supply in the long run, and thus may earn 'temporary' economic rents until supply is able to adjust fully to demand. The economic rents accruing to such factors of production are termed 'quasi-rents', and they tend to disappear in the long run as supply catches up with demand. For example, in the case of particular types of work where a lengthy training period is required, a sudden increase in the demand for such work would enable persons already possessing the appropriate skills to secure large quasi-rents through high wage rates.

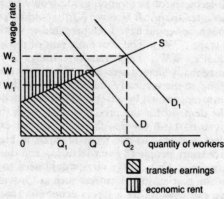

Fig. 51. Economic rent.

economics the study of the problem of using available FACTORS OF PRODUCTION as efficiently as possible so as to attain the maximum fulfilment of society's unlimited demands for GOODS and SERVICES. The ultimate purpose of economic endeavour is to satisfy human wants for goods and services. The problem is that whereas wants are virtually without limit, the resources – NATURAL RESOURCES, LABOUR and CAPITAL – available at any one time to produce goods and services, are limited in supply; i.e., resources are scarce (see SCARCITY) relative to the demands they are called upon to satisfy. The fact of scarcity means that we must always be making CHOICES. If, to take a simple example, more resources are devoted to producing motor cars, fewer resources are then available for providing hospitals and other goods. Various ECONOMIC SYSTEMS may be employed to allocate resources and deal with such choices.

Economics has a microeconomic and a macroeconomic dimension. Microeconomics is concerned with the efficient supply of *particular* products. Macroeconomics is concerned with the *overall* efficiency of resource use in the economy, in particular the achievement of FULL EMPLOYMENT of current resources and the growth of output over time.

See OPPORTUNITY COSTS, PRODUCTION POSSIBILITY BOUNDARY, EFFICIENCY, PRICE SYSTEM, ECONOMIC GROWTH.

economic sanctions bilateral or multinational prohibitions (embargoes) on the EXPORT and IMPORT of goods, services and capital to and from a particular country. Economic sanctions are applied as an adjunct to political pressure being brought to bear on a country by the international community for that country to change its political/economic policies.

economic statistics the statistics collected by government and other bodies concerning levels of output and income in an economy, exports and imports, unemployment levels, rates of inflation, etc.

Economic statistics may be used to show trends in economic variables over time and to facilitate comparisons between countries or regions within a country. This data may be analysed by conventional statistical methods or by ECONOMETRICS to establish significant relationships between the variables involved as a basis for formulating ECONOMIC POLICY.

Economic statistics are contained in government publications such as the *UK National Accounts* (Blue Book), *UK Balance of Payments* (Pink Book), and the *Department of Employment Gazette*. International statistics appear in such publications as the *United Nations Yearbook*, *OECD Main Economic Indicators*, and *EC Statistical Digest*.

economic system a mechanism for tackling the twin problems of SCARCITY and CHOICE. Because economic resources are limited relative to society's demand for goods and services, some means of allocating resources between alternative ends is required. In the modern world three basic allocative mechanisms perform this function: PRIVATE ENTERPRISE ECONOMY in which resources are allocated through markets; CENTRALLY PLANNED ECONOMY in which resources are allocated by the State; MIXED ECONOMY in which resources are allocated both by the market and by the State.

See NATIONALIZATION, PRIVATIZATION.

economic theory the formulation of ECONOMIC MODELS about the relationships between economic variables in order to generate testable hypotheses from these models. Where a HYPOTHESIS conflicts with real world data then the hypothesis will be amended or abandoned in favour of a better one; where the hypothesis is confirmed by the data then it can form a valuable guide in the specification of ECONOMIC POLICY. Economic theory aims to produce simplified economic models of real-world economic phenomena by employing a process of logical deduction from sets of initial assumptions about the behaviour of consumers, producers, etc. (often using mathematical analysis). Having specified a hypothesis based upon the economic model, it is then possible to test the hypothesis against empirical data. See HYPOTHESIS TESTING.

economic union a form of TRADE INTEGRATION between a number of countries, that provides not only the COMMON MARKET features of free trade and factor movements but also the unification of members' general economic objectives in respect of economic growth, employment, etc., and the harmonization of monetary, fiscal and other policies.

Economic union is one of the long-term objectives of the EUROPEAN COMMUNITY.

economies of scale the LONG RUN reduction in AVERAGE (or unit) COSTS that occurs as the scale of the firm's output is increased (all FACTOR INPUTS being variable). There are available in most industries 'economies of scale', so that when producing a greater quantity of a product, average or unit costs are reduced. See Fig. 52.

Economies of scale may operate both at the level of the individual plant and the firm (operating a number of plants) and arise due to: (a) indivisibilities in machinery and equipment especially where a number of processes are linked together; (b) economies of increased dimensions – for many types of capital equipment (tankers, boilers) both set-up and operating costs increase less rapidly than capacity; (c) economies of SPECIALIZATION – at larger outputs there is more scope for using specialist labour and capital equipment; (d) superior techniques or organization of production – as scale is increased automatic machinery may be used instead of manually operated items, or it may be possible to substitute continuous MASS PRODUCTION for BATCH PRODUCTION; (e) economies of bulk-buying of raw materials and supplies; (f) marketing economies resulting from the use of mass advertising media and greater density of deployment of sales forces; (g) financial economies which arise from the ability of large firms to raise capital on more advantageous terms; (h) managerial economies from the use of specialist management techniques like work study, operational research and critical path analysis.

Unit costs may not fall continuously as the scale of the firm's operations is increased and they may level off at some point – the MINIMUM EFFICIENT SCALE of operation (OX in Fig. 52) and remain relatively constant thereafter (bd in Fig. 52); or they may rise because of the growing complexities of managing a larger organization – diseconomies of scale (bc in Fig. 52).

The potential to realize economies of scale can be limited for a variety of reasons. In some industries the nature of the product and the processes of manufacture, or technology, may be such that DIS-ECONOMIES OF SCALE are encountered at modest output levels. On the demand side, total market demand may be insufficient to permit firms to attain minimal efficient scale, or firms' individual market shares may be too small. Where consumers demand a wide variety of products this mitigates against standardization and long production runs.

Where economies of scale are substantial, SELLER CONCENTRATION tends to be high, as for example in petro-chemicals and motor vehicles, for only in this way can industry output be produced as efficiently as possible. In such industries firms may undertake HORIZONTAL INTEGRATION, particularly through mergers and takeovers, to eliminate high-cost plants and to rationalize production so as fully to exploit economies of scale.

In some industries FLEXIBLE MANUFACTURING SYSTEMS can enable small quantities of a variety of products to be manufactured at unit costs which match those achievable with large-scale production, thus lowering the minimum efficient scale and leading possibly to a reduction in the level of SELLER CONCENTRATION.

See EXTERNAL ECONOMIES OF SCALE, NATURAL MONOPOLY.

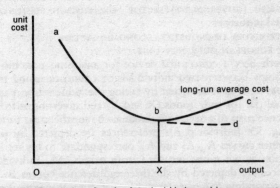

Fig. 52. **Economies of scale**. A typical U-shaped long-run average cost curve for a plant. OX is the scale of output at which average cost is minimized and economies of scale exhausted. Thereafter DISECONOMIES OF SCALE may set in (bc), although this is not always the case (bd) (see MINIMUM EFFICIENT SCALE).

economies of scope the LONG RUN reduction in AVERAGE (or unit) COSTS that occurs as the scope of the firm's activities increases. A firm can achieve economies of scope by sharing common inputs over a range of its activities or by jointly promoting or distributing its products. For example, a building society could use its existing branches and staff not only to sell mortgages but also to offer customers other financial services such as banking and insurance.

Economies of scope are often an important motive for firms undertaking 'concentric' DIVERSIFICATION.

economize, *vb.* to produce: (a) a *given* OUTPUT of a product using less FACTOR INPUTS than previously; (b) *more* output than before from the *same* amount of factor inputs; (c) a given output of a product at lower cost than before by substituting cheaper factor inputs for more expensive ones in the production process (the 'ideal' or optimum position is attained when the largest possible output is produced from a given volume of factor inputs using available technology); (d) a given output at the least possible factor cost.

See PRODUCTIVITY, EFFICIENCY, ECONOMICS, PRODUCTION POSSIBILITY BOUNDARY.

economy a country defined in terms of the total and composition of its economic activities. The total value of goods and services produced in an economy in any one year is called GROSS DOMESTIC PRODUCT (GDP). The contribution made to GDP by the various subdivisions or sectors of the economy can be viewed in a variety of ways: for example, either by broad sectors (the PERSONAL or household SECTOR, the CORPORATE or business SECTOR, the FINANCIAL SECTOR, PUBLIC (GOVERNMENT) SECTOR, the FOREIGN SECTOR), or by individual industries.

See STRUCTURE OF INDUSTRY, ECONOMIC SYSTEM.

ECU see EUROPEAN CURRENCY UNIT.

Edgeworth box a conceptual device for analysing possible trading relationships between two individuals or countries, using INDIFFERENCE CURVES. It is constructed by taking the indifference map of one individual (B) for two goods (X and Y) and inverting it to face the indifference map of a second individual (A) for the same two goods, as in Fig. 53. Individual A's preferences are depicted by the three indifference curves A_1, A_2 and A_3, corresponding to higher levels of satisfaction as we move outward from origin OA. Individuals B's preferences are depicted by the three indifference curves B_1, B_2 and B_3, corresponding to higher levels of satisfaction as we move outward from origin OB. Both consumers' preferences as between the two products X and Y are reflected in the slopes of their indifference curves, with the slope of a curve at any point reflecting the MARGINAL RATE OF SUBSTITUTION of X for Y.

Only where individual A's indifference curves are tangential to individual B's indifference curves (points E, F and G in Fig. 53), will A's marginal rate of substitution of product X for product Y be the same as B's marginal rate of substitution of X for Y, so that their relative valuations of the two products are the same. Starting from any other point, say Z, the two can gain by trading with one another.

At point Z individual A has a lot of product X and little of product Y; consequently he values product Y more highly than product X, being prepared to give up a lot of product X ($X_1 X_3$) to gain just a little of product Y ($Y_1 Y_2$). This is why his indifference curve A_1 is relatively flat at point Z. On the other hand, at point Z individual B has a lot of product Y and little product X; consequently he values product X more highly than product Y, being prepared to give up a lot of product Y ($Y_1 Y_3$) to gain just a little of product X ($X_2 X_3$). This is why his indifference curve B_2 is relatively steep at point Z.

These two sets of relative valuations of product X and product Y offer the promise of mutually beneficial exchange. If individual A offers some of his plentiful and low-valued product X in exchange for extra units of scarce and high-valued product Y he can gain from trade. Similarly if individual B offers some of his plentiful and low-valued product Y in exchange for extra units of scarce and high-valued product X he can also gain from trade. The two will continue to exchange product X in return for product Y (individual A) and product Y in return for product X (individual B), until they reach a point such as E or F where the indifference curves have the same slope, so that their marginal rates of substitution of the two products are the same.

The *contract curve* or *offer curve* in Fig. 53 traces out the path of all the points such as E, F and G, where the indifference curves are tangential, and if individuals A and B start with any combination of products X and Y other than ones lying along the contract curve, then they have an incentive to redistribute products X and Y between

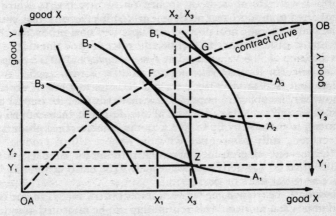

Fig. 53. **Edgeworth box**. See entry.

themselves through exchange. Where they come to lie along the contract curve will depend upon their relative bargaining strength and skills. If individual A is the stronger they may end up at a point like G far from A's origin OA and putting individual A on a high indifference curve A_3; while individual B ends up on a low indifference curve B_1 near his origin OB. On the other hand, if individual B is the stronger, they may end up at a point like E far from B's origin OB and putting individual B on a high indifference curve B_3; while individual A ends up on a low indifference curve A_1 near his origin OA.

See also PARETO OPTIMALITY, THEORY OF CONSUMER BEHAVIOUR, THEORY OF INTERNATIONAL TRADE.

EEC see ECONOMIC COMMUNITY.

effective demand see DEMAND.

effective interest rate the INTEREST RATE payable on the purchase price of a BOND. For example, a bond with a face value of £100 and a NOMINAL (COUPON) INTEREST RATE of 5% generates a nominal return of £5 per year. If, however, the bond can be purchased for £50 on the open market, then the effective interest rate now rises to 10% representing a 10% return on the £50 invested. The lower the purchase price of a bond with a given nominal rate of interest the higher its effective rate of interest will be, and vice-versa. There is thus an inverse relationship between the price paid for a bond and its effective rate of interest.

The effective interest rate is sometimes called the interest YIELD.

effective rate of protection the real amount of PROTECTION accorded to domestic suppliers of a final product when a TARIFF is applied to a competing imported final product (see IMPORTS) but either no tariff, or a lower rate of tariff, is applied on FACTOR INPUTS which are imported to produce that product. For example, assume that initially the same domestic final product and imported final product are both priced at £100. Assume further that the price of the domestic product is made up of 50% value added by *domestic inputs* and 50% by *imported raw materials*. If an *ad valorem* tariff of 10% is now applied to the imported final product, its price will increase to £110. If no tariff, however, is applied to imported raw materials then the import price of these will remain at £50. This allows domestic VALUE ADDED (and prices) to increase by up to £10 with the domestic final product still remaining fully competitive with the imported final product. The effective rate of protection accorded to domestic suppliers is thus 20% (that is, £10 additional value added/£50 existing value added). See NOMINAL RATE OF PROTECTION.

efficiency the relationship between scarce FACTOR INPUTS and OUTPUTS of goods and services. This relationship can be measured in physical terms (TECHNOLOGICAL EFFICIENCY) or cost terms (ECONOMIC EFFICI-

ENCY). The concept of efficiency is used as a criterion in judging how well MARKETS have allocated resources. See MARKET PERFORMANCE, RESOURCE ALLOCATION, ECONOMIZE.

efficient-markets hypothesis the proposition that an efficient market exists where all available information which may influence the price of a PRODUCT or FINANCIAL SECURITY is reflected in that price. This implies that there exists PERFECT COMPETITION within such a market, so that changes in the price of products or securities would only be affected by the acquisition of new information. The hypothesis suggests that due to the rapid assimilation of this new information by the market, expectations of future price changes are revised randomly about the product's or security's intrinsic value. Statisticians term such occurrences a *random walk*. For example, if a SHARE has an initial price of £1, the next change in price has an equal chance of being an increase or a decrease in value. If it goes up to, say, £1.10p, the next change in price has an equal chance of going up or down. The implication that STOCK and share prices follow a random walk implies that price changes are independent of one another.

In practice, it is unlikely that share prices reflect *all* information since it is most difficult to be in possession of *all* necessary information, though share prices may reflect all publicly available information. See STOCK EXCHANGE.

EFTA see EUROPEAN FREE TRADE ASSOCIATION.

elastic, *adj.* relatively responsive to change. See PRICE-ELASTICITY OF DEMAND, PRICE-ELASTICITY OF SUPPLY, INCOME-ELASTICITY OF DEMAND, CROSS-ELASTICITY OF DEMAND.

elasticity of demand or **demand elasticity** a measure of the degree of responsiveness of quantity demanded of a particular product (see DEMAND) to a given change in one of the INDEPENDENT VARIABLES which affect demand for that product. The responsiveness of demand to a change in price is referred to as PRICE-ELASTICITY OF DEMAND; the responsiveness of demand to a change in income is known as INCOME-ELASTICITY OF DEMAND; and the responsiveness of demand for a particular product to changes in the prices of other related products is called CROSS-ELASTICITY OF DEMAND.

elasticity of supply the degree of responsiveness of quantity supplied of a particular product (see SUPPLY) to changes in the product's PRICE (PRICE ELASTICITY OF SUPPLY).

elasticity of technical substitution the rate at which one FACTOR INPUT can be substituted for another with OUTPUT remaining constant. For example, the rate of substitution between CAPITAL and LABOUR may be expressed as:

$$e = \frac{\% \text{ change in the ratio of amounts of factors of production employed}}{\% \text{ change in the ratio of their marginal physical products}}$$

The denominator in the above expression is known as the MARGINAL RATE OF TECHNICAL SUBSTITUTION. Essentially, the elasticity of substitution is the change in factor proportions used (the numerator) in relation to their substitutability (the denominator). The above expressions may be illustrated graphically using ISOQUANT CURVES (equal product curves) and PROCESS RAYS (see Fig. 54).

The elasticity of substitution between factor inputs is not infinite. Where no substitution is possible ($e = 0$) inputs must be used in fixed proportions; where factors are perfect substitutes $e = \infty$. The actual measure will lie somewhere between the two. Where it is one (as exhibited in the COBB-DOUGLAS PRODUCTION FUNCTION) there exists constant returns to scale, i.e., labour can be substituted for capital in any given proportions and vice versa, without affecting output.

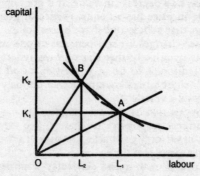

Fig. 54. **Elasticity of technical substitution**. The numerator of the expression is the percentage change in factors employed when moving from process ray OA to process ray OB. The denominator is the change in each factor's relative MARGINAL PHYSICAL PRODUCT, given by the slope of the isoquent curve at the points of tangency A and B.

emerging country/market see DEVELOPING COUNTRY.

embargo the prohibition of the IMPORT and EXPORT of particular types of product (for example, military equipment) or a complete ban on trade with a particular country as an adjunct to the political policies pursued by the government.

empirical testing the process of testing economic theories against empirical data. See HYPOTHESIS, HYPOTHESIS TESTING.

employee a person who is hired (employed) by another person or FIRM to provide LABOUR services as a FACTOR INPUT in the production of a good or service.

Compare EMPLOYER, SELF-EMPLOYED. See WORKING POPULATION.

employee share ownership plan (ESOP) a scheme whereby employees acquire SHARES in the company in which they are employed. Employees can, of course, purchase shares in their company on the open market, or companies can simply choose to donate shares to them. However, in recent years many companies have set up employee share ownership plans which formally transfer a proportion of the company's shares to employees, a movement encouraged in the UK by government tax concessions.

ESOPs are seen as a means of increasing employee loyalty and commitment to the firm, serving to reduce labour turnover and providing incentives to improve PRODUCTIVITY.

See PROFIT SHARING, WORKER PARTICIPATION.

employer a person or FIRM which hires (employs) LABOUR as a FACTOR INPUT in the production of a good or service.

Compare EMPLOYEE.

employment the use of LABOUR as a FACTOR INPUT in the production of a good or service.

employment contract a contract between an EMPLOYEE and the company for which he works, specifying the terms and conditions governing his employment. Employment contracts of directors and senior executives are called *service contracts*, and these often contain provision for generous severance payments in the event of early dismissal.

employment exchange or **job centre** a government agency which facilitates the smooth operation of LABOUR MARKETS by collecting and publicizing information about job vacancies.

See REGISTERED UNEMPLOYMENT.

employment laws the body of legislation providing for the regulation of relations between employers and employees and the conduct of INDUSTRIAL DISPUTES. UK employment law provides for the protection of individual employees' rights such as the right to protection from unfair dismissal, the right to statutory redundancy payments, etc. UK employment law embodies ARBITRATION and CONCILIATION mechanisms for settling industrial disputes, and proscribes certain courses of action which parties might employ in furtherance of an industrial dispute, such as certain forms of PICKETING.

Recent UK employment legislation, such as the Employment Acts of 1980, 1982, 1988 and 1989, have limited the effect of TRADE UNION power, for example, by making trade unions legally liable for certain losses caused to employers in an industrial dispute; and by forcing trade unions to conduct 'secret ballots' prior to taking strike action, and protecting the rights of trade union members who refuse to go on strike. These measures have been taken in order to reduce the monopoly power of trade unions as suppliers of labour, thereby making for more flexible LABOUR MARKETS.

See SUPPLY-SIDE ECONOMICS.

endogenous money or **inside money** that part of the MONEY SUPPLY which is created inside the economic system by the banking sector, as opposed to being 'put into' the system from outside by the government (EXOGENOUS MONEY). See BANK DEPOSIT CREATION, MONEY SUPPLY SCHEDULE.

endogenous variable a VARIABLE in an ECONOMIC MODEL which both affects and is itself affected by the relationship depicted in the model. For example, in the EQUILIBRIUM LEVEL OF NATIONAL INCOME model an increase in consumption spending increases aggregate demand and raises the level of national income. By the same token, an increase in the level of national income (which results, say, from an increase in investment) will induce an increase in consumption spending. Compare EXOGENOUS VARIABLE.

endowment see FACTOR ENDOWMENT.

Engel's law a principle that states that consumers will tend to spend an increasing proportion of any additional income upon LUXURY GOODS and a smaller proportion on STAPLE GOODS; so that a rise in income will lower the overall share of consumer expenditures spent on staple goods (such as basic foodstuffs) and increase the share of consumer expenditures on luxury goods (such as motor cars).

See INFERIOR PRODUCTS, INCOME ELASTICITY OF DEMAND, INCOME CONSUMPTION CURVE, AGRICULTURAL POLICY.

enterprise zone a small area scheduled by the British authorities for special financial assistance (for example, 100% capital allowance, exemption from rates, etc, for investing firms) and other forms of assistance to encourage industrial expansion.

Although not formally part of REGIONAL POLICY, enterprise zones like their larger brethren the DEVELOPMENT AREAS are clearly intended to act as a magnet for new investment and job creation.

entrepôt trade a commercial operation whereby goods are imported into a country and re-exported without distribution within the importing country (see IMPORTS, EXPORTS).

Entrepôt transactions are confined in the main to COMMODITIES such as tea and tin, where a MIDDLEMAN located in a particular commodity centre (London, for example, in the case of tea and tin), can arrange for the sale of the commodity and its world-wide shipment to customer countries.

entrepreneur an individual who assembles and organizes FACTORS OF PRODUCTION to undertake a venture with a view to PROFIT. The individual may supply one or more of the three factors of production (NATURAL RESOURCES, LABOUR, CAPITAL) himself, or may hire or buy any or all factors in the expectation of future profits. The entrepreneurial function is sometimes called a *fourth factor of production*.

The entrepreneur was seen in the 19th century as an individual proprietor who supplied most or all of the factors of production but especially managerial expertise. The advent of the JOINT-STOCK COMPANY led to the division of management and the supply of capital, so that the term entrepreneur became a more hypothetical abstract term attached to any individual or group who performs the risk-bearing and organizing functions above. The traditional THEORY OF THE FIRM suggests that entrepreneurs attempt to maximize profit, but since the 1930s there has been growing awareness that the DIVORCE OF OWNERSHIP FROM CONTROL in large joint-stock companies influences the behavioural attitudes of groups of individuals within organizations, which may lead to corporations following objectives other than PROFIT MAXIMIZATION.

See BEHAVIOURAL THEORY OF THE FIRM, MANAGERIAL THEORIES OF THE FIRM, RISK AND UNCERTAINTY.

entry see MARKET ENTRY, CONDITION OF ENTRY, BARRIERS TO ENTRY, POTENTIAL ENTRANT.

entry-forestalling price see LIMIT PRICING.

envelope curve see AVERAGE COST (LONG-RUN).

environmental audit an assessment of the environmental impact of a firm or public agency in the process of supplying goods or services. This usually involves an independent investigation of the way in which the firm or public agency organizes itself to supply products and the resulting environmental costs. Environmental audits are often undertaken with a view to reducing or eliminating POLLUTION associated with the production, packaging or distribution of products.

See SOCIAL COSTS, COST-BENEFIT ANALYSIS.

environmental impact assessment an assessment of the environmental impact of a proposed INVESTMENT project such as a new road or by-pass to determine the extent of any POLLUTION effects and destruction of natural habitats. Government authorities in the European Community are now required to undertake an environmental impact assessment of a proposed public investment project.

See COST-BENEFIT ANALYSIS.

EPOS (electronic point of sale) a system for recording sales using sophisticated cash tills which record the total amount to be paid by a customer, provide him or her with itemized bills, and simultaneously adjust the firm's STOCK records to assist the firm to plan its reordering of goods. EPOS is increasingly being used in retail outlets such as supermarkets.

equal pay the principle that people performing the *same* JOB or work task should receive the same rate of PAY regardless of their age, gender or race. This principle is enshrined in the UK Equal Pay Act 1970 and has been extended to include equal pay for different jobs that are judged to be of equal value.

equation a means of portraying arithmetically the relationship between VARIABLES. For example, the equation: $C = 1,000 + 0.9Y$

suggests a particular relationship between consumer expenditure (C) and disposable income (Y), which would be true for certain values of C and Y (such as 10,000 and 10,000 respectively), but not true of other values of C and Y (such as 6,000 and 10,000 respectively). Equations are generally written with a two-bar equals sign (=) with the value to the left of the sign being equal to the value to the right of the sign. The validity of an equation can be tested statistically by collecting paired observations of the variables involved and testing whether or not these observations conform with the equation formulated. See IDENTITY.

equilibrium a state of balance with no tendency to change. See EQUILIBRIUM MARKET PRICE, EQUILIBRIUM LEVEL OF NATIONAL INCOME.

equilibrium level of national income 1. the level of NATIONAL INCOME at which the purchasing and production plans of the economy are synchronized. This occurs at the point of intersection of the AGGREGATE DEMAND SCHEDULE with the AGGREGATE SUPPLY SCHEDULE, which is Point E in Fig. 55a. Equilibrium income is not necessarily the level of income at which FULL EMPLOYMENT is attained, for an equilibrium level of income can occur at any level of economic activity. Full employment equilibrium is a special case where aggregate demand exactly corresponds with POTENTIAL GROSS NATIONAL PRODUCT, leaving no INFLATIONARY GAP or DEFLATIONARY GAP. For example, aggregate demand 2 in Fig. 55b represents a full employment equilibrium where E_2 corresponds with full employment output.

2. the level of national income at which total INJECTIONS (investment + government expenditure + exports) is exactly equal to WITHDRAWALS (saving + taxes + imports). Also called *injections-withdrawals approach to national income determination*. In the CIRCULAR FLOW OF NATIONAL INCOME MODEL, income = consumption + withdrawals, spending = consumption + injections. See Fig. 55c, d.

3. the level of real national income at which aggregate demand is exactly equal to aggregate supply as shown by the intersection of the aggregate demand curve and the aggregate supply curve at a particular PRICE LEVEL. See Fig. 55e, f, and g.

equilibrium market price the PRICE at which the quantity demanded of a good is exactly equal to the quantity supplied (see DEMAND, SUPPLY). The DEMAND CURVE depicts the quantity that consumers are prepared to buy at particular prices; the SUPPLY CURVE depicts the quantity that producers are prepared to sell at particular prices. See Fig. 56 on page 171.

equilibrium market price (changes in) an increase or decrease in PRICE resulting from a shift in the DEMAND CURVE or SUPPLY CURVE. See Fig. 57 on page 172.

See DEMAND CURVE, (SHIFT IN), SUPPLY CURVE, (SHIFT IN).

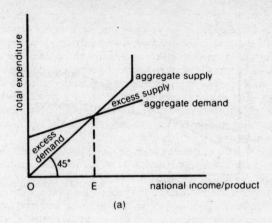

(a)

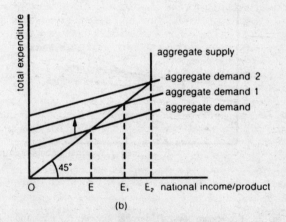

(b)

Fig. 55. **Equilibrium level of national income.** (a) Income levels above point E are not sustainable because total spending is insufficient to buy up all of the output being produced. Businesses find themselves with unplanned stocks on their hands and thus cut back production. Conversely, at income levels below point E aggregate demand exceeds aggregate supply. Businesses find that they can sell all of their current output and are encouraged to expand production. (b) The equilibrium level of national income will change if there is a shift in the aggregate demand schedule. For example, if aggregate demand rises from AD to AD_1 this results in an increase in the equilibrium income level from E to E_1. (See MULTIPLIER).

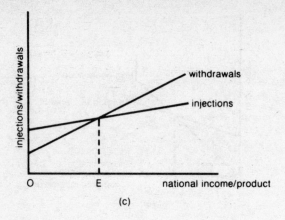

(c)

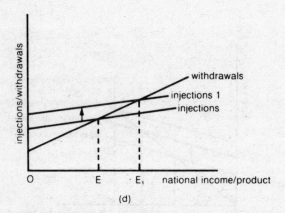

(d)

Fig. 55. **Equilibrium level of national income**. (c) Equilibrium is achieved where withdrawals = injections, i.e. point E which is the same as point E in the aggregate demand/aggregate supply schedules in (b). If withdrawals exceed injections then total expenditure will fall, resulting in a contraction of income and output. Conversely, if injections exceed withdrawals then total expenditure will rise, resulting in an increase in income and output. Only when injections and withdrawals are equal will income and output remain unchanged. (d) The equilibrium level of national income will change if there is a shift in either the injections or withdrawals schedules. For example, an increase in investment spending will shift the injections schedule from I to I₁ resulting in an increase in the equilibrium income level from E to E₁ (see also PARADOX OF THRIFT).

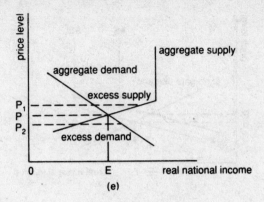

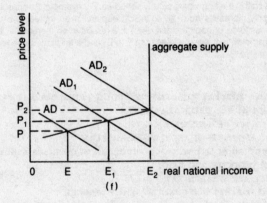

Fig. 55. **Equilibrium level of national income.** (e) Aggregate demand equals aggregate supply at the equilibrium price level P. At any price level above this, say P_1, aggregate supply exceeds aggregate demand and the resulting excess supply will force the price level down to P. At price levels below P, say P_2, aggregate demand exceeds aggregate supply and this excess demand will force the price level up to P. (f) The equilibrium level of real national income and the price level will change if there is a shift in the aggregate demand schedule. For example, if aggregate demand rises from AD to AD_1, this results in an increase in the equilibrium real income level from E to E_1 and an increase in the price level from P to P_1.

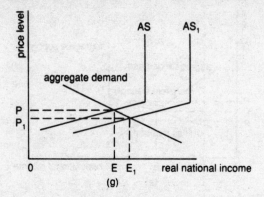

Fig. 55. **Equilibrium level of national income.** (g) The equilibrium level of real national income and the price level will also change if there is a shift in the aggregate supply schedule. For example, if aggregate supply increases from AS to AS_1 (because of an increase in the labour force or capital stock, etc.) this results in an increase in the equilibrium real income level from E to E_1 and a fall in the price level from P to P_1.

equilibrium market quantity see EQUILIBRIUM MARKET PRICE.

equity capital see ORDINARY SHARES.

error term see REGRESSION ANALYSIS.

ESOP see EMPLOYEE SHARE OWNERSHIP PLAN.

estate agent an AGENT who acts on behalf of clients in selling houses, industrial property and land.

estate duty see WEALTH TAX.

Eurobond market see EUROCURRENCY MARKET.

Eurocurrency market or **Eurobond market** a market based primarily in Europe that is engaged in the lending and borrowing of US DOLLARS and other major foreign currencies outside their countries of origin to finance international trade and investment.

The main financial instrument used in the Eurocurrency market for long-term investment purposes is the Eurobond (see BOND), a form of fixed-interest security denominated in a particular currency or currencies. Depositers in the eurocurrency market include commercial banks, industrial companies and central banks. Borrowers for the most part are companies, who have resorted to Eurofinance during times of domestic credit restrictions and/or when domestic interest rates have been high in comparison to those prevailing in the Eurocurrency market. See FOREIGN EXCHANGE MARKET.

Eurodollar see EUROCURRENCY MARKET.

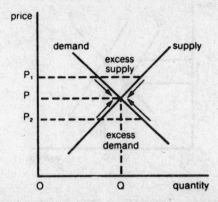

Fig. 56. **Equilibrium market price**. The equilibrium market price, OP, is generated by the intersection of the demand and supply curves. A higher initial price such as OP_1 results in EXCESS SUPPLY which forces price down; a lower initial price such as OP_2 results in EXCESS DEMAND which forces the price up. Only at price OP are buying and supply intentions fully synchronized.

European Atomic Energy Community (Euratom) an organization established by member countries of the EUROPEAN COMMUNITY to develop the Community's nuclear energy capabilities for industrial and commercial purposes.

European Coal and Steel Community (ECSC) a regional alliance established in 1951 to promote free trade in coal and steel. Its founding members were West Germany, France, Italy, Belgium and Luxembourg, five of the six countries who later went on to build on the spirit of cooperation kindled by the ECSC to establish the broader-based EUROPEAN COMMUNITY. One of the main rôles of the ECSC is the regulation of the industry's capacity to ensure that long-run supply is kept in line with demand potential, and that individual suppliers, including nationalized concerns, are prevented from dominating the market.

European Commission the central body which is responsible for the day-to-day administration and coordination of the affairs of the EUROPEAN COMMUNITY (EC), the control of the EC's general budget finances, and which, together with the various specialist agencies set up to run particular programmes (for example, the Common Agricultural Policy), is involved in the detailed implementation of Community policies.

European Community (EC) or (formerly) **European Economic Community (EEC)** a regional alliance established by the Treaty of

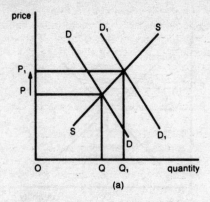

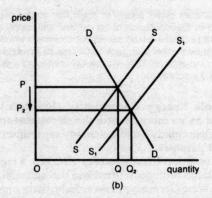

Fig. 57. **Equilibrium market price (changes in)**, (a) If there is a shift in the demand curve from DD to D_1D_1, with supply unchanged, the equilibrium price will rise from OP to OP_1. (b) If there is a shift in the supply curve from SS to S_1S_1, with demand unchanged, the equilibrium price will fall from OP to OP_2.

Rome in 1958, and which is now part of the EUROPEAN UNION, with the general objective of integrating the economies of member countries. There were six founding countries of the EC: West Germany, France, Italy, Netherlands, Belgium and Luxembourg, who had previously cooperated (with the exception of the Netherlands) in the EUROPEAN COAL AND STEEL COMMUNITY. Further countries have since joined the EC: the UK, Eire and Denmark in 1973, Greece (1981), Spain and Portugal (1986). Austria, Sweden and Finland joined the EC in 1995.

The strategic and main operational policies of the EC are formulated by member country governments acting through the Council of Ministers (one appointed member per country, one vote) and the European Parliament (democratically elected). The EUROPEAN COMMISSION is responsible for overseeing the day-to-day administration of Community policy and in controlling its general budget finances (see Fig. 58), while various other bodies are charged with running specific programmes such as the Common Agricultural Policy.

The primary economic developments within the EC to date include:

(a) the creation of a COMMON MARKET providing for free trade in goods and services and the free movement of labour and capital resources across national boundaries. Member countries are committed to removing TARIFFS, QUOTAS and other obstacles to trade within the Community and to maintaining the EC's common external tariff against nonmember countries. Import restrictions by the six original members against each other were dismantled and their external barriers harmonized, in stages between 1958 and 1968. The EC has concluded a number of trade preference agreements with nonmember countries, including the multilateral LOMÉ AGREEMENT with over 40 less-developed countries, most of them former colonies of EC members, and bilateral pacts with members of the EUROPEAN FREE TRADE ASSOCIATION (see GAINS FROM TRADE, TRADE CREATION, TRADE DIVERSION). See also EUROPEAN ECONOMIC ASSOCIATION.

(b) a *competition policy* providing for the prohibition of price-fixing and market-sharing agreements between firms, etc., and the abuse of a dominant market position, which have the effect of reducing or eliminating intra-EC trade (see COMPETITION POLICY EC).

(c) a *common agricultural policy* providing for the subsidization and protection of the farm sector (see COMMON AGRICULTURAL POLICY).

(d) a *regional policy* providing financial assistance for the removal of regional imbalances both within and between member countries (see EUROPEAN REGIONAL DEVELOPMENT FUND, EUROPEAN INVESTMENT BANK).

(e) the establishment of the EUROPEAN MONETARY SYSTEM to provide a closer coordination of member countries' exchange rates and settlement of payments imbalances.

(f) the creation of a special monetary unit, the EUROPEAN CURRENCY UNIT to provide a common basis for intercountry settlements under the Common Agricultural Policy, European Monetary System, etc.

Over the longer term it is hoped to work towards a full ECONOMIC UNION, involving a closer harmonization of member countries' general economic policies and the centralization of fiscal and monetary control procedures (see MAASTRICHT TREATY, 1991). In the interim, the SINGLE EUROPEAN MARKET ACT (the '1992' initiative) embodies some 400 detailed directives providing for the implementation, by

EUROPEAN CURRENCY UNIT

1992, of *common* value-added tax rates, road haulage regulations, descriptions of products, etc., in order to establish a unified, barrier-free European market.

See EUROPEAN ECONOMIC AREA.

	European currency units* (in millions)
Farm price support	40,828
Structural policies (social, regional)	29,131
Industry, Education, R&D	6,025
Administration	5,281
Aid and development	5,261
	86,526

* 1 ECU = £0.82

Fig. 58. **European Community**. The EC budget for 1996.

European Currency Unit (ECU) a monetary asset used by member countries of the EUROPEAN MONETARY SYSTEM (EMS) to value the EXCHANGE RATES of members' currencies and which are held as part of their INTERNATIONAL RESERVES to settle payments imbalances between members. Unlike other reserve assets such as gold, ECUs have no tangible life of their own. They are 'created' by the EMS's European Monetary Cooperation Fund in exchange for the in-payment of GOLD and other reserve assets by members and take the form of bookkeeping entries in a special account managed by the Fund. The value at the ECU is based on a weighted basket of members' national currencies. In sterling terms it is (currently) worth around 82 pence.

European Economic Area (EEA) a FREE TRADE alliance established in 1991 between the member countries of the EUROPEAN COMMUNITY (EC) and the EUROPEAN FREE TRADE ASSOCIATION (EFTA). The EEA's aim is to extend the EC's four 'single market freedoms' in the flow of goods, services, capital and labour to include EFTA. EFTA countries will adopt the harmonization directives currently being implemented under the SINGLE EUROPEAN MARKET ACT, 1986.

European Economic Community see EUROPEAN COMMUNITY.

European Free Trade Association (EFTA) a regional alliance established by the Stockholm Treaty, 1959, with the general objective of securing the benefits of FREE TRADE for its member countries. EFTA came about following the breakdown of attempts in the latter half of the 1950s to create a large European-based CUSTOMS UNION. Those countries in favour of the customs union approach, with its detailed commitment to long-term economic integration duly formed the EUROPEAN COMMUNITY (EC) in 1958. The remainder, for a variety of reasons such as colonial connections and a political preference for neutrality, chose the FREE TRADE AREA route and formed EFTA.

There were seven original members of EFTA: Austria, the UK, Denmark, Norway, Portugal, Sweden and Switzerland. Finland joined in 1961, Iceland in 1970 and Liechtenstein in 1991. In 1973, however, the UK and Denmark left and joined the EC, and Finland, Sweden and Austria joined the EC in 1995.

Import restrictions on trade between member countries, were abolished in stages over the period 1960–66, while each country continued to operate its own separate TARIFFS, etc., against non-members. See EUROPEAN ECONOMIC AREA, GAINS FROM TRADE.

European Investment Bank an institution established in 1958 with the formation of the EUROPEAN COMMUNITY to provide financial assistance for the schemes and projects considered to be beneficial in promoting the economic integration of the Community. Together with the EUROPEAN REGIONAL DEVELOPMENT FUND, the Bank is an important source of funds for the development of the more impoverished areas of the Community. The Bank also makes finance available to less developed countries. See REGIONAL POLICY.

European Monetary Cooperation Fund see EUROPEAN MONETARY SYSTEM.

European Monetary System (EMS) an institutional arrangement, established in 1979, for coordinating and stabilizing the EXCHANGE RATES of member countries of the EUROPEAN COMMUNITY (EC). The EMS is based on a FIXED EXCHANGE RATE mechanism and the EUROPEAN CURRENCY UNIT (ECU), which is used to value, on a common basis, exchange rates and which also acts as a reserve asset which members can use, alongside their other INTERNATIONAL RESERVE holdings, to settle payments imbalances between themselves. The EMS is managed by the European Monetary Cooperation Fund (EMCF).

Under the EMS 'exchange rate mechanism' (ERM) each country's currency is given a fixed central par value specified in terms of the ECU and the exchange rate between currencies can move to a limited degree around these par values, being controlled by a 'parity grid' and 'divergence indicator'. The parity grid originally permitted a currency to move up to a limit of 2.25% either side of its central rate. As a currency moves towards its outer limit, the divergence indicator comes into play, requiring the country's central bank to intervene in the foreign exchange market or adopt appropriate domestic measures (e.g. alter interest rates) in order to stabilize the rate. If in the view of the EMCF the central rate itself appears to be overvalued or under-valued against other currencies, a country can devalue (see DEVALUATION) or revalue (see REVALUATION) its currency, refixing it at a new central parity rate. At the present time (1996) Greece, the UK, Italy and Sweden are outside the ERM arrangements.

The European Currency Unit, unlike other reserve assets such as gold, has no tangible life of its own. ECUs are 'created' by the Fund in exchange for the in-payment of gold and other reserve assets and take the form of book-keeping entries recorded in a special account managed by the Fund. The value of the ECU is based on a weighted 'basket' of members' currencies. In sterling terms it is (currently) worth around 82 pence.

Initially, the UK declined to join the Exchange Rate Mechanism (ERM) but did so eventually in October 1990, establishing a central rate against the German DM (the leading currency in the ERM) of £1 = 2.95 DM. The UK withdrew from the ERM in September 1992 after prolonged speculation against the £ had pushed it down to its 'floor' limit of 2.77 DM, rejecting the devaluation option within the ERM in favour of a market-driven 'floating' of the currency (see FLOATING EXCHANGE RATE SYSTEM). In August 1993, after the French franc came under pressure, ERM currency bands were widened to 15%. These episodes, together with the earlier withdrawal of the Italian lira from the ERM, illustrate one of the major drawbacks of a fixed exchange rate system, namely, the tendency for 'pegged' rates to get out of line with underlying market tendencies and so fuel excessive speculation against weak currencies.

In the long term, however, it is planned (under the MAASTRICHT TREATY) that the EC will move towards an eventual *monetary unification (EMU)* through (a) initially, greater exchange rate harmonization requiring all member countries to join the exchange rate mechanism, (b) the establishment in 1994 of a European Monetary Institute to provide for coordinated monetary policies leading ultimately to (c) the replacement of individual members' currencies by a single community currency, the 'euro'.

European Regional Development Fund an organization established by the EUROPEAN COMMUNITY in 1975 to provide financial assistance for the removal of intra and interregional imbalances.

European Union (EU) the 'new' European regional bloc established following the final ratification in 1993 by all twelve members of the EUROPEAN COMMUNITY of the MAASTRICHT TREATY which provides for a closer unification of the economic, social and political systems of member countries. Responsibilities of the EU include (a) the European Community with its long-term commitment to economic, monetary and social integration; and two new areas of common responsibilities: (b) foreign policy and defence and (c) co-operation in law enforcement and immigration.

ex ante, *adj.* being applied from before an action. The concept of an 'ex ante' approach to economics, together with that of *ex post* (from after) is widely employed in economic analysis to examine the change in some economic phenomenon as it moves from a state of DISEQUI-

Keynesian model of national income determination planned investment may be greater than planned saving so that the economic system
is in a state of disequilibrium. The excess of investment, however,
serves to inject additional income into the economy and, via the
MULTIPLIER effect, increases both income and saving, bringing about
an eventual 'ex post' equilibrium where realized investment equals
realized savings.

See EQUILIBRIUM LEVEL OF NATIONAL INCOME.

excess capacity 1. a situation where a firm or industry has more plant
to supply a product than is currently being demanded. As a result a
proportion of the firm or industry's CAPACITY is left idle. Excess capacity
can result from a temporary (short-run) downturn in demand, a secular
(long-run) fall in demand, or from the industry having overinvested
in new plant relative to long-run demand potential. In the latter two
instances, excess capacity may be eliminated by an intensification of
competitive pressures (see EXCESS SUPPLY) which forces the more inefficient suppliers to exit the industry, or by RATIONALIZATION schemes.

2. in economic theory, the cost structures of firms operating in
imperfect markets. Industry output is maximized (that is, full capacity
attained) when all firms produce at the minimum point on their
long-run average total cost curves (see PERFECT COMPETITION). See
Fig. 59 for the effect of MONOPOLISTIC COMPETITION.

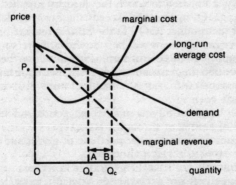

Fig. 59. **Excess capacity**. Under the imperfect market conditions of
monopolistic competition, the equilibrium (PROFIT MAXIMIZING) position
for the firm is at a point (Q_e) to the left of the cost-minimizing point
(Q_c) on the long-run average total cost curve; industry output is less,
and costs are higher than the optimum position. Thus 'excess
capacity' is measured as the difference between actual industry output and the cost-minimizing level of industry output (distance AB).

excess demand or **shortages** a situation in which the quantity demanded (see DEMAND) of a product (OQ_2 in Fig. 60) exceeds the quantity supplied (see SUPPLY) (OQ_1) at the *existing* market price (OP). In competitive markets there will be an upward pressure on price reflecting a shortage of the product, but where the price is controlled the excess could persist. See EQUILIBRIUM MARKET PRICE, EXCESS SUPPLY, PRICE CONTROLS.

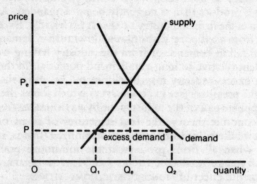

Fig. 60. **Excess demand**. See entry.

excess profit see ABOVE-NORMAL PROFIT.

excess supply a situation in which the quantity supplied (see SUPPLY) of a product (OQ_2 in Fig. 61) exceeds the quantity demanded (see DEMAND) of the product (OQ_1) at the *existing* market-price (OP). In a competitive market there will be a downward pressure on price as suppliers compete to dispose of surpluses, but where there is government intervention the situation could persist. See EQUILIBRIUM MARKET PRICE, EXCESS DEMAND, PRICE CONTROLS, PRICE SUPPORT, COMMON AGRICULTURAL POLICY.

exchange 1. the act of buying and selling goods and services either in the form of BARTER or through a MARKET.

2. the means of financing the purchase of goods and services in a market. See MONEY, FOREIGN EXCHANGE.

exchange controls see FOREIGN EXCHANGE CONTROLS.

exchange equalization account see FOREIGN EXCHANGE EQUALIZATION ACCOUNT.

exchange rate the price of one CURRENCY expressed in terms of some other currency. Fig. 62a shows the rate, or price, at which dollars (\$s) might be exchanged for pounds (£s). The demand curve (D) for £s is downwards-sloping, reflecting the fact that if £s become less expensive to Americans, British goods, services and assets will

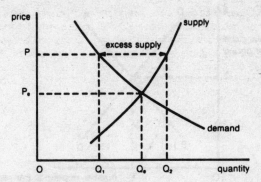

Fig. 61. **Excess supply**. See entry.

become cheaper to them. This causes Americans to demand greater quantities of British goods, etc. and therefore greater amounts of £s with which to buy those items. The supply curve (S) of £s is upwards-sloping, reflecting the fact that as the dollar price of £s rises, American goods, services and assets become cheaper to the British. This causes the British to demand greater quantities of American goods, etc. and hence the greater the supply of £s offered in exchange for $s with which to purchase those items. The equilibrium rate of exchange between the two currencies is determined by the intersection of the demand and supply schedules ($2 = £1, in Fig. 62a) overleaf.

Under a FIXED EXCHANGE-RATE SYSTEM the exchange rate, once established, will remain unchanged for longish periods. If the exchange rate gets too much out of line with underlying market conditions, however, and becomes overvalued, resulting in a country being persistently in BALANCE OF PAYMENTS deficit, the exchange rate can be devalued; i.e., refixed at a new lower value, which makes IMPORTS more expensive and its EXPORTS cheaper. (see DEVALUATION). By the same token, if the exchange rate becomes undervalued, resulting in a country being persistently in balance of payments surplus the exchange rate can be revalued; i.e., refixed at a new higher value, which makes imports cheaper and its exports more expensive (see REVALUATION). However, governments often tend to delay altering the exchange rate, particularly in respect of devaluing, so that the pegged rate gets seriously out of line with underlying market tendencies. When this happens SPECULATION against the currency builds up, leading to highly disruptive HOT MONEY flows which destabilize currency markets.

Over time, exchange rates, if left unregulated by the authorities,

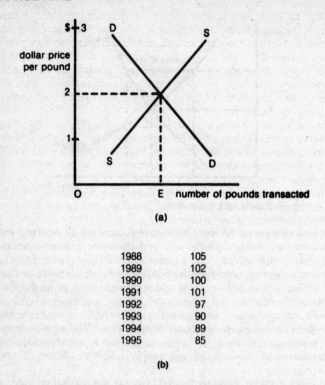

$3

dollar price
per pound

2

1

O   E   number of pounds transacted

(a)

1988	105
1989	102
1990	100
1991	101
1992	97
1993	90
1994	89
1995	85

(b)

Fig. 62. **Exchange rate.** (a) The graph shows the interaction of demand (D) and supply (S) in determining the exchange rate between pounds and dollars. (b) The effective exchange rate of sterling. 1990 = 100.

will fluctuate according to changes in underlying market conditions, reflecting such things as differences in INFLATION rates and INTEREST RATES between countries. For example, if the prices of UK goods rise faster than the prices of equivalent American goods, people will tend to buy more American goods, causing the $ to appreciate and the £ to depreciate. On the other hand, if UK interest rates are higher than American interest rates, this will encourage American investors to deposit money in the UK money markets, causing the £ to appreciate against the $.

Under a FLOATING EXCHANGE-RATE SYSTEM, the exchange rate is free to fluctuate day-by-day and will fall (see DEPRECIATION) or rise (see APPRECIATION) in line with changing market conditions, serving (in theory) to keep a country's balance of payments more or less in equilibrium on a continuous basis. In practice, however, the uncertainties and speculation associated with 'free' floats tend to produce erratic and random exchange rate movements which tend to inhibit trade as well as producing destabilizing domestic effects. For these reasons countries often prefer to 'manage' their exchange rates, both to moderate the degree of short-run fluctuation and to 'smooth out' the long-run trend line.

As a result of regional economic alliances (e.g. the EUROPEAN COMMUNITY) some countries are involved in both fixed and floating exchange rate systems. For example, France is a member of the fixed exchange rate mechanism of the EUROPEAN MONETARY SYSTEM which allows only small, short-term variations around the central par value of the franc against other members' currencies. By contrast, the franc 'floats' against the US $ etc., so that the franc rate against the $ tends to fluctuate much more widely.

The term *effective exchange rate* is used to describe a given currency's value in terms of a trade-weighted average of a 'basket' of other currencies where the weight attached to each currency in the basket depends upon its share of total INTERNATIONAL TRADE. Fig. 62b depicts the 'effective exchange rate' over time of the £ against other major countries' currencies, for example, the US $, Japanese yen, German deutschmark, French franc, etc. A fall (depreciation) in the effective (nominal) exchange rate indicates a general improvement in the price competitiveness of a country's products vis-a-vis trade partners. (See TERMS OF TRADE, REAL EXCHANGE RATE.)

In FOREIGN EXCHANGE MARKETS the exchange rate may be quoted either in terms of how many units of a foreign currency may be bought or sold per unit of the domestic currency (an 'indirect quotation'), or in terms of how many units of domestic currency may be bought or sold per unit of a particular foreign currency (a 'direct quotation'). For example, in the UK an indirect quotation of the exchange rate between the £ and the US $ might be £1 = $2, whereas a direct quotation would be $1 = 50 pence.

Exchange rates are usually quoted by dealers as a 'pair' of rates, the 'offer' or sell rate and the 'bid' or buy rate, the difference between the two (the 'spread') representing the dealers' profit margin. Currencies which are traded in large volumes, such as the US $ and German D-mark, usually have a narrower spread than currencies which are little used in international dealings. Similarly, the spread on current exchange rates quoted in the SPOT MARKET for currencies is usually narrower than the spread on forward prices quoted in the FUTURES MARKET.

See EXCHANGE RATE EXPOSURE, BALANCE OF PAYMENTS EQUILIBRIUM, PURCHASING-POWER PARITY THEORY, ASSET VALUE THEORY.

exchange rate exposure the extent of a firm's potential losses/gains on its overseas operations (measured in domestic currency terms) as a result of EXCHANGE RATE changes. The firm can be exposed to variations in exchange rates in two main ways:

(a) *transactions exposure* arises when a firm exports and imports products and borrows funds from abroad or invests overseas. For example, when a firm exports a product, invoicing the customer in terms of the customer's own local currency, and granting the customer 60 days' credit, then the firm is exposed to the effects of exchange rate variations during the 60-day credit period, which may decrease or increase the domestic currency value of the money due. Were the exchange rate of the foreign currency to fall dramatically vis-a-vis the domestic currency, then the exchange rate loss may completely eliminate any expected profit on the transactions;

(b) *economic* or *cash flow exposure* is concerned with the impact of exchange rate variations on the future cash flows generated by a company's production and marketing operations. Long-term or dramatic changes in exchange rates may well force a firm to rethink its FOREIGN MARKET SERVICING STRATEGY and raw material SOURCING strategy. For instance, a firm which serviced its overseas markets by direct exporting from domestic plants might decide to establish local production units to supply these markets instead, if an exchange rate appreciation were to render its export prices uncompetitive.

There are a number of mechanisms whereby a firm can reduce its exposure to potential losses resulting from exchange rate changes. First, a firm can seek to prevent an exposed position from arising by using such internal exposure management techniques as *currency matching* (matching foreign currency holdings with equal foreign currency borrowings); *leading and lagging* (accelerating or delaying foreign currency payments and receipts where the exchange rate of the currency is expected to change); and *netting* of currency receipts and payments between subsidiaries of a MULTINATIONAL COMPANY (offsetting receipts and payments with each other so as to leave only a single net intra-company balance to be settled in foreign currency). Second, the firm can use external contractual arrangements to reduce or eliminate whatever exposure remains, hedging risks by: entering into forward exchange contracts to buy and sell currencies as appropriate (see FUTURES MARKET); FACTORING (selling the firm's trade debts); buying and selling foreign exchange OPTIONS; foreign currency borrowing; the use of export credit guarantees (see EXPORT CREDIT GUARANTEE DEPARTMENT), SWAPS and BACK-TO-BACK LOANS.

exchange rate mechanism (ERM) see EUROPEAN MONETARY SYSTEM.

Exchequer a UK government office within the TREASURY responsible for the receipt, custody and issue of government funds.

excise duty an INDIRECT TAX levied by the government on certain goods, most notably tobacco, oil and alcoholic drink. Demand for these goods is price inelastic (see PRICE ELASTICITY OF DEMAND) so that duty increases, implemented as part of FISCAL POLICY, will not only raise government revenue but also leave customers with less money to spend on other goods. See TAXATION.

exclusive dealing a practice whereby a supplier contracts distributors to deal only in his products to the exclusion of competitor's products. Exclusive dealing may be beneficial in some cases by allowing distribution costs to be lowered but, if exclusive dealing is pursued by several large firms in a market, the access of smaller suppliers and potential entrants to established distributive outlets may be severely restricted. See RESTRICTIVE TRADE PRACTICE, COMPETITION POLICY, OFFICE OF FAIR TRADING.

ex-dividend, *adj.* (of a particular SHARE) excluding entitlement to the DIVIDEND which attaches to the share. If shares are purchased on the STOCK EXCHANGE 'ex. div.', the purchaser would not be entitled to the dividend accruing to that share when the dividend is next paid. Compare CUM-DIVIDEND.

exhaustable natural resources see NATURAL RESOURCES.

exit see MARKET EXIT.

exogenous money that part of the MONEY SUPPLY which is 'put into' the economic system from outside by the government, as opposed to being created inside the system by the banking sector (ENDOGENOUS MONEY). See MONEY SUPPLY SCHEDULE.

exogenous variable a VARIABLE that affects the operation of an ECONOMIC MODEL but which itself is not affected by any of the relationships depicted in the model. For example, in the EQUILIBRIUM LEVEL OF NATIONAL INCOME model, an increase in exports will increase AGGREGATE DEMAND and induce an increase in the level of national income, but the volume of exports itself is determined by any other country's propensity to import and not by the level of its own national income. Compare ENDOGENOUS VARIABLE.

expectations anticipations of future events which influence present economic behaviour. A major unresolved problem in economics is how to deal with the uncertainty the future holds, especially when each individual has a different subjective perception of that future. (See RISK AND UNCERTAINTY.)

Consequently much economic analysis incorporates expectations into the various models as a given variable, usually under the heading CETERIS PARIBUS, or by assuming that an individual acts in accordance with the RATIONAL EXPECTATIONS HYPOTHESIS. A further problem is that expectations involve a time period and much economic analysis is static, i.e., points of equilibrium may be observed but the route between them is considered irrelevant. (See COMPARATIVE STATIC ANALYSIS.)

Nevertheless, expectations have played a significant part in economic theory, most notably in the work of Keynes. Expectations are a major variable, it is argued, in determining BUSINESS CYCLES, and affecting the SPECULATIVE DEMAND for money. Expectations are also influential when dealing with the TERM STRUCTURE OF INTEREST RATES.

To incorporate expectations into economic theory it is possible to treat individual behaviour as adaptive, as illustrated in the ADAPATIVE EXPECTATIONS HYPOTHESIS. Although the concept is straightforward, future expectations being adapted from past and present experiences, the attempts to reflect reality have led to complex structures being formulated.

See KEYNESIAN ECONOMICS, EXPECTATIONS-ADJUSTED/AUGMENTED PHILLIPS CURVE, SPECULATOR, ANTICIPATED INFLATION.

expectations–adjusted/augmented Phillips curve a reformulated PHILLIPS CURVE that allows for the effects of price EXPECTATIONS on money wage increases. In the expectations-adjusted Phillips curve (see Fig. 63) U^* is the 'natural' rate of unemployment or NON-ACCELERATING INFLATION RATE OF UNEMPLOYMENT (NAIRU) (i.e., the rate of UNEMPLOYMENT at which INFLATION is neither accelerating nor decelerating). If the authorities attempt to reduce unemployment below the 'natural' rate to, say, U_1 the inflation rate rises from point A to point B on Phillips curve PC_1.

Assuming that the increase in money wages exceeds the growth of output per man then labour 'prices itself out of jobs', and unemployment reverts to its 'natural level' (point C) on a 'new' Phillips curve (PC_2) which is based on a higher 'expected' rate of inflation. Starting now at point C, if the authorities again attempt to reduce unemployment (to U_1), this will produce an acceleration in the inflation rate to point D, but again the higher rate of money wages will cause unemployment to revert back to its natural level (point E) on a 'new' Phillips curve (PC_3) which is based on a yet higher 'expected' rate of inflation.

To get the inflation rate down the authorities need to force unemployment above the 'natural' rate temporarily (from point E to point F on Phillips curve (PC_3) so as to reduce public expectations about the expected rate of inflation. As money wage rates fall people are 'priced back into jobs' and unemployment falls to its 'natural' level (at point C) on PC_2. See also INFLATIONARY SPIRAL.

expenditure spending by buyers on PRODUCTS or ASSETS. Expenditure on a particular product or asset is equal to product or asset price times quantity bought, that is, TOTAL REVENUE.

In aggregate terms expenditure by households, businesses and government (see CONSUMPTION, INVESTMENT, GOVERNMENT EXPENDITURE) constitutes the AGGREGATE DEMAND which (in conjunction with AGGREGATE SUPPLY) determines the level of activity in the economy.

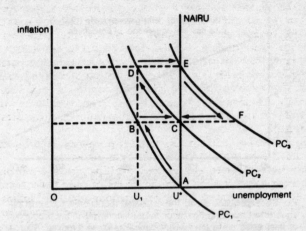

Fig. 63. Expectations-adjusted/augmented Phillips curve. See entry.

expenditure approach to GDP see NATIONAL INCOME ACCOUNTS.

expenditure tax a form of INDIRECT TAX that is incorporated into the selling price of a product and which is borne by the consumer.

In raising revenue and in applying FISCAL POLICY governments have two broad choices: the use of taxes on expenditure and the use of taxes on INCOME (DIRECT TAXES). Taxes on income, such as INCOME TAX, deduct tax at source whereas taxes on expenditure are levied at the point of sale. Direct taxes tend to be PROGRESSIVE TAXES in so far as the amount of tax paid is related to a person's income, whereas expenditure taxes are REGRESSIVE TAXES in so far as consumers pay tax in proportion to their spending regardless of income.

In the UK, VALUE ADDED TAX, EXCISE DUTIES and CUSTOMS DUTIES are the main types of expenditure tax. See TAXATION, BUDGET (GOVERNMENT).

experience curve or **learning curve** the process whereby managers and operators learn from experience how to operate new technologies more effectively over time such that a growing familiarity with, and the repetitive operation of, a new technology enables unit costs of production to be progressively reduced. See Fig. 64 (overleaf). See PRODUCTIVITY.

explicit cost a payment made by a firm for the use of FACTOR INPUTS (labour, capital) not owned by the firm. Unlike IMPLICIT COSTS (which represent payments for the use of factor inputs owned by the firm itself), explicit costs involve the firm in purchasing inputs from outside FACTOR MARKETS.

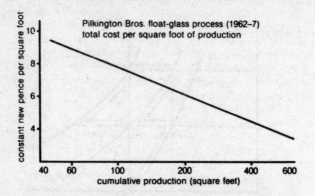

Fig. 64. **Experience curve**. The estimated reduction in total cost per square foot accruing from accumulated increases in the production of float glass using the revolutionary 'float glass' process. Source: Monopolies Commission, *Float Glass* report, HMSO, 1968.

exponential smoothing see TIME SERIES ANALYSIS.

export a good, service or capital asset which is sold to foreign countries.

(i) A good which is produced in the home country and which is then physically transported to, and sold in, an overseas market earning foreign exchange for the home country is called a *visible export*.

(ii) A service which is provided for foreigners either in the home country (for example, visits by tourists) or overseas (for example, banking, insurance) which likewise generates foreign exchange for the home country is called an *invisible export*.

(iii) Capital which is placed abroad in the form of portfolio investment, foreign direct investment in physical assets and banking deposits is called a *capital export*.

Exports are important in two main respects: (a) together with IMPORTS they make up a country's BALANCE OF PAYMENTS (a country must export in order to finance ('pay for' in foreign currency terms) its imports); (b) they represent an 'injection' into the CIRCULAR FLOW OF NATIONAL INCOME, serving to raise real income and output.

See INTERNATIONAL TRADE, EXPORT MULTIPLIER, C.I.F. (COST-INSURANCE-FREIGHT), F.O.B. (FREE-ON-BOARD), CERTIFICATE OF ORIGIN, INSURANCE, FACTORING, FORFAITING, EXPORT SUBSIDY, EXPORT RESTRAINT AGREEMENT, FOREIGN INVESTMENT, EXCHANGE RATE, EXCHANGE RATE EXPOSURE, TERMS OF TRADE.

Export Credit Guarantee Department (ECGD) a UK government office which provides insurance cover for British exporters against the risk of nonpayment by overseas customers as a means of encouraging exports.

export incentives the financial assistance given to domestic firms by the government as a means of promoting EXPORTS and assisting the country's balance of payments. Export incentives include direct subsidies to lower export prices (EXPORT SUBSIDY), tax concessions (remission of profits earned on exports), credit facilities (cheap export finance) and financial guarantees (provision for bad debts, etc).

Export incentives are often viewed as an 'unfair' trade practice by other countries and frequently result in retaliatory action being taken by them.

See COUNTERVAILING DUTY, BEGGAR–MY–NEIGHBOUR POLICY.

export–led growth an expansion of the economy with EXPORTS serving as a 'leading sector'. As exports rise they inject additional income into the domestic economy and increase total demand for domestically-produced output (see EXPORT MULTIPLIER). Equally importantly, the increase in exports enables a higher level of import absorption to be accommodated so that there is no BALANCE OF PAYMENTS contraint on the achievement of sustained ECONOMIC GROWTH. See CIRCULAR FLOW OF NATIONAL INCOME MODEL.

export multiplier the ratio of the increase in a country's NATIONAL INCOME to the increase in the demand for the country's EXPORTS that brought it about. The INJECTION of increased exports into the CIRCULAR FLOW OF NATIONAL INCOME raises national income by some multiple of the original increase in exports. The value of the export multiplier depends on the country's MARGINAL PROPENSITY TO SAVE, MARGINAL PROPENSITY TO IMPORT and MARGINAL PROPENSITY TO TAXATION. The larger these propensities – the larger, that is, the 'WITHDRAWALS' from the income flow – the smaller will be the value of the export multiplier. See Fig. 65 (overleaf). See also MULTIPLIER, FOREIGN TRADE MULTIPLIER, EXPORT–LED GROWTH.

export restraint agreement a voluntary arrangement between an exporting country and an importing country that limits the volume of trade in a particular product (or products). Specifically, EXPORTS/IMPORTS between the two countries are limited to an agreed number of units, or percentage share of the importing country's domestic sales. An export restraint agreement is thus a protectionist measure (see PROTECTIONISM) designed to shield domestic producers in the importing country from foreign competition and assist that country's balance of payments.

See MULTIFIBRE ARRANGEMENT.

export subsidy a direct payment, or tax concession, or low-interest 'soft loan' made by the government to domestic firms to enable them to reduce their EXPORT prices. Although the widespread use of export subsidies by a country can increase its exports and assist its balance

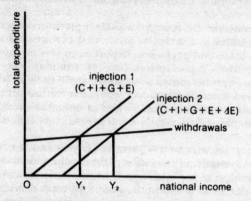

Fig. 65. **Export multiplier.** The effect of an increase in exports on national income. The additional exports (ΔE) serve to increase total injections and shift the injection schedule to the right, increasing national income by Y_1Y_2.

of payments, such subsidies are viewed as an 'unfair' trade practice by the GENERAL AGREEMENT ON TARIFFS AND TRADE, and are likely to lead to retaliatory action by other countries. See COUNTERVAILING DUTY, BEGGAR-MY-NEIGHBOUR POLICY.

ex post see EX ANTE.

external balance a situation of BALANCE-OF PAYMENTS EQUILIBRIUM that, over a number of years, results in a country spending and investing abroad no more than other countries spend and invest in it. The achievement of external balance is one of the macroeconomic objectives of the government. Compare INTERNAL BALANCE. See also DEMAND MANAGEMENT, EXCHANGE RATES, MACROECONOMIC POLICY, INTERNAL-EXTERNAL BALANCE MODEL.

external benefits see EXTERNALITIES.

external costs see EXTERNALITIES.

external diseconomies of scale the factors outside the influence of a single firm that lead to increasing long run AVERAGE COSTS for firms within an industry as a whole. For example, if a large number of firms settle in a particular area then the additional road congestion which they cause could slow up deliveries for any particular firm, increasing its own (internal) transport costs. See EXTERNAL ECONOMICS OF SCALE, DISECONOMIES OF SCALE.

external economies of scale the factors outside the influence of a single firm that lead to decreasing long run AVERAGE COSTS for firms within an industry as a whole. For example, if a college concentrated on training large numbers of, say, computer programmers to serve the needs of local computer business nearby, then the individual employer would have a supply of trained programmers available with a resulting reduction in the firm's own (internal) training costs.

See EXTERNAL DISECONOMIES OF SCALE, ECONOMIES OF SCALE, INTERNAL ECONOMIES OF SCALE.

external growth a mode of business growth which involves a firm in expanding its activities by MERGER, TAKEOVER or JOINT VENTURES, rather than through ORGANIC GROWTH (i.e. internal expansion). External growth may take the form of horizontal, vertical or diversified expansion (see HORIZONTAL INTEGRATION, VERTICAL INTEGRATION, DIVERSIFICATION).

In general terms, external growth allows a firm to expand more rapidly and in a more cost-effective way than internal expansion, while augmenting and widening the firm's resource base. Additionally, external growth has some specific attractions. For example, in the case of horizontal growth, a merger with, or takeover of, a competitor can enable a firm significantly to increase its market share while providing scope for exploiting economies of scale through rationalization of the two firms' operations. The alternative of attempting to improve market share through price and product differentiation competition may be prohibitively expensive by comparison. Likewise, in the case of conglomerate expansion, the firm may simply not have the expertise to develop products in non-related areas, whereas external growth allows a firm to move into new activities by acquiring a cusomized operation and related resource capabilities.

External growth, however, is not without its complications. For example, the merged or acquired firms have to be integrated into the one controlling organization which may require a major streamlining of operations and the creation of new management structures. If this is not done effectively, efficiency may be impaired and financial resources strained.

See BUSINESS STRATEGY, PRODUCT-MARKET MATRIX, FRANCHISE.

externalities factors that are not included in GROSS NATIONAL PRODUCT but which have an effect on human welfare. POLLUTION is a prime example of an external cost imposed on society: national output may only be maintained by allowing a certain degree of pollution which detracts from the quality of life. A firm will include the PRIVATE COSTS of materials, labour and capital used in producing goods and services but will not count the SOCIAL COSTS of pollution involved. On the other hand, positive externalities such as the social benefits conferred by firms in training workers who become available for employment elsewhere, are again not counted in national output.

See WELFARE ECONOMICS, COST-BENEFIT ANALYSIS.

extrapolate, *vb.* to estimate an unknown (future) value by projecting from known (past) values (in TIME-SERIES ANALYSIS). This involves predicting a value for the DEPENDENT VARIABLE from a value of the INDEPENDENT VARIABLE which is beyond the range of observed independent variables, and outside the range the trend line may be inaccurate because the underlying relationship may be different over the broader range. By contrast, if we *interpolate*, i.e., predict a value for the dependent variable from a value of the independent variable which lies within the range of observed independent variables, then the prediction is likely to be more reliable. See FORECASTING.

F

factor 1. a FACTOR INPUT which is used in production (see NATURAL RESOURCES, LABOUR, CAPITAL).

2. a business that buys in bulk and performs a WHOLESALING function.

3. a business that buys trade debts from client firms (at some agreed price below the nominal value of the debts) and then arranges to recover them for itself.

See FACTOR MARKET, FACTORING.

factor cost the value of goods and services produced measured in terms of the cost of the FACTOR INPUTS (materials, labour, etc.) used to produce them, that is, excluding any indirect taxes levied on products and any subsidies offered on products. For example, a product costing £10 to produce (including profit) and with a £1 indirect tax levied on it would have a market price of £11 and a factor cost of £10. See FACTORS OF PRODUCTION.

factor endowment the FACTORS OF PRODUCTION which a country has available to produce goods and services. The size and quality of a country's resource base (natural resources, labour and capital) determines the amount of goods and services it can produce (see GROSS NATIONAL PRODUCT) and the rate at which it can raise living standards over time (see ECONOMIC GROWTH). Differences between countries in terms of the availability and sophistication of their resource inputs provide an incentive for them to engage in INTERNATIONAL TRADE in order to obtain products which they cannot make efficiently for themselves.

factor income see NATIONAL INCOME.

factoring a financial arrangement whereby a specialist finance company (the factor) purchases a firm's DEBTORS for an amount less than the book value of those debts. The factor's profit derives from the difference between monies collected from the DEBTS purchased and the actual purchase price of those debts. The firm benefits by receiving immediate cash from the factor rather than having to wait until trade debtors eventually pay their debts, and avoids the trouble and expense of pursuing tardy debtors.

See CREDIT CONTROL.

factor inputs FACTORS OF PRODUCTION (labour, capital, etc.) which are combined to produce OUTPUT of goods and services. See PRODUCTION FUNCTION, COST FUNCTION.

factor market a market in which FACTORS OF PRODUCTION are bought and sold, and in which the prices of labour and other FACTOR INPUTS

191

are determined by the interplay of demand and supply forces. See LABOUR MARKET, CAPITAL MARKET, COMMODITY MARKET, DERIVED DEMAND, MARGINAL PHYSICAL PRODUCT, MARGINAL REVENUE PRODUCT, PRICE SYSTEM.

factors of production the resources that are used by firms as FACTOR INPUTS in producing a good or service. There are three main groups of factor inputs: NATURAL RESOURCES, LABOUR and CAPITAL. Factors of production can be combined together in different proportions to produce a given output (see PRODUCTION FUNCTION); it is assumed in the THEORY OF THE FIRM that firms will select that combination of inputs for any given level of output which minimizes the cost of producing that output (see COST FUNCTION). See ENTREPRENEUR, MOBILITY.

Fair Trading Act, 1973 an Act which consolidated and extended UK competition law by controlling MONOPOLIES, MERGERS AND TAKEOVERS, RESTRICTIVE TRADE AGREEMENTS and RESALE PRICES. The Act established a new regulatory authority, the OFFICE OF FAIR TRADING (headed by the Director-General of Fair Trading) with powers to supervise all aspects of COMPETITION POLICY, including the monitoring of changes in market structure, companies' commercial policies, the registration of restrictive trade agreements, and the referral, where appropriate, of cases for investigation and report by the MONOPOLIES AND MERGERS COMMISSION and RESTRICTIVE PRACTICES COURT. The Act also gave the OFT specific responsibilities to oversee other matters affecting consumers' interests, including weights and measures, trade descriptions and voluntary codes of good practice.
See CONSUMER PROTECTION.

fallacy of composition an error in economic thinking that often arises when it is assumed that what hold true for an individual or part must also hold true for a group or whole. For example, if a small number of people save more of their income, this might be considered to be a 'good thing' because more funds can be made available to finance investment. But if everybody attempts to save more this will reduce total spending and income and result in a fall in total saving. See PARADOX OF THRIFT.

family expenditure survey an annual UK government survey of households' expenditure patterns. The survey provides information which is used by the government to select a typical 'basket' of goods and services bought by consumers, the prices of which can then be noted in compiling a retail PRICE INDEX.

feasible region see LINEAR PROGRAMMING.

Federal Reserve Bank the CENTRAL BANK of the US.

fees the payments to professional persons such as lawyers and accountants for performing services on behalf of clients.

fiat currency see FIDUCIARY ISSUE.

fiduciary issue or **fiat currency** CURRENCY issued by a government that is not matched by government holdings of GOLD or other securities. In the 19th century most currency issues were backed by gold, and people could exchange their BANK NOTES for gold on demand. Nowadays most governments have only minimal holdings of gold and other securities to redeem their currency so that most of their currency issues are fiduciary. See MONEY SUPPLY.

FIMBRA see FINANCIAL INTERMEDIARIES, MANAGERS AND BROKERS REGULATORY ASSOCIATION.

final income the INCOME received by a household (or person) after allowing for any payment of INCOME TAX and other taxes, and the receipt of various TRANSFER PAYMENTS (social security benefits, etc.).

Compare ORIGINAL INCOME. See REDISTRIBUTION OF INCOME PRINCIPLE OF TAXATION.

final products GOODS and SERVICES which are consumed by end-users, as opposed to INTERMEDIATE PRODUCTS which are used as FACTOR INPUTS in producing other goods and services. Thus purchases of bread count as part of final demand but not the flour used to make this bread.

The total market value of all final products (which corresponds with total expenditure in the NATIONAL INCOME ACCOUNTS) corresponds with the total VALUE ADDED at each product stage for all products in the economy.

Finance Corporation for Industry see INVESTORS IN INDUSTRY.

finance house a financial institution that accepts deposits from savers and which specializes in the lending of money by way of INSTALMENT CREDIT (hire purchase loans) and LEASING for private consumption and business investment purposes. See FINANCIAL SYSTEM.

financial accounting the accounting activities directed towards the preparation of annual PROFIT-AND-LOSS ACCOUNTS and BALANCE SHEETS in order to report to shareholders on their company's overall (profit) performance. See MANAGEMENT ACCOUNTING.

financial innovation the development by FINANCIAL INSTITUTIONS of new financial products and processes for the transmission of money and the lending and borrowing of funds, for example, telephone banking services, direct debit systems, credit cards, etc. These developments have augmented the traditional means of transmitting money (cash, cheques) and may have served to increase the velocity of circulation of money. They have also increased the availability of CREDIT and by creating new 'NEAR MONEY' assets have served to extend the liquidity base of the economy. This has tended to make the application of MONETARY POLICY by the authorities more complex.

financial institution an institution that acts primarily as a FINANCIAL INTERMEDIARY in channelling funds from LENDERS to BORROWERS (e.g., COMMERCIAL BANKS, BUILDING SOCIETIES), or from SAVERS to INVESTORS (e.g., PENSION FUNDS, INSURANCE COMPANIES). See FINANCIAL SYSTEM.

Financial Intermediaries, Managers and Brokers Regulatory Association (FIMBRA) a body which is responsible for regulating firms which advise and act on behalf of members of the general public in financial dealings such as life assurance policies, unit trusts, etc. See SELF–REGULATORY ORGANIZATION.

financial intermediary an organization that operates in financial markets linking LENDERS and BORROWERS or SAVERS and INVESTORS. See FINANCIAL SYSTEM, COMMERCIAL BANK, SAVINGS BANK, BUILDING SOCIETY, PENSION FUND, INSURANCE COMPANY, UNIT TRUST, INVESTMENT TRUST COMPANY, INTERMEDIATION.

financial sector that part of the ECONOMY concerned with the transactions of FINANCIAL INSTITUTIONS. Financial institutions provide money transmission services and loan facilities, and influence the workings of the 'real' economy by acting as intermediaries in channelling SAVINGS and other funds into INVESTMENT uses. The financial sector, together with the CORPORATE SECTOR and PERSONAL SECTOR constitute the PRIVATE SECTOR. The private sector, PUBLIC (GOVERNMENT) SECTOR and FOREIGN SECTOR make up the national economy. See FINANCIAL SYSTEM.

financial security a financial instrument issued by companies, financial institutions and the government as a means of borrowing money and raising new capital. The most commonly used financial securities are SHARES, STOCKS, DEBENTURES, BILLS OF EXCHANGE, TREASURY BILLS and BONDS. Once issued, these securities can be bought and sold either on the MONEY MARKETS or on the STOCK EXCHANGE. See WARRANT, CERTIFICATE OF DEPOSIT, CONSOL.

Financial Services Act, 1986 a UK Act which provides a regulatory system for the FINANCIAL SECURITIES and INVESTMENT industry. The Act covers the businesses of securities dealing and investment, commodities and financial futures, unit trusts and some insurance (excluding the Lloyds insurance market). Also excluded from its remit is commercial banking, which is supervised by the Bank of England, and mortgage and other business of the building societies, which is regulated separately by the BUILDING SOCIETY ACT, 1986.

The main areas covered by the Act are the authorization of securities and investment businesses, and the establishment and enforcement of rules of good and fair business practice. The DEPARTMENT OF TRADE AND INDUSTRY, together with its appointed agency, the Securities and Investment Board (SIB), is responsible for the overall administration of the Act, in conjunction with various SELF–REGULATORY ORGANIZATIONS (SROs), RECOGNIZED INVESTMENT EXCHANGES (RIEs) and RECOGNIZED PROFESSIONAL BODIES (RPBs).

The general objective of the legislation is to ensure that only persons deemed to be 'fit and proper' are authorized to undertake securities and investment business, and that they conduct their business according to standards laid down by the SIBs, SROs, RIEs and RPBs; leading, for example, to the clarification of the relationship between the firm and its clients, especially as regards disclosure of fees and charges.

financial system a network of financial institutions (BANKS, COMMERCIAL BANKS, BUILDING SOCIETIES, etc.) and markets (MONEY MARKET, STOCK EXCHANGE) dealing in a variety of financial instruments (BANK DEPOSITS, TREASURY BILLS, STOCKS and SHARES etc.) that are engaged in money transmission and the lending and borrowing of funds.

The financial institutions and markets occupy a key position in the economy as intermediaries in channelling SAVINGS and other funds to BORROWERS. In so doing one of their principal tasks is to reconcile the different requirements of savers and borrowers, thereby facilitating a higher level of saving and INVESTMENT than would otherwise be the case. Savers in general are looking for a safe and relatively risk-free repository for their monies, which combines some degree of liquidity (i.e., ready access to their money) with a longer-term investment return which protects the real value of their wealth as well as providing current income. Borrowers, in general, require access to funds of varying amounts to finance current, medium-term and long-term financial and capital commitments often, as is especially the case with business investments, under conditions of unavoidable uncertainty and high degrees of risk. The financial institutions help to reconcile these different requirements in the following three main ways:

(a) by pooling together the savings of a large number of individuals, so making it possible in turn to make single loans running into millions of pounds;

(b) by holding a diversified portfolio of assets and lending for a variety of purposes to gain economies of scale by spreading their risks while still keeping profitability high;

(c) by combining the resources of a large number of savers to provide both for an individual to remove his funds at short notice, and for their own deposits to remain stable as a base for long-term lending.

Financial Times All-Share Index see SHARE PRICE INDEX.

fine-tuning a short-run interventionist approach to the economy that uses monetary and fiscal measures to control fluctuations in the level of AGGREGATE DEMAND, with the aim of minimizing deviations from MACROECONOMIC POLICY objectives. The application of 'fine-tuning', however, is beset with problems of accurately FORECASTING fluctuations in economic activity and in gauging the magnitude and timing of counter-cyclical measures.

See DEMAND MANAGEMENT, MONETARY POLICY, FISCAL POLICY.

firm or **company** or **supplier** a transformation unit concerned with converting FACTOR INPUTS into higher-valued intermediate and final GOODS or SERVICES. The firm or BUSINESS is the basic producing/supplying unit and is a vital building block in constructing a theory of the market to explain how firms interact and how their pricing and output decisions influence market supply and price (see THEORY OF THE FIRM, THEORY OF MARKETS).

The legal form of a firm consists of:

(a) a *sole proprietorship*, a firm owned and controlled (managed) by a single person, i.e., the type of firm that most closely approximates to that of the 'firm' in economic theory.

(b) a *partnership*, a firm owned and controlled by two or more persons who are parties to a partnership agreement.

(c) a JOINT-STOCK COMPANY, a firm owned by a group of ordinary shareholders and whose capital is divided-up into a number of SHARES. See COOPERATIVE.

The economic form of a firm consists of:

(a) a *horizontal firm*, a firm that is engaged in a single productive activity; e.g., motor-car assembly.

(b) a *vertical firm*, a firm that undertakes two or more vertically-linked productive activities; e.g., the production of car components (clutches, steel body shells) and car assembly.

(c) a *diversified* or *conglomerate firm*, a firm that is engaged in a number of unrelated productive activities; e.g., car assembly and the production of bread.

See HORIZONTAL INTEGRATION, VERTICAL INTEGRATION, DIVERSIFICATION.

firm location the area where a firm chooses to locate its business. In principle a profit-maximizing firm will locate where its production and distribution costs are minimized relative to revenues earned. Often firms are faced with competing pulls of nearness to their market (to reduce product distribution costs), and nearness to their raw material supplies (to reduce materials transport costs), and must seek to balance these costs. Some firms have little choice in this regard, service companies being forced to locate near customers, and mineral extraction companies having to locate near materials sources. Many firms are relatively footloose, though, and are free to locate anywhere, influenced by the general attractiveness of an area; the quality of its transport, communications and education infrastructure; skills and reputation of its workforce, etc. See REGIONAL POLICY.

firm objectives an element of MARKET CONDUCT that denotes the goals of the firm in supplying GOODS and SERVICES. In the traditional THEORY OF THE FIRM and the THEORY OF MARKETS, in order to facilitate intermarket comparisons of performance, *all* firms, whether operating under conditions of PERFECT COMPETITION, MONOPOLISTIC COMPETITION, OLIGOPOLY or MONOPOLY, are assumed to be seeking

PROFIT MAXIMIZATION. More recent contributions to this body of theory have postulated a number of alternative firm objectives, including SALES-REVENUE MAXIMIZATION and ASSET-GROWTH MAXIMIZATION. In these formulations profits are seen as contributing to the attainment of some other objective rather than as an end in themselves.

See MANAGERIAL THEORIES OF THE FIRM, DIVORCE OF OWNERSHIP FROM CONTROL, BEHAVIOURAL THEORY OF THE FIRM, SATISFICING THEORY, MANAGEMENT UTILITY MAXIMIZATION.

first-in first-out (FIFO) STOCK VALUATION.

fiscal drag the restraining effect of PROGRESSIVE TAXATION on economic expansion. As NATIONAL INCOME rises, people move from lower to higher tax brackets, thereby increasing government TAXATION receipts. The increase in taxation constitutes a 'leakage' (from the CIRCULAR FLOW OF NATIONAL INCOME) which will reduce the rate of expansion of AGGREGATE DEMAND below that which would otherwise be the case. Governments may choose as part of FISCAL POLICY to adjust for the effects of fiscal drag by regularly increasing personal tax allowances.

Fiscal drag can also serve to automatically constrain the effect of the pressure of INFLATION in the economy, for with a high rate of inflation people will tend to move into higher tax brackets thereby increasing their total taxation payments, decreasing their disposal income, and reducing aggregate demand. This has the effect of reducing the pressure of DEMAND-PULL INFLATION. See AUTOMATIC (BUILT-IN) STABILIZERS.

fiscal policy an instrument of DEMAND MANAGEMENT which seeks to influence the level of economic activity in an economy through the control of TAXATION and GOVERNMENT EXPENDITURE.

The fiscal authorities (principally the TREASURY in the UK) can employ a number of taxation measures to control AGGREGATE DEMAND or spending: DIRECT TAXES on individuals (INCOME TAX) and companies (CORPORATION TAX) can be increased if spending needs to be reduced, for example, to control INFLATION; i.e. an increase in income tax reduces people's disposable income, and similarly an increase in corporation tax leaves companies with less profit available to pay dividends and reinvest. Alternatively, spending can be reduced by increasing INDIRECT TAXES: an increase in VALUE ADDED TAXES on products in general, or an increase in EXCISE DUTIES on particular products such as petrol and cigarettes will, by increasing their price, lead to a reduction in purchasing power.

The government can use changes in its own expenditure to affect spending levels; for example, a cut in current purchases of products or capital investment by the government again serves to reduce total spending in the economy.

Taxation and government expenditure are linked together in terms of the government's overall fiscal or BUDGET position: total spending in the economy is reduced by the twin effects of increased taxation and expenditure cuts with the government running a budget surplus. If the objective is to increase spending, then the government operates a budget deficit, reducing taxation and increasing its expenditure.

A decrease in government spending and an increase in taxes (a WITHDRAWAL from the CIRCULAR FLOW OF NATIONAL INCOME) reduces aggregate demand and through the MULTIPLIER process serves to reduce inflationary pressures when the economy is 'over-heating'. By contrast, an increase in government spending and/or decrease in taxes (an INJECTION into the circular flow of national income) stimulates aggregate demand and via the multiplier effect creates additional jobs to counteract UNEMPLOYMENT. Fig. 66 shows the effect of an increase in government expenditure and/or cuts in taxes in raising aggregate demand from AD to AD_1 and national income from Y to Y_1, and the effect of a decrease in government expenditure and/or increases in taxes, lowering aggregate demand from AD to AD_2 and national income from Y to Y_2.

The use of budget deficits was first advocated by KEYNES as a means of counteracting the mass unemployment of the 1920s and 1930s. With the widespread acceptance of Keynesian ideas by Western governments in the period since 1945, fiscal policy was used as the main means of 'fine-tuning' the economy to achieve full employment.

In practice the application of fiscal policy as a *short-term* stabilization technique encounters a number of problems which reduce its effectiveness. Taxation rate changes, particularly alterations to income tax, are administratively cumbersome to initiate and take time to implement; likewise, a substantial proportion of government expenditure on, for example, schools, roads, hospitals and defence reflects *longer-term* economic and social commitments and cannot easily be reversed without lengthy political lobbying. Also, changes in taxes or expenditure produce 'multiplier' effects (i.e. some initial change in spending is magnified and transmitted around the economy), but to an indeterminate extent.

Moreover, the use of fiscal policy to keep the economy operating at high levels of aggregate demand so as to achieve full employment often leads to DEMAND-PULL INFLATION.

Experience of fiscal policy has indicated that the short-termism approach to economic management has not in fact been especially successful in stabilizing the economy. As a result, *medium-term* management of the economy has, in recent years, assumed a greater degree of significance. (See MEDIUM-TERM FINANCIAL STRATEGY).

See FISCAL STANCE, DEFLATIONARY GAP, INFLATIONARY GAP, KEYNESIAN ECONOMICS, MONETARISM, MONETARY POLICY, SUPPLY-SIDE

ECONOMICS, BUSINESS CYCLE, PUBLIC FINANCE, BUDGET, CROWDING-OUT EFFECT.

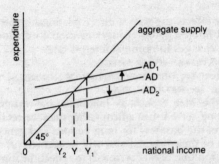

Fig. 66. **Fiscal policy**. The effect of (a) an increase in government spending/tax cuts (AD₁) and (b) a decrease in government spending/tax increases (AD₂).

fiscal stance the government's underlying position in applying FISCAL POLICY, that is, whether it plans to match its expenditure and taxation revenues (a planned BALANCED BUDGET); or deliberately plans to spend more than it expects to receive in taxation revenues (a planned BUDGET DEFICIT); or deliberately plans to spend less than it receives in taxation revenues (a planned BUDGET SURPLUS). The government's actual budgetary position, however, can deviate from its fiscal stance insofar as, for example, recession will cause taxable incomes and expenditures to fall below expected levels and unemployment and other social security payments to increase above the expected level. Thus, without any actual change in the government's fiscal stance and tax rates set, the government's budget position and borrowing requirements can vary with the level of economic activity.

See PUBLIC SECTOR BORROWING REQUIREMENT.

fiscal year the government's accounting year which, in the UK, runs from 6 April to 5 April the following year. Different countries frequently have a fiscal year different to the normal calendar year. In the US the fiscal year runs up to 30th June. See BUDGET (GOVERNMENT).

Fisher effect an expression which formally allows for the effects of INFLATION upon the INTEREST RATE of a LOAN or BOND. The Fisher equation, devised by Irving Fisher (1867–1947), expresses the nominal interest rate on a loan as the sum of the REAL INTEREST RATE and the rate of inflation expected over the duration of the loan: $R = r + F$, where R = nominal interest rate, r = real interest rate and F = rate of annual inflation. For example, if inflation is 6% in one year and the real interest rate required by lenders is 4%, then the nominal interest rate will be 10%. The inflation premium of 6% incorporated in the nominal interest rate serves to compensate lenders for the reduced value of the currency loaned when it is returned by borrowers.

The Fisher effects suggests a direct relationship between inflation and nominal interest rates, changes in annual inflation rates leading to matching changes in nominal interest rates.

See INTERNATIONAL FISHER EFFECT.

Fisher equation see QUANTITY THEORY OF MONEY.

five-year plan see NATIONAL PLAN.

fixed assets the ASSETS such as buildings and machinery that are bought for long-term use in a firm rather than for resale. Fixed assets are retained in the business for long periods and generally each year a proportion of their original cost will be written off against PROFITS for amortization (see DEPRECIATION 2) to reflect the diminishing value of the asset. In a BALANCE SHEET fixed assets are usually shown at cost less depreciation charged to date. Certain fixed assets such as property tend to appreciate in value (see APPRECIATION 2) and need to be revalued periodically to help keep their BALANCE SHEET values in line with market values. See CURRENT ASSETS, RESERVE.

fixed costs any costs that, in the SHORT RUN, do not vary with the level of output of a product. They include such items as rent and depreciation of fixed assets, whose total cost remains unchanged regardless of changes in the level of activity. Consequently, fixed cost per unit of product will fall as output increases as total fixed costs are spread over a larger output. See Fig. 67.

In the THEORY OF MARKETS, a firm will leave a product market if in the LONG RUN it cannot earn sufficient TOTAL REVENUE to cover both total fixed costs and total VARIABLE COSTS. However, it will remain in a market in the short run as long as it can generate sufficient total revenue to cover total variable cost and make some CONTRIBUTION towards total fixed costs even though it is still making a loss, on the assumption that this loss-making situation is merely a temporary one. See MARKET EXIT.

fixed exchange-rate system a mechanism for synchronizing and coordinating the EXCHANGE RATES of participating countries' CURRENCIES. Under this system, currencies are assigned a central fixed par value in terms of the other currencies in the system and countries are committed to maintaining this value by support buying and selling. For example, between 1949 and 1967, under the INTERNATIONAL MONETARY FUND's *former* fixed exchange rate system, the UK maintained a rate of exchange at £1 = \$2.80 with the US dollar. If the price of the £ rose (appreciated) in the FOREIGN EXCHANGE MARKET the UK CENTRAL BANK bought dollars and sold pounds; if the price

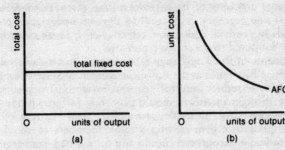

Fig. 67. **Fixed costs**. (a) The graph represents payments made for the use of FIXED FACTOR INPUTS (plant and equipment, etc.) which must be met irrespective of whether output is high or low. (b) The graph represents the continuous decline in average fixed cost (AFC) as output rises as a given amount of fixed cost is spread over a greater number of units.

of the £ fell (depreciated) the central bank sold dollars and bought pounds. See Fig. 68. Because of the technical difficulties of hitting the central rate with complete accuracy on a day-to-day basis, most fixed exchange rate systems operate with a 'band of tolerance' around the central rate: for example, the *current* EUROPEAN MONETARY SYSTEM allows members' currencies to fluctuate 2.25% either side of the central par value.

Once an exchange rate is fixed, countries are expected to maintain this rate for fairly lengthy periods of time, but are allowed to devalue their currencies (that is, refix the exchange rate at a new, lower value; see DEVALUATION) or revalue it (that is, refix it at a new, higher value; see REVALUATION) if their BALANCE OF PAYMENTS are, respectively, in chronic deficit or surplus.

Generally speaking, the business and financial community prefer relatively fixed exchange rates to FLOATING EXCHANGE RATES, since it enables them to enter into trade (EXPORT, IMPORT contracts) and financial transactions (FOREIGN INVESTMENT) at known foreign exchange prices so that the profit and loss implications of these deals can be calculated in advance. The chief disadvantage with such a system is that governments often tend to delay altering the exchange rate, either because of political factors (e.g. the 'bad publicity' surrounding devaluations) or because they may choose to deal with the balance of payments difficulties by using other measures, so that the pegged rate gets seriously out of line with underlying market tendencies. When this happens SPECULATION against the currency tends to build up, leading to highly disruptive HOT MONEY flows, which destabilizes currency markets and force the central bank to spend large amounts of its INTERNATIONAL RESERVES to defend the parity. If one currency is 'forced' to devalue under such pressure, this tends to produce a 'domino' effect as other weak currencies are likewise subjected to speculative pressure.

Proponents of fixed exchange rate systems (particularly relatively small-group blocs such as the European Monetary System) emphasize that in order to reduce 'internal' tensions between participants, economically stronger members should play their full part in the adjustment process (for example, revaluing their currencies when appropriate) rather than leaving weaker members to shoulder the entire burden; and countries should aim for a broad 'convergence' in their economic policies both with respect to objectives (e.g. low inflation rates) and instruments (e.g. similar interest rate structures).

See BALANCE OF PAYMENTS EQUILIBRIUM, ADJUSTABLE PEG EXCHANGE RATE SYSTEM, CRAWLING PEG EXCHANGE RATE SYSTEM, GOLD STANDARD, FOREIGN EXCHANGE EQUALIZATION ACCOUNT.

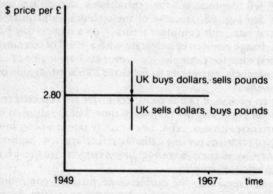

Fig. 68. **Fixed exchange-rate system.** The exchange rate between the pound and the dollar between 1949 and 1967.

fixed factor input a FACTOR INPUT to the production process that cannot be increased or reduced in the SHORT RUN. This applies particularly to capital inputs such as (given) plant and equipment. See VARIABLE FACTOR INPUT, RETURNS TO THE VARIABLE FACTOR INPUT, FIXED COSTS.

fixed-interest financial securities any FINANCIAL SECURITIES that have a predetermined fixed INTEREST RATE attached to their PAR VALUE. For example, TREASURY BILLS, DEBENTURES and PREFERENCE SHARES. A debenture with a par value of £100 at 5% will pay out a fixed rate of interest of £5 per annum until the expiry of the debenture, that is, the date of redemption. See BONDS.

fixed investment any INVESTMENT in plant, machinery, equipment and other durable CAPITAL GOODS.

Fixed investment in the provision of social products like roads, hospitals and schools is undertaken by central and local government as part of government expenditure. Fixed investment in plant, equipment and machinery in the private sector will be influenced by the expected returns on such investments and the cost of capital needed to finance planned investments.

Investment is a component of AGGREGATE DEMAND and so affects the level of economic activity in the short-run, while fixed investment serves to add to the economic INFRASTRUCTURE and raise POTENTIAL GROSS NATIONAL PRODUCT over the longer term.

In the short run expected returns from an investment in plant will depend upon business confidence about sales prospects and therefore plant utilization. The volatility of business EXPECTATIONS means that planned levels of investment can vary significantly over time, leading to large changes in the demand for capital goods (see ACCELERATOR), that is, large fluctuations in the investment component of aggregate demand leading to larger fluctuations in output and employment through the MULTIPLIER effect.

See BUSINESS CYCLE, INVENTORY INVESTMENT, MARGINAL EFFICIENCY OF CAPITAL/INVESTMENT.

fixed targets an approach to macroeconomic policy that sets specific target values in respect of the objectives of FULL EMPLOYMENT, PRICE STABILITY, ECONOMIC GROWTH and BALANCE OF PAYMENTS EQUILIBRIUM.

The essence of this approach can be illustrated, to simplify matters, by reference to the PHILLIPS CURVE 'trade-off' between unemployment and inflation illustrated in Fig. 69 (overleaf).

See MACROECONOMIC POLICY, OPTIMIZING.

flat yield see YIELD.

flexible exchange rate see FLOATING EXCHANGE RATE.

flexible manufacturing system (FMS) a means of PRODUCTION which makes extensive use of 'programmed' AUTOMATION and COMPUTERS to achieve rapid production of small batches of components or products whilst maintaining flexibility in manufacturing a wide range of these items.

Flexible manufacturing systems enable small batches of a product to be produced at the same unit cost as would be achievable with large-scale production, thus diminishing the cost advantages associated with ECONOMIES OF SCALE and lowering the MINIMUM EFFICIENT SCALE. This enables small firms to compete in cost terms with large firms and may lead to a lowering of SELLER CONCENTRATION.

See BARRIERS TO ENTRY.

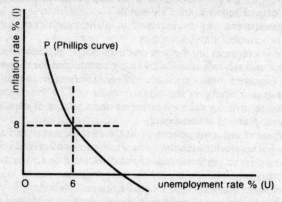

Fig. 69. **Fixed targets.** The Phillips curve shows that as unemployment (U) falls, inflation (I) increases, and vice-versa. The Phillips curve is drawn as P. Ideally, the authorities would like the economy to be at the origin, point O, for here full employment and complete price stability are simultaneously attained. The Phillips curve, however, sets a limit to the combinations of U and I which can be achieved in practice. Given this constraint, the task of the authorities is to specify 'acceptable' target values for the two objectives. They could, for example, set a fixed target value on unemployment at 6% and a target value for inflation at 8%, or, alternatively a lower value for I and a higher value for U.

floating exchange-rate system a mechanism for coordinating EXCHANGE RATES between countries' CURRENCIES which involves the value of each country's currency in terms of other currencies being determined by the forces of the demand for, and supply of, currencies in the FOREIGN EXCHANGE MARKET. Over time the exchange rate of a particular currency may rise (APPRECIATION) or fall (DEPRECIATION) depending, respectively, on the strength or weakness of the country's underlying BALANCE OF PAYMENTS position and exposure to speculative activity (see SPECULATOR), as shown in Fig. 70a. In theory, this should always result in an equilibrium exchange rate (i.e. a rate which ensures that a country achieves a BALANCE-OF-PAYMENTS EQUILIBRIUM), leaving the country more freedom to pursue desirable domestic policies without external restraints. In practice, however, 'unregulated', free-floating exchange rates tend to produce erratic and destabilizing exchange rate movements, often fuelled by speculative HOT MONEY flows, which makes it difficult to enter into meaningful trade (EXPORT, IMPORT contracts) and investment transactions (FOREIGN INVESTMENT deals) because of the uncertainties surrounding the profit and loss implications of such deals when exchange rates are fluctuating wildly. For this reason countries often prefer to 'manage' their exchange rates, as shown in Fig. 70b, with their CENTRAL BANKS buying and selling currencies, as appropriate, in the foreign exchange market.

While this creates a more settled and controlled environment in which to operate, nonetheless firms are usually forced to cover their currency requirements by, for example, taking out OPTIONS in the FUTURES MARKET (see EXCHANGE RATE EXPOSURE).

Moreover, a country's intervention in currency markets sometimes goes beyond merely 'smoothing' its exchange rate and may involve a deliberate attempt to 'manipulate' the exchange rate so as to gain a trading advantage over other countries (a so-called 'dirty float').

Contrast FIXED EXCHANGE RATE SYSTEM. See PURCHASING-POWER PARITY THEORY, ASSET VALUE THEORY, INTERNATIONAL MONETARY FUND, FOREIGN EXCHANGE EQUALIZATION ACCOUNT.

flow a measurement of quantity over a specified period of time.

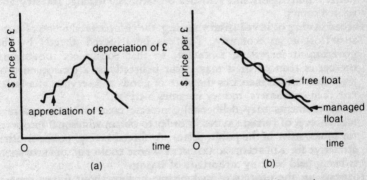

Fig. 70. **Floating exchange-rate system**. (a) If the UK's imports from the US rise faster than the UK's exports to the US, then, in currency terms, the UK's demand for dollars will increase relative to the demand in the US for pounds. This will cause the pound to fall (see DEPRECIATION 1) against the dollar, making imports from the US to the UK more expensive and exports from the UK to the US cheaper. By contrast, if the UK's imports from the US rise more slowly than its exports to the US, then, in currency terms, its demand for dollars will be relatively smaller than the US demand for pounds. This will cause the pound to rise (see APPRECIATION sense 1), making imports from the US to the UK cheaper and exports from the UK to the US more expensive. (b) The graph shows how nations can manage the float by intervening in the currency market to buy and sell currencies, using their national currency reserves to moderate the degree of short-term fluctuation and smooth out the long-term trend line.

F.O.B.

Unlike a STOCK, which is not a function of time, a flow measures quantity passing per minute, hour, day or whatever. A common analogy is to a reservoir. The water entering and leaving the reservoir is a flow, but that water actually in the reservoir at any one point in time is a stock. INCOME is a flow but WEALTH is a stock.

f.o.b. *abbrev.* for free-on-board. In BALANCE OF PAYMENTS terms, f.o.b. means that only the basic prices of imports and exports of goods (plus loading charges) are counted while the 'cost-insurance-freight' (C.I.F) charges incurred in transporting the goods from one country to another are excluded.

Food and Agricultural Organization (FAO) an international agency of the UNITED NATIONS, established in 1945. Its primary objective is to improve agricultural productivity and hence the nutritional standards of agrarian countries throughout the world. It achieves this objective through undertaking research on all aspects of farming, fishing and forestry and by offering technical assistance to those countries which require it. In addition, the FAO continually surveys world agricultural conditions, collects and issues statistics on human nutritional requirements and statistics on farming, fishing, forestry and related topics.

forced saving or **involuntary saving** the enforced reduction of CONSUMPTION in an economy. This can be achieved directly by the government increasing TAXATION so that consumers' DISPOSABLE INCOME is reduced or it may occur indirectly as a consequence of INFLATION which increases the price of goods and services at a faster rate than consumers' money incomes increase.

Governments may deliberately increase taxes so as to secure a higher level of forced SAVING in order to obtain additional resources for INVESTMENT in the public sector. A 'forced saving' policy is often attractive for a DEVELOPING COUNTRY whose ECONOMIC DEVELOPMENT is being held back by a shortage of savings.

forecasting the process of making predictions about future general economic and market conditions as a basis for decision-making by government and business. Various forecasting methods can be used to estimate future economic conditions, varying greatly in terms of their subjectivity, sophistication, data requirements and cost:

(a) survey techniques involving the use of interviews or mailed questionnaires asking consumers or industrial buyers about their future (buying) intentions. Alternatively, members of the sales force may provide estimates of future market sales; or industry experts can offer scenario-type forecasts about future market developments.

(b) experimental methods providing demand forecasts for new products, etc, based on either the buying responses of small samples of panel consumers, or large samples in test markets.

(c) EXTRAPOLATION methods employing TIME-SERIES ANALYSIS, using past economic data to predict future economic trends. These methods implicitly assume that the historical relationships which have held in the past will continue to hold in the future, without examining causal relationships between the variables involved. Time-series data usually comprises: a long run secular trend, with certain medium-term cyclical fluctuations; and short-term seasonal variations, affected by irregular, random influences. Techniques such as moving averages or exponential smoothing can be used to analyse and project such time series, though they are generally unable to predict sharp upturns or downturns in economic variables.

(d) *Barometric forecasts* to predict the future value of economic variables from the present values of particular statistical indicators which have a consistent relationship with these economic variables. Such LEADING INDICATORS as business capital investment plans and new housebuilding starts can be used as a barometer for forecasting values like economic activity levels or product demand, and they can be useful for predicting sharp changes in these values.

(e) INPUT–OUTPUT methods using input–output tables to show interrelationships between industries, and to analyse how changes in demand conditions in one industry will be affected by changes in demand and supply conditions in other industries related to it. For example, car component manufacturers will need to estimate the future demand for cars and the future production plans of motor car manufacturers who are their major customers.

(f) ECONOMETRIC methods predicting future values of economic variables by examining other variables which are causally related to it. Econometric models link variables in the form of equations which can be estimated statistically and then used as a basis for forecasting. Judgement has to be exercised in identifying the INDEPENDENT VARIABLES which causally affect the DEPENDENT VARIABLE to be forecast. For example, in order to predict future quantity of a product demanded (Qd) we would formulate an equation linking it to product price (P) and disposable income (Y):

$$Qd = a + bP + cY$$

then use past data to estimate the regression coefficients a, b and c (see REGRESSION ANALYSIS). Econometric models may consist of just one equation like this, but often in complex economic situations the independent variables in one equation are themselves influenced by other variables, so that many equations may be necessary to represent all the casual relationships involved. For example, the macroeconomic forecasting model used by the British Treasury to predict future economic activity levels has over 600 equations.

No forecasting method will generate completely accurate predictions, so when making any forecast we must allow for a *margin of error* in that forecast. In the situation illustrated in Fig. 71, we cannot make a precise estimate of the future value of an economic variable, rather we must allow that there is a range of possible future outcomes centred around the forecast value, showing a range of values with their associated probability distribution. Consequently forecasters need to exercise judgement in predicting future economic conditions both in choosing which forecasting methods to use and in combining information from different forecasts.

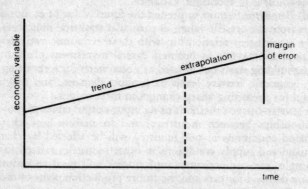

Fig. 71. **Forecasting**. The margin of error expected in economic forecasts.

foreclosure the refusal by a VERTICALLY INTEGRATED firm to supply inputs to non-integrated rivals, or distribute their products, as a means of putting them at a competitive disadvantage. In market situations where there are a substantial number of alternative independent supply sources and outlets, rival suppliers are unlikely to be inconvenienced. However, the control by a DOMINANT FIRM of the majority of input sources and outlets, combined with limitations on the establishment of new ones, could have serious anti-competitive consequences. Under UK COMPETITION POLICY cases of vertical integration may be referred to the MONOPOLIES AND MERGERS COMMISSION for investigation.

See REFUSAL TO SUPPLY.

foreign currency or **foreign exchange** the CURRENCY of an overseas country, which is purchased by a particular country in exchange for its own currency. This foreign currency is then used to finance INTERNATIONAL TRADE and FOREIGN INVESTMENT between the two countries.

See FOREIGN EXCHANGE MARKET, FOREIGN EXCHANGE CONTROLS.

foreign exchange see FOREIGN CURRENCY.

foreign exchange controls restrictions on the availability of FOREIGN CURRENCIES by a country's CENTRAL BANK, to assist in the removal of a BALANCE OF PAYMENTS deficit and to control disruptive short-run capital flows (HOT MONEY) which tend to destabilize the country's EXCHANGE RATE. Where importers can only purchase foreign currencies from the country's central bank (via their commercial banks) in order to buy products from overseas suppliers, by cutting off the supply of foreign currencies the authorities can reduce the amount of IMPORTS to a level compatible with the foreign currency earned by the country's EXPORTS. Exchange controls may be applied not only to limit the total amount of currency available but can also be used to discriminate against particular types of imports, thus serving as a form of PROTECTIONISM.

See FOREIGN EXCHANGE MARKET.

Foreign Exchange Equalization Account FOREIGN CURRENCIES held by a country's CENTRAL BANK (for example, the Bank of England) which are used to intervene in the FOREIGN EXCHANGE MARKET in order to stabilize the EXCHANGE RATE of that country's currency.

See FIXED EXCHANGE RATE SYSTEM, EUROPEAN MONETARY SYSTEM, INTERNATIONAL MONETARY FUND.

foreign exchange market a MARKET engaged in the buying and selling of FOREIGN CURRENCIES. Such a market is required because each country involved in INTERNATIONAL TRADE and FOREIGN INVESTMENT has its own domestic currency and this needs to be exchanged for other currencies in order to finance trade and capital transactions. This function is undertaken by a network of private foreign exchange dealers and a country's monetary authorities acting through its central banks.

The foreign exchange market by its very nature is multinational in scope. The leading centres for foreign exchange dealings are London, New York and Tokyo.

Foreign currencies can be transacted on a 'spot' basis for immediate delivery (see SPOT MARKET), or can be bought and sold for future delivery (see FUTURES MARKET). Some two-thirds of London's foreign exchange dealings in 1995 were spot transactions.

The foreign exchange market may be left unregulated by governments, with EXCHANGE RATES between currencies being determined by the free interplay of the forces of demand and supply (see FLOATING EXCHANGE RATE SYSTEM) or they may be subjected to support buying and selling by countries' CENTRAL BANKS in order to fix them at particular rates (see FIXED EXCHANGE RATE SYSTEM).

foreign exchange reserves INTERNATIONAL RESERVES.

foreign investment INVESTMENT by domestic residents (individuals, companies, financial institutions and governments) in the acquisition of overseas FINANCIAL SECURITIES and physical assets. Overseas investment in financial assets, in particular by institutional investors, is undertaken primarily to diversify risk and to obtain higher returns than would be achievable on comparable domestic investments. Physical foreign direct investment (FDI) in new manufacturing plants and sales subsidiaries, or the acquisition of established businesses, provide the MULTINATIONAL COMPANY with a more flexible approach to supplying foreign markets.

Interest, profit and dividends gained on these foreign investments count as 'invisible earnings' in the BALANCE OF PAYMENTS, though some of this income may be reinvested overseas rather than repatriated.

See CAPITAL MOVEMENT, FOREIGN MARKET SERVICING STRATEGY.

foreign sector that part of the ECONOMY concerned with transactions with overseas countries. The foreign sector includes IMPORTS and EXPORTS of goods and services as well as CAPITAL MOVEMENTS in connection with investment and banking transactions. The net balance of foreign transactions influences the level and composition of domestic economic activity and the state of the country's BALANCE OF PAYMENTS. The foreign sector, together with the PERSONAL SECTOR, CORPORATE SECTOR, FINANCIAL SECTOR, PUBLIC (GOVERNMENT) SECTOR make up the national economy. See also CIRCULAR FLOW OF NATIONAL INCOME MODEL.

foreign trade multiplier the increase in a country's foreign trade resulting from an expansion of domestic demand. The increase in domestic demand has a twofold effect. As well as directly increasing the demand for domestic products it will also (a) *directly* increase the demand for IMPORTS by an amount determined by the country's MARGINAL PROPENSITY TO IMPORT, (b) *indirectly* it may also increase overseas demand for the country's EXPORTS by those countries whose own incomes have now been increased by being able to export more to the country concerned.

The latter effect, however, is usually much less than the former so that the overall effect is to 'dampen' down the value of the domestic MULTIPLIER; i.e., the increase in net imports serves to partially offset the extra income created by increased spending on domestic products.

See CIRCULAR FLOW OF NATIONAL INCOME MODEL, LOCOMOTIVE PRINCIPLE.

forex, *abbrev. for* foreign exchange. See FOREIGN CURRENCY, FOREIGN CURRENCY MARKET.

forfaiting the provision of finance by one firm (the forfaiter) to another firm (the client) by purchasing goods the client has pre-sold to a customer but for which he has not yet been paid. The forfaiter (which often is a subsidiary of a commercial bank, or a specialist firm) buys the client's goods at a discounted cash price, thus releasing ready money for the client to use to finance his WORKING CAPITAL requirements. The forfaiter then arranges to collect the payment when due from the customer to whom the goods have been sold, thus also saving the client the paperwork involved.

forward contract see FUTURES MARKET.

forward exchange market see FUTURES MARKET.

forward integration the joining together in one FIRM of two or more successive stages in a vertically-related production/distribution process, for example, flour millers acquiring their own outlets for flour, such as bakeries. The main motives for forward integration by a firm are to secure the market for the firm's output and to obtain cost savings. See VERTICAL INTEGRATION, BACKWARD INTEGRATION.

fractional banking a BANKING SYSTEM in which banks maintain a minimum RESERVE ASSET RATIO in order to ensure that they have adequate liquidity to meet customers' cash demands.
See COMMERCIAL BANK.

franchise the assignment by one FIRM to another firm (*exclusive franchise*) or others (*nonexclusive franchise*) of the right/s to supply its product. A franchise is a contractual arrangement (see CONTRACT) which is entered into for a specified period of time, with the franchisee paying a ROYALTY to the franchisor for the rights assigned. Examples of franchises include the Kentucky Fried Chicken and McDonald Burger diner and 'take-away' chains. Individual franchisees are usually required to put up a large capital stake with the franchisor providing back-up technical assistance, specialized equipment and advertising and promotion. Franchises allow the franchisor to develop his business without having to raise large amounts of capital.

freedom of entry see CONDITION OF ENTRY.

free enterprise economy see PRIVATE ENTERPRISE ECONOMY.

free goods goods such as air and water which are abundant and thus not regarded as scarce economic goods. Such goods will be consumed in large quantities because they have a zero supply price and there is thus a tendency to overuse these goods causing environmental POLLUTION.

freehold property a property which is legally owned outright by a person or firm. Contrast LEASEHOLD PROPERTY.

free market economy see PRIVATE ENTERPRISE ECONOMY.

free port see FREE TRADE ZONE.

free rider a CONSUMER who deliberately understates his preference for a COLLECTIVE PRODUCT in the hope of being able to consume the product without having to pay the full economic price for it.

For example, where a number of householders seek to resurface their common private road, an individual householder might deliberately understate the value of the resurfaced road to himself, on the grounds that the other householders will pay to have all the road resurfaced anyhow, and that he will therefore enjoy the benefit of it without having to pay towards its resurfacing. See CLUB PRINCIPLE.

free trade the INTERNATIONAL TRADE that takes place without barriers such as TARIFFS, QUOTAS and FOREIGN EXCHANGE CONTROLS, being placed on the free movement of goods and services between countries. The aim of free trade is to secure the benefits of international SPECIALIZATION. Free trade as a policy objective of the international community has been fostered both generally by the GENERAL AGREEMENT ON TARIFFS AND TRADE (GATT), and on a more limited regional basis by the establishment of various FREE TRADE AREAS, CUSTOM UNIONS and COMMON MARKETS. See GAINS FROM TRADE, EUROPEAN COMMUNITY, EUROPEAN FREE TRADE ASSOCIATION, TRADE INTEGRATION.

free trade area a form of TRADE INTEGRATION between a number of countries, in which members eliminate all trade barriers (TARIFFS, etc.) among themselves on goods and services, but each continues to operate its own particular barriers against trade with the rest of the world. The aim of a free trade area is to secure the benefits of international SPECIALIZATION, thereby improving members' real living standards. The EUROPEAN FREE TRADE AREA is one example of a free trade area. See GAINS FROM TRADE, LATIN AMERICAN FREE TRADE AREA, NORTH AMERICAN FREE TRADE AGREEMENT.

free trade zone or **freeport** a designated area within the immediate hinterland of an air or shipping port into which IMPORTS are allowed without payment of IMPORT DUTY (TARIFFS), provided the goods are to be subsequently exported (see EXPORTS) either in their original form or as intermediate products within a final good. See ENTREPÔT TRADE.

freight or **cargo** goods that are in the process of being physically transported from a factory or depot to a customer by road, rail, sea or air, involving both domestically and internationally traded goods. The movement of goods may be done by the supplier's own distribution division or by independent fleet operators and FREIGHT FORWARDERS. See C.I.F., F.O.B..

freight forwarder or **forwarding agent** a firm which specializes in the physical movement of goods in transit, arranging the collection of goods from factory, depot, etc. and delivering them direct to the customer in the case of domestic consignments and to seaports, airports, etc. in the case of exported goods. In the latter case the forwarder also handles the documentation required by the customs authorities and booking arrangements.

frictional unemployment or **transitional unemployment** UNEMPLOYMENT associated with people changing jobs. In some cases people who leave one job may start another job the next day. In other cases, people may be temporarily unemployed between jobs while they explore possible job opportunities. The latter case constitutes 'frictional' unemployment insofar as labour markets do not operate immediately in matching the supply of, and demand for, labour. Some frictional unemployment may be regarded as 'voluntary' because people choose to leave their current jobs to look for better ones; whereas other frictional unemployment is 'involuntary', where people have been dismissed from their current jobs and are forced to look for an alternative one.

Friedman, Milton (1912–) an American economist who advocates the virtues of the free market system and the need to minimize government regulations of markets in his book, *Capitalism and Freedom* (1962).

Friedman has attacked Keynesian policies of government fine tuning of aggregate demand, arguing that such policies accentuate business uncertainty and can destabilize the economy. Instead he suggests that governments should gradually expand the MONEY SUPPLY at a rate equal to the long-run increase in national output, in order to eliminate inflationary tendencies in the economy. In an economy experiencing a high inflation rate Friedman acknowledges that a sharp reduction in the rate of growth of money supply would deflate demand and cause unemployment to rise. However, he argues that such a rise in unemployment would be temporary, for once people lower their expectations about future inflation rates full employment can be restored. Friedman's monetarist ideas have had considerable influence among governments in the 1980s.

Friedman also looked at the relationship between consumption and income, rejecting the Keynesian idea that as peoples' incomes rise they will spend a smaller proportion of them and save a larger share. Instead he argued that consumption is a constant fraction of the consumer's PERMANENT INCOME, and that as long-term income rises the proportion of it spent remains the same. See MONETARISM.

friendly society an association of individuals (members) who made regular voluntary contributions into a fund upon which they could draw in times of need or to provide themselves with houses. These friendly societies were the forerunner of the modern INSURANCE COMPANIES and BUILDING SOCIETIES. See REGISTRAR OF FRIENDLY SOCIETIES, BUILDING SOCIETIES ACT, 1986.

fringe benefits any additional benefits offered to employees such as the use of a company car, free meals or luncheon vouchers, interest-free or low-interest loans, private health care subscriptions, subsidized holidays and share purchase schemes. In the case of senior managers such benefits or perquisites (perks) can be quite substantial in relation to wages and salaries. Companies offer fringe benefits to attract employees and because such benefits provide a low tax or no-tax means of rewarding employees compared with normally-taxed salaries.

front door the formal mechanism whereby the Bank of England makes loans to the DISCOUNT HOUSES when the discount houses experience temporary liquidity shortages. In this capacity as LENDER OF LAST RESORT the Bank of England charges a penal interest rate on the loans which it makes (called BILL DISCOUNTING rate). Compared with BACK DOOR operations, where the Bank of England makes funds available to discount houses at prevailing market interest rates, a front-door operation seeks deliberately to increase interest rates across the whole banking sector. See MONETARY POLICY.

full capacity see CAPACITY.

full-cost pricing a pricing method which sets the PRICE of a product by adding a percentage profit mark-up to AVERAGE COST or unit total cost, where unit total cost is composed of average or unit variable cost and average or unit fixed cost. See Fig. 72. A key element in full-cost pricing is the estimate of sales volume which is necessary to calculate average fixed cost and required unit contribution, though inevitably the price charged will *itself* affect sales volume. The full-cost pricing method is also called AVERAGE-COST PRICING. Though this pricing method is based upon costs, in practice managers take into account demand and competition by varying the target profit mark-up over time and between products.

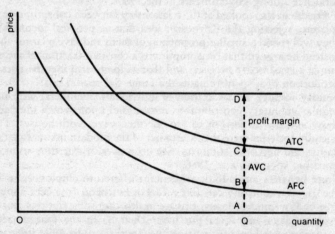

Fig. 72. **Full-cost pricing**. The price (OP) is made up of three elements: a contribution to cover part of the firm's overhead costs (average FIXED COST) – AB; the actual unit cost (average VARIABLE COST) of producing a planned output of OQ units – BC; a PROFIT MARGIN expressed as a fixed percentage of total unit costs (average variable cost plus average fixed cost) – CD.

Compare MARGINAL-COST PRICING. See COST-PLUS PRICING.

full employment the full utilization of all available labour (and capital) resources so that the economy is able to produce at the limits of its POTENTIAL GROSS NATIONAL PRODUCT. Full employment is one of the main objectives of MACROECONOMIC POLICY.

In practice, of course, 100% employment cannot be achieved. Inevitably there will always be some unemployment present due to labour turnover and people spending time in searching for and selecting new jobs; and because of structural changes in the economy – job losses in declining trades which require people to transfer to new jobs created in expanding sectors. Accordingly, a more realistic interpretation of full employment suggests itself: full employment is achieved when the number of registered unemployed (see UNEMPLOYMENT RATE) is equal to the number of job vacancies (see VACANCY RATE). However, even these measures do not give an accurate estimate because many groups like housewives and older workers may fail to register as unemployed when job prospects are bleak even though they wish to work (DISGUISED UNEMPLOYMENT).

For macroeconomic purposes, however, most governments tend to specify their full employment objectives in terms of some 'targeted' level of unemployment (for example, 5% of the total labour force), though the exact target level is rarely publicly disclosed.

See UNEMPLOYMENT, FIXED TARGETS (APPROACH TO MACROECONOMIC POLICY), SUPPLY-SIDE ECONOMICS.

full employment equilibrium see EQUILIBRIUM LEVEL OF NATIONAL INCOME, POTENTIAL GROSS NATIONAL PRODUCT.

full line forcing a type of RESTRICTIVE TRADE PRACTICE whereby a supplier requires a retailer to take all of the items making up a particular product line, thereby restricting the freedom of the retailer to select the product mix, including items from competing suppliers, which best suits his own requirements. See COMPETITION POLICY, OFFICE OF FAIR TRADING.

functional distribution of income the distribution of NATIONAL INCOME classified according to type of FACTOR INPUT: LABOUR, CAPITAL, etc. Here income is seen as a payment for the various factor inputs in contributing to the output of the economy. WAGES constitute the largest single element in factor payments, as Fig. 73 (overleaf) shows. See PERSONAL DISTRIBUTION OF INCOME.

fundamental disequilibrium a situation under a FIXED-EXCHANGE-RATE SYSTEM where a country is in a position of *persistent* (long-run) BALANCE OF PAYMENTS deficit or surplus at a particular (fixed) exchange rate against other countries. The only practical course of action, given the inadequacy of internal measures such as DEFLATION and REFLATION to remedy the situation, is a DEVALUATION to a lower exchange rate value to eliminate a deficit, and a REVALUATION to a

	Percentage
Wages	74
Profits	16
Rent	10

Fig. 73. **Functional distribution of income**. The functional distribution of national income for the UK, 1995. Source: *UK National Accounts* (Blue Book), CSO 1996.

higher exchange rate value to eliminate a surplus. See BALANCE-OF-PAYMENTS EQUILIBRIUM, INTERNAL-EXTERNAL BALANCE MODEL.

funding the process by which a government or company converts its short-term, fixed-interest DEBTS into long-term, fixed-interest debts. This involves persuading holders of short-term FIXED-INTEREST FINANCIAL SECURITIES to relinquish these in return for an equivalent amount of long-term, fixed-interest financial securities and this usually can only be done by offering a more attractive rate of interest on the latter.

Funding is undertaken by the monetary authorities as a means of reducing the liquidity of the banking system, and by companies as a means of improving their short-term liquidity. See PUBLIC SECTOR BORROWING REQUIREMENT, MATURITY STRUCTURE.

futures market or **forward exchange market** a market which provides for the buying and selling of COMMODITIES (rubber, tin, etc.) and FOREIGN CURRENCIES for delivery at some future point in time, as opposed to a SPOT MARKET which provides for immediate delivery. Forward positions are taken by traders in a particular financial asset or commodity whose price can fluctuate greatly over time, in order to minimize the risk and uncertainty surrounding their business dealings in the immediate future (i.e. 'hedge' against adverse price movements), and by dealers and speculators (see SPECULATION) hoping to earn windfall profits from correctly anticipating price movements.

Traders seek to minimize uncertainty about future prices by buying or selling *futures*, particularly OPTIONS, i.e. contracts that promise to buy or sell a commodity or financial asset at a price agreed upon now for delivery at some later point in time, usually within a three-month period. For example, a producer of chocolate could contract to buy a given amount of cocoa at today's price plus a percentage risk premium for delivery in two months' time. Even if the price of cocoa were to go up markedly, the manufacturer knows that he is still able to buy at the (lower) contract price, and is thus able to plan his raw material outlays accordingly. Similarly, the growers of cocoa can contract to sell the commodity at an agreed price now for delivery in the near future in order to cover themselves against adverse price changes. Unlike the spot market, where commodities are traded in the physical sense, in the futures market it is only these contracts which are bought and sold.

In between the original buyers and producers, using futures as a hedge to minimize risk, stand the various dealers and speculators who buy or sell the paper contracts to such items according to their view of probable price movements in the hope of securing windfall profits.

Forward prices reflect anticipated future demand and supply conditions for a commodity, financial security or foreign currency being traded.

Specifically, the forward prices will be based partially on current spot prices but will also take into account interest rate and inflation rate trends. The difference between the current spot price of a commodity and the forward price constitutes the 'forward margin'. The forward margin can be at either a discount or a premium to the spot price. Forward margins for a particular commodity such as cocoa in different commodity markets in London, Chicago, etc. tend to be similar as a result of the buying and selling of futures contracts between these markets (ARBITRAGE).

The LONDON INTERNATIONAL FINANCIAL FUTURES MARKET (LIFFE) constitutes the largest European Community centre for forward dealings in securities and commodities. The forward markets in the UK are regulated by The Securities Association in accordance with various standards of good practice laid down under the FINANCIAL SERVICES ACT, 1986.

See COMMODITY MARKET, FOREIGN EXCHANGE MARKET, STOCK EXCHANGE, COVERED INTEREST ARBITRAGE, EXCHANGE RATE EXPOSURE.

G

gains from trade the extra production and consumption benefits that countries can achieve through INTERNATIONAL TRADE. Countries trade with one another basically for the same reasons that individuals, firms and regions engaged in the exchange of goods and services – to obtain the benefits of SPECIALIZATION. By exchanging some of its own products for those of other nations, a country can enjoy a much wider range of commodities, and obtain them more cheaply than would otherwise be the case. International division of labour, with each country specializing in the production of only some of the commodities that it is capable of producing, enables total world output to be increased and raises countries' real standards of living.

A country's choice of which commodities to specialize in will be determined in large measure by the advantages it possesses over others in the production of these things. Such advantages can arise because the country can produce particular commodities more efficiently, at lower cost, than can others. The static, or 'pure' theory of international trade emphasizes that opportunities for mutually beneficial trade occur as the result of differences in comparative costs or COMPARATIVE ADVANTAGE. Countries will gain from trade if each country EXPORTS those commodities in which its costs of production are comparatively lower, and IMPORTS commodities in which its costs are comparatively higher.

This proposition is demonstrated in Fig. 74a on page 220 for a simple two country (A and B) and two product (X and Y) world economy. The same given resource input in both countries enables them to produce either the quantity of X or the quantity of Y. In the absence of trade between the two, X and Y exchange in country A is in the ratio 1X/1Y, and, in country B in the ratio 1X/3Y. These exchange ratios indicate the marginal OPPORTUNITY COST of one commodity in terms of the other. Thus, in country A the opportunity cost of producing one more unit of X is 1Y.

It can be seen that country B is absolutely more efficient than country A in the production of Y and just as efficient in the production of X. However, it is *comparative advantage*, not ABSOLUTE ADVANTAGE, which determines whether trade is advantageous or not. Country B's comparative advantage is greatest in the production of commodity Y of which it can produce three times as much as country A. Alternatively, we can say that country B's relative efficiency is greatest in producing commodity Y because the resource or opportunity cost of producing an additional unit of Y is one-third of one unit of X in country B, but 1X in country A. Country A, by concentrating on the commodity it can produce with least relative inefficiency, has a comparative advantage in the production of X; i.e., the resource or opportunity cost of producing an additional unit of X in country A is only 1Y, while in country B it is 3Y. Thus, in terms of real factor costs commodity X can be produced more cheaply in country A, and commodity Y can be produced more cheaply in country B.

This combination of comparative advantages opens up the possibility of mutually beneficial trade. Domestically, in country A, 1X can be exchanged for 1Y, but abroad it can be exchanged for anything up to 3Y. Trade will be advantageous to it if it can obtain more than 1Y for 1X. Domestically, in country B, 1Y can be exchanged for one-third of 1X, but abroad it can be exchanged for anything up to 1X. It will be to B's advantage if it can obtain through trade more than one-third of X for 1Y.

The limits to mutually beneficial trade are set by the opportunity cost ratios. Within these limits, specialization and trade on the basis of comparative advantage will enable both countries to attain higher consumption levels. This possibility is indicated in Fig. 74b assuming the exchange ratio to be 1X = 2Y. Using its entire resources, country B can produce 600Y, of which it consumes, say, 400 and exports 200. Country A can produce 200X, of which it consumes 100 and exports 100. With trade, the 200Y can be exchanged for 100X, enabling country B to consume 400Y and 100X, and country A to consume 200Y and 100X. Without trade, country B can transform (at an internal exchange ratio of 1X/3Y) 200Y into only 662/3X, while country A can transform (at an internal exchange ratio of 1X/1Y) 100X into only 100Y. Thus both countries gain by specialization and trade. How the gain is shared between countries A and B depends essentially upon the strength of demand in the two countries for the goods they import. If country A's demand for commodity Y increases, the trading ratio of 1X to 2Y would be likely to move against country A. Thus it might require 2½Y exports to obtain 1X imports, pushing country B nearer to the limit to mutually beneficial trade.

Obviously, in a more complex multicountry, multiproduct 'real' world situation it is less easy to be categorical about who gains from international trade and by how much. Some countries may possess a comparative advantage in a large number of products, others may possess few such advantages; countries differ in the quantity and quality of their factor endowments, and are at different stages of ECONOMIC DEVELOPMENT. DEVELOPING COUNTRIES, in particular, may find themselves at a disadvantage in international trade, especially those that are over-reliant on a narrow range of volatile commodity exports.

See THEORY OF INTERNATIONAL TRADE, TRADE INTEGRATION, TRADE CREATION.

Country	Commodity X	Y	Opportunity cost ratios X : Y
A	200	200	1 : 1
B	200	600	1 : 3

(a)

	Country B	Country A
Production	600Y	200X
Consumption with trade	400Y	200Y
	100X	100X
Consumption without trade	400Y	100Y
	66⅔X	100X

(b)

Fig. 74. **Gains from trade.** (a) The physical output of commodity X and commodity Y from a given factor input. (b) Production and consumption possibilities with and without trade (internal exchange rates are 1X/1Y in A, 1X/3Y in B, and the international exchange 1X/2Y).

Galbraith, John Kenneth (1908–   ) Canadian economist whose radical views about the workings of the market economy have been expressed in a series of books such as *The Affluent Society* (1958) and *The New Industrial State* (1967). Galbraith suggests that advanced industrial economies comprise a competitive sector of small owner-managed businesses and a monopoly sector of large industrial companies managed by salaried technocrats and he concentrates on the workings of the latter.

Galbraith argues that large companies plan their activities so as to minimize market uncertainty and that they seek through advertising to create demand for new products before manufacturing them: a REVISED SEQUENCE, compared with the conventional economic view that consumers express innate wants then see resources allocated to satisfying these wants. Nevertheless, Galbraith acknowledges that such large firms help to foster technical innovation and scale-economies which have yielded large gains in incomes. Furthermore he sees the growth of large companies leading to the growth of trade unions as a COUNTERVAILING POWER to secure a share of efficiency gains for workers. Consequently, Galbraith argues that large companies should not be broken up but controlled by government to prevent abuse of their monopoly power, with attempts to increase the countervailing power of consumers and small businesses.

Galbraith also attacked the American market economy for devoting too few resources to the public sector whilst allowing private sector activities to dominate, creating a situation of private affluence and public squalor.

game theory a technique that uses logical deduction to explore the consequences of various strategies which might be adopted by competing game players. Game theory can be used in economics to represent the problems involved in formulating marketing strategy by small numbers of interdependent competitors.

An oligopolist (see OLIGOPOLY) needs to assess competitors' reactions to his own marketing policies to ensure that the 'payoff' from any particular marketing strategy may be estimated. For example, consider a struggle for market share between two firms (X and Y) where total market-size is fixed, so that every percentage increase in the market share of one firm is necessarily lost to the other (that is, a ZERO-SUM GAME situation). Suppose company X has two strategy choices available, a price reduction (P) or a new advertising campaign (A), and that company Y has the same two strategies available. Any pair of strategies open to the two firms would result in a particular division of the market between them: if firm X were to adopt strategy P, and firm Y were to adopt its strategy P, then firm X would gain 50% of the market leaving 50% for firm Y. This 50% market share is firm X's payoff and all such market share information can be summarized in the form of a *payoff matrix* as in Fig. 75.

Each firm must decide on its own best strategy, using the information in the table. If firm X adopts a cautious approach then it would assume that in response to its strategy P, firm Y would counter with strategy A, reducing firm X's payoff from its strategy P to its minimum value 40% (underlined). Similarly the fatalistic view of firm X's strategy A is that firm Y will counter with strategy P, reducing firm X's payoff from strategy A to its minimum value 55% (underlined). Following this pessimistic view firm X can make the best of the situation by aiming at the highest of these (underlined) minimum payoffs, in this case 55% yielded by strategy A (a *maximum strategy*).

Firm Y could employ a similar strategy, though for Y to assume the worst means that firm X receives a large market share so that firm Y, residually, receives very little. Thus, if firm Y employs its strategy P, its worst possible payoff is 45% of the market (55% going to firm X) and this is marked by circling 55% on the matrix. If firm Y were to employ its strategy A, its worst possible payoff would be 40% of the market (60% going to firm X) and this 60% is similarly marked by a circle. The best of these pessimistic payoffs for firm Y is the smallest of these circled figures, in this case 55% of the market going to firm X (a *minimax strategy*).

The outcome of this situation is that firm X will choose its strategy A and firm Y its strategy P and neither would be inclined to alter its choice of strategy.

Firm Y's strategy

		P	A
Firm X's strategy	P	50	40
	A	⑤⑤	⑥⓪

Fig. 75. **Game theory**. The payoff matrix between firm X and firm Y.

GATT see GENERAL AGREEMENT ON TARIFFS AND TRADE.
GDP see GROSS DOMESTIC PRODUCT.
gearing see CAPITAL GEARING.
General Agreement on Tariffs and Trade (GATT) an international organization established in 1947 to promote the expansion of INTERNATIONAL TRADE through the removal of TARIFFS and other restrictions on cross-frontier trade. GATT operates in two principal ways:

(a) by arranging for countries to receive foreign tariff reductions in return for tariff cuts of their own (reciprocity);

(b) by requiring that a country should apply its lowest tariff for any particular product to all of its suppliers (the 'most favoured nation' rule).

GATT has supervised 11 major multilateral rounds of tariff negotiations, including the 'Kennedy Round' of 1962–67 which secured an average cut in tariff rates of around 35% and the 'Tokyo Round' of 1973–79 which provided further significant reductions in tariffs. In the main, tariff cuts have applied only to manufactured goods. The present 'Uruguay Round' (1988–) is also concerned with manufactures but emphasis has been placed on the possibility of major tariff reductions in agricultural produce and also the liberalization of international trade in services.

The GATT initiatives, together with the work of the INTERNATIONAL MONETARY FUND, the formation of FREE TRADE BLOCS (in particular, the EUROPEAN COMMUNITY and the EUROPEAN FREE TRADE ASSOCIATION) and high growth rates in industrial countries, led to a record expansion of world trade up to the 1970s. The OPEC oil price increase of 1973 and the subsequent onset of recessionary conditions in the world economy, however, has reduced the impact of GATT and has led to a renaissance of PROTECTIONISM based on national self-interest. The 'new protectionism', as it is referred to, is based not on tariffs but on various measures which are much less transparent and diffuse and therefore more difficult to control on a uniform basis, including EXPORT RESTRAINT AGREEMENTS, LOCAL CONTENT RULES, import licensing restrictions, subsidies given to domestic industries, etc. In 1995 GATT was replaced by the World Trade Organization.

See DUMPING.

general equilibrium analysis the analysis of the interrelationships that exist between subsectors of an ECONOMY. General equilibrium analysis proceeds on the basis that events in one sector can have such a significant impact on other sectors that feed-back effects, in turn, are likely to affect the functioning of the first. See Fig. 76.

Thus, in general equilibrium analysis, an attempt is made to determine the nature and strength of intersectoral linkages using, for example, INPUT–OUTPUT analysis. See PARTIAL EQUILIBRIUM ANALYSIS.

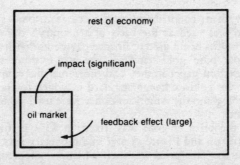

Fig. 76. **General equilibrium analysis**. An increase in the price of oil is likely to increase the cost structures of many other industrial sectors, and hence serve to raise the general price level and related wage rates. This increase in prices and wages, in turn, increases input costs to the oil industry.

Giffen good a GOOD for which quantity demanded increases as its PRICE increases, rather than falls, as predicted by the general theory of DEMAND. It only applies in the highly exceptional case of a good (see INFERIOR PRODUCT) which accounts for such a high proportion of households' budgets that an increase in price produces a large negative INCOME EFFECT which completely overcomes the normal SUBSTITUTION EFFECT. See PRICE EFFECT, UPWARD–SLOPING DEMAND CURVE.

gilt-edged security or **government bond** a financial security (see BOND) issued by the government as a means of borrowing money. The term 'gilt-edged' denotes the fact that such securities are a very safe ASSET for people to hold in so far as governments are usually able to honour their debts. In addition, the monetary authorities use gilt-edged securities as a means of regulating the MONEY SUPPLY. See OPEN MARKET OPERATION.

Gini coefficient see CONCENTRATION MEASURES.

GNP see GROSS NATIONAL PRODUCT.

GNP deflator a PRICE INDEX that is used as a means of adjusting money GROSS NATIONAL PRODUCT values to obtain *real* GNP values (see REAL VALUES). Real GNP is important because this represents output of physical goods and services not their money values. An economy may appear to produce more goods and services (ECONOMIC GROWTH) because money GNP has increased, but this may simply reflect price increases (INFLATION) without any increase in physical output. The GNP deflator is thus designed to remove the influence of price changes and record only real changes.

gold a monetary ASSET that is held by countries as part of their INTERNATIONAL RESERVES and used to finance BALANCE OF PAYMENTS deficits.

Formerly, many countries operated a GOLD STANDARD system under which gold was used as the basis of a country's domestic MONEY SUPPLY, as well as being used to finance payments deficits. Gradually, however, the 'pure' gold standard gave way to domestic monetary systems based on paper money and other metallic coins and, internationally, the gold-exchange standard in which foreign currencies such as sterling and the American dollar were used alongside gold as reserve assets.

In 1935 the price of gold was 'fixed' at $35 per fine ounce by America, Britain and France as part of a monetary pact between the three countries. This price was then 'officially' adopted by member countries of the INTERNATIONAL MONETARY FUND on its formation in 1947; gold was used as the numeraire of the Fund's fixed exchange rate system in setting par values for members' currencies, and members were required to pay one quarter of their 'quota' subscriptions to the Fund in gold. Gold continued to serve as the linchpin of the IMF system, and its 'official' price remained pegged at $35 per ounce, down to 1971, when the Fund's fixed exchange-rate system gave way to floating exchange rates. Countries had, however, found it increasingly difficult to hold the price of gold at the $35 per ounce level as world demand for gold as an industrial metal and for ornamental purposes continued to expand. In 1961 a 'gold pool' was set up to regulate dealings in the metal, but in 1968 Fund members bowed to the inevitable and a 'two-tier' price structure was established: gold continued to be priced at $35 per ounce for 'official' transactions between countries' central banks and the Fund, while the 'free' market price of gold was left to be determined by market forces.

In 1972, gold was dropped as the numeraire of the Fund and replaced by the SPECIAL DRAWING RIGHT unit; the Fund's existing gold holdings were sold off and members were required to subscribe their quotas in a nongold form.

Outside the Fund, however, gold has continued to hold on to its status as the single most important component of international reserves. The attractiveness of gold as a reserve asset is underpinned by the fact that unlike national paper currencies (which are intrinsically worthless) it has a value in exchange as a commodity related to its use as an industrial base metal and for ornamental purposes. Gold holdings, however, suffer from the disadvantage that compared with other assets such as STOCKS and SHARES they yield no interest return.

golden handshake a generous severance payment made to a director or worker of a company who is dismissed prior to the expiry of his service contract.

golden hello a large lump-sum payment made to a new director or worker of a company to attract him to join that company.

golden parachute see TAKEOVER BID.

gold-exchange standard a modified version of the 'pure' GOLD STANDARD in which CURRENCIES such as the US DOLLAR are used by countries in addition to GOLD to settle BALANCE OF PAYMENTS deficits. See INTERNATIONAL RESERVES.

gold standard an INTERNATIONAL MONETARY SYSTEM in which GOLD forms the basis of countries' domestic MONEY SUPPLY and is used to finance INTERNATIONAL TRADE and BALANCE OF PAYMENTS deficits.

Under the gold standard EXCHANGE RATES were rigidly fixed in terms of gold. (The gold standard was widely adopted in the 19th century and operated down to the early 1930s). In theory, the gold standard provided an 'automatic' ADJUSTMENT MECHANISM for eliminating payments imbalances between countries: deficits were financed by outward gold transfers which reduced the domestic MONEY SUPPLY. This in turn deflated (see DEFLATION) the domestic price level, making IMPORTS relatively more expensive and EXPORTS relatively cheaper, thereby reducing the volume of imports and increasing the volume of exports. Surpluses were financed by inward gold transfers which increased the domestic money supply. This in turn inflated (see INFLATION) the domestic price level making imports relatively cheaper and exports relatively more expensive, resulting in a fall in the volume of exports and an increase in the volume of imports. In this way both deficits and surpluses were removed and BALANCE-OF PAYMENTS EQUILIBRIUM restored. In practice, however, countries found that a combination of rigidly fixed exchange rates and the complete subordination of domestic economic policy to the external situation was too onerous and opted for more flexible arrangements.

See FIXED EXCHANGE RATE SYSTEM, INTERNATIONAL MONETARY FUND.

Goodhart's law the proposition that attempts by a CENTRAL BANK to regulate the level of lending by commercial banks through the imposition of controls over certain types of lending can be circumvented by the banks which find alternative methods of lending which are not subject to regulation.

See MONETARY POLICY, FINANCIAL INNOVATION.

goodness of fit see REGRESSION ANALYSIS.

goods or **commodities** any tangible economic products (cars, soap powders, tools, machines, etc.) that contribute directly (see FINAL PRODUCTS) or indirectly (see INTERMEDIATE PRODUCTS) to the satisfaction of human wants. CONSUMER GOODS and PRODUCERS' GOODS are an important component of GROSS NATIONAL PRODUCT.

goodwill the difference at a particular point in time between the market valuation of a FIRM and the sum of its (net) ASSETS recorded in a BALANCE SHEET. If another firm wishes to acquire this firm, goodwill represents the premium which the buyer must be prepared to pay for the firm, over and above its asset value, because of the firm's trade contacts, reputation, BRAND NAMES, management expertise and general 'know-how'. Where a firm has a poor trading record its market value as a going concern to a potential buyer may be less than the BALANCE SHEET value of its assets, in which case goodwill is negative.

government the primary decision-making body in a nation state which is responsible for national defence, maintaining law and order, etc. Government's economic rôle in the State depends upon the socio-political system the country has adopted, the two extremes being a CENTRALLY PLANNED ECONOMY and a PRIVATE ENTERPRISE ECONOMY. In the former case, governments play an all-embracing rôle, often owning most economic resources and determining what products to produce. In the latter case, where resources are held privately and markets are the main mechanism for allocating resources, governments play a more restricted rôle, merely influencing the general level of economic activity through DEMAND MANAGEMENT policies and redistribution of income and wealth.

See MIXED ECONOMY, GOVERNMENT (PUBLIC) EXPENDITURE.

government bond see GILT-EDGED SECURITY, BOND.

government broker the firm formerly appointed by the government to handle issues of government securities. In 1986 the Bank of England itself undertook the sale of such securities through a network of 'approved' dealing firms.

See CAPITAL MARKET, STOCK EXCHANGE.

government debt see NATIONAL DEBT.

government (public) expenditure the current spending and INVESTMENT by central government and local authorities on the provision of SOCIAL GOODS and services (health, education, defence, roads, etc.), marketed goods and services (coal, postal services, etc.) and TRANSFER

PAYMENTS (unemployment benefit, state pensions, etc.). In the CIRCULAR FLOW OF INCOME MODEL, transfer payments are excluded from government spending because these are not made in return for productive services (that is, add to total output) but merely transfer taxation receipts from one household to another.

Government expenditure is financed by TAXATION and by borrowing (see PUBLIC SECTOR BORROWING REQUIREMENT).

Government expenditure is an important component of AGGREGATE DEMAND in the circular flow of income/expenditure, and is used as an instrument of FISCAL POLICY in regulating the level of spending in the economy. However, short-term changes in government expenditure may be difficult to achieve because of administrative and political difficulties, especially where cuts in expenditure are being made with a view to contracting aggregate demand. For example, short-term cuts can be difficult to achieve in health, education, etc. expenditures, given the labour-intensive nature of these activities, without heavy redundancies and disruption of public services; whilst cuts in transfer payments to poorer members of the community are politically unpopular. Furthermore, where the brunt of changes fall upon public investment expenditures this can severely disrupt long-term investment projects, while cuts serve to deplete the social infrastructure. In addition, where government expenditure includes spending on goods and services bought in from businesses, changes can have dramatic effects on the prosperity of the private sector.

See SOCIAL PRODUCTS, BUDGET (GOVERNMENT), COLLECTIVE PRODUCTS, CROWDING-OUT EFFECT.

government sector see PUBLIC SECTOR.

graph a means of portraying data in pictorial form that shows the relationship between an INDEPENDENT VARIABLE and a DEPENDENT VARIABLE by labelling and scaling the two axes of the graph to represent the two variables, plotting joint values of the two in the space between the axes, and joining these values with a line. Frequently graphs show time as the independent variable, depicting by means of a line how the dependent variable has changed over time.

'green' consumers buyers who are influenced by environmental considerations in purchasing products. For example, a typical green consumer of petrol would favour the purchase of a lead-free brand. Pressures from green consumer groups like Friends of the Earth or Greenpeace have on occasions forced companies to adopt production and waste disposal methods which reduce pollution levels.

See CONSUMERISM.

greenfield investment the establishment of a new manufacturing plant, workshop, office, etc. by a firm. Greenfield investment is undertaken by a 'start-up' (i.e. new) business and by existing firms as a means of expanding their activities (see ORGANIC GROWTH). Estab-

227

lishing a new plant may be preferred to inheriting existing plants through takeovers and mergers (see EXTERNAL GROWTH) because it gives the firm greater flexibility in choosing an appropriate location. It enables it to build a scale of plant most appropriate to its operations and to instal modern manufacturing processes, techniques and work practices, thus avoiding, for example, various problems associated with the rationalization and reorganization of existing plants and the removal of restrictive labour practices.

See MARKET ENTRY, BARRIERS TO ENTRY.

greenmail see TAKEOVER BID.

green money see MONETARY COMPENSATION AMOUNTS.

'green' product a product which is designed and manufactured in such a manner as to minimize the adverse environmental impact involved in its production, distribution and consumption. This could involve the use of recyclable materials, bio-degradable elements and components such as catalytic converters in motor-cars which reduce sulphur emissions.

See RECYCLING, POLLUTION.

Gresham's law the economic hypothesis that 'bad' MONEY forces 'good' money out of circulation. The principle applies only to economies whose domestic money system is based upon metal coinage which embodies a proportion of intrinsically valuable metals such as silver and gold. Where governments issue new coins embodying a lower proportion of valuable metals, people are tempted to hoard the older coins for the commodity value of their metal content so that the 'good' money ceases to circulate as currency.

grey market an 'unofficial' market in newly issued shares prior to their being formally listed and traded on the STOCK EXCHANGE.

See SHARE ISSUE.

gross domestic-fixed-capital formation the total spending on FIXED INVESTMENT (plant, equipment, etc.) in an economy over a one-year period. Gross domestic-fixed-capital formation is one component of GROSS NATIONAL PRODUCT. However, because of CAPITAL CONSUMPTION (fixed capital lost due to wear and tear) *net domestic-fixed-capital formation* may be considerably less than gross investment. In this case the net addition to the CAPITAL STOCK would be much smaller than the total figure unadjusted for capital DEPRECIATION. See NET NATIONAL PRODUCT.

gross domestic product (GDP) the total money value of all final GOODS and SERVICES produced in an economy over a one-year period. Gross domestic product can be measured in three ways:

(a) the sum of the value added by each industry in producing the year's output (the output method).

(b) the sum of factor incomes received from producing the year's output (the income method).

(c) the sum of expenditures on the year's domestic output of goods and services (the expenditure method).

See NATIONAL INCOME ACCOUNTS.

gross national product (GNP) the total money value of all final goods and services produced in an economy over a one-year period (GROSS DOMESTIC PRODUCT) plus net property income from abroad (interest, rent, dividends and profits). See NATIONAL INCOME ACCOUNTS.

GNP is an important measure of a country's *general* economic prosperity, while GNP per head (see INCOME PER HEAD) provides a measure of the *average* monetary STANDARD OF LIVING of the populace. By converting GNP data in several countries into a common currency (such as the US dollar) it is possible to make international comparisons of countries' general economic well-being, as Fig. 77 shows.

See ACTUAL GROSS NATIONAL PRODUCT, ECONOMIC GROWTH, GNP (DEFLATOR).

GNP 1994

(in US $ millions)

Developed countries	
UK	1,063,720
Germany	2,071,900
Japan	4,320,750
USA	6,754,680

Developing countries	
Egypt	41,040
Mozambique	1,390
Rwanda	620
Ethiopia	5,500

Fig. 77. **Gross national product for selected countries.** Source: *World Development Report*, World Bank, 1996.

gross profit the difference between SALES REVENUE and the COST OF GOODS SOLD. Gross profit less the operating expenses of the business equals NET PROFIT.

group bonus scheme see BONUS SCHEME.

Group of 7 (G7) an informal group of seven major industrial countries who meet regularly to discuss matters of mutual interest, in particular the promotion of more stable world economic conditions in the face of potentially disruptive floating exchange rates (see FLOATING EXCHANGE RATE SYSTEM) and growing trade PROTECTIONISM. The group consists of the finance ministers and central bank governors of the US, Japan, Germany, France, the UK, Italy and Canada.

growth see ECONOMIC GROWTH.

H

hard currency a FOREIGN CURRENCY that is in strong demand, but in short supply on the FOREIGN EXCHANGE MARKET. Hard-currency status is usually associated with an economically-strong country which is running a large surplus on its balance of payments; demand for the currency is high to finance purchases of its exports, but the supply of the currency is relatively limited because the amount of it being made available through the purchase of imports is much lower. However, under a FLOATING-EXCHANGE-RATE SYSTEM, the demand for, and supply of, the currency should be, in theory, brought into balance by an APPRECIATION of its EXCHANGE RATE value. Compare SOFT CURRENCY.

Harrod economic-growth model a theoretical construct that examines the growth path of the economy. Specifically, the model is concerned with the rate at which NATIONAL INCOME (Y) must grow in order to satisfy the Keynesian EQUILIBRIUM NATIONAL INCOME condition:

$$\text{saving } (S_t) = \text{investment } (I_t) \qquad (1)$$

where t denotes a time period.

$$S_t = s Y_t \qquad (2)$$

In the model, S_t depends on national income:
i.e., saving in each period depends on the income of the same period; s represents the AVERAGE PROPENSITY TO SAVE and MARGINAL PROPENSITY TO SAVE.

I_t depends on the *rate of change of income* from one period to the next, notationally Y_t (income in current time period), Y_{t-1} (income in previous time period), i.e:

$$I_t = \propto (Y_t - Y_{t-1}) \qquad (3)$$

i.e., investment is INDUCED INVESTMENT with the symbol '$\propto$' representing the ACCELERATOR.

Given this assumed saving and investment behaviour, the equilibrium condition represented in equation (1) can be shown to require that:

$$\frac{\varDelta Y_t}{Y_t} = \frac{s}{\propto} \qquad (4)$$

The left-hand expression is the percentage change in income; the right-hand side is the ratio of the marginal propensity to save to the accelerator. Since this is deducted from the condition for maintaining equilibrium in each time period, Harrod called the rate of change in income the 'warranted' rate of growth.

If the 'actual' rate of growth exceeds (or is lower than) the warranted rate, income will be raised more (or lowered more) than is appropriate for maintaining equilibrium, causing a cumulative deviation from the equilibrium path.

Equation (4) determines the warranted rate of growth. The actual rate of growth is determined in the model, by the rate of growth of the LABOUR FORCE and the rate of growth of labour PRODUCTIVITY. Suppose that the labour force is growing at the rate of 1% per year and labour productivity at the rate of 2% per year; the actual (or the 'natural' rate of growth, as Harrod called it) attainable rate of growth of national income and output is thus 3% per year.

If the natural rate of growth exceeds the warranted rate of growth then the economy will experience a cumulative deviation from the warranted rate, income growing at an excessive rate and causing secular expansion. By contrast, if the natural rate falls below that of the warranted rate, then there will be SECULAR STAGNATION.

See DOMAR ECONOMIC GROWTH MODEL, SOLOW ECONOMIC GROWTH MODEL.

Heckscher-Ohlin factor proportions theory an explanation of COMPARATIVE ADVANTAGE in INTERNATIONAL TRADE which is based on differences in factor endowments between countries.

Consider a situation in which two countries (A and B) produce two goods (X and Y). Country A, let us assume, possesses an abundance of labour but a scarcity of capital; by contrast, country B possesses an abundance of capital but a shortage of labour. Thus, the cost of labour is low relative to capital in country A, whereas the cost of capital is low relative to labour in country B. The production of good X, let us assume, is capital-intensive; while the production of good Y is labour-intensive.

Given these differences in labour and capital intensities the following hypothesis about the structure of trade suggests itself: Country A has a comparative advantage in the production of good Y because this uses much of its relatively cheap factor (labour). It will specialize in the production of good Y, exporting Y in exchange for imports of X, the good in which it has a comparative disadvantage.

Country B has a comparative advantage in the production of good X because this uses much of its relatively cheap factor (capital). It will specialize in the production of good X, exporting X in exchange for imports of Y, the good in which it has a comparative disadvantage.

The Heckscher-Ohlin theory presents a *static* supply-orientated interpretation of international trade which assumes that production functions are the same in all countries. The theory takes no account of the influence of dynamic technological change on comparative advantage; nor does it consider the effect of DEMAND and PRODUCT DIFFERENTIATION on the pattern of international trade flows.

See GAINS FROM TRADE, THEORY OF INTERNATIONAL TRADE.

hedging the act of reducing uncertainty about future (unknown) price movements in a COMMODITY (rubber, tea, etc.), FINANCIAL SECURITY (share, stock, etc.) or FOREIGN CURRENCY. This can be done by undertaking forward sales or purchases of the commodity, security or currency in the FUTURES MARKET, or by taking out an OPTION which limits the option-holder's exposure to price fluctuations.

See EXCHANGE RATE EXPOSURE.

Herfindahl index a measure of the degree of SELLER CONCENTRATION in a MARKET that takes into account the total number of firms in the market and their *relative* size distribution (share of total market output). See Fig. 78.

See CONCENTRATION MEASURES.

	Leading firm's share of market output (%)	5-firm concentration ratio (%)	Market share % per firm of remaining firms	Herfindahl index (H)
Firms	1 2 3 4 5			
Market A	12 12 12 12 12	60	5 8	0.104
Market B	40 5 5 5 5	60	8 5	0.190

Fig. 78. **Herfindahl index**. The Herfindahl index (H) is the sum of the squared firm sizes, all measured as a proportion of total market size. In the Fig., for market A, $H = (0.12)^2 \times 5 + (0.08)^2 \times 5 = 0.104$. If all firms in the market are the same size, then the value of the index is equal to the reciprocal of the number of firms; thus, if there are 10 firms all of the same size, $H = 0.1$. The upper limit of the index is 1, which occurs when there is a monopoly. The fig. shows that market B ($H = 0.190$), with a single dominant firm, is almost twice as concentrated as market A despite the latter having fewer firms.

hidden economy see BLACK ECONOMY.

hidden price reduction an increase in the amount or quality of a product offered at an unchanged PRICE, e.g., an increase in the weight of crisps per packet sold at the same price as before. Compare HIDDEN PRICE RISE.

hidden price rise a reduction in the quality or amount of a product offered at an unchanged PRICE, e.g., a reduction in the weight of a bar of chocolate sold at the same price as before. Compare HIDDEN PRICE REDUCTION.

hidden reserve the undervaluation of the ASSETS, or overvaluation of the LIABILITIES of a firm in its BALANCE SHEET. For example, the value of a firm's land and buildings may be shown in the balance sheet at HISTORIC COST or original cost, whereas the current market price of those assets may be considerably higher. Thus, if the assets were to be revalued to reflect current market values the difference would be formally recorded in the balance sheet as an addition to capital RESERVES. See INFLATION ACCOUNTING.

hidden tax an INDIRECT TAX that is incorporated into the PRICE of a good or service, but the consumer is not made fully aware of its existence or magnitude; for example, the amount of EXCISE DUTY included in the price of cigarettes and beer is not normally made known to the consumer. VALUE-ADDED TAX, by contrast, is incorporated into the price of a product at specified rates.

hidden unemployment a situation in which although people are technically in employment, their PRODUCTIVITY is negligible or zero. This can occur when powerful trade unions are able to operate restrictive labour practices such as OVERMANNING, or where governments employ vast bureaucracies of civil servants.

hierarchy the ORGANIZATION of economic activities *within* the FIRM. The internal hierarchy of management levels within the firm can, under certain circumstances, take responsibility for economic transactions rather than conduct them at arms' length through external MARKET relationships.

See INTERNALIZATION.

high-powered money see MONETARY BASE.

hire the use by an individual or business of an asset which is leased to them by the owner of the asset in return for a financial payment (the hire charge). Hiring provides a means for consumers or firms to make use of assets without having to make large cash payments to purchase them.

See LEASING.

hire purchase see INSTALMENT CREDIT.

histogram see BAR CHART.

historic cost the original cost of purchasing an ASSET (such as an item of machinery). For accountancy purposes, the asset is entered in a firm's BALANCE SHEET at historic cost. However, allowance has to be made for the REPLACEMENT COST of the asset which, because of INFLATION, may well be considerably greater than the original price paid. Thus, DEPRECIATION provisions may be inadequate in a period of rapidly rising prices. See INFLATION ACCOUNTING.

hoarding the nonproductive retention of MONEY or PRODUCTS. A certain amount of money is held in currency form to finance day-to-day transactions but this is turned-over on a regular basis. Hoarding involves a deliberate abstention from current spending and investing, and may occur because of an increase in LIQUIDITY PREFERENCE. Hoarding often occurs in less-developed countries where people are unfamiliar with, or suspicious of, using the banking system as a savings repository.

holding company a company that controls another company or companies. Ownership may be complete (100%) or partial (ownership of 51% + of the voting shares in the company). Such ownership confers powers to control the policies of subsidiary companies. The holding company will report the accounting results of these subsidiary companies as part of the accounting results for the group of companies.

Holding companies are most frequently used as a means of achieving diversified or conglomerate growth, with the firm operating separate companies in different lines of production activity, but with each company subject to varying degrees of centralized control by the 'parent company'.

See DIVERSIFICATION.

homogeneous products any identical goods offered in a market by competing suppliers. Given complete knowledge, buyers will regard the products as perfect substitutes for one another and will have no 'preference' for the products of particular suppliers. Homogeneity results in all suppliers having no ability to charge other than a common price for their products. See PERFECT COMPETITION, PRODUCT DIFFERENTIATION.

horizontal firm see FIRM.

horizontal integration 1. the tendency for firms to SPECIALIZE at a particular level in the production and distribution of a product rather than engage in a number of successive stages (VERTICAL INTEGRATION). Also called *lateral integration*.

2. the MERGER of firms making the same product. From the firm's point of view, expansion through horizontal integration may be advantageous because it enables the firm to reduce its production and distribution costs by securing ECONOMIES OF SCALE, or because it removes or reduces competitive pressures and increases the firm's control over the market.

In terms of its wider impact on the operation of market processes, horizontal integration may, on the one hand, promote greater efficiency in resource use, and reduce market supply costs and prices, or, on the other hand, by reducing competition and increasing the level of SELLER CONCENTRATION in the market, it may result in a less efficient allocation of resources and the danger of monopolistic exploitation.

Thus, horizontal integration may produce, simultaneously, both beneficial and detrimental effects. Under UK COMPETITION POLICY, horizontal integration by an established monopoly firm, or a proposed merger (TAKEOVER) between two competing firms involving a market share in the product concerned of over 25%, can be referred to the MONOPOLIES AND MERGERS COMMISSION to determine whether or not it operates against the public interest.

See MONOPOLY, OLIGOPOLY, OFFICE OF FAIR TRADING, DIVERSIFICATION.

hot money short-term and volatile CAPITAL MOVEMENTS between countries which take place primarily in response to interest rate differentials between financial centres (ARBITRAGE), or in anticipation of likely DEVALUATIONS or DEPRECIATIONS and REVALUATIONS or APPRECIATIONS of foreign currencies (SPECULATION). Speculative hot money flows are especially disruptive to the conduct of 'orderly' exchange rate management and the maintenance of balance-of-payments equilibrium, and are thus sometimes subjected to FOREIGN EXCHANGE CONTROL regulation by the authorities. See CAPITAL INFLOW, CAPITAL OUTFLOW.

household a group of individuals whose economic decision-making is interrelated. In economic theory households perform two rôles. On the one hand, they enter the market place as buyers or CONSUMERS of goods and services produced by firms; on the other hand, they provide FACTOR INPUTS to firms in order to produce those goods and services. The term 'households' is used primarily in macro- (national income) analysis, while the term 'consumers' is used in micro- (supply and demand) analysis. See CIRCULAR FLOW OF NATIONAL INCOME MODEL, PERSONAL SECTOR.

human capital the body of human knowledge that contributes 'know how' to productive activity. The knowledge base of a nation is added to by research and disseminated by teaching through general education and vocational training. INVESTMENT in human capital results in new, technically improved, products and production processes which improve ECONOMIC EFFICIENCY, and it can be as significant as physical CAPITAL in promoting ECONOMIC GROWTH. See ECONOMIC DEVELOPMENT.

hyperinflation a situation of high and accelerating rates of INFLATION. Unlike CREEPING INFLATION, which usually has little ill-effect on the functioning of the economy, hyperinflation reflects a situation where people begin to lose confidence in the value of MONEY and revert to BARTER. At this point there is a serious danger of economic collapse accompanied by growing social disorder. Hyperinflation is a rare phenomenon, but when it does occur its causes are as much political as economic; for example, the excessive printing of money to finance government spending (wars, in particular), or an acute shortage of goods and services combined with a large pent-up demand, as in periods immediately following the ending of a war.

hypermarket see SUPERMARKET.

hypothesis a prediction derived from theoretical analysis that is couched in a form precise enough to be subjected to testing against empirical data. In economics, hypotheses are generated by a process of logical deduction from sets of initial assumptions about the behaviour of consumers, producers, etc., and are generally tested by collecting economic data and using statistical techniques to analyse them. This testing can lead to modification of the economic theory in the light of the new economic data; or to abandonment of that theory in favour of an alternative theory which better explains the facts. See HYPOTHESIS TESTING.

hypothesis testing the development and use of statistical criteria to aid in taking decisions about the validity of a HYPOTHESIS in uncertain conditions. In any decision about the validity of a hypothesis, there is a chance of making a correct choice and a risk of making a wrong choice. Hypothesis testing is concerned with evaluating these chances and providing criteria that minimize the likelihood of making wrong decisions.

For example, suppose we wanted to decide whether or not company size determines management remuneration, and formulated the hypothesis that average management remuneration, is larger in bigger firms. This hypothesis can be either true or false and will be either accepted or rejected; these options are shown in the matrix below:

	Hypothesis is true	*Hypothesis is false*
Accept Hypothesis	correct decision	error (type 2)
Reject Hypothesis	error (type 1)	correct decision

If the hypothesis is true and we accept it, and if the hypothesis is false and we reject it, our decision will be correct. On the other hand, we could reject the hypothesis when it should be accepted (a *type 1 error*), or we could accept a hypothesis which should be rejected (a *type 2 error*). The risk of making such errors in testing a hypothesis using available sample data can be minimized. To avoid the risk of making a type 2 error, and to establish clear probabilities for the risk of committing a type 1 error, careful formulation of the hypothesis is necessary. Often this involves formulating a *null hypothesis* which assumes the exact opposite of what we want to prove. For example, in place of the earlier hypothesis that average management remuneration is larger in bigger firms, we would formulate the null hypothesis that average management remuneration is the same in large and small companies. Rejection of this null hypothesis is equivalent to acceptance of the original hypothesis. This null hypothesis can then be tested against sample data.

If repeated samples are taken from the population of firms then these samples can be used to assess the PROBABILITY of making a type 1 error. This probability of making a type 1 error is called the *level of significance* at which a test of the significance of the null hypothesis will be conducted (customarily 0.01, 0.05 or 0.10). This level of significance is always specified before any test is made.

The final step involves the test of significance: average management remuneration is calculated from sample data for small and large firms and compared with expected management remuneration which, according to our null hypothesis, should be the same in both small and big companies. If the difference between what we expect to find (average remuneration the same), and what we get, is so large that it cannot reasonably be attributed to chance, we reject the null hypothesis on which our expectation is based. On the other hand, if the difference between what we expect (average remuneration the same), and what we get, is so small that it reasonably may be attributed to chance, the results are not statistically significant. In the former case we would reject the null hypothesis and accept its mirror image, namely that management remuneration is larger in bigger firms. In the latter case we would reserve judgement on the issue of company size and management remuneration since no clear link is either proved or disproved.

The statistical techniques of hypothesis testing are widely employed in empirical economic research.

I

identity a means of portraying arithmetically the enduring equality between two (or more) VARIABLES which are equal by definition. For example, £1 = 100p (or $1 = 100c), and no matter how many pounds (or dollars) we have, they can always be converted into pennies (or cents) by multiplying by one hundred. Identities are generally given a three-bar 'identity' sign ($\equiv$) to indicate that the value to the left of the three bars is identical to the value to the right of the sign. The QUANTITY THEORY OF MONEY is one of the best known examples of an identity in economics, written as

$$M.V \equiv P.T$$

where M is the money stock, V is the velocity of circulation of money, P is the general price level, and T is the number of transactions undertaken. See EQUATION.

illegal activities any activities which because they are prohibited by law are excluded from a country's NATIONAL INCOME ACCOUNTS. Drug smuggling, for example, is illegal and therefore not included as part of legitimate economic activity.

See BLACK ECONOMY, BLACK MARKET.

IMF see INTERNATIONAL MONETARY FUND.

immiserizing growth a situation in which a DEVELOPING COUNTRY'S ATTEMPT TO INCREASE ITS GROWTH POTENTIAL THROUGH EXPORTS actually results in a retardation of that potential. This is very much an exceptional situation confined only in *theory* to a country whose export speciality (some mineral or agricultural crop) accounts for a preponderant share of world trade in the product. The country needs to export more to earn the foreign exchange to finance the capital imports which it requires to underpin domestic growth. If all its export effort is concentrated on its speciality, this could lead to an 'oversupply' of product resulting in a deterioration of the country's TERMS OF TRADE. As a result the country's foreign exchange earnings will now buy fewer imports and domestic growth potential will be impaired. See ECONOMIC DEVELOPMENT.

imperfect competition see MONOPOLISTIC COMPETITION.

imperfect market see MONOPOLISTIC COMPETITION.

implicit cost or **imputed cost** the OPPORTUNITY COST to a FIRM of using resources owned by the firm itself to produce its output. For example, if a firm occupies a building that it owns, it foregoes the opportunity of renting it out for some other alternative use. Thus, implicit costs represent the sacrifice of income that could have been earned by renting out (or selling) the firm's resources to others.

To achieve an accurate measure of the total cost of producing goods or services the firm must *impute* a rent to itself based upon the current market rates for renting the property.

See PROFIT, EXPLICIT COST, SHADOW PRICE.

import (i) a good which is produced in a foreign country and which is then physically transported to and sold in the 'home' market leading to an outflow of foreign exchange from the home country ('visible' import).

(ii) a service which is provided for the 'home' country by foreign interests, either in the home country (banking, insurance) or overseas (for example, travel abroad), again leading to an outflow of foreign exchange from the home country ('invisible' import).

(iii) capital which is invested in the home country in the form of portfolio investment, foreign direct investment in physical assets and banking deposits (capital imports).

Imports are important in two main respects. (a) Together with EXPORTS they make up a country's BALANCE OF TRADE. Imports must be financed ('paid for' in foreign currency terms) by an equivalent value of exports in order to maintain a payments equilibrium. (b) They represent a 'WITHDRAWAL' from the CIRCULAR FLOW OF NATIONAL INCOME, serving to reduce real income and output. (See PROPENSITY TO IMPORT).

On the one hand imports are seen as beneficial in that they allow a country to enjoy the benefits of INTERNATIONAL TRADE (obtain goods and services at lower prices), but on the other hand, as indicated by (b) above, detrimental because they reduce income and output. It is important to maintain a *balance* between imports and exports. Imports are beneficial provided that they are matched by exports – i.e., 'lost' income on imports is restored by income 'gained' on exports to maintain domestic income and output levels, and, as indicated by (a) above, imports are financed by exports to preserve a BALANCE-OF-PAYMENTS EQUILIBRIUM.

See BALANCE OF PAYMENTS, INTERNAL-EXTERNAL BALANCE MODEL, GAINS FROM TRADE, IMPORT PENETRATION, IMPORT RESTRICTIONS, IMPORT SCHEDULE, IMPORT SUBSTITUTION, PARALLEL IMPORT.

import deposit the requirement that importers of a product (see IMPORT) pay to the government a specified sum of money (calculated as a percentage of the value of the product) on arrival of the product in the domestic market prior to its eventual sale. Import deposits are used primarily as a means of assisting in the removal of a BALANCE-OF-PAYMENTS deficit. See BALANCE-OF-PAYMENTS EQUILIBRIUM, IMPORT RESTRICTIONS.

import duty a TAX levied by the government on imported products (see IMPORT). Import duties are used to raise revenue for the government and as a means of protecting domestic industries from foreign competition. See TARIFF, IMPORT RESTRICTIONS, PROTECTIONISM.

import levy see TARIFF.

import penetration an increase in the proportion of domestic CONSUMPTION accounted for by IMPORTS. In particular cases the displacement of domestic supply by imports may be beneficial in so far as it reflects COMPARATIVE ADVANTAGE (imports cheaper than domestic goods). Widespread import penetration across the economy, however, not matched by an equivalent amount of EXPORTS can result in balance-of-payments difficulties and a fall in domestic income and output levels.

In the case of the UK, import penetration in the manufacturing sector has increased markedly in the period since 1955 as Fig. 79 shows.

See PROPENSITY TO IMPORT, DEINDUSTRIALIZATION.

	Percentage of domestic consumption
1955	7
1965	9
1975	16
1995	38

Fig. 79. **Import penetration.** The UK import penetration ratio for manufactured goods. Source: NIESR, 1978; *Business Monitor*, 1996.

import quota see QUOTA.

import restrictions or **trade barriers** the limitation of IMPORTS into a country by a variety of techniques, e.g., TARIFFS, QUOTAS, IMPORT SURCHARGES, IMPORT DEPOSITS, EXPORT RESTRAINT AGREEMENTS and FOREIGN EXCHANGE CONTROLS. The aim of import restrictions is to assist in the removal of a BALANCE OF PAYMENTS deficit and as a means of protecting domestic industries against foreign competition. In general these practices are contrary to the rules of the GENERAL AGREEMENT ON TARIFFS AND TRADE, but GATT has been powerless to stop them in many cases (see, for example, the MULTI-FIBRE ARRANGEMENT.)

See PROTECTIONISM, BALANCE-OF-PAYMENTS EQUILIBRIUM.

import schedule a schedule depicting the relationship between NATIONAL INCOME and the proportion of income spent on IMPORTS, as shown in Fig. 80. See AVERAGE PROPENSITY TO IMPORT. The slope of the import schedule equals the MARGINAL PROPENSITY TO IMPORT.

import substitution a strategy aimed at reducing IMPORTS in order to encourage the production of domestic substitutes. Import substitution is pursued in particular by DEVELOPING COUNTRIES as a means of promoting domestic INDUSTRIALIZATION and conserving scarce

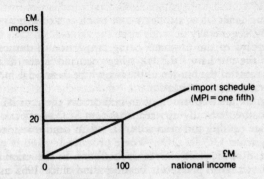

Fig. 80. Import schedule. See entry.

FOREIGN CURRENCY resources. By limiting or removing competing IMPORTS through the use of QUOTAS, TARIFFS, etc., the country aims to establish its own manufacturing industries which, initially, can be expanded to cater for the domestic market, and at a later stage develop an EXPORT trade. See INFANT INDUSTRY, ECONOMIC DEVELOPMENT.

import surcharge a special TAX levied on IMPORTS (over and above existing TARIFF rates). Import surcharges are employed primarily as a (temporary) means of assisting in the removal of a balance of payments deficit. See IMPORT RESTRICTIONS, BALANCE-OF-PAYMENTS EQUILIBRIUM.

imputed cost see IMPLICIT COST.

IMRO see INVESTMENT MANAGEMENT REGULATORY ORGANIZATION.

incentive pay scheme any form of PAY system which rewards an employee or group of workers in such a way as to induce increased effort or production. Such reward systems include PIECEWORK PAYMENTS which are geared to an individual's or group's effort and output; BONUS SCHEMES which provide bonuses for reaching stipulated levels of production or sales; PROFIT-RELATED PAY systems and PROFIT SHARING schemes which provide for employees to receive a proportion of the firm's profits.

See PRODUCTIVITY, X-INEFFICIENCY, SUPPLY-SIDE ECONOMICS.

incidence of taxation the location of the ultimate bearer (i.e., payer) of a TAX. For example, in the case of personal INCOME TAX it is the individual taxpayer concerned who bears the tax. In other cases, due account must be taken of shifts in tax. For example, suppose the tax authorities impose a PAYROLL TAX on firms who treat the tax as an increase in their input costs and put up their prices by an equivalent amount. Then, assuming there is no fall in sales, it is the buyers of the firm's product who bear the full burden of the tax, not the firm itself.

The incidence of an INDIRECT TAX (such as EXCISE DUTY or VALUE ADDED TAX) generally depends upon the PRICE-ELASTICITY OF DEMAND (and supply) of the products being taxed, with producers bearing most of the burden of the tax where demand is elastic and buyers bearing most of the burden of the tax where demand is inelastic. Fig. 81 contrasts the two situations.

In Fig. 81 the imposition of an indirect tax equal to BE_1 shifts the supply curve vertically upward from S to S_1. The effect of the tax is to increase equilibrium price from OP to OP_1 and reduce equilibrium quantity from OQ to OQ_1. Where product demand is price-elastic as in Fig. 81a, the price increase is small and the reduction in quantity sold is large, with producers bearing most of the burden of the tax in lost sales and reduced profit margins. By contrast, where product demand is price-inelastic as in Fig. 81b, the price increase is large and the reduction in quantity sold is small, with buyers bearing most of the burden of the tax in the form of a higher price. The relative burden of the tax borne by consumers is CE_1 and that borne by producers is BC in both (a) and (b).

In choosing which products to levy indirect taxes upon, governments usually select products such as cigarettes and alcohol, demand for which is highly price-inelastic, in order to ensure that buyers bear the burden of the tax and that the effects upon suppliers and employment are minimized.

See TAXATION, VALUE-ADDED TAX, PRINCIPLES OF TAXATION, LUMP SUM TAXES.

income money received by individuals and firms in the form of WAGES, SALARIES, RENT, INTEREST, PROFIT, etc., together with unemployment benefit, old age pensions, etc. In microeconomic analysis the term income is used specifically to refer to the flow of returns over a period of time from providing FACTORS OF PRODUCTION (NATURAL RESOURCES, LABOUR and CAPITAL) in the form of rent, wages and interest/profit, respectively. In macroeconomic analysis, the term NATIONAL INCOME is used to refer to the aggregate income of a country from rents, wages, interest and payments, excluding TRANSFER PAYMENTS (unemployment benefit, old age pensions, etc.).

More generally, from the point of view of the individuals concerned, any money received counts as income (whether it be from providing factors of production, or takes the form of an old age pension, unemployment benefit or other transfer payment). Any such FINAL INCOME is an important determinant of an individual's spending capabilities in the THEORY OF DEMAND.

See CIRCULAR FLOW OF NATIONAL INCOME MODEL, DISPOSABLE

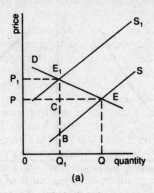

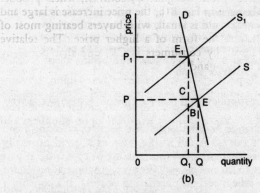

Fig. 81. Incidence of taxation. See entry.

INCOME, FUNCTIONAL DISTRIBUTION OF INCOME, PERSONAL DISTRI-
BUTION OF INCOME.

income approach to GDP see NATIONAL INCOME ACCOUNTS.

income-consumption curve a line that depicts the relationship
between consumer INCOME and the quantity of a product demanded
(see DEMAND) on a graph. See Fig. 82. The slope of the income-
consumption curve reflects the INCOME-ELASTICITY OF DEMAND, a
steeply-sloping curve indicating inelastic demand with small changes
in quantity demanded resulting from large changes in income, and
vice-versa.

income determination, theory of see EQUILIBRIUM LEVEL OF
NATIONAL INCOME.

income distribution the share-out of NATIONAL INCOME between the
various FACTOR INPUTS (FUNCTIONAL DISTRIBUTION OF INCOME), or

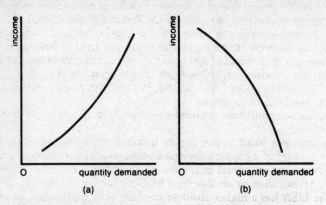

Fig. 82. **Income-consumption curve**. (a) An income-consumption curve for a NORMAL PRODUCT where, as income rises, the demand for the product also rises. (b) An income-consumption curve for an INFERIOR PRODUCT where, as income rises, buyers purchase less of the product, generally because they can now afford to buy more expensive alternatives. See INCOME-ELASTICITY OF DEMAND.

between factor input suppliers and other recipients (PERSONAL DISTRIBUTION OF INCOME).

income effect the change in CONSUMERS' real INCOME resulting from a change in product PRICES. A fall in the price of a good normally results in more of it being demanded (See THEORY OF DEMAND). A part of this increase is due to the *real income* effect (i.e., income adjusted for changes in prices to reflect current purchasing power). If a consumer has a money income of, say, £10 and the price of good X is £1, he can buy 10 units of the product; if the price of good X now falls to 50 pence, he can buy the same 10 units for only £5. The consumer now has an 'extra' £5 to spend on buying more of good X and other goods. The income effect, together with the SUBSTITUTION EFFECT, provides an explanation of why DEMAND CURVES are usually downward sloping.

See CONSUMER EQUILIBRIUM, REVEALED PREFERENCE, PRICE EFFECT.

income–elasticity of demand a measure of the degree of responsiveness of DEMAND to a given change in INCOME:

$$\text{income–elasticity of demand} = \frac{\% \text{ change in quantity demanded}}{\% \text{ change in income}}$$

If a given change in income results in a more than proportional change in quantity demanded then demand is said to be *income-elastic*, while if a given change in income results in a less than proportional change in quantity demanded then demand is *income-inelastic*.

Income-elasticity is positive for a NORMAL PRODUCT and negative for an INFERIOR PRODUCT. STAPLE PRODUCTS tend to have an income-elasticity of demand of less than 1, whereas LUXURY PRODUCTS generally tend to have an income-elasticity of more than 1.

See ENGEL'S LAW, INCOME EFFECT, INCOME-CONSUMPTION CURVE, DEMAND CURVE (SHIFT IN).

income-expenditure model see EQUILIBRIUM LEVEL OF NATIONAL INCOME.

income per head or **per capita income** the GROSS NATIONAL PRODUCT (GNP) of a country divided by its POPULATION. Income per head gives a more general indication of a country's monetary STANDARD OF LIVING than its *absolute* level of GNP: as Fig. 83 shows, although the USA has a higher absolute level of GNP than Japan, its income per head is much lower. However, an income per head measure of people's standard of living is itself also flawed as an indicator of typical living standards because, in practice, the *distribution* of income is not equal and non-monetary elements of lifestyle quality differ as between different people.

See PERSONAL DISTRIBUTION OF INCOME.

	GNP 1994	
	Total *(in US $ millions)*	*Per Head* *(US $)*
Developed countries		
UK	1,063,720	18,340
Germany	2,071,900	25,580
Japan	4,320,750	34,630
USA	6,754,680	25,880
Developing Countries		
Egypt	41,040	720
Mozambique	1,390	90
Rwanda	620	80
Ethiopia	5,500	100

Fig. 83. Income per head. GNP, total and per capita, for selected countries. Source: *World Development Report*, World Bank, 1996.

income redistribution a policy concerned with altering the pattern of the PERSONAL DISTRIBUTION OF INCOME in an economy, mainly with social rather than economic objectives in mind. The general aim of such a policy is to achieve a more equitable distribution of income as between the various sections of the community so as to ensure that everybody is provided with some minimum STANDARD OF LIVING. The transfer of income from one section of the community to another is achieved primarily by the use of a PROGRESSIVE TAXATION system and a variety of welfare provisions (subsidised housing, old-age pensions, etc.)

See ABILITY-TO-PAY PRINCIPLE OF TAXATION, REDISTRIBUTION OF INCOME PRINCIPLE OF TAXATION, WEALTH TAX.

incomes policy see PRICES AND INCOMES POLICY.

income support 1. a means of supplementing the INCOMES of poorer members of the community by means of TRANSFER PAYMENTS such as supplementary benefits, unemployment benefit, etc. See NEGATIVE INCOME TAX, REDISTRIBUTION OF INCOME PRINCIPLE OF TAXATION.

2. a method of supporting the incomes of certain producers by providing direct payment where market prices are felt to yield insufficient income. See Fig. 84.

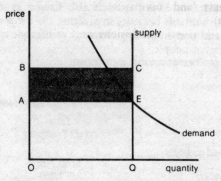

Fig. 84. **Income support**. In many countries income-support systems are used specifically to assist the agricultural sector. In the graph, the equilibrium market price is OA. If this price is considered too low to adequately remunerate farmers the government will set a guaranteed or SHADOW PRICE, say OB, and thus supplement farm incomes by a deficiency payment equal in the aggregate to the shaded area ABCE. Note, in contrast to the PRICE-SUPPORT method, consumers still pay the market-determined price OA and producers sell market-determined output OQ. The UK used the income-support method to assist its agricultural sector prior to joining the EUROPEAN COMMUNITY'S COMMON AGRICULTURAL POLICY scheme in 1973. See AGRICULTURAL POLICY.

income tax a DIRECT TAX levied by the government on the INCOME (wages, rent, dividends) received by households in order to raise revenue and as an instrument of FISCAL POLICY. Income tax is usually paid on a progressive scale (see PROGRESSIVE TAX). In the UK, the INLAND REVENUE assesses and collects taxes on behalf of the government for a fiscal year starting 6th April to the following 5th April. Taxes such as CAPITAL GAINS TAX and WEALTH TAX also impinge upon individuals but are quite separate in their scope and calculation.

Changes in income tax rates can be used as part of fiscal policy to regulate the level of AGGREGATE DEMAND, increases in tax serving to reduce DISPOSABLE INCOME available for consumption spending, while decreases in tax increase disposable income. Income taxes can also be used to affect the distribution of incomes in society in line with the government's social policy.

See TAXATION, PRINCIPLES OF TAXATION, INCOME-TAX SCHEDULES.

income-tax schedules the classification by the INLAND REVENUE in the UK of various sources of INCOME to facilitate the assessment of TAXATION liability upon an individual. There are 6 schedules lettered A to F. Briefly, the income source of each schedule is:

A: land and property

B: woodlands run as a business

C: INTEREST and DIVIDENDS from public bodies (including government)

D: trades, business, professions and vocations, interest received gross

E: WAGES from employment (collected under the PAY-AS-YOU-EARN system – PAYE)

F: company distributions

There are considerable rules and regulations concerning INCOME TAX and the expenses allowable against it.

income velocity of circulation see QUANTITY THEORY OF MONEY.**incorporation** see COMPANY FORMATION.

increasing returns to scale see ECONOMIES OF SCALE.

increasing returns to the variable-factor input see RETURNS TO THE VARIABLE FACTOR INPUT.

independent variable a variable which affects some other variable in a model. For example, the price of a product (the independent variable) will influence the demand for it (the DEPENDENT VARIABLE). It is conventional to place the independent variable on the right-hand side of an EQUATION.

See DEMAND FUNCTION, SUPPLY FUNCTION.

indexation the automatic adjustment of an INCOME payment (e.g., wages) or a value (for example, household contents insurance value) in proportion to changes in a general PRICE INDEX. Indexation is commonly used as a means of countering the effects of persistant price increases (INFLATION). See BASE YEAR, INDEX-LINKED, INDEX NUMBER.

index-linked, *adj.* (of a VARIABLE) having a value determined in proportion to a specified index. For example, many pension schemes are linked to the retail price index so that as retail prices increase year by year, pensions increase by the same proportion so as to maintain their value in real terms. See BASE YEAR, INDEXATION, INDEX NUMBER, PRICE INDEX, REAL VALUES.

index number a single numerical value that reflects the relative size of a VARIABLE in the period under review compared with its size in some predetermined BASE YEAR. For example, a retail price index takes the same sample of goods and services in each period and measures the average price of this typical basket of goods and services, showing this average price in the form of a single index number.

The base period of an index is, by convention, given an index number of 100. For the British Retail Price Index, this period is (currently) 1987 and subsequent percentage changes commence from that year. In 1995 the Retail Price Index was 149, suggesting that retail prices have increased by 49% on average between 1987 and 1995.

Regardless of whether the index is in terms of price, volume or value, the principle of index numbers remains the same, to exhibit simply and concisely the measured change in a variable from one period to another.

See PRICE INDEX, INDEXATION, INDEX-LINKED.

indicative planning a method of controlling the economy that involves the setting of long-term objectives and the mapping-out of programmes of action designed to fulfill these objectives, using techniques such as INPUT-OUTPUT ANALYSIS. Unlike a CENTRALLY-PLANNED ECONOMY indicative planning works through the market (PRICE SYSTEM) rather than replaces it. To this end the planning process specifically brings together both sides of industry (the trade unions and management) and the government.

The only occasion when indicative planning was attempted in the UK was in 1965 when a 'NATIONAL PLAN' was formulated (which set a target economic growth for the UK economy of 3.8% over the period 1964–70), and employed a variety of planning agencies (the NATIONAL ECONOMIC DEVELOPMENT COUNCIL and Economic Development Committees (EDCs) for individual industries) to provide national as well as industry-by-industry coordination. The National Plan itself, however, was abandoned in 1966 after being overtaken by events (a balance of payments crisis resulting in a deflationary package of measures) but the NEDC and the EDCs have continued to function on a less formal basis. By contrast the French and Japanese have used indicative planning continuously since the 1950s.

See INDUSTRIAL POLICY.

indifference curve a curve showing alternative combinations of two products, each of which gives the same UTILITY or satisfaction. See Fig. 85. Indifference curves are used (along with BUDGET LINES) to determine a consumer's equilibrium purchases of two products and to analyse the effect of changes in the relative prices of these two

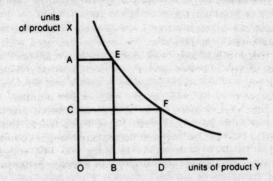

Fig. 85. **Indifference curve**. A combination of OA units of product X, and OB units of product Y, yields exactly as much satisfaction to the consumer as does the combination of OC units of product X and OD units of product Y.

Indifference curves always slope downwards because, rationally, consumers will always prefer more of both products and so would not be indifferent between two combinations of products where one combination offers more of both. Specifically, they would only give up one product if they receive more of another for it, being indifferent as between combination E, which offers a lot of product X and little of product Y, and combination F which offers less product X and more product Y (see ECONOMIC MAN).

products upon quantities demanded (see PRICE EFFECT). See CONSUMER EQUILIBRIUM, INDIFFERENCE MAP.

indifference map a collection of ranked INDIFFERENCE CURVES which exhibit graphically an individual's increasing UTILITY, or satisfaction, when moving outwards from the origin, consuming larger quantities of two products. See Fig. 86 (overleaf). Indifference curves are an ORDINAL measure and the numbers on the indifference curves in Fig. 86 *do not* indicate an absolute level of utility. Indifference curves never cross because two crossing curves would imply inconsistent or irrational choices between the two products by the consumer (see ECONOMIC MAN).

indirect costs see OVERHEADS.

indirect investment any expenditure on FINANCIAL SECURITIES such as STOCKS and SHARES. This is sometimes referred to as *financial* or *portfolio investment*. See INVESTMENT.

indirect labour that part of the labour force in a firm which is not directly concerned with the manufacture of a good but who provide support services, for example, supervision and clerical work. Contrast DIRECT LABOUR.

INDIRECT MATERIALS

indirect materials any raw materials which, while they are not incorporated in a product, are nonetheless consumed in the production process, for example, lubricants and moulds for metal castings.

Contrast DIRECT MATERIALS.

indirect tax a TAX levied by the government on goods and services in order to raise revenue and as an instrument of FISCAL POLICY. Examples of an indirect tax are VALUE ADDED TAX and EXCISE DUTY.

Changes in indirect tax can be used as part of fiscal policy to regulate the level of AGGREGATE DEMAND, increases in tax serving to reduce disposable income available for consumption spending, while decreases in tax increase disposable income. Indirect taxes can be used to affect the shape of demand as well as its level, increases in indirect tax serving to discourage consumption of socially disapproved products like cigarettes or alcoholic drinks, while reductions in indirect taxes encourage consumption of socially-approved products like basic foodstuffs or books.

Unlike a DIRECT TAX which varies according to the income of the taxpayer (PROGRESSIVE TAXATION), indirect taxes are regressive, insofar as the same amount is paid by each taxpaying consumer regardless of their income.

See TAXATION, REGRESSIVE TAXATION, INCIDENCE OF TAXATION.

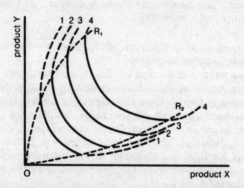

Fig. 86. **Indifference map.** In principle, indifference curves 1,2,3, etc., can take the full form indicated in the map, though in practice only the solid-line segment of each curve is relevant, because once the curves become vertical, and the consumer is fully sated with product Y, he will not be prepared to give up extra units of product X to get extra Y; and once the curves become horizontal, and the consumer is fully sated with product X, he will not be prepared to give up extra units of product Y to get extra X. The ridge lines R_1 and R_2 mark the boundaries of the effective segments of the indifference curves.

250

indivisibilities the minimum physical or technical size limitations on FACTOR INPUTS. For example, a company wants to purchase a machine which can undertake 5,000 operations a day. Due to design and technical difficulties the minimum-size machine available optimally carries out 10,000 operations a day. The machine is indivisible since it cannot be reduced to two optimal half-machines. The AVERAGE COST of each unit of output is consequently greater than it would be if the manufacturer could produce at an output level where the machine was optimally employed.

The manufacturer could achieve ECONOMIES OF SCALE by attaining a large volue of production, but this can give rise to problems of combining large, indivisible inputs with different capacities. For example, if the manufacturer above needs to combine process A machines capable of carrying out 10,000 operations a day and process B machines capable of carrying out 4,000 operations a day then only by producing 20,000 units a day in two process A machines and five process B machines would he be able to use both types of machine in an economically-feasible way. Any other output level would result in a degree of under-utilization of one or other machine.

See PRODUCTION FUNCTION.

induced consumption that part of an increase, or decrease, in total CONSUMPTION expenditure which is brought about by a change in the level of NATIONAL INCOME or DISPOSABLE INCOME. In the short term consumption expenditure consists of AUTONOMOUS CONSUMPTION (consumption expenditure which does not vary with income) and induced consumption.

See CONSUMPTION SCHEDULE.

induced investment that part of an increase, or decrease, in real INVESTMENT which is brought about by a change in the level of NATIONAL INCOME. For example, a rise in national income accompanied by increased consumption spending which puts pressure on existing supply capacity will encourage businesses to invest in new plant and machinery. See ACCELERATOR, INVESTMENT SCHEDULE, AUTONOMOUS INVESTMENT.

Industrial and Commercial Finance Corporation see INVESTORS IN INDUSTRY.

industrial classification the grouping of economic activities of a similar nature into INDUSTRIES or MARKETS. Such a classification begins by identifying a wide spectrum of related activities (for example, the 'manufacturing sector'), each group of activities then being subdivided into progressively narrower groups so that the classification can be used with varying amounts of detail for different purposes. In the UK, a *Standard Industrial Classification* (*SIC*) codifies and measures groups of economic activity at various levels of aggregation and disaggregation. The Standard Industrial Classification comprises 10 major Divisions (for example, Metal Goods/Engineering); 60 Classes (for example, Metal Manufacturing); 222 Groups (for example, Non-Ferrous Metals); and 334 Activities (for example, Copper).

Activities, or their equivalent 'industries' (see INDUSTRY), are derived on the basis of their *supply* characteristics, in particular the use of common raw materials and processes of manufacture. Such a classification provides a useful source of information on industry structure and statistical details of employment, output and investment by the industrial sector. However, for purposes of market analysis, SIC data usually needs to be reinterpreted in order to provide more meaningful specifications of markets defined in terms of groups of products which are regarded by *buyers* as close substitute products. To illustrate, glass jars and metal cans are assigned to different industries by the SIC (Division 2, Activity 'glass containers'; Division 3, 'packaging products of metal', respectively), but would be regarded by a user of packaging materials such as a coffee manufacturer as substitute products.

Industrial classifications are used for macroeconomic planning and COMPETITION POLICY purposes, and to obtain statistical information on output and employment.

See STRUCTURE OF INDUSTRY, CROSS-ELASTICITY OF DEMAND.

industrial democracy the participation of the workforce in the corporate decision-making process alongside management. See WORKER PARTICIPATION, TRADE UNION, EMPLOYEE SHARE OWNERSHIP PLAN.

industrial development certificate an instrument of REGIONAL POLICY that is used to control the location of firms and industries.

industrial dispute a dispute between one or more employers, or organizations of employers, and one or more workers or organizations of workers (TRADE UNIONS), where the dispute relates wholly or mainly to matters of trade. Such matters may comprise terms and/or conditions of employment; the engagement, termination or suspension of employment of workers; the allocation of work between workers; matters of discipline, and so forth.

Serious industrial disputes are often characterized by STRIKE action on the part of workers and/or the LOCK-OUT of workers by management. Industrial disputes may be settled in a number of ways, including voluntary agreement between the parties concerned, or by recourse to an independent arbiter.

See INDUSTRIAL RELATIONS, COLLECTIVE BARGAINING, ARBITRATION, MEDIATION, CONCILIATION.

industrial economics or **industrial organization** the branch of economics concerned with the functioning of the PRICE SYSTEM. Industrial economics examines the interrelationships between MARKET STRUCTURE, MARKET CONDUCT and MARKET PERFORMANCE, utilizing the analytical framework of the THEORY OF MARKETS but within an empirical and dynamic setting. See MARKET STRUCTURE-CONDUCT-PERFORMANCE SCHEMA.

industrial estate a formally-planned area designated for commercial and industrial use separate from residential accommodation. Industrial estates initially offered low cost work space for light and medium size engineering companies and warehouse distribution facilities. Such estates may be financed privately or by government. In the UK, current attempts to attract high-technology firms into one convenient area, often referred to as *science parks*, situated close to university facilities, follow a similar theme.

industrialization the extensive development of organized economic activity for the purpose of manufacture. Industrialization is characterized by the transformation of a primarily agrarian economy into a more specialized, capital-intensive economy. Such a transformation was termed the *Industrial Revolution* in Western Europe and North America during the 18th and 19th centuries. Compare DEINDUSTRIALIZATION. See STRUCTURE OF INDUSTRY, ECONOMIC DEVELOPMENT.

industrial location the geographical site or sites selected by a firm to perform its economic function. The choice of an appropriate location is influenced by a range of considerations but two are particularly important: (a) the nature and characteristics of the industrial activity that the firm performs (raw material extraction or crop cultivation, the manufacture of intermediate or final products, the provision of a service), and (b) the relative costs of production at different locations 'balanced' against the cost of physical distribution to target markets, and the importance of 'closeness' to customers as a basis for establishing COMPETITIVE ADVANTAGES over rival suppliers.

Some activities are highly locational-specific. For example, the extraction of iron ore can only occur where there are deposits of the metal. Likewise, many service activities, for example retailing, have to be located in and around customer catchment areas, while some suppliers of components may find it advantageous to operate alongside their key customers in order better to synchronize the latter's input-production requirements. The manufacture of final products tends to be more 'footloose'. Certain locations may be preferred because of their production advantages, either because, for example, of lower labour costs or the availability of investment subsidies (see REGIONAL POLICY), or because of the availability of skilled workers and access to related facilities. On the other hand, high distribution costs, especially in the case of bulky, low value-added products, or, in the international context, the imposition of tariffs and quotas on imports, tend to favour a market-oriented location.

See GREENFIELD INVESTMENT, INDUSTRIAL ESTATE, MULTINATIONAL COMPANY, LOCATION OF INDUSTRY.

industrial organization see INDUSTRIAL ECONOMICS.

industrial policy a policy concerned with promoting industrial efficiency and competitiveness, industrial regeneration and expansion and the creation of employment opportunities. Industrial policy can be broadly based, encompassing, for example, measures to increase competition (see COMPETITION POLICY) and promote regional development (see REGIONAL POLICY) as well as specific across-the-board measures to stimulate efficiency and the adoption of new technology; or it can be more narrowly focused involving selective intervention in particular industries or support for particular projects and firms. Industrial policy in most countries is both *reactive* (responding, for example, to cases of market failure by acting to restructure and rationalize declining industries or support failing, 'lame-duck' firms), and *proactive* (acting as a catalyst for change by encouraging, for example, the establishment of new businesses and the development of new technologies).

In the UK, industrial policy in its broadest sense has been implemented until recently through the NATIONAL ECONOMIC DEVELOPMENT COUNCIL(NEDC) and its satellites, the Economic Development Committees. The main work of NEDC had been to formulate programmes for improving efficiency and international competitiveness and to identify the threats and opportunities facing particular industrial sectors. NEDC was abolished in 1992.

Examples of general programmes to assist industry include support for small business start-ups and development (Business Expansion Scheme); the adoption of advanced technologies (Micro-Processor Applications Scheme); and vocational training.

Examples of selective intervention in British industry include the RATIONALIZATION of declining industries; support for high-technology growth industries; support for firms in temporary financial difficulties; support for INVENTIONS and INNOVATIONS; support for strategic MERGERS.

A number of bodies have been established to sponsor and provide financial assistance in this area, including the National Research and Development Corporation (established 1948), the Industrial Reorganization Corporation (1966–71), the National Enterprise Board (1975), and (currently) the British Technology Group, formed through the merger of the National Research and Development Corporation and the National Enterprise Board in 1981.

In some countries (most notably the UK), industrial policy has developed on a piecemeal basis and has varied in the degree of enthusiasm accorded to it by the government of the day. In others, for example Japan and France, industrial policy has been seen as an arm of INDICATIVE PLANNING and has been applied on a more continuous and coordinated basis.

industrial property rights see INTELLECTUAL PROPERTY RIGHT.

industrial relations the relationships between employers in terms of day-to-day worker-manager dealings and the more formal procedures and institutions through which the two groups determine PAY and conditions of employment. COLLECTIVE BARGAINING is the main means used to determine pay and conditions, and where employers and workers are unable to settle these matters through negotiation, INDUSTRIAL DISPUTES, in particular STRIKES and LOCK-OUTS may ensue, unless the two parties can find alternative means of settling their disputes, such as CONCILIATION, MEDIATION and ARBITRATION.

The general state of relationships between managers and their employees, often represented as a group by TRADE UNIONS, can have significant implications for the effectiveness and competitiveness of the organization and the general health of the economy. Poor industrial relations can lead to an inefficient use of labour resources with poor labour flexibility and RESTRICTIVE LABOUR PRACTICES (overmanning, demarcation restrictions) resulting in reduced PRODUCTIVITY. In addition, strikes involving the loss of working days can seriously disrupt production and lower output. The potential conflict between employers and workers over pay and employment conditions is part of the continuing 'tug of war' over the share of NATIONAL INCOME going to CAPITAL and LABOUR respectively.

Because of the importance of good industrial relations in enhancing economic performance, governments have attempted to foster collaborative arrangements between employers and employees through, for example, EMPLOYEE SHARE OWNERSHIP PLANS and WORKER PARTICIPATION.

Industrial Reorganization Corporation a UK organization whose particular rôle from 1966 to 1971 was to promote and financially assist RATIONALIZATION, MERGERS and industrial projects. See INDUSTRIAL POLICY.

Industrial Revolution see INDUSTRIALIZATION.

industrial sector that part of the economy concerned with the production of INTERMEDIATE PRODUCTS (iron and steel, machinery and equipment, etc.) and FINAL PRODUCTS (washing machines, furniture, etc.) The industrial sector, together with the PRIMARY SECTOR and SERVICE SECTOR form an interlocking chain of economic activities which constitute a modern economy. See STRUCTURE OF INDUSTRY.

industry a group of related economic activities classified according to the type of good or service supplied. For example, the beer/brewing industry might be defined as all those firms that produce bitter and mild ales, lagers, stouts and ciders. However, beer production might be seen also as constituting part of a wider and bigger industry, the 'alcoholic beverages industry', which includes the production of spirits and wines as well as beer. Thus, there are specification problems with respect to how widely or narrowly a particular industry is defined. Moreover, INDUSTRIAL CLASSIFICATIONS typically group together products on the basis of their *supply* characteristics such as the use of common raw materials and manufacturing processes. This may or may not coincide with how goods and services are grouped together to define MARKETS, which requires account to be taken also of how products are seen from the point of view of buyers (that is, their *demand* characteristics). Thus although men's and women's shoes are produced using the same materials and manufacturing processes, and often by the same firms, they are not considered by buyers as close *substitutes*, and hence, from a buyer's point of view, they must be treated as constituting separate markets.

See STRUCTURE OF INDUSTRY, CROSS-ELASTICITY OF DEMAND, MARKET STRUCTURE.

inelastic, *adj.* relatively unresponsive to change. See PRICE-ELASTICITY OF DEMAND, PRICE-ELASTICITY OF SUPPLY, INCOME-ELASTICITY OF DEMAND, CROSS-ELASTICITY OF DEMAND.

infant industry a newly-established industry, developed either by private-enterprise interests or set up by the government, often in DEVELOPING COUNTRIES, as part of their INDUSTRIALIZATION programmes. New industries are often subsidized by the government and/or protected from import competition in the hope that in due course they can exploit economies of scale and thus eventually withstand foreign competition.

Infant industries are often cited as a 'legitimate' area for the application of PROTECTIONISM, but policy in this area is often open to abuse. See ECONOMIC DEVELOPMENT.

inferior product a good or service for which the INCOME ELASTICITY OF DEMAND is negative; i.e., as income rises, buyers purchase less of the product. Consequently, when the price of such a product falls thereby effectively increasing consumers' real income, then that price cut will have the INCOME EFFECT of tending to decrease the quantity demanded. This will tend to partially offset the SUBSTITUTION EFFECT of a price cut which causes consumers to buy more of the product because it is now relatively cheaper. This applies to a very limited range of products. See PRICE EFFECT, NORMAL PRODUCT, INCOME-CONSUMPTION CURVE, ENGEL'S LAW.

inflation an increase in the general level of prices in an economy that is sustained over a period of time. The annual increases in prices may be small or gradual (creeping inflation), or large and accelerating (hyperinflation). The rate of inflation can be measured using, for example, a consumers' PRICE INDEX which shows the annual percentage change in consumer prices. See Fig. 87a on page 258. Inflation reduces the PURCHASING POWER of money (see REAL VALUES).

The avoidance of inflation has long been one of the main objectives of MACROECONOMIC POLICY. Inflation is considered to be undesirable because of its adverse effects on income distribution (people on fixed incomes suffer) lending and borrowing (lenders lose, borrowers gain), speculation (diversion of saving away from industry into property and commodity speculation), and international trade competitiveness (exports become relatively more expensive, imports cheaper). Hyperinflation is particularly serious because people lose confidence in the use of money for exchange purposes and the economic system is liable to collapse.

There are two main explanations of why inflation occurs: (a) the presence of excess demand at the full employment level of national output which 'pulls-up' prices (DEMAND-PULL INFLATION); (b) an increase in FACTOR INPUT costs (wages and raw materials) which 'pushes-up' prices (COST-PUSH INFLATION).

According to the monetarist school (see MONETARISM), demand-pull inflation is caused by the excessive creation of money, and they prescribe strict controls on the MONEY SUPPLY as a means of reducing excess spending (see MONETARY POLICY). Likewise, the Keynesian school advocates cuts in spending as the way of tackling excess demand, but in their case mainly by increasing taxes and reducing government expenditure (see FISCAL POLICY). Cost-push inflation tends to be associated particularly with excessive increases in money wage rates (i.e. wage rates greater than can be paid for by increases in the underlying rate of productivity growth) and with occasional explosions in commodity prices (the OPEC oil price increases of 1973 and 1979 being a case in point). Cost-push inflation caused by excessive wage demands can be modified or eliminated either directly by the use of controls on prices and incomes (see PRICES AND INCOMES POLICY) or more indirectly by 'moral suasion' and measures to reduce the monopoly power of trade unions.

See INFLATIONARY SPIRAL, PURCHASING POWER, PHILLIPS CURVE, EXPECTATIONS-ADJUSTED AUGMENTED PHILLIPS CURVE, ADAPTIVE EXPECTATIONS HYPOTHESIS, QUANTITY THEORY OF MONEY, INDEXATION, INTERNAL-EXTERNAL BALANCE MODEL.

inflation accounting any adjustments to a firm's accounts to allow for the effects of INFLATION and arrive at a view of the real profitability of the firm. In a period of rising prices when the purchasing power of the money unit is declining, profit calculations based upon the HISTORIC COST of STOCKS and FIXED ASSETS are likely to overstate the real profit position in the PROFIT-AND-LOSS ACCOUNT and BALANCE SHEET.

inflation-adjusted PSBR see PUBLIC-SECTOR BORROWING REQUIREMENT.

inflationary gap the excess of total spending (AGGREGATE DEMAND) at the full employment level of national income (POTENTIAL GROSS

Average annual inflation rate (%)

	1965–80	1980–90	1991	1992	1993	1994	1995
UK	11.2	5.8	6.8	4.7	3.0	2.6	2.7
USA	6.5	3.7	4.2	3.0	3.0	2.4	3.0
Japan	7.7	1.5	3.3	1.7	1.3	0.7	0.2
Germany	5.2	2.7	4.5	4.9	4.7	3.1	1.8

(a)

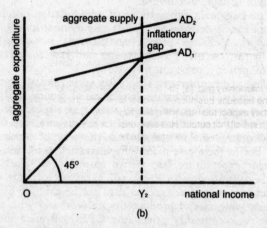

(b)

Fig. 87. **Inflation.** (a) National inflation rates, 1965–1995. Source: *World Development Report*, World Bank and IMF. (b) In the EQUILIBRIUM LEVEL OF NATIONAL INCOME model inflation occurs whenever AGGREGATE DEMAND exceeds full employment aggregate supply (POTENTIAL GROSS NATIONAL PRODUCT): equilibrium national income in the Fig. is OY_2, and if aggregate demand AD_2 exceeds full employment demand AD_1, an INFLATIONARY GAP develops. The traditional prescription for this situation is for the authorities to reduce spending by deflationary FISCAL POLICY and MONETARY POLICY measures – to shift aggregate demand from AD_2 to AD_1.

NATIONAL PRODUCT). As it is not possible to increase output further the excess demand will cause prices to rise, i.e., real output remains the same but the money or nominal value of that output will be inflated. To counter this excess spending the authorities can use FISCAL POLICY and MONETARY POLICY to reduce aggregate demand. See Fig. 88.

inflationary spiral or **price-wage spiral** a self-sustained increase in the rate of INFLATION brought about by the interaction of rising final prices and rising input costs. For example, an initial sharp increase in the prices of goods and services caused by an increase in raw

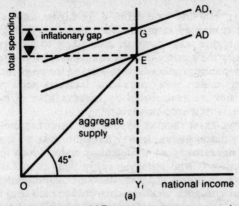

Fig. 88. **Inflationary gap.** (a) The AGGREGATE SUPPLY SCHEDULE is drawn as a 45° line because businesses will offer any particular level of output only if they expect total spending (aggregate demand) to be just sufficient to sell all that output. However, once the economy reaches the full employment level of national income (OY_t) then output cannot expand further and at this level of output the aggregate supply schedule becomes vertical. If aggregate demand was at the level indicated by AD the economy would be operating at full employment without inflation (at point E). However if aggregate demand was at a higher level like AD_1 this excess aggregate demand would create an inflationary gap (equal to EG), pulling price upward.

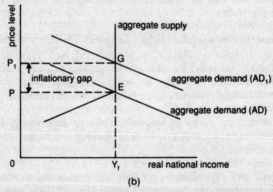

(b) Alternatively, where aggregate demand and aggregate supply are expressed in terms of real national income and price levels, an inflationary gap shows up as the difference between the price level (OP) corresponding to the full employment level of aggregate demand (AD) and the price level (OP_1) corresponding to the higher level of aggregate demand (AD_1) at real national income level OY_t. See DEMAND-PULL INFLATION.

material costs, can lead to a demand for higher MONEY WAGES by trade unions concerned to protect their members' living standards. If conceded, higher wage costs are soon likely to prompt manufacturers to put up their prices in order to maintain profit margins. The higher prices in turn produce further demand for wage increases, and so on. Once under way, price-cost increases tend to be self-reinforcing, and are exacerbated by EXPECTATIONS of even further increases (see ANTICIPATED INFLATION).

See ADAPTIVE-EXPECTATIONS HYPOTHESIS, EXPECTATIONS-ADJUSTED/ AUGMENTED PHILLIPS CURVE, MONEY ILLUSION, REAL WAGES.

information agreement an arrangement under which firms undertake to furnish a central agency, usually their TRADE ASSOCIATION, with data on such things as prices, discounts, conditions of sale, etc. These data are compiled and then circulated to each firm involved in the agreement. Information exchanges can take place either on a post- or prenotification basis. In the former case, information is only made available to other firms after, for example, a change in prices, while in the case of prenotification schemes, firms are notified of proposed price changes etc in advance of a definite commitment being made. It will be readily apparent that such information exchanges, particularly prenotification exchanges, provide a cloak for COLLUSION between competitors.

In the UK, information agreements covering prices and conditions of sale of goods are required to be registered with the OFFICE OF FAIR TRADING, and can be referred for investigation to the RESTRICTIVE PRACTICES COURT.

See COMPETITION POLICY.

infrastructure or **social overhead capital** a nation's roads, railways, housing, hospitals, schools, water supply, etc., accumulated from INVESTMENT, usually by the government or local authorities, in previous periods. It also includes intangible items such as an educated/trained labour force created by investment in HUMAN CAPITAL.

Infrastructure plays an important rôle in improving a country's general living standards and in contributing to a higher rate of ECONOMIC GROWTH.

inheritance tax see WEALTH TAX.

injections any expenditures on domestic goods and services originating from outside the household sector. In the basic CIRCULAR FLOW OF NATIONAL INCOME MODEL all spending is done by households (CONSUMPTION expenditure). In the extended circular flow of income model, domestic output is also purchased by businesses, government and overseas buyers. Thus, INVESTMENT, GOVERNMENT EXPENDITURE and EXPORTS, respectively, constitute 'injections' into the income-spending flow. Compare WITHDRAWALS.

injections-withdrawals approach to national income determination see EQUILIBRIUM LEVEL OF NATIONAL INCOME.

Inland Revenue a UK government department that is responsible for assessing individual and corporate TAXATION liabilities (H.M. Inspector of Taxes), and for the collection of taxation monies due (H.M. Collector of Taxes). In the US the Internal Revenue Service performs similar functions.

innovation the practical refinement and development of an original INVENTION into a usable technique (process innovation) or product (product innovation). Innovation is an important means for a firm to improve its competitive position over rival suppliers by enhancing its PRODUCT DIFFERENTIATION advantages, and for improving MARKET PERFORMANCE (by, for example, lowering supply costs and enhancing product quality). Certain kinds of MARKET STRUCTURE may be more conducive to innovation insofar as they offer better incentives and resources for undertaking RESEARCH AND DEVELOPMENT (see MONOPOLY for further discussion). Innovation can be a lengthy and expensive process. For example, the original invention of the Xerox photocopying process was made in 1948, but it took a further 10 years of development work before the first commercial version of the product was put on the market.

In a more general way, innovation can contribute to faster ECONOMIC GROWTH.

See TECHNOLOGICAL PROGRESSIVENESS, PRODUCT LIFE CYCLE, PRODUCT DEVELOPMENT, PATENT, FINANCIAL INNOVATION.

inputs see FACTOR INPUTS.

input-output analysis or **interindustry analysis** the study and empirical measurement of the structural interrelationships between PRODUCTION sectors within an economy. The technique was devised by Wassily Leontief (1906–) to measure the FACTOR INPUT required by different industries to achieve a given OUTPUT. A particular sector of the economy requires inputs from other sectors, be it raw materials, intermediate goods and services, or labour, in order to produce output. The interdependence between industries, or sectors, is not linear but complex. That is, one sector does not produce, say, coal, for other sectors independent of the requirements of the coal industry for inputs from other sectors. For the mining sector coal is an output. But coal is an input for the electricity industry. By the same token, the coal industry requires inputs (including electricity) in order to produce the coal. The complexity of an economy can be gauged from this simple example.

See VERTICAL INTEGRATION, INDICATIVE PLANNING, GENERAL EQUILIBRIUM ANALYSIS.

inside money see ENDOGENOUS MONEY.

insider trading any transactions in securities such as STOCKS and

SHARES by persons having access to privileged (confidential) information not as yet available to the general investing public, and who in consequence stand to gain financially from this knowledge. For example, a person who is employed by a merchant bank and is involved in working out details of a prospective TAKEOVER by a client firm of another firm may himself or through other people arrange to purchase shares in the target firm prior to the public announcement of the takeover. See CITY CODE.

insolvency or **bankruptcy** a condition under which an individual or firm's LIABILITIES to CREDITORS exceed ASSETS. The individual or firm is therefore unable to discharge all accumulated liabilities from realizable assets.

Insolvency occurs after a period in which an individual's expenditure has exceeded his income; or a firm's costs have exceeded its sales revenues (LOSSES are made). Frequently an insolvent individual or firm will become bankrupt and arrange for the LIQUIDATION of available assets, the proceeds being distributed amongst creditors.

See INSOLVENCY ACT, 1986.

Insolvency Act, 1986 a UK Act which sets out the procedures for dealing with insolvent companies (see INSOLVENCY). This involves a number of possible steps: (a) a *voluntary arrangement* under which the company and its creditors agree to a schedule of reduced or delayed debt repayments. If the company continues to make losses, then (b) the company may ask the bankruptcy court to appoint an Administrator to try to reorganize the company and rehabilitate it. If the Administrator is unable to revive the company, then (c) he will put the company into *receivership*, selling company assets to pay off creditors; (d) should the company continue to deteriorate, the Administrator will *wind-up* the company, adopting the rôle of *liquidator* selling off remaining company assets and using the proceeds to pay back creditors, with ORDINARY SHAREHOLDERS receiving any funds that remain.

instalment credit a contractual means of purchasing a product over an extended period of time using a CREDIT facility provided either by a financial institution such as a FINANCE HOUSE, or by the firm selling the product concerned. An initial down payment is usually required followed by monthly fixed payments (including interest charges) over a specified repayment period (e.g. 12 months, 24 months, etc.).

One popular form of instalment credit is a *hire purchase* agreement under which a purchaser takes immediate possession of a product but does not have legal title to that product until all the instalment payments have been made.

See CREDIT CONTROLS, MONETARY POLICY, CONSUMER CREDIT ACT, 1974.

institutional investors the financial institutions that collect SAVINGS and other deposits and invest (see INVESTMENT) long-term in company STOCKS and SHARES, government BONDS, property and overseas securities. In Britain, the main investing institutions are the INSURANCE COMPANIES, PENSION FUNDS, INVESTMENT TRUST COMPANIES and UNIT TRUSTS. In many other countries the commercial banks are also major long-term investors. In most of these countries the lack of an established STOCK EXCHANGE and the availability of private capital from individuals was the main historical reason for their close tie-in with industrial companies.

Institutional investors have grown rapidly in Britain and elsewhere since the 1950s, encouraged both by the favourable tax concessions granted by the government to contractual pension and life insurance schemes, and the opportunities which financial institutions provide to pool risks by investing in a variety of financial securities.

Institutional investors now occupy a prominent position in the FINANCIAL SYSTEM and form the primary conduit for channelling personal savings into industrial and commercial investment, displacing direct investment by individual savers. In Britain institutional investors now own around 60% of the ordinary SHARE CAPITAL of British companies. The collective interests of the institutional investors are represented by the Institutional Investors Committee, which provides a forum for discussion of matters of mutual concern to members and acts on behalf of members in dealings with other bodies and the government.

Institutional Investors Committee the body which represents the collective interests of the PENSION FUNDS, INSURANCE COMPANIES, UNIT TRUSTS and INVESTMENT TRUST COMPANIES in the UK.

insurance a method of protecting a person or firm against financial loss resulting from damage to, or theft of, personal and business assets (general insurance), and death and injury (life and accident insurance). Insurance may be obtained directly from an INSURANCE COMPANY or through an intermediary such as an INSURANCE BROKER/ AGENT. In return for an insurance premium the person or firm obtains insurance cover against financial risks.

The term *assurance* is frequently used interchangeably with that of insurance to describe certain kinds of life insurance.

See RISK AND UNCERTAINTY.

insurance broker/agent a person or firm which acts as an intermediary in bringing together clients seeking INSURANCE cover and INSURANCE COMPANIES offering suitable policies. In some cases the agent may be employed by a particular insurance company to sell insurance policies on its behalf and handle claims, receiving a commission on sales. Alternatively, insurance brokers may act as independent intermediaries who negotiate with a number of insurance companies on behalf of clients. Insurance brokers are regulated by FIMBRA in accordance with various standards of good practice laid down under the FINANCIAL SERVICES ACT, 1986.

insurance company a financial institution that provides a range of INSURANCE policies to protect individuals and businesses against the RISK of financial losses in return for regular payments of PREMIUMS. An insurance company operates by pooling risks amongst a large number of policyholders. From its past claims record, the company actuary can ascertain the probability of a particular event occurring, for example, a fire, and can assess the average financial loss associated with each event. Using this information he attempts to calculate appropriate premiums for policyholders and from the collective pool of premium income to meet outstanding financial claims.

For very large insurance risks an insurance company may resort to *reinsurance*, sharing the insurance premium with other insurers in proportion to the share of potential claim which they are prepared to accept. In addition, many insurance companies offer contractual savings schemes.

Insurance companies use the premiums they receive not only to settle day-to-day claims but also to generate additional income and profit by investing their funds in FINANCIAL SECURITIES (see INSTITUTIONAL INVESTORS). Life insurance business, in particular, because of its long-term contractual nature, is especially conducive to offering long-term investment returns to policyholders as well as the insurance company. *With profit* life insurance policies are now commonplace, as are life insurance policies linked to the provision of MORTGAGE finance for house purchase.

Most insurance companies are members of Lloyd's, a corporation of insurers. Insurance companies in the UK are represented by the Association of British Insurers, which provides a forum for the discussion of matters of general concern to members and acts on behalf of members in dealings with other institutional bodies such as the Institutional Investors Committee and the government. The investment and management of funds by insurance companies is regulated by IMRO and LAUTRO in accordance with various standards of good practice laid down under the Financial Services Act, 1986.

See FINANCIAL SYSTEM.

intangible assets nonphysical assets such as GOODWILL, PATENTS and TRADEMARKS which have a money value. Compare TANGIBLE ASSETS.

intangibles costs and benefits usually associated with an INVESTMENT project that either cannot be quantified, or which can be quantified but cannot easily be valued in money terms. Examples of the former include the scenic effects of projects such as airport runways in rural areas; examples of the latter might include reductions in accident deaths, associated with road building projects which give problems setting a money value per life saved. Such intangibles are important though they cannot easily be incorporated into an investment appraisal. See COST-BENEFIT ANALYSIS.

integration see HORIZONTAL INTEGRATION, VERTICAL INTEGRATION, DIVERSIFICATION, TRADE INTEGRATION.

intellectual property right the legal ownership by a person or business of a COPYRIGHT, DESIGN, PATENT, TRADE MARK attached to a particular product or process which protects the owner against unauthorized copying or imitation. Such property rights are an important element of PRODUCT DIFFERENTIATION and confer temporary MONOPOLY advantages to suppliers.

interbank clearing interest rate the INTEREST RATE at which the COMMERCIAL BANKS in Britain lend short-term funds to one another. The interbank rate of interest influences the BILL-DISCOUNTING RATE at which the Bank of England is prepared to loan money to the DISCOUNT HOUSES. In turn, the interbank rate of interest influences the BASE RATE which is used by commercial banks to calculate rates of interest to be charged to their customers. See also BANK RATE.

interest the charge made for borrowing money in the form of a LOAN. Interest is payable on a number of short-term and long-term borrowing forms including BANK LOANS, MORTGAGES, INSTALMENT CREDIT, LEASING, LOAN STOCK, DEBENTURES, BONDS, TREASURY BILLS and BILLS OF EXCHANGE. Lenders require a NOMINAL INTEREST RATE which compensates them for the effects of INFLATION in reducing the PURCHASING POWER of any sums that they lend, so that the real or EFFECTIVE INTEREST RATE provides an adequate 'reward' to lenders for forgoing current consumption and for the risk of default introduced in lending out money.

In aggregate terms, interest is a source of income and is thus included as part of NATIONAL INCOME. In the THEORY OF SUPPLY interest is a payment for the use of CAPITAL as a FACTOR OF PRODUCTION. See INTEREST RATE.

interest cover an accounting measure of the extent to which a firm's earnings cover INTEREST payments due on LOANS; which expresses profit after tax as a ratio of interest due.

interest rate the particular amount of INTEREST which a household or business borrower is required to pay to a lender for borrowing a particular sum of money to finance spending on CONSUMPTION and INVESTMENT.

The level of interest rates is determined by the forces of demand and supply for finance in the MONEY MARKET. The cheaper the cost of borrowing money, the more money will be demanded by households and businesses. The higher the rate of interest the greater the supply of loanable funds. The 'equilibrium' rate of interest is determined by the intersection of the demand for (D_m), and supply of (S_m), loanable funds – interest rate R in Fig. 89. In theory, the monetary authorities can control the rate of interest by changes in the MONEY SUPPLY. If the money supply is increased from S_m to S_m^1, the effect would be to lower the equilibrium rate of interest from R to R^1, and through the rate of interest the level of total spending (AGGREGATE DEMAND) in the economy. (See MONEY SUPPLY/SPENDING LINKAGES.)

There is some controversy about the interest sensitivity of the demand for money and supply of money schedules. Keynesians (see KEYNESIAN ECONOMICS) would argue that saving is largely a function of the level of income rather than the rate of interest so that the supply of loanable funds is relatively interest-inelastic. Keynesians also argue that investment plans are primarily determined by businessmen's expectations about future levels of economic activity, with the cost of capital being of secondary importance, so that the demand for loanable funds is also relatively interest-inelastic. This means that even quite large changes in interest rates are unlikely to have much effect upon the amounts of money demanded and supplied, and thus upon levels of consumer and investment spending. By contrast, monetarists (see MONETARISM) would argue that both the supply of and demand for loanable funds are relatively interest-elastic so that only small changes in interest rates can have a large effect on consumer and investment spending.

A number of key short-term interest rates may be identified in the UK, including the INTERBANK CLEARING INTEREST RATE (at which the COMMERCIAL BANKS lend short-term sterling funds to one another); BILL-DISCOUNTING INTEREST RATE (at which the CENTRAL BANK (Bank of England) is prepared to lend money to the DISCOUNT HOUSES in its capacity as 'lender of last resort'); BASE RATE (the 'floor' rate which is used by the commercial banks as the basis for charging interest on loans and overdrafts to their customers). These rates of interest (and others) are highly interrelated and subject to manipulation by the Bank of England as part of its application of MONETARY POLICY. Formerly, base rates, etc. were linked directly to 'bank rate', but at the present time the authorities seek to control the level of interest rates more indirectly by 'open market operations', buying or selling monetary instruments such as Treasury Bills to reduce or increase the availability of loanable funds.

The rate of interest or COST OF CAPITAL is an important factor in relation to companies' investment decisions (see INVESTMENT APPRAISAL). The rate of interest charged for any particular transaction will depend on such considerations as the purpose and duration of the loan, the amount of money borrowed, the COLLATERAL SECURITY offered (if any), and the creditworthiness of the borrower, all factors influencing the degree of perceived 'risk' involved in making the loan as seen by the lender.

In a situation of INFLATION where prices are rising rapidly, it is important to distinguish between the NOMINAL INTEREST RATE stipulated in a LOAN contract and the 'real' or EFFECTIVE INTEREST RATE which allows for the effects of inflation in reducing the REAL VALUE or PURCHASING POWER of the interest received (see REAL INTEREST RATE).

See MONEY DEMAND SCHEDULE, MONEY SUPPLY SCHEDULE, MARGINAL EFFICIENCY OF CAPITAL/INVESTMENT, APR, LIBOR.

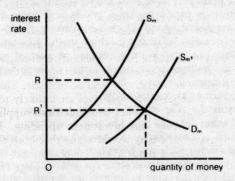

Fig. 89. **Interest rate**. See entry.

interest rate sensitivity of investment see MARGINAL EFFICIENCY OF CAPITAL/INVESTMENT, INTEREST RATE.

interest rate swap see SWAP.

interest yield the INTEREST paid on a BOND expressed as a fraction of the current market price of the bond. For example, a bond offering an interest payment of £5 per year and having a current market price of £50 would have flat YIELD of 10%.

interfirm conduct an element of MARKET CONDUCT that denotes the ways in which firms interact in the market. Two main patterns of behaviour may be identified:

(a) independent behaviour. Each firm formulates its competitive strategy with respect to price, advertising, etc., unilaterally without considering the actions of other firms. This pattern of behaviour is usually associated with markets consisting of a large number of small suppliers each of which contributes an insignificant proportion of total market supply (see PERFECT COMPETITION; MONOPOLISTIC COMPETITION).

(b) interdependent behaviour. Firms recognize that they are MUTUALLY INTERDEPENDENT (i.e., that their own actions directly affect the position of other firms) and thus they explicitly take into account the likely effects of their own competitive strategies on other firms).

Interdependency is associated with an OLIGOPOLY, where the bulk of market supply is in the hands of a few large firms, often resulting in COLLUSION as a means of coordinating their pricing, production and selling policies.

intermediate area a moderately DEPRESSED AREA scheduled under UK REGIONAL POLICY as in need of industrial regeneration. Firms prepared to undertake new investment in such areas may be eligible for REGIONAL SELECTIVE ASSISTANCE. See DEVELOPMENT AREA.

intermediate products the goods and services that are used as FACTOR INPUTS by firms in producing other goods or services. For example, steel is an intermediate good which has a variety of end-uses, including motor car bodies, washing machine shells, nuts and bolts, etc.

Intermediate products are not counted as part of gross national product in the NATIONAL INCOME ACCOUNTS where final goods and services are measured.

See FINAL PRODUCTS, VALUE ADDED.

intermediation the rôle of the financial institutions in channelling SAVINGS and other deposits by LENDERS to BORROWERS. Financial intermediaries such as COMMERCIAL BANKS and BUILDING SOCIETIES accept deposits from individuals and businesses and use these funds to make LOANS to creditworthy customers. An intermediary's profit is the difference between INTEREST RATES paid for deposits and interest rates on loans. See FINANCIAL SYSTEM, DISINTERMEDIATION.

internal balance a situation where the economy is operating at FULL EMPLOYMENT and the general level of prices is constant (PRICE STABILITY). The achievement of full employment and price stability are two important macroeconomic objectives of the government. In practice, it is difficult to secure both objectives simultaneously (see PHILLIPS CURVE).

Compare EXTERNAL BALANCE. See also DEMAND MANAGEMENT, INTERNAL-EXTERNAL BALANCE MODEL, MACROECONOMIC POLICY.

internal economies of scale the reduction in the individual firm's AVERAGE COSTS of production as OUTPUT increases. Emphasis is often placed on technical economies such as using plant at a greater capacity to reduce unit costs. A larger plant may facilitate a greater division of labour. However, economies within the marketing, managerial and financial spheres may be similarly obtained.

Compare EXTERNAL ECONOMIES OF SCALE. See ECONOMIES OF SCALE, DISECONOMIES OF SCALE.

internal-external balance model a theoretical construct that seeks to integrate the achievement of the MACROECONOMIC POLICY objectives of FULL EMPLOYMENT and PRICE STABILITY (internal balance) and BALANCE-OF-PAYMENTS EQUILIBRIUM (external balance).

A brief illustration of the model is given in Fig. 90a. The vertical axis shows the ratio of international prices to domestic prices. This

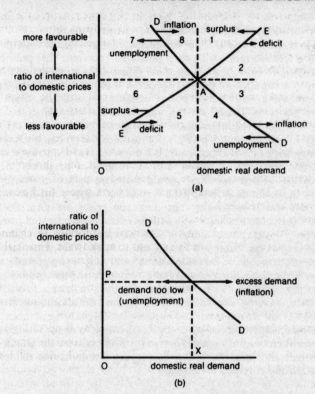

Fig. 90. **Internal-external balance model.** (a) See entry. (b) Given the ratio of international to domestic prices (P), domestic demand must be at level X to secure internal balance. If it is not, the result is unemployment or inflation.

is an index of the country's foreign competitive position: the higher one moves up the scale, the larger are exports and the smaller are imports. On the horizontal axis is domestic real demand, which increases from left to right. The two curves shown in the figure represent, respectively external balance (EE) and internal balance (DD). The EE curve has a positive slope, indicating that the more unfavourable the international price ratio becomes, the lower domestic real demand must be to maintain balance-of-payments equilibrium. Positions to the left and above the curve represent payments surplus; to the right and below, deficit. The DD curve has a negative slope indicating that the more unfavourable the international price ratio becomes, the higher domestic real demand must be to maintain full employment. Positions to the right and above the curve represent price inflation; to the left and below, unemployment.

Where the EE and DD curves intersect (point A), the country is in general equilibrium. All other positions represent disequilibrium. However, from only a few of these disequilibrium positions can the country attain the two policy objectives of internal and external equilibrium using just a single policy variable – specifically, from only those positions located on the horizontal and vertical dotted lines drawn through the intersection. In the situations shown by the horizontal line to the right of point A, for instance, the ratio of international to domestic prices is appropriate, but domestic real demand is too high resulting in both inflation and a balance-of-payments deficit. DEFLATION of demand alone would therefore suffice to realize both goals. In situations shown by the vertical line below point A, domestic real demand is just right, but domestic prices are uncompetitive resulting in both a balance-of-payments deficit and unemployment. A currency DEVALUATION alone would therefore suffice to realize both goals. However, these are special cases. In all other situations both domestic demand and the international price ratio are inappropriate. As a result, the two policy objectives are in conflict, and the separate policy variables must be combined to be effective. In zones 1 and 2, for instance, varying combinations of demand-deflation and currency REVALUATION are required, and in zones 3 and 4, varying combinations of demand-deflation and currency devaluation. In zones 5 and 6, varying combinations of demand REFLATION and currency devaluation are required; and in zones 7 and 8, varying combinations of demand reflation and currency revaluation.

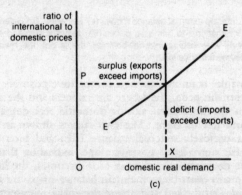

Fig. 90. **Internal-external balance model.** (c) Given the level of domestic demand (X), the ratio of international to domestic prices must be at level P to secure external balance. If it is not, the result is a surplus or deficit balance of payments.

internal financing the ability to finance a firm's growth from retained earnings. A company's NET PROFIT can be paid out in DIVIDENDS or retained for internal financing or some mixture of these two. Generally, shareholders look for some immediate income in the form of dividends and some growth in the capital value of their shares (which depends on growth). By paying out more dividends, growth is slowed. Achieving the optimum solution between two conflicting objectives is an important area of study in managerial finance.

See COST OF CAPITAL, RESERVES.

internalization the combining in one firm of two or more related activities, as opposed to these activities being conducted separately in different firms and then being synchronized through arms-length MARKET transactions. Economic theory postulates that a PROFIT-MAXIMIZING firm will internalize a sequence of activities if the costs of doing so are lower than transacting the same activities through the market.

The most common example of internalization is that of VERTICAL INTEGRATION, where a series of vertically-related activities are combined. Cost advantages accruing through vertical internalization include reduced production costs by linking together successive processes of manufacture (e.g., iron and steel mills, to avoid reheating), and the avoidance of TRANSACTION COSTS incurred in imperfect markets (e.g., monopoly surcharges imposed by input suppliers, unreliable sources of supply, and restrictions on sales outlets).

The concept of internalization is also relevant to HORIZONTAL INTEGRATION by multiplant domestic firms and MULTINATIONAL COMPANIES. In the case of multinational firms the establishment of production plants in overseas markets, instead of servicing those markets by direct exporting, occurs because of the transaction costs of market imperfections such as TARIFFS, QUOTAS and exchange rate restrictions and the fact that monopolistic advantages (a patented product, know-how or a unique product) can be better exploited and protected by direct control.

The principle of internalization is also relevant to the funding of capital investment programmes by diversified firms. Such conglomerates are able to recycle funds from some of their operating divisions to headquarters, which are then reallocated to other operating divisions. This avoids the need for these divisions to bear the costs of raising funds externally through the stock exchange.

See TRANSFER PRICE.

internal rate of return see DISCOUNTED CASH FLOW.

International Bank for Reconstruction and Development see WORLD BANK.

international commodity agreement an agreement that attempts to stabilize the prices of some internationally-traded COMMODITIES such as cocoa and tin, with the objective of stabilizing foreign exchange earnings and producers' incomes, primarily in the DEVELOPING COUNTRIES. Although international commodity agreements are established to further the interests of producing countries, they may also benefit consumers by removing the uncertainties and inconveniences associated with erratic price movements.

International commodity agreements vary in format but one typical approach involves the establishment of an 'official' price for the commodity, agreed on by member countries, which is then maintained over a period of time by the use of a BUFFER STOCK mechanism: surplus output is bought in if market supply exceeds demand at the official price and sold off if demand exceeds market supply.

International commodity agreements have been promoted by the UNITED NATIONS CONFERENCE ON TRADE AND DEVELOPMENT as a means of enhancing the economic interests of the developing countries (see NEW INTERNATIONAL ECONOMIC ORDER), but there are often serious difficulties encountered in ensuring their viability. For example, disagreements can occur between member countries on what particular official prices to set arising out of differences in the degree of importance of the commodity to individual members' economies; and often the temptation is to set prices above market-determined rates, which places a financial strain on the buffer stock which may then eventually run out of money.

international competitiveness the ability of a country to compete successfully against other countries in INTERNATIONAL TRADE. Countries which are successful will maintain or increase their share of world exports and, by the same token, limit the extent of IMPORT PENETRATION into their domestic economies.

International competitiveness is reflected in two things: (a) price competitiveness; it is important that domestic suppliers are efficient and cost-effective and that governments can control domestic rates of INFLATION and maintain 'realistic' EXCHANGE RATES for their currencies. (b) nonprice competitiveness; it is equally important that domestic suppliers offer export customers attractive new products, improve the quality and performance of their products, meet delivery dates, etc.

See TERMS OF TRADE.

international debt the money owed to the international community by borrowing countries. In the main, debtor countries consist of DEVELOPING COUNTRIES who have borrowed foreign exchange from the WORLD BANK, the governments of advanced countries and private banks to finance their long-term ECONOMIC DEVELOPMENT programmes, and from the INTERNATIONAL MONETARY FUND to cover balance of payments deficits.

The problem of 'debt servicing' (interest charges and repayment of loans) has been especially acute for a number of poorer countries who, in recent years, because of a decline in their foreign exchange earnings, have been forced to renege on, or reschedule, their foreign debts. In 1995, outstanding loans to the developing countries totalled around $1800 billion and interest payments on this debt amounted to some $232 billion.

See ECONOMIC AID.

International Development Association see WORLD BANK.

International Finance Corporation see WORLD BANK.

international Fisher effect a situation where NOMINAL INTEREST RATE differentials between countries reflect anticipated rates of change in the EXCHANGE RATE of their currencies.

For example, if British investors anticipate that the US dollar will appreciate by, say, 5% per annum against sterling, then in order to offset the expected change in parity between the two countries, they would be prepared to accept an interest rate approximately 5% per annum less on a dollar-denominated financial security than that which could be expected on an equivalent investment denominated in sterling. From a borrower's viewpoint, when the international Fisher effect holds, the cost of equivalent loans in alternative currencies will be the same, regardless of the rate of interest.

The International Fisher effect can be contrasted with the *domestic Fisher effect* where nominal interest rates reflect the anticipated real rate of interest and the anticipated rate of change in prices (INFLATION). The international equivalent of inflation is therefore changing exchange rates.

See COVERED INTEREST ARBITRAGE.

International Labour Organization (ILO) a special agency of the UNITED NATIONS, whose objective is to promote an improvement in living standards and working conditions throughout the world, thereby facilitating social justice as a basis for securing world peace.

The functions of the ILO encompass all aspects of social and economic conditions affecting employment throughout the world. It promotes national labour standards and work practices, but only in an advisory capacity, as it has no legislative powers. It provides technical assistance in manpower training, social policy and administration, and encourages cooperation between labour groups. The ILO is also concerned with the collection and dissemination of international labour statistics and undertakes research on a variety of labour-related problems.

international liquidity or **international money** monetary assets that are generally acceptable as a means of financing INTERNATIONAL TRADE and/or as an INTERNATIONAL RESERVE asset with which to finance BALANCE-OF-PAYMENTS deficits. For example, the US DOLLAR is used as the NUMERAIRE of the oil trade and also serves as an important reserve asset; the SPECIAL DRAWING RIGHT is used only as a reserve asset.

International Monetary Fund (IMF) a multinational institution set up in 1947 (following the Bretton Woods Conference, 1944) to supervise the operation of a new international monetary regime – the 'ADJUSTABLE-PEG' EXCHANGE RATE SYSTEM. The Fund seeks to maintain co-operative and orderly currency arrangements between member countries with the aim of promoting increased INTERNATIONAL TRADE and BALANCE-OF-PAYMENTS EQUILIBRIUM. The Fund is active in two main areas:

(a) EXCHANGE RATES. Down to 1971 countries established FIXED EXCHANGE-RATES for their currencies which provided pivotal values for concluding trade transactions. A country, provided it first obtained the approval of the Fund, could alter its exchange rate, adjusting the rate upwards (REVALUATION) or downwards (DEVALUATION) to a new fixed level to correct a FUNDAMENTAL DISEQUILIBRIUM in its balance of payments – a situation of either chronic payments surplus or deficit. This procedure ensured that currency realignments were decided by multilateral agreement rather than initiated as a unilateral act. In the early 1970s, however, with a continued weakening of the US dollar, the pivotal currency in the Fund's operations, and the onset of a world recession, a large number of currencies were 'floated' to provide a greater degree of exchange rate flexibility (see FLOATING EXCHANGE RATE SYSTEM). Most major currencies have continued to float, although fixed exchange rate arrangements have been reintroduced on a limited basis (see EUROPEAN MONETARY SYSTEM). This has resulted in the Fund losing formal control over exchange rate movements, but member countries are still obligated to abide by certain 'rules of good conduct' laid down by the Fund, avoiding in particular EXCHANGE CONTROLS and BEGGAR-MY-NEIGHBOUR tactics.

(b) INTERNATIONAL LIQUIDITY. The Fund's resources consist of a pool of currencies and INTERNATIONAL RESERVE assets (excluding GOLD) subscribed by its members according to their allocated 'quotas'. Each country pays 75% of its quota in its own currency and 25% in international reserve assets. Countries are given *borrowing* or *drawing rights* with the Fund which they can use, together with their own nationally-held international reserves, to finance a balance-of-payments deficit.

Under the Fund's ordinary drawing-right facilities members with balance of payments difficulties may 'draw' (i.e., purchase foreign currencies from the Fund with their own currencies) up to 125% of their quota. The first 25% (the 'reserve tranche') may be drawn on demand; the remaining 100% is divided up into four 'credit tranches' of 25% each, and drawings here are 'conditional' on members agreeing with the Fund a programme of measures (for example,

DEFLATION, DEVALUATION) for removing their payments deficit. Members are required to repay their drawings over a three to five year period.

In 1970 the Fund created a new international reserve asset, the SPECIAL DRAWING RIGHT (SDR) to augment the supply of international liquidity, and it has also provided additional borrowing facilities for its poorer members. See also DOMESTIC CREDIT EXPANSION.

international monetary system a system for promoting INTERNATIONAL TRADE and SPECIALIZATION, while at the same time ensuring long-run individual BALANCE-OF-PAYMENTS EQUILIBRIUM. To be effective an international monetary system must be able to: (a) provide a system of EXCHANGE RATES between national currencies, (b) provide an ADJUSTMENT MECHANISM capable of removing payments imbalances, (c) provide a quantum of INTERNATIONAL RESERVES to finance payments deficits. Various international monetary systems have been tried, including the GOLD STANDARD and, currently, the INTERNATIONAL MONETARY FUND system.

See FIXED EXCHANGE-RATE SYSTEM, FLOATING EXCHANGE-RATE SYSTEM, EUROPEAN MONETARY SYSTEM.

international money see INTERNATIONAL LIQUIDITY, INTERNATIONAL RESERVES.

international reserves or **foreign exchange reserves** monetary assets that are used to settle BALANCE-OF-PAYMENTS deficits between countries. International reserves are made up of GOLD, FOREIGN EXCHANGE, INTERNATIONAL MONETARY FUND Drawing Rights, and SPECIAL DRAWING RIGHTS (SDRs). As Fig. 91 shows, gold and foreign exchange (particularly the US dollar) are the most important reserve assets. See EUROPEAN CURRENCY UNIT.

Reserve assets	Percentage of international reserves
Gold	48
Foreign exchange	47
Reserve position in International Monetary Fund	3
Special drawing rights	2

Fig. 91. **International reserves**. International reserves for 1995.

International Securities Regulatory Organization see STOCK EXCHANGE.

International Standards Organization (SIO) an international organization established to promote common technical standards in all spheres of operations including science and commerce.

international trade the EXCHANGE of goods and services between countries through EXPORTS and IMPORTS. Such cross-frontier trade is generally based on the COMPARATIVE ADVANTAGES which countries have in supplying particular products, providing the basis of an international division of labour (location of production).

Inter-country variations in comparative advantage are reflected both in terms of their differential cost structures (i.e. price competitiveness) and different skill levels (i.e. product differentiation competitiveness). These, in turn, are determined in large measure by the country's basic factor endowments (natural resources, labour and capital) and degree of economic maturity (level of per capita income, general cost and price levels, scientific and technical skills, etc.). Resource availability and skills indicate the product range which a country is technically capable of supplying, while *relative* cost, price and product differentiation factors dictate which of these products it is economically appropriate for the country to produce, i.e. those products in which it has a comparative advantage over other countries. The way countries have evolved as political states takes no account of their economic strengths and weaknesses. Through international trade, countries can capitalize on their economic strengths, thereby improving their real living standards.

International trade can bring both consumption and production gains to a country. Such trade enables countries to consume some goods and services more cheaply by importing them, and also to obtain some resources and products from other countries which would otherwise be totally unavailable because domestic producers are unable to supply them (for example, a scarce raw material or high-technology product). International trade promotes productive efficiency by encouraging a reallocation of resources away from areas of the economy best served by imports into industries where the country itself has a comparative advantage over trade partners.

Consideration of the benefits of international trade suggests that the optimization of such benefits is best achieved by conditions of FREE TRADE (i.e. the absence of restrictions on trade such as TARIFFS and QUOTAS), a view given operational validity by the international community by the establishment of the GENERAL AGREEMENT ON TARIFFS AND TRADE and the formation of various regional FREE TRADE AREAS. In practice, however, the benefits of international trade are often unequally divided between countries, and this inevitably tends to produce situations where national self-interest is put before international obligations, resulting in the unilateral imposition of protectionist measures (see PROTECTIONISM). In addition, the manner in which world trading patterns have developed has not benefited certain DEVELOPING COUNTRIES who have specialized in a narrow range of commodities for which world demand has grown slowly.

A country's international trade dealings affect its BALANCE OF PAYMENTS insofar as exports earn foreign exchange whilst imports require financing in terms of foreign exchange. The FOREIGN EXCHANGE MARKET acts as a conduit for the purchase and sale of foreign currency used to finance trade. A country's international trade performance will affect the value of its domestic currency when traded against other countries' currencies, that is, its EXCHANGE RATE.

See GAINS FROM TRADE, THEORY OF INTERNATIONAL TRADE, TRADE INTEGRATION, COUNTERTRADE, DUMPING.

interpersonal comparison see WELFARE ECONOMICS.

interpolate see EXTRAPOLATE.

intertemporal substitution the substitution of present for future production and consumption, and vice versa. For example, an economy which consumes a large proportion of its NATIONAL INCOME and saves and invests only a small proportion will tend, as a consequence, to experience slower ECONOMIC GROWTH and smaller consumption in future years than an economy which consumes a low proportion of its national income and saves and invests a high proportion. These trade-offs reflect the TIME PREFERENCE of consumers for current as opposed to future consumption.

intra-industry specialization a situation where different firms specialize in particular products within the *same* industry (see SPECIALIZATION). For example, in the textile industry, one firm may specialize in the production of expensive mohair suits, another in cheap casual wear. Specialization enables firms both to exploit ECONOMIES OF SCALE in production, thereby lowering supply costs, and to accommodate consumers' demands for greater product variety. See INTRA-INDUSTRY TRADE.

intra-industry trade a situation where firms operating in the *same* industry but in *different* countries SPECIALIZE in particular products and engage in INTERNATIONAL TRADE. For example, in the textile industry a firm in the UK may specialize in the production and EXPORT of expensive mohair suits, while another firm in Taiwan may specialize in the production and export of cheap casual wear. Thus, Britain may export textile products to Taiwan, and by the same token import textiles from Taiwan.

See PREFERENCE-SIMILARITY THEORY (OF INTERNATIONAL TRADE), INTRA-INDUSTRY SPECIALIZATION.

introduction a method of raising new SHARE CAPITAL by issuing company shares to STOCKBROKERS and MARKET MAKERS at an agreed price rather than to the general public. See SHARE ISSUE.

invention the creation of new production techniques and processes and new products which can be developed into usable processes and products through INNOVATION. Invention is an important means for a firm to improve its competitive position over rival suppliers by enabling it to lower supply costs and prices to consumers and to provide consumers with improved products. These benefits also improve overall MARKET PERFORMANCE. Certain kinds of MARKET STRUCTURE may be more conducive to invention insofar as they offer better incentives and resources for undertaking RESEARCH AND DEVELOPMENT (see MONOPOLY for further discussion).

In a more general way, invention can add to the growth of national income and output (see ECONOMIC GROWTH) by the qualitative improvement of a country's CAPITAL STOCK as investment in new technologies improves PRODUCTIVITY.

See TECHNOLOGICAL PROGRESSIVENESS, PATENT.

inventory the STOCKS of finished goods, WORK-IN-PROGRESS and raw materials held by businesses. See INVENTORY INVESTMENT.

inventory investment the INVESTMENT in raw materials, WORK-IN-PROGRESS, and finished STOCK. In contrast to FIXED INVESTMENT, inventories are constantly being 'turned over' as the production cycle repeats itself, with raw materials being purchased, converted first into work-in-progress, then finished goods, then finally being sold.

The level of inventory investment made by a firm will depend upon its forecasts about future demand and its resulting output plans, and the amount of stock it needs to allow for delivery delays on raw materials and production delays in serving customers, with appropriate buffer stocks to cover unforeseen contingencies. A firm can minimize these buffer stocks by negotiating JUST-IN-TIME delivery arrangements with suppliers.

Frequently a firm finds that actual levels of demand differ from its forecasts, so that demand is less than expected and the firm finds that stocks of unsold goods build up (unintended inventory investment); or that demand exceeds expectations so that stocks run down (unintended inventory disinvestment). Such inventory investment and disinvestment tends to occur with downturns and upturns in the BUSINESS CYCLE.

In aggregate terms the rate at which *all* firms accumulate and run down their stocks influences the level of economic activity. The increase and decrease in stocks operates on the same ACCELERATOR principle as fixed investment, so that widespread changes in business confidence or EXPECTATIONS about future levels of demand influence current stockbuilding decisions which, in turn, have a magnified influence on levels of output and employment through the MULTIPLIER effect.

investment 1. expenditure on the purchase of FINANCIAL SECURITIES such as STOCKS and SHARES. Also called *financial investment*. PORTFOLIO investment is undertaken by persons, firms and financial institutions in the expectation of earning a return in the form of INTEREST or DIVIDENDS, or an appreciation in the capital value of the securities. **2**. capital expenditure on the purchase of physical ASSETS such as plant, machinery and equipment (FIXED INVESTMENT) and STOCKS (INVEN-

TORY INVESTMENT), i.e., *physical* or *real investment*. In economic analysis, the term investment relates specifically to physical investment. Physical investment creates *new* assets thereby adding to the country's productive capacity, whereas financial investment only transfers the ownership of *existing* assets from one person or institution to another.

Investment requires that an amount of current CONSUMPTION is foregone (i.e., saved, see SAVINGS) so as to release the resources to finance it. Investment expenditure is a component of AGGREGATE DEMAND and an INJECTION into the CIRCULAR FLOW OF NATIONAL INCOME. In NATIONAL INCOME analysis, investment in the provision of SOCIAL PRODUCTS such as roads, hospitals and schools undertaken by the government is counted as part of GOVERNMENT EXPENDITURE; thus, investment expenditure is normally defined as consisting only of private sector investment spending.

Investment can be split up into gross and net investment: (a) gross investment is the total amount of investment that is undertaken in an economy over a specified time period (usually one year); (b) net investment is gross investment less replacement investment or CAPITAL CONSUMPTION, i.e., investment which is necessary to replace that part of the economy's existing capital stock which is used up in producing this year's output. (See DEPRECIATION (2).)

The amount of fixed investment undertaken is dependent on a number of factors other than capital consumption considerations. In national income analysis, the MARGINAL EFFICIENCY OF CAPITAL/ INVESTMENT and the INTEREST RATE are important determinants of the level of investment.

The marginal efficiency of capital/investment itself is dependent upon business confidence and expectations about future demand levels and therefore plant utilization. The volatility of business expectations in the short run means that planned levels of fixed investment can vary significantly over time, leading to large changes in the demand for capital goods (see ACCELERATOR), that is, large fluctuations in the investment component of aggregate demand leading to larger fluctuations in output and employment through the MULTIPLIER effect (see BUSINESS CYCLE).

Similar considerations apply to inventory investment with stock levels being increased or decreased over time with changing business expectations.

The long-term significance of investment lies in the contribution it makes to economic prosperity. Building new factories, adding new machinery and equipment, and investing in new techniques and products enables industry to supply a greater quantity of more sophisticated products and services to the consuming public, while similar investments in the provision of social capital (schools, health, etc.) contribute vitally to the up-grading of general living standards.

At the micro-level a firm's investment decisions depend upon the profitability or cash flow implications of particular investment projects (see DISCOUNTED CASH FLOW) and are considered as part of its CAPITAL BUDGETING procedures.

Compare DISINVESTMENT. See ECONOMIC GROWTH, CAPITAL ACCUMULATION, CAPITAL DEEPENING, CAPITAL GOODS, CAPITAL STOCK, CAPITAL WIDENING, INVESTMENT SCHEDULE, AUTONOMOUS INVESTMENT, INDUCED INVESTMENT, GROSS DOMESTIC-FIXED CAPITAL FORMATION, FOREIGN INVESTMENT, INVESTMENT INCENTIVES, INVESTMENT APPRAISAL, GREENFIELD INVESTMENT, RISK PREMIUM.

investment appraisal the process of evaluating the desirability of INVESTMENT proposals covering such things as the replacement of worn-out plant and machinery, the establishment of a new factory, the takeover of another company, new product development, a sales promotion campaign, a new road or hospital.

Generally the desirability of a private sector investment will be considered in terms of the PROFIT it might yield, and managers will prefer those investments which promise the largest profit. Alternatively, managers could estimate the CASH FLOWS associated with a project and award priority to projects which promise the best contribution towards future cash flows. There are several techniques which can be used to assess investment opportunities in terms of cash flow, including the PAYBACK PERIOD method and the DISCOUNTED CASH FLOW METHOD. Public sector investment projects can also be assessed in terms of their cash flows, though for such projects the broader SOCIAL COSTS, such as any POLLUTION caused, need to be considered as well as private costs borne by the government (see COST-BENEFIT ANALYSIS).

In making investment decisions, managers will undertake an investment which promises a rate of return greater than the COST OF CAPITAL that is needed to finance it. This involves estimating the cash outflows and inflows associated with an investment and allowing for the different timing of these flows by converting them into their equivalent present values using an appropriate DISCOUNT RATE.

All investment projects are concerned with future costs/cash flows and future revenues/cash inflows and thus there is inevitably some uncertainty about whether cash flows will turn out to be as estimated at the time a project is assessed (see RISK AND UNCERTAINTY).

investment bank a bank whose particular function is the provision of long-term equity and loan finance for industrial companies. See EUROPEAN INVESTMENT BANK.

investment centre an organizational sub-unit of a firm which is fully independent with full control over its costs and revenues (that is, a PROFIT CENTRE) but which also has the responsibility for raising capital and for long-term investment.

investment cycle see ACCELERATOR.

investment demand curve see MARGINAL EFFICIENCY OF CAPITAL/
INVESTMENT.

investment incentives inducements offered by the government or
local authorities to encourage capital INVESTMENT by the PRIVATE SEC-
TOR either generally or in a specific area. Government inducements
may take the form of capital grants towards the cost of equipment
or tax reliefs on any profits earned. Local authority inducements
usually take the form of reductions or exemptions from local taxes
and organizing the local infrastructure for the convenience of potential investors. The rationale for such incentives depends primarily
upon the government's objectives. It may want to reduce UNEMPLOY-
MENT, in which case investment through the MULTIPLIER effect will
help, or it may want to give certain DEVELOPMENT AREAS additional
help in tackling local problems of unemployment or urban
renewal.

See REGIONAL POLICY, INDUSTRIAL POLICY.

Investment Management Regulatory Organization (IMRO) a
body responsible for regulating firms involved in the management
and trusteeship of collective investment schemes and pension funds.

See SELF-REGULATORY ORGANIZATION.

investment schedule a schedule that depicts the relationship between
INVESTMENT and the level of NATIONAL INCOME. In the short and
medium term the investment schedule would tend to have a positive
slope and a positive intercept with the vertical axis as indicated by
the solid line in Fig. 92 insofar as some investment (*Autonomous investment*) will take place even when national income is zero.

As shown in Fig. 92, the investment schedule is made up of a
number of elements: (a) *Autonomous* investment which is related to
non-income factors such as technological change and cost-cutting
will be undertaken irrespective of the level of income.

(b) *Replacement* investment which is required to maintain the economy's existing capital stock and which tends to vary in line with
changes in levels of national income insofar as a greater amount (in
absolute terms) of replacement investment is required to maintain
the economy's existing capital stock as national income and output
rises, viz:

	£	£
national income	1,000	2,000
capital stock	100	200
replacement investment	10	20

(c) *Induced* investment which takes place as rising demand puts
pressure on existing capacity and raises profitability, thereby encouraging businesses to invest more. Thus, the more rapid the rate of

growth of national income, the higher the level of induced investment.

See ACCELERATOR, EQUILIBRIUM LEVEL OF NATIONAL INCOME.

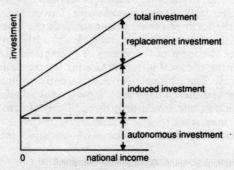

Fig. 92. **Investment schedule**. See entry.

investment trust company a financial institution which issues its own shares to the investing public and which specializes in investment in FINANCIAL SECURITIES, mainly UK and overseas corporate stocks and shares and government fixed-interest securities. Investment trust company shares themselves are bought and sold on the STOCK EXCHANGE.

They tend to be attractive to smaller investors who wish to secure a wider spread of risk than they could achieve for themselves by direct investment in a limited number of securities, or who require professional management of their investments.

Investment trust companies in the UK are represented by the Association of Investment Trust Companies (AITC), which acts on behalf of members in dealings with other institutional bodies such as the Institutional Investors Committee and the government. The investment and management of funds by investment trust companies is regulated by IMRO in accordance with various standards of good practice laid down under the FINANCIAL SERVICES ACT, 1986.

See INSTITUTIONAL INVESTORS, FINANCIAL SYSTEM.

Investors in Industry see THREE I'S.

invisible balance a statement of a country's trade in SERVICES (invisibles) with the rest of the world over a particular period of time. The term 'invisible balance' specifically excludes trade in GOODS (visibles) and concentrates on the foreign currency earnings and payments associated with banking, insurance, tourism, together with interest and profits on foreign investments. Unlike visible transactions (which can be seen and recorded by a country's customs authorities as they cross national frontiers) invisible receipts and payments are recorded from data supplied by companies and financial institutions to a country's central bank.

See BALANCE OF PAYMENTS.

invisible export and import any service such as banking, insurance and tourism, which cannot be seen and recorded as it crosses boundaries between countries. Invisible exports and imports, together with VISIBLE EXPORTS AND IMPORTS make up the CURRENT ACCOUNT of a country's BALANCE OF PAYMENTS.

See EXPORT, IMPORT.

invisible hand a term devised by Adam SMITH to denote the way in which the market mechanism (PRICE SYSTEM) is capable of coordinating the independent decisions of buyers and sellers without anyone being consciously involved in the process. As the automatic equilibrating mechanism of the competitive market, Smith held that the 'invisible hand' maximizes individual welfare and economic efficiency. See PRIVATE-ENTERPRISE ECONOMY.

invoice a document sent by a supplier to a customer that itemizes the products supplied to the customer, their prices, and the total amount of money owed by the customer for these products. An invoice is usually sent after the products have been shipped with their associated DELIVERY NOTE, and serves to inform the customer that payment is required.

See STATEMENT OF ACCOUNT.

involuntary saving see FORCED SAVING.

involuntary unemployment UNEMPLOYMENT which is due to workers being unable to find paid jobs even though they are prepared to work at current wage rates because there are insufficient jobs available due to recession, or because they do not have the necessary skills to perform available work.

Contrast VOLUNTARY UNEMPLOYMENT. See SUPPLY-SIDE ECONOMICS.

irredeemable financial security or **undated security** a financial security such as a PREFERENCE SHARE or CONSOL that is issued for an indefinite period of time and is never repayable.

Contrast REDEEMABLE FINANCIAL SECURITY.

irregular variations see TIME-SERIES ANALYSIS.

I-S (investment-saving) schedule a schedule displaying the combinations of levels of NATIONAL INCOME and INTEREST RATE where the equilibrium condition for the real economy (INVESTMENT = SAVINGS) holds (see EQUILIBRIUM LEVEL OF NATIONAL INCOME).

As shown in Fig. 93, the I.S. schedule is downward-sloping: a lower rate of interest stimulates a higher volume of investment (see MARGINAL EFFICIENCY OF CAPITAL/INVESTMENT) which in turn generates a higher level of output and income through a MULTIPLIER process. However, a higher volume of investment requires a higher volume of saving to keep the real economy in equilibrium (S = I). A higher volume of saving will only be forthcoming at a higher level of income; therefore a lower rate of interest requires a higher equilibrium level of income.

The I.S. schedule interacts with the L.M. SCHEDULE in determining a general equilibrium position for the economy as a whole.

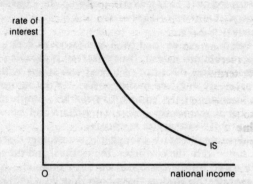

Fig. 93. I.S. (investment saving) schedule. See entry.

I.S./L.M. model a theoretical construct that integrates the real, I.S. (investment-saving), and the monetary, L.M. (demand for, and supply of money), sides of the economy simultaneously to present a determinate general equilibrium position for the economy as a whole.

In the model, SAVING is a function of the level of NATIONAL INCOME and INVESTMENT is a function of the INTEREST RATE and the MARGINAL EFFICIENCY OF CAPITAL/INVESTMENT. The I.S. SCHEDULE shows the combinations of levels of national income and rates of interest where the equilibrium condition for the real economy I = S holds (see EQUILIBRIUM LEVEL OF NATIONAL INCOME).

The demand for money L is a function of the level of national income (TRANSACTIONS DEMAND) and the rate of interest (SPECULATIVE DEMAND). The MONEY SUPPLY, M, is given exogenously. The L.M. SCHEDULE shows the combinations of levels of national income and rates of interest where the equilibrium condition for the monetary economy L = M holds (see RATE OF INTEREST).

As shown in Fig. 94a (overleaf), the I.S. schedule interacts with the L.M. schedule to determine a general equilibrium position, Y_c, for the economy as a whole.

The I.S./L.M. model can be used to illustrate how FISCAL POLICY and MONETARY POLICY can be employed to alter the level of national income. If the authorities wish to increase national income they can, for example, increase the money supply. The increase in the money supply lowers the interest rate. The fall in the rate of interest, in turn, increases the volume of investment (see MARGINAL EFFICIENCY OF CAPITAL/INVESTMENT) which then, via MULTIPLIER effects serves to increase the level of national income. In terms of the I.S./L.M. model depicted in Fig. 94b, the increase in the money supply shifts the L.M. schedule from LM_1 to LM_2, lowering the interest rates from r_1 to r_2 and bringing about an increase in national income from Y_1 to Y_2.

Alternatively, the authorities could increase national income by, for example, increasing government investment, this increase in investment serving to raise the level of national income via multiplier effects. In terms of the I.S./L.M. model depicted in Fig. 94c, the increase in investment shifts the I.S. schedule from IS_1 to IS_2 bringing about an increase in national income from Y_1 to Y_2.

See also MONEY-SUPPLY/SPENDING LINKAGES.

isocost line a line showing combinations of FACTOR INPUTS that can be purchased for the same total money outlay. See ISOQUANT CURVE.

isoquant curve a curve that shows the varying combinations of FACTORS OF PRODUCTION such as labour and capital which can be used to prc luce a given quantity of a product with a given state of technology (where FACTOR INPUTS can be substituted for one another in the production process). See Fig. 95 on page 287.

If the isoquant in Fig. 95 reflects 100 units of production per period, then anywhere along that curve it is possible to determine the combination of factors required to produce 100 units. The slope of the isoquant reflects the 'substitutability' of one factor for the other in the production process (see MARGINAL RATE OF TECHNICAL SUBSTITUTION).

Isoquants slope downward to the right because the two inputs can be substituted for one another in the production process. The isoquants are convex to the origin, because although the inputs can be substituted for one another, they are not perfect substitutes, so that the MRTS of X for Y declines as we move down any equal product curve from left to right.

Isoquants bear a marked similarity with INDIFFERENCE CURVES: combinations of two commodities yielding equal satisfaction to the consumer. But while there is no way of measuring satisfaction in physical units (so that we can only talk of 'higher' or 'lower' indifference curves), we can measure physical output and say by how much production is greater on one equal-product contour than on another.

The ISOCOST LINE shows the combinations of the two factor inputs which can be purchased for the same total money outlay. Its slope reflects the *relative prices* of the two factors of production. Point A, where the isoquant is tangential to the isocost line, shows the least-

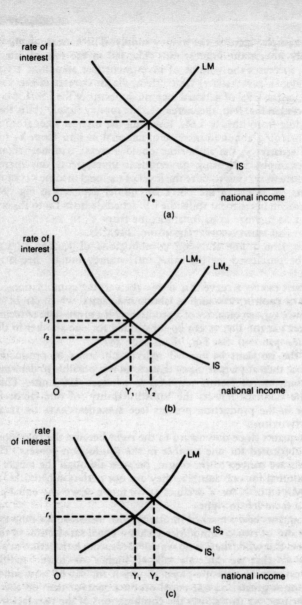

Fig. 94. I.S./L.M. model. (a) The general equilibrium position. (b) The effect of a shift in the L.M. schedule. (c). The effect of a shift in the I.S. schedule.

cost combination of inputs for producing 100 units of input. See
PROCESS RAY, PRODUCTION FUNCTION, COST FUNCTION.

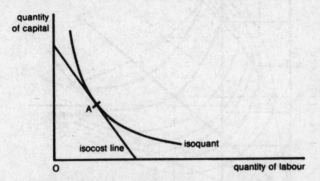

Fig. 95. **Isoquant curve**. The isoquant curve and isocost line.

isoquant map a collection of ranked ISOQUANT CURVES that exhibits,
graphically, a producer's increasing output per period when moving
outward from the origin using larger quantities of two FACTOR
INPUTS, as in Fig. 96a. Isoquant curves are a cardinal measure and the
numbers on the isoquant curves in Fig. 96a indicate the absolute
level of output per period. Isoquant curves never cross because two
crossing curves would imply inconsistent or irrational choices
between the two factor inputs by the producer (see ECONOMIC
MAN).

Although it is often possible to substitute factor inputs in the production process, such substitution cannot continue indefinitely. Some
minimum amount of both factors is required if production is to be
maintained at a given level: for example, in order to produce 300
units in Fig. 96a at least VL of X is required, and at least UT of Y.
For at point T the isoquant is horizontal, indicating that at T the
MARGINAL RATE OF TECHNICAL SUBSTITUTION of X for Y is zero. Similarly at point L the isoquant is vertical, showing that beyond this
point the substitution of Y for X would result in a decrease in output
(indicated by the fact that the isoquant sheers away from the Y axis).

The ridge lines in Fig. 96a delineate those portions of the isoquants
from which the firm will make its choice of resource combinations.
The top one joins all points at which isoquants become vertical, while
the bottom one is the locus of all points at which isoquants become
horizontal. The typical relations that will obtain between one isoquant and another can be shown by taking a cross-section of the production 'contour' map along the line MN. As we move up this line

287

ISOQUANT MAP

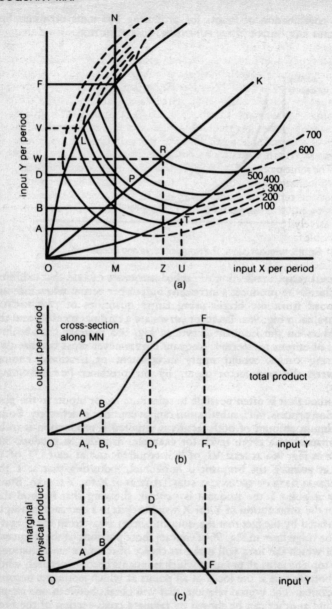

Fig. 96. **Isoquant map**. See entry.

from M, we can read of the outputs that will be produced by increasing quantities of input Y, when used with the firm's plant and the given quantity OM of input X.

Not only does output increase as we move along MN but the rate at which output rises follows a general pattern. In Fig. 96b, at output BB_1 an increase in input Y promises larger than proportional increases in output; at output DD_1 small percentage increases in the use of Y promise equal percentage changes in output; at output FF_1 increases in factor Y promise less than proportional increases in output. This pattern is recognizable as the 'law of variable factor proportions' (see RETURNS TO THE VARIABLE-FACTOR INPUT).

The same pattern would be recognizable if we traced the behavior of output along a line such as OK. Here the distances between successive isoquants reduce as we move towards K, until point P is reached. After this point, the distance between successive isoquants becomes progressively larger. Along the line OK, increasing quantities of the two variable factors X and Y are being combined with the firm's fixed plant and equipment.

The MARGINAL PHYSICAL PRODUCT curve for input Y shown in Fig. 96c is derived from the total product curve in Fig. 96b. As the amount of factor Y used increases from OA_1 to OD_1, its marginal physical product is rising. Then, for further increases in the use of factor Y, its marginal physical product is falling, becoming negative if more than OF_1 of Y is applied.

issued share capital the amount of its AUTHORIZED SHARE CAPITAL that a JOINT-STOCK COMPANY has issued to SHAREHOLDERS in order to raise CAPITAL. Where a company issues shares with phased payment terms, then the amount of PAID-UP CAPITAL may be less than the issued share capital in the short term.

See SHARE ISSUE.

issuing house a financial institution (often a part of a MERCHANT BANK) that arranges and underwrites the issue of new STOCKS and SHARES on behalf of corporate clients on the STOCK EXCHANGE.

See SHARE ISSUE.

J

J-curve effect the tendency for a country's BALANCE-OF-PAYMENTS deficit to initially worsen following a DEVALUATION of its currency before then moving into surplus. This is because the full adjustment of trade volumes to devaluation involves a time lag: there is an immediate fall in export prices and a rise in import prices so that current exports earn less foreign exchange and current imports absorb more foreign exchange thereby increasing the size of the payment deficit (the downturn of the J-curve). Over time, however, the lower export prices will increase overseas demand and export earnings will rise, while higher import prices will reduce domestic demand for imports, leading to an improvement in the balance of payments (the upturn of the J-curve). See BALANCE-OF-PAYMENTS EQUILIBRIUM.

Jevons, William Stanley (1835–82) an English economist who developed UTILITY theory in his book *The Theory of Political Economy* (1871). Jevons rejected the idea that the value of a good depends upon the labour needed to produce it, and argued instead that value depends upon the individual consumer's subjective evaluation of the utility of a good. He suggested that goods are valuable only if they provide utility and that labour and other factors of production become valuable when they are used to produce these goods. Specifically, he showed that a consumer will increase purchases of goods until the MARGINAL UTILITY gained from the last pennyworth of one good equals the marginal quality of the last pennyworth of every other good.

Jevons was also particularly interested in linking statistical analysis with theoretical analysis in economics, and he developed statistical series on production in Britain over a long period to try and determine the cause of BUSINESS CYCLES.

job a work task or series of work tasks to be performed in order to produce a good or service. Jobs differ in terms of skills, physical fitness, personality, etc. requirements, and in terms of the decision-making autonomy and responsibilities involved. Some jobs involve a wide-ranging set of work tasks whilst others may be broken down into a number of narrowly defined activities through a 'division of labour'. Such SPECIALIZATION is often conducive to achieving high levels of labour PRODUCTIVITY in industries such as motor-car assembly which utilize mass production techniques. In other cases, productivity may be enhanced by grouping together larger numbers of work tasks to form individual jobs. Job design has an important effect on *job satisfaction* and thus levels of absenteeism, labour turnover, industrial disputes, etc., which affect productivity. In some instances the process of specialization has been partially reversed by programmes of '*job enlargement*' (adding additional tasks to provide greater variety); '*job rotation*' (where workers rotate jobs to reduce monotony); and '*job enrichment*' (where workers are given greater scope in deciding how tasks should be performed).

jobber a dealer who acts as a principal in buying and selling FINANCIAL SECURITIES such as STOCKS, SHARES and BONDS, thereby 'making a market' in these securities.

    See MARKET MAKER, STOCK EXCHANGE.

job centre see EMPLOYMENT EXCHANGE.

job enlargement see JOB.

job enrichment see JOB.

job rotation see JOB.

joint costs the COSTS involved in producing several products which are in JOINT SUPPLY, for example, petrol, diesel, tar, etc. produced from a common oil-refining process. Joint costs such as oil-refinery running costs are difficult to allocate precisely between the different products in determining the exact cost of each.

joint demand see COMPLEMENTARY PRODUCTS.

joint-profit maximization the possible situation of the optimization of industry profits by firms who coordinate their price and output policies rather than compete against each other. Joint-profit maximization is typically associated with oligopolistic markets (see OLIGOPOLY) where firms, recognizing their MUTUAL INTERDEPENDENCE operate PRICE LEADERSHIP systems and CARTELS.

joint-stock company a form of company in which a number of people contribute funds to finance a FIRM in return for SHARES in the company. Joint-stock companies are able to raise funds by issuing shares to large numbers of SHAREHOLDERS and thus are able to raise more capital to finance their operations than could a sole proprietor or even a partnership. Once a joint-stock company is formed then it becomes a separate legal entity apart from its shareholders, able to enter into contracts with suppliers and customers. Joint-stock companies are managed by the board of directors appointed by shareholders. The directors must report on the progress of the company to the shareholders at an ANNUAL GENERAL MEETING where shareholders can in principle vote to remove existing directors if they are dissatisfied with their performance.

    The development of joint stock companies was given a considerable boost by the introduction of the principle of LIMITED LIABILITY which limited the maximum loss which a shareholder was liable for in the event of company failure. This protection for shareholders encouraged many more of them to invest in companies.

    There are two main forms of joint stock company:

(a) *private company*. Under UK Company Law the maximum number of shareholders in a private company is limited to 50 and the shares the company issues cannot be bought and sold on the STOCK EXCHANGE. Such companies carry the term limited (Ltd) after their name.

(b) *public company*. Under UK Company Law there must be a minimum of 7 shareholders in a public company, but otherwise a company can have an unlimited number of shareholders. Shares in a public company can be bought and sold on the stock exchange and so can be bought by the general public. Such companies carry the term public limited company (Plc) after their name.

Most big firms (OLIGOPOLISTS) are public companies since this is the only practical way of obtaining access to large amounts of capital. Although the shareholders are the owners of a public company very often it is the company's management which effectively controls its affairs. See FIRM, DIVORCE OF OWNERSHIP FROM CONTROL, SHARE ISSUE.

joint supply a situation where the increase or decrease in PRODUCTION of one good is inextricably linked to a greater or lesser extent with the production of another. An example of joint supply is wool and mutton. An increase in the DEMAND for wool increases the SUPPLY of sheep, which in turn brings about an autonomous shift (increase) in the SUPPLY CURVE of mutton. As a result, if the demand for mutton remains unchanged, the PRICE of mutton will fall. See COMPLEMENTARY PRODUCTS.

joint venture a business owned jointly by two or more independent firms who continue to function separately in all other respects but pool their resources in a particular line of activity. Firms set up joint ventures for a variety of reasons. The combining of the resources of the two firms may facilitate the establishment of a larger-scale operation giving the joint venture access to ECONOMIES OF SCALE and increasing its penetration of the market. A joint venture is often a particularly effective way of exploiting complementary resources and skills, with one firm, for example, contributing new technology and products and the other providing marketing expertise and distribution channels. In the international context, joint ventures with local partners are often used by MULTINATIONAL COMPANIES as a means of entering unfamiliar foreign markets.

Joint ventures are usually a less expensive way of expanding a firm's business interests than undertaking full mergers and takeovers (see EXTERNAL GROWTH). The main problem with joint ventures centres on the need to secure agreement between the two partners (especially if it is a 50–50 arrangement) as to how the business should be managed and developed.

junk bond or **mezzanine debt** colloquial terms used to describe financial securities such as forms of high-risk, high-interest LOAN

CAPITAL which are issued by a company as a means of borrowing money to finance a TAKEOVER BID or MANAGEMENT BUY-OUT. A so-called 'leveraged' takeover bid or buy-out involves the company in increasing the proportion of its debt capital to equity capital, that is, increasing its CAPITAL GEARING.

just-in-time (JIT) system a system in which products are delivered to customers, and materials and components are purchased for the next stage of production, at the exact time they are needed. JIT seeks to economize on finished product stocks by matching the final production of goods with the rate of customers' orders, and to economize on work-in-progress stocks by synchronizing the flow of materials between production processes. Operation of JIT systems requires a higher degree of cooperation between suppliers and customers, providing most of the advantages of VERTICAL INTEGRATION whilst permitting firms to remain independent and trade through MARKETS.

K

Keynes, John Maynard (1883–1946) an English economist who offered an explanation of mass UNEMPLOYMENT and suggestions for government policy to cure unemployment in his influential book: *The General Theory of Employment, Interest and Money* (1936). Prior to Keynes, CLASSICAL ECONOMICS had maintained that in a market economy the economic system would spontaneously tend to produce full employment of resources because the exchange mechanism would ensure a correspondence between supply and demand (SAY'S LAW). Consequently the classicists were confident that business recessions would cure themselves, with interest rates falling under the pressure of accumulating savings so encouraging businessmen to borrow and invest more; and with wage rates falling, so reducing production costs and encouraging businessmen to employ more workers. Keynes' concern about the extent and duration of the world-wide interwar DEPRESSION led him to look for other explanations of recession.

Keynes argued that classical political economists were concerned with the relative shares in national output of the different factors of production, rather than the forces which determine the level of general economic activity, so that their theories of value and distribution related only to the special case of full employment. Concentrating upon the economic aggregates of NATIONAL INCOME, CONSUMPTION, SAVINGS and INVESTMENT, Keynes provided a general theory for explaining the level of economic activity. He argued that there is no assurance that savings would accumulate during a depression and depress interest rates, since savings depend on income and with high unemployment incomes are low.

Furthermore, he argued that investment depends primarily on business confidence which would be low during a depression so the investment would be unlikely to rise even if interest rate fell. Finally, he argued that the wage rate would be unlikely to fall much during a depression given its 'stickiness', and even if it did fall, this would merely exacerbate the depression by reducing consumption.

Keynes saw the cause of a depression as reduced AGGREGATE DEMAND, and in the absence of any automatic stimulus to demand he argued that governments must intervene to increase aggregate demand and end depression. He suggested that governments stimulate consumption by putting money into consumers' pockets through tax cuts or directly increase governments' own expenditure to add to aggregate demand. See EQUILIBRIUM LEVEL OF NATIONAL INCOME.

Keynesian economics the view held by KEYNES of the way in which the aggregate economy works, subsequently refined and developed by his successors.

Much of what is today called Keynesian economics originated from Keynes' book: *The General Theory of Employment, Interest and Money* (1936). Keynes gave economics a new direction and an explanation of the phenomenon of mass unemployment so prevalent in the 1930s. Economic doctrine before Keynes was based primarily upon what is now termed MICROECONOMICS. Keynes switched from the classical concentration on individual prices and markets and individual demand functions to aggregate analysis, introducing new concepts such as the CONSUMPTION FUNCTION.

The classical economists argued (and were officially supported by the monetary authorities, up to the time of accepting Keynes' arguments) that FULL EMPLOYMENT is the result of a smooth-working PRIVATE-ENTERPRISE ECONOMY. If UNEMPLOYMENT occurred, then WAGES would fall (due to competition in labour markets), to such an extent that unemployed labour would be re-employed (the neoclassical analysis that marginal productivity of labour would now exceed or equal its marginal cost). Keynes introduced the possibility of 'rigid wages' in an attempt to explain what was inconceivable to classical and neoclassical economists, general equilibrium within the economy at less than full employment.

Keynes argued that INCOME depends upon the volume of employment. The relationship between income and CONSUMPTION is defined by the PROPENSITY TO CONSUME.

Therefore, consumption is dependent upon the interrelated functions of income and employment. Anticipated expenditure on consumption and INVESTMENT is termed AGGREGATE DEMAND and in a situation of equilibrium, equals AGGREGATE SUPPLY. Keynes was of the opinion that in a state of equilibrium, the volume of employment was dependent upon the aggregate-supply function, the propensity to consume, and the amount of investment. The level of employment would therefore increase if either the propensity to consume increased or the level of investment increased, i.e., greater demand for consumer and producer goods leads to an increase in supply. Increasing supply tends to lead to higher levels of employment.

The difficulty of reducing wages, (because of trade union pressure to maintain living standards), means that 'rigidity of wages' or WAGE STICKINESS may lead to a situation of equilibrium at less than full employment. Where this occurs, the government as a buyer of both consumer and producer goods, can influence the level of aggregate demand in the economy. Aggregate demand may be increased by FISCAL POLICY or MONETARY POLICY. Keynes placed the emphasis on fiscal policy whereby the government spends more on investment

projects than it collects from taxes. This is known as DEFICIT FINANC-
ING and stimulates aggregate demand when the economy finds itself
in a condition of DEPRESSION. Through the MULTIPLIER effect the
stimulus to aggregate demand is a number of times larger than the
initial investment. The effect is to move the economy towards a
situation of full employment.

Certain Western countries began to question Keynesian economic
ideas in the 1970s as they embraced MONETARISM and began to revert
to the classical economic idea that government intervention is
unnecessary and that markets can ensure prosperity, provided that
market rigidities are removed.

See EQUILIBRIUM LEVEL OF NATIONAL INCOME, BUSINESS CYCLE, CIRCU-
LAR FLOW OF NATIONAL INCOME, CLASSICAL ECONOMICS, DEFLATIONARY
GAP, MONEY SUPPLYSPENDING LINKAGES, QUANTITY THEORY OF MONEY,
I.S./L.M. MODEL, SAY'S LAW, INFLATIONARY GAP, SUPPLY-SIDE
ECONOMICS.

kinked demand curve a curve that explains why the PRICES charged
by competing oligopolists (see OLIGOPOLY), once established, tend to
be stable. In Fig. 97, DD is the DEMAND CURVE if all firms charge the
same price. Starting from point K, if one firm felt that if it were to
charge a higher (unmatched) price than its rivals it would lose sales
to these rivals, then its relevant perceived demand curve becomes
$D_H K$. On the other hand, the firm may feel that if it were to charge
a lower price it would not gain sales from rivals, because rivals would
not let this happen – they would match price cuts along DD. Both
price increases and decreases are thus seen to be self-defeating, and

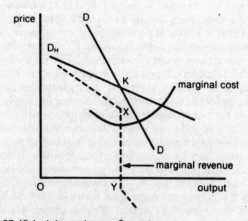

Fig. 97. Kinked demand curve. See entry.

this produces a 'kinked demand curve' with prices tending to settle at K. The theory suggests that price K is likely to 'stick' even though costs may change.

It can be seen that there is a sharp step in the marginal revenue curve corresponding to the kink in the demand curve. In consequence, for a wide range of vertical shifts in the marginal cost curve (between points X and Y) K remains the profit maximizing selling price. See GAME THEORY, MUTUAL INTERDEPENDENCE, PRICE LEADERSHIP.

know-how expertise and trade contacts developed by a firm over time which enhance its competitiveness.

Kondratief cycle or **long-wave cycle** a theoretical long-term cycle ranging from boom to recession over a period of fifty years or so upon which shorter-term BUSINESS CYCLES are superimposed. Based upon statistical observations by Kondratief, explanations for these long waves in economic activity usually rely upon a 'bunching' of significant INNOVATIONS like petrol engines, the motor car, etc., which give an impetus to economic activity for several decades before their impact wanes.

L

labour the contribution to productive activity made by the workforce
both by hand (for example, the assembly of a car) and mentally (for
example, devising a stock-control system). Labour is one of the three
main FACTORS OF PRODUCTION, the others being NATURAL RESOURCES
and CAPITAL. See also ECONOMIC GROWTH, HUMAN CAPITAL.

labour force or **working population** the total number of workers
available for employment in an country. The labour force comprises
those people currently working as EMPLOYEES, the SELF-EMPLOYED and
people currently unemployed. The size of the labour force depends
upon the country's total POPULATION and the proportion of that population offering themselves for work (see ACTIVITY RATE).

   The labour force, together with the CAPITAL STOCK, determine a
country's AGGREGATE SUPPLY potential. Fig. 98 gives details of the
labour force for four major industrial countries.

   The structure of the labour force as well as its size can be important
in aᶠecting an economy's supply potential, in particular the age distribution of the labour force. A country with a predominantly young
labour force will tend to find it easier to train workers in the changing
skills needed to take advantage of new technologies.

   See LABOUR MARKET, POTENTIAL GROSS NATIONAL PRODUCT, ECON-
OMIC GROWTH.

Number of persons making up the labour force, 1995

(000s)

UK	28,000
Germany	40,000
Japan	66,000
USA	132,000

Fig. 98. **Labour force** for selected countries, 1995. Source: OECD.

labour-intensive firm/industry a firm or industry that produces its
output of goods or services using proportionately large inputs of
LABOUR and relatively small amounts of CAPITAL.

   The proportions of labour and capital which a firm uses in production depends mainly on the relative prices of labour and capital
inputs and their relative productivities. This in turn depends upon
the degree of standardization of the product in so far as fragmented
markets where consumers demand product variety are not amenable

to the use of large-scale capital-intensive production methods which facilitate ECONOMIES OF SCALE.

Clothing manufacture, plumbing and hairdressing are examples of labour-intensive industries. See BATCH PRODUCTION, CAPITAL-LABOUR RATIO.

labour market a FACTOR MARKET that provides for an exchange of work for WAGES. The SUPPLY side of the market is represented by individual workers, or, more commonly, TRADE UNIONS bargaining on a collective basis. The DEMAND side of the market is represented by firms who are requiring labour as a FACTOR INPUT in the production process (see MARGINAL-PHYSICAL PRODUCT, MARGINAL-REVENUE PRODUCT).

The labour market has certain characteristics which distinguish it from other factor markets. Unlike other FACTORS OF PRODUCTION such as capital, once workers are hired the rate at which they produce output can vary considerably depending upon the efficiency with which employers organize work tasks and the extent to which workers themselves are motivated to achieve work targets (see X-INEFFICIENCY). Furthermore, work is often performed by groups of workers who themselves develop group norms about what is an appropriate work rate.

The determination of wage rates in labour markets depends upon the supply of, and demand for, labour. The supply of labour depends upon the size of the POPULATION, school-leaving and retirement ages, geographic mobility, skills, training and experience (HUMAN CAPITAL); entry barriers to professions and jobs through qualifications requirements, 'closed-shop' agreements, etc.; occupational mobility which depends upon training and retraining facilities; RESTRICTIVE LABOUR PRACTICES and demarcation barriers which limit the tasks which workers can perform; hours worked which may be influenced by workers' willingness to work overtime and the effects of marginal income tax rates (see LAFFER CURVE). Also, workers may be influenced by non-monetary factors such as congenial working conditions in deciding where to work. In addition, trade unions can act as monopoly sellers of labour and restrict the supply of labour in the interests of raising wage rates. The demand for labour is influenced by, for example, the size and strength of demand for the goods and services produced by workers, the proportion of total production costs accounted for by wages, and the degree of substitutability of capital for labour in the production process. In addition, employers' associations may act as monopsony buyers of labour, restricting the demand for labour in the interests of lowering wage rates.

As a consequence of these factors, the labour market cannot be regarded as a single homogeneous market but must be seen as a number of separate labour markets each with its own particular

LABOUR THEORY OF VALUE

characteristics. For example, as Fig. 99 shows, a group of workers such as surgeons, whose skills are in limited supply and the demand for whose services is high, will receive a high wage rate; by contrast, office cleaners, who require little or no training or skills, are usually in plentiful supply in relation to the demand for their services, so their wage rates are comparatively low. The WAGE DIFFERENTIAL between these two group is Ws-Wo.

Labour markets often operate imperfectly because it is costly for workers to collect information about new employments and for firms to seek new workers. Furthermore, individual workers within any occupational group are not homogeneous units, requiring employers to assess the relative skills and capabilities of individual workers in recruiting labour. In addition, redundancy payments and the desire to 'hoard' scarce labour skills may encourage firms to retain surplus labour during short-term downturns in economic activity even when the supply of labour exceeds demand, providing a downward 'stickiness' in wages. A similar 'stickiness' in wages may occur because of the activities of powerful trade unions who are able to establish national wage rates which prevail even in regions where the supply of labour exceeds demand.

Such imperfections mean that the labour market consists of fragmented, non-competing labour groups between which there may be only limited movement of workers. In these circumstances the wages paid to a worker may exceed the earnings which he or she could command in the 'next best' employment, that is, his or her transfer earnings. The difference between such a worker's current earnings and his or her transfer earnings is often termed ECONOMIC RENT and reflects the particular knowledge and skills the worker possesses and which enhance his or her value to the employer compared with using an alternative worker.

At the aggregate level there is a potential conflict between labour and capital as to which 'should' receive the largest share of national income (see FUNCTIONAL DISTRIBUTION OF INCOME, LABOUR THEORY OF VALUE).

See COLLECTIVE BARGAINING, SUPPLY–SIDE ECONOMICS, PRICE SYSTEM, EMPLOYMENT LAWS, LABOUR FORCE, ACTIVITY RATE, PART–TIME WORK, MINIMUM WAGE RATE.

labour theory of value a doctrine developed by the classical economists, (particularly Adam SMITH and David RICARDO) that states that the value of a GOOD is determined by the amount of LABOUR input needed to produce that good. Thus, the ratio of the equilibrium prices of two commodities is directly proportional to the ratio of labour required to produce them.

Smith was the first to tentatively suggest a labour theory of value, though he acknowledged that the value of a good must be determined

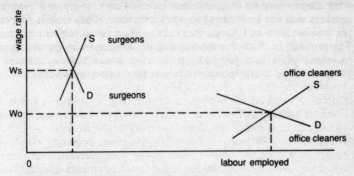

Fig. 99. **Labour market** and wage rates.

by a number of input costs: RENT, WAGES and PROFIT, even if labour did constitute the greatest part of final value. Ricardo accepted that profits and rent may have to be taken into account but that it did not detract from his main argument of relative values between two goods being fundamentally determined by labour cost. Karl MARX developed Ricardo's ideas, decomposing labour value into three constituent parts. The three parts are 'constant capital' (the capital used up in production), 'variable capital' (human labour input), and 'surplus value' (the excess value over and above labour and capital used in the production process). Where surplus value exists there is exploitation of the labour input insomuch as they are being paid less than their full input value.

The labour theory of value was replaced towards the end of the 19th century by the MARGINAL-PRODUCTIVITY THEORY OF DISTRIBUTION, which took into account the contribution of all factor inputs into the production process not just labour. See CLASSICAL ECONOMICS.

labour turnover the proportion of a firm's labour force which leaves its employment over a given period. Labour turnover occurs as a result of retirement, voluntary resignations, redundancies, etc. In general, labour turnover is strongly influenced by the BUSINESS CYCLE, being particularly high during periods of boom, when there are plentiful job opportunities available, or periods of depression, when widespread redundancies occur.

Laffer curve a curve depicting the possible relationship between INCOME TAX rates and total TAX revenue received by the government. Fig. 100 shows a typical Laffer curve. As tax rates per pound of income are raised by the government, total tax revenue or yield initially increases. However, if tax rate is increased beyond OR, then this higher tax rate has a disincentive effect so that fewer people will offer themselves for employment (see POVERTY TRAP) and existing workers will not be inclined to work overtime. The result is that the tax base declines and government tax receipts fall at higher tax rates. The possible Laffer curve relationship has been used by governments in recent years as a justification for cuts in tax rates as part of a programme of work incentives (see SUPPLY-SIDE ECONOMICS).

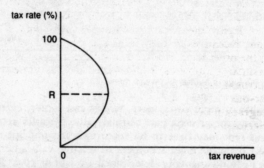

Fig. 100. **Laffer curve.** See entry.

LAFTA see LATIN AMERICAN FREE TRADE ASSOCIATION.

lagged relationship the relationship between two or more VARIABLES in different time periods. For example, the current value of a variable like consumption expenditure will depend upon income in the previous time period. Time is denoted by the letter t, with t − 1 being one period back and t + 1 being one period forward. Such a relationship between income and consumption can be written in the notational form:

$$C_t = f(Y_{t-1})$$

where C_t = consumption in present period, Y_{t-1} = income in the previous period.

See also LEADS AND LAGS, COBWEB THEOREM.

lagging indicator a run of statistical data that past experience has shown tends to reflect earlier changes in some related area of the economy, and which can thus be forecast from information about these changes because they follow the changes in a consistent manner and by a relatively constant time interval. For example, unemployment and company bankruptcies statistics both tend to change after a lag as a result of changes in economic activity as measured by changes in GROSS NATIONAL PRODUCT and thus can be forecast from changes in GNP.

See LEADING INDICATOR, FORECASTING, TIME-SERIES ANALYSIS.

lags see LEADS AND LAGS.

laissez-faire an economic doctrine which emphasizes the superiority of 'free' markets (see PRICE SYSTEM) over State regulation of individual markets and of the economy in general. Proponents of laissez-faire argue that a PRIVATE-ENTERPRISE ECONOMY will achieve a more efficient allocation and use of scarce economic resources and greater economic growth than will a CENTRALLY PLANNED ECONOMY where the government owns and directs the use of resources. This inference is based on the rationale that private ownership of resources and maximum freedom to deploy these resources in line with profit signals will create strong incentives to work hard and take risks. State bureaucracies, on the other hand, can tend to stifle enterprise and initiative.

See CLASSICAL ECONOMICS, RATIONALIZATION, PRIVATIZATION.

land see NATURAL RESOURCES.

last-in-first-out (LIFO) see STOCK VALUATION.

lateral integration see HORIZONTAL INTEGRATION.

Latin American Free Trade Association (LAFTA) the former regional alliance established in 1960 with the general objective of spurring the INDUSTRIALIZATION of member countries by creating a FREE TRADE AREA. There were seven original members of LAFTA: Argentina, Brazil, Peru, Chile, Mexico, Paraguay and Uruguay, with three other countries joining later: Columbia, Ecuador and Venezuela.

However, because of an initial difference in the level of economic development between the various members and serious nationalistic (sovereignty) differences on policy issues, progress towards trade liberalization has been limited. In 1995 a new trade bloc, Mercosur, was established, creating a CUSTOMS UNION between Brazil, Uruguay, Argentina and Paraguay. Mercosur provides for the tariff-free movement of products between member countries and operates a common external tariff against imports from non-members. Mexico is now a member of NAFTA.

LAUTRO see LIFE ASSURANCE AND UNIT TRUST REGULATORY ORGANIZATION.

law of diminishing marginal returns see DIMINISHING RETURNS.

law of large numbers the law that states that large groups tend to behave more uniformly than a single individual. For example, an individual consumer might buy more of a product whose price has risen, whereas most consumers would buy less. See DEMAND CURVE.

law of variable-factor proportions see RETURNS TO THE VARIABLE-FACTOR INPUT.

leading indicator a run of statistical data that past experience has shown tends to reflect later changes in some related areas of the economy, and which thus can be used to forecast these changes because they precede the changes in a consistent manner and by a relatively constant time interval. For example, current birth statistics would provide a firm basis for predicting primary school admissions five or six years ahead. Leading indicators like orders for new machine tools, overtime/short-time working in manufacturing and house-building starts are frequently used to forecast cyclical changes in macro-economic variables like GNP.

See FORECASTING, TIME-SERIES ANALYSIS, LAGGING INDICATOR.

leads and lags 1. the timing differences that exist between peaks and troughs of LEADING INDICATORS and LAGGING INDICATORS, and the overall BUSINESS CYCLE. Thus, in a seven-year business cycle, if the peak of the cycle occurred in the middle year (year four), then a leading indicator, such as starts on new houses, may have peaked in year three. This indicator leads the business cycle by one year. Similarly lagged variables will have peaks or troughs after the business cycle.

2. the time variation from standard payment practice when settling foreign trade debts. The variation from standard practice results from the expectations of traders which may influence the profitability of settling the debt early (lead) or late (lag). The commonest factor which contributes to this practice is expectations of a change in the EXCHANGE RATE. Traders in an importing country have an incentive to postpone settlement to manufacturers in the exporting nation if there is an expectation of a foreseeable devaluation in the rate of exchange of the exporting country's currency. Similarly, if a revaluation (that is, an increase in exchange rate) is in prospect, traders in the debtor nation can be expected to settle early.

See also J-CURVE, LAGGED RELATIONSHIP, EXCHANGE RATE EXPOSURE.

leakages see WITHDRAWALS.

learning curve see EXPERIENCE CURVE.

lease a legal contract under which the owner of an ASSET (such as buildings and machinery) grants to someone else the right to use that asset for a specified period of time in return for periodic payments of RENT. See LEASING, LEASEBACK.

leaseback an arrangement whereby the owner of an ASSET agrees to sell it to another person or company on condition that the asset can be leased to its original owner for a fixed term at a prearranged RENT. Leaseback is normally undertaken to enable companies with large assets such as property to realise cash for use elsewhere in their business. See LEASE, LEASING.

leasehold property a property which is LEASED to a person or firm from its legal owners for an agreed period of time.

Contrast FREEHOLD PROPERTY.

leasing the purchase of an ASSET (mostly buildings, machinery and vehicles) by a leasing company which retains the ownership of the assets, and which then hires out the item for use by clients who pay an agreed RENT. Leasing is a useful source of INVESTMENT in so far as it enables individuals or companies to use assets without having to tie up large amounts of capital. See LEASE, OFF-BALANCE SHEET FINANCING.

least-cost supply an assumption within the THEORY OF SUPPLY that PROFIT MAXIMIZING firms will always employ that combination of FACTOR INPUTS which minimizes the TOTAL COST of producing a given output.

See COST FUNCTION, ISOQUANT CURVE.

least-squares estimation see REGRESSION ANALYSIS.

legal tender that part of a country's MONEY SUPPLY which is, in the eyes of the law, totally acceptable in payment for a purchase of a good or service or repayment of a debt. CURRENCY (BANKNOTES and COINS) issued by the government fulfil this requirement. By contrast, a trader is within his legal rights to refuse to accept as payment a cheque drawn against a BANK DEPOSIT.

See MINT.

lender a person, firm or institution that makes a LOAN to a BORROWER to enable the borrower to finance CONSUMPTION or INVESTMENT. Lenders frequently require borrowers to offer some COLLATERAL SECURITY, for example, property deeds, which lenders may retain in the event of borrowers failing to repay the loan.

See also CREDIT, FINANCIAL SYSTEM.

lender of last resort the rôle of the CENTRAL BANK in the UK of making money available to the DISCOUNT HOUSES when they are short of funds. When the COMMERCIAL BANKS find themselves with fewer liquid assets than they feel it is commercially prudent for them to hold, (that is, when they fall below their RESERVE-ASSET RATIO requirement), then they must improve their liquidity. They can do this either by selling off TREASURY BILLS to the central bank or calling in their short-term loans to the discount houses who in turn are then forced to borrow from the central bank. To ensure that discount houses turn to the central bank for funds only as a last resort, the central bank generally makes funds available at a higher cost than prevailing market interest rates. This penal rate of interest is presently called the BILL-DISCOUNTING INTEREST RATE (formerly, minimum lending rate). The discount house must offer collateral such as government bonds as security for the loan.

The central bank's rôle as lender of last resort provides a guarantee that adequate liquidity will be provided for commercial banks and thus helps to maintain public confidence in the BANKING SYSTEM.

See FRONT DOOR, BACK DOOR.

less developed country (LDC) see DEVELOPING COUNTRY.

level of significance see HYPOTHESIS TESTING.

leverage see CAPITAL GEARING.

leveraged bid see TAKE-OVER BID.

Lewis, Sir W. Arthur (1915–) a West Indian economist who has contributed to the theory of ECONOMIC DEVELOPMENT and whose seminal text is *The Theory of Economic Growth* (1955). He argued that though growth can bring positive benefits in improving living standards in DEVELOPING COUNTRIES, it can also disrupt those countries' cultures especially where growth is too rapid. Lewis has emphasized the importance of economic infrastructure in developing countries, and stressed the need for such social overhead capital as transport networks, communications systems and educational facilities as prerequisites for growth.

liability a claim on the resources of an individual or business in respect of monies borrowed. A liability is thus a form of DEBT, for example, a bank overdraft or LOAN, a building society MORTGAGE. See ASSET, BALANCE SHEET.

LIBOR (London Interbank Offered Rate) the INTEREST RATE on dollar and other foreign currency deposits at which larger banks are prepared to borrow and lend these currencies in the EUROCURRENCY MARKET. The LIBOR rates reflect market conditions for international funds and are widely used by the banks as a basis for determining the interest rates charged on dollar and foreign currency loans to business customers.

licence, *n*. **1**. The grant by one FIRM to another firm (*exclusive licence*) or others (*nonexclusive licence*) of the right(s) to manufacture its product, or to use its technology or distribution facilities. Similarly, the grant by the government to an authority (for example, a gas corporation) or firm of the rights to supply a particular good or provide a particular service. The granting of a licence in these cases is a CONTRACTUAL arrangement which is entered into usually for a specified period of time, with the licensee usually paying a ROYALTY or FEE for the rights assigned.

2. a document that shows proof of legal ownership (or entitlement) and compliance with a statutory or private requirement for a payment thereon, for example, a television licence issued by the government or a private fishing licence. Such licences are issued primarily for the purpose of raising revenue.

3. a document issued as a means of ensuring that premises or persons are 'fit and proper' for the purposes in which they are engaged, for example, a licensed casino, a licensed dealer in securities.

licensed deposit taker a COMMERCIAL BANK, SAVINGS BANK, FINANCE HOUSE or other financial institution that is recognized by the Bank of England as being allowed to operate a banking service and which is therefore subject to credit controls.

Life Assurance and Unit Trust Regulatory Organization (LAUTRO) a body which is responsible for regulating firms involved in the provision of life assurance and unit trust management. See SELF-REGULATORY ORGANIZATION.

life-cycle hypothesis the hypothesis that states that current CON-SUMPTION is not dependent solely on current DISPOSABLE INCOME, but is related to a person's anticipated lifetime INCOME. For example, a young worker may purchase products such as a house on extended CREDIT because he expects his future income to rise as he moves up a salary scale or obtains increases in basic wage rates and thus will be able to pay future interest and repayment charges. By contrast, an older worker nearing retirement may limit his consumption from current income in anticipation that his income will fall after retirement. Long-term consumption may also be related to changes in a person's WEALTH, in particular the value of their house over time.

The economic significance of the life-cycle hypothesis is that in the *short term* the level of consumption may be higher (or lower) than that indicated by the level of current disposable income.

See KEYNESIAN ECONOMICS, CONSUMPTION FUNCTION, PERMANENT INCOME HYPOTHESIS.

LIFFE see LONDON INTERNATIONAL FINANCIAL FUTURES EXCHANGE.

limited liability a liability that limits the maximum LOSS which a SHAREHOLDER is liable for in the event of company failure to the SHARE CAPITAL which he originally subscribed.

The principle of limited liability limits a shareholder's maximum loss in the event of his company failing to the original share capital which he invested, no further claims by creditors against the shareholder's other assets being permitted. In protecting shareholders in this way many more people were encouraged to invest in companies and JOINT-STOCK COMPANIES grew rapidly. To warn potential creditors that any claims by creditors will be limited in total to the amount of the company's share capital, such companies carry the term: 'Limited' (Ltd.) or 'Public Limited Company' (Plc) after their names.

When a business is subject to *unlimited liability*, as is the case with sole proprietors, unlimited partnerships and unlimited companies then the owners of the business are liable in full for the debts of the business if it fails. This may involve them losing not only the capital that they have put into the business, but also most of their personal assets.

limit pricing or **entry-forestalling price** a pricing strategy employed by established oligopolists (see OLIGOPOLY) in a market to exploit BARRIERS TO ENTRY in order to forestall new entry. A limit-pricing model is shown in Fig. 101, where the barrier to entry is assumed to be ECONOMIES OF SCALE. Established firms produce a total output of OQ_1, which is sold at price OP_1. The MINIMUM EFFICIENT SCALE of output for the entrant to be just as cost-effective as established firms is Q_1Q_2 (equal to OQ). It will be seen that as a result of the addition of this 'extra' output to existing market supply OQ_1, the market price is lowered to OP_2, a price at which entry is unprofitable. Established firms are thus able to set an entry-limiting price of OP_1, thereby securing ABOVE-NORMAL PROFITS of the order AB.

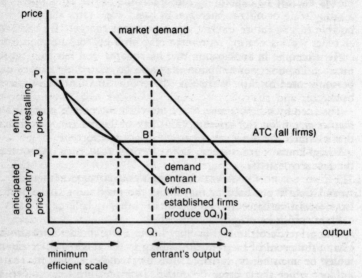

Fig. 101. **Limit pricing**. See entry.

linear programming a mathematical technique for utilizing limited resources to meet a desired objective, such as minimizing cost or maximizing profit, where the resource limits are expressed as constraints.

For example, consider a firm making only two products: bookcases and chairs, and trying to decide how many of each to make. The company's output will be limited by the productive resources which it has available, and these are depicted graphically in Fig. 102, where quantities of bookcases are represented on the horizontal axis and quantities of chairs on the vertical axis. If the company has only 80 hours of machine time available each week, while a bookcase needs 5 hours of machine time to make and a chair 5 hours of machine time, then the maximum output with the available machine would be represented by line XY. Again, if there were only 84 man hours of direct labour hours available, and each bookcase needs 7 hours work while each chair needs 3 hours work, then the maximum output with the available direct labour force would be represented by line RT.

The area OXZT represents all feasible combinations of bookcases and chairs which can be produced with the limited machine hours and man hours available (the *feasible region*).

If each bookcase (b) sold makes a profit of £5, and each chair (c) £4, then in order to maximize profit the firm would seek to maximize output:

$$5b + 4c.$$

For example, in order to earn a profit of £60 the company could produce 12 bookcases or 15 chairs or some combination of the two, as represented by the broken line MT in Fig. 102. Combinations of bookcases and chairs corresponding to larger total profits can be represented by other lines such as LN, which are parallel to MT, but further out from the origin 0. The line LN represents the largest profit which the firm can earn with its available man-hours and machine-hours, since it is the highest broken line which just touches the resource constraints represented by the feasible region OXZT. The firm will therefore settle at point Z producing OV chairs per week and OW bookcases each week in order to maximize its profits from available resources.

Linear programming also provides information about the value of additional resources to a company. For example, it shows how much extra profit could be earned by increasing the amount of machine-hours or man-hours available, and thus indicate the maximum amount which the company should pay for additional units of these resources. These maximum amounts which the company could afford to pay for additional resources without prejudicing profitability are called SHADOW PRICES of the machine-hours and man-hour resources.

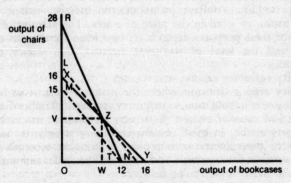

Fig. 102. **Linear programming**. See entry.

LIQUIDATION

See PRODUCTION POSSIBILITY BOUNDARY.

liquidation the process by which a JOINT-STOCK COMPANY's existence as a legal entity ceases by 'winding up' the company. Such a process can be initiated at the behest of the CREDITORS where the company is insolvent (a compulsory winding up), or by the company directors or SHAREHOLDERS, in which case it is known as a voluntary winding up.

The person appointed liquidator, either by the company directors/ shareholders or the creditors, sells off the company's ASSETS for as much as they will realize. The proceeds of the sale are used to discharge any outstanding liabilities to the creditors of the company. If there are insufficient funds to pay all creditors (INSOLVENCY), preferential creditors are paid first (for example, the INLAND REVENUE for tax due), then ordinary creditors pro rata. If there is a surplus after payment of all creditors this is distributed pro rata amongst the shareholders of the company. See also LIMITED LIABILITY, SHAREHOLDERS CAPITAL.

liquid asset a monetary ASSET (such as CURRENCY) which can be used directly as a means of payment. See MONEY, MONEY-SUPPLY DEFINITIONS, LIQUIDITY PREFERENCE.

liquidity the extent to which an ASSET can be quickly and completely converted into CURRENCY (notes and coin) in order to be used as a means of payment. Monetary assets (see MONEY) are the most liquid since they are widely acceptable as a medium of exchange; while durable and highly specific assets such as a machine are the least liquid since such assets can only be converted into money after a willing buyer can be found and a money value placed on the asset.

liquidity preference a preference for holding MONEY instead of investing it. KEYNES identifies three motives for holding money: (a) TRANSACTIONS DEMAND – money held on a day-to-day basis to finance current purchases; (b) PRECAUTIONARY DEMAND – money held to meet unexpected future outlays; (c) SPECULATIVE DEMAND – money held in anticipation of a fall in the price of assets. The amount of money held for these purposes depends on two main factors: the INTEREST RATE and the level of NATIONAL INCOME. See MONEY DEMAND SCHEDULE.

liquidity ratio see RESERVE-ASSET RATIO.

liquidity trap a situation where the INTEREST RATE is so low that people prefer to hold money (LIQUIDITY PREFERENCE) rather than invest it. At low rates of interest the MONEY DEMAND SCHEDULE becomes infinitely elastic. In these circumstances any attempt by monetary policy to lower interest rates in order to stimulate more INVESTMENT (see MONEY SUPPLYSPENDING LINKAGES) will be futile, and will simply result in more money being held.

KEYNES argued that in a depressed economy which is experiencing a liquidity trap the only way to stimulate investment is to increase GOVERNMENT EXPENDITURE or reduce TAXES in order to increase AGGREGATE DEMAND and improve business confidence about future prosperity, encouraging them to invest.

listed company a public JOINT-STOCK COMPANY whose shares are traded on the main STOCK EXCHANGE. To obtain a full listing on the main stock exchange a company is required to provide comprehensive information about its activities. See QUOTED COMPANY, UNLISTED SECURITIES MARKET.

list price the published PRICE of a good or service. The actual price paid by the buyer is often less than this because suppliers are prepared to offer cash and trade DISCOUNTS. Many suppliers specify RECOMMENDED RETAIL PRICES for their products, but again the actual price paid can be much less than that recommended depending upon the strength of retail competition.

See BULK BUYING.

L.M. (liquidity-money) schedule a schedule that shows the combinations of levels of NATIONAL INCOME and INTEREST RATES where the equilibrium condition for the monetary economy L = M holds. See Fig. 103 (overleaf).

The L.M. schedule interacts with the I.S. SCHEDULE in determining a general equilibrium position for the economy as a whole.

See also I.S./L.M. MODEL, SPECULATIVE DEMAND, TRANSACTIONS DEMAND.

loan the advance of a specified sum of MONEY to a person or business (the BORROWER) by other persons or businesses, or more particularly by a specialist financial institution (the LENDER), which makes its profits from the INTEREST charged on loans. The provision of loans by COMMERCIAL BANKS, FINANCE HOUSES, BUILDING SOCIETIES, etc. is an important source of CREDIT in the economy, serving to underpin a substantial amount of spending on current consumption and the acquisition of personal and business assets.

Loans may be advanced on an *unsecured* or *secured* basis; in the latter case the lender requires the borrower to offer some form of COLLATERAL SECURITY (for example, property deeds) which the lender may retain in the event of the borrower defaulting on the repayment of the loan.

See BANK LOAN, INSTALMENT CREDIT, MORTGAGE, LOAN CAPITAL, DEBENTURE, LOAN GUARANTEE SCHEME, INTEREST RATE, SOFT LOAN, BOND.

loan capital or **debt capital** the money employed in a company that has been borrowed from external sources for fixed periods of time by the issue of fixed-interest financial securities. The providers of loan capital do not normally share in the profits of the company as do providers of SHARE CAPITAL but are rewarded by means of regular

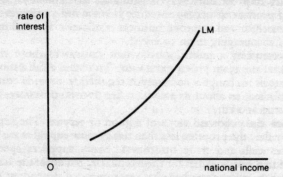

Fig. 103. **L.M. (liquidity-money) schedule**. The L.M. schedule is upward-sloping: with a given money stock, a higher rate of interest leads to a smaller demand for speculative balances leaving more money available for transaction balances (see MONEY DEMAND SCHEDULE). If these transaction balances are to be demanded, national income will have to be higher (the transaction demand for money is a function of the level of national income). Hence, to ensure that people will willingly take up these balances at a higher rate of interest, a higher level of national income is required.

INTEREST payments which must be paid under the terms of the loan contract. Lenders take precedence over shareholders both for receipt of interest payments out of profits and the repayment of the capital sums subscribed in the event of company INSOLVENCY. Loans carry various degrees of risk if the borrower defaults on the loan. Least risky are DEBENTURES secured by means of a 'fixed' charge on a specific company asset such as a particular machine which the lender could claim in the event of default. Next come debentures secured by means of a 'floating' charge against all company assets in the event of default. Finally, holders of 'subordinated' loans (often referred to colloquially as 'junk bonds') would only receive repayment of their loans after the claims of other lenders have been met. These increasing degrees of risk are reflected in the interest rates paid to lenders, holders of unsubordinated loans generally being offered higher interest rates than debenture holders.

See CAPITAL GEARING.

lobbying the process of bringing pressure to bear on governments to persuade them to adopt policies or allocate resources in ways which are favourable to special-interest groups, for example, farmers pressuring their agricultural ministers for higher agricultural support prices and environmental groups pressing for tougher pollution controls.

local content rule or **rule of origin** the stipulation by a country that for a product to qualify as an authentic domestically manufactured product (that is, originating in that country) the product must be manufactured predominantly from locally supplied as opposed to imported components. Local content rules are used by governments mainly to prevent the operation of so-called 'screwdriver' plants (plants producing final products from mainly imported components) established to circumvent TARIFFS, QUOTAS and COUNTERVAILING DUTIES imposed on imported final products.

The application of local content rules poses various problems – in particular, the proportion of the final product that has to be sourced domestically (see SOURCING) for the product to qualify as a locally produced one, and how the extent of local content is to be measured (number, value of components, etc.).

See PROTECTIONISM, CERTIFICATE OF ORIGIN.

local tax a TAX on property or persons by local authorities/councils which, together with central government grants, is used to finance the provision of various local services. Before 1990, in the UK, 'rates' were levied on eligible *properties*; between April 1990 and April 1993 a 'community charge' ('poll tax') was levied on eligible *persons*; since April 1993 a 'council tax' has been levied on eligible *properties*. The current means of raising local taxes, the 'council tax' is based on the rateable value of local properties, the amount payable in the case of residential dwellings being adjusted to take into account such things as the number of people living in the property, their incomes, and any disabilities they suffer.

See UNIFORM BUSINESS RATE.

location of industry the geographical spread of economic activity within an economy. A multitude of factors influence the location decisions of firms and industries including proximity to raw material supplies, availability of labour, good communications and nearness to markets. Once an industry becomes established in a particular location it tends to act as a focal point for further economic expansion, attracting, directly, the establishment of ancillary trades (component suppliers, back-up services, etc.,) and, indirectly, other firms and industries through EXTERNAL ECONOMIES OF SCALE and regional MULTIPLIER effects. REGIONAL POLICY also has a significant effect on INDUSTRIAL LOCATION.

lockout an action taken by an employer that involves the exclusion of the workforce from their place of work as part of an INDUSTRIAL DISPUTE. See INDUSTRIAL RELATIONS, STRIKE.

locomotive principle the principle that in a world-wide RECESSION, one country, by expanding its AGGREGATE DEMAND, will increase its demand for IMPORTS, stimulating the EXPORTS of other countries and so increasing economic activity in these other countries. In this way one country can act as a locomotive to pull other countries out of recession, at some expense to its balance of payments.

See FOREIGN TRADE MULTIPLIER.

Lomé agreements the agreements of 1975 and 1979 entered into between the EUROPEAN COMMUNITY and 58 African, Caribbean and Pacific (ACP) countries that provide for TARIFF-free entry into the EC market of a wide range of ACP primary products and manufacturers. The agreements also cover the provision of ECONOMIC AID to the ACPs through the EUROPEAN REGIONAL DEVELOPMENT FUND and the EUROPEAN INVESTMENT BANK, and established the Stabex and Minex schemes to stabilize the export earnings of those ACPs especially dependent on volatile agricultural and mineral products.

London International Financial Futures Exchange (LIFFE) a FUTURES MARKET which is engaged in the buying and selling of FINANCIAL SECURITIES and COMMODITIES. LIFFE's operations have been expanded by the absorption of two other exchanges, the London Traded Options Market and the London Commodity Market. See FINANCIAL SERVICES ACT, 1986.

London Traded Option Market see LONDON INTERNATIONAL FINANCIAL FUTURES EXCHANGE.

long position a situation in which a dealer or MARKET MAKER in a particular COMMODITY, FINANCIAL SECURITY or FOREIGN CURRENCY is selling less than he is buying, so that his working stock of the item increases (i.e. becomes 'long').

Contrast SHORT POSITION.

long run an abstract time period (in the THEORY OF SUPPLY) long enough for all FACTOR INPUTS to be varied, but within an existing technological framework (known production methods). Thus, the firm's plant size, which is fixed in the short run, can now be altered to allow for an increased scale of operations.

In the VERY LONG RUN, the technological framework itself changes as a result of new INVENTIONS and knowledge. Compare SHORT RUN. See also ECONOMIES OF SCALE, DISECONOMIES OF SCALE, RETURNS TO SCALE.

long-term capital-employed or **net worth** any long-term funds (see FUNDING) employed in a firm. For companies this takes the form of SHAREHOLDERS' CAPITAL-EMPLOYED plus long-term loans such as DEBENTURES.

Lorenz curve see CONCENTRATION MEASURES.

loss the difference that arises when a firm's TOTAL REVENUES are less than TOTAL COSTS. In the SHORT RUN, where firms' total revenues are insufficient to cover VARIABLE COSTS, then they will exit from the market unless they perceive this situation as being temporary. In these circumstances, where firms' total revenues are sufficient to cover variable costs and make some CONTRIBUTION towards FIXED COSTS, then they will continue to produce despite overall losses. In the LONG RUN, however, unless firms' revenues are sufficient to cover both variable and fixed costs, then their overall losses will cause them to exit from the market.

See MARKET EXIT, LOSS MINIMIZATION, PROFIT–AND–LOSS ACCOUNT.

loss-leading the practice of retailers in selling a particular product at a price below bought-in cost in order to attract customers into the store hoping that they will then be encouraged to make other purchases. This constitutes a form of retailer discrimination against manufacturers, and is usually outlawed by RESTRICTIVE TRADE PRACTICES legislation.

See COMPETITION POLICY, RESALE–PRICE MAINTENANCE.

loss minimization the objective of the FIRM in the SHORT RUN when confronted with adverse market conditions which prevent PROFIT MAXIMIZATION. Profit maximization or loss minimization requires the firm to produce at that level of output where MARGINAL COST equals MARGINAL REVENUE. For example, a firm under PERFECT COMPETITION would produce output OQ in Fig. 104. However, adverse short-run conditions may mean that at this level of output, price (OP) is insufficient to cover average total cost (OC) so that the firm makes losses (equal to area PCXY in Fig. 104). In the short run, the firm will continue to produce this level of output as long as price is sufficient to cover AVERAGE VARIABLE COST (OC_1) and make some CONTRIBUTION (equal to area PC_1ZY) towards FIXED COSTS, though in the LONG RUN a continuation of this situation of loss-making would force the firm to leave the market.

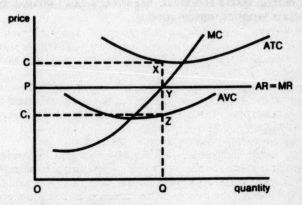

Fig. 104. **Loss minimization**. See entry.

Ltd see LIMITED LIABILITY.

lump of labour the proposition that there is only so much work to be done in the economy, so if fewer people are needed to produce any given output, UNEMPLOYMENT must rise. It follows that labour-saving technological change will inevitably lead to higher unemployment. The proposition is fallacious for the following reasons: (a) it assumes that the economy is already producing all the products society could possibly want, making no allowance for the fact that labour displaced in one area of the economy can now be redeployed to produce *more* goods and services elsewhere in the economy; (b) technological advance creates its own demand – it leads to higher PRODUCTIVITY and the payment of higher wages thereby increasing purchasing power in the economy which in turn generates more output and employment.

lump-sum taxes the taxes that raise revenue for the government without distorting resource allocation patterns. INDIRECT TAXES have a distorting effect because they cause consumers to rearrange their consumption patterns and this rearrangement represents a loss to consumers without any corresponding gain to the government. Similarly, INCOME TAXES can distort choice patterns in affecting the choice between work and leisure. In practice there are few taxes which do not affect resource allocation other than poll taxes which simply levy a tax per head of population.

See TAXATION, INCIDENCE OF TAXATION, PRINCIPLES OF TAXATION.

luxury product any product whose consumption varies considerably with changes in INCOME – for example, electrical appliances, holidays and entertainment. Luxury products have an INCOME ELASTICITY OF DEMAND much greater than 1. This means that as incomes rise, proportionally more income is spent on such products.

Contrast STAPLE PRODUCTS. See ENGEL'S LAW, NORMAL PRODUCT, INFERIOR PRODUCT, GIFFEN GOOD.

M

M0, M1, M2, M3, M4, M5 see MONEY-SUPPLY DEFINITIONS.

Maastricht Treaty, 1991 a *provisional* agreement between member countries of the EUROPEAN COMMUNITY which is designed to provide for a closer unification of the economic and political systems of member countries.

The Treaty contains three main elements: economic and monetary union, political union, and a reform of the structures and present functioning of the Community. In the case of economic and monetary union the Treaty proposes a three-stage plan for the irrevocable change to a single currency. The plan (arising from the 'Delors proposals') makes participation in the 'exchange rate mechanism' (ERM) of the EUROPEAN MONETARY SYSTEM a prerequisite for all countries participating in the first stage (1991–94). In the second transitional stage, starting in 1994, a 'European Monetary Institute' was created, as the forerunner to a European CENTRAL BANK. In 1996, the Institute and the European Commission will report on the 'fitness' of each country for inclusion in the ECU zone, based on stiff criteria of 'economic convergence', which includes low inflation rates (under 3%) and small budget deficits (under 3% of GNP).

The third stage, locking all currencies together and placing monetary policy under the control of an independent central bank, will begin if, by 1996, a majority of seven members have met the 'convergence' criteria and vote to decide on a starting date. Otherwise, the central bank will begin work in 1998 and the third stage will start on 1 January 1999. However, the overall plan is behind schedule and has been put in jeopardy by the political indecisiveness of a number of countries who dislike the idea of a single currency.

macroeconomic equilibrium see EQUILIBRIUM LEVEL OF NATIONAL INCOME.

macroeconomic policy the setting of broad objectives by the government for the economy as a whole and the use of control instruments to achieve those objectives. Macroeconomic objectives include: FULL EMPLOYMENT; the avoidance of INFLATION; ECONOMIC GROWTH; and BALANCE-OF-PAYMENTS EQUILIBRIUM. FISCAL POLICY and MONETARY POLICY are the main instruments used to regulate the economy.

See also DEMAND MANAGEMENT, PRICES AND INCOMES POLICY, INTERNAL–EXTERNAL BALANCE MODEL, FIXED TARGETS, OPTIMIZING, BUSINESS CYCLE, EQUILIBRIUM LEVEL OF NATIONAL INCOME, DEFLATION-

ARY GAP, INFLATIONARY GAP, MEDIUM-TERM FINANCIAL STRATEGY, ECONOMIC POLICY, MICROECONOMIC POLICY.

macroeconomics the branch of economics concerned with the study of aggregate economic activity. Macroeconomic analysis investigates how the economy as a whole 'works', and seeks to identify strategic determinants of the levels of national income and output, employment and prices.

See also CIRCULAR FLOW OF NATIONAL INCOME MODEL, EQUILIBRIUM LEVEL OF NATIONAL INCOME, INTERNAL-EXTERNAL BALANCE MODEL, MACROECONOMIC POLICY, MICROECONOMICS.

mail order a form of WHOLESALER/RETAILER operation that is involved in the sale of products to consumers through the post. The mail order firm appoints agents whose task it is to canvas potential customers. Customers are supplied with a catalogue from which they make purchases directly through the post, by telephone or through their agent.

Malthus, Thomas (1766–1834) an English clergyman whose pessimistic ideas on POPULATION growth were published in his *Essay on the Principle of Population as it Affects the Future Improvement of Society* (1798). Malthus argued that land is finite and that its productivity can, at best, increase only arithmetically (1,2,3,4, etc.); while population increases geometrically (1,2,4,8, etc.), so that the increase in population tends to outrun the increase in food supply. Consequently most people would be condemned to live in misery and poverty with wars, epidemics and famines serving to slow the growth of population.

Malthus's gloomy view of population growth contrasted sharply with the optimistic views about long-term economic development held by his contemporaries and contributed to the belief that economics was the 'dismal science'. Though Malthus did not foresee the dramatic improvements of agricultural techniques which have occurred, nor the tendency for population growth to slow in industrialized countries, his ideas still cause concern, especially in DEVELOPING COUNTRIES. See DEMOGRAPHIC TRANSITION.

managed exchange rate see FLOATING EXCHANGE-RATE SYSTEM, FIXED EXCHANGE-RATE SYSTEM.

management accounting any accounting activities geared to the preparation of information for managers to help them plan and control a company's operations. Management accounts generally provide more detailed information than financial accounts, for example, breaking down revenues and costs between different products, or factories or departments to provide comparative data and to help reveal profitable and unprofitable activities. Management accounts also tend to provide information about performance more frequently than financial accounts, with monthly or even weekly management accounts rather than annual accounts, to give managers prompt

feedback and to enable them to act quickly to check inefficiencies.
Compare FINANCIAL ACCOUNTING.

management buy-in the purchase of a company, or division of a
company, by a small group of shareholders (often ex-managers of
the company) who then form the nucleus of a new management team
to run the company or division.
See MANAGEMENT BUY-OUT.

management buy-out the purchase of a FIRM or division of a firm
by its present management. In the former case, the shareholders of
the firm may be prepared to accept management's financial terms of
purchase because they are better than an outside takeover bidder
or merger partner is prepared to offer. In these cases, management
buy-outs are often 'defensively' motivated, with the existing management fearing loss of office following a hostile takeover. The sale of
a subsidiary or division of a firm to its incumbent management is
often undertaken as a means of DIVESTMENT by the parent firm from
a particular line of business rather than resulting from a takeover or
merger approach. Again, in the interests of the shareholders of the
firm, the financial details of such deals need to be carefully gone
into. Management buy-outs are usually financed by outside interests,
including VENTURE CAPITAL specialists and banks.

management-utility maximization a company objective in the
THEORY OF THE FIRM which is used as an alternative to the traditional
assumption of PROFIT-MAXIMIZATION. The FIRM is assumed to seek to
maximize management's utility or satisfactions, and the managerial
preference function comprises three principal components: utility =
F (staff, emoluments, investments).

Salaried managers prefer spending company money on these three
things (an 'expense preference' for them, as Oliver Williamson puts
it) because:

(a) additional staff can lead to managers getting more salary since
extra staff generally necessitates more tiers in the organization's hierarchy and so, (given the traditional salary differentials between tiers)
will increase the salaries of those at the top of the organization. In
addition, extra staff are a source of power, status and prestige and
may contribute to job security, insofar as larger departments in a
company are less likely to be closed down.

(b) managerial emoluments or 'perks' such as big expense accounts,
generous travel budgets and company cars are valued as both (low-
taxed) sources of indirect material income and because they boost
status and prestige.

(c) discretionary investments over and above those which are
strictly economically essential allow managers to pursue 'pet projects'
and afford them status, prestige and security through the amount of
physical plant and equipment which they control.

See also MANAGERIAL THEORIES OF THE FIRM, DIVORCE OF OWNERSHIP FROM CONTROL.

managerial theories of the firm the theories of the FIRM that substitute firm objectives such as SALES-REVENUE MAXIMIZATION and ASSET-GROWTH MAXIMIZATION for the traditional hypothesis of PROFIT MAXIMIZATION. These theories are based on two assumptions: (a) that for large oligopolistic firms there is a DIVORCE OF OWNERSHIP FROM CONTROL which allows the firm's management to set the firm's objectives rather than its shareholders; (b) managers are more interested in sales and assets goals than profit maximization because the size of their salaries and their power and status (managerial utility) are chiefly linked to the size of the firm. Profits are still important but they are seen as contributory to the attainment of some other objective rather than as an end in themselves.

The significance of the managerial theories as an extension of the THEORY OF THE FIRM lies in their prediction of higher output levels and lower prices in comparison with the profit-maximizing theory.

See MANAGEMENT-UTILITY MAXIMIZATION, BEHAVIOURAL THEORY OF THE FIRM, SATISFICING THEORY.

manpower planning the continuing managerial process of identifying the requirement for human resources and implementing a strategy to optimally utilize and develop labour resources in line with strategic objectives. Manpower planning can be undertaken at corporate level, or it may be done at industry or national level. Manpower planning or human-resource planning seeks to identify future manpower requirements and also embodies other personnel management activities, such as recruitment, training, promotion, etc.

marginal analysis the examination of the effects of adding one extra unit to, or taking away one unit from, some economic VARIABLE. See also MARGINAL COST, MARGINAL REVENUE, MARGINAL UTILITY, MARGINAL PHYSICAL PRODUCT, MARGINAL REVENUE PRODUCT, MARGINAL PROPENSITY TO CONSUME, MARGINAL PROPENSITY TO SAVE, MARGINAL PROPENSITY TO IMPORT, MARGINAL PROPENSITY TO TAX, MARGINAL RATE OF TAX, MARGINAL RATE OF SUBSTITUTION, MARGINAL RATE OF TRANSFORMATION, MARGINAL-COST PRICING, MARGINAL EFFICIENCY OF CAPITAL/INVESTMENT, DIFFERENTIAL CALCULUS.

marginal cost the extra cost (addition to TOTAL COST) that is incurred in the SHORT RUN in increasing OUTPUT by one unit. Given that FIXED COSTS do not vary with output, marginal costs (MC) are entirely marginal VARIABLE COSTS. MC falls at first reflecting increasing RETURNS TO THE VARIABLE-FACTOR INPUT so that costs increase more slowly than output, as shown in Fig. 105. However, MC then rises as decreasing returns set in so that costs increase faster than output.

MC together with MARGINAL REVENUE determines the level of output at which the firm attains PROFIT MAXIMIZATION.

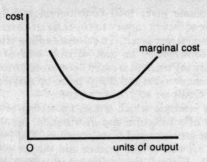

Fig. 105. **Marginal cost**. See entry.

marginal-cost/average-cost relationship the mathematical relationship between MARGINAL COST and AVERAGE COST. See Fig. 106. When average cost (AC) is falling, marginal cost (MC) is always below it; that is, if the cost of an extra unit of output lowers AC, it must itself be less than AC in order to drag the average down. When AC is rising, MC is above it; that is, if an extra unit of output increases AC, its cost must be more than AC in order to pull the average up. The MC curve cuts the AC curve at the minimum point on that curve, as shown in Fig. 106.

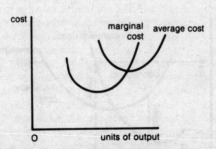

Fig. 106. **Marginal-cost/average-cost relationship**. See entry.

marginal-cost pricing the setting of a PRICE for a product which is based upon the MARGINAL COST of producing and distributing it.

1. a pricing method which sets the price for a product based upon the CONTRIBUTION (i.e. price less unit VARIABLE COST or marginal cost) needed for the product to BREAK-EVEN or provide a predetermined target level of PROFIT. Unit contribution when multiplied by sales/

production volume gives total contribution and this contribution should provide sufficient money to cover FIXED COSTS (to break-even) or fixed costs and target profit. To calculate selling price it is necessary to add unit contribution to unit variable cost or marginal cost. Though this pricing method is based upon costs, in practice managers take into account demand and competition by varying the target unit contribution. Compare FULL-COST PRICING.

2. a pricing principle which argues for setting prices equal to the marginal cost of production and distribution, ignoring whether or not fixed costs are recouped from revenues. The principle has been advocated as a guide to the pricing and output policies of PUBLIC UTILITIES on the grounds that prices which reflect the marginal cost to society of producing an extra unit of output are more socially desirable. The principle is particularly appealing when used for public utilities where marginal costs are effectively zero, such as parks, bridges and museums, because here society can be made better off by lowering the price of these facilities until they are fully used.

However, the marginal-cost pricing principle deals only with the short-run problem of generating an optimum price and output with existing capacity and ignores the long-run problem of ideal investment in new capacity. See Fig. 107.

S e also AVERAGE-COST PRICING, TWO-PART TARIFF.

marginal efficiency of capital/investment the RATE OF RETURN

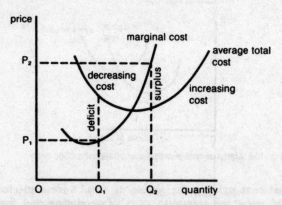

Fig. 107. **Marginal-cost pricing.** In decreasing-cost industries where marginal costs are below average total costs, setting a price equal to the marginal cost would result in losses which would have to be met from taxes or other sources (price OP$_1$); while in increasing-cost industries where marginal costs are greater than average total costs, marginal cost pricing would result in a surplus (price OP$_2$).

(PROFITS) expected on an extra pounds worth of INVESTMENT. The marginal efficiency of investment decreases as the amount of investment increases (see Fig. 108a). This is because initial investments are concentrated on the 'best' opportunities and yield high rates of return; later investments are less productive and secure progressively lower returns.

The amount of investment undertaken depends not only on expected returns but also on the cost of capital, that is, the INTEREST RATE. Investment will be profitable up to the point where the marginal efficiency of investment is equal to the COST OF CAPITAL. In Fig. 108a, at an interest rate of 20% only OX amount of investment is

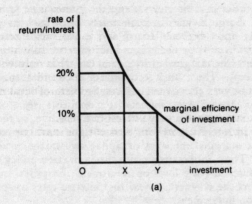

(a)

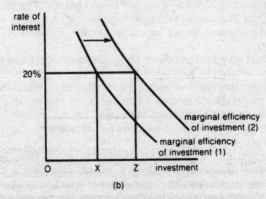

(b)

Fig. 108. **Marginal efficiency of capital/investment**. See entry.

worthwhile. A fall in the interest rate to 10% increases the amount of profitable investment to OY.

It will be readily apparent from Fig. 108a that there is a link between the monetary side of the economy and the real economy: a fall in interest rates will stimulate more investment, which in turn will result in a higher level of national income. (See MONEY SUPPLY/SPENDING LINKAGES).

If EXPECTATIONS change and investors expect to receive better returns from each investment because, for example, of technological progress then at any given rate of interest (such as 20%) more investment will be undertaken than before; that is, the marginal efficiency of investment schedule will shift to the right, as shown in Fig. 108b, and investment will increase from OX to OZ.

Economists differ in their views about the interest rate sensitivity of investment. Some Keynesian economists argue that investment depends largely upon expected return and is not very interest rate sensitive, so that even large changes in interest rates have little effect upon investment (the marginal efficiency of capital/investment curve being very steep). Thus, such economists claim that MONETARY POLICY will not be very effective in influencing the level of investment in the economy. By contrast, monetarist economists (see MONETARISM) argue that investment is very interest rate sensitive, so that even small changes in interest rates will have a significant impact upon investment (the marginal efficiency of capital/investment curve being very shallow). Thus, monetarists claim that monetary policy will be effective in influencing the level of investment. Empirical evidence tends to support the Keynesian view that interest rates have only a limited effect on investment.

marginal factor cost (MFC) the extra cost incurred by a firm in using one more unit of a FACTOR INPUT. Marginal factor cost together with the MARGINAL REVENUE PRODUCT of a factor, indicates to a firm how many factor inputs to employ in order to maximize its profits.

marginal physical product the quantity of OUTPUT in the SHORT RUN theory of supply produced by each extra unit of VARIABLE-FACTOR INPUT (in conjunction with a given amount of FIXED-FACTOR INPUT). The marginal physical-product curve, as shown in Fig. 109, rises steeply at first, reflecting increasing returns to the variable-factor input, but then falls as DIMINISHING RETURNS to the variable-factor input set in.

See RETURNS TO THE VARIABLE-FACTOR INPUT, ISOQUANT MAP.

marginal productivity theory of distribution a theory of the FUNCTIONAL DISTRIBUTION OF INCOME in which FACTOR INPUTS (labour, etc.) receive a payment for their services (wages, etc.) which is equal to their MARGINAL REVENUE PRODUCT.

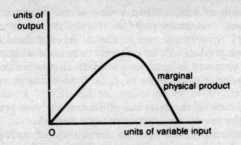

Fig. 109. **Marginal physical product**. See entry.

marginal propensity to consume (MPC) the fraction of any change in NATIONAL INCOME which is spent on consumption:

$$MPC = \frac{\text{change in consumption}}{\text{change in income}}$$

Alternatively, the change in consumption can be expressed as a proportion of the change in DISPOSABLE INCOME.

See CONSUMPTON EXPENDITURE, PROPENSITY TO CONSUME, MULTIPLIER.

marginal propensity to import (MPM) the fraction of any change in NATIONAL INCOME which is spent on IMPORTS:

$$MPM = \frac{\text{change in imports}}{\text{change in income}}$$

Alternatively, the change in imports can be expressed as a proportion of the change in DISPOSABLE INCOME.

See PROPENSITY TO IMPORT, MULTIPLIER.

marginal propensity to save (MPS) the fraction of any change in NATIONAL INCOME which is saved (see SAVING):

$$MPS = \frac{\text{change in savings}}{\text{change in income}}$$

Alternatively, the change in savings can be expressed as a proportion of the change in DISPOSABLE INCOME.

See PROPENSITY TO SAVE, MULTIPLIER.

marginal propensity to tax (MPT) the fraction of any change in NATIONAL INCOME which is taken in TAXATION:

$$MPT = \frac{\text{change in tax}}{\text{change in income}}$$

See PROPENSITY TO TAX, MULTIPLIER, MARGINAL RATE OF TAX.

marginal rate of substitution a ratio of the MARGINAL UTILITIES of two products. It is measured by the slope of the consumer's INDIFFERENCE CURVE between the two products. As an individual consumes more of one product (A), he will tend to become satiated with it and would be prepared to give up less of an alternative product (B) in order to acquire more units of A (a diminishing marginal rate of substitution). In order to maximize his utility, a consumer must equate the ratio of the marginal utilities of the two products to the ratio of their prices (see CONSUMER EQUILIBRIUM).

For an economy, the optimal distribution of national output is achieved when the marginal rate of substitution for all consumers is equal.

See PARETO OPTIMALITY, EDGEWORTH BOX.

marginal rate of taxation the rate of TAXATION an individual would pay on an incremental unit of INCOME. For example, in a PROGRESSIVE TAXATION structure, if an individual paid tax at 30% up to a limit of £15,000, at which point the rate changed to 40%, the marginal rate of taxation on an income of £15,001 is 40%. The incremental rate of taxation on the last pound earned is 40%. See STANDARD RATE OF TAXATION, AVERAGE RATE OF TAXATION, PROPENSITY TO TAX, PROPORTIONAL TAXATION, REGRESSIVE TAXATION.

marginal rate of technical substitution the ratio of the MARGINAL PHYSICAL PRODUCTS of two FACTOR INPUTS in the production process, that is, the amount by which it is possible to reduce factor input X and maintain output by substituting an extra unit of factor input Y. It is measured by the slope of the producer's ISOQUANT CURVE. In order to minimize his production costs a producer must equate the ratio of the marginal physical products of the two factor inputs (shown by the isoquant curve) to the ratio of their factor prices (shown by the ISOCOST LINE). See ISOQUANT MAP.

marginal rate of transformation a ratio of the MARGINAL COSTS of producing two products. It is measured by the slope of the PRODUCTION-POSSIBILITY BOUNDARY which indicates the rate at which the production of one product can be replaced by the production of the other as a result of the reallocation of inputs.

For an economy, the optimum composition of national output is achieved when the marginal rate of transformation of the goods produced equals the ratio of their prices. See PARETO OPTIMALITY.

marginal revenue the addition to TOTAL REVENUE from the sale of one extra unit of output. Under conditions of PERFECT COMPETITION, the firm faces a horizontal DEMAND CURVE at the going market price (marginal revenue = price). See Fig. 110a. Marginal revenue interacts with MARGINAL COST in determining the level of output at which the firm achieves its objective of PROFIT MAXIMIZATION.

See AVERAGE REVENUE, ELASTICITY OF DEMAND, KINKED DEMAND CURVE, MONOPOLY.

marginal revenue product (MRP) the extra REVENUE obtained from using one more FACTOR INPUT to produce and sell additional units of OUTPUT. The marginal revenue product of a factor is given by the factor's MARGINAL PHYSICAL PRODUCT (MPP) multiplied by the MARGINAL REVENUE of the product. (In the case of products sold in per-

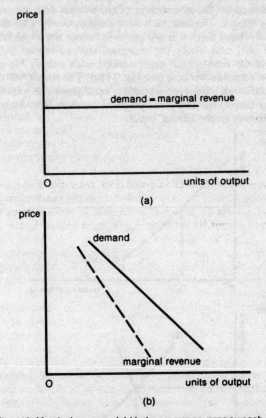

Fig. 110. **Marginal revenue.** (a) Under PERFECT COMPETITION each extra unit of output sold adds exactly the same amount to total revenue as previous units. (b) Under conditions of imperfect competition (for example, MONOPOLISTIC COMPETITION) the firm faces a downward sloping demand curve and price has to be lowered in order to sell more units. Marginal revenue is less than price: as price is lowered each extra unit sold adds successively smaller amounts than previous units.

fectly competitive markets, marginal revenue equals price so that MRP is equal to MPP × price.)

The marginal revenue product, together with the MARGINAL FACTOR COST, indicates to a firm how many factor inputs to employ in order to maximize its profits. This can be illustrated by reference to the utilization of the labour input under PERFECT COMPETITION market conditions. In a competitive LABOUR MARKET, the equilibrium WAGE RATE and numbers employed (W_e and Q_e^*, respectively, in Fig. 111b), are determined by the intersection of the market demand and supply curves for labour. Because each firm employs only a small fraction of the total labour force it is unable to influence the wage rate. Thus, the wage rate, and hence the marginal cost of labour (MFC), are constant to the firm – each extra worker adds exactly his wage rate to the firm's total factor cost (see Fig. 111a). The firm's MRP declines because although under competitive conditions the product price remains constant, the marginal physical product falls due to DIMINISHING RETURNS to the labour input.

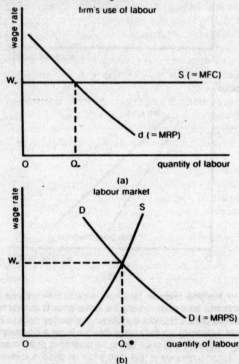

Fig. 111. **Marginal revenue product**. See entry.

The firm will maximize its profits by employing additional workers up to the point (Q_e in Fig. 111a), where the last worker's contribution to revenue (MRP), is equal to the going wage rate (MFC).

marginal tax rate the fraction of the last pound of a person's income which is paid in TAX. High marginal tax rates may act as a disincentive to working longer hours when the incremental DISPOSABLE INCOME from such extra effort is small.

See LAFFER CURVE, POVERTY TRAP.

marginal utility the increase in satisfaction (UTILITY) a consumer derives from the use or CONSUMPTION of one additional (incremental) unit of a good or service in a particular time period. For example, if a consumer, having consumed three bars of chocolate, then eats a fourth bar, then his TOTAL UTILITY will increase, and if he then eats a fifth bar his total utility will increase further. However, the marginal (incremental) utility derived from consuming the fifth bar of chocolate would tend not to be as great as the marginal utility from consuming the fourth bar, the consumer experiencing DIMINISHING MARGINAL UTILITY as he becomes sated with the product.

Most goods and services are subject to diminishing marginal utility, with consumers being prepared to pay less for successive units of these products since they are yielding lower levels of satisfaction. This explains why the DEMAND CURVE for such products slopes downwards.

See CARDINAL UTILITY, ORDINAL UTILITY, CONSUMER EQUILIBRIUM, PARETO OPTIMALITY, PARADOX OF VALUE.

marginal utility of money the increase in satisfaction (UTILITY) an individual derives from spending one incremental unit of MONEY on goods or services.

margin of error see FORECASTING.

market an EXCHANGE mechanism that brings together sellers and buyers of a PRODUCT, FACTOR OF PRODUCTION or FINANCIAL SECURITY. Markets embrace a number of product, spatial and physical dimensions. In terms of product, a market can be defined as consisting of a group of goods or services which are viewed as *substitute* products by buyers. Thus, from a buyer's point of view, women's shoes and men's shoes would be represented as constituting separate markets, that is, markets catering for the needs of different buyers.

Spatially, a market may be local, regional, national or international in scope, depending on such considerations as transport costs, product characteristics and the homogeneity of buyer tastes. For example, because of a high ratio of transport costs to value added, cement and plasterboard markets tend to be localized. Likewise, Bavarian beer caters for a specialized regional taste, while Coca Cola, by contrast, is sold worldwide as a global brand.

Physically, seller and buyer exchanges may be transacted in a well-defined market-place (for example, a local fish market or wool exchange), or in a much more amorphous way (for example, the buying and selling of stocks and shares by telephone through a nexus of international dealing offices). Finally, in some markets sellers deal directly with final buyers, while in others transactions are conducted through a chain of intermediaries such as wholesalers and retailers, brokers and banks.

Economists generally define a market as a group of products which consumers view as being substitutes for one another (that is, they have a high CROSS-ELASTICITY OF DEMAND). This concept of the market may not correspond exactly with INDUSTRIAL CLASSIFICATIONS which group products into industries (see INDUSTRY) in terms of their technical or production characteristics rather than consumer substitutability. For example, glass bottles and metal cans would be regarded by users as substitute packaging materials but are in fact allocated to different industrial classifications (the glass and metal industries respectively). By contrast, the industrial-classification category of 'steel products', for example, can encompass such diverse users as civil engineers (reinforcing bars), car manufacturers (car bodies) and white-goods manufacturers (washing machine shells). However, in the absence of reliable cross-elasticity of demand data, economists are often forced to fall back on industrial classifications as a best approximation of markets in empirical analysis.

The THEORY OF MARKETS distinguishes between markets according to their structural characteristics, in particular the number of sellers and buyers involved. A number of 'market' situations can be identified, including:

PERFECT COMPETITION	=	many sellers, many buyers
OLIGOPOLY	=	few sellers, many buyers
OLIGOPSONY	=	many sellers, few buyers
BILATERAL OLIGOPOLY	=	few sellers, few buyers
DUOPOLY	=	two sellers, many buyers
DUOPSONY	=	many sellers, two buyers
MONOPOLY	=	one seller, many buyers
MONOPSONY	=	many sellers, one buyer
BILATERAL MONOPOLY	=	one seller, one buyer

Such a classification serves well for theoretical analysis, and there is no need to make 'fine' distinctions relating to the boundaries of the market under consideration. However, from the point of view of applying policy, how widely or narrowly a market is defined depends largely upon the particular issue the policy is concerned with and the degree of precision appropriate for that policy. For example, for macroplanning purposes it may be appropriate to refer broadly to the 'drinks' market or 'food' market. From the point of view of applying COMPETITION POLICY, however, a disaggregation of such groupings into submarkets is necessary. Thus, the drinks market could be divided as between alcoholic and non-alcoholic drinks, and further divided as between the various types of alcoholic beverage – beer, spirits, wines, etc.

See also LABOUR MARKET, FOREIGN-EXCHANGE MARKET, STOCK EXCHANGE, CAPITAL MARKET, COMMODITY MARKET, MONEY MARKET, FUTURES MARKET.

market concentration the extent to which the production of a particular good or service is controlled by the leading suppliers (SELLER CONCENTRATION), and the extent to which the purchase of a product is controlled by the leading buyers (BUYER CONCENTRATION). The degree of seller (or buyer) concentration in a MARKET is often measured by a CONCENTRATION RATIO which shows the proportion of market sales (or purchases) accounted for by the largest five, or 10, suppliers (or buyers).

The significance of market concentration for market analysis lies in its effect on the nature and intensity of competition. Structurally, as the level of seller concentration in a market progressively increases, 'competition between the many' becomes 'competition between the few' until, at the extreme, the market is totally monopolized by a single supplier (see MARKET STRUCTURE). In terms of MARKET CONDUCT, as supply becomes concentrated in fewer and fewer hands (OLIGOPOLY), suppliers may seek to avoid mutually ruinous price competition and channel their main marketing efforts into sales promotion and product innovation, activities which offer a more profitable and effective way of establishing COMPETITIVE ADVANTAGE over rivals.

Buyer concentration can also affect the competitive situation. In many markets (particularly end-consumer markets) buyers are too small to influence supply conditions, but in others (particularly in intermediary goods markets and in retailing), buying power is concentrated and purchasers are able to obtain BULK BUYING discounts from suppliers.

See ECONOMIES OF SCALE, HORIZONTAL INTEGRATION, COMPETITION POLICY, MONOPOLY.

market conduct the 'things done' by firms in their capacity as suppliers (and buyers) of goods and services. Key elements of market conduct include:

(a) FIRM OBJECTIVES, for example profit, sales and asset growth targets;

(b) the COMPETITION METHODS deployed by firms to achieve their objectives, in particular their policies on PRICE and output levels and PRODUCT DIFFERENTIATION;

(c) INTERFIRM CONDUCT, specifically the extent to which firms in a market compete against each other or seek to coordinate their pricing behaviour (see COLLUSION).

In the THEORY OF MARKETS, market conduct interacts with MARKET STRUCTURE in determining MARKET PERFORMANCE, while market structure and market performance, in turn, affect market conduct.

See MARKET STRUCTURE–CONDUCT–PERFORMANCE SCHEMA, PERFECT COMPETITION, MONOPOLISTIC COMPETITION, OLIGOPOLY, MONOPOLY.

market entry the entry into a MARKET of a new FIRM or firms. In the THEORY OF MARKETS, entrants are assumed to come into the market by establishing a new plant, thereby adding to the number of competing suppliers in the market (see GREENFIELD INVESTMENT). New entry into a market occurs when established firms are earning ABOVE-NORMAL PROFITS. The entry of new firms plays an important rôle in enlarging the supply capacity of a market and in removing above-normal profits. In practice, new entry also takes place through TAKEOVER of, or MERGER with an established firm.

Most markets are characterized by BARRIERS TO ENTRY which impede or prevent entry, protecting established firms from new competitors.

See CONDITION OF ENTRY, POTENTIAL ENTRANT, CONTESTABLE MARKET, PERFECT COMPETITION, MONOPOLISTIC COMPETITION, OLIGOPOLY, MONOPOLY, LIMIT PRICING.

market exit or **exit** the withdrawal from a MARKET of a firm or firms. In the THEORY OF MARKETS, a firm will leave a market if it is unable to earn a NORMAL PROFIT in the long run. Firm exit plays an important rôle in removing EXCESS CAPACITY and reducing total market supply.
See also LOSS, AVERAGE COST (SHORT-RUN), CONTRIBUTION.

market failure the failure of MARKETS to achieve an optimum RESOURCE ALLOCATION. This may occur in particular where markets are dominated by MONOPOLY suppliers or where the production/consumption of products causes POLLUTION. See EXTERNALITIES. Market failure may necessitate government intervention to regulate markets through COMPETITION POLICY, REGIONAL POLICY, INDUSTRIAL POLICY and PRICE SUPPORT systems.
See PRICE SYSTEM.

marketing the managerial process of identifying customer requirements and satisfying them by providing customers with appropriate products in order to achieve the organization's objectives. Marketing goes beyond merely selling what the firm produces, but starts by identifying underlying consumer needs through MARKET RESEARCH; generating products which satisfy these needs through NEW PRODUCT DEVELOPMENT; promoting these products to consumers through various MARKETING MIX policies (pricing, advertising, sales promotion,

etc.); and physically distributing products to customers through DIS-
TRIBUTION CHANNELS.

market maker a firm attached to the STOCK EXCHANGE which is
engaged in the buying and selling of FINANCIAL SECURITIES such as
STOCKS, SHARES and BONDS and by so doing acts to establish a market
for these securities. Market-making firms in the UK have (since the
1986 stock market reforms) combined the rôles of jobber (acting as
a *principal* in the buying and selling of securities) and stockbroker
(acting as an *agent* on behalf of clients wishing to sell or buy securities), although the stockbroking function is still performed by firms
specializing in that activity alone.

A market-making firm usually specializes in a small group of
securities, for example the shares of companies in a particular industry. The firm makes its profit out of the difference between the 'bid'
price at which it buys a security and the (higher) 'offer' price at which
it sells. The firm marks its buying and selling prices upwards or
downwards according to whether its holding of a security is falling
or increasing. For example, if there is a strong demand for a particular
share then as the firm sells some of its holdings it will mark the share
price up to reflect its growing security value.

See BID PRICE, SHARE PURCHASE/SALE, DUAL CAPACITY, CHINESE WALL.

marketing mix the range of competitive dimensions along which
FIRMS promote their products to customers and potential consumers,
including the styling, quality, etc., of the goods and services themselves, their prices, their advertising and promotion, their packaging,
their distribution, their selling and their servicing. Management can
manipulate all these variables, and if the mix is to be effective each
dimension must be developed as one aspect of the total marketing
effort. No one dimension should be emphasized in isolation otherwise
effort is wasted, for example, pricing decisions should not be div-
orced from consideration of product and promotion policies.

See COMPETITION METHODS, PRODUCT DIFFERENTIATION, PRODUCT
MIX.

marketing research the systematic collection, assimilation and analysis of data about BUYERS and MARKETS as a means of identifying market
opportunities for a firm's existing or potential goods and/or services.
See TEST MARKET.

market mechanism see PRICE SYSTEM.

market performance the efficiency of a MARKET in utilizing scarce
resources to meet consumers' demands for goods and services; that is,
how well a market has contributed to the optimization of economic
welfare. Key elements of market performance include:

(a) PRODUCTIVE EFFICIENCY and (b) DISTRIBUTIVE EFFICIENCY, that is,
the ability of a market to produce and distribute its products at the
lowest possible cost;

(c) ALLOCATIVE EFFICIENCY, that is, the extent to which the market prices charged to buyers are consistent with supply costs, including a NORMAL PROFIT return to suppliers;

(d) TECHNOLOGICAL PROGRESSIVENESS, the ability of suppliers to introduce new cost-cutting production and distribution techniques, and superior products over time;

(e) PRODUCT PERFORMANCE, that is, the quality and variety of products offered by suppliers.

In the THEORY OF MARKETS, market performance is determined by the interaction of MARKET STRUCTURE and MARKET CONDUCT, while market performance itself has an affect on market structure and conduct.

See PARETO OPTIMALITY, RESOURCE ALLOCATION, MARKET STRUCTURE-CONDUCT-PERFORMANCE SCHEMA, PERFECT COMPETITION, MONOPOLISTIC COMPETITION, OLIGOPOLY, MONOPOLY.

market power the ability of a FIRM to administer (within limits) the supply price and terms of sale of its product without immediate competitive encroachment. Market power brings with it the particular danger of exploitation of the consumer by the supplier. The exercise of market power is typically associated with an OLIGOPOLY or a MONOPOLY.

See also ADMINISTERED PRICE, COMPETITION POLICY, SELLER CONCENTRATION, CONDITION OF ENTRY.

market price the PRICE that consumers pay for a product. For most products the market price will be the EQUILIBRIUM MARKET PRICE established by the interaction of market DEMAND and SUPPLY, though INDIRECT TAXES such as VALUE-ADDED TAX or SUBSIDIES may modify the equilibrium market price.

See INCIDENCE OF TAXATION.

market segmentation the division of a MARKET into particular subgroups of customers, each with their own buying characteristics, for example, men and women. Firms are thus able to adopt PRODUCT DIFFERENTIATION strategies to cater for the needs of different groups of buyers, enlarging their sales potential. See also PRICE DISCRIMINATION.

market share the proportion of total MARKET output or sales accounted for by an individual FIRM. Market-share data is used to measure the degree of SELLER CONCENTRATION in a market. See CONCENTRATION RATIO, CONCENTRATION MEASURES.

market structure the way in which a MARKET is organized. The THEORY OF MARKETS focuses especially on those aspects of market structure which have an important influence on the behaviour of firms and buyers and on MARKET PERFORMANCE. Structural features having a major strategic importance in relation to MARKET CONDUCT and performance include: (a) the degree of SELLER CONCENTRATION and BUYER CONCENTRATION as measured by the number of sellers and buyers (whether there are many sellers/buyers in the market, or a few, or only one), and their relative size distribution; (b) the CONDITION OF ENTRY to the market (the extent to which established suppliers have advantages over potential new entrants because of BARRIERS TO ENTRY); (c) the nature of the product supplied (whether it is a HOMOGENEOUS PRODUCT or subject to PRODUCT DIFFERENTIATION); (d) the extent to which firms produce their own input requirements, or own distribution outlets for their products (VERTICAL INTEGRATION); (e) the extent to which firms operate in a number of markets rather than just one market (DIVERSIFICATION).

Market structure, in turn, is affected by market conduct and performance.

See CONCENTRATION MEASURES, MARKET STRUCTURE-CONDUCT-PERFORMANCE SCHEMA, PERFECT COMPETITION, MONOPOLISTIC COMPETITION, OLIGOPOLY, MONOPOLY.

market structure-conduct-performance schema an analytical framework for investigating the operation of market processes. MARKETS are ultimately judged in terms of their economic performance, that is, how well they have contributed to the achievement of optimal economic efficiency. MARKET PERFORMANCE (see Fig. 112) is determined fundamentally by the interaction of MARKET STRUCTURE and MARKET CONDUCT. The schema attempts to identify those structural and conduct parameters which have a strategic influence on market performance. These relationships have been formalized in the THEORY OF MARKETS.

The market structure-conduct-performance schema highlights the interdependency of structure, conduct and performance and the extent to which each element can affect the others. Structure can influence conduct and performance; for example, a monopolistic market structure (see MONOPOLY) often leads to exploitative market conduct and poor market performance in the form of excessive prices and output restriction. Alternatively, conduct can influence structure and performance; for example, firms seeking to increase their market shares by mergers and takeovers can raise the level of SELLER CONCENTRATION which in turn will affect market performance. Again, performance can influence structure and conduct; for example, where established firms earn ABOVE NORMAL PROFITS this may induce other firms to enter the market thereby decreasing market concentration and removing excess profits. Thus, rather than these relationships being sequential and deterministic, it is more accurate to view them as being circular.

The schema is useful to public-policy makers (see COMPETITION POLICY, INDUSTRIAL POLICY) in framing measures designed to improve market performance.

Such measures can operate on market structure, for example, by prohibiting mergers which increase market concentration or by encouraging mergers in industries suffering excess capacity. Alternatively, such measures may operate on market conduct, for example, by seeking to eliminate excess profits by prohibiting price-fixing agreements between firms. Additionally, the authorities may operate directly on market performance by regulating the prices charged by monopolistic suppliers.

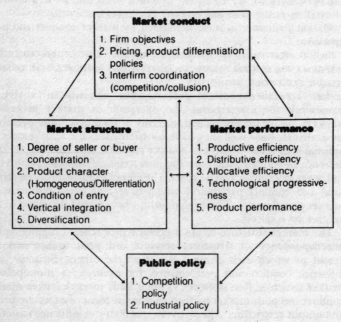

Fig. 112. **Market structure-conduct-performance schema**. See entry.

market system see PRICE SYSTEM.

Marshall, Alfred (1842–1924) an English economist who depicted precise mathematical relationships between economic variables in his textbook *Principles of Economics* (1890). Using calculus, Marshall was able to show how value is partly determined by the MARGINAL UTILITY of a good and how the intensity of wants decrease with each unit acquired. Thus, Marshall was able to explain the PARADOX OF VALUE, showing how luxuries like diamonds have a higher price than essentials like water because consumers have few diamonds whilst water is generally plentiful. This analysis enabled Marshall to explain downward-sloping DEMAND CURVES and CONSUMER SURPLUS (the surplus satisfaction derived by a consumer whenever he can buy a good at a lower price than that which he would be prepared to pay rather than go without the good). Marshall also developed the concept of ELASTICITY OF DEMAND.

Marshall argued that the forces of both demand and supply determine value, with demand determining price and output in the short run and, changes in resource inputs and production costs influencing price in the long run. He suggested that supply prices would depend upon production costs and in analysing short-run production cost showed how the marginal product of all resources tends to diminish as variable factor inputs are combined with fixed amounts of other resources (DIMINISHING RETURNS to the variable factor input). In the long run, Marshall suggested that industries would experience reducing costs and prices because of ECONOMIES OF SCALE resulting from greater specialization.

See 'REPRESENTATIVE FIRM'.

Marshall-Lerner condition the PRICE-ELASTICITY OF DEMAND for IMPORTS and EXPORTS condition which must be satisfied if an EXCHANGE-RATE alteration (DEVALUATION or REVALUATION) is to be successful in removing a balance of payments deficit or surplus.

Specifically, the elasticity values for a successful devaluation, for example, are:

demand for imports is price-elastic $(e \geqslant 1)$
demand for exports is price-elastic $(e \geqslant 1)$

How successful the devaluation is thus depends critically on the reaction of import and export volumes to the change in prices implied by the devaluation. If trade volumes are relatively elastic to price changes the devaluation will be successful; that is, an increase in import prices results in a more than proportionate fall in import volume, reducing the total amount of foreign currency required to finance the import bill, while the decrease in export prices results in a more than proportionate increase in export volume, bringing about an increase in total foreign currency earnings on exports.

By contrast, if trade volumes are relatively inelastic to price changes the devaluation will not succeed; that is, an increase in import prices results in a less than proportionate fall in import volume, increasing the total amount of foreign currency required to finance the import bill, while the decrease in export prices results in a less than proportionate increase in export volume, bringing about a fall in total foreign currency earnings on exports.

There are, however, a number of other factors which influence the eventual outcome of a devaluation, in particular the extent to which domestic resources are sufficiently mobile to be switched into export-producing and import-substitution industries.

See DEVALUATION, BALANCE-OF-PAYMENTS EQUILIBRIUM, PRICE-ELASTICITY OF SUPPLY.

Marx, Karl (1818–1883) a German philosopher who produced a new theory about historical change based upon conflict between competing groups in his book: *Das Kapital*. The first volume was published in 1867, with the remaining volumes, edited by Friedrich Engels, being published posthumously in 1885 and 1894. Marx argued that at each stage in history one particular class in society would become powerful because of its ownership of the means of production. However, in the meanwhile, another class would be developing whose interests clashed with those of the dominant class. Finally the new class would overturn the old and set itself up as a new dominant group. For example, under feudalism the aristocracy predominated because of their control of the land; then they gave way to the capitalists who gained ascendancy because of their control of capital.

Capitalists were able to drive a hard bargain with workers over wage rates, and the low-paid exploitation of the working class permitted factory owners to accumulate even greater wealth and gain monopoly power. Workers produce goods and services of value, but because they are paid so little, capitalists are able to appropriate much of this value for themselves in the form of high profits. Marx predicted that this exploitation would eventually provoke a revolution in which the 'property-less proletariat' would overthrow the dominant capitalist class and take over the means of production. Initially, under socialism, the nation's productive assets would be acquired and controlled by the State but eventually under COMMUNISM the workers themselves would collectively own the means of production, with goods and services being distributed according to peoples' needs.

See also CENTRALLY-PLANNED ECONOMY, LABOUR THEORY OF VALUE.

mass production the manufacture of a PRODUCT in very large quantities using continuous flow capital-intensive methods of production. Mass production is typically found in industries where the product supplied is highly standardized, which enables automated machinery and processes to be substituted for labour. Mass-production industries are usually characterized by high levels of SELLER CONCENTRATION, difficult CONDITIONS OF ENTRY and the exploitation of ECONOMIES OF SCALE which results in low unit costs of supply.

Compare BATCH PRODUCTION. See PRODUCTION, AUTOMATION, COMPUTER.

maturity structure the distribution of future dates on which BILLS, BONDS and REDEEMABLE FINANCIAL SECURITIES are due to be redeemed. An investor may seek to have a 'phased' PORTFOLIO of such securities which will generate a planned pattern of cash inflows as these various securities mature. Similarly, firms and governments will seek to have a phased portfolio of borrowings which will generate a planned pattern of cash outflows as these various borrowings become repayable.

See FUNDING, PUBLIC SECTOR BORROWING REQUIREMENT, TERM STRUCTURE OF INTEREST RATES.

maximin strategy see GAME THEORY.

means test an examination of the personal and financial circumstances of an individual to assess his or her eligibility for benefits under a country's system of SOCIAL SECURITY BENEFITS. The benefits which are being claimed are not regarded as a universal right, but are assessed under rules and regulations as laid down by legislation and the government department concerned. The payment of the welfare benefit is a right only if an individual is within the limits of income, personal circumstance, etc., for the period of the claim. Many poverty-action groups argue for the abolition of means-tested benefits because of the indignities which an examination of circumstances imposes and because they discourage proud but needy individuals from applying. Others argue for their retention as a means of limiting TRANSFER PAYMENTS and curbing GOVERNMENT EXPENDITURE.

media the channels of communication (commercial television and radio, newspapers and magazines, poster sites, etc.) through which a firm's product can be advertised to prospective buyers.

See ADVERTISEMENT, ADVERTISING.

mediation a procedure for settling disputes, most notably INDUSTRIAL DISPUTES in which a neutral third party meets with the disputants and endeavours to help them resolve their differences and reach agreement through continued negotiation. In some countries 'conciliation' is distinguished from 'mediation', according to the degree of intervention exercised by the conciliator or mediator in the process of encouraging the parties to settle their differences with a conciliator refraining from advancing, and the mediator expected to advance, proposals of his own for possible settlements. Both forms of intervention leave the bargaining process intact with any resultant settlement being agreed upon by all disputing parties.

In the UK, the ADVISORY, CONCILIATORY AND ARBITRATION SERVICE acts in this capacity.

See also ARBITRATION, COLLECTIVE BARGAINING, INDUSTRIAL RELATIONS.

medium of exchange an attribute of MONEY, enabling people to price goods and services and exchange them using money as a common denominator rather than exchanging one good directly for another (as in BARTER).

medium-term financial strategy a financial policy which sets out a target range for the growth of the MONEY SUPPLY, and target values for the PUBLIC-SECTOR BORROWING REQUIREMENT expressed as a percentage of GROSS DOMESTIC PRODUCT. The first UK medium-term financial strategy was introduced in 1980 and covered a period of five years ahead, and was revised and extended at annual intervals to provide a set of rolling plans for the economy. The purpose of the medium-term financial strategy was to provide a known firm base for the operation of government MONETARY POLICY, to assist in the control of public expenditure and to influence the public's expectations about future rates of INFLATION.

See also MACROECONOMIC POLICY, MONEY SUPPLY/SPENDING LINKAGES, MONETARISM.

memorandum of association a legal document which must be filed with the Register of Companies before a JOINT-STOCK COMPANY can be incorporated, and which governs the external relationship between the company and third parties. The Memorandum must contain certain compulsory clauses stating: (a) the name of the company; (b) the objects of the company; (c) the country in which the company is situated; (d) whether it is limited by shares or other means; (e) the amount and division of share capital; (e) the signature of the subscribers forming the company, each of whom must take at least one share. See ARTICLES OF ASSOCIATION.

mercantilism a set of economic ideas and policies which became established in England during the 17th century, accompanying the rise of commercial capitalism. The mercantilists stressed the importance of trade and commerce as the source of the nation's wealth, and advocated policies to increase a nation's wealth and power by encouraging exports and discouraging imports in order to allow the country to amass quantities of GOLD. These protectionist ideas (see PROTECTIONISM) were criticized by later classical economists like Adam SMITH.

merchandizing see SALES PROMOTION AND MERCHANDIZING.

merchant bank a BANK which offers a range of financial facilities and services to clients. The merchant banks are still involved in what was their original business, namely the provision of merchandise finance in the form of 'acceptance' notes on BILLS OF EXCHANGE to importers and exporters to cover products in transit. They have variously extended their interests into investment management, stockbroking, MARKET MAKING and corporate finance (see VENTURE CAPITAL). In the latter capacity, merchant banks arrange new stock and share issues on behalf of corporate clients (see SHARE ISSUES) and UNDERWRITE such issues. Merchant banks nowadays play a particularly prominent rôle in advising corporate clients on MERGERS and TAKEOVER BID TACTICS and in putting together the financial terms and details of such deals. See BANKING SYSTEM.

Mercosur see LATIN AMERICAN FREE TRADE ASSOCIATION

merger or **amalgamation** the combining together of two or more firms. Unlike a TAKEOVER, which involves one firm mounting a 'hostile' TAKEOVER BID for the other firm without the agreement of the victim firm's management, a merger is usually concluded by mutual agreement. Three broad categories of merger may be identified: (a) horizontal mergers between firms that are direct competitors in the same market; (b) vertical mergers between firms which stand in a supplier-customer relationship; (c) conglomerate mergers between firms operating in unrelated markets which are seeking to diversify their activities.

From the firm's point of view a merger may be advantageous because it may enable the firm to reduce production and distribution costs, enable it to expand its existing activities or move into new areas, or remove unwanted competition and increase its market power.

In terms of their wider impact on the operation of market processes, mergers may, on the one hand, promote greater efficiency in resource use, or, on the other hand, by reducing competition, lead to a less efficient allocation of resources.

Usually, any benefit that comes from a merger will depend upon the achievement of greater efficiency in some branch of the enlarged firm's operations. Several important sources of greater efficiency may be distinguished. Horizontal mergers frequently allow firms to secure low cost operation by realizing ECONOMIES OF SCALE in manufacture and distribution, and RATIONALIZATION opportunities. In addition, the combined organization may have access to superior technical knowhow and financial resources, previously available to only one of the firms. Vertical mergers may make possible benefits in efficiency of production by making possible more comprehensive production planning, particularly where successive processes are closely linked, and permit economies in stock holding and distribution of goods. Conglomerate mergers may yield economies in overheads (finance, administration and marketing expenditure) and may lead to an important cross-fertilization of ideas and attitudes, particularly where the acquiring company is notably well managed and cost-conscious.

While mergers may result in greater efficiency, thereby enhancing consumer welfare, they may also serve to increase MONOPOLY power. This is most clearly seen in the case of horizontal and vertical mergers. Horizontal mergers *prima facie* increase the level of SELLER CONCENTRATION in the market by reducing the number of independent sources of supply. Where the merging firms are already substantial suppliers this may reduce effective competition and permit the enlarged group more control over the market and discretion over prices. A vertical merger can produce an increase in market power in a variety of ways. If a customer firm, for example, takes over a supplier, and if the supplier is large in relation to other suppliers, other (nonintegrated) customers may find themselves forced to buy from the merged supplier and then sell their products in competition with the merged customer firm. This puts the merged group in a powerful position to discriminate in prices and availability of supplies and so 'squeeze' the profits of other nonintegrated suppliers. Superficially, conglomerate mergers appear to have little relevance to the monopoly power issue, but it is to be noted that the conglomerate may have an opportunity to affect the state of competition in a number of separate markets, by internal transfers of resources, and thus to exercise a larger degree of market power against rival companies than its market share in individual markets would otherwise permit.

In sum, mergers may involve, simultaneously, both benefits and detriments. In the UK, since 1965, mergers which create or extend a firm's market share of a particular product in excess of 25%, or where the value of assets acquired is over £70 million can be referred to the MONOPOLIES AND MERGERS COMMISSION to determine whether or not it is in the public interest.

See also COMPETITION POLICY, OFFICE OF FAIR TRADING, WILLIAMSON TRADE-OFF MODEL, HORIZONTAL INTEGRATION, VERTICAL INTEGRATION, DIVERSIFICATION, CITY CODE, DE-MERGER.

merit goods see SOCIAL PRODUCTS.

mezzanine debt see JUNK BOND.

M-form (multidivisional-form) organization an organizational structure adopted by firms in which the management of a firm is decentralized, with separate groups or divisions of the firm responsible for groups of similar products or serving separate markets. Each group or division will have its own autonomous management team and its own separate marketing, production, etc., functions. With such a structure, the top managers at head office leave the day-to-day running of the divisions to the managers responsible, though they monitor the profitability performance of the divisional managers and generally retain power over the allocation of investment funds to the divisions. Oliver Williamson coined the term 'M-form', and he argued that firms with M-form organizations were less likely to pursue nonprofit goals (MANAGEMENT-UTILITY MAXIMIZING), than firms with U-FORM (UNITARY-FORM) ORGANIZATIONS, because top managers could set clear profit goals for divisions and so suffer little control-loss over their subordinates, compared with U-form firms.

See also MANAGERIAL THEORIES OF THE FIRM, BEHAVIOURAL THEORY OF THE FIRM.

microeconomic policy the setting of specific objectives by the government for particular markets or industries and the use of control instruments to achieve those objectives. Microeconomic objectives focus upon the efficiency with which resources are allocated and ways in which impediments to efficient resource allocation such as, for example, monopoly distortions or the slow adjustment of industry capacity to market demand might be overcome through COMPETITION POLICY and INDUSTRIAL POLICY.

See REGIONAL POLICY, ECONOMIC POLICY, MACROECONOMIC POLICY.

microeconomics the branch of economics concerned with the study of the behaviour of CONSUMERS and FIRMS and the determination of the market prices and quantities transacted of FACTOR INPUTS and GOODS and SERVICES. Microeconomic analysis investigates how scarce economic resources are allocated between alternative ends and seeks to identify the strategic determinants of an optimally efficient use of resources.

See also THEORY OF CONSUMER BEHAVIOUR, THEORY OF THE FIRM, THEORY OF MARKETS, THEORY OF DEMAND, THEORY OF SUPPLY, MACRO-ECONOMICS.

middleman a trader or firm who provide a service by acting as inter-mediaries between two parties, frequently producer to consumer or seller to purchaser. WHOLESALERS may be considered middlemen for they frequently act as distributors from producers to retailers on a COMMISSION or mark-up basis. ESTATE AGENTS or insurance brokers are further examples.

middle price the price of a FINANCIAL SECURITY, FOREIGN CURRENCY or COMMODITY which lies halfway between the bid (buy) and offer (sell) price quoted by market makers or dealers.

Share prices, commodity prices and exchange rates published in newspapers are generally middle prices.

See BID PRICE.

migration the movement of people into (immigration) and out of (emigration) a country which serves to increase or decrease the country's POPULATION and labour force. For example, immigration was an important factor in the early colonization of Australia and New Zealand, and the USA and Canada.

Mill, John Stuart (1806–1873) an English economist who helped develop CLASSICAL ECONOMIC theory in his book *Principles of Political Economy with some of their Applications to Social Philosophy* (1848). Mill was a social reformer, and though he preferred to see the production and exchange of goods taking place in free markets, he argued that government intervention could improve the material well-being of the people through REDISTRIBUTION OF INCOME. Mill was the first to argue that educational barriers to labour mobility could create noncompeting groups of labour with permanent differences in wage rates between groups. He was also the first to analyse costs where two or more joint products are produced in fixed proportions.

minimax strategy see GAME THEORY.

minimum efficient scale the point on the firm's long-run AVERAGE COST curve at which ECONOMIES OF SCALE are exhausted and constant returns to scale begin.

In the theory of costs the long-run average cost is conventionally depicted as being U-shaped, with economies of scale serving to reduce average cost as output increases to begin with, but then DIS-ECONOMIES OF SCALE set in and average cost rises as output increases. However, statistical studies suggest that for many industries long-run average cost curves are L-shaped, as shown in Fig. 113.

In industries where the minimum efficient scale is large relative to the total size of the market we would expect to find high degrees of SELLER CONCENTRATION, for the market may only support a few firms of minimum efficient scale size. The potential cost disadvantage to firms seeking to enter a market on a small scale viz-a-viz large estab-lished firms can also serve as a BARRIER TO ENTRY in certain industries.

See NATURAL MONOPOLY, FLEXIBLE MANUFACTURING SYSTEM.

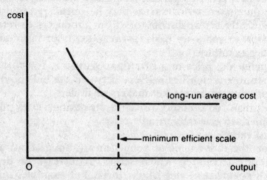

Fig. 113. **Minimum efficient scale**. See entry.

minimum lending rate see BANK RATE.

minimum wage rate the minimum rate of PAY for LABOUR either decreed by the government or voluntarily agreed between trade unions and employers. Minimum WAGE RATES are designed to ensure that workers are able to enjoy some basic standard of living, although (as shown in Fig. 114), if wage rates are set much above the 'equilib-rium rate', W_e, the effect is to reduce the demand for labour (from Q_e to Q_m). Thus, although those who remain in work (OQ_m) are now better off, those persons who are made unemployed as wages rise (Q_mQ_e) are worse off.

See TRADE UNION, SUPPLY-SIDE ECONOMICS, MARGINAL-REVENUE PRODUCT, PROFIT-RELATED PAY.

Ministry of International Trade and Industry (MITI) the Japanese equivalent of the UK DEPARTMENT OF TRADE AND INDUSTRY which is responsible for stimulating Japanese industrial development.

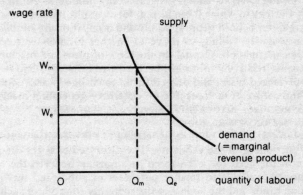

Fig. 114. **Minimum wage rate**. See entry.

minority interest that part of a subsidiary company's issued SHARE CAPITAL which is not owned by the HOLDING COMPANY. Where the holding company owns more than 50% of the shares of a subsidiary company then it is able to control that company, but where it owns less than 100% of the shares then the minority interest of other shareholders in the subsidiary company must be recognized, in particular their entitlements to a share in the profits of subsidiary companies.

mint the organization which has the exclusive right to manufacture and issue BANK NOTES and COINS on the instructions of the government's monetary authorities. In the UK this function is performed by the Royal Mint.

mixed economy a method of organizing the economy to produce goods and services. Under this ECONOMIC SYSTEM some goods and services are supplied by private enterprise, and others, typically basic INFRASTRUCTURE goods and services such as electricity, postal services, water supply, are provided by the State.

The mixed economy is a characteristic feature of most present-day developed and developing countries, 'pure' or totally PRIVATE-ENTERPRISE ECONOMIES and CENTRALLY-PLANNED ECONOMIES being rarely encountered. The precise 'mix' of private enterprise and State activities to be found in particular countries, however, does vary substantially between these two extremes and is very much influenced by the political philosophies of the country concerned. See NATIONALIZATION, PRIVATIZATION.

mobility the degree to which a FACTOR OF PRODUCTION is willing or able to move between different locations or uses.

Of the three factors of production i.e., NATURAL RESOURCES (land), LABOUR and CAPITAL, land is geographically immobile, but not necessarily the uses to which it can be put, for example, industry or agriculture. Labour is both geographically and occupationally mobile but is not necessarily willing to move to another location or retrain for another occupation. Capital (in the form of plant and machinery) is frequently relatively immobile because it is difficult to find new uses for specialized plant, and often difficult to change location due to the size and nature of such plant (e.g., electricity-generating machinery). See RESOURCE ALLOCATION, SUPPLY-SIDE ECONOMICS.

model see ECONOMIC MODEL.

monetarism a body of analysis relating to the influence of MONEY in the functioning of the economy. The theory emphasizes the importance of the need for a 'balanced' relationship between the amount of money available to finance purchases of goods and services, on the one hand, and the ability of the economy to produce such goods and services, on the other.

The theory provides an explanation of INFLATION centred on excessive increases in the MONEY SUPPLY. Specifically, the monetarists argue that if the government spends more than it receives in taxes, increasing the PUBLIC-SECTOR BORROWING REQUIREMENT to finance the shortfall, then the increase in the money supply which results from financing the increase in the public-sector borrowing requirement will increase the rate of inflation. The 'pure' QUANTITY THEORY OF MONEY (MV ≡ PT) suggests that the ultimate cause of inflation is excessive monetary creation (that is, 'too much money chasing too little output') – thus it is seen as a source of DEMAND-PULL INFLATION.

Monetarists suggest that 'cost-push' is not a truly independent theory of inflation – it has to be 'financed' by money supply increases. Suppose, initially a given stock of money and given levels of output and prices. Assume now that costs increase (for example, higher wage rates) and this causes suppliers to put up prices. Monetarists argue that this increase in prices will not turn into an inflationary process (that is, a persistent tendency for prices to rise) unless the money supply is increased. The given stock of money will buy fewer goods at the higher price level and real demand will fall; but if the government increases the money supply then this enables the same volume of goods to be purchased at the higher price level. If this process continues, COST-PUSH INFLATION is validated.

See also MONEY SUPPLY/SPENDING LINKAGES, MONETARY POLICY, MEDIUM-TERM FINANCIAL STRATEGY, CHICAGO SCHOOL.

monetary accommodation the use of MONETARY POLICY to 'accommodate' sudden supply-side changes in the economy, for example, an increase in nominal money supply to offset the deflationary impact of an oil price or other major cost increase. In the absence of monetary accommodation the cost-push inflation associated with an increase in oil prices would act to reduce the real money supply, increase interest rates and cause AGGREGATE DEMAND to fall. To avoid such recessionary tendencies, the authorities need to increase the rate of monetary growth to restore lost purchasing power.

monetary base or **high-powered money** that part of the MONEY SUPPLY that is directly under the control of a country's CENTRAL BANK. In the UK this consists of CURRENCY (BANK NOTES and COINS) in circulation plus commercial banks' TILL MONEY and their OPERATIONAL BALANCES AT THE BANK OF ENGLAND – equal to the 'M0' definition of money.

See MONEY SUPPLY DEFINITIONS, MONETARY POLICY.

monetary base control the control of the MONETARY BASE of the banking system as a means of regulating a nation's MONEY SUPPLY. If the COMMERCIAL BANKS adhere to a well-defined CASH RESERVE RATIO, then the monetary authorities, by controlling this narrow monetary base, can regulate monetary growth.

See BANK–DEPOSIT CREATION, RESERVE–ASSET RATIO, MONEY SUPPLY DEFINITIONS, MONETARY POLICY.

monetary compensatory amounts (MCAs) or **green money** the system used by the COMMON AGRICULTURAL POLICY of the EUROPEAN COMMUNITY to convert the common prices agreed for farm products into the national currencies of member countries and to realign prices when the EXCHANGE RATES of those currencies change.

The Council of Ministers meets annually and fixes common prices for individual farm products such as milk, beef, etc., for the coming year. These prices are converted into national currency values on the basis of prevailing exchange rates. Should, however, a member alter its exchange rate then the 'common link' is broken and its farm prices will either be more, or less expensive than the other member depending upon whether its exchange rate has fallen or increased. To counter this border taxes and subsidies on food IMPORTS and EXPORTS (monetary compensatory amounts) are deployed. For example, if the exchange rate rises (see APPRECIATION 1) the general effect is to cheapen food imports and make food exports more expensive. To 'compensate' for this movement, that is to ensure 'green money' values and domestic farm incomes remain stable, then food imports are taxed and food exports are subsidized. In contrast, if the exchange rate falls (see DEPRECIATION sense 1) the general effect is to cheapen food exports and make food imports more expensive. To stabilize the situation, food imports are subsidized and food exports are taxed.

monetary economy an economy that is characterized by the use of MONEY as a medium of exchange and store of value. Contrast BARTER.

monetary policy a tool of MACROECONOMIC POLICY which involves the regulation of the MONEY SUPPLY, CREDIT and INTEREST RATES in order to control the level of spending in the economy. (See DEMAND MANAGEMENT).

The monetary authorities (principally the Bank of England in the UK) can employ a number of measures to regulate the money supply, in particular that part of it which is used to underpin the provision of credit, including open market operations in government BONDS and TREASURY BILLS, special deposits and directives (see CENTRAL BANK).

Open market operations are targeted at the liquidity base of the banking system and involve the sale or purchase of bonds and Treasury bills, which alters the amount of bank deposits held by the COMMERCIAL BANKS and thus their capacity to advance LOANS and OVERDRAFTS to customers. For example, if authorities wish to reduce the money supply they can sell long-dated bonds to the general public. Buyers pay for these bonds by running down their bank deposits – an important constituent of the money supply – which forces the banks in turn to reduce the volume of their lending (see BANK DEPOSIT CREATION).

A *special deposit* call by the authorities requires the banks to place a specified portion of their liquid assets on deposit with the Bank of England which are then 'frozen', i.e. they cannot be used by the banks as the basis for advancing loans and overdrafts to customers, again reducing the money supply. A *directive* is a request by the Bank of England to the banks to keep their total lending below a specified global ceiling or to reduce their lending for particular purposes (for example, car purchase).

The authorities can also operate *instalment credit* controls on lending by FINANCE HOUSES to limit spending. They can, for example, discourage potential borrowers from using instalment facilities by increasing the down payment required and by reducing the time period of the loan; the former stipulation requires the borrower to find more ready cash, while the latter increases the effective interest charge payable.

The authorities may seek to influence interest rates more widely rather than just on particular categories of borrowing. By reducing the supply of money relative to the demand for it, the authorities can increase the price of money, i.e. the interest rate, with a view to deterring borrowing in general. For example, if the central bank wishes to raise the interest rate, say, from Or_1 to Or_2 in Fig. 115, then they can do so by reducing the money supply from OM_1 to OM_2. With the given demand curve for money this would have the effect of raising interest rates as required.

In practice, the application of monetary policy is fraught with difficulties. One problem is that there is no single reliable definition of the money supply (see MONEY SUPPLY for details), so that any attempt to target a particular specification of the money supply tends to be undermined by asset-switching from other categories. To illustrate briefly: if the authorities target M3 (mainly currency plus bank

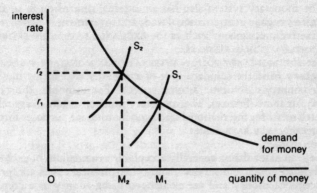

Fig. 115. **Monetary policy**. See entry.

deposits) for control purposes and use the various instruments noted above to reduce the level of bank deposits, this may not be sufficient in itself to reduce spending. Spenders may simply switch to 'M4' type money, running down their building society deposits to finance current purchases.

In addition, the 'openness' of national economies to inflows and outflows of foreign currencies makes it difficult for a government to operate domestic monetary policy without having to consider the international implications of their policy. For example, a country pursuing a policy of domestic credit contraction, leading to higher interest rates, would tend to attract inflows of foreign currencies which serve to increase the EXCHANGE RATE value of its currency.

For most of the period since 1945, monetary policy has been used as a short-term stabilization technique, but has largely taken second place to FISCAL POLICY. However, with the recent upsurge in monetarist ideas, control of the money supply on a longer-term basis has taken centre-stage in the application of economic policy.

See ECONOMIC POLICY, MONEY–DEMAND SCHEDULE, MONEY SUPPLY/ SPENDING LINKAGES, MONETARISM, QUANTITY THEORY OF MONEY, MEDIUM–TERM FINANCIAL STRATEGY, FINANCIAL INNOVATION, MONETARY ACCOMMODATION.

monetary system the policies and instruments employed by a country to regulate its MONEY SUPPLY. The physical form of the money supply (bank notes, coins, etc.), the denomination of the values of monetary units (pounds and pence, etc.), and the total size of the money supply are basic policy issues.

The instruments that can be used to control the money supply include OPEN MARKET OPERATIONS, SPECIAL DEPOSITS, DIRECTIVES and INTEREST RATE.

The monetary system also has an external dimension in so far as countries engage in international trade and investment which involves interactive mechanisms such as the EXCHANGE RATE, CONVERTIBILITY and INTERNATIONAL RESERVES.

See also MONETARY POLICY, INTERNATIONAL MONETARY SYSTEM.

monetary unit the standard unit of CURRENCY that forms the basis of a country's domestic MONEY SUPPLY. For example, the pound (UK), or franc (France). The monetary units of countries are related to each other for international trade and investment purposes through their EXCHANGE RATE values.

See MONEY.

money an ASSET that is generally acceptable as a medium of exchange. Individual goods and services, and other physical assets are 'priced' in terms of money and are exchanged using money as a common denominator rather than one GOOD, etc., being exchanged for another (as in BARTER). The use of money as a means of payment enables an economy to produce more output because it facilitates SPECIALIZATION in production and reduces the time spent by sellers and buyers in arranging exchanges. Other important functions of money are its use as a store of value or purchasing power (money can be held over a period of time and used to finance future payments), a standard of deferred payment (money is used as an agreed measure of future receipts and payments in contracts), and as a unit of account (money is used to measure and record the value of goods or services, for example, GROSS NATIONAL PRODUCT, over time). See LEGAL TENDER.

money-at-call and short notice see CALL MONEY.

money-demand schedule a schedule that depicts the relationship between the quantity of MONEY demanded, Qd (LIQUIDITY PREFERENCE) and the INTEREST RATE (i) at a given level of NATIONAL INCOME (Y):

$$Qd = f(i, Y)$$

The money-demand schedule has three components: (i) the TRANSACTION DEMAND FOR MONEY (that is, money held on a day-to-day basis to finance current expenditures on goods and services); (ii) the PRECAUTIONARY DEMAND FOR MONEY (that is, money held to cover for unforeseen contingencies); and (iii) the SPECULATIVE DEMAND FOR MONEY (that is, money held to purchase BONDS in anticipation of a fall in their price).

If the rate of interest falls this increases the speculative demand for money. The rate of interest varies inversely with the price of bonds, for example, if the nominal return on a bond is 10p and the price of the bond is £1 then the effective interest rate is 10%; if the price of

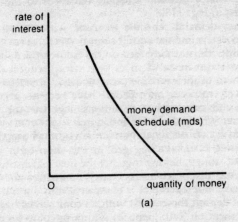

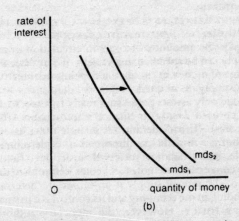

Fig. 116. **Money-demand schedule.** (a) With assumed constant national income. (b) The effect of an increase in national income.

the bond falls to 50p, the effective interest rate increases to 20%. Consequently the lower the rate of interest is the higher will be the price of bonds. The higher the price of bonds the less likely it is that bond prices will continue to rise and the greater the chances that they will fall. Thus, as shown in Fig. 116a, the lower the rate of interest the greater is the inducement to hold cash for speculative purposes.

An increase in national income increases the TRANSACTION-DEMAND FOR MONEY and may increase the PRECAUTIONARY DEMAND for money, shifting the money demand schedule outwards to the right, from mds$_1$ to mds$_2$ in Fig. 116b.

The money-demand schedule interacts with the MONEY-SUPPLY SCHEDULE to determine the equilibrium INTEREST RATE.

money illusion the illusion based on the failure of people to appreciate that a general increase in prices (INFLATION) reduces the real PURCHASING POWER of their income (REAL WAGES). In practice, however, this is unlikely to occur once people have become 'accustomed' to living with inflation, and trade unions negotiate for increases in MONEY WAGES which allow for inflationary EXPECTATIONS. See also ADAPTIVE-EXPECTATIONS HYPOTHESIS, INFLATIONARY SPIRAL.

money market a MARKET engaged in the short-term lending and borrowing of MONEY, linking together the financial institutions (COMMERCIAL BANKS, DISCOUNT HOUSES, etc.), companies and the government. To take one example: a company with surplus short-term funds might deposit these funds with its commercial bank, which in turn places them on 'call' (deposit) with a discount house. The discount house in turn uses the money to purchase TREASURY BILLS issued by the government.

See DISCOUNT MARKET, BILLS OF EXCHANGE, CERTIFICATES OF DEPOSIT.

money multiplier see BANK DEPOSIT CREATION.

money supply the amount of MONEY in circulation in an economy. Money supply can be specified in a variety of ways (see Fig. 117) and the total value of money in circulation depends on which definition of the money supply is adopted. 'Narrow' definitions of the money supply include only assests possessing ready LIQUIDITY (that is, assets which can be used *directly* to finance a transaction – for example, notes and coins). 'Broad' definitions include other assets which are less liquid but are nonetheless important in underpinning spending (for example, many building society deposits have first to be withdrawn and 'converted' into notes and coins before they can be spent).

The size of the money supply is an important determinant of the level of spending in the economy and its control is a particular concern of MONETARY POLICY. However, the monetary authorities have a problem because, given the number of possible definitions of the money supply, it is difficult for them to decide which is the most appropriate money supply category to target for control purposes. Moreover, having targeted a particular definition, they face the added difficulty of actually controlling it because of the potential for asset-switching from one category of money to another. For example, if the authorities target M3 (mainly currency plus bank deposits) for control purposes, this may not be sufficient in itself to reduce spending. Spenders may simply use their building society deposits (M4 type money) or national savings (M5 type money) to finance current purchases.

In the 1980s the UK government, as part of its MEDIUM–TERM FINANCIAL STRATEGY, set 'target bands' for the growth of, initially, sterling M3 and later M0. In recent years formal targeting of the money supply has been abandoned, although the authorities have continued to 'monitor' M0, together with M4, as 'indicators' of general monetary conditions in the economy.

See LEGAL TENDER.

money-supply definitions the definitions of MONEY SUPPLY in terms of their 'narrowness' or 'broadness'. 'Narrow' definitions include only assets possessing ready LIQUIDITY (that is, assets which can be used *directly* to finance a transaction – for example, notes and coins). 'Broad' definitions include other assets which are less liquid but are nonetheless important in underpinning spending (for example, many

Initials	Definition	Amount £bn. July 1996
	'Narrow' money (Money held predominantly for spending)	
	Bank notes and coin in circulation	22
M0	Currency plus banks' till money and operational balances at Bank of England	24
M1	M0 plus UK private sector sight bank deposits	325
M2	M1 plus UK private sector deposits in banks and building societies	452
'Broad' Money	*(Money held for spending and/or as a store of value)*	
M3 (formerly Sterling M₃)	M1 plus UK private sector time bank deposits and UK public sector sterling deposits	537
M4	M3 plus net building society deposits.	652
M5 (formerly Private Sector Liquidity)	M4 plus UK private sector holdings of money market instruments (e.g. Treasury Bills), plus National Savings	682

Fig. 117. **Money-supply definitions**. Source: Bank of England *Quarterly Bulletin*, October 1996.

building society deposits have first to be withdrawn and 'converted' into notes and coins before they can be spent). See Fig. 117.

money-supply schedule a schedule that depicts the amount of MONEY supplied and the INTEREST RATE. In some analyses the MONEY SUPPLY is drawn as a vertical straight line; that is, the money supply is exogenously determined, being put into the economic system 'from outside' by the government (for example, government-issued notes and coins which form part of 'narrow' M0 money). However, a significant part of the 'wider' money supply (M3 money), is endogenously determined – for example, bank deposits are 'created' by the banking system and these are highly interest-rate sensitive. Thus, as a general proposition, the higher the rate of interest (the higher the return on loanable funds), the greater the quantity of money supplied (see Fig. 118).

The money-supply schedule interacts with the MONEY-DEMAND SCHEDULE to determine the equilibrium rate of interest. See MONEY SUPPLY/SPENDING LINKAGES, BANK DEPOSIT CREATION.

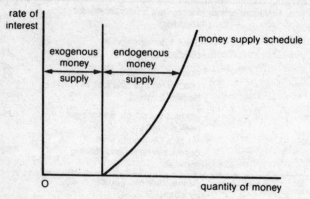

Fig. 118. **Money-supply schedule**. See entry.

money-supply/spending linkages 1. the *indirect* link (in the Keynesian view) between MONEY SUPPLY and AGGREGATE DEMAND through the INTEREST RATE. In brief, an increase in the money supply (from M to M¹ in Fig. 119a on page 356), brings about a fall in the rate of interest (from *r* to *r*¹), which results in an increase in planned INVESTMENT from I to I¹ (Fig. 119b). The rise in investment, in turn, increases aggregate demand and, via the MULTIPLIER effect, raises national income from Y to Y¹ (Fig. 119c). The fall in interest rates can also be shown to increase consumption expenditure (the lower cost of borrowing encourages people to use more LOAN finance to buy cars, televisions, etc.).

See KEYNES, KEYNESIAN ECONOMICS, EQUILIBRIUM LEVEL OF NATIONAL INCOME, LIQUIDITY TRAP.

2. the *direct* link (in the monetarist view) between the money supply and the level of aggregate demand. In brief, an increase in the money supply feeds directly into an increase in demand for final goods and services, and not just for investment goods. This proposition is based on the assumption that when households and businesses have more money than they need to hold, they will spend the excess on currently produced goods and services. See also QUANTITY THEORY OF MONEY, MONETARISM, CROWDING-OUT EFFECT.

money transmissions mechanism see MONEY SUPPLY/SPENDING LINKAGES.

money wages WAGE RATES expressed in terms of current MONEY values. An increase in the general level of prices which is not matched by an equivalent rise in money wages either because of MONEY ILLUSION on the part of the labour force or because employers refuse to grant money wage increases, will cause REAL WAGES to fall; that is, an unchanged money-wage rate will now buy fewer goods and services at the higher level of prices.

Monopolies and Mergers Commission (MMC) a commission established in 1948, and responsible, in part, for the implementation of UK COMPETITION POLICY. The basic task of the Commission is to investigate and report on cases of MONOPOLY, MERGER and ANTI-COMPETITIVE PRACTICES referred to it by the OFFICE OF FAIR TRADING to determine whether or not they operate against the PUBLIC INTEREST.

Under UK competition law, a monopoly is defined as a situation where at least one-quarter of a reference good or service is supplied by one firm (dominant-firm monopoly), or a number of suppliers who restrict competition between themselves (complex monopoly). Mergers falling within the scope of the legislation are those which create or intensify a monopoly situation (defined by the one-quarter market share rule), or where the value of assets taken over exceeds £70 million. Anticompetitive practices are those which distort, restrict or eliminate competition in a market.

The criterion of the public interest is used to evaluate monopolies, mergers and anticompetitive practices. The term 'public interest' is not expressly defined in monopoly law, so it has been left to the MMC itself to determine what constitutes offence to the public interest in each case. In monopoly cases the MMC scrutinizes the 'things done' by dominant firms for evidence of the 'abuse' of market power, and invariably condemns predatory pricing policies which result in monopoly profits. Practices such as EXCLUSIVE DEALING, AGGREGATED REBATES, TIE-IN SALES which yield very little in the way of economic benefit and whose main effect is to restrict competition have been

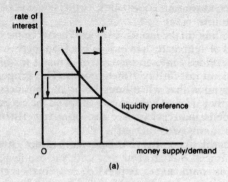

(a)

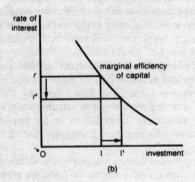

(b)

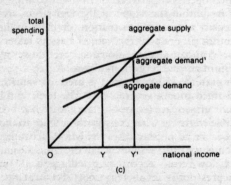

(c)

Fig. 119. **Money-supply/spending linkages**. See entry. (a) Rate of interest. (b) Planned investment. (c) National income.

invariably condemned by the MMC, especially when employed by a dominant firm to erect barriers to entry and to undermine the market positions of smaller rivals. In merger cases, the MMC is involved in weighing up the possible benefits of the merger (for example, the scope for reducing costs and better research and development) against possible detriments (for example, increased market power bringing with it the danger of higher prices). Under present law, however, parties to mergers are not required to show *net* benefit and can only be opposed if they are judged to reduce competition seriously or to impair efficiency.

In all cases the Commission has powers only of recommendation. It can recommend price cuts to deal with the problem of monopoly profits, the discontinuance of offending practices and the prohibition of offending mergers, but it is up to the Office of Fair Trading to implement the recommendations, or otherwise, as it sees fit.

monopolistic competition or **imperfect competition** or **imperfect market** a type of MARKET STRUCTURE. A monopolistically-competitive market is one that is characterized by:

(a) *many firms and buyers*, that is, the market is comprised of a large number of independently-acting firms and buyers.

(b) *differentiated products*, that is, the products offered by competing firms are differentiated from each other in one or more respects. These differences may be of a physical nature, involving functional features, or may be purely 'imaginary' in the sense that artificial differences are created through ADVERTISING and SALES PROMOTION (see PRODUCT DIFFERENTIATION).

(c) *free market entry and exit*, that is, there are no BARRIERS TO ENTRY preventing new firms entering the market or obstacles in the way of existing firms leaving the market. (No allowance is made in the 'theory' of monopolistic competition for the fact that product differentiation by establishing strong BRAND LOYALTIES to established firm's products may act as a barrier to entry).

Apart from the product-differentiation aspects, monopolistic competition is very similar structurally to PERFECT COMPETITION.

The analysis of individual firm equilibrium in monopolistic competition can be presented in terms of a 'representative' firm, that is, all firms are assumed to face *identical* cost and demand conditions, and each is a profit maximizer (see PROFIT MAXIMIZATION), from which it is then possible to derive a market-equilibrium position.

The significance of product differentiation is: (a) each firm has a market which is partially distinct from its competitors; that is, each firm faces a downward-sloping demand curve (D in Fig. 120a), although the presence of close-competing substitute products (a high CROSS-ELASTICITY OF DEMAND) will cause this curve to be relatively elastic; (b) the firms' cost structures (MARGINAL COST and AVERAGE

COSTS) are raised as a result of incurring differentiation expenditures (SELLING COSTS).

The firm being a profit maximizer will aim to produce at that price (OP)–output (OQ) combination, shown in Fig. 120a, which equates marginal cost (MC) and MARGINAL REVENUE (MR). In the short run this may result in firms securing ABOVE-NORMAL PROFITS.

In the long run, above-normal profits will induce new firms to enter the market and this will have the effect of depressing the demand curve faced by established firms (that is, push the demand curve leftwards, thereby reducing the volume of sales associated with each price level). The process of new entry will continue until the excess profits have been competed away. Fig. 120b shows the long-run equilibrium position of the 'representative' firm. The firm continues to maximize its profits at a price (OP$_e$)–output (OQ$_e$) combination where marginal cost equals marginal revenue, but now secures only a NORMAL PROFIT return. This normal profit position for the firm in the long run is similar to the long-run equilibrium position for the firm in perfect competition. But monopolistic competition results in a less efficient MARKET PERFORMANCE when compared to perfect competition. Specifically, monopolistically competitive firms produce lower rates of output and sell these outputs at higher prices than perfectly competitive firms. Since the demand curve is downwards sloping, it is necessarily tangent to the long-run average cost curve (which is higher than the perfectly competitive firms cost curve because of the addition of selling costs) to the left of the latter's minimum point. Firms thus operate a less than optimum scale of plant and as a result there is EXCESS CAPACITY in the market.

monopoly a type of MARKET STRUCTURE characterized by: (a) *one firm and many buyers*, that is, a market comprised of a single supplier selling to a multitude of small, independently-acting buyers; (b) *a lack of substitute products*, that is, there are no close substitutes for the monopolist's product (CROSS-ELASTICITY OF DEMAND is zero); (c) *blockaded entry*, that is, BARRIERS TO ENTRY are so severe that is impossible for new firms to enter the market.

In *static monopoly* the monopolist is in a position to set the market price. However, unlike a perfectly competitive producer (see PERFECT COMPETITION), the monopolist's marginal and average revenue curves are not identical. The monopolist faces a downward-sloping demand curve (D in Fig. 121a) and the sale of additional units of his product forces down the price at which all units must be sold. The objective of the monopolist, like that of the competitive firm, is assumed to be PROFIT MAXIMIZATION and he operates with complete knowledge of relevant cost and demand data. Accordingly, the monopolist will aim to produce at that price-output combination which equates MARGINAL COST and MARGINAL REVENUE. Fig. 121a indicates the short-run

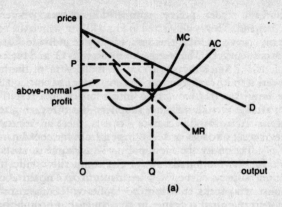

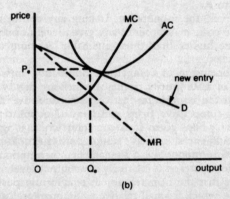

Fig. 120. **Monopolistic competition.** See entry. (a) Short-run equilibrium. (b) Long-run equilibrium.

equilibrium position for the monopolist. The monopolist will supply Q_e output at a price of P_e. At the equilibrium price, the monopolist secures ABOVE-NORMAL PROFITS. Unlike the competitive firm situation, where entry is unfettered, entry barriers in monopoly are assumed to be so great as to preclude new suppliers. There is thus no possibility of additional productive resources entering the industry and in consequence the monopolist will continue to earn above-normal profits over the long-term (until such time that supply and demand conditions radically change.) Market theory predicts that given identical cost and demand conditions, monopoly leads to a higher price and a lower output than does perfect competition.

359

Equilibrium under perfect competition occurs where supply equates demand. This is illustrated in Fig. 121b in which the competitive supply curve is MC (the sum of all the individual suppliers' marginal cost curves). The competitive output is Q_c and the competitive price is P_c. Since the supply curve is the sum of the marginal cost curves, it follows that in equilibrium, marginal cost equals price. Assume now that this industry is monopolized as a result, say, of one firm taking over all the other suppliers, but that each plant's cost curve is unaffected by this change – that is, there are *no* ECONOMIES OF SCALE or DISECONOMIES OF SCALE arising from the coordinated planning of production by the monopolist. Thus marginal costs will be the same for the monopolist as for the competitive industry, and, hence, their supply curves will be identical. As noted above, the monopolist who seeks to maximize profits will equate cost not to price, but to marginal revenue. In consequence, in equilibrium, the output of the industry falls from Q_c to Q_m and market price rises from P_c to P_m.

Moreover, the monopolist, lacking any competitive pressure to minimize cost, may produce any given level of output at unit costs which are higher than those attainable, without any penalty (see X-INEFFICIENCY).

The conclusion of competitive optimality, however, rests on a number of assumptions, some of which are highly questionable, in particular the assumption that cost structures are identical for small perfectly-competitive firms and large oligopolistic and monopoly suppliers, while, given its static framework, it ignores important *dynamic* influences, such as TECHNOLOGICAL PROGRESS.

In a static monopoly, a fundamental assumption is that costs of production increase at relatively low output levels. The implication of this is that the firm reaches an equilibrium position at a size of operation which is small relative to the market. Suppose, however, that production in a particular industry is characterized by significant economies of scale. That is, individual firms can continue to lower unit costs by producing much larger quantities. We shall illustrate this by assuming that a perfectly competitive industry is taken over by a monopolist. It is very unlikely in this instance that costs would be unaffected by the change in the scale of operations. Fig. 121c illustrates the case where the reduction in unit costs as a result of the economies of single ownership give rise to greater output and lower price than the original perfect competition situation.

The fall in unit costs as a result of monopolization moves the marginal cost curve of the monopolist (MC_m) to the right of the original supply curve (S_{pc}) so that more is produced (Q_m) at the lower price (P_m). We still make the assumption that marginal costs are rising over the relevant range of output. In the long run, this expectation follows from the proposition that at some size economies of large scale are exhausted and diseconomies of scale set in. The diseconomies are usually associated with the administrative and managerial difficulties that arise in very large complex organizations. However, there is growing evidence to the effect that the long-run average cost curve (and hence MC curve) for many capital-intensive industries is L-shaped. In these industries total demand and individual market shares, not cost considerations, are the factors limiting the size of the firm. The firm may thus grow and find a level of output such that further expansion would be unprofitable. But in doing so it may become so large relative to the market that it attains a degree of power over price. This is not to deny that the monopolist could further increase output and lower price were he not trying to maximize his profit. Such a position would not, however, be the result of a return to perfect competition. What has happened is that the firm, seeking its best profit position, has abandoned the status of an insignificant small competitor. It has not necessarily done so through a systematic attempt to dominate the market. On the contrary, it is the underlying cost conditions of the market that have impelled this growth. In such an industry it is possible that small 'competitive-sized' firms cannot survive. Moreover, to the extent that the unit costs are lower at higher production levels, the large firm is a *technically more efficient* entity.

The case of significant economies of scale, then, may be characterized as one in which atomistic competition becomes technically impossible and under an efficiency criterion, undesirable. The demonstration of competitive optimality implicitly assumes away this kind of complication.

The analysis developed above also neglects dynamic aspects of the market system. According to an influential group of writers, major improvements in consumer welfare occur largely as a result of technological INNOVATIONS, that is the growth of resources and development of new techniques and products over time rather than adjustments to provide maximum output from a given (static) input, and that monopolistic elements function as a precondition and protection of innovating effort. Perfectly competitive firms certainly have the motivation to employ the most efficient known production techniques, since this is necessary to their survival. But their inability to sustain above-normal profits limits both their resources and incentive to develop new technology. By contrast, the pure monopolist, earning above normal profits, will have greater financial resources to promote technical advance but his *incentive* to innovate may be weak given the lack of effective competition. However, technological advance is a means of lowering unit costs and thereby expanding profits; and these profits will not be of a transitory nature, given barriers to entry. Moreover, technical superiority may itself be one of the monopolist's barriers to entry; hence, the monopolist must persist and succeed in the area of technological advance to maintain his dominant position.

One of the most important advocates of the possibility that an industry exhibiting strong monopolistic elements may employ productive techniques superior to those of its competitive counterpart, was SCHUMPETER. To the extent that invention and introduction of new processes and products is centred in the large oligopolistic firm, a comparison of oligopoly/monopoly with perfect competition at a fixed technological position systematically understates the social contribution of the former.

Diagrammatically, the Schumpeterian contention may be illustrated by using Fig. 121c. The competitive market produces Q_{pc} where short-run marginal cost equals price. If this industry were monopolized, the ordinary expectation would be a price rise to P_m^1 and output decrease to Q_m^1. However, if the monopolist in such an industry introduces cost-saving innovations, the entire marginal cost curve may fall so that the monopolist may actually produce more (Q_m) at a lower price (P_m) than the original competitive industry, even if the monopolist fully exploits his market power.

It is, of course, possible that society will remain worse off under monopoly, even if the monopoly innovates; the benefits of innovation may not outweigh the costs of monopolistic exploitation.

See also OLIGOPOLY, MONOPOLISTIC COMPETITION, DISCRIMINATING MONOPOLY, COMPETITION POLICY, CONSUMER SURPLUS, CONCENTRATION MEASURES, REVISED SEQUENCE.

monopoly firm see DOMINANT FIRM.

monopoly laws see COMPETITION LAWS.

monopoly of scale see DOMINANT FIRM.

monopoly policy a policy concerned with the regulation of MONOPOLIES, MERGERS and TAKEOVERS, RESTRICTIVE TRADE AGREEMENTS, CARTELS, RESALE PRICES and ANTI-COMPETITIVE PRACTICES.

See COMPETITION POLICY for further discussion of these areas.

monopoly profit the long-term ABOVE-NORMAL PROFIT accruing to a monopolist. See MONOPOLY.

monopoly tax a levy imposed by the government on the ABOVE-NORMAL PROFIT earned by a monopolist. Unlike an order to cut prices or RATE-OF-RETURN REGULATION such a tax does nothing to restore the loss of the CONSUMERS' SURPLUS imposed by the monopoly back to the consumer. The immediate beneficiary is the government itself who may decide to use the tax as a means of raising revenue rather than as an antimonopoly device. See COMPETITION POLICY.

monopsony a form of BUYER CONCENTRATION, that is, a MARKET situ-

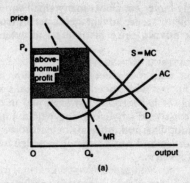

(a)

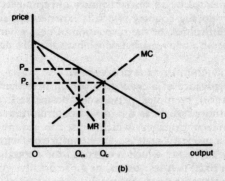

(b)

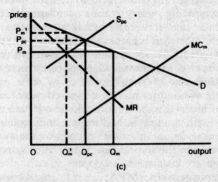

(c)

Fig. 121. **Monopoly**. See entry.

ation in which a single buyer confronts many small suppliers. Monopsonists are often able to secure advantageous terms from suppliers in the form of BULK BUYING price discounts and extended CREDIT terms.

See MONOPOLY, BILATERAL MONOPOLY.

moonlighter a person who is registered as unemployed and draws unemployment benefit, but who nonetheless takes paid work 'on the side' to supplement his or her income. For example, an out-of-work painter may decorate a friend's house, being paid a sum of money for undertaking the job. This and other BLACK ECONOMY transactions are not officially recorded and hence are not included in a country's NATIONAL-INCOME ACCOUNTS.

See TAX EVASION.

moratorium the suspension of repayment of DEBT, or INTEREST, for a specified period of time. For example, the freezing of debt repayment obligations extended by advanced country governments and private banks to a developing country which is experiencing acute balance of payments difficulties, or the suspension of debt payments owing to dealers in a commodity market which has suffered a dramatic price collapse.

See DEBT SERVICING, INTERNATIONAL DEBT.

mortgage the advance of a LOAN to a person or business (the borrower/mortgagor) by other persons or businesses, in particular financial institutions such as BUILDING SOCIETIES and COMMERCIAL BANKS (the lender/mortgagee) which is used to acquire some asset, most notably a property such as a house, office or factory. A mortgage is a form of CREDIT which is extended for a specified period of time either on fixed INTEREST terms, or more usually, given the long duration of most mortgages, on variable interest terms.

The asset is 'conveyed' by the borrower to the lender as security for the loan. The deeds giving entitlement to ownership of the property remain with the building society or bank as collateral security (against default on the loan) until it is repaid in full, when they are transferred to the mortgagor who then becomes the legal owner of the property.

most-favoured nation clause an underlying principle of the GENERAL AGREEMENT ON TARIFFS AND TRADE whereby each country undertakes to apply the same rate of TARIFF to *all* of its trade partners. This general principle of nondiscrimination evolved out of earlier GATT endorsement of bilateral trade treaties whereby if country A negotiated a tariff cut with country B, and subsequently country B negotiated an even more favourable tariff cut with country C, then the tariff rate applying in the second case would also be extended to A.

moving average see TIME-SERIES ANALYSIS.

Multi-Fibre Arrangement (MFA) a trade pact between some 80 developed and DEVELOPING COUNTRIES which regulates INTERNATIONAL

TRADE in textiles and clothing through the use of QUOTAS on imports. Its purpose is to give poor countries guaranteed and growing access to markets in Europe and North America, but at the same time to ensure this growth does not disrupt the older established textile clothing industries of the developed countries.

The MFA is a form of PROTECTIONISM which discriminates against the interests of the less-developed countries, many of whom are highly dependent on the textile industries as a leading sector in promoting their ECONOMIC DEVELOPMENT; it is contrary to the principles of the GENERAL AGREEMENT ON TARIFFS AND TRADE, but has been conveniently 'exempted' from that body's rules of good conduct.

multilateral trade the INTERNATIONAL TRADE between all countries engaged in the exporting and importing of goods and services. Compare BILATERAL TRADE.

multinational company (MNC) or **multinational enterprise (MNE)** a firm that *owns* production, sales and other revenue-generating assets in a number of countries. Foreign direct investment by MNCs in the establishment or acquisition of overseas raw material and components operations, production plants and sales subsidiaries occurs because of the potentially greater cost-effectiveness and profitability in obtaining inputs and servicing markets through a direct presence in a number of locations, rather than sole reliance on a single home base and IMPORTS and EXPORTS as the basis of the firm's international operations.

A firm may possess various COMPETITIVE ADVANTAGES over rival suppliers ('firm-specific advantages') in the form of patented process technology or a unique branded product which it can better exploit and protect by establishing overseas supply facilities. Direct investment may enable a firm to reduce its distribution costs and keep in touch more closely with local market conditions – changes in consumer tastes, competitors' actions, etc. Moreover, direct investment enables a firm both to avoid governmental restrictions on market access such as TARIFFS and QUOTAS and to benefit from other 'country-specific advantages' such as the availability of government cash grants and subsidies on inward investment. In the case of inputs, direct investment allows the MNC to take advantage of some countries' lower labour costs or provides access to superior technological know-how.

See FOREIGN INVESTMENT, INTERNALIZATION, TRANSFER PRICE, EXCHANGE RATE EXPOSURE.

multinational enterprise (MNE) see MULTINATIONAL COMPANY.

multiplier the ratio of an induced change in the EQUILIBRIUM LEVEL OF NATIONAL INCOME to an initial change in the level of spending. The 'multiplier effect' denotes the phenomenon whereby some initial increase (or decrease) in the rate of spending will bring about a more than proportionate increase (or decrease) in national income.

Two important features of the multiplier need to be noted: (a) it is a cumulative process rather than instantaneous effect, and as such is best viewed in terms of a series of successive 'rounds' of additions to income; (b) the value of the multiplier depends on the fraction of extra INCOME that is spent on CONSUMPTION (the MARGINAL PROPENSITY TO CONSUME) (MPC) at each successive round.

For simplicity, let us assume that all income is either consumed or 'withdrawn' as SAVINGS. (That is, the MPC and MARGINAL PROPENSITY TO SAVE (MPS) together = 1.) The value of the multiplier (K) is then given by the formula:

$$K = \frac{1}{1 - MPC} \text{ or } \frac{1}{MPS}$$

The larger an increase in consumption from an increment of income, the larger the multiplier. Thus, if MPC is 0.9 and MPS is 0.1, the multiplier value is 10; if MPC is 0.75 and MPS is 0.25, the multiplier value is only 4.

The multiplier effect is illustrated in Fig. 122a and b. With a multiplier value of 4, an initial £500 million of extra spending results in a £2 billion increase in national income, as Fig. 122a shows. In each round a proportion of the additional income created is saved and so leaks from the circular flow, failing to get passed on as additional consumption expenditure in the next round. When the cumulative total of these savings leakages is equal to the initial increase in spending the multiplier process ceases and the economy reaches a new equilibrium.

Fig. 122b demonstrates the multiplier effect in graphical form. Starting at national income level OY_1, if AGGREGATE DEMAND increases from AD to AD_1, then the initial injection of extra spending AB would serve to increase output and income by Y_1Y_2. This additional income would induce yet more spending (CD) which would in turn increase output and income by Y_2Y_3. This additional income would induce yet more spending (EF) which would in turn increase output and income yet further, and so on. The process ends when the new equilibrium level of income Y_e is reached.

In addition, of course, to the savings 'withdrawal' from the income flow there are also TAXATION and IMPORT withdrawals which further reduce the value of the multiplier. Thus the more sophisticated multiplier is given by the formula:

$$K = \frac{1}{MPS + MPT + MPM}$$

where MPT is the MARGINAL PROPENSITY TO TAX and MPM is the

MARGINAL PROPENSITY TO IMPORT. See also CIRCULAR FLOW OF NATIONAL INCOME MODEL, ACCELERATOR.

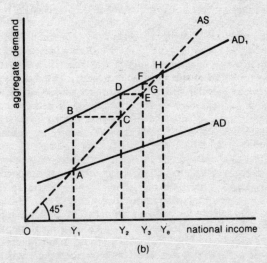

Round	Change in national income (in £ millions)	Change in consumption MPC = 0.75	Change in saving MPS = 0.25
1. Initial Increase in Spending	500	375	125
2.	375	281	94
3.	281	211	70
4.	211	158	53
5.	158	119	39
All later Rounds	475	356	119
Totals	2,000	1,500	500

(a)

(b)

Fig. 122. **Multiplier**. See entry. (a) The multiplier process. (b) The multiplier effect of increased spending on national income.

multiproduct firm a FIRM that produces a number of products. Basic economic theory concentrates on the single-product firm to simplify analysis though in practice firms can produce different varieties of the same product (product development) or several different products (DIVERSIFICATION). See PRODUCT-MARKET MATRIX.

mutual interdependence a form of INTERFIRM CONDUCT pattern in which some or all of the firms in a market formulate their competitive strategy in the light of anticipated reactions and countermoves of rival firms. The actions of firms both affect and are affected by each other – the situation is circular. A price cut, for example, may appear to be advantageous to one firm considered in isolation, but if this results in other firms cutting their prices also to protect their sales then all firms may suffer reduced profits. Accordingly, firms may seek to avoid price competition, employing such mechanisms as PRICE LEADERSHIP to coordinate their prices. The same mutual interdependency considerations may apply to other areas of competition; for example, if one firm increases its advertising expenditures other firms may follow suit to protect their market shares.

Such interdependency exists in market situations, typically in an oligopolistic market (see OLIGOPOLY), where the leading firms each supply a significant proportion of total market supply.

See also CARTEL, PRICE WAR, DUOPOLY, PRODUCT DIFFERENTIATION, GAME THEORY, KINKED–DEMAND CURVE THEORY, LIMIT PRICING.

N

NAFTA see NORTH AMERICAN FREE TRADE AGREEMENT.

National Board for Prices and Incomes a UK regulatory body which acted to control prices, wages etc. under the government's PRICES AND INCOMES POLICY from 1965 to 1970.

national debt or **government debt** the money owed by central government to domestic and foreign lenders. A national debt arises as a result of the government spending more than it receives in taxation and other receipts (BUDGET DEFICIT). This may arise due to, for example, a 'one-off' event (the financing of a war), or reflects the governments commitment to an expansionary FISCAL POLICY.

National debt in the UK is made up of a number of financial instruments primarily short-dated TREASURY BILLS and long-dated BONDS, together with national savings certificates. INTEREST on the national debt is paid out of current budget receipts.

Concern is sometimes expressed at the size of the national debt. In 1995, for example, the UK's net national debt stood at £307,000 million compared to current GROSS DOMESTIC PRODUCT of £700,900 million. However, provided that the bulk of the debt is held by domestic residents and institutions there is no cause for alarm. In terms of the CIRCULAR FLOW OF NATIONAL INCOME MODEL, the interest paid on the national debt to domestic lenders is only a TRANSFER PAYMENT and does not represent a net reduction in the real resources of the economy or compromise the ability of the economy to provide goods and services. In 1995, 94% of the UK's national debt was held domestically and interest payments accounted for only 9% of total GOVERNMENT EXPENDITURE.

See BUDGET (GOVERNMENT), PUBLIC SECTOR BORROWING REQUIRE-MENT, PUBLIC SECTOR DEBT REPAYMENT.

National Economic Development Council (NEDC) an organization which operated in the UK from 1962 to 1992 whose objective was to improve the country's poor economic performance compared to other advanced industrial countries. NEDC was created as a form of economic-planning agency, bringing together the government and both sides of industry, management and the trade unions, with a general remit to identify obstacles to the attainment of improved efficiency and growth and to formulate appropriate means of over-coming them. At the 'grass roots' level, NEDC was represented by various subcommittees (Economic Development Committees) each covering a particular industrial sector, with the main NEDC body playing a supportive and coordinating rôle. See also INDICATIVE PLAN-NING, NATIONAL PLAN.

National Enterprise Board a UK organization that promoted and financially assisted industrial RATIONALIZATION, MERGERS and industrial projects from 1975 to 1981. See also BRITISH TECHNOLOGY GROUP, INDUSTRIAL POLICY.

national income or **factor income** the total money income received by households in return for supplying FACTOR INPUTS to business over a given period of time. National income is equal to NET NATIONAL PRODUCT, and consists of the total money value of goods and services produced over the given time period (GROSS NATIONAL PRODUCT) less CAPITAL CONSUMPTION. See NATIONAL INCOME ACCOUNTS, CIRCULAR FLOW OF NATIONAL INCOME.

national income accounts the national economic statistics that show the state of the economy over a period of time (usually one year). NATIONAL INCOME is the net value of all goods and services (NATIONAL PRODUCT) produced annually in a nation: it provides a useful money measure of economic activity, and by calculating national-income per head of population, serves as a useful indicator of living standards. In this latter use it is possible to compare living standards over time or to make international comparisons of living standards.

National income can be considered in three ways, as Fig. 123 on page 372 suggests:

(a) the *domestic product/output* of goods and services produced by enterprises within the country. (*value-added approach to GDP*). This total output does not include the value of imported goods and services. To avoid overstating the value of output produced by double-counting both the final output of goods and services and the output of intermediate components and services which are eventually absorbed in final output, only the VALUE ADDED at each stage of the production process is counted. The sum of all the value added by various sections of the economy (agriculture, manufacturing, etc.) is known as the GROSS DOMESTIC PRODUCT; and to arrive at the GROSS NATIONAL PRODUCT it is necessary to add net property income from abroad (defined as net income in the form of interest, rent, profits and dividends accruing to a nation's citizens from their ownership of assets abroad).

(b) the total INCOME of residents of the country derived from the current production of goods and services (*income approach to GDP*). Such incomes are called FACTOR INCOMES because they accrue to factors of production, and they exclude TRANSFER PAYMENTS like sickness or unemployment benefit for which no goods or services are received in return. The sum of all these factor incomes (wages and salaries, incomes of the self-employed, etc.) should exactly match the gross domestic product, since each £1's worth of goods and services produced should simultaneously produce £1 of factor income for their producers. To get from gross domestic factor incomes (= gross domestic product) to gross national factor incomes (= gross national product) it is necessary to add net property income from abroad.

(c) the *total domestic expenditure* by residents of a country on consumption and investment goods (*expenditure approach to GDP*). This includes expenditure on *final* goods and services (excluding expenditure on intermediate products), and includes goods which are unsold and added to stock (inventory investment). However, some domestic expenditure will be channelled to imported goods, while expenditure by nonresidents on goods and services produced by domestic residents will add to the factor incomes of these residents. Thus, to get from total domestic expenditure to total national expenditure (= gross national product) it is necessary to deduct imports and add exports.

All three measures outlined above show the gross money value of goods and services produced – the gross national product. However, in the process of producing these goods and services the nation's capital stock will be subject to wear and tear, and so we must allow for the net money value of goods and services produced (allowing for the depreciation of the capital stock or CAPITAL CONSUMPTION) – the NET NATIONAL PRODUCT. This net national product is called national income.

In practice, data-collection problems mean that the three measures of national income give slightly different figures, necessitating the introduction of a residual error term in the national income accounts which reflects these differences. Additionally, in order to highlight the difference in the money and REAL VALUE of national income it is necessary to take account of the effects of INFLATION upon GNP by applying a broad-based PRICE INDEX called the GNP-DEFLATOR. See also BLACK ECONOMY.

national insurance contributions the payments made by employers and their employees to the UK government, on a two-thirds and one-thirds basis respectively, up to a specified maximum limit. National insurance contributions, together with other government budgetary receipts, are used to finance state pensions, sick pay, unemployment benefits, etc. See BUDGET (GOVERNMENT).

nationalization the public ownership of industry. In a CENTRALLY PLANNED ECONOMY most or all of the country's industries are owned by the State, and resources are allocated, and the supply of goods and services determined, in accordance with a NATIONAL PLAN. In a MIXED ECONOMY some industries are owned by the State but the supply of the majority of goods and services is undertaken by PRIVATE-ENTERPRISE industries operating through the MARKET mechanism. The extent of public ownership of industry depends very

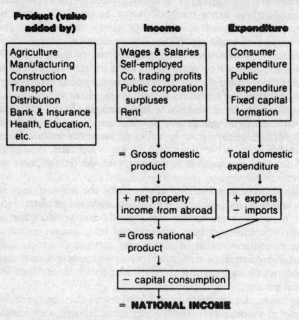

Product (value added by)	Income	Expenditure
Agriculture Manufacturing Construction Transport Distribution Bank & Insurance Health, Education, etc.	Wages & Salaries Self-employed Co. trading profits Public corporation surpluses Rent	Consumer expenditure Public expenditure Fixed capital formation
↓	↓	↓
	= Gross domestic product	Total domestic expenditure
	↓	↓
	+ net property income from abroad	+ exports − imports
	↓	
	= Gross national product	
	↓	
	− capital consumption	
	↓	
	= **NATIONAL INCOME**	

Fig. 123. **National income accounts**. See entry.

much on political ideology with centrally planned economy advocates seeking more nationalization, and private-enterprise proponents favouring little or no nationalization. For example, in the UK a Labour government nationalized the iron and steel industry in 1949, having previously nationalized the Bank of England, civil aviation, transport, electricity, coal and gas industries; the iron and steel industry was denationalized by a Conservative government in 1953, but later a large part of the industry was renationalized by a Labour government in 1967. Since 1980 a Conservative government has embarked on a major denationalization programme, including British Steel (see PRIVATIZATION).

The main economic justification for nationalization relies heavily on the NATURAL MONOPOLY argument: the provision of some goods and services can be more efficiently undertaken by a monopoly supplier, because ECONOMIES OF SCALE are so great that only by organizing the industry on a single-supplier basis can full advantage be taken of cost savings. Natural monopolies are particularly likely to arise where the provision of a good or service requires an interlocking supply network as, for example, in gas, electricity and water distribution, and railway and telephone services. In these cases laying down competing pipelines and carriage ways would involve unnecessary duplication of resources and extra expense. Significant production economies of scale are associated with capital-intensive industries such as iron and steel, gas and electricity generation. In other instances, however, the economic case for nationalization is far less convincing: industries or individual firms may be taken over because they are making losses and need to be reorganized, or a political concern with preserving jobs. For example, in the UK, the British Leyland car firm and British Shipbuilders were nationalized in 1975 and 1977 respectively, only to be returned to private enterprise in the 1980s.

A private-enterprise MONOPOLY could, of course, also secure the same efficiency gains in production and distribution as a state monopoly, but the danger exists that it might abuse its position of market power by monopoly pricing. The state monopolist, by contrast, would seek to promote the interests of consumers by charging 'fair' prices. Opponents of nationalization argue, however, that State monopolists are likely to dissipate the cost savings arising from economies of scale by internal inefficiencies (bureaucratic rigidities and control problems giving rise to X-INEFFICIENCY), and the danger is that such inefficiencies could be exacerbated over time by governments subsidizing loss-making activities.

The problem of reconciling supply efficiency with various other economic and social objectives of governments further complicates the picture. For example, the government may force nationalized industries to hold down their prices to help in the control of inflation, but by squeezing the industries' cash flow the longer term effects of this might be to reduce their investment programmes. Many of the nationalized industries are charged with social obligations; for example, they may be required by the government to provide railway and postal services to remote rural communities even though these are totally uneconomic.

Thus, assessing the relative merits and demerits of nationalization in the round is a difficult matter. From an economic efficiency point of view, under British COMPETITION POLICY, nationalized industries can be referred for investigation to the MONOPOLIES AND MERGERS COMMISSION to determine whether or not they are operating in the public interest.

See MARGINAL COST PRICING, AVERAGE COST PRICING, TWO-PART TARIFF, PUBLIC UTILITY, RATE-OF-RETURN REGULATION, PRIVATIZATION.

nationalized industry an industry that is owned by the State.

See NATIONALIZATION.

national plan a long-term plan for the development of an economy.

Such plans usually cover a period of five years or more and attempt to remove bottlenecks to economic development by co-ordinating the growth of different sectors of the economy by making appropriate investment and manpower planning arrangements. National plans are formulated by government agencies in CENTRALLY-PLANNED ECONOMIES, and by collaboration between government, industry and trade unions in MIXED ECONOMIES.

See also INDICATIVE PLANNING, NATIONAL ECONOMIC DEVELOPMENT COUNCIL.

national product the total money value of goods and services produced in a country over a given time period (GROSS NATIONAL PRODUCT). Gross national product less CAPITAL CONSUMPTION or depreciation is called NET NATIONAL PRODUCT which is equal to NATIONAL INCOME. See NATIONAL-INCOME ACCOUNTS.

National Research and Development Corporation a UK organization that promoted and financially assisted the development and industrial application of INVENTIONS from 1948 to 1981. See INDUSTRIAL POLICY.

natural monopoly a situation where ECONOMIES OF SCALE are so significant that costs are only minimized when the entire output of an industry is supplied by a single producer so that supply costs are lower under MONOPOLY than under conditions of PERFECT COMPETITION and OLIGOPOLY. The natural monopoly proposition is the principal justification for the NATIONALIZATION of industries such as the railways. See MINIMUM EFFICIENT SCALE.

natural rate of economic growth see HARROD ECONOMIC-GROWTH MODEL.

natural rate of unemployment the general rate of UNEMPLOYMENT which is consistent with a stable rate of INFLATION. The term natural rate of unemployment is often used synonymously with NONACCELERATING INFLATION RATE OF UNEMPLOYMENT (NAIRU).

See EXPECTATIONS-ADJUSTED/AUGMENTED PHILLIPS CURVE.

natural resources the contribution to productive activity made by land (for example, a factory site or farm) and basic raw materials such as iron-ore, timber, oil, corn, etc. Some natural resources, such as wheat, are renewable, whilst others, such as iron ore, are finite and will eventually be exhausted. However, as stocks of exhaustable natural resources begin to deplete their price will tend to rise, providing an incentive to seek other natural or synthetic substitutes for them. Natural resources are one of the three main FACTORS OF PRODUCTION, the other two being LABOUR and CAPITAL.

near money any easily saleable (liquid) ASSET that performs the function of MONEY as a STORE OF VALUE, but not that of a universally acceptable MEDIUM OF EXCHANGE. CURRENCY (notes and coins) serves as a store of value and being the most liquid of all assets is universally accepted as a means of PAYMENT. However, building society deposits, National Savings deposits and Treasury Bills are, respectively, less and less readily acceptable in their present form for making payments, and thus function as 'near money'.

See MONEY-SUPPLY DEFINITION.

necessary condition a condition that is indispensable for the achievement of an objective. A necessary condition is usually contrasted with *sufficient condition*, which is viewed as the adequacy of a condition to achieve an objective.

For example, an increase in INVESTMENT is a necessary condition in the achievement of higher rates of ECONOMIC GROWTH but it is not a sufficient condition to generate growth in so far as other factors, such as an increase in the LABOUR FORCE, also contribute to raising growth rates.

NEDC see NATIONAL ECONOMIC DEVELOPMENT COUNCIL.

negative income tax a proposed TAX system aimed at linking the TAXATION and SOCIAL-SECURITY BENEFITS systems for low income or no income members of society. This is done by replacing the separate systems for collecting PROGRESSIVE TAXATION and for paying social security benefits, by a single system which links the two together by establishing a common stipulated minimum income level, taxing those above it and giving *tax credits* to those below it.

Proponents of the negative income-tax system point to its advantages in assisting in the removal of the POVERTY TRAP and in making labour markets more flexible.

See SUPPLY-SIDE ECONOMICS.

neoclassical economics a school of economic ideas based on the writings of MARSHALL, etc., that superseded CLASSICAL ECONOMIC doctrines towards the end of the 19th century. Frequently referred to as the 'marginal revolution', neoclassical economics involved a shift in emphasis away from classical economic concern with the source of wealth and its division between labour, landowners and capitalists, towards a study of the principles that govern the optimal allocation of scarce resources to given wants. The principles of DIMINISHING MARGINAL UTILITY and STATIC EQUILIBRIUM ANALYSIS were founded in this new school of economic thought.

neoKeynesians those economists who tend to support, to a greater or lesser degree, the main thrust of KEYNES' arguments and who have subsequently revised and built upon the theory Keynes propounded.

See DOMAR ECONOMIC-GROWTH MODEL, HARROD ECONOMIC-GROWTH MODEL.

net book value the accounting value of a FIXED ASSET in a firm's BALANCE SHEET that represents its original cost less cumulative DEPRECIATION charged to date.

net domestic-fixed-capital formation see GROSS DOMESTIC-FIXED-CAPITAL FORMATION.

net domestic product the money value of a nation's annual output of goods and services, less CAPITAL CONSUMPTION experienced in producing that output. See NATIONAL-INCOME ACCOUNTS.

net national product the GROSS NATIONAL PRODUCT less CAPITAL CONSUMPTION or depreciation. It takes into account the fact that a proportion of a country's CAPITAL STOCK is used up in producing this year's output. See NATIONAL-INCOME ACCOUNTS.

net present value see DISCOUNTED CASH FLOW.

net profit the difference between a firm's TOTAL REVENUE and all EXPLICIT COSTS. In accounting terms net profit is the difference between GROSS PROFIT and the costs involved in running a firm. See PROFIT, PROFIT-AND-LOSS ACCOUNT.

net worth see LONG-TERM CAPITAL-EMPLOYED.

New International Economic Order (NIEO) an economic and political concept that advocates the need for fundamental changes in the conduct of INTERNATIONAL TRADE and ECONOMIC DEVELOPMENT to redress the economic imbalance between the DEVELOPED COUNTRIES and the DEVELOPING COUNTRIES. The UNITED NATIONS responded to the call of developing countries for such a change by issuing the Declaration and Programme of Action on the Establishment of a New International Economic Order in 1974, which laid down principles and measures designed to improve the relative position of the developing countries. These initiatives have centred on the promotion of schemes such as: (a) INTERNATIONAL COMMODITY AGREEMENTS to support developing countries' primary-produce exports; (b) the negotiation of special trade concessions to enable developing countries' manufactured exports to gain greater access to the markets of the developed countries; (c) the encouragement of a financial and real resource transfer programme of ECONOMIC AID; (d) an increase in economic cooperation between the developing countries.

These aspirations have been pursued primarily through the UNITED NATIONS CONFERENCE ON TRADE AND DEVELOPMENT, but as yet have met with little success.

new-issue market see CAPITAL MARKET.

newly industrializing country a DEVELOPING COUNTRY that has moved away from exclusive reliance on primary economic activities (mineral extraction and agricultural and animal produce) by establishing manufacturing capabilities as a part of a long-term programme of INDUSTRIALIZATION. Brazil, Mexico and Hong Kong are examples of a newly industrializing country. See STRUCTURE OF INDUSTRY, ECONOMIC DEVELOPMENT.

new product a good or service which is sufficiently different from existing products to be regarded as 'new' by consumers. The degree of 'newness' of a product depends upon the extent of its novelty and whether it embodies product attributes not previously available, and can range from relatively minor adaptations of existing products to entirely different product offerings like microwave ovens. A product which is significantly novel can give a supplier a major PRODUCT DIFFERENTIATION advantage over competitors. As such NEW PRODUCT DEVELOPMENT is an important area of non-price competition in OLIGOPOLY.

new product development see PRODUCT DEVELOPMENT.

new protectionism the use of various devices such as EXPORT RESTRAINT AGREEMENTS, local content requirements and import licensing arrangements which serve to restrict INTERNATIONAL TRADE. See GENERAL AGREEMENT ON TARIFFS AND TRADE, PROTECTIONISM, BEGGAR-MY-NEIGBOUR POLICY.

NIC see NEWLY INDUSTRIALIZING COUNTRY.

nineteen ninety-two (1992) see EUROPEAN COMMUNITY, SINGLE EUROPEAN MARKET ACT.

nominal exchange rate the EXCHANGE RATE of a currency expressed in current price terms, that is, making no allowance for the effects of INFLATION.

Contrast REAL EXCHANGE RATE.

nominal interest rate the INTEREST RATE paid on a LOAN without making any adjustment for the effects of INFLATION.

Contrast REAL INTEREST RATE.

nominal price the PRICE of a PRODUCT or FINANCIAL SECURITY measured in terms of current prevailing price levels, that is, making no allowance for the effects of INFLATION.

Contrast REAL PRICE. See PAR VALUE.

nominal rate of protection the actual amount of PROTECTION accorded to domestic suppliers of a final product when a TARIFF is applied to a competing imported final product. For example, assume that initially the same domestic product and imported product are both priced at £100. If an AD VALOREM TAX of 10% is now applied to the imported product its price will increase to £110. This allows domestic VALUE ADDED (and prices) to rise by up to £10 with the domestic product still remaining fully competitive with the imported product. The nominal rate of protection accorded to domestic suppliers is thus 10% of the price of the imports. Compare EFFECTIVE RATE OF PROTECTION.

nominal values the measurement of an economic aggregate (for example GROSS DOMESTIC PRODUCT) in terms of current prices. Because of price changes from year to year observations based on current prices can obscure the underlying real trend.

Contrast REAL VALUES.

nominee holding the SHARES in a JOINT-STOCK COMPANY that are held under the names of a token shareholder on behalf of their ultimate owners. Nominee holdings are used where a person or institution wishes to keep secret the extent of their shareholding in a company, often as a prelude to a TAKEOVER initiative.

nonaccelerating inflation rate of unemployment (NAIRU) the underlying level of UNEMPLOYMENT that is consistent with a stable rate of INFLATION. This underlying rate of unemployment is often termed the NATURAL RATE OF UNEMPLOYMENT. The natural rate of unemployment reflects the demand for, and supply of, labour and should result in labour market forces which neither accelerate nor decelerate the current rate of inflation insofar as it produces inflationary EXPECTATIONS among wage bargainers which are consistent with the current inflation rate.

However, there is nothing immutable about the 'natural' rate of unemployment, which can vary between countries as well as within countries over time as a result of:

(a) government measures which seek to reduce inflationary expectations directly through such devices as PRICES AND INCOMES POLICY norms which aim to establish lower wage and price increases;

(b) various supply-side measures, for example improved training which, by affecting skill levels and occupational labour mobility, serve to increase the supply of products in relation to current demand. This can either reduce the unemployment rate in relation to the current inflation rate, or lead to lower inflation rates for a given rate of unemployment.

See EXPECTATIONS-ADJUSTED/AUGMENTED PHILLIPS CURVE, SUPPLY-SIDE ECONOMICS.

nondiscretionary competition policy an approach to the control of MONOPOLY that involves the stipulation of 'acceptable' standards of MARKET STRUCTURE and MARKET CONDUCT and which prohibits outright any breach of these standards.

See COMPETITION POLICY.

nondurable good a CONSUMER GOOD, such as a vegetable, and some CAPITAL GOODS, such as a casting mould, which is used up in a single time period rather than over a relatively long time period.

Contrast DURABLE GOOD.

non-exhaustable natural resources see NATURAL RESOURCES.

nonmarketed economic activity any economic activity that, although usually legal, is not recorded in the NATIONAL INCOME ACCOUNTS of a nation. The labour and other inputs used in such activities are not paid a cash price for the work done and are therefore unrecorded. Examples of such activities are unpaid cooking and cleaning by housewives and unpaid charity work by voluntary organizations. Such omissions distort international comparisons of gross national income figures not least because rural areas tend to be more self-sufficient whilst urbanized countries tend to purchase what they need rather than making it themselves (e.g., milk, bread, etc.).

See BLACK ECONOMY.

nonprice competition see COMPETITION METHODS, PRODUCT DIFFERENTIATION.

non-profit making organization any organization which has primary objectives other than the making of PROFIT, for example a charitable trust.

non-tariff barrier see IMPORT RESTRICTION.

nontraded product 1. a product that cannot be traded under any circumstance because no markets for such products exist, for example COLLECTIVE PRODUCTS like defence.

2. a product which cannot be traded outside a certain limited geographic area because its bulk or weight make it prohibitively expensive to transport and trade internationally, for example gravel and bricks.

normal product a good or sevice for which the INCOME-ELASTICITY OF DEMAND is positive; that is, as income rises, buyers purchase more of the product. Consequently, when the price of such a product falls thereby effectively increasing consumers' real income, then that price cut will have the INCOME EFFECT of tending to increase quantity demanded. This will tend to reinforce the SUBSTITUTION EFFECT of a price cut which will cause consumers to buy more of the product because it is now relatively cheaper.

This applies to most products with the exception of INFERIOR PRODUCTS where the income effect is negative. See PRICE EFFECT.

normal profit a PROFIT that is just sufficient to ensure that a firm will continue to supply its existing good or service. In the THEORY OF MARKETS, firms' COST curves thus include normal profit as an integral part of supply costs (see ALLOCATIVE EFFICIENCY).

If the level of profit earned in a particular market is too low to generate a return on capital employed comparable to that obtainable in other equally risky markets, then the firm's resources will be transferred to some other use.

See OPPORTUNITY COST, MARKET EXIT, ABOVE-NORMAL PROFIT.

normative economics the study of what 'ought to be' in economics, rather than what 'is'. For example, the statement that 'people who earn high incomes *ought* to pay more income tax than people who earn low incomes' is a normative statement. Normative statements reflect peoples' subjective value judgements of what is good or bad and depend on ethical considerations such as 'fairness' rather than strict economic rationale. The actual economic effects of a taxation structure which taxes the rich more heavily than the poor (on spending and saving, for example) is a matter for POSITIVE ECONOMICS. See WELFARE ECONOMICS.

North American Free Trade Agreement (NAFTA) a regional FREE
TRADE AREA established in 1989 by the USA and Canada. NAFTA
aims to remove trade barriers for most manufactured goods, raw
materials and agricultural produce over a 10-year period, as well as
restrictions on cross-border investment, banking and financial services. Mexico joined NAFTA in 1993.

null hypothesis see HYPOTHESIS TESTING.

numeraire a monetary unit that is used as the basis for denominating
international exchanges in a product or commodity, and financial
settlements, on a common basis. For example, the US DOLLAR is used
as the numeraire of the oil trade; the SPECIAL DRAWING UNIT is used
as the numeraire of the internal financial transactions of the INTER-
NATIONAL MONETARY FUND and the EUROPEAN CURRENCY UNIT is used
to denominate financial transactions within the EUROPEAN MONETARY
SYSTEM.

O

OECD see ORGANIZATION FOR ECONOMIC COOPERATION AND DEVELOPMENT.

off-balance sheet financing the payment for use of an ASSET by hiring (LEASING) it rather than buying it. If a company wishes to instal a new £50,000 photocopier it may enter into a lease agreement and agree to pay £12,000 per year over 5 years rather than buy the copier. Each year £12,000 is charged against profits in the company's PROFIT-AND-LOSS ACCOUNT. The copier does not appear in the BALANCE SHEET as a FIXED ASSET because the firm does not own it, but shows up as an annual operating cost which may be offset against PROFIT for TAXATION purposes. Off-balance sheet financing enables a company to make use of expensive assets without having to invest large sums of money to buy them. It also enables a company to keep its LONG-TERM CAPITAL EMPLOYED as small as possible, improving its measured RETURN ON CAPITAL-EMPLOYED.

See LEASE-BACK.

offer curve see EDGEWORTH BOX.

offer for sale a method of raising new SHARE CAPITAL by issuing company shares to the general public at a prearranged fixed price.

See SHARE ISSUE.

offer-for-sale by tender a method of raising new SHARE CAPITAL by issuing company shares to the general public at a price which is determined by the strength of investment demand for it, subject to a minimum price bid.

See SHARE ISSUE.

Office of Fair Trading (OFT) an authority established by the FAIR TRADING ACT, 1973 to administer all aspects of UK COMPETITION POLICY, specifically the control of MONOPOLIES, MERGERS and TAKEOVERS, RESTRICTIVE TRADE AGREEMENTS, RESALE PRICES and ANTICOMPETITIVE PRACTICES. The OFT, headed by the Director General of Fair Trading, collects data on industrial structure, monitors changes in market concentration and merger and takeover activity, and investigates and acts on information received from interested parties concerning allegedly 'abusive' behaviour in respect of trade practices, prices, discounts and other terms and conditions of sale. Where appropriate, the OFT may decide to refer particular cases for further investigation and report to the MONOPOLIES AND MERGERS COMMISSION and the RESTRICTIVE PRACTICES COURT. The OFT also has other main responsibilities with regard to the protection of consumers' interests generally, including taking action against unscrupulous trade prac-

OFFICIAL FINANCING

tices such as false descriptions of goods and inaccurate weights and measures, and the regulation of consumer credit.

See CONSUMER PROTECTION, TRADE DESCRIPTIONS ACTS, 1968 and 1972, WEIGHTS AND MEASURES ACT, 1963, CONSUMER CREDIT ACT, 1974.

official financing see BALANCE OF PAYMENTS.

Official List the prices of STOCKS and SHARES published daily by the UK STOCK EXCHANGE. The prices quoted are the prices ruling at the close of the day's trading and are based on the average of the bid and offer prices.

See BID PRICE.

OFT see OFFICE OF FAIR TRADING.

oligopoly a type of MARKET STRUCTURE that is characterized by:

(a) *few firms and many buyers*, that is, the bulk of market supply is in the hands of a relatively few large firms who sell to many small buyers.

(b) *homogenous or differentiated* products, that is, the products offered by suppliers may be identical or, more commonly, differentiated from each other in one or more respects. These differences may be of a physical nature, involving functional features, or may be purely 'imaginary' in the sense that artificial differences are created through ADVERTISING and SALES PROMOTION (see PRODUCT DIFFERENTIATION).

(c) *difficult market entry*, that is, high BARRIERS OF ENTRY which make it difficult for new firms to enter the market.

The primary characteristic associated with the condition of 'fewness' is known as MUTUAL INTERDEPENDENCE. Basically, each firm when deciding upon its price and other market strategies must explicitly take into account the likely reactions and countermoves of its competitors in response to its own moves. A price cut, for example, may appear to be advantageous to one firm considered in isolation, but if this results in other firms cutting their prices also to protect sales then all firms may suffer reduced profits. Accordingly, oligopolists tend to avoid price competition, employing various mechanisms (PRICE LEADERSHIP, CARTELS) to coordinate their prices.

Oligopolists compete against each other using various product-differentiation strategies (advertising and sales promotion, new product launches) because this preserves and enhances profitability – price cuts are easily matched whereas product differentiation is more difficult to duplicate, thereby offering the chance of a more permanent increase in market share; differentiation expands sales at existing prices, or the extra costs involved can be 'passed on' to consumers; differentiation by developing brand loyalty to existing suppliers makes it difficult for new firms to enter the market.

Traditional (static) market theory shows oligopoly to result in a 'MONOPOLY-like' suboptimal MARKET PERFORMANCE: output is restricted to leve's below cost minimization; inefficient firms are cushioned by a 'reluctance' to engage in price competition; differentiation competition increases supply costs; prices are set above minimum supply costs yielding oligopolists ABOVE-NORMAL PROFITS which are protected by barriers to entry. As with monopoly, however, this analysis makes no allowance for the contribution that ECONOMIES OF SCALE may make to the reduction of industry costs and prices and the important contribution of oligopolistic competition to INNOVATION and NEW PRODUCT development.

See KINKED-DEMAND CURVE, LIMIT-PRICING, PERFECT COMPETITION, MONOPOLISTIC COMPETITION, DUOPOLY, GAME THEORY, REVISED SEQUENCE.

oligopsony a form of BUYER CONCENTRATION, that is, a MARKET situation in which a few large buyers confront many small suppliers. Powerful buyers are often able to secure advantageous terms from suppliers in the form of BULK BUYING price discounts and extended credit terms.

See also OLIGOPOLY, BILATERAL OLIGOPOLY, COUNTERVAILING POWER.

OPEC see ORGANIZATION OF PETROLEUM EXPORTING COUNTRIES.

open economy an economy that is heavily dependent on INTERNATIONAL TRADE, EXPORTS and IMPORTS being large in relation to the size of that economy's NATIONAL INCOME. For such economies, analysis of the CIRCULAR FLOW OF NATIONAL INCOME must allow for the influence of exports and imports. Compare CLOSED ECONOMY.

open-market operation an instrument of MONETARY POLICY involving the sale or purchase of government TREASURY BILLS and BONDS as a means of controlling the MONEY SUPPLY. If, for example, the monetary authorities wish to *increase* the money supply, then they will buy bonds from the general public. The money paid out to the public will increase their bank balances. As money flows into the banking system the banks' liquidity is increased enabling them to increase their lending. This results in the multiple creation of new bank deposits and, hence, an expansion of the money supply.

See BANK-DEPOSIT CREATION, RESERVE-ASSET RATIO.

opportunity cost or **economic cost** a measure of the economic cost of using scarce resources (FACTOR INPUTS) to produce one particular good or service in terms of the alternatives thereby foregone. To take an example, if more resources are used to produce food fewer resources are then available to provide drinks. Thus, in Fig. 124, the PRODUCTION-POSSIBILITY BOUNDARY (PP) shows the quantity of food and drink which can be produced with society's scarce resources. If society decides to increase production of food from OF_1 to OF_2 then it will have less resources to produce drinks, so that drink production will decline from OD_1 to OD_2. The slope of the production-possibility boundary shows the MARGINAL RATE OF TRANSFORMATION (the ratio between the MARGINAL COST of producing one good and the marginal cost of producing the other). In practice, not all resources can be readily switched from one end use to another (see SUNK COSTS).

In the same way, if a customer with limited income chooses to buy more of one good or service he can only do so by foregoing the consumption of other goods or services. His preference between food and drink are reflected in his INDIFFERENCE CURVE II in Fig. 124. The slope of the indifference curve shows the consumer's MARGINAL RATE OF SUBSTITUTION (how much of one good he is prepared to give up in order to release income which can be used to acquire an extra unit of the other good).

If the indifference curve II is typical of all consumers' preferences between food and drink then society would settle for OF_1 of food and OD_1 of drinks, for only at point A would the opportunity cost of deploying resources (the slope of PP) correspond with the opportunity cost of spending limited income (the slope of II).

See also PARETO OPTIMALITY, ECONOMIC RENT.

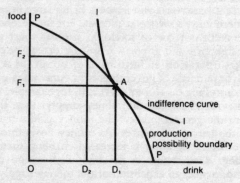

Fig. 124. **Opportunity cost**. See entry.

optimal factor combination see DIMINISHING RETURNS.
optimal scale see PRODUCTIVE EFFICIENCY.
optimizing the maximization of society's economic welfare in respect of the macroeconomic objectives of FULL EMPLOYMENT, PRICE STABILITY, ECONOMIC GROWTH and BALANCE-OF-PAYMENTS EQUILIBRIUM.

The essence of this approach can be illustrated, to simplify matters, by reference to the PHILLIPS CURVE 'trade-off' between unemployment (U) and inflation (I). The Phillips curve in Fig. 125 shows that as unemployment falls inflation increases, and vice-versa.

See MACROECONOMIC POLICY, FIXED TARGETS, INTERNAL-EXTERNAL
BALANCE MODEL.

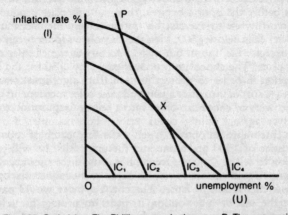

Fig. 125. **Optimizing**. The Phillips curve is drawn as P. The economic
welfare of society is represented by a family of INDIFFERENCE CURVES IC_1,
IC_2, IC_3, IC_4, each indicating successively higher levels of economic
welfare as the origin, O, is approached. The optimum point is at the
origin, because here full employment and complete price stability
are theoretically simultaneously attained. However, the Phillips curve
sets a limit to the combinations of U and I which can be achieved
in practice. Given this constraint, the task of the authorities is to
select that combination of U and I which maximizes society's economic welfare. This occurs at point X where the Phillips curve is tangential to indifference curve IC_3.

optimum the best possible outcome within a given set of circumstances. For example, in the theory of CONSUMER EQUILIBRIUM a consumer with a given income and facing set prices for products will
adjust the purchases of these products so as to maximize the utility
or satisfaction to be derived from spending his limited income. Similarly, in the THEORY OF THE FIRM, a business confronted by a given
market price for its product will adjust its output of that product so
as to maximize its profits.

See also PROFIT MAXIMIZATION, OPTIMIZING, PARETO OPTIMALITY.

optimum order quantity see STOCKHOLDING COSTS.

option a contractual right to buy or sell a COMMODITY (rubber, tin,
etc.), a FINANCIAL SECURITY (share, stock, etc.) or a FOREIGN CURRENCY
at an agreed (predetermined) price at any time within three months
of the contract date. Options are used by buyers and sellers of commodities, financial securities and foreign currencies to offset the
effects of adverse price movements of these items. For example, a

producer of chocolate could purchase an option to buy a standard batch of cocoa at an agreed price of, say, £500 per tonne. If the market price of cocoa rises above £500 per tonne over the next three months before the option expires, then the chocolate producer will find it worthwhile to exercise his option to buy the cocoa at £500. If the price falls below £500, then the chocolate producer can choose not to exercise the option but instead to buy at the cheaper current market price. The chocolate producer pays, say, £50 for the buy or 'call' option in order to protect himself from significant price rises for cocoa (a sort of insurance against adverse price movements). Similarly, growers of cocoa can enter into a sell or 'put' option to cover themselves against falling cocoa prices. For example, if a cocoa grower enters into an option to sell a standard batch of cocoa at an agreed price of £500 per tonne and the price falls, he will exercise his option to sell at £500 per tonne; but if the price rises above £500 per tonne, he will choose to sell his cocoa at the higher market price and allow the option to lapse. The cocoa grower would pay, say, £50 for the sell or 'put' option in order to protect himself from significant price falls in cocoa. In between the buyers and producers of cocoa are the specialist dealers who draw up option contracts and decide option prices in the light of current and anticipated prices of cocoa.

In addition to options which are bought and sold to underpin a normal trading transaction, some options are bought and sold by speculators (see SPECULATION) seeking to secure windfall profits. Options are traded on the FUTURES MARKET. The LONDON DERIVATIVES EXCHANGE is the largest European Community centre for dealings in options.

ordinal utility the (subjective) UTILITY or satisfaction that a consumer derives from consuming a product, measured on a *relative* scale. Ordinal utility measures acknowledge that the *exact* amount of utility derived from consuming products cannot be measured in discrete units as implied by CARDINAL UTILITY measures. Ordinal measures instead involve the consumer ordering his or her preference for products, ranking products in terms of which product yields the greatest satisfaction (1st choice), which product then yields the next greatest satisfaction (2nd choice), and the product which then yields the next greatest satisfaction (3rd choice), and so on. Such ordinal rankings give a clear indication about consumer preferences between products, but do not indicate the precise magnitude of satisfaction as between the 1st and 2nd choices and the 2nd and 3rd choices, etc.

Ordinal utility measures permit consumer preferences between two products to be shown in the form of INDIFFERENCE CURVES which depict various combinations of the two products which yield equal satisfaction to the consumer. Assuming 'rational' consumer behaviour (see

ECONOMIC MAN) a consumer will always choose to be on the highest possible indifference curve, though the increase in satisfaction to be derived from moving from a lower to a higher indifference curve cannot be exactly determined. Nevertheless, INDIFFERENCE MAPS can be used to construct DEMAND CURVES.

See DIMINISHING MARGINAL UTILITY.

ordinary least squares see REGRESSION ANALYSIS.

ordinary shares or **equity** a FINANCIAL SECURITY issued to those individuals and institutions who provide long-term finance for JOINT-STOCK COMPANIES. Ordinary SHAREHOLDERS are entitled to any net profits made by their company after all expenses (including interest charges and tax) have been paid and they generally receive some or all of these profits in the form of DIVIDENDS. In the event of the company being would up (see INSOLVENCY) they are entitled to any remaining ASSETS of the business after all debts and the claims of PREFERENCE SHAREHOLDERS have been discharged. Ordinary shareholders generally have voting rights at company ANNUAL GENERAL MEETINGS which depend upon the number of shares which they hold. See also SHARE CAPITAL.

organic growth (internal growth) a mode of business growth which is self-generated (that is, expansion from within) rather than achieved externally through MERGERS and TAKEOVERS. Organic growth typically involves a firm in improving its market share by developing new products and generally outperforming competitors (see HORIZONTAL INTEGRATION), and through market development (that is, finding new markets for existing products). Organic growth may also involve firms in expanding vertically into supply sources and market outlets (see VERTICAL INTEGRATION), as well as DIVERSIFICATION into new product areas.

The advantages of organic growth include the ability to capitalize on the firm's existing core skills and knowledge, use up spare production capacity and more closely match available resources to the firm's expansion rate over time. Internal growth may be the only alternative where no suitable acquisition exists or where the product is in the early phase of the PRODUCT LIFE CYCLE. The disadvantages of organic growth are that in relying too extensively on internally generated resources, the firm may fail to develop acceptable products to sustain its position in existing markets, while existing skills and know-how may be too limited to support a broader-based expansion programme.

For this reason, firms often rely on a combination of internal and external growth modes to internationalize their operations and undertake product/market diversifications.

See EXTERNAL GROWTH, BUSINESS STRATEGY, PRODUCT-MARKET MATRIX, NEW PRODUCT DEVELOPMENT.

organization the structure of authority or power within a FIRM or public body. Generally there will be a number of management levels in an organization, with a chief executive at the top of the pyramid-shaped organization and increasing numbers of senior, middle and junior managers further down the hierarchy, operatives, sales people and clerks forming the base of the pyramid. Lines of authority are established by the organization's structure with orders being transmitted downward in increasing detail and information feedback being transmitted upward.

In the traditional THEORY OF THE FIRM such organizational details are ignored, the firm being portrayed as a simple decision-making unit which responds exactly to orders initiated by its controlling ENTREPRENEUR. In practice, the structure and operations of large, complex organizations themselves will affect the decision-making process and the specification of organization objectives.

See ORGANIZATION THEORY, BEHAVIOURAL THEORY OF THE FIRM.

organizational slack any organizational resources devoted to the satisfaction of claims by sub-units within the business organization in excess of the resources which these subunits need to complete company tasks. Organizations tend to build up a degree of 'organizational slack' where they operate in less competitive, oligopolistic markets (see OLIGOPOLY), in the form of excess staffing, etc., and this slack provides a pool of emergency resources which the organization can draw upon during bad times. When confronted with a deterioration in the economic environment the organization can exert pressure on subunits within the organization to trim organizational slack and allow the organization to continue to achieve its main goals. Faced with increasing market competition the organization will increasingly be run as a 'tight ship' as slack is trimmed, until in the limiting case of PERFECT COMPETITION organizational slack will be zero and PROFIT MAXIMIZATION becomes the rule.

The concept of organizational slack is a particular feature of the BEHAVIOURAL THEORY OF THE FIRM and is similar in many respects to the concept of X-INEFFICIENCY. See also PRODUCTIVITY.

Organization for Economic Cooperation and Development (OECD) an international organization whose membership comprises mainly the economically advanced countries of the world. The OECD provides a regular forum for discussions amongst government finance and trade ministers on economic matters affecting their mutual interests, particularly the promotion of economic growth and international trade, and it coordinates the provision of ECONOMIC AID to the less developed countries. The OECD is a main source of international economic data and regularly compiles and publishes standardized inter-country statistics.

Organization of Petroleum Exporting Countries (OPEC) an

organization established in 1960 to look after the oil interests of five countries: Iran, Iraq, Kuwait, Saudi Arabia and Venezuela. By 1973 a further eight countries had joined the OPEC ranks: Qatar, Indonesia, Libya, Abu Dhabi, Algeria, Nigeria, Ecuador and Gabon.

In 1973 OPEC used its power to wrest the initiative in administering oil prices away from the American oil corporations and the price of oil quadrupled from $2.5 (American dollars) a barrel to over $11.50 a barrel. The effect of this was to produce balance-of-payments deficits in most oil-consuming countries and with it a period of protracted world recession. As the recession bit, oil revenues began to fall, to which OPEC responded by increasing prices sharply again in 1979 from under $15 a barrel to around $28 a barrel.

OPEC is often cited as an example of a successful producers' CARTEL. In a 'classical' cartel market supply is deliberately restrained in order to force prices up by allocating production QUOTAS to each member. Interestingly, in OPEC's case because of political difficulties formal quotas have not been used to cut production until very recently. The main reason it has been able to successfully increase prices in the past has been that the demand for oil is highly price-inelastic. Recently, however, OPEC has been under pressure for two reasons: (a) the total demand for oil has fallen, partly due to the world recession but also due to the fact that its high price has made it economical to substitute alternative forms of energy (coal, in particular) so that oil is now less price inelastic than formerly; (b) the increased profitability of oil production has led to a high rate of investment in new oil fields (the North Sea, in particular) and this has weakened the control of OPEC over world supplies. These factors led to the introduction of limited production quotas which have raised oil prices in the early 1990s.

organization theory a behavioural framework for the analysis of decision-making processes within large complex ORGANIZATIONS. Economic analysis frequently considers a FIRM to be a single autonomous decision-making unit seeking to maximize profit. By contrast, organization theory suggests that in large organizations decisions are often decentralized, that decisions are influenced by other than economic motives; and that the decision process is influenced by the company's internal structure, or organization. Nonoptimal or satisficing decisions are the result, rather than profit maximizing.

See PROFIT-MAXIMIZATION, FIRM OBJECTIVES, SATISFICING THEORY, BEHAVIOURAL THEORY OF THE FIRM.

original income the INCOME received by a household (or person) before allowing for any payment of INCOME TAX and other taxes, and the receipt of various TRANSFER PAYMENTS (social security benefits, etc.).

Compare FINAL INCOME. See PERSONAL DISTRIBUTION OF INCOME, REDISTRIBUTION OF INCOME PRINCIPLE OF TAXATION.

output the GOODS and SERVICES that are produced using a combination of FACTOR INPUTS.

output-approach to GDP see NATIONAL INCOME ACCOUNTS.

output gap see DEFLATIONARY GAP.

output per man-hour see PRODUCTIVITY.

outside money see EXOGENOUS MONEY.

overcapacity see EXCESS CAPACITY.

overdraft see BANK LOAN.

overheads or **indirect costs** any COSTS that are not directly associated with a product, that is, all costs other than DIRECT MATERIALS cost and DIRECT LABOUR cost. Production overheads (factory overheads) include the cost of other production expenses like factory heat, light and power, and depreciation of plant and machinery. The cost of factory departments such as maintenance, materials stores and the canteen which render services to producing departments are similarly part of production overheads. SELLING COSTS and DISTRIBUTION COSTS, and all administration costs are also counted as overheads since they cannot be directly related to units of product.

See also FIXED COST.

overmanning the employment of more LABOUR than is strictly required to efficiently undertake a particular economic activity. This can arise through bad work organization on the part of management, or through trade union-instigated RESTRICTIVE LABOUR PRACTICES.

overseas investment see FOREIGN INVESTMENT.

oversubscription a situation in which the number of SHARES applied for in a new share issue exceeds the numbers to be issued. This requires the ISSUING HOUSE responsible for handling the share issue to devise some formula for allocating the shares. By contrast, *undersubscription* occurs when the number of shares applied for falls short of the number on offer, requiring the issuing house which has underwritten the shares to buy the surplus shares itself. See CAPITAL MARKET.

overtime the hours of work that are additional to those formally agreed with the labour force as constituting the basic working week. Employers resort to overtime working to meet sudden increases in business activity, viewing overtime by the existing labour force as a more flexible alternative to taking on extra workers. Overtime pay rates can be two to three times basic hourly rates.

See PAY.

overtrading a situation where a FIRM expands its production and sales without making sufficient provision for additional funds to finance the extra WORKING CAPITAL needed. Where this happens the firm will run into LIQUIDITY problems and can find itself unable to find the cash to pay suppliers or wages.

See CASH FLOW.

overutilized capacity a situation in which a plant is operated at output levels beyond the output level at which short-run AVERAGE COST is at a minimum.

See DIMINISHING RETURNS, RETURNS TO THE VARIABLE FACTOR INPUT.

'own-label' brand a product which is sold by a RETAILER which bears the retailer's OWN BRAND NAME. In some cases own-label brands are manufactured by the retailer as part of a vertically integrated manufacturing-retailing operation (Boots the Chemist, for instance, both produces and retails a large number of its own pharmaceutical and cosmetic products). More usually, however, retailers' own-labels are produced by independent manufacturers on a contract basis. Retailers use own-label brands in order to provide greater control and flexibility over their product/price mixes and to build up customer loyalty to their stores, so that customers will tend to frequent the one store rather than 'shop around'.

P

pac-man defence see TAKEOVER BID.

packaging the means of protecting and selling a product. Function-ally, packaging protects products whilst they are in transit and being stored, enables products to be sold in convenient retail packs, and identifies the contents of the package by means of labelling.

In addition, packaging may play an important part in marketing a product, particularly when products are being sold on a SELF-SERVICE basis. The attractiveness of the colour and design of the package is important in attracting the attention of the buyer. In addition, the use of BRAND NAMES on packaging reinforces the perceptions of the brand at the point of sale.

See PRODUCT DIFFERENTIATION.

paid-up capital the amount of CALLED-UP CAPITAL which shareholders have paid to date, where a JOINT-STOCK COMPANY issues shares with phased payment terms. Where some shareholders fail to pay an instal-ment (CALLS IN ARREARS) paid-up capital will be less than called-up capital.

See SHARE ISSUE.

paradox of thrift the proposition that there is an inconsistency between the apparently virtuous nature of household SAVING and the potentially undesirable consequences of such saving. If most house-holds decide to save a larger proportion of their incomes then they will consume less and this reduced expenditure will lower AGGREGATE DEMAND and so lead to lower levels of output and employment. Thus, an increase in savings will reduce the level of national income.

Thriftiness or saving is beneficial to the economy as it releases resources from the production of consumer goods to be used for producing investment goods. However, if households attempt to save more than businesses plan to invest at a given level of income (i.e., 'withdrawals' exceed 'injections' in the CIRCULAR FLOW OF NATIONAL INCOME MODEL) this will cause the EQUILIBRIUM LEVEL OF NATIONAL INCOME to decline, reducing also the actual amounts saved and invested. See Fig. 126.

paradox of value the proposition that the value (PRICE) of a good is determined by its relative scarcity rather than by its usefulness. Water is extremely useful and its TOTAL UTILITY is high but, because it is generally so abundant, its MARGINAL UTILITY (and hence, price) is low. Diamonds, by contrast, are much less useful than water but their great scarcity makes their marginal utility (and hence, price) high.

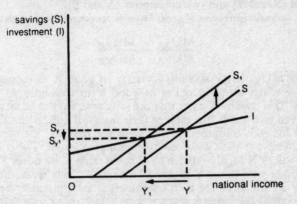

savings (S), investment (I)

Fig. 126. **Paradox of thrift.** The savings schedule rises from S to S_1 but this serves to reduce the equilibrium level of national income from Y to Y_1, and the actual amount saved from S_y to S_{y1}.

parallel importing a form of ARBITRAGE whereby an independent importer buys a particular supplier's product at a low price in one country and resells it in direct competition with the supplier's appointed distributors in another national market where prices are higher.

Parallel importing helps promote FREE TRADE and competition by breaking down barriers to INTERNATIONAL TRADE and undermines PRICE DISCRIMINATION between markets by suppliers.

See IMPORT.

parallel loan see BACK-TO-BACK LOAN.

Pareto, Vilfredo (1848–1923) an Italian economist who used the mathematical principles applicable to equilibrium in mechanical systems to construct a general theory of economic equilibrium in his book: *Mannuale di Economica Politica* (1906). Pareto acknowledged that utility was not measurable but argued that a purely ordinal conception of utility (see ORDINAL UTILITY) was sufficient to formulate a theory of choice. This led Pareto to use INDIFFERENCE CURVES to show how an individual's scale of preferences can be represented by an indifference map. Pareto was also known for his ideas on income distribution.

See PARETO OPTIMALITY.

Pareto optimality the maximization of the economic welfare of the community.

There are three conditions which must hold in order for a Pareto optimum to be attained.

Consider a simplified economy in which there are two goods produced (X and Y) and two consumers (A and B).

(a) *optimal distribution of goods between consumers* requires that:

$$\frac{MU_{XA}}{MU_{YA}} = \frac{MU_{XB}}{MU_{YB}}$$

where MU_{XA} is the MARGINAL UTILITY of good X to consumer A, MU_{YA} is the marginal utility of good Y to consumer A, and so forth. This condition states that the MARGINAL RATE OF SUBSTITUTION between two goods (the ratio of their marginal utilities) must be the same for each consumer. If this were not the case, the consumers could improve their positions by exchanging goods. The consumer who values X highly relative to Y could trade some of his Y to the consumer who values Y highly relative to X. Only when the utility ratios are the same for both consumers is such mutually beneficial trade impossible. INDIFFERENCE CURVES which show combinations of goods which yield satisfaction to consumers can be used to depict marginal rates of substitution insofar as their slopes reflect these trade-offs.

(b) *optimal allocation of inputs in productive uses* where two inputs i and j are used in the production of goods X and Y. Optimal utilization of inputs requires that the ratio of the MARGINAL PHYSICAL PRODUCTS of i and j employed in the production of X be the same as the ratio of their marginal physical products in the production of Y. That is:

$$\frac{MP_{iX}}{MP_{jX}} = \frac{MP_{iY}}{MP_{jY}}$$

If this equality is not satisfied, one input is relatively more efficient in the production of one output (and the other input is thus relatively less efficient in the production of the same output). It will thus benefit the community to divert more of the first input into its more efficient use (and to divert the other input from that use). This will permit the community to expand the production of one output at a constant level of resource use. Only when the marginal product ratios are the same can the community not gain by reallocating its inputs among competing uses. Production ISOQUANTS which show combinations of inputs which produce a given output can be used to depict MARGINAL RATES OF TECHNICAL SUBSTITUTION insofar as their slopes reflect these trade-offs.

(c) *optimal amounts of output* (illustrated in Fig. 127, which depicts a transformation curve (PRODUCTION POSSIBILITY BOUNDARY) that shows the quantities of goods X and Y that can be produced by utilizing fully the resources of the community). The slope of this transformation curve represents the MARGINAL RATE OF TRANSFORMATION, that is, the ratio of the MARGINAL COST of good X to the marginal cost of good Y. Optimal output for any pair of goods, X and Y, requires that the goods be produced in quantities such that:

$$\frac{MU_X}{MC_X} = \frac{MU_Y}{MC_Y}$$

That is, the ratio of marginal cost to marginal utility must be the same for each good, so that the last £'s worth of good X generates the same utility as the last £'s worth of good Y, etc. This condition will be satisfied if the slope of the transformation curve (the marginal cost ratio between X and Y) is equal to the marginal utility ratio between X and Y (the marginal rate of substitution). If the ratios were unequal the community would benefit by producing more of the good that yields the higher marginal utility per unit of marginal cost. The optimal combination of goods is depicted as OX_1 and OY_1 in Fig. 127 where the indifference curve (IC) is tangential to the production possibility boundary (PP). However, it should be noted that Pareto optimality indicates only the optimum allocation of resources for a *given* pattern of demand which itself reflects the present PERSONAL DISTRIBUTION OF INCOME. Any change in the distribution of personal income, say from rich to poor (SEE REDISTRIBUTION OF INCOME), would change demand patterns for products and lead to a different Pareto optimum.

If all these conditions are met, then it would be impossible to improve the welfare of one or more individuals without simultaneously reducing the welfare of another or others.

See EDGEWORTH BOX, WELFARE ECONOMICS.

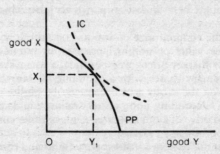

Fig. 127. **Pareto optimality**. The transformation curve or production possibility boundary.

Parkinson's law an observation by Professor C. Northcote Parkinson suggesting that work expands according to the time available in which to do it. If this observation holds then the inefficiency it creates poses a serious organizational problem for businesses of any significant size. See ORGANIZATION THEORY, X-INEFFICIENCY.

partial equilibrium analysis the analysis of relationships within a particular subsector of an economy (for example, an individual market) that proceeds on the basis that events in this sector have such an insignificant impact on other sectors that feedback effects will be negligible or nonexistent. For example, an increase in the price of carrots is unlikely to have much effect on the general price level so that any possible feedback effects can be safely ignored for purposes of analysing the market for carrots. Thus, in partial equilibrium analysis each subsector is treated as a selfcontained entity. See GENERAL EQUILIBRIUM ANALYSIS.

participation rate see ACTIVITY RATE.

partnership. see FIRM.

part-time work employment where the hours of work are substantially less than the usual working week. In the UK, part-time work is officially defined as that which is under 30 hours each week. Below this number, national insurance contributions do not have to be paid.

The advantage of part-time working to employers is that it can be relatively cheap and it also enables them to adapt production or the provision of services to variations in demand, e.g. a shop may stay open into the evening by employing part-time workers to cover the evening work. Part-time work can also be advantageous to employees themselves insofar as it allows them to fit work in with other commitments.

In the UK in recent years growth in part-time work has formed a large part of the growth in employment. Approximately 25% of the employed labour force is now in part-time jobs. Most of these are women.

par value 1. the coupon price of a FINANCIAL SECURITY, for example, the initial face value or nominal price of an ORDINARY SHARE (as opposed to its market price). For example, a JOINT-STOCK COMPANY may issue ordinary shares with a par value of, say, 25p though its market price on the STOCK EXCHANGE may be higher or lower than this par value, depending upon current demand and supply for it.

2. The fixed price of a CURRENCY in terms of other currencies under a FIXED EXCHANGE-RATE SYSTEM.

patent the grant of temporary MONOPOLY rights and control over new products, processes and techniques to their INVENTORS by the government. Patent protection is seen as an important means of fostering TECHNOLOGICAL PROGRESS by providing an opportunity for inventors and INNOVATORS to recoup development expenses and secure a profit reward for risk-taking. To minimize the danger of monopolistic exploitation, patents are granted for limited time periods only. In the

UK, under the COPYRIGHT, DESIGNS AND PATENTS ACT, 1988, the PAT-ENT OFFICE can grant a patent for a maximum of 20 years.

See INTELLECTUAL PROPERTY RIGHTS, RESEARCH AND DEVELOPMENT.

Patent Office a UK government department that administers matters relating to PATENTS, TRADEMARKS and other INTELLECTUAL PROPERTY RIGHTS. The Patent Office is the sole authority for the granting of patent rights on product and process INVENTIONS and for the registration of industrial designs and trademarks.

pawnbroker a person or firm who makes LOANS taking temporary possession of borrowers' personal ASSETS as security for the loan. Borrowers can reclaim their assets by repaying the loan and interest charges in full, although if they default the pawnbroker is entitled to sell their assets.

pay the money paid to an employee for performing specified work tasks or jobs. Payment to employees for the labour they provide takes two main forms:

(a) payment by time, principally weekly WAGES and OVERTIME, together with monthly SALARIES.

(b) payment by results, principally PIECEWORK PAYMENTS, bonuses (see BONUS SCHEME) and PROFIT-RELATED PAY.

The main distinction between the two is that 'payment by time' systems remunerate workers for the amount of labour supplied (i.e. the *input* of labour) per time period (hourly, weekly, etc.) irrespective of the amount of output produced; whereas 'payment by results' systems remunerate workers specifically for the amount or value of the *output* produced in a given time period. 'Payment by results' is favoured by many firms because it is thought to provide a strong financial incentive for workers to strive to maximize their output rather than work at a more leisurely pace, but the firm may be required to instal appropriate inspection systems to ensure that extra output has not been achieved at the expense of product quality and reliability.

Pay rates are determined by a number of factors including the forces of supply and demand for particular types of job in the LABOUR MARKET (see WAGE RATE), the bargaining power of TRADE UNIONS (see COLLECTIVE BARGAINING), and the general economic climate (see, for example, PRICES AND INCOMES POLICY).

In addition to receipt of money, employees may receive various other work-related benefits such as free or subsidized meals, travel allowances, a company car, etc. (see FRINGE BENEFITS).

See EMPLOYEE SHARE OWNERSHIP, PROFIT SHARING.

pay-as-you-earn (PAYE) a scheme for collecting INCOME TAX due from a person's earnings by deducting the tax owing before that person's employer pays WAGES OR SALARIES. PAYE is *not* a tax, merely a scheme for the collection of tax. See INCOME TAX SCHEDULES.

payback period or **payback method** the period it takes for an INVESTMENT to generate sufficient cash to recover in full its original capital outlay. For example, a machine which cost £1,000 and generated a net cash inflow of £250 per year would have a payback period of four years.

See also DISCOUNTED CASH FLOW, INVESTMENT APPRAISAL.

payback method see PAYBACK PERIOD.

Pay Board a UK regulatory body which acted to control wages under the government's PRICES AND INCOMES POLICY from 1973 to 1980.

payment by results see INCENTIVE PAY SCHEME, PAY.

payment by time see PAY.

payoff matrix see GAME THEORY.

payroll tax a TAX on a firm's total WAGE bill. The tax may be paid wholly by the firm, or on some shared basis with employees. In so far as such a tax alters the relative price of LABOUR and CAPITAL, it may result in the firm substituting capital for labour.

peace dividend the additional resources which may be made available as a result of cuts in national defence budgets following improved political relationships between Western industrial countries and the former Eastern bloc countries.

peak see BUSINESS CYCLE.

peak-load pricing the principle of charging higher PRICES for certain products (which cannot be stored) at times of peak demand to reflect the higher MARGINAL COSTS of supplying products at peak times. Peak-load pricing is designed to encourage consumers to spread their demand more evenly so as to avoid the need to invest in plant which is then grossly underutilized at off-peak times. Peak-load pricing is used in electricity supply, railways, etc. using multipart tariffs.

See TWO-PART TARIFF.

penetration price a pricing policy that involves charging a comparatively low PRICE for a product in order to secure growing sales and a high market share. This policy will be adopted by a firm where consumers are expected to be price sensitive, that is, demand is price elastic.

See PRICE-ELASTICITY OF DEMAND, PRODUCT LIFE CYCLE, SKIMMING PRICE.

pension a payment received by individuals who have retired from paid employment or have reached the government's pensionable age in the form of a regular weekly or monthly income, or as a lump sum. There are three main types of pension scheme: (a) state retirement pensions operated by the government whereby the employee pays NATIONAL INSURANCE CONTRIBUTIONS over his working life, giving entitlement to an old-age pension on retirement of an amount considered to provide some minimum standard of living; (b) occupational pensions operated by private sector employers whereby the employee and employer each make regular contributions to a PENSION FUND or INSURANCE COMPANY scheme, the pensioner then receiving a pension which is related to the amount of his contributions (annual contributions × number of years worked); (c) personal pension plans (PPP) operated by insurance companies, pension funds and other financial institutions which provide 'customized' pension arrangements for individuals depending on their personal circumstances. Since a PPP scheme is not tied to a particular employer the problem of transferring pension rights should the person move job is much reduced.

pension fund a financial institution which specializes in the management and administration of personal and corporate PENSION schemes. Pension funds collect regular contributions from individuals, employees and employers in the case of occupational pension schemes, and make payments to retired beneficiaries.

Pension funds use the monies they receive not only to make day-to-day disbursements to pensioners, but also to generate additional income and profit by investing their funds in FINANCIAL SECURITIES, mainly UK and overseas government fixed-interest bonds, corporate stocks and shares, and property bonds (see INSTITUTIONAL INVESTORS). Their portfolios attempt to maintain a careful balance between immediate liquidity needs and longer-term investment returns.

The investment and management of monies by pension funds are regulated by IMRO in accordance with various standards of good practice laid down under the FINANCIAL SERVICES ACT, 1986.

See FINANCIAL SYSTEM.

per capita income see INCOME PER HEAD.

perfect competition or **atomistic competition** a type of MARKET STRUCTURE characterized by: (a) *many firms and buyers*, that is, a large number of independently-acting firms and buyers, each firm and buyer being sufficiently small to be unable to influence the price of the product transacted; (b) *homogeneous products*, that is, the products offered by the competing firms are identical not only in physical attributes but are also regarded as identical by buyers who have no preference between the products of various producers; (c) *free market-entry and exit*, that is, there are no BARRIERS TO ENTRY (hindrances to the entry of new firms) or impediments to the exit of existing sellers; (d) *perfect knowledge* of the market by buyers and sellers.

In a perfectly competitive market, individual sellers have no control over the price at which they sell, the price being determined by aggregate market demand and supply conditions. Each firm produces such a small fraction of total industry output that an increase or decrease in its own output will have no perceptible influence upon total supply and, hence, price. Further, given the infinite CROSS-ELASTICITY OF DEMAND between the homogeneous outputs of the com-

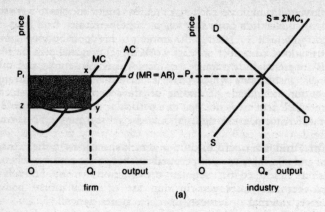

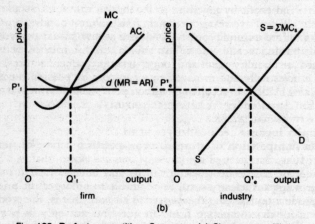

Fig. 128. **Perfect competition.** See entry. (a) Short-run equilibrium.
(b) Long-run equilibrium.

peting sellers, no seller can increase his price above the ruling market
price without losing all of his custom. Thus, the demand curve facing
the firm will be a horizontal straight line at the ruling market price.
In consequence, marginal revenue (MR) equals average revenue
(AR). The competitive firm is a *price taker*, accepting price as something completely outside its control, and will simply adjust its output
independently to the most profitable level at that price; that is, the
firm will continue to produce additional units of output so long as
price (= MR = AR) exceeds marginal cost. When these are equated

the firm will maximize profits. Fig. 128a shows the short-run competitive-equilibrium position for a 'representative' firm and the industry.

The individual supply schedules (MCs) of 'x' number of identical firms are summed horizontally to obtain the industry supply curve (SS). Given industry demand (DD), the short-run equilibrium price and output are P_e and Q_e. Taking the equilibrium price as given, the competitive firm establishes its profit maximizing output at the level $Q_f (P = MC)$ and, in this case, realizes ABOVE-NORMAL PROFITS ($P_f$xyz).

The long-run equilibrium position can also be ascertained. It is deduced from the assumptions of profit maximization, perfect knowledge and free entry and exit, that unless the returns to the productive resources employed in the industry are at a level that could be derived from alternative uses elsewhere in the economy, there will be resources entering or leaving this industry. In general, outputs will be adjusted to demand until market output is extended (or reduced) and price reduced (or increased) to the point where the average cost of supplying that output is just equal to the price at which that output sells.

If, as in the example above, established sellers are earning above-normal profits then new resources will be attracted into the industry thereby increasing total market supply and reducing market price. This process will continue until the excess profits have been competed away. Fig. 128b shows the long-run competitive equilibrium position for the 'representative' firm and the industry. Given an unchanged industry demand (DD) the long-run equilibrium price and output for the industry are P^1_e and Q^1_e. Given the equilibrium price, the firm establishes its profit maximizing output at the point Q^1_f, where $P = MC$ at the point of minimum long run average cost.

Static market theory shows perfect competition to result in a more efficient MARKET PERFORMANCE than other forms of market organization (see especially the comparison with MONOPOLY). Specifically, market output is optimized at a level equal to minimum supply costs; consumers are charged a price just equal to minimum supply costs, with suppliers receiving a NORMAL PROFIT return. The conclusion of competitive optimality, however, rests on a number of assumptions, some of which are highly questionable, in particular the assumption that cost structures are *identical* for small perfectly competitive firms and large oligopolistic and monopoly suppliers (see OLIGOPOLY, ECONOMIES OF SCALE); while given its static framework it ignores important dynamic influences, such as TECHNOLOGICAL PROGRESS. See also MONOPOLISTIC COMPETITION.

perfect market SEE PERFECT COMPETITION.

perks SEE FRINGE BENEFITS.

permanent-income hypothesis the hypothesis that states that current CONSUMPTION is not dependent solely on current DISPOSABLE INCOME but also on whether or not that income is expected to be permanent or transitory. The permanent income hypothesis argues that both income and consumption are split into two parts, permanent and transitory.

A person's permanent income is comprised of such things as their *long-term* earnings from employment (WAGES, SALARIES), retirement PENSIONS and income derived from the possession of capital assets (INTEREST, DIVIDENDS). The amount of a person's permanent income will determine their permanent consumption plans, for example the size and quality of the house they buy and thus their *long-term* expenditure on mortgage repayments, etc.

Transitory income comprises *short-term* temporary overtime payments, bonuses, and 'windfall' gains from winnings and inheritances, and short-term reductions in income arising from temporary unemployment and illness. Transitory consumption such as additional holidays, clothes, etc. will depend upon the amount of this extra income.

Long-term consumption may also be related to changes in a person's WEALTH, in particular the value of their house over time.

The economic significance of the permanent-income hypothesis is that in the *short term* the level of consumption may be higher (or lower) than that indicated by the level of current disposable income.

See LIFE-CYCLE HYPOTHESIS, KEYNESIAN ECONOMICS, CONSUMPTION FUNCTION.

per se illegality the outright prohibition of elements of MARKET CONDUCT (for example, RESTRICTIVE TRADE AGREEMENTS) and MARKET STRUCTURE (for example, MERGERS which would reduce competition) under a NONDISCRETIONARY COMPETITION POLICY.

personal distribution of income the distribution of NATIONAL INCOME classified according to the size of income received by individuals or households. The size of people's incomes differ for a variety of reasons including differences in natural abilities, educational attainments, special skills, and differences in the ownership of WEALTH. The personal distribution of 'original' income is very unequal, as Fig. 129 shows.

See also REDISTRIBUTION OF INCOME, PRINCIPLES OF TAXATION, FUNCTIONAL DISTRIBUTION OF INCOME, INCOME PER HEAD.

personal equity plan (PEP) a scheme introduced by the UK government in 1987 to encourage small savers to invest in UK ORDINARY SHARES. An individual can invest up to (currently) £9,000 per year in shares and, provided the sums involved remain invested for a calendar year, any income or capital gain received is exempt from tax.

personal pension plan see PENSION.

Quintile groups of households	Original income %
Bottom fifth	2
Second fifth	7
Third fifth	16
Fourth fifth	27
Top fifth	48

Fig. 129. **Personal distribution of income**. The personal distribution of original income in the UK, 1994. Original income = income before payment of tax and receipts of state benefits in cash (e.g. pensions) and kind (e.g. health, education). Source: *Social Trends*, 1996.

personal savings ratio the proportion of households' DISPOSABLE INCOME that is saved. Savings ratios can vary over time depending upon households' confidence about their future employment prospects and their WEALTH, though contractual saving through insurance and pension contributions tends to be more stable.

In the CIRCULAR FLOW OF NATIONAL INCOME MODEL, increases in the personal savings ratio will cause CONSUMPTION spending to fall, and unless this is offset by an increase in investment spending or net exports, AGGREGATE DEMAND will decline.

See SAVING RATIO.

personal sector that part of the economy concerned with the transactions of HOUSEHOLDS. Households receive INCOME from supplying factor-inputs to other sectors of the economy and influence the workings of the economy through their spending (CONSUMPTION of goods and services) and SAVING decisions. The personal sector, together with the CORPORATE SECTOR and FINANCIAL SECTOR constitute the PRIVATE SECTOR. The private sector, PUBLIC (GOVERNMENT) SECTOR and FOREIGN SECTOR make up the national economy. See also CIRCULAR FLOW OF NATIONAL INCOME MODEL.

personal selling a means of increasing the sales of a firm's product which involves direct contact between the firm's sales representatives and prospective customers. Unlike 'passive' means of communicating with buyers, such as ADVERTISING, face-to-face meetings with customers facilitate a more proactive approach, with sales representatives being able to explain fully the details of a product, advise and answer customer queries about the product, and, where appropriate, demonstrate the workings of the product.

Phillips curve a curve depicting an empirical observation (based on the work of the British economist A. W. Phillips) of the relationship between the level of UNEMPLOYMENT and the rate of change of MONEY WAGES and, by inference, the rate of change of prices (INFLATION). A fall in unemployment (from A to B in Fig. 130) due to an increase in the level of AGGREGATE DEMAND brings about an acceleration in the rate of increase of money wages (from C to D) reflecting employers' greater willingness to grant wage increases as the demand for their products expands. By contrast, rising unemployment and falling demand leads to a slowing down in the rate of increase of money wages. The 'curve' thus suggests that there is a 'trade-off' between unemployment and DEMAND-PULL INFLATION. However, while there has been strong empirical support of the Phillips curve relationship in the past, in recent years unemployment and inflation have tended to co-exist (see STAGFLATION). This has led to attempts to reformulate the Phillips curve to allow, for example, for the effect of price expectations on money wage increases.

See also EXPECTATIONS-ADJUSTED/AUGMENTED PHILLIPS CURVE.

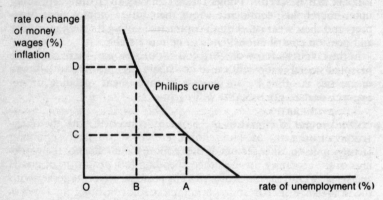

Fig. 130. Phillips curve. See entry.

physiocracy a school of thought or set of economic ideas based on the writings of QUESNAY and other 18th century French economists and philosophers. The physiocrats felt that land was the single source of income and wealth in society, capable of producing a 'net product'. They also believed in the idea of a 'natural order' in society which harmonized the particular interests of individual citizens with the common interests of society. This made them strong proponents of individual liberty and strong opponents of government intervention in society, other than to protect the individual and his property rights. Adam SMITH was strongly influenced by physiocratic ideas and in his hands the 'natural order' was spelled out in the form of the workings of the market mechanism. See also PRIVATE-ENTERPRISE ECONOMY.

picket a person either on STRIKE or supporting that strike, who seeks to prevent other persons from gaining access to a place of work during the course of an INDUSTRIAL DISPUTE. In the UK, picketing one's own place of work is lawful; picketing other people's places of work (*secondary picketing*) is unlawful.

piecework a system of PAY in which an individual's WAGE is related to his or her output. In some industries this type of 'payment by results' system is used because of its potential beneficial impact upon worker motivation and PRODUCTIVITY; other industries make little use of it because of their particular difficulties in determining appropriate piece-rates per unit of output.

pie chart a chart that portrays data in pictorial form, and shows the relative share of each category in a total by means of the relative size of its 'slice' of a circular 'pie'.

Pigou, Arthur Cecil (1877–1959) an English economist who developed the theory of WELFARE ECONOMICS in his book *The Economics of Welfare* (1919). Pigou preferred to accept market prices as indicators of the relative utilities of different goods, but he argued that divergence between private returns and social returns could necessitate taxes and subsidies to achieve an optimal allocation of resources. This distinction between marginal private net product and marginal social net product provided a case for State intervention to increase the efficiency of resource allocation. Pigou thought that interpersonal comparisons have to be made in formulating policy, and he made out a case for a more equitable DISTRIBUTION OF INCOME on the ground of diminishing marginal utility of income. See REAL BALANCE EFFECT.

placing a means of raising new SHARE CAPITAL by issuing company shares to a 'selected' group of investors rather than the investing public at large.

See SHARE ISSUE.

planned economy see CENTRALLY PLANNED ECONOMY.

planning see CENTRALLY PLANNED ECONOMY, INDICATIVE PLANNING, PLANNING–PROGRAMMING–BUDGETING SYSTEM, CORPORATE PLANNING.

planning-programming-budgeting system a framework for the presentation and analysis of information to assist in reaching decisions about resource allocation in the public sector. Planning, programming, budgeting, seeks to establish what a government department is aiming to achieve in terms of: (a) what its objectives are, (b) what activities contribute to these objectives, (c) what resources or inputs contribute to those activities, (c) what the outputs are (what is being achieved). This contrasts with the manner in which governments traditionally account for expenditure in terms of who does the spending (local/central government, which government department, etc.), and how the money is spent (salaries, equipment, etc.). Instead expenditure is classified according to the policy ends which the expenditure is designed to achieve (programme budgets).

See VALUE FOR MONEY AUDIT, GOVERNMENT PUBLIC EXPENDITURE.

Plc see LIMITED LIABILITY.

plough back see RETAINED PROFIT.

point elasticity a precise measure of the responsiveness of DEMAND or SUPPLY to changes in PRICE, INCOME, etc. Taking PRICE-ELASTICITY OF DEMAND (E), point elasticity may be defined as:

$$E = (-1) \frac{\% \triangle Q}{\% \triangle P}$$

where E = price-elasticity of demand, $\% \triangle Q$ = percentage change in quantity demanded, $\% \triangle P$ = percentage change in price.

Since the DEMAND CURVE slopes downwards from left to right, the $\triangle Q$ has the opposite sign to $\triangle P$, so (-1) is added to the equation to generate a positive value for the elasticity figure. The numerical value of E signifies the degree of elasticity, that is, it lies between zero and infinity. An example of the measurement of point elasticity is given in Fig. 131.

In order to measure elasticity at a particular price, P, we need to measure the slope of the demand curve at point T where the demand curve is tangential to the straight line LL. The slope of the tangent LL is equal to $\triangle Q/\triangle P$ where the increment in output ($\triangle Q$) is very small. This gives the formula for point elasticity:

$$E = \frac{\triangle Q}{\triangle P} \times \frac{P}{Q}$$

Where the calculated value of E is greater than 1, demand is described as elastic; where E is less than one, but greater than zero, demand is inelastic. See also ARC ELASTICITY.

poison pill see TAKEOVER BID.

poll tax a TAX that is levied at a fixed rate per head of population. Poll tax was also used as a colloquial term to describe the UK's COMMUNITY CHARGE.

See LUMP-SUM TAXES, LOCAL TAX.

pollution the contamination of the environment with dirty or harmful substances. In economics, pollution problems such as smoke from factory chimneys, hazardous chemical waste and the dumping of waste materials and products are treated as EXTERNALITIES. Pollution is considered to be a cost of economic growth and a negative input into the measure of economic welfare (see SOCIAL COST, WELFARE ECONOMICS).

Increasingly, governments have passed more onerous regulations covering the use and disposal of industrial materials and production methods. As a consequence, industry itself is being forced to invest in appropriate pollution control and limitation systems, and take a

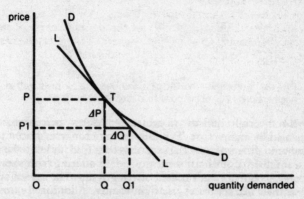

Fig. 131. Point elasticity. See entry.

more proactive approach to the production and marketing of products which are environment-friendly.

See GREEN CONSUMER, GREEN PRODUCT, ENVIRONMENTAL AUDIT, POLLUTOR PAYS PRINCIPLE.

pollutor pays principle the principle that pollutors should bear the SOCIAL COSTS of any POLLUTION which they cause. Adoption of this principle as part of government policy toward the environment involves intervening in markets to protect the environment by placing the onus of responsibility for dealing with pollution on pollutors.

See WELFARE ECONOMICS.

population the total number of people resident in a country. The size of the population is determined by past and present BIRTH RATES and DEATH RATES, and MIGRATION trends. In most advanced industrial countries, both birth and death rates have declined over the long-run (see DEMOGRAPHIC TRANSITION), which has produced slow-growing populations. See Fig. 132 (overleaf). The size and growth of a country's population determines the size of the LABOUR FORCE which is available to produce output.

population census see CENSUS.

population trap a situation in which a country's rate of POPULATION growth is greater than its attainable rate of ECONOMIC GROWTH. As a consequence INCOME PER HEAD declines and the problem of alleviating mass poverty is made worse. To remedy this situation it may be necessary for the government to introduce birth control programmes. This problem is sometimes found in a DEVELOPING COUNTRY. See DEMOGRAPHIC TRANSITION.

porcupine see TAKEOVER BID.

PORTFOLIO

	Birth rate	Death rate	Total population (millions)
1740	37	36	7
1800	37	25	11
1900	26	17	38
1995	13	12	58

Fig. 132. **Population**. The UK birth and death rates, measured in numbers per 1,000 of the population, from 1740 to 1995.

portfolio the collection of FINANCIAL SECURITIES such as shares and bonds held by an investor. Typically an investor would want to hold a number of different financial securities to spread his RISK, and would seek a mixture of financial securities, some offering high short-term DIVIDEND payments with others offering long-term capital appreciation as their market prices rise significantly. Additionally, investors may plan to hold various financial securities which have a particular MATURITY STRUCTURE so that they can achieve a predetermined pattern of cash flows.

See PORTFOLIO THEORY.

portfolio theory the study of the way in which an individual investor may theoretically achieve the maximum expected return from a varied PORTFOLIO of FINANCIAL SECURITIES which has attached to it a given level of RISK. Alternatively, the portfolio may achieve for the investor a minimum amount of risk for a given level of expected return. Return on a security comprises INTEREST or DIVIDEND, plus or minus any CAPITAL GAIN or loss from holding the security over a given time period. The *expected* return on the collection of securities within the portfolio is the weighted average of the expected returns on the individual INVESTMENTS that comprise the portfolio. However, the important thing is that the risk attaching to a portfolio is less than the weighted average risk of each individual investment.

See also EFFICIENT MARKET HYPOTHESIS, RISK AND UNCERTAINTY.

positive economics the study of what 'is' in economics, rather than what 'ought to be'. For example, the statement that 'a cut in personal taxes increases consumption spending in the economy', is a factual statement that can be confirmed or refuted by examining the available empirical evidence on the effects of taxation on spending. Positive economics seeks to identify relationships between economic variables, to quantify and measure these relationships, and to make predictions of what will happen if a variable changes. Compare NORMATIVE ECONOMICS.

potential entrant a FIRM that is willing and able to enter a MARKET given the right conditions. In the THEORY OF MARKETS, potential entry turns into actual entry into a market when (a) existing firms in the market are earning ABOVE-NORMAL PROFITS, (b) newcomers are able to overcome any BARRIERS TO ENTRY.

'Actual' new entry plays an important regulatory rôle in a market in removing above-normal profits and in expanding market supply (see, for example, PERFECT COMPETITION). However, the mere 'threat' of potential entry may in itself be sufficient to ensure that existing firms supply the market efficiently and set prices which are consistent with supply costs.

Potential entrants to a market may be newly established firms; firms who currently supply the market with inputs, or who are currently its customers (vertical entry); or firms who currently operate in other markets and which are looking to expand their activities in new directions (diversified entry).

See also CONDITION OF ENTRY, MARKET ENTRY, VERTICAL INTEGRATION, DIVERSIFICATION, CONTESTABLE MARKET.

potential gross national product the maximum level of real OUTPUT an economy is capable of producing at a point in time by fully utilizing all available FACTOR INPUTS. Productive potential depends upon the size of the LABOUR FORCE and the average level of labour PRODUCTIVITY (that is, output per man). The level of productivity itself is dependent on the current state of technology, the amount of CAPITAL STOCK per worker, and the CAPITAL-OUTPUT RATIO.

Potential GNP interacts with the level of AGGREGATE DEMAND to determine the level of ACTUAL GROSS NATIONAL PRODUCT in an economy. If aggregate demand falls short of potential GNP at any point in time then actual GNP will be equal to aggregate demand leaving a DEFLATIONARY GAP (output gap) between actual and potential GNP. However, at high levels of aggregate demand (in excess of potential GNP), potential GNP sets a ceiling on actual output, any excess of aggregate demand over potential GNP showing up as an INFLATIONARY GAP.

Potential GNP will tend to grow over time as a result of increases in the labour force and labour productivity (see SUPPLY-SIDE ECONOMICS). Fig. 133 shows the (hypothetical) path followed by potential GNP over time in the form of a broken line. The rate of growth of actual output (GNP) over time (ECONOMIC GROWTH), shown by the solid line, will depend upon both potential GNP and the rate of growth of aggregate demand. When aggregate demand matches (or exceeds) potential GNP, as at points A and C in the figure, the economy's resources are fully employed and maximum output of goods and services is achieved. When aggregate demand falls short of potential GNP, as at points B and D, some of the economy's resources are left unemployed (see UNEMPLOYMENT) or underemployed. When aggregate demand exactly matches potential GNP, a full employment equilibrium level of aggregate demand exists.

In practice the level and rate of growth of potential GNP are difficult to measure. See also BUSINESS CYCLE.

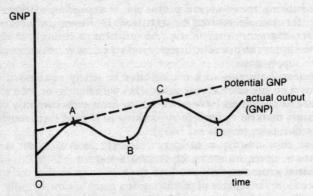

Fig. 133. **Potential gross national product**. The difference between potential GNP and actual GNP.

pound the standard CURRENCY unit of the UK and a number of other countries, mainly current and former members of the British Commonwealth. When used in international transactions the UK pound is referred to as STERLING to distinguish it from other country's pounds, such as the Lebanese or Egyptian pound.

poverty trap a situation where an unemployed person receiving SOCIAL-SECURITY BENEFITS is not encouraged to seek work because his or her after tax earnings potential in work is *less* than the benefits currently obtained by not working. Given that social security benefits represent the 'bottom line' (that is, the provision of some socially and politically 'acceptable' minimum standard of living) the problem is how to reconcile this with the 'work ethic'. One suggested way is for the government to provide employers with employment subsidies which allow them to pay wages higher than the minimum level of social security, even though the MARGINAL REVENUE PRODUCT of the work undertaken does not warrant it. It will thus be to people's economic advantage to obtain employment, and hopefully in so doing they will acquire work experience and skills which will improve their long-run earnings potential.

Alternatively, the overlap between entitlement to social security benefits (based on one set of income scales) and the threshold level of income at which people start to pay tax (based on a different set of income scales) can be removed by the introduction of a NEGATIVE INCOME TAX. A negative income tax system replaces means-tested social security benefits on the one hand, and PROGRESSIVE TAXES on the other, with a single unitary tax system. Under this unitary tax system people pay taxes when they are in employment and earning more than a stipulated minimum income and receive a tax rebate to bring their income up to the stipulated minimum level when they are either unemployed or earning less than the minimum. See also SUPPLY-SIDE ECONOMICS.

precautionary demand for money the demand for MONEY balances which are held to cover for unforeseen contingencies, for example loss of earnings due to illness. The amount of money held for such purposes is broadly dependent on the level of INCOME and expenditure. The precautionary demand for money, together with the TRANS-ACTIONS DEMAND FOR MONEY (that is, money held on a day-to-day basis to finance current expenditures on goods and services) and the SPECULATIVE DEMAND FOR MONEY (that is, money held to purchase BONDS in anticipation of a fall in their price), constitute the MONEY-DEMAND SCHEDULE.

See LIQUIDITY PREFERENCE, L.M. SCHEDULE.

predatory pricing a pricing policy pursued by a firm (or firms) with the express purpose of harming rival suppliers or exploiting the consumer. Examples of the former include PRICE SQUEEZING and 'selective' price cuts to drive competitors out of the market, while exploitation of the consumer comes about through over pricing by MONOPOLY suppliers and CARTELS.

See also COMPETITION POLICY.

preferences the CHOICES made by consumers as to which products to consume. The strength of consumer preferences will determine which products they buy from their limited disposable income and thus the DEMAND for products. As well as choosing which products to buy, consumers will also express preferences as to which particular BRAND of a product to purchase.

See CONSUMER EQUILIBRIUM, PRICE SYSTEM.

preferred stock see PREFERENCE SHARE.

preference share or **preferred stock** a FINANCIAL SECURITY issued to those individuals and institutions who provide long-term finance for JOINT-STOCK COMPANIES. Preference shares pay a fixed rate of DIVI-DEND and are generally given priority over ORDINARY SHARES in receiving dividend. In the event of the company being wound up (see INSOLVENCY) they also have first claim on any remaining ASSETS of the business after all debts have been discharged. Generally, preference SHAREHOLDERS have no voting rights at company ANNUAL GENERAL MEETINGS. See also SHARE CAPITAL.

preference/similarity theory an explanation of INTERNATIONAL TRADE in manufactured products which is based on consumers' demands for product variety, for example, the EXPORT from the UK of cars to, and the import of cars from, Germany.

The theory postulates that domestic suppliers specialize in the manufacture of the kinds of product demanded by the majority of domestic consumers, but are able to export some of their output to countries where such products appeal to a minority of consumers. By the same token, the minority of domestic consumers have slightly different demands, demands which can be satisfied by imports from those countries where such tastes are those of the majority. Since the kinds of product demanded in a country are determined in large measure by the level of income per head, most exchanges of manufactures take place between countries of a similar industrial structure, each exporting and importing essentially similar products. Through trade the variety of manufactured products available to consumers is extended and the gain from trade derives, not from lower prices as emphasized by the conventional theory of COMPARATIVE ADVANTAGE, but from the choice of being able to consume the precise brand or variety of product demanded.

See also INTRA-INDUSTRY TRADE, THEORY OF INTERNATIONAL TRADE.

premium 1. an addition to the published LIST PRICE of a good or service charged by a supplier to customers. The premium could be charged for express delivery of the product, or could reflect the temporary scarcity of the product. A 'premium price' for a product over similar products might be charged by a supplier who is able to convince buyers that his product is superior in some respect to competitors' offerings (see PRODUCT DIFFERENTIATION). **2.** the sale of new STOCKS and SHARES at an enhanced price. In the UK this involves the issue of a new share at a price above its nominal value. In other countries where shares have no nominal value it involves the sale of new shares above their current market price. **3.** the purchase of a particular company's issued stock or share at a price above the average market price of those of other companies operating in the same area. The price is higher, reflecting investors' optimism about that company's prospects. **4.** a general rise in the prices of all stocks and shares to higher levels in anticipation of an upturn in the economy. **5.** the purchase of a BOND for more than its nominal value. The price which people are prepared to pay for a bond can be more than its nominal value if the nominal rate of interest on that bond exceeds current market interest rates. **6.** the extent to which a foreign currency's market EXCHANGE RATE rises above its 'official' exchange rate under a FIXED EXCHANGE-RATE SYSTEM. **7.** the annual payment made to an INSURANCE COMPANY for an insurance policy.

See also SPECULATIVE DEMAND FOR MONEY.

premium bond a FINANCIAL SECURITY issued by the UK government as a means of raising money for the government and encouraging private SAVING. Premium bonds are issued in small denominations, but do not pay interest, nor can a capital gain be obtained on redemption, since they are issued and redeemed at their face value. Their appeal lies in the prospect of a 'gambler's chance' of winning a substantial lump sum of money in a monthly prize lottery (numbers being drawn electronically by 'ERNIE').

present value SEE DISCOUNTED CASH FLOW.

price the money value of a unit of a GOOD, SERVICE, ASSET or FACTOR INPUT. In some markets (for example, see PERFECT COMPETITION), price will be determined entirely by the forces of DEMAND and SUPPLY. By contrast, in other markets (for example, MONOPOLY markets) powerful suppliers have considerable discretion over the price which they charge. In certain circumstances prices may be subjected to governmental PRICE CONTROL or regulated by means of PRICES-AND-INCOMES POLICY. See also EQUILIBRIUM MARKET PRICE, ADMINISTERED PRICE.

price ceiling the maximum PRICE that can be charged for a PRODUCT as determined by the government.

Contrast PRICE FLOOR. See PRICE CONTROLS, PRICES AND INCOMES POLICY.

Price Commission a UK regulatory body which acted to control prices from 1973 to 1980, under the government's PRICES AND INCOMES POLICY.

price competition a form of rivalry between suppliers which involves an attempt to win customers by offering a product at a lower PRICE than competitors.

Price competition is especially beneficial to consumers in so far as it results in the establishment of prices which are consistent with the real costs of supplying the product, and serves to improve the RESOURCE ALLOCATION efficiency of the market by eliminating inefficient, high cost suppliers (see PERFECT COMPETITION). From the suppliers' point of view price competition is often something to be resisted because it reduces the profitability of the market, and, where conditions permit (for example, OLIGOPOLY) suppliers may attempt to avoid price competition.

See PRICE LEADERSHIP, PRICE PARALLELISM, COLLUSION, COMPETITION METHODS.

price controls the specification by the government of minimum and/or maximum PRICES for goods and services. The price may be fixed at a level below the market EQUILIBRIUM PRICE or above it depending on the objective in mind. In the former case, for example, the government may wish to keep the price of some essential good (for example, food) down as a means of assisting poor consumers. In the latter case, the aim may be to ensure that producers receive an adequate return (see PRICE SUPPORT). More generally, price controls may be applied across a wide range of goods and services as part of a PRICES

PRICE DISCRIMINATION

AND INCOMES POLICY aimed at combating INFLATION. See also
RATIONING.

price discrimination the ability of a supplier to sell the *same* product
in a number of separate MARKETS at *different* PRICES. Markets can be
separated in a number of ways, including different geographical locations (e.g., domestic and foreign), the nature of the product itself
(e.g., original and replacement parts for motor cars) and users'
requirements (e.g., industrial and household electricity consumption).

Price discrimination can be both beneficial and detrimental, for
example, discriminating prices may be used as a means of ensuring
a plant produces at full capacity thereby enabling economies of large-
scale production to be attained. On the other hand, price discrimination may be used as a means of enlarging monopoly profits. See
DISCRIMINATING MONOPOLIST.

price-earnings ratio a ratio used to appraise a quoted public
company's profit performance, which expresses the market PRICE
of the company's SHARES as a multiple of its PROFIT. For example,
if a company's profit amounted to £1 per share and the price
of its shares was £10 each on the STOCK EXCHANGE, then its price-
earnings ratio would be 10:1. Where a company's prospects are
considered by the stock exchange to be good, then it is likely
that the company's share price will rise, producing a higher price-
earnings ratio. The price-earnings ratio is the mirror image of
EARNINGS YIELD.

See EARNINGS PER SHARE.

price effect the effect of a change in price upon the quantity
demanded of a product. In the THEORY OF DEMAND the price effect can
be subdivided into the SUBSTITUTION EFFECT and the INCOME EFFECT. In
Fig. 134, a consumer has an initial BUDGET LINE XY (which shows
the different combinations of the products A and B which he can
buy given the relative prices of the two products). I_1 and I_2 are INDIF-
FERENCE CURVES (which show the alternative combinations of the two
products, each of which yields him the same UTILITY or satisfaction).
The point (L) where I_2 is tangential to the budget line XY denotes
the initial equilibrium position for the consumer, who maximizes his
satisfaction by purchasing a combination of O_d of product A and O_e
of product B. Assume now that the price of product B increases so
that the consumer is now unable to buy as much of product B as
before. This new situation is reflected in an inward shift in the budget
line from XY to XZ. The consumer will move to a new equilibrium
position (point M) where I_1 is tangential to the budget line XZ,
purchasing O_f of product A and O_g of product B.

The consumer's real income has been decreased by the rise in the
price of product B. However, the movement from L to M and the

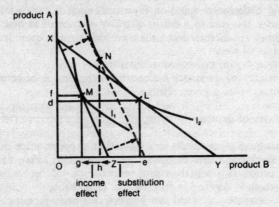

Fig. 134. **Price effect**. See entry.

reduction in the quantity purchased of B, from O_e to O_g, is a result of the combination of an income and substitution effect. To isolate the substitution effect, it is necessary to increase the consumer's income just enough to compensate him for his loss in purchasing power; that is, the budget line is moved to the right parallel to itself until it becomes tangent to his original indifference curve I_2 at point N (Combination N yields the same satisfaction as Combination L).

But the consumer has cut his consumption of product B (whose price has risen relative to product A) and increased his consumption of product A. Hence the movement from L to N, or the decrease in quantity demanded of product B from O_e to O_h is the substitution effect.

The income effect alone is determined by taking the compensating increase in income away from the consumer, that is, we revert back to budget line XZ which cuts indifference curve I_1 at point M yielding the optimal combination of O_f of product A and O_g of product B. The movement from N to M is the income effect and reduces the quantity demanded of product B from O_h to O_g.

For NORMAL PRODUCTS the income effect and the substitution effect reinforce each other so that an increase in price will result in a decrease in quantity demanded. However, in the case of INFERIOR PRODUCTS the income and substitution effects work in opposite directions making it difficult to predict the effect of a change in price on quantity demanded. In extreme cases where a product accounts for a large proportion of household budgets the income effect of a price change may be so large as to swamp the substitution effect so that a decrease in price leads (perversely) to a decrease in quantity demanded. For example, in developing countries where a high proportion of (small) household budgets are spent on foodstuffs such as rice, a fall in the price of rice can lead to a fall in quantity consumed as households' real incomes are increased and they are able to buy more meat and fish in place of rice.

See GIFFEN GOOD, CONSUMER EQUILIBRIUM.

price-elasticity of demand a measure of the degree of responsiveness of DEMAND to a given change in PRICE:

$$\text{elasticity of demand} = \frac{\%\ \text{change in quantity demanded}}{\%\ \text{change in price}}$$

If a change in price results in a more than proportionate change in quantity demanded, then demand is *price-elastic* (Fig. 135a); if a change in price produces a less than proportionate change in the quantity demanded, then demand is *price-inelastic* (Fig. 135b).

At the extremes, demand can be perfectly price-inelastic, that is, price changes have no effect at all on quantity demanded, which shows up as a straight-line vertical demand curve; or demand can be perfectly price-elastic, that is, any amount will be demanded at the prevailing price, which shows up as a straight-line horizontal demand curve.

TOTAL REVENUE (price times quantity demanded) will be affected by price changes. Where demand is price-elastic a small cut in price will generate a large increase in quantity demanded so that the price cut will serve to increase total revenue (while a price rise serves to reduce total revenue). By contrast, where demand is price-inelastic a large cut in price will generate only a small increase in quantity demanded so that the price cut will serve to reduce total revenue (while a price rise serves to increase total revenue). Where demand has *unitary elasticity* then the percentage price cut will be matched by an exactly offsetting percentage change in quantity demanded so that total revenue remains the same.

It must be stressed, however, that the price-elasticity of demand can vary along the length of a given demand curve. For example, although in Fig. 135a the demand curve as a whole is elastic in configuration, it is more elastic at point X than it is at point Y.

The concept of demand elasticity is useful to firms in setting product prices (including PRICE DISCRIMINATION), and the government in setting rates of indirect taxes such as EXCISE DUTY to raise revenue.

See also ARC ELASTICITY, POINT ELASTICITY, INCIDENCE OF TAXATION, TARIFF, PENETRATION PRICE, SKIMMING PRICE, MARSHALL–LERNER CONDITION.

price-elasticity of supply a measure of the degree of responsiveness of SUPPLY to a given change in PRICE:

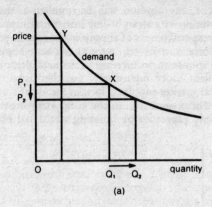

(a)

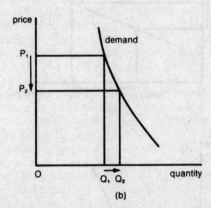

(b)

Fig. 135. **Price-elasticity of demand.** See entry. (a) Elastic demand.
(b) Inelastic demand.

$$\text{elasticity of supply} = \frac{\%\ \text{change in quantity supplied}}{\%\ \text{change in price}}$$

If a change in price results in a more than proportionate change in quantity supplied then supply is price-elastic (Fig. 136a); if a change in price produces a less than proportionate change in the quantity supplied, then supply is price-inelastic (Fig. 136b).

At the extremes, supply can be perfectly price-inelastic, that is, price changes have no effect at all on quantity supplied, which shows up as a straight-line vertical supply curve; or supply can be perfectly price-elastic, that is, any amount will be supplied at the prevailing price, which shows up as a straight-line horizontal supply curve.

The degree of responsiveness of supply to changes in price is affected by the time horizon involved. In the SHORT RUN, supply can only be increased in response to an increase in demand/price by working firms' existing plant more intensively, but this usually adds only marginally to total market supply. Thus, in the short run the supply curve tends to be price-inelastic. In the LONG RUN, firms are able to enlarge their supply capacities by building additional plants and by

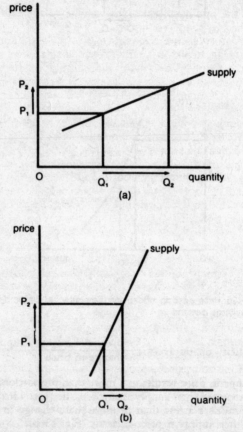

Fig. 136. **Price-elasticity of supply.** See entry. (a) Elastic supply. (b) Inelastic supply.

extending existing ones so that supply conditions in the long run tend to be more price-elastic. However, in some cases, for example petrochemicals, the long-run supply responses can be five years or more.

price equilibrium see EQUILIBRIUM MARKET PRICE.

price fixing the establishment of a common PRICE for a good or service by a group of suppliers acting together, as opposed to each supplier setting his own price independently. Price fixing is often a feature of an unregulated OLIGOPOLY market.

See RESTRICTIVE TRADE AGREEMENT, COLLUSION, CARTEL, ADMINISTERED PRICE.

price floor the minimum PRICE that can be charged for a PRODUCT as determined by the government.

Contrast PRICE CEILING. See PRICE CONTROLS, PRICE SUPPORT, MINIMUM WAGE RATE, COMMON AGRICULTURAL POLICY.

price index a weighted average of the PRICES of selected goods, services, commodities or financial assets measured over time. One commonly used price index is the *Retail Price Index (RPI)*, which measures the average level of the prices of a general 'basket' of goods and services bought by final consumers. Each item in the index is weighted according to its relative importance in total consumers' expenditure. Starting from a selected BASE YEAR (index value = 100), price changes are then reflected in changes in the index value over time. Thus, taking the example of the UK *Retail Price Index (RPI)*, the current RPI base year is 1987 = 100; in 1995 the index value stood at 149, indicating that retail prices, on average, had risen 49% between the two dates. Such price indices can be used to measure the rate of INFLATION and as a GNP DEFLATOR. Another commonly used index of prices is the *Wholesale Price Index* which records the price of a 'basket' of goods measured in terms of wholesale prices.

In similar fashion a SHARE PRICE INDEX is used to measure changes in the prices of STOCKS and SHARES over time. The TERMS OF TRADE index is used to measure the average prices of EXPORTS relative to IMPORTS over time.

See PURCHASING POWER, FAMILY EXPENDITURE SURVEY, TRADE-WEIGHTED INDEX.

price leader a FIRM that establishes the market PRICE for a good or service and initiates price changes which are then followed by competing suppliers. Two forms of price leadership have been identified. (a) DOMINANT FIRMS who are able to secure compliance to their prices by smaller rivals because of their powerful positions in the market. (b) *barometric price leaders* whose price changes are accepted by other suppliers because of their recognized adeptness at establishing prices fully reflective of changing market conditions.

Price leader-follower relationships are a typical feature of OLIGO-

POLY markets in coordinating price changes, and tend to result in a strong degree of PRICE PARALLELISM. See PRICE LEADERSHIP.

price leadership a means of coordinating oligopolistic price behaviour (see OLIGOPOLY), allowing firms whose fortunes are MUTU- ALLY INTERDEPENDENT to secure high profits. One example of price leadership is that of leadership by a DOMINANT FIRM (a *dominant firm- price leader*) possessing cost advantages over his competitors. In Fig. 137, firm A is the low cost supplier with a MARGINAL COST curve MC_A; firm B has higher costs with a marginal cost curve MC_B. The individual demand curve of each firm is dd when they set *identical* prices (that is, it is assumed that total industry sales at each price are divided equally between the two firms); mr is the associated MAR- GINAL REVENUE curve. Firm A is able to maximize his profits by producing output OQ_A (where $MC_A = mr$) at a price of OP_A. Firm B would like to charge a higher price (OP_B), but the best he can do is to 'accept' the price set by firm A, although this means less than maximum profit. For given firm B's conjecture about the reactions of firm A to any price change by himself, any alternative course of action would mean even less profit. If he were to charge a higher price than P_A he would lose sales to firm A (whose price is unchanged), moving left along a new 'kinked' demand curve segment KP_B; if he were to cut his price below P_A, this would force firm A to undertake matching price cuts, moving right along the demand–curve segment Kd. Firm B could not hope to win such a 'PRICE WAR' because of his higher costs. Thus, firm B's best course of action is to charge the same price as that established by firm A.

Though price leadership systems are used by suppliers to avoid ruinous price competition they may, however, act as a cloak for COLLUSION leading to higher prices which exploit consumers.

See COMPETITION POLICY.

price level the general level of prices in an economy, as measured by a PRICE INDEX. Price levels in two consecutive time periods are often compared as an indication of INFLATION rates.

Price Marking (Bargain Offers) Order, 1979 a UK directive (made under the PRICES ACT, 1974) which prohibits traders from making vague or misleading PRICE claims such as 'worth £10 our price £5' and 'reductions of up to 50%', and comparisons with prices of other unspecified traders. 'Genuine' bargain offer price claims must be related to the seller's previous prices (specifically a price the trader has charged for at least 28 consecutive days during the previous six months) or to the manufacturer's RECOMMENDED RETAIL PRICE.

See CONSUMER PROTECTION.

price parallelism the tendency in an OLIGOPOLY market for suppliers to charge identical PRICES. Parallel prices may come about because suppliers, recognizing their MUTUAL INTERDEPENDENCE, desire to

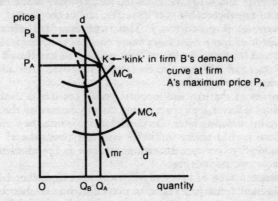

Fig. 137. **Price leadership**. Price leadership by a low-cost firm. See entry.

avoid price competition which reduces their profits, or they may come about as a result of deliberate COLLUSION between suppliers to 'fix' prices which maximize their joint profits.

See also PRICE LEADERSHIP, CARTEL.

prices and incomes policy a policy concerned with controlling INFLATION by *directly* attempting to halt or slow down the INFLATION-ARY SPIRAL of price-wage rises, in contrast to deflationary MONETARY POLICY and FISCAL POLICY which work *indirectly* to achieve the same result. The basic rationale for a prices and incomes policy is that whereas deflationary monetary and fiscal policies can only control inflation by increasing the rate of unemployment, a prices and incomes policy, if applied rigorously, can check inflation *and* maintain high levels of employment.

A prices and incomes policy can be operated on a voluntary or a statutory (compulsory) basis. In the former case, an appeal is made to the collective responsibilities of firms not to increase their prices 'unduly' and for trade unions to 'moderate' their demands for wage increases. The very vagueness of such exhortations, however, is usually given short shrift by vested interests. A statutory policy has more chance of success, certainly in the medium term if it is backed by strong penalties for non-compliance. Typical elements of the statutory approach include: (a) an initial, brief (6 months–1 year) standstill or 'freeze' on all price, wage, dividend, etc., increases; (b) a following period (usually 'phased' to allow for a progressive relaxation of controls) in which either (i) general 'norms' are laid down for permitted price and wages, for example, limiting them to say, 3% per annum, or (ii) more specifically, the establishment of formulas for linking

PRICE-SQUEEZE

permitted price and wage increases to, for example, in the case of a price rise to nonabsorbable cost increases, and in the case of a wage rise to increases in productivity. This latter approach requires the establishment of some regulatory body (such as the National Board for Prices and Incomes, the Price Commission, the Pay Board, which formerly operated in Britain) to ensure that proposed price and wage increases are indeed justified.

Proponents of a prices and incomes policy see it as a useful way of 'defusing' inflationary expectations, thereby removing the danger of accelerating inflation rates. On the debit side it must be recognized that because such a policy interferes with the operation of market forces it is likely to produce distortions in factor and product markets. See MACROECONOMIC POLICY.

price-squeeze a type of RESTRICTIVE TRADE PRACTICE whereby vertically integrated firms (see VERTICAL INTEGRATION) are able to injure nonintegrated competitors. This arises when the integrated firms produce both a raw material and the finished good, while the nonintegrated firms produce only the finished good but have to rely on the integrated firms for their raw material supplies. A 'squeeze' is applied if the integrated firms charge the nonintegrated firms a high price for the raw material and sell the finished product at a price which allows nonintegrated firms only minimal profits or forces losses on them.

Situations can also arise where the integrated firms produce raw materials and finished goods, while the nonintegrated firms produce only the raw material but have to rely on the integrated firms as a market for their raw materials. A 'squeeze' can be applied if the integrated firms pay a low price for the raw material from nonintegrated firms, but a high price for the raw material from integrated firms, allowing the nonintegrated firms only minimal profits or forcing losses on them.

price stability the maintenance of an unchanged general level of prices over time in an economy. Price stability, especially the avoidance of rising prices (INFLATION) is one of the main objectives of MACROECONOMIC POLICY.

See INTERNAL-EXTERNAL BALANCE MODEL.

price stickiness the tendency for PRICES to adjust slowly in response to EXCESS SUPPLY and EXCESS DEMAND in product markets. Price stickiness is often encountered in oligopolistic markets where interdependence between suppliers makes each supplier cautious about making price changes.

See KINKED DEMAND CURVE.

price support a means of supporting the incomes of certain producers by administratively maintaining the PRICES of their products above market price. In many countries, price support systems are used specifically to assist the agricultural sector by ensuring an adequate level of total farm incomes. In Fig. 138, the EQUILIBRIUM MARKET PRICE is OA. If this price is considered too low to adequately remunerate farmers the government will set a support price, say OB, at which it is prepared to buy up any unsold output. At the support price of OB, the government is then committed to acquiring the unsold output of CF at a total cost equal to the shaded area CFGH. The main problems with the price support method are that it penalizes consumers and results in wasteful over production. The price support method is used as the basis of the COMMON AGRICULTURAL POLICY of the EC.

Compare INCOME SUPPORT. See also AGRICULTURAL POLICY, BUFFER STOCK.

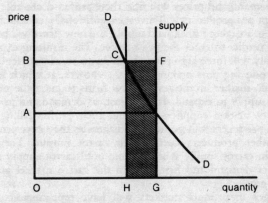

Fig. 138. **Price support**. See entry.

price system or **market mechanism** a characteristic of an economy in which basic decisions about what to produce, how to produce it and how products (incomes) are to be distributed are determined by the interaction of buyers and sellers in product and factor markets, as indicated in Fig. 139a on page 426.

In a PRIVATE-ENTERPRISE ECONOMY, or a MIXED ECONOMY with a significant private sector, the current levels of output and consumption of products are the result of the varied decisions of households and firms being put into operation through the price system as they carry out transactions in markets. The firm is a key element in the market system operating in product markets where it sells products and factor markets where it buys or hires resources. The price system embraces both types of market and broadly operates so as to ensure that resources are allocated in accordance with consumer demand.

For example, suppose initially that carrot and pea prices were such as to equate supply and demand for these products in their respective markets but then there was a change in consumer demand away from carrots and towards peas, as indicated in Fig. 139b. The increased demand for peas, coupled with unchanged pea supply in the short run, would result in an excess demand for peas at the prevailing price and price would rise to ration the scarce peas amongst consumers. The decreased demand for carrots, coupled with unchanged carrot supply in the short run, would initially give rise to an excess market supply at the prevailing price and the price of carrots would fall as suppliers sought to clear unsold stocks.

These changes in prices will affect the profits of carrot and pea suppliers. As demand and prices rise in the pea market, pea growers will experience increased profits, while carrot growers faced with falling demand and prices will find their profits declining. Over the long term pea producers will invest in additional land and machinery and hire more labour to expand supply and new firms will be tempted by high profits to enter the pea market. The resulting expansion in pea supply will force high prices back down to a lower level, leaving firms producing peas making NORMAL PROFITS, at which level there will be no further incentives for new firms to enter the pea market or total supply to expand. By contrast, as demand and prices fall in the carrot market suppliers will find their profits falling and less efficient producers will go out of business as they experience losses, while other producers curtail their carrot output. The resulting decline in carrot supply will continue until carrot supply adjusts to the lower demand and firms left in the carrot market are earning normal profit.

Changes in product markets will have repercussions in factor markets as Fig. 139b indicates. In order to expand pea supply, extra natural, human and capital resources must be drawn into pea production and this can only be achieved by offering them a higher return than they receive elsewhere. The increased demand for peas will result in an increased derived demand for FACTOR INPUTS in pea production and this excess demand for factor inputs in the pea industry will increase the returns to factors employed there. By contrast, the carrot industry will be releasing resources as firms leave the industry, and unemployment of factors of production in the carrot trade will reduce factor returns as the derived demand for them falls. These forces serve to shape the distribution of income between those working in pea and carrot production.

The above example shows how the price system results in a reallocation of resources in response to signals given out by consumers about their changed demand for products which in turn affect the prices of factor inputs. However, autonomous changes in the prices of factor inputs can themselves affect product prices and consumer demand patterns through the price system. For example, assume that carrot production is a relatively labour-intensive process while the growing and picking of peas is highly automated. Consequently, a sharp upward shift in wage rates would affect the two industries differently, the cost and price of carrots rising substantially while pea costs and prices change little. Since carrots are now more expensive while peas are much the same price, consumers will tend to alter their consumption patterns buying less relatively expensive carrots and more relatively cheap peas. Consequently output and employment in the carrot industry will tend to fall while output of peas expands, and a reallocation of resources from carrots to peas might be expected. The process of reallocation may be more direct than this though, for, as firms seek to produce carrots at minimum cost through the most efficient combination of factor inputs, faced then with an increase in wage rates they will alter production methods using less relatively expensive labour inputs and more relatively cheap capital. Increasing wage rates are thus likely to accelerate automation in the carrot industry reducing the demand for labour there.

The price system can provide a sophisticated mechanism for allocating resources in an automatic way. However, it is not necessarily as perfect a resource allocator as it may appear. First, the response of supply within the price system to changes in consumer demand may be very slow and painful, because less efficient firms are not eliminated quickly but linger on making losses. Second, resources are not always as occupationally or geographically mobile as the model implies, especially where workers require significant training to acquire appropriate skills. Third, the price system cannot ensure the provision of certain COLLECTIVE PRODUCTS like defence which are enjoyed in common by all consumers, because no markets for such products exist. Fourth, the price system only takes into account the private costs incurred by suppliers in producing and distributing products, ignoring the SOCIAL COSTS of pollution EXTERNALITIES. Finally, the efficient functioning of the price system depends crucially upon the structural characteristics of product and factor markets. With PERFECT COMPETITION in product and factor markets, the price system might well operate along the lines of the previous example. By contrast, where markets are characterized by MONOPOLY or OLIGO-POLY with high BARRIERS TO ENTRY and BARRIERS TO EXIT, then firms are not free to enter or leave product markets at will in response to profit opportunities. For example, if our earlier pea market was dominated by a monopoly supplier, then faced with an increase in demand the monopolist may decide not to expand pea supply but exploit the increased demand by raising selling price. Consequently in the long run the monopolist earns above normal profit and no

(a)

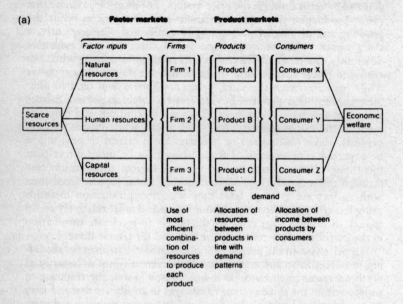

(b)

	Product markets		Factor markets	
	Pea market	Carrot market	Pea inputs	Carrot inputs
Short Run	D = S	D = S	DF = SF	DF = SF
	D↑	D↓		
	D > S	D < S		
	P↑	P↓		
	Pr↑	Pr↓		
Long Run	market entry	market exit	DF↑	DF↓
	S↑	S↓	DF > SF	DF < SF
	P↓	P↑	Pf↑	Pf↓
	Pr↓	Pr↑		
	D = S	D = S		

Key: D = product demand; S = product supply; P = price of products;
Pr = profits of suppliers; Pf = price of factor input; SF = factor
supply; DF = factor demand

Fig. 139. **Price system**. See entry.

extra factor inputs are devoted to pea production as consumer demand requires.

See CENTRALLY PLANNED ECONOMY, THEORY OF MARKETS, CONSUMER SOVEREIGNTY, REVISED SEQUENCE.

price taker a FIRM that sells its output at a fixed PRICE that is determined by market forces (as in PERFECT COMPETITION) or by government-imposed PRICE CONTROLS.

price theory an integrative body of MICROECONOMIC theory concerned with the determination of the EQUILIBRIUM MARKET PRICES and quantities transacted of goods and services.

See THEORY OF DEMAND, THEORY OF SUPPLY, THEORY OF MARKETS, THEORY OF CONSUMER BEHAVIOUR, THEORY OF THE FIRM.

price-wage spiral see INFLATIONARY SPIRAL.

price war any competition between rival suppliers centred on aggressive PRICE cutting. Price wars often break out when demand for a product is depressed and there is EXCESS SUPPLY capacity in the market. If FIXED COSTS are a high proportion of total costs, suppliers may be tempted to cut their prices to maintain full capacity working.

Price warfare is beneficial to the consumer and to RESOURCE ALLOCATION within the market in so far as it serves to eliminate inefficient, high cost suppliers. The problem from the suppliers' point of view is that cut throat price competition reduces the profitability of the market and everybody finishes up worse off. For this reason suppliers, particularly OLIGOPOLY suppliers, will normally try to avoid price wars and direct their competitive efforts into PRODUCT-DIFFERENTIATION activities.

See COMPETITION METHODS, PRICE LEADERSHIP.

primary sector the part of the economy concerned with the extraction of raw materials and the provision of agricultural crops and animal produce. The primary sector, together with INDUSTRIAL SECTOR and the SERVICE SECTOR form an interlocking chain of economic activities which constitute a modern economy. See STRUCTURE OF INDUSTRY.

prime rate the INTEREST RATE charged by COMMERCIAL BANKS for short-term LOANS to their most preferential customers. The prime rate is somewhat lower than other commercial borrowing rates but only applies to what may be called 'blue-chip' companies, generally large companies with the highest credit ratings.

See BANK LOAN, BASE RATE.

principles of taxation the rationale underlying the use of different methods of TAXATION. There are three main principles of taxation: ABILITY-TO-PAY PRINCIPLE, BENEFITS-RECEIVED PRINCIPLE, REDISTRIBUTION OF INCOME PRINCIPLE.

private company see JOINT-STOCK COMPANY.

private costs the costs (EXPLICIT COSTS and IMPLICIT COSTS) incurred

PRIVATE-ENTERPRISE ECONOMY

by firms for the use of FACTOR INPUTS in producing their OUTPUTS. Compare SOCIAL COSTS.

private-enterprise economy or **free-market economy** or **capitalism** a method of organizing the economy to produce GOODS and SERVICES. Under this ECONOMIC SYSTEM the means of production are privately held by individuals and firms. Economic decision-making is highly decentralized with resources being allocated through a large number of goods and services markets. The MARKET synchronizes the decisions of buyers and sellers and by establishing an EQUILIBRIUM PRICE determines how much of a good will be produced and sold.

Free enterprise advocates argue that a decentralized, MARKET-based system leads to a more efficient allocation of productive resources in line with the demands of buyers, and that in pursuit of individual self-interest (the profit motive) it will produce economic results (lower costs and prices, innovative new products) which are beneficial to society as a whole. Critics of private-enterprise economies argue, however, that market-based economies may not fully respond to the demands of buyers where supply is in the hands of powerful suppliers (see MONOPOLY); that it cannot ensure the provision of COLLECTIVE PRODUCTS for which no market exists; that it can generate POLLUTION and other EXTERNALITIES; and that it leads to gross inequalities in INCOME DISTRIBUTION. (See PRICE SYSTEM.)

See CENTRALLY PLANNED ECONOMY, MIXED ECONOMY, NATIONALIZATION, PRIVATIZATION, LAISSEZ-FAIRE.

private products the goods and services that are purchased and paid for by individual consumers for their own personal benefit. Compare SOCIAL PRODUCTS.

private property ASSETS which are held by individuals as part of their personal WEALTH. The protection of private property through legal title to assets and the enforcement of legal contracts relating to private property are a crucial foundation of a PRIVATE-ENTERPRISE ECONOMY.

private sector that part of the economy concerned with the transactions of private individuals, businesses and institutions (the PERSONAL SECTOR, the CORPORATE SECTOR and the FINANCIAL SECTOR, respectively). The private sector together with the PUBLIC SECTOR makes up the domestic economy, and together with the FOREIGN SECTOR make up the national economy.

private time preference see DISCOUNT RATE.

privatization the denationalization of an industry, transferring it from public to private ownership. The extent of State ownership of industry depends very much on political ideology, with CENTRALLY PLANNED ECONOMY proponents seeking more NATIONALIZATION, and PRIVATE-ENTERPRISE ECONOMY advocates favouring little or no nationalization. Thus, in the UK, the wide-ranging programme of privatization embarked upon by a Conservative government since

1980 can be interpreted partly as a political preference for the private enterprise system. Advocates of privatization, however, also espouse the economic virtues of free enterprise over State control. Specifically, they argue that firms left to fend for themselves in a competitive market environment are likely to allocate resources more efficiently and meet changing consumers' demands more effectively than a bureaucratic State monopolist (see PRICE SYSTEM).

In this regard it is pertinent to distinguish between industries which can be considered NATURAL MONOPOLIES and those where, in theory, a more fragmented industrial structure could be recreated. In the former category come those industries such as gas and electricity distribution, railway and telephone services where ECONOMIES OF SCALE are so great that only a monopoly supplier is in a position to fully maximize supply efficiency. There could be a serious loss of efficiency through unnecessary duplication of resources if these activities were to be fragmented. The alternative of a private-enterprise MONOPOLY is not appealing either, critics argue, because of the dangers of monopolistic abuse.

In the latter category come industries such as iron and steel, gas and electricity generation, shipbuilding and car manufacture, where because production usually takes place on a multiplant basis, the scope exists for placing each plant under a different ownership interest, thereby creating a more competitive supply situation. However, because these activities are capital-intensive, and, like natural monopolies, are characterized by significant economies of scale, the most that can be hoped for is the creation of a high seller concentration OLIGOPOLY. By contrast, the removal from the public sector of those *individual* firms (as distinct from whole industries) nationalized because they were making losses and needing reorganizing (for example, Ferranti, International Computers, Rolls-Royce, Jaguar, British Leyland, British Shipbuilders) can be more easily justified.

The main problem with privatization is the extent to which competition can in fact be introduced into sectors hitherto confined to State monopolies, either by breaking up an existing State corporation into a number of separate private companies (as for electricity) or by encouraging new entry (as in gas and telecommunications). Because of this it has been necessary in some cases to establish a regulatory authority (Ofgas and Oftel respectively for gas and telecommunications), backed up by the possibility of a reference to the MONOPOLIES AND MERGERS COMMISSION, to control the industry.

See DEREGULATION.

probability the likelihood of a particular uncertain event occurring, measured on a scale from 0.0 (such an event is impossible) to 1.0 (such an event is certain to occur). People generally estimate probabilities on the basis of the relative frequency with which an event has occurred in the past under given circumstances, and generalize from this past experience. In some circumstances it is easy to estimate the proportion of occasions on which an event occurs, for example, the probability of getting 'heads' when flipping a balanced coin is 0.5 because with such a coin in the long run we would get 50% 'heads' and 50% 'tails'. In estimating probabilities in business situations though, there may be no or only a few previous experiences which can be used to gauge the relative frequency of an event occurring. See also RISK AND UNCERTAINTY.

process ray a line depicting the path which a firm can follow in expanding OUTPUT where technical constraints mean that FACTOR INPUTS must be used in fixed proportions in a given production process. Fig. 140 shows the production options open to a firm which has a choice between just three processes A, B and C each of which uses capital and labour in fixed proportions. If this firm wanted to produce, say, 100 units of output per period then it could produce 100 units by settling at point d using process A, or point e using process B, or point f using process C. However, it cannot choose any combination of inputs along the lines joining d, e and f because such intermediate combinations are not technically feasible.

See ISOQUANT CURVE, ISOQUANT MAP, PRODUCTION FUNCTION.

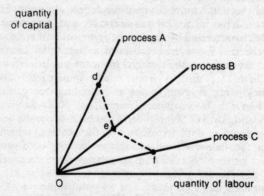

Fig. 140. Process ray. See entry.

producer or **supplier** the basic producing-supplying unit of economic theory. In economic theory, a producing unit is usually a FIRM though government organizations also produce goods and services.

producer goods CAPITAL GOODS and other goods such as fuel and lubricants which are used as FACTOR INPUTS in the production of other products, as opposed to being sold directly to consumers. Compare CONSUMER GOODS.

producers' surplus the extra earnings obtained by a producer from receiving a price for a good which is higher than the price at which he would have been prepared to supply.

Since producers are not equally efficient in supplying goods, a market price which is just sufficient to induce the 'intra-marginal' producer (i.e. the least efficient producer) to remain a supplier will simultaneously result in more efficient producers earning a producers' surplus.

Producers' surplus is directly analagous to CONSUMERS' SURPLUS and is shown in Fig. 141 where the EQUILIBRIUM MARKET PRICE is OP_e. At any point along the segment of the supply curve AE producers would be willing to supply the appropriate quantity and would receive a greater price OP_e than the price that they would be prepared to sell at. For example, one producer would be prepared to supply the intra-marginal quantity OQ_1 at a price of OP_1, though in fact he receives the market price OP_e, giving a producers' surplus P_1P_e. The total of all such producers' surpluses is indicated by the shaded area AP_eE.

In PERFECTLY COMPETITIVE markets only the most efficient producers are able to survive, and since the equilibrium market price is only just sufficient to cover suppliers' costs (including a NORMAL PROFIT return) the producers' surplus is zero. By contrast, in imperfect markets such as OLIGOPOLY the tendency for market prices to be higher than the costs of the intra-marginal supplier may enable *some* suppliers to secure a producers' surplus.

product a generic term covering both GOODS and SERVICES.

product characteristics model a THEORY OF CONSUMER BEHAVIOUR

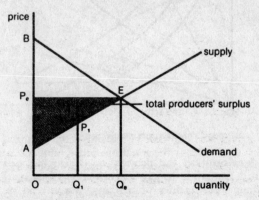

Fig. 141. **Producers' surplus**. See entry.

that shows how CONSUMERS choose between a number of BRANDS of a product each of which offer particular product characteristics in fixed proportions. For example, consumers buying blackcurrant juice may be looking for two principal product characteristics – flavour and vitamin content. Three brands of blackcurrant juice are available – Brand A, Brand B and Brand C – each of which is differentiated insofar as it places a different emphasis on the two product characteristics. The three brands are represented by the rays in Fig. 142 which show the fixed proportions of product characteristics in each brand. Brand A, for example, has a high vitamin content but has little flavour while Brand C, by contrast, has a lot of flavour but a low vitamin content.

Points a, b and c on these rays show how much of each brand of juice can be bought for a given unit of expenditure at the prevailing prices of the three brands. To find the consumer's utility-maximizing brand purchases it is necessary to introduce a set of indifference curves, I_1, I_2 and I_3, showing the consumer's preferences between the two product characteristics. The consumer's final choice will be brand B, as he settles at point b on the highest indifference curve (I_3) consistent with his limited expenditure.

See CONSUMER EQUILIBRIUM, INDIFFERENCE CURVES, PRODUCT DIFFER-ENTIATION.

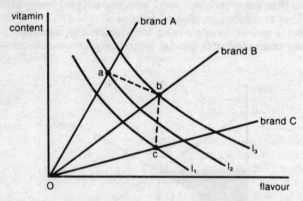

Fig. 142. Product characteristics model. See entry.

product development the process of developing new products which a firm can sell in its existing markets or new markets. Given the dynamic characteristics of markets, which tend to grow and decline over time (see PRODUCT LIFE CYCLE), it is important for firms to develop new brands to supersede those that are beginning to decline in popularity. Furthermore, the ability of a firm to introduce new products embodying superior product and performance attributes can improve its competitive position over rival suppliers in OLIGOPOLY markets where suppliers compete mainly in terms of PRODUCT DIFFERENTIATION.

See PRODUCT MATRIX, RESEARCH AND DEVELOPMENT.

product differentiation an element of MARKET CONDUCT that denotes the ways in which suppliers attempt to distinguish their own product from those of competitors. Product differentiation is a form of non-price competition (see MARKET COMPETITION). On the 'supply side' products may be differentiated according to differences in quality, performance, innovatory or novelty features, design, styling and packaging. On the 'demand side', 'imaginary' differences may be cultivated between products by the use of ADVERTISING emphasizing imputed or subjective qualities: 'better than', 'cleaner and whiter than', etc. The more ignorant buyers are of the relative qualities and performance of competing brands, the more susceptible they are likely to be to persuasive advertising.

The purpose of such differentiating activity is to secure an initial demand for the firm's products and, by cultivating BRAND LOYALTIES, to ensure that sales are increased or at least maintained. The significance of product differentiation is that it widens the parameters of competitive action, with firms competing against each other in quality, advertising, etc., rather than on price alone.

Product differentiation is an important means of establishing COMPETITIVE ADVANTAGE over rival suppliers, and in some market structures, most notably OLIGOPOLY, it is regarded as constituting a more effective competitive strategy than price competition. The attraction of product differentiation competition over price competition lies in the fact that whereas price cuts, for example, can be quickly and completely matched by competitors, a successful advertising campaign or the introduction of an innovatory product is less easily imitated. Moreover, whereas price competition lowers firms' profitability, product differentiation tends to preserve and even enhance profit returns. In particular, the establishment of product uniqueness may allow firms to command premium prices over competitors' offerings. Finally, product differentiation may serve to act as a BARRIER TO ENTRY, thereby protecting existing market shares against new competition.

Although product differentiation is often referred to as a form of 'market imperfection', this should not be interpreted to mean that heterogeneity is bad. Genuine differences among products, in particular, imply great diversity and more choices for consumers.

See also MARKET-MIX, PRODUCT CHARACTERISTICS MODEL, MONOPOLISTIC COMPETITION, OLIGOPOLY, HOMOGENEOUS PRODUCTS, MARKET

STRUCTURE, PRODUCT DEVELOPMENT, RESEARCH AND DEVELOPMENT, COMPETITIVE METHODS, INTELLECTUAL PROPERTY RIGHTS.

production the act of combining FACTORS OF PRODUCTION (labour, capital, etc.) by FIRMS to produce OUTPUTS of goods and services. The relationship between inputs and outputs in physical terms is shown by the PRODUCTION FUNCTION and in cost terms by the COST FUNCTION.

See BATCH PRODUCTION, MASS PRODUCTION, FLEXIBLE MANUFACTURING SYSTEM.

production census see CENSUS.

production costs the costs of converting FACTOR INPUTS into higher-value OUTPUTS of goods and services. The costs of manufacturing products include costs of raw materials, labour costs, depreciation and maintenance of plant and equipment, and rent, rates, lighting and heating of factory buildings. See also PRODUCTION FUNCTION, COST FUNCTION.

production function a function that shows for a given state of technological knowledge the relationship between physical quantities of FACTOR INPUTS and the physical quantities of OUTPUT involved in producing a good or service. Since the quantity of output depends upon the quantities of inputs used, the relationship can be depicted in the form of FUNCTIONAL NOTATION:

$$Q = f(1_1, I_2 . . . I_n)$$

where Q = output of a product and I_1, I_2, etc., are quantities of the various factor inputs 1, 2 etc., used in producing that output.

It is important to emphasize that factor inputs can be combined in a number of different ways to produce the same amount of output. One method which is technically the most efficient is the one which uses the only small amounts of labour, while another method may employ large quantities of labour and only a little capital. In physical terms, the method which is *technically the most efficient* is the one which uses the fewest inputs. Economists, however, are more concerned with the cost aspects of the input–output relationship (see COST FUNCTION), specifically the least costly way of producing a given output. Such relationships can be analysed using ISOQUANT CURVES, ISOQUANT MAPS and PROCESS RAYS.

production possibility boundary or **transformation curve** a method of illustrating the economic problem of SCARCITY. The production possibility boundary shows the maximum amount of goods and services that can be produced by an economy at a given point in time with available resources and technology. Fig. 143 shows a production-possibility boundary for motor cars and hospitals, assuming that all resources are fully employed in the most efficient way. Point A represents the maximum production of motor cars if no hospitals are produced, while point B represents the maximum production of hospitals if no motor cars are produced. At any point along the boundary, such as C, there is a trade-off between the two goods. Motor car production can be expanded *only* by taking resources away from the production of hospitals.

The boundary is curved rather than a straight line because not all resources are equally efficient in production of the two goods. Thus, near point A where a large number of cars are being produced and few hospitals, large numbers of construction workers have been diverted from hospital construction to make cars, and as it is unlikely that they will be as efficient working in engineering as in construction, as we move from point C to point A the production possibility curve flattens. By contrast, near point B where large numbers of hospitals are being built and few cars, large numbers of engineering workers have been diverted from car making to construction work, and since they are likely to be less efficient at the latter than the former, as we move from point C to point B the boundary steepens.

The point labelled U indicates UNEMPLOYMENT. More of both goods can be produced as idle resources are employed up to the limit set by the production possibility boundary. The broken line A^1B^1 shows how the production possibility boundary tends to move outwards over time as a result of long-term ECONOMIC GROWTH which increases POTENTIAL OUTPUT. How far outward the boundary moves and how quickly depends upon the rate of economic growth.

See OPPORTUNITY COST, LINEAR PROGRAMMING, SUPPLY-SIDE ECONOMICS, PARETO OPTIMALITY, INTERTEMPORAL SUBSTITUTION.

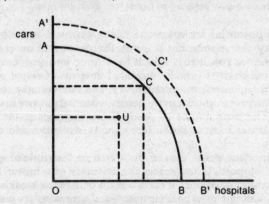

Fig. 143. **Production possibility boundary**. See entry.

productive efficiency an aspect of MARKET PERFORMANCE that denotes the efficiency of a market in producing current products at the lowest possible cost in the long run, using existing technology. Productive efficiency is achieved when output is produced in plants of optimal scale and when there is a long-run balance of market supply and demand. See Fig. 144.

See also MINIMUM EFFICIENT SCALE, TECHNOLOGICAL PROGRESS-IVENESS, EXCESS CAPACITY, RATIONALIZATION.

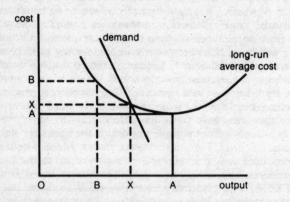

Fig. 144. **Productive efficiency**. In the graph, which assumes a long-run AVERAGE COST curve which is U-shaped, plant size OA results in minimum cost. If plant sizes are suboptimal (OB), or if optimal-sized plants (OA) are underutilized because of a shortfall in demand (OX), then actual supply costs will be higher than attainable costs.

productive potential SEE POTENTIAL GROSS NATIONAL PRODUCT.

productivity the relationship between the OUTPUT of an economic unit and the FACTOR INPUTS which have gone into producing that output. Productivity is usually measured in terms of *output per man-hour* to facilitate interfirm, interindustry, and intercountry comparisons. An increase in productivity occurs when output per man-hour is raised. The main source of productivity increases is the use of more and better CAPITAL STOCK (see CAPITAL WIDENING and CAPITAL DEEPENING).

This important point can be illustrated in the following three stages. (a) Suppose, initially, that the assembly of a motor car is a labour-intensive operation; it takes a team of 10 men working with a minimal amount of capital (spanners and screwdrivers only) one whole day to assemble one car. (b) The firm now invests in hydraulic lifting gear (CAPITAL DEEPENING) and this cuts down considerably the amount of time in aligning parts for assembly, reducing the time it takes to complete the assembly operation to, say, one tenth of a day.

The same team of men are now able to assemble 10 cars a day – their productivity has gone up tenfold. (c) The firm introduces a continuous flow assembly line with automatically controlled machines (again, capital deepening), which one man can operate. Output increases to say, 50 cars a day; the productivity of the remaining man has increased from 1 car a day (a one-tenth part of 10 cars) to 50.

Just as importantly, 9 men have been 'released' from the team. Either they too could all be put to work on a similar automated assembly line (capital widening), in which case the total output of the 10 men is now 500 cars per day (10 × 50), compared to 50 before. Alternatively, they could be redeployed outside the car industry, thereby helping to increase output in other sectors of the economy.

Increased productivity thus makes an important contribution to the achievement of higher rates of ECONOMIC GROWTH.

See JOB, CAPITAL–OUTPUT RATIO, SPECIALIZATION, QUALITY CONTROL, RESTRICTIVE LABOUR PRACTICE, WORK STUDY, X-INEFFICIENCY, ORGAN-IZATIONAL SLACK, SUPPLY–SIDE ECONOMICS, COLLECTIVE BARGAINING.

productivity bargaining a form of COLLECTIVE BARGAINING which deals with ways of improving productivity alongside WAGES and con-ditions of work. It can involve both changes in existing work prac-tices (see RESTRICTIVE LABOUR PRACTICES) and the introduction of new work methods which call upon the work force to be more flexible and adaptable in exchange for improved pay prospects.

Productivity bargaining can help firms to become more efficient and more responsive to changes in market conditions. More gener-ally, productivity bargaining can improve the supply-side efficiency of the economy and counter COST–PUSH INFLATION.

See SUPPLY–SIDE ECONOMICS.

product life-cycle the typical sales pattern followed by a product over time as changing consumer tastes and technological INNOVATION cause new products to emerge which supersede existing products. The typical life-cycle followed by a product introduced into a market is depicted in Fig. 145. It consists of four main phases:

(a) product launch/introduction, which follows the successful development of a new product and its national launch. When the product is first put on the market sales volume will be low until consumer resistance has been overcome, and at this stage the market is frequently limited to high-income consumers with more adventur-ous buying habits.

(b) product growth phase, where the product gains market accept-ance and sales grow rapidly as the product reaches the mass market. During this phase competitors may begin to enter the field with rival products, so that the distinctiveness of the original product fades.

(c) product maturity/saturation, where sales are largely limited to repeat purchases by existing customers, since the majority of potential customers have already made their first purchases. At this stage the market is saturated, so that competitors are unable to benefit from market growth and must compete intensely to maintain or increase their share of the constant market.

(d) product decline, where sales begin to decline as consumer tastes change or superior products are launched. If left to follow this downward trend the product will eventually die as sales fall to low levels, though long before this managers may decide to phase out the product.

Most companies market a number of different products and must formulate a product-range strategy, providing for a regulated process of new product launches, with new products like B in Fig. 145 growing as older products like A reach maturity, so as to maintain an appropriate PRODUCT MIX of newly-launched products, growth products and mature lines.

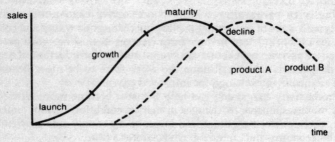

Fig. 145. **Product life-cycle**. See entry.

A company's pricing policy for a product may be related to the stages of the product's life-cycle. During the launch phase, managers will tend to opt for a high *skimming price* which capitalizes on the new and distinctive nature of the product and the temporary monopoly power which this conveys. In this early stage demand for the product is likely to be less price-elastic (see PRICE-ELASTICITY OF DEMAND), for high prices will not deter high-income pioneer consumers. Furthermore, a high price will reinforce the quality image of the largely untried product as well as recouping research and development and heavy promotion expenditures. During the growth phase managers may change to a low *penetration price*, lowering price to bring the product within reach of the mass of consumers. At this stage demand is likely to be more price-elastic, for the average consumer is more price-conscious than the pioneer consumer. By lowering price the firm can expand sales appreciably, gaining cost-savings from large-scale production and can maintain a large market share in the face of entry by competitors. Once the maturity phase is reached with several similar products firmly established in the market then prices will tend to stay in line with one another, for any attempt by one firm to reduce its price and expand its market-share will provoke retaliation as competitors fight to maintain their market share.

Similarly, other elements of the MARKETING MIX such as advertising and sales promotion need to be adapted to the phases of the product life cycle.

See also BOSTON MATRIX, PRODUCT PERFORMANCE.

product life-cycle theory a theory that seeks to explain changes in the pattern of INTERNATIONAL TRADE over time, which is based on a dynamic sequence of product INNOVATION and diffusion. Four 'phases' of the cycle can be postulated. (a) To begin with, as new products are introduced, the consuming country is likely to be the producing country because of the close association between innovation and demand. This original producing country – typically an advanced industrial country – becomes an exporter to other high-income countries. (b) Production begins in other leading industrial countries, and the innovating country's exports to these markets are displaced. (c) As these countries' own demand for the product reaches sufficient size to enable producers to take advantage of economies of scale, they too become net exporters, thereby displacing the innovating country's exports in nonproducing countries. (d) Finally, as the technology and product become increasingly standardized to the point where relatively unskilled labour can be used in the production process, DEVELOPING COUNTRIES with lower costs become exporters of the product, further displacing the innovating country's exports. Meanwhile, however, the innovating country has moved on to the production of new products.

See also TECHNOLOGICAL-GAP THEORY, THEORY OF INTERNATIONAL TRADE.

product market a MARKET in which products are bought and sold, and in which the prices of goods and services are determined by the interplay of demand and supply forces.

See PRICE SYSTEM, EQUILIBRIUM MARKET PRICE.

product-market matrix a matrix for analysing the scope for change in a firm's product-market strategy. Fig. 146 shows the matrix, which depicts products on one axis and markets on the other. A firm seeking to achieve profit and growth in changing market conditions has four major strategies available: (a) more effective penetration of existing markets by existing products, increasing the firm's market share; (b) development of new markets for its existing products, capitalizing on the firm's production strengths; (c) development of new products

PRODUCT MIX

for its existing markets, exploiting the firm's marketing strengths; (d) development of new products for new markets, that is, DIVERSIFICATION. This is generally the highest-risk strategy since it takes the firm furthest from its production and marketing expertise.

See also BOSTON MATRIX, PRODUCT MIX.

		Market	
		Present	New
Product	Present	1. market penetration	2. market development
	New	3. product development	4. diversification

Fig. 146. Product-market matrix. See entry.

product mix the mixture of PRODUCTS offered by a FIRM. Since most products tend to follow a typical PRODUCT LIFE-CYCLE it is expedient for companies to maintain an appropriate mix of newly-launched products, growth products and mature lines. In addition, the firm may choose to offer a range of similar products to appeal to different sectors of the market as part of a MARKET-SEGMENTATION strategy. A firm will generally consider its product mix in the context of its broader MARKETING MIX (embracing price, advertising, etc.). See also PRODUCT-MARKET MATRIX.

product performance an aspect of MARKET PERFORMANCE that denotes the quality and performance of existing products and firms' record with respect to the development of new products. The introduction of new products and the qualitative improvement of existing products may enhance consumer welfare by providing consumers with 'better-value-for-money' in terms of price/quality trade-offs. See Fig. 147.

See also PRODUCT DIFFERENTIATION, TECHNOLOGICAL PROGRESSIVENESS, INVENTION, INNOVATION, RESEARCH AND DEVELOPMENT, PRODUCT LIFE-CYCLE.

product standards minimum national standards of product design and construction which are legally enforced in order to protect the health and safety of consumers. Complex, nationally established product standards which have to be met by IMPORTS can serve as a form of PROTECTIONISM.

profit the difference that arises when a firm's TOTAL REVENUE is greater than its TOTAL COSTS. This definition of 'economic profit' differs from that used conventionally by businessmen (*accounting profit*) in that accounting profit only takes into account explicit costs. Economic profit can be viewed in terms of:

(a) the return accruing to enterprise owners (entrepreneurs) after the payment of all EXPLICIT COSTS (payments such as wages to outside

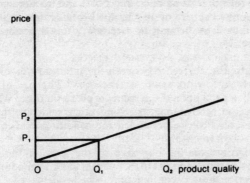

Fig. 147. **Product performance**. An improvement in product quality from OQ_1 to OQ_2 can allow the firm producing the product to charge a higher price to reflect this improvement, increasing price from OP_1 to OP_2. If price is raised by only P_1P_2, which is less than proportionate to the increase in product quality Q_1Q_2 (as in the Fig.), then the consumer receives a net benefit from product improvement.

factor-input suppliers) and all IMPLICIT COSTS (payments for the use of factor inputs – capital, labour – supplied by the owners themselves).

(b) a residual return to the owner(s) of a firm (an individual ENTREPRENEUR or group of SHAREHOLDERS) for providing capital and for risk-bearing.

(c) the 'reward' to entrepreneurs for organizing productive activity, for innovating new products, etc., and for risk taking.

(d) the prime mover of a PRIVATE-ENTERPRISE ECONOMY serving to allocate resources between competing end uses in line with consumer demands.

(e) in aggregate terms, a source of income and thus included as part of NATIONAL INCOME.

See also PROFIT MAXIMIZATION, NORMAL PROFIT, ABOVE-NORMAL PROFIT, RISK AND UNCERTAINTY, NATIONAL INCOME ACCOUNTS.

profitability the PROFIT earned by a firm in relation to the size of the firm, measured in terms of total ASSETS employed, long term capital or number of employees. See RETURN ON CAPITAL-EMPLOYED.

profit-and-loss account an accounting statement that shows a firm's SALES REVENUE generated over a trading period and all the relevant EXPLICIT COSTS incurred in earning that revenue. In the account, the COST-OF-GOODS SOLD is deducted from sales revenue to calculate GROSS PROFIT then the other costs involved are deducted from the gross profit to show any NET PROFIT earned.

PROFIT CENTRE

profit centre an organizational subunit of a firm which is given responsibility for minimizing operating COSTS and maximizing REVENUE within its limited sphere of operations. Profit centres facilitate management control by helping to ascertain a unit's performance and profitability.

See also COST CENTRE, INVESTMENT CENTRE.

profit margin the difference between the SELLING PRICE of a product and its PRODUCTION COST and SELLING COST. The size of the profit margin will depend upon the percentage profit mark-up which a firm adds to costs in determining its selling price, which in turn may be varied in response to changes in demand conditions and competition.

See FULL-COST PRICING.

profit maximization the objective of the firm in the traditional THEORY OF THE FIRM and the THEORY OF MARKETS. Firms seek to establish that price-output combination which yields the maximum amount of profit. The achievement of profit maximization can be depicted in two ways.

(a) Firstly, where TOTAL REVENUE (TR) exceeds TOTAL COST (TC) by the greatest amount. In Fig. 148, this occurs at the output level where the slope of the two curves is identical, and tangents to each curve are consequently parallel as at Q_e. At any output level below Q_e the relevant tangents would be diverging – the TR and TC curves would still be moving further apart and profits would still be rising. At any output level beyond Q_e, on the other hand, the relevant tangents would be converging and the profit surplus of TR over TC would be falling. Thus, Q_e is the optimum point, for here the distance between the total revenue and total cost curves is maximized (equal to AB). The difference between the two curves shows up in the total profit curve which becomes positive at output OQ_1, reaches a maximum at output OQ_e (where profit CD = AB), and becomes negative beyond output OQ_2.

(b) Secondly, profit maximization can be shown to occur where MARGINAL REVENUE (MR) equals MARGINAL COST (MC) – at output OQ_e in the figure. At all output rates above OQ_e additional units add more to cost than revenue so that total profits are reduced. At all output rates less than OQ_e additional units add more to revenue than cost, thereby expanding total profits. Only where MR = MC are profits maximized.

See FIRM OBJECTIVES.

profit motive the objective of a FIRM to ensure that revenue exceeds costs. The term is usually associated with the FIRM OBJECTIVE of PROFIT MAXIMIZATION, but a profit motive would still exist where only satisfactory profits were aimed for. See also PROFIT, SATISFICING THEORY.

profit-related pay a PAY system whereby employees receive a proportion of their pay in the form of PROFIT-related payments. Advo-

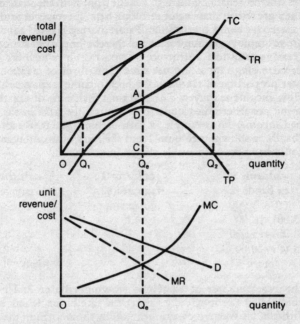

Fig. 148. **Profit maximization**. See entry.

cates of such schemes suggest that they can help to reduce UNEMPLOYMENT by making WAGES more variable. They hold that unemployment occurs because the price of labour is stuck at too high a level and argue that profit-related income schemes can build some flexibility into labour markets. Specifically, they argue that because of the automatic profit-related cushion, employers will be slower to lay off workers during a recession and quicker to hire workers when conditions are good. In addition, it is held that profit-sharing workers are better motivated than wage earners to improve PRODUCTIVITY within their companies, since they share in any additional profits created.

See also SUPPLY-SIDE ECONOMICS, WAGE RATE, MINIMUM WAGE RATE.

profit sharing the distribution of some portion of PROFITS to the employees of a company. It can take the form of an annual cash bonus based on the previous year's profits or it can form an element of weekly or monthly pay (see PROFIT-RELATED PAY). Less direct forms of profit sharing include allocation to employees of shares in the company, paid for out of company profits, and providing employees with the option to buy shares at some point in the future at current

PROGRESSIVE TAXATION

prices, thereby enabling them to benefit from both the share dividend and any growth in share value resulting from increases in profitability (see EMPLOYEE SHARE OWNERSHIP). Profit sharing is often advocated to improve employee commitment and thereby improve PRODUCTIVITY.

progressive taxation a structure of TAXATION in which tax is levied at an increasing rate as INCOME rises. This form of taxation takes a greater proportion of tax from the high-income taxpayer than from the low-income taxpayer. The marginal incidence of taxation rises to some pre-determined upper limit, currently 40% in the UK on earned income. For example, a man earning £20,000 with current tax bands as shown in column 1 and the rates of taxation in column 2 would have the tax payable shown in column 3:

column 1 tax bands (£)	column 2 tax rates(%)	column 3 tax payable (£)
0– 5,000	tax exempt	nil
5,001–10,000	20	1,000
10,001–15,000	30	1,500
15,001–20,000	40	2,000
etc.		total 4,500

The increasing rate of taxation is shown in column 2. The greater the individual's earnings, the greater the rate of tax which is levied.

Virtually all Western economies exhibit some form of progressive taxation structure as a means of redistributing income from the more affluent members of society to the poorer. This type of ABILITY-TO-PAY PRINCIPLE is regarded, as far as earned personal incomes are concerned, as the most equitable form of taxation. Ideally, however, a progressive income tax structure should not only promote social equity by redistributing income, but should also encourage enterprise by avoiding penal rates of taxation at the upper end of the income scale and, together with SOCIAL SECURITY BENEFITS, provide suitable incentives to work at the lower end of the income scale.

Compare REGRESSIVE TAXATION, PROPORTIONAL TAXATION. See also INCIDENCE OF TAXATION, REDISTRIBUTION–OF–INCOME PRINCIPLE OF TAXATION, SUPPLY–SIDE ECONOMICS, LAFFER CURVE, MARGINAL RATE OF TAXATION.

progress payments a contractual arrangement common to large construction projects whereby payment for work done is made at predetermined stages along the route to completion.

propensity to consume the proportion of NATIONAL INCOME which is spent by households on consumption of final goods and services. The average propensity to consume (APC) is given by:

$$\frac{\text{total consumption}}{\text{total income.}}$$

The marginal propensity to consume (MPC) is the fraction of any change in income which is spent:

$$\text{marginal propensity to consume (MPC)} = \frac{\text{change in consumption}}{\text{change in income.}}$$

Alternatively, consumption can be expressed as a proportion of DISPOSABLE INCOME.

In the simple CIRCULAR FLOW OF NATIONAL INCOME MODEL all disposable income is either consumed or saved. It follows that the sum of the MPC and the MARGINAL PROPENSITY TO SAVE always adds up to one.

A rise in the propensity to consume increases consumption expenditure for a given income level, for example from OC to OC₁ at income level Y in Fig. 149. This increases the consumption injection into the circular flow of national income and results in an increase in aggregate demand and national income.

See MULTIPLIER, CONSUMPTION EXPENDITURE.

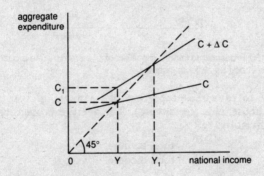

Fig. 149. **Propensity to consume.** The effect of an increase in the propensity to consume on national income.

propensity to import the proportion of NATIONAL INCOME which is spent on IMPORTS. The average propensity to import (APM) is given by:

$$\frac{\text{total imports}}{\text{total income.}}$$

The marginal propensity to import (MPM) is the fraction of any change in income spent on imports:

$$\text{marginal propensity to import (MPM)} = \frac{\text{change in imports}}{\text{change in income.}}$$

PROPENSITY TO SAVE

Alternatively, imports can be expressed as a proportion of DISPOS-ABLE INCOME.

A rise in the propensity to import decreases consumption expenditure on domestically produced output for a given income level, for example from OC to OC_1 in Fig. 150. This increases the imports withdrawal from the CIRCULAR FLOW OF NATIONAL INCOME and reduces national income from OY to OY_1.

See MULTIPLIER, IMPORT PENETRATION.

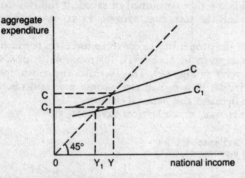

Fig. 150. **Propensity to import.** The effect of an increase in the propensity to import on national income.

propensity to save the proportion of NATIONAL INCOME which is saved by households (see SAVING). The average propensity to save (APS) is given by:

$$\frac{\text{total saving}}{\text{total income.}}$$

The marginal propensity to save (MPS) is the fraction of any change in income which is saved:

$$\text{marginal propensity to save (MPS)} = \frac{\text{change in saving}}{\text{change in income.}}$$

Alternatively, saving can be expressed as a proportion of DISPOS-ABLE INCOME.

In the simple CIRCULAR FLOW OF NATIONAL INCOME MODEL all disposable income is either consumed or saved by households. It follows that the sum of the MARGINAL PROPENSITY TO CONSUME and the MPS add up to one (note that saving is defined as all disposable income which is not spent by consumers regardless of whether savings are placed in banks, hidden under the bed, or whatever).

A rise in the propensity to save decreases consumption expenditure for a given income level, for example from OC to OC₁ at income level Y in Fig. 151. This increases the savings withdrawal from the circular flow of national income resulting in a decrease in aggregate demand and national income.

See MULTIPLIER.

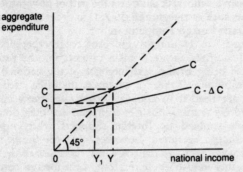

Fig. 151. **Propensity to save**. The effect of an increase in the propensity to save on national income.

propensity to tax the proportion of NATIONAL INCOME which is taken in TAXATION by government. The average propensity to tax (APT) is given by:

$$\frac{\text{total taxation}}{\text{total income.}}$$

The marginal propensity to tax (MPT) is the fraction of any change in income which is taken in taxation:

$$\text{marginal propensity to tax (MPT)} = \frac{\text{change in taxation}}{\text{change in income.}}$$

Direct taxes reduce total income to (net of tax) DISPOSABLE INCOME. Thereafter a proportion of this disposable income will be spent, and indirect taxes on goods and services bought will reduce still further the proportion of income returned to the business sector as factor returns.

See MULTIPLIER.

A rise in the propensity to tax decreases disposable income for a given income level (increases the taxation withdrawal from the CIRCULAR FLOW OF NATIONAL INCOME), decreasing consumption expenditure, which results in a decrease in AGGREGATE DEMAND and NATIONAL INCOME.

property see ASSET.

proportional taxation a structure of TAXATION in which tax is levied at a constant rate as INCOME rises, for example, 10% of each increment of income as income rises. This form of taxation takes the same proportion of tax from a low-income taxpayer as from a high-income taxpayer. Compare PROGRESSIVE TAXATION, REGRESSIVE TAXATION.

protectionism a deliberate policy on the part of governments to erect trade barriers such as TARIFFS and QUOTAS in order to protect domestic industries from foreign competition.

While there are arguments for protection especially appealing to sectional interests, protectionism cannot, for the most part, be vindicated as being in the best interests of the national and international community. Take, for example, the often cited contention that tariffs are needed to equalize wage rates between countries. The UK and US textile industries complain that their domestic positions are undermined by foreign suppliers who employ 'cheap labour'. It should be noted, however, that for the economy as a whole high wage rates are the *result*, not the cause of the productive efficiency, other industries successfully meet foreign competition in both domestic and foreign markets despite higher wages. This is because they rank higher in the order of COMPARATIVE ADVANTAGE. Protection of industries which come low in the order of comparative advantage distorts the industrial ranking and leads to inefficient resource utilization. Foreign competition would force contraction of the textile industries, and the resources released from it could then be devoted to products in which the country has a comparative advantage.

Protection might be necessary, it is suggested, in the short term to facilitate an orderly restructuring of industries (particularly where manpower resources are highly localized), but there is the danger that such protection might become permanent in the face of vested interests.

Other arguments for protection, while superficially appealing, can usually be achieved more effectively by alternative means. Thus selective tariffs and quotas may assist in restoring BALANCE-OF-PAYMENTS EQUILIBRIUM, but distort the ordering of industries by comparative advantage. By contrast, aggregate fiscal and monetary policies and exchange-rate adjustments affect all foreign transactions.

There are, however, some seemingly respectable arguments for protection. From the viewpoint of the welfare of the world as a whole the most popular claim made for tariffs, etc., is the so-called INFANT-INDUSTRY argument. Protection can be an effective means of stimulating the development of an industry that is well suited to a country (in terms of potential comparative advantage) but which finds it impossible to get started unless it is protected from imports. Over time, suitably protected, such an industry is able to acquire internal economies of scale (i.e., lower costs through exploiting a larger domestic market) and take advantage of various external economies (a well-trained labour force or the 'learning-by-doing' effect). Eventually the new industry is able to become equally or more efficient than its older competitors. The tariff can then be removed, leaving behind a viable and competitive industry.

Such temporary protection of industries does not conflict with the goal of free traders: maximum specialization on the basis of comparative advantage. It is only through the temporary equalization of competitive conditions that the industry is able to reach that stage of development which allows it to fully realize its potential.

There are problems, however. Industries are frequently selected for protection not on the basis of a favourable comparative advantage but for nationalistic reasons (e.g. diversification of the economy); 'infant industry' becomes a slogan to justify promiscuous protection without regard to merit. The protection afforded may be over-excessive and continued for longer than is strictly necessary.

In some circumstances, tariffs can be employed to improve a country's TERMS OF TRADE by forcing down prices in exporting countries. This applies especially to major importers who are large enough to exercise buying power. It is to be noticed, however, that the gain from lower-priced imports may be offset by two adverse effects of tariffs: their diversion of resources to less productive uses, and the fact that trade partners are likely to retaliate by imposing tariffs of their own.

See also IMPORT RESTRICTIONS, NOMINAL RATE OF PROTECTION, EFFECTIVE RATE OF PROTECTION, BEGGAR-MY-NEIGHBOUR POLICY, GENERAL AGREEMENT ON TARIFFS AND TRADE, MULTI-FIBRE ARRANGEMENT, DUMPING, LOCAL CONTENT RULE.

proxy an authorization to a person or firm to act in place of another. During a JOINT-STOCK COMPANY'S ANNUAL GENERAL MEETING, for example, a SHAREHOLDER may be unable to attend and vote on items contained in the agenda. The shareholder may therefore give written authorization for someone else to attend and vote at the meeting in his stead. A shareholders proxy is frequently given to the incumbent board of directors to vote with as they think fit, hence the term 'proxy vote'.

PSBR see PUBLIC-SECTOR BORROWING REQUIREMENT.

PSDR see PUBLIC-SECTOR DEBT REPAYMENT.

PSL$_2$ see MONEY SUPPLY DEFINITIONS.

public company see JOINT-STOCK COMPANY.

public corporation a company which is owned by the State. See NATIONALIZATION.

public debt the NATIONAL DEBT and other miscellaneous debt for which the government is ultimately accountable. Such debt includes, for example, the accumulated debts of nationalized industries and local authorities.

public expenditure see GOVERNMENT EXPENDITURE.

public finance the branch of economics concerned with the income and expenditure of public authorities and its effect upon the economy in general. When the CLASSICAL ECONOMISTS wrote upon the subject of public finance they concentrated upon the income side, TAXATION. Since the Keynesian era of the 1930s much more emphasis has been given to the expenditure side and the effect FISCAL POLICY has on the economy.

The PUBLIC SECTOR is so large a part of most economies that it influences virtually every aspect of economic life either through its own expenditure on goods and services provided by the private sector; its wage payments to public-sector employees; or its social security payments (pensions, sickness and unemployment benefits). Similarly, the financing of these expenditures by means of various taxes (income tax, value added tax, corporation tax, etc.) affects the size and pattern of spending by individuals and businesses.

Governments plan their revenues and expenditures each fiscal year by preparing a budget (see BUDGET (GOVERNMENT)). They may plan to match their expenditures with their revenues, aiming for a BALANCED BUDGET; or they may plan to spend less than they raise in taxation, running a BUDGET SURPLUS and using this surplus to repay former public debts (see NATIONAL DEBT); or they may plan to spend more than they raise in taxation, running a BUDGET DEFICIT which has to be financed by borrowing (see PUBLIC-SECTOR BORROWING REQUIREMENT).

As well as serving as the instrument of government planning of its own economic and social commitments, the budget plays an integral rôle in the application of fiscal policy, specifically the operation of DEMAND MANAGEMENT policies to reduce unemployment and inflation.

See KEYNESIAN ECONOMICS, PROGRESSIVE TAXATION.

public goods see SOCIAL PRODUCTS.

public interest a 'benchmark' used in the application of COMPETITION POLICY (in the UK) to judge whether or not a particular action or policy pursued by a supplier or by a group of suppliers, or a change in the structure of a market, is 'good' or 'bad' in terms of its effects on economic efficiency and the consumer. For example, it is clearly in the public interest if a firm prices its product at a level which yields it only a 'fair' profit return – that is, a profit reward which is just adequate to secure the efficient supply of the product (see NORMAL PROFIT). By the same token, it is clearly against the public interest if a firm profiteers at the expense of the consumer by charging excessive prices (see ABOVE-NORMAL PROFIT). In practice, however, the issue is complicated by difficulties in interpreting data: for example, low profits may reflect a conservative pricing policy or result from the fact that the firm is grossly inefficient. Moreover, there are further complications arising from the fact that particular actions may produce, simultaneously, both beneficial and detrimental effects. In this case a 'trade-off' assessment is required to form a balanced judgement.

See WILLIAMSON 'TRADE-OFF' MODEL, MONOPOLIES AND MERGERS COMMISSION, RESTRICTIVE PRACTICES COURT.

public ownership see NATIONALIZATION.

public sector or **government sector** that part of the economy concerned with the transactions of the government. Government receives income from TAXATION and other receipts and influences the workings of the economy through its own spending and investment decisions (GOVERNMENT EXPENDITURE) and through its control (via MONETARY POLICY and FISCAL POLICY) of the spending and investment decisions of other sectors of the economy. The public sector, together with the PERSONAL SECTOR, FINANCIAL SECTOR, CORPORATE SECTOR and FOREIGN SECTOR make up the national economy. See CIRCULAR FLOW OF NATIONAL INCOME MODEL.

public-sector borrowing requirement (PSBR) the excess of GOVERNMENT EXPENDITURE over TAXATION receipts, requiring the government to make good the difference by borrowing money from the banking system (TREASURY BILLS) or from the general public (long-dated BONDS). BUDGET DEFICITS are used as an instrument of FISCAL POLICY as a means of increasing total spending (AGGREGATE DEMAND) in the economy.

The size of the nominal public-sector borrowing requirement (PSBR) depends not only on the government's fundamental spending and taxation plans (its underlying FISCAL STANCE) but also on the level of economic activity and the rate of inflation.

Fluctuations in economic activity lead to movements in the PSBR, for the PSBR tends to increase in a recession as total tax revenues fall and social security payments rise in response to lower incomes and higher unemployment, and to fall in a boom as tax revenues rise and social security payments fall in response to higher incomes and lower unemployment (see AUTOMATIC (BUILT-IN) STABILIZERS). In order to remove the impact of cyclical fluctuations in economic activity associated with BUSINESS CYCLES upon the PSBR, it is necessary to calculate the *cyclically-adjusted PSBR*. By removing from the PSBR figure the effect of cyclical variations on the budget balance, the cyclically-adjusted PSBR measures what the PSBR would be if economic activity levels were 'on trend'.

INFLATION also has an effect on the nominal PSBR, because since most public-sector debt is denominated in nominal terms, its real value falls with the rate of inflation, reducing the real value of the government's liabilities. The real PSBR is defined as the actual PSBR less the erosion by inflation of the real value of the stock of public-sector debt (*inflation-adjusted PSBR*). So for a given real PSBR, a higher rate of inflation implies a higher nominal PSBR. When the effects of inflation rates of the 1970s are allowed for, the high nominal PSBR figures (indicating a large fiscal deficit) show a modest real PSBR (indicating a fiscal surplus). The public sector has been adding to its nominal stock of debt at a slower rate than that at which inflation has been eroding the value of past borrowing.

There are three main ways in which a government can finance its borrowing requirement:

(a) by borrowing funds from individuals, firms and financial institutions in the private sector by selling government bonds and bills. This requires high interest rates to make government debt attractive to lenders.

(b) by borrowing funds from overseas lenders by selling government securities. This overseas borrowing has effects on the balance of payments.

(c) by borrowing short-term from the commercial banking system by issuing Treasury bills to them. This has the effect of increasing the banks' reserve assets allowing them in turn to expand their lending.

The first two methods of financing the public-sector borrowing requirement by selling bonds to the nonbank private sector are likely to raise interest rates but because they provide stable (generally long-term) funding for government borrowing they do not affect the MONEY SUPPLY. By contrast, to the extent that the government cannot fund all its borrowing needs from the first two sources it must resort to borrowing from the banking system. This is akin to printing additional money and serves to increase the money supply.

Public-sector borrowing may contribute to 'crowding out' (see CROWDING-OUT EFFECTS) the private sector in two main ways. First by facilitating larger government expenditure it may cause real crowding out as the public sector uses more of the nation's resources, leaving less for private consumption spending and investment and for exports. Second, the additional borrowing by government will tend to raise interest rates thereby causing financial crowding out, as private investment is discouraged by the high interest rates.

Since 1980 the British government has published a MEDIUM-TERM FINANCIAL STRATEGY which lays down targets each year for the public-sector borrowing requirement expressed as a percentage of GROSS DOMESTIC PRODUCT, though in the 1990s this strategy has received less emphasis.

Where a government's taxation receipts exceed its expenditures, this results in negative PSBR or a 'public sector debt repayment' position, enabling it to repay some past borrowings.

See MONEY SUPPLY/SPENDING LINKAGES, MONETARISM, PUBLIC FINANCE, BUDGET (GOVERNMENT), MATURITY STRUCTURE, NATIONAL DEBT.

public-sector debt repayment (PSDR) the excess of TAXATION receipts over GOVERNMENT EXPENDITURE enabling the government to use the difference to repay past borrowings. BUDGET SURPLUSES are used as an instrument of FISCAL POLICY as a means of decreasing total spending (AGGREGATE DEMAND) in the economy. See PUBLIC-SECTOR BORROWING REQUIREMENT PSBR for further discussion of how fluctuations in economic activity levels and inflation rates affect the government's budgetary position.

See NATIONAL DEBT.

public utility an enterprise that provides certain essential goods or services like water, electricity and gas. In some countries such as the US and the UK, most of these goods and services are provided by privately-owned (but publicly regulated) companies. In other countries, for instance, France, most of these products are provided by publicly-owned corporations (nationalized industries).

See RATE-OF-RETURN REGULATION, MARGINAL-COST PRICING, TWO-PART TARIFF, NATIONALIZATION.

public works any expenditure by government on social INFRASTRUCTURE such as roads, houses, hospitals, sewers, etc. Such expenditure was strongly advocated by KEYNES during the DEPRESSION of the 1930s to alleviate the problem of UNEMPLOYMENT and stimulate AGGREGATE DEMAND, via the MULTIPLIER. See KEYNESIAN ECONOMICS, MACRO-ECONOMIC POLICY, GOVERNMENT EXPENDITURE.

pump priming spending by the government on PUBLIC WORKS, etc. which is aimed at increasing AGGREGATE DEMAND in order to stimulate economic activity and raise NATIONAL INCOME. Increased government spending will, through MULTIPLIER effects, enlarge spending in other sectors of the economy, serving to reduce UNEMPLOYMENT and increasing output of goods and services.

See DEMAND MANAGEMENT, GOVERNMENT EXPENDITURE.

purchasing power the extent to which a given monetary unit can buy goods and services. The greater the amount of goods and services purchased with say, £10, the greater is its purchasing power. Purchasing power is directly linked to the retail PRICE INDEX and can be used to compare the material wealth of an average individual from a previous time period to the present.

See INFLATION, PURCHASING-POWER PARITY THEORY.

purchasing-power parity theory a theory of EXCHANGE-RATE determination that postulates that under a FLOATING EXCHANGE-RATE SYSTEM, exchange rates adjust to offset differential rates of INFLATION between countries who are trade partners in such a way as to restore BALANCE-OF-PAYMENTS EQUILIBRIUM. Differential rates of inflation can bring about exchange rate changes in two principal ways. The first relates to the effect of changes of relative prices on import and export demand. As the price of country A's products rise relative to those of country B, demanders of these products tend to substitute away from A and toward B, decreasing the demand for A's currency and increasing the demand for B's currency. This leads to a DEPRECIATION of the bilateral exchange rate of currency A for currency B. Thus, a higher level of domestic prices in country A is 'offset' by a fall in the external value of its currency.

A second way that exchange rates can change in response to differential rates of inflation is through SPECULATION about future exchange rate movements. As prices rise in country A relative to country B, managers of foreign-currency portfolios and speculators anticipate an eventual lowering of the real value of the currency in terms of its purchasing power over tradeable products and tend to substitute away from it in their holdings, again causing a depreciation of currency A.

This theory therefore predicts that differential rates of inflation leads to compensating exchange rate changes. However, it is also possible that exchange-rate changes themselves can lead to differential rates of inflation; if, for example, import demand is highly price-inelastic, an exchange rate depreciation may lead to an increase in domestic inflation. There is thus a problem in respect of causality (see DEPRECIATION).

See also ASSET-VALUE THEORY.

put option see OPTION.

Q

quality the totality of the attributes of a good or service which meet the requirements of buyers or customers. The materials which make up the product, the design and engineering of the product, product performance and reliability are all important characteristics of the 'quality package' which ultimately influence customers to buy a product and repeat-purchase it.

Product quality is an important source of PRODUCT DIFFERENTIATION, enabling firms to establish BRAND LOYALTY and COMPETITIVE ADVANTAGE over rival suppliers. See QUALITY CONTROL.

quality circle a body of employees who meet periodically, usually under the guidance of a supervisor, to discuss ways in which the QUALITY of the organization's products or service can be improved. See PRODUCTIVITY.

quality control a discipline concerned with improving the QUALITY of goods and services produced. The object of quality control is to prevent faulty components or finished goods from being produced and it uses a variety of devices to help achieve this aim. Techniques of statistical sampling and testing can be used to identify faulty materials and products. Statistical variability limits can be used to ensure, for example, that machines are continuing to hold their tolerances in producing goods. Quality circles can be employed to involve work-groups in the task of quality assurance, by generating discussion about the cause of quality problems and how workers themselves can deal with such problems.

See also PRODUCTIVITY, PRODUCT PERFORMANCE, PRODUCT DIFFERENTIATION.

quantity demanded the amount of a PRODUCT (or FACTOR OF PRODUCTION) that consumers (or firms) buy in a given time period. The quantity demanded of a product depends upon the product's own price, consumers' income, price of substitute products, etc. See DEMAND FUNCTION, DEMAND CURVE, DERIVED DEMAND.

quantity of money see MONEY SUPPLY.

quantity supplied the amount of a PRODUCT (or FACTOR OF PRODUCTION) that suppliers offer for sale in a given time. The quantity supplied of a product depends upon the product's own price, prices of factor inputs, the state of technology, etc. See SUPPLY FUNCTION, SUPPLY CURVE.

quantity theory of money a theory that posits a direct relationship between the MONEY SUPPLY and the general PRICE LEVEL in an economy.

QUANTITY THEORY OF MONEY

The basic identity underlying the quantity theory was first developed by Irving Fisher (1867–1947) in 1911. The Fisher equation states that:

$$MV \equiv PT$$

where M is the money stock; V is the VELOCITY OF CIRCULATION of money (the average number of times each £ or $ changes hands in financing transactions during a year); P is the general price level; and T is the number of transactions or the total amount of goods and services supplied.

The above relationship is true by definition because total money expenditure on goods and services (MV) in a period must equal the money value of goods and services produced (PT), and the four terms are defined in such a way that the identity must hold. However, the identity can be converted into a testable equation by assuming that the velocity of circulation of money is constant or changes slowly.

Economists at Cambridge University reformulated the traditional quantity theory of money to emphasize the relationship between the stock of money in an economy (M) and final income (Y), of the form $MV \equiv Y$. The income velocity of circulation (Cambridge equation) is thus:

$$V = \frac{PT}{M}$$

where V is the average number of times the money stock of an economy changes hands in the purchase of final goods and services. For example, taking Y as gross national product, if a country has a GNP of £5,000m and an average money stock (M) over a year of £1,000m, then V is 5. Velocity cannot be observed directly and is thus determined using Y and M, figures which may be calculated from government statistics.

The term V in the Cambridge equation is not the same as V in Fisher's traditional quantity theory of money. In Fisher's equation, $MV \equiv PT$, rearranged to give:

$$V = \frac{Y}{M}$$

the number of transactions in the period, T, includes *all* transactions for real goods and services plus financial transactions. In the Cambridge equation, PT (where P = average price level) is replaced by Y which contains not *all* transactions, but only those generating final income. This formulation allowed the Cambridge economists to emphasize real income (that is, final goods and services).

The classical economists argued that velocity of circulation was constant because consumers have relatively constant spending habits and so turn over money at a steady rate. This argument converts the identity into an equation that leads to the quantity theory which expresses a relationship between the supply of money and the general price level. If V and T are constant then:

$$M = P \text{ and } \Delta M = \Delta P.$$

The modern exponents of the quantity theory (see MONETARISM) do not necessarily hold that the velocity of circulation is fixed, but they argue that it will change only slowly over time as a result of financial innovations like the spread of bank accounts and cheque payments, and the growing use of credit cards. They also point out that in a fully employed economy there is a maximum amount of goods and services being produced and which therefore can be exchanged, so that the number of transactions, T, is determined by real supply-wide considerations like productivity trends. With V and T fixed or slowly changing, then the price level is determined by the stock of money M. Any increase in the money supply feeds directly into an increase in demand for goods and services (aggregate demand). It follows that if the money supply (M), and hence aggregate demand, increase *over time* faster than the supply capacity of the economy (T), the result will be a rise in the general price level, P (INFLATION). By contrast, Keynesian economists argue that the velocity of circulation is unstable and changes rapidly and may offset changes in the money stock.

See also MONEY-SUPPLY/SPENDING LINKAGES, MONETARY POLICY.

quantity traded the amount of a PRODUCT (or FACTOR OF PRODUCTION) that is bought/sold. In most markets the quantity traded will depend upon the interaction of DEMAND and SUPPLY in determining the product's EQUILIBRIUM MARKET PRICE.

quasi-rent see ECONOMIC RENT.

Quesnay, François (1694–1774) a French economist whose writings helped to lay the basis for the physiocratic school of thought (see PHYSIOCRACY). Quesnay suggested that agriculture was the source of wealth, with the productive class (tenant farmers) creating an economic surplus over and above what they need for their own subsistence. This 'net product' is then available to meet the needs of landowners, and the artisans and merchants. Quesnay wrote *Tableau Économique* (1758), a work designed to show how the net product is produced and circulates between farmers, landlords and merchants, which was, in effect, an INPUT-OUTPUT table.

quota an administrative device to limit (a) output or (b) trade.

(a) Under a producer's CARTEL arrangement each supplier is given a fixed output to produce. Quotas are used by the cartel to establish monopoly prices by ensuring that the total of the firms' output quotas is restricted relative to market demand.

(b) Under a trade quota system, the government directly restricts the volume of permissible IMPORTS to a specified maximum level (the *import quota*) in order to protect domestic industries against foreign competition. As a protectionist device, a quota is much more effective than TARIFFS, especially when import demand is price-inelastic (when import demand is price-inelastic, increasing import prices has little effect on the volume of imports). In these cases the only certain way of limiting imports are physical controls. See also PROTECTIONISM.

quoted company a public JOINT-STOCK COMPANY whose shares are traded either on the main STOCK EXCHANGE or related secondary markets such as the UNLISTED-SECURITIES MARKET. See LISTED COMPANY.

R

R and D see RESEARCH AND DEVELOPMENT.

random walk see EFFICIENT-MARKETS HYPOTHESIS.

rate of exchange see EXCHANGE RATE.

rate of interest see INTEREST RATE.

rate of return the PROFITS earned by a business, measured as a percentage of the ASSETS employed in the business.

See NORMAL PROFIT, ABOVE-NORMAL PROFIT, RATE-OF-RETURN REGULATION, RETURN ON CAPITAL-EMPLOYED.

rate-of-return regulation the stipulation by the government of maximum permitted levels of PROFIT accruing to a MONOPOLY supplier. Profit regulation is commonly used in the US and the UK to control the pricing policies of (privately owned) PUBLIC UTILITIES.

rates see LOCAL TAX, UNIFORM BUSINESS RATE.

rational behaviour see ECONOMIC MAN.

rational-expectations hypothesis a HYPOTHESIS that suggests that firms and individuals predict future events without bias and with full access to relevant information at the time the decision is to be made. Only 'new' information will have an effect on EXPECTATIONS or behaviour.

Business expenditure on investment and stocks is affected greatly by the expectations that businessmen have of the future. These expectations, for instance, are major contributory elements in determining the BUSINESS CYCLE. If businessmen operated under conditions of total knowledge, then the business cycle in its present form would cease to exist. Expectations play a major part in wage-bargaining whereby each side (employers and employees) have to anticipate future events such as the rate of inflation. MONEY ILLUSION would not exist and employment would be based on real wages at all times.

The rational-expectation model is perhaps more applicable to markets approaching perfect competition and is rather less successful when applied to modern macroeconomic problems.

See also ECONOMIC MAN.

rationalization the reorganization of an industry (or firm) in order to enable it to use its resources more efficiently. Rationalization usually involves the closure of high-cost plants (either through the merging of firms or their exit from the industry) which then allows output to be concentrated in plants of MINIMUM EFFICIENT SCALE and enables a better 'balance' to be achieved between industry supply and demand by eliminating EXCESS CAPACITY. Within a firm, rationalization may involve streamlining its organizational structure in order to reduce overhead costs.

See also PRODUCTIVE EFFICIENCY, ORGANIZATIONAL SLACK.

rationing a physical method of allocating a product which is in short supply relative to demand (EXCESS DEMAND). In a free market this situation would not arise – the excess demand would be 'choked off' and additional supply encouraged by an increase in the price of the product (see EQUILIBRIUM MARKET PRICE). But if the price is fixed below its equilibrium rate (for example, by the government wishing to hold down the prices of key products such as food) the use of ration tickets provides one practical means of allocating the available supply between consumers on an equitable basis.

In Fig. 152, for example, if the price of a product is fixed by the government at O_r then it is necessary to ration the amount of output which producers are willing to supply, OQ_r, at this price amongst consumers who are demanding the greater amount of OQ_s.

See also BLACK MARKET, PRICE CONTROLS.

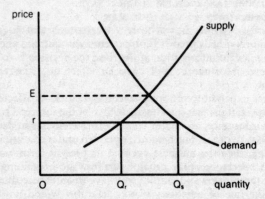

Fig. 152. **Rationing**. See entry.

real balance the real PURCHASING POWER of a MONEY balance. The true value of money lies not in its nominal denomination but in its ability to purchase goods to satisfy wants. If prices doubled the REAL VALUE of money balances held would be halved.

See REAL BALANCE EFFECT.

real balance effect or **Pigou effect** the mechanism by which a change in the real value of money balances leads to a change in AGGREGATE DEMAND. If prices are flexible in an economy, a decrease in prices, for example, will increase the real value of a household's cash holdings. The increase in a household's money wealth increases its PURCHASING POWER, thereby stimulating consumption. By contrast, a rise in prices will decrease the real value of a household's cash holdings and by reducing its purchasing power cause it to consume less. Since prices are most likely to fall during a recession, then the Pigou effect will serve partially to offset the fall in consumption associated with the recession. However, if the Pigou mechanism occurred at a point of full employment, then the increase in consumer demand associated with the increase in real money wealth could not be satisfied because the economy would already be operating at full capacity. Here prices would rise until real money balances were restored to their original level.

real exchange rate the EXCHANGE RATE of a currency expressed in constant price terms to make allowance for the effects of INFLATION. For example, where a country experiences a higher rate of domestic inflation than its trade competitors, then its exports will become more expensive than those of competitors' exports and its imports cheaper than domestic products, unless its exchange rate depreciates to offset fully the inflation differential. In situations where exchange rates are fixed by international agreement or determined by market forces which do not reflect relative inflation rates, then *nominal* exchange rates can differ significantly from real exchange rates. A country's real exchange rate is the more important measure of that country's INTERNATIONAL COMPETITIVENESS.

See PURCHASING–POWER PARITY THEORY.

real income see REAL WAGES.

real interest rate the INTEREST RATE paid on a LOAN, adjusted for the effects of INFLATION. Thus, for example, if a borrower were to pay a 10% NOMINAL INTEREST RATE on a loan during a year when the inflation rate was 6%, then the 'real' interest rate would be only 4%. Inflation reduces the real burden of interest payments to borrowers whilst reducing the real return to lenders.

real price the PRICE of a PRODUCT or FINANCIAL SECURITY measured in constant price terms to make allowance for the effects of INFLATION. For example, though the price of a product increases from, say, £1 to £1.10 (a 10% increase) between 1990 and 1992, if during this period the general price level had risen by 20%, then the real price of the product would have fallen.

Contrast NOMINAL PRICE. See PRICE INDEX.

real values the measurement of an economic aggregate (for example GROSS DOMESTIC PRODUCT corrected for changes in the PRICE LEVEL over time; that is, expressing the value in terms of constant prices. Thus, Fig. 153 shows that the UK's GDP (real income) declined in real terms between 1990 and 1992, whereas using current, INFLATION-affected prices, GDP is shown to have increased.

See GNP DEFLATOR.

REAL WAGE

UK Gross domestic product

	Constant (1990) prices £ billion	Current prices £ billion
1990	551	551
1991	540	576
1992	537	599
1993	548	631

Fig. 153. **Real values**. See entry.

real wage or **real income** the MONEY WAGE rate divided by the general PRICE LEVEL of products. Notationally this is written W/P. If wages and prices both rise by, say, 10% from an initial index number of, say, 100, the original ratio of W/P is 100/100 = 1, and the new ratio of 110/110 is also 1. An increase in real wages occurs where wages rise more quickly than prices, or prices remains constant. In the later instance, a rise in wages of 10% would give the ratio 110/100 = 1.1, thus making the wage earner 10% better off because he is capable of purchasing 10% more products with his new wage.

The analysis of real and money wages in relation to employment and output is a continuing central theme within economics although it is generally thought to be real wages which determines the level of employment rather than money wages.

See CLASSICAL ECONOMICS, KEYNESIAN ECONOMICS, MONEY ILLUSION.

recession a phase of the BUSINESS CYCLE characterized by a modest downturn in the level of economic activity (ACTUAL GROSS NATIONAL PRODUCT). Real output and investment fall, resulting in rising UNEMPLOYMENT. A recession is usually caused by a fall in AGGREGATE DEMAND, and provided that the authorities evoke expansionary FISCAL POLICY and MONETARY POLICY it can be reversed.

See DEFLATIONARY GAP, DEMAND MANAGEMENT.

Recognized Investment Exchange (RIE) a body such as the STOCK EXCHANGE which provides an organized framework for dealings in financial assets or securities, including monitoring and reporting completed transactions and providing for settlement and delivery through an appropriate clearing system. Only investment exchanges which meet the regulatory requirements of the FINANCIAL SERVICES ACT, 1986 are recognized for this purpose.

Recognized Professional Body (RPB) a professional body such as the Chartered Accountants of England and Wales which is recognized as a regulating organization under the terms of the UK FINANCIAL SERVICES ACT, 1986. RPBs are responsible for regulating their members in relation to their work in advising clients about investments.

recommended retail price the practice of manufacturers in indicating a resale PRICE for their products. Unlike RESALE PRICE MAINTEN-ANCE, the recommended retail price is seen merely as acting as a 'reference point' for retailers in setting their own price. Subject to competitive conditions the actual price paid by consumers is in most cases much less than the recommended price.

See LIST PRICE, COMPETITION POLICY (UK).

recovery a phase of the BUSINESS CYCLE characterized by an upturn in the level of economic activity (ACTUAL GROSS NATIONAL PRODUCT). Real output and investment increase and UNEMPLOYMENT falls. A recovery in economic activity is usually dependent on there being an increase in AGGREGATE DEMAND which may come about autonomously or be induced by expansionary FISCAL POLICY and MONETARY POLICY.

See also DEMAND MANAGEMENT.

recycling the reprocessing of materials, containers and goods which would otherwise have been thrown away to be used in the manufacture of some other product, for example the pulping of old newspapers to produce egg boxes and writing paper; the melting down of used metal drinks cans to make new containers.

Recycling can help businesses keep their production costs down since materials which are recycled are generally less expensive than using primary raw materials, and it helps the economy by serving to conserve scarce natural resources and save on energy costs: recycling paper preserves forests and is estimated to result in a 70% energy saving compared to processing new timber. Recycling also helps control environmental POLLUTION by reducing the need for waste dumps.

redeemable financial security a financial security such as a BOND, DEBENTURE or PREFERENCE SHARE which is issued for a fixed period of time and repayable on maturity at its redemption value.

Contrast IRREDEEMABLE FINANCIAL SECURITY.

redemption yield see YIELD.

redeployment of labour the movement of LABOUR from one firm to another, or from one industry to another, usually made necessary by technical change (the introduction of labour-saving machinery, for example) or by structural change (the decline of an industry, for example). Redeployment often requires a high degree of labour MOBILITY both geographically and in terms of acquiring new job skills. See also RESOURCE ALLOCATION.

rediscounting the purchase and sale of BILLS OF EXCHANGE, TREASURY BILLS and BONDS between their issue and redemption dates. For example, if a bond with a nominal value of £1,000 redeemable in one year's time is sold initially for £900 (giving a £100 discount on its formal redemption value), then it might be resold or rediscounted for £950 after 6 months. See also DISCOUNT, DISCOUNT MARKET.

redistribution-of-income principle of taxation the principle that the TAXATION system, together with the provision of state welfare programmes, should be used to benefit poorer households at the expense of richer households. Fig. 154 shows the extent of income redistribution brought about by taxation and state spending. Thus, the poorest 20% of the population receives only 2% of total original income, but after taxation and state benefits they receive 10% of total final income.

See also PROGRESSIVE TAXATION, ABILITY-TO-PAY PRINCIPLE OF TAXATION.

Quintile groups of households	Original income %	Final income %
Bottom fifth	2	10
Second fifth	7	13
Third fifth	16	17
Fourth fifth	27	23
Top fifth	48	37
	100	100

Fig. 154. **Redistribution-of-income principle of taxation**. The personal distribution of original and final income in the UK, 1994. Final income = original income less taxes paid, plus state spending on education, health, social security benefits. Source: *Social Trends*, 1996.

redundancy the loss of jobs by employees brought about by company RATIONALIZATION and reorganization which results from falling demand or PRODUCTIVITY improvement.

See UNEMPLOYMENT.

reflation an increase in the level of NATIONAL INCOME and output. A reflation is often deliberately brought about by the authorities in order to secure FULL EMPLOYMENT and to increase the rate of ECONOMIC GROWTH. Instruments of reflationary policy include fiscal measures (for example, tax cuts) and monetary measures (for example, lower interest rates).

See also FISCAL POLICY, MONETARY POLICY, DEFLATIONARY GAP, DEMAND MANAGEMENT.

refusal to supply a type of RESTRICTIVE TRADE PRACTICE whereby a seller deliberately withholds supplies to customers as a means of enforcing EXCLUSIVE DEALING, TIE-IN SALES arrangements, and RESALE PRICE MAINTENANCE.

See COMPETITION POLICY.

regional policy a policy concerned with removing significant imbalances between the regions of an economy in respect of UNEMPLOYMENT rates and levels of INCOME PER HEAD. The main approach adopted is that of spreading industrial activity around the regions so as to avoid unemployment of labour and capital resources in the DEPRESSED AREAS and undue congestion in the more prosperous ones. A particular emphasis of regional policy is the regeneration of areas which have fallen into industrial decline by encouraging new firms and industries to locate and invest in these areas (the 'inward investment' approach, which involves taking work to the workers). The rationale behind this approach is that the problems of the depressed areas stem largely from overspecialization in industries which have gone into decline (for example, coal mining in South Wales, shipbuilding in North-East England, cotton in Lancashire, etc.), rather than any fundamental economic disadvantage. Accordingly, what is required is a diversification of the industrial base of such areas so as to provide new employment opportunities, which increases investment-boosting local spending and, via MULTIPLIER effects, increasing income levels.

The 'inward investment' approach to regional policy is implemented in three main ways:

(a) the provision of financial inducements (investment grants, low-interest 'soft loans', tax relief, rent and rate-free factories, etc.) to firms prepared to locate in designated DEVELOPMENT AREAS, or INTER-MEDIATE AREAS;

(b) the use of physical controls on factory and office buildings to prevent firms from locating to any great extent outside these development areas through the issue of industrial development certificates;

(c) investment by the government in INFRASTRUCTURE capital, particularly good road and rail networks and general amenities.

Critics of this approach to regional policy argue that 'forcing' firms to locate in areas which might not suit them and 'subsidizing' their activities might impair economic efficiency. However, there is little evidence to suggest this has been a serious matter.

In the UK, REGIONAL SELECTIVE ASSISTANCE is the main means used to provide help to firms investing in development and intermediate areas.

A possible alternative approach, that of encouraging people to move out of depressed regions (the 'taking the workers to the work' approach) has not found favour because not only does it tend to accentuate the problems of the depressed areas themselves (the loss of skilled workers, reduced local spending and incomes, etc.), but it also creates difficulties for 'receiving' areas, particularly if they are already over-congested with respect to housing, schools, etc.

See ENTERPRISE ZONE, EUROPEAN REGIONAL DEVELOPMENT FUND, STRUCTURAL UNEMPLOYMENT, DEINDUSTRIALIZATION, LOCATION OF INDUSTRY, FIRM LOCATION.

regional selective assistance an instrument of REGIONAL POLICY used in Britain as a means of encouraging new INVESTMENT in DEVELOPMENT

AREAS and INTERMEDIATE AREAS. *Regional selective* assistance in the form of cash grants is potentially available to *all* firms undertaking investments in the development and intermediate areas. Such aid, however, is discretionary – 'selectivity' requires that the investment project should have a good chance of paying its way, that assistance is vital for the project to go ahead (i.e. without the grant the project could not go ahead at all, or only on a smaller scale), and that the project should contribute to both the regional and the national economy. A project grant is based on the fixed capital costs of a project and the number of jobs it is expected to create or safeguard. The amount of grant is negotiated for the minimum necessary for the project to go ahead on the basis proposed. This is obviously open to manipulation, but has been useful in enabling the authorities to attract foreign firms into the UK, for example the location of the Nissan car assembly plant in Washington, Tyne and Wear.

regional unemployment a form of STRUCTURAL UNEMPLOYMENT associated with the decline of certain industrial activities such as ship-building and steel production which are heavily concentrated in particular regions of the country.

See REGIONAL POLICY.

registered company a JOINT-STOCK COMPANY that is registered in the UK with the REGISTRAR OF COMPANIES.

registered unemployment the number of people who register with employment exchanges or job centres as being unemployed and available for work.

The numbers of unemployed people who register will depend upon whether or not unemployment benefit and other social security payments are made only to those who register.

See UNEMPLOYMENT.

Registrar of Companies a government official who maintains a record of all JOINT-STOCK COMPANIES operating in the UK. All joint-stock companies must lodge a copy of their MEMORANDUM OF ASSOCIATION and ARTICLES OF ASSOCIATION with the Registrar when they are first formed, and larger companies must continue to file their ANNUAL REPORT AND ACCOUNTS with the Registrar each year. Any potential lender or investor can inspect the company register to gain background information about a particular company.

Registrar of Friendly Societies the official (responsible to the DEPARTMENT OF TRADE AND INDUSTRY) who maintains a register of all FRIENDLY SOCIETIES in the UK and supervises their activities.

regression analysis a statistical technique used in ECONOMETRICS for estimating the EQUATION which best fits sets of observations of DEPENDENT VARIABLES and INDEPENDENT VARIABLES, so generating the best estimate of the true underlying relationship between these variables. From this estimated equation it is then possible to predict what the (unknown) dependent variable(s) will be for a given value of the (known) independent variable(s).

Taking the simplest example of a linear equation with just one independent variable and a dependent variable (disposable income and consumption expenditure), the problem is to fit a straight line to a set of data consisting of pairs of observations of income (Y) and consumption (C). Fig. 155 shows such a set of paired observations plotted in graph form, and we need to find the equation of the line which provides the best possible fit to our data, for this line will yield the best predictions of the dependent variable. The line of best fit to the data should be chosen so that the sum of the squares of the vertical deviations (distances) between the points and the line should be a minimum. This method of *ordinary least squares* is applied in most regressions. The *goodness of fit* of the regression line to the sample observations is measured by the CORRELATION COEFFICIENT.

In arithmetic terms the line depicted in Fig. 155 is a linear equation of the form:

$$C = a + bY$$

where the coefficients of the equation, a and b, are estimates (based on single observations) of the true population parameters. These constants, a and b, obtained with the method of ordinary least squares, are called the estimated regression coefficients, and once their numerical values have been determined then they can be used to predict values of the dependent variable (C) from values of the independent variable (Y). For example, if the estimated regression coefficient of a and b were 1,000 and 0.9 respectively then the regression equation would be $C = 1,000 + 0.9\ Y$ and we could predict that for a disposable income of £10,000, consumer expenditure would be:

$$C = a + bY$$
$$C = 1,000 + 0.9Y$$
$$= 1,000 + 0.9\ 10,000$$
$$= 10,000$$

The regression coefficient of the slope of the linear regression, b, is particularly important in economics for it shows the change in the dependent variable (here consumption) associated with a unit change in the independent variable (here income). For example, in this case a b value of 0.9 suggests that consumers will spend 90% of any extra disposable income.

The regression equation will not provide an exact prediction of the dependent variable for any given value of the independent variable, because the regression coefficients estimated from sample observations are merely the best estimate of the true population parameters, and are subject to chance variations.

REGRESSION ANALYSIS

To acknowledge the imperfections in any estimated regression equation based on a sample in depicting the true underlying relationship in the population as a whole, the regression equation is generally written as:

$$C = a + bY + e$$

with the addition of a *residual* or *error term, e*, to reflect the residual effect of chance variations and the effects of other independent variables (such as, say, interest rates on consumer credit) which influence consumption spending but which are not explicitly included in the regression equation.

Where it is felt that more than one independent variable has a significant effect upon the dependent variable, then the technique of *multiple linear regression* will be employed. The technique involves formulating a multiple linear regression equation involving two or more independent variables, such as:

$$C = a + bY + dI + e$$

where I is the interest rate on consumer credit and d is an additional regression coefficient attached to this extra independent variable. Estimation of this multiple linear regression equation by the method of ordinary least squares involves fitting a three-dimensional plane or surface to a set of sample observations of consumer spending, disposable income and interest rates in such a way as to minimize the squared deviations of the observations from the plane. In arithmetic terms the sample observations can be used to generate numerical

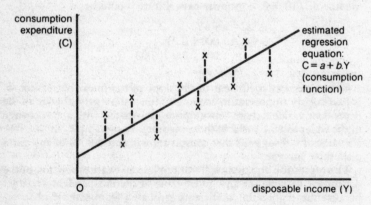

Fig. 155. **Regression analysis**. See entry.

estimates of the three regression coefficients (a, b and d) in the above equation.

See FORECASTING.

regressive taxation a structure of TAXATION in which tax is levied at a decreasing rate as INCOME rises. This form of taxation takes a greater proportion of tax from the low-income taxpayer than from the high-income taxpayer. INDIRECT TAXES such as value added tax or excise duty become regressive when taken as a proportion of total net income. For example, if an item costs £100 and value added tax is 15%, then £15 in relation to £200 per week net pay (7½%) is greater than £15 to another person earning £600 per week net (2½%). The burden of taxation is therefore proportionately greater on the less affluent members of society and cannot be considered an equitable tax. Compare PROGRESSIVE TAXATION, PROPORTIONAL TAXATION.

See also ABILITY-TO-PAY PRINCIPLE OF TAXATION, INCIDENCE OF TAXATION, REDISTRIBUTION-OF-INCOME PRINCIPLE OF TAXATION.

regulation the control of economic activities by the government or some other regulatory body, for example an industry trade association. Regulation can include PRICE CONTROLS to regulate inflation; FOREIGN EXCHANGE CONTROLS to regulate currency flows; and COMPETITION POLICY to regulate the operation of particular markets. More specific regulation may be imposed upon individual industries or activities, for example price control of privately owned PUBLIC UTILITIES (e.g. Oftel, which regulates telecommunication prices in the UK); and the regulation of financial services by the Bank of England and the Securities and Investment Board.

See DEREGULATION.

relative-concentration measure see CONCENTRATION MEASURES.

relative-income hypothesis the hypothesis that it is not a person's or nation's absolute income which matters but his or its relative income. If this is so, then since all individuals or countries cannot become *relatively* better off, the pursuit of growth for growth's sake becomes futile. See also CONSPICUOUS CONSUMPTION.

relative price see INDIFFERENCE CURVE, ISOQUANT CURVE.

relativities any comparisons between the WAGES or SALARIES of workers in the same firm, the same industry, or between different industries. Such relativities reflect differences in training requirements, skill levels and responsibilities. See also WAGE DIFFERENTIALS.

rent the periodic payments made to the owners of ASSETS for the use of their land or other assets as either FACTORS OF PRODUCTION or for consumption. In aggregate terms, rents are a source of income and they are included as a part of NATIONAL INCOME.

See also ECONOMIC RENT, NATIONAL INCOME ACCOUNTS.

rent controls the regulation by government of the RENT payable on a leasehold property by a tenant. Rent controls are used to establish maximum rent levels to assist tenants on low incomes. However, such controls can distort the housing market, discouraging the supply of rented properties and reducing the incentive to maintain rented properties in good repair. Rent controls may also reduce the geographical MOBILITY of labour insofar as 'sitting tenants' will be reluctant to move from rent-controlled tenancies.

replacement cost the cost of replacing an ASSET (such as an item of machinery). Unlike HISTORIC COST – the original cost of acquiring an asset – replacement cost makes due allowance for the effects of INFLATION in increasing asset prices over time.

See also INFLATION ACCOUNTING, APPRECIATION (2).

replacement investment the INVESTMENT that is undertaken to replace a firm's plant and equipment or an economy's CAPITAL STOCK which has become worn out or obsolete. See CAPITAL CONSUMPTION.

'representative firm' the typical supplying firm in a market. The concept of the 'representative' firm is used specifically in the analysis of supply conditions in PERFECT COMPETITION and MONOPOLISTIC COMPETITION to identify the equilibrium price and output of the individual firm.

resale price maintenance (rpm) a type of RESTRICTIVE TRADE PRACTICE whereby a supplier prescribes the PRICE at which all retailers are to sell the product to final buyers. The main objection to rpm centres on the fact that it restricts or eliminates retail price competition and by prescribing uniform retail margins it serves to cushion inefficient retailers.

The practice of rpm (except in very special circumstances) was made illegal in the UK in 1964 and this led to the rapid expansion of mass retailers such as supermarket chains.

See also COMPETITION POLICY, OFFICE OF FAIR TRADING, RECOMMENDED RETAIL PRICES.

Resale Prices Acts, 1964, 1976 a body of UK legislation providing for the control of RESALE PRICE MAINTENANCE (RPM) by suppliers of a product. The Acts make the practice of rpm illegal unless it is specifically exempted by the OFFICE OF FAIR TRADING, usually after investigation by the RESTRICTIVE PRACTICES COURT. Under the Acts, suppliers must satisfy the Court that not only does RPM benefit buyers in one or more specified ways (for example, through greater convenience, the provision of after-sales services) but that, *on balance*, these benefits are greater than any detriments (for example, higher prices resulting from the elimination of retail price competition). The Acts make one concession to manufacturers, allowing them legally to prevent a retailer from pricing their products as a 'LOSS LEADER' (i.e. selling the product at below bought-in cost).

See COMPETITION POLICY UK, RECOMMENDED RESALE PRICE.

research and development (R & D) the commitment of resources by a firm to scientific research (both 'pure' and 'applied') and the refinement and modification of research ideas and prototypes aimed at the ultimate development of commercially viable processes and products. Thus, R & D is concerned both with INVENTION (the act of discovering new methods and techniques of manufacture and new products) and INNOVATION (the task of bringing these inventions to the market-place.

Though invention is often an 'inspirational' act which can be undertaken with limited facilities, innovation is very resource-intensive. The substantial capital outlays required to pursue development work, coupled with a high risk of failure to come up with a marketable product, tend to favour the larger firm which is able to finance R & D out of current profits and also pool risks by undertaking a number of research projects. Thus, it might be argued that MONOPOLY or OLIGOPOLY market structures tend to be more conducive to R & D since they are associated with the generation of ABOVE-NORMAL PROFITS. However, though a monopolist has the resources to fund R & D, it may not have the incentive to do so, since its present market position is secure. By contrast, oligopolists have both the resources and the incentive to undertake R & D, since the ability to develop new processes which lower supply costs and introduce innovative NEW PRODUCTS is often a critical factor in establishing COMPETITIVE ADVANTAGE over rival suppliers.

R & D can also be an important factor in promoting a higher rate of ECONOMIC GROWTH, and in order to foster TECHNOLOGICAL PROGRESSIVENESS many countries grant temporary PATENT rights to reward inventors.

See PRODUCT PERFORMANCE, PRODUCT LIFE-CYCLE.

reserve asset ratio or **liquidity ratio** the proportion of a COMMERCIAL BANK's total assets which it keeps in the form of liquid assets to meet day-to-day currency withdrawals by its customers and other financial commitments. In Britain assets held as part of a bank's reserve asset ratio include: TILL MONEY (notes and coins) and BALANCES WITH THE BANK OF ENGLAND which together comprise the CASH RESERVE RATIO; CALL MONEY (short term deposits with the DISCOUNT MARKET); and near-mature BILLS OF EXCHANGE and TREASURY BILLS.

The ratio of liquid assets to total assets held can be dictated by reasons of commercial prudence to maintain customers' confidence in the banks' ability to repay their deposits on demand. This is a matter of individual discretion. In some countries, however, the monetary authorities prescribe mandatory and uniform minimum reserve-asset ratios for the banking sector. This is because the reserve-asset ratio of the banking sector determines the amount of new bank deposits that can be created and, hence, has an important influence on the size of the MONEY SUPPLY.

RESERVES

See also BANK DEPOSIT CREATION, MONETARY POLICY, OPEN MARKET OPERATIONS.

reserves 1. any additional claims of company shareholders which reflect increases in the value of company ASSETS in the BALANCE SHEET. Reserves arise when some after-tax profit is retained in the business to finance the acquisition of extra assets, rather than being paid out as DIVIDENDS; or when company assets such as buildings are revalued to reflect their increased market value due to inflation. Reserves serve to increase SHAREHOLDERS' CAPITAL EMPLOYED in a company. See also RETAINED PROFITS, CAPITALIZATION ISSUE, APPRECIATION (2), INFLATION ACCOUNTING.

2. the proportion of a bank's total assets which it keeps in the form of liquid assets. See RESERVE-ASSET RATIO.

3. monetary assets held by countries to finance balance of payments deficits. See INTERNATIONAL RESERVES.

reserve tranche see INTERNATIONAL MONETARY FUND.

residual see REGRESSION ANALYSIS.

residual unemployment the UNEMPLOYMENT of certain members of society who cannot locate economically viable employment even in times of full employment. The costs of employing a severely handicapped person, for example, may far outweigh the productivity obtained. Residual unemployment may be reduced in terms of numbers by government subsidies to offset a firm's costs of employment but such unemployment is not easily removed.

resource allocation the allocation of an economy's FACTORS OF PRODUCTION between alternative uses in line with patterns of consumer demand (which in turn reflect a given size and distribution of national income). Resources are optimally allocated when the proportions in which factor inputs are combined to produce GOODS and SERVICES reflect their relative costs so as to minimize costs of production, and when the output of goods and services fully reflects the distribution of consumer preferences as between those goods and services. (See PARETO OPTIMALITY.)

More specifically, resources are optimally allocated when in each market the price paid for the good or service fully reflects the *lowest* economic cost of supplying it.

See ALLOCATIVE EFFICIENCY, PRODUCTIVE EFFICIENCY, DISTRIBUTIVE EFFICIENCY, MOBILITY, PRICE SYSTEM, THEORY OF MARKETS, PRODUCTION POSSIBILITY BOUNDARY.

resources see FACTORS OF PRODUCTION.

restraint of trade see RESTRICTIVE TRADE AGREEMENT, RESTRICTIVE TRADE PRACTICE.

restrictive labour practice a practice, usually operated by a TRADE UNION in the interests of its members, that has the effect of reducing productive efficiency. For example, a union may insist that a specified number of men work on a particular activity even though this involves employing more men than is strictly required to undertake the activity efficiently (overmanning); different unions operating in the same plant may lay down demarcation rules specifying what tasks their members can work on and what they cannot, which has the effect of limiting job interchangeability; unions may resist the installation of new machinery, especially if this results in job losses. See also PRODUCTIVITY, X-INEFFICIENCY, INDUSTRIAL RELATIONS, SUPPLY-SIDE ECONOMICS.

Restrictive Practices Court (RPC) a regulatory body responsible, in part, for the implementation of UK COMPETITION POLICY. The basic task of the RPC is to investigate and report on cases of RESTRICTIVE TRADE AGREEMENTS, INFORMATION AGREEMENTS and RESALE PRICE MAINTENANCE referred to it by the OFFICE OF FAIR TRADING to determine whether or not they operate against the public interest.

The public interest can be broadly equated with the cause of promoting effective competition in the sense that the legislation in this area contains a presumption that competition is generally preferable to COLLUSION. In the case of restrictive agreements and information agreements all such agreements are presumed to operate *against* the public interest unless the parties to them can prove otherwise by satisfying one or more of eight 'gateways' (that the agreement is beneficial, for example, because it improves efficiency, increases exports, or creates employment), and only then if the benefits, on balance, outweigh any detriments. Agreements found by the Court to be contrary to the public interest are automatically null and void.

Very few agreements have been successfully defended; less than 15 in fact. The vast majority of agreements (over 9000) registered with the OFT have been abandoned voluntarily without a formal Court trial. Thus, on the surface the attack on collusion between suppliers appears to have been highly successful. However, there is growing evidence to suggest that many agreements have simply been driven underground and are now being operated 'secretly'.

restrictive trade agreement a form of COLLUSION between suppliers aimed at removing competition wholly or in part. For the most part such agreements concentrate on fixing common prices and discounts, but may also stipulate production quotas, market-sharing and coordinated capacity adjustments. The main objection to restrictive agreements is that they tend to raise prices above competitive levels and serve to protect inefficient suppliers from the rigours of competition. COMPETITION POLICY in most countries takes a tough line on restrictive agreements, either prohibiting them outright, or only allowing them to continue in exceptional circumstances.

See also OFFICE OF FAIR TRADING, RESTRICTIVE PRACTICES COURT.

restrictive trade practice a means of reducing or eliminating competition between rival suppliers. Examples of restrictive practices include EXCLUSIVE DEALING, REFUSAL TO SUPPLY, PRICE SQUEEZING, TIE-IN SALES, AGGREGATED REBATES, RESALE PRICE MAINTENANCE and LOSS LEADING. As part of COMPETITION POLICY such practices are either prohibited outright, or allowed to continue only if they can be shown to operate in the 'public interest'.

See also OFFICE OF FAIR TRADING, MONOPOLIES AND MERGERS COMMISSION.

Restrictive Trade Practices Acts, 1956, 1968, 1976 a body of UK legislation providing for the control of RESTRICTIVE TRADE AGREEMENTS between rival suppliers. The Acts make the operation of a restrictive trade agreement illegal unless it is specifically exempted by the OFFICE OF FAIR TRADING, usually after investigation by the RESTRICTIVE PRACTICES COURT. Under the Acts, parties to such an agreement must satisfy the Court that not only do the restrictions contained in the agreement confer benefits in one or more specified ways (for example, by reducing costs and prices through greater specialization, or by helping exports and reducing unemployment) but that, *on balance*, these benefits are greater than any detriments (for example, higher prices resulting from the elimination of price competition or the protection of inefficient producers).

See COMPETITION POLICY (UK).

retailer a business which stocks a particular type of product (such as a shoe shop) or an extensive range of products (such as a DEPARTMENT STORE) for sale to consumers. Retailers operate at the final end of a DISTRIBUTION CHANNEL for a product or products which also involves PRODUCERS and WHOLESALERS.

Although some retailers are involved in the preparation and packaging of products before their final sale (for example, butchers), most retailers are engaged in selling pre-packed, complete items. Formerly in the UK and elsewhere, retailers played a relatively 'passive' rôle in the distribution channel, merely providing a convenient point of sale for manufacturers' products (in many trades, at prices controlled by the manufacturers through RESALE PRICE MAINTENANCE (RPM)). However, with the emergence of large CHAIN STORE retailers (SUPERMARKET, DO-IT-YOURSELF groups) the 'balance of power' in the channel has switched towards retailers. Retailers have been able to use their BULK BUYING power to obtain substantial price discounts from manufacturers, and this, together with the demise of rpm, has given retailers greater discretion in the use of price as a competitive weapon (see DISCOUNT STORE). Moreover, the larger retailer groups have established an extensive 'OWN-LABEL' BRAND business in direct competition with manufacturers' brands, which has also increased their MARKETING MIX opportunities to compete against other retailers.

See SPECIALIST SHOP, MAIL ORDER.

retail outlet a business premise or facility for selling products to CONSUMERS. A retail outlet may take the form of a SHOP or store which buyers visit to make purchases, or it could be an AUTOMATIC VENDING machine or kiosk located in a hotel or restaurant. Apart from 'points of sale' geographically located within easy reach of prospective customers, retail sales can be made by direct delivery or through the post to a buyer's home as, for example, in MAIL ORDER selling.

See RETAILER, DISTRIBUTION CHANNEL, EPOS, CHAIN STORE, DEPARTMENT STORE, DISCOUNT STORE, DO-IT-YOURSELF STORE, SPECIALIST SHOP, SUPERMARKET.

retail price index see PRICE INDEX.

retained profits or **undistributed profits** any after-tax PROFITS that are reinvested (*ploughed back*) in the firm rather than being paid out to the owners of the company in DIVIDENDS. Such retained earnings form a valuable source of capital to be invested in additional FIXED ASSETS and CURRENT ASSETS. They serve to swell the value of the company to the shareholders and increase SHAREHOLDERS' CAPITAL-EMPLOYED by adding to revenue RESERVES. Retained profits are a form of business savings.

See SAVINGS RATIO.

return on capital employed an accounting measure of a firm's PROFITABILITY, which expresses the firm's PROFITS for a time period as a percentage of its period-end capital employed. Generally, profit is taken before deduction of tax and is related to long-term capital employed, though broader comparisons are possible, which relate profit before tax and interest payments to all ASSETS employed, and narrower comparisons which relate after-tax profit to shareholders' capital.

Under COMPETITION POLICY, return on capital employed is used to ascertain whether a firm is earning NORMAL PROFIT or ABOVE-NORMAL PROFIT.

See also ALLOCATIVE EFFICIENCY, PUBLIC INTEREST.

returns to scale the relationship between OUTPUT of a product and the quantities of FACTOR INPUTS used to produce it in the LONG RUN. Where, for example, doubling the quantity of factor inputs used results in a doubling of output then constant 'returns to scale' are experienced. Where ECONOMIES OF SCALE are present a doubling of factor inputs results in a more than proportionate increase in output. By contrast, where DISECONOMIES OF SCALE are encountered a doubling of factor inputs results in a less than proportionate increase in output.

returns to the variable factor input the rate of change of OUTPUT within the SHORT RUN theory of supply, resulting from changes in the VARIABLE-FACTOR INPUT in a plant of a given (fixed) size. In the short run, some FACTOR INPUTS are variable but other inputs are fixed.

A firm can change its rate of output only by combining more or less of the variable factors with the fixed factors; that is, by changing the proportions in which the factor inputs are used. As more and more of a variable input is used in conjunction with a given quantity of fixed input:

(a) initially, as Fig. 156a shows, there are *increasing returns* to the variable input: output increases more than proportionately to the increase in the variable input so that the TOTAL PHYSICAL PRODUCT curve rises steadily and both MARGINAL PHYSICAL PRODUCT and AVERAGE PHYSICAL PRODUCT also increase.

(b) CONSTANT RETURNS are then experienced, with the increase in output being exactly proportional to the increase in the variable input (marginal physical product and average physical product being constant).

(c) DIMINISHING RETURNS to the variable input are then experienced (see Fig. 156b), with the increase in output being less than proportional to the increase in the variable input (the total physical product curve flattens out and both marginal physical product and average physical product decrease).

(d) finally, *negative returns* may be experienced with an increase in the variable input bringing about a fall in total output (the total physical product curve turns down and both marginal physical product and average physical product become negative).

See ISOQUANT MAP.

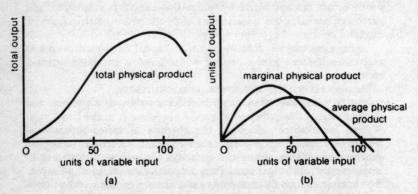

Fig. 156. **Returns to the variable factor input.** See entry. (a) The total physical product. (b) The marginal and average physical product.

revaluation an administered increase in the value of one CURRENCY against other currencies under a FIXED EXCHANGE-RATE SYSTEM, for example, as in Fig. 157, an increase in the value of the UK pound against the US dollar from one fixed value to another higher value, say, from £1 = $2.40 to £1 = $2.80. The objectives of a revaluation are to assist in the removal of a surplus in a country's BALANCE OF PAYMENTS and the excessive accumulation of INTERNATIONAL RESERVES. A revaluation makes IMPORTS (in the local currency) cheaper and EXPORTS (in the local currency) more expensive, thereby encouraging additional imports and lowering export demand.

How successful a revaluation is in removing a payments surplus depends on the reactions of export and import volumes to the change in relative prices, that is, the PRICE-ELASTICITY OF DEMAND for exports and imports. If these values are low, that is, demand is inelastic, trade volumes will not change very much and the revaluation may in fact make the surplus larger. On the other hand, if export and import demand is elastic then the change in trade volumes will operate to remove the surplus. BALANCE-OF-PAYMENTS EQUILIBRIUM will be restored if the sum of export and import elasticities is greater than unity (the MARSHALL-LERNER CONDITION).

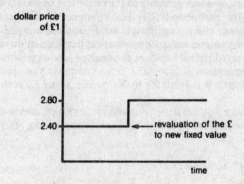

Fig. 157. **Revaluation**. A revaluation of the pound against the dollar.

Also, whether or not a revaluation 'works' in restoring balance of payments equilibrium depends on a number of factors, including the reaction of domestic firms and the effect of the government's other policies over the longer term (for example, the control of inflation). For business, a revaluation makes imports more price-competitive, putting pressure on domestic producers either to cut their prices or, alternatively, depend more on advertising and sales promotion. Likewise, in export markets, a firm may choose to hold its prices, accepting lower profit margins, rather than increase them, in order to maintain market share. Thus, in the short run, revaluations threaten firms' current profitability and market position, putting firms under pressure to cut costs by improving productivity and generally placing a greater emphasis on PRODUCT DIFFERENTIATION as a means of remaining competitive against overseas suppliers.

Contrast DEVALUATION. See EXTERNAL-INTERNAL BALANCE MODEL.

revealed preference theory an alternative explanation for an individual consumer's downward-sloping DEMAND CURVE, requiring the consumer to reveal what his preferences are in given sets of circumstances. The preferences given may be between two or more goods, but where more than two goods exist money is taken to represent all other goods for ease of graphical analysis, as in Fig. 158.

If a consumer decides he prefers a combination of money (OM_1) and good X (OX_1) he will be at point a on the BUDGET LINE (or relative price line) MX. If good X becomes cheaper so more can be had, his *real* income increases and he can move to budget line MX_2. The combination of goods the consumer prefers is now at, say, b.

However, not all the change is due to increasing real income caused by the fall in the price of good X. Some of it is due to the substitution of the now-cheaper good X for others, and this effect is always positive, that is, it is not possible to purchase less of the now-cheaper good X after the change to MX_2, than when on the budget line MX.

If the consumer's new configuration of goods at b is reduced proportionately, by introducing a hypothetical decrease in income in the form of an inward parallel shift of the budget line to position $M_2 X_3$, then the consumer will choose a new position, say, point c; the SUBSTITUTION EFFECT is from X_1 to X_5, while X_5 to X_4 is the INCOME EFFECT.

See CONSUMER EQUILIBRIUM, INDIFFERENCE CURVE, PRICE EFFECT.

revenue the money received by a firm from selling its output of

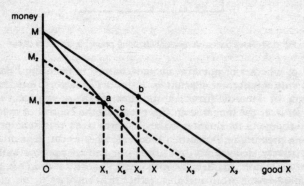

Fig. 158. **Revealed preference theory**. See entry.

GOODS or SERVICES (SALES REVENUE), or money received by government from TAXATION. See AVERAGE REVENUE, MARGINAL REVENUE, TOTAL REVENUE.

reverse takeover a situation in which a smaller but dynamic company wishing to expand rapidly, takes over a larger but unprogressive company, issuing SHARES or FIXED-INTEREST FINANCIAL SECURITIES to raise the necessary finance to purchase the shares of the larger company. See TAKEOVER.

revised sequence the proposition that it is suppliers who *actively* determine what products are offered to consumers, rather than *passively* responding to the demands of buyers (see CONSUMER SOVEREIGNTY). This proposition was advanced by GALBRAITH, who suggested that large monopolistic and oligopolistic firms have the means and ability to influence consumers' market behaviour through their NEW PRODUCT DEVELOPMENT and ADVERTISING policies. To the extent that large suppliers are able to shape consumer choices and effectively 'create' the demand for products over time, they are able to make the PRICE SYSTEM producer-driven. This poses a challenge to the 'conventional sequence' whereby competitive firms merely serve the innate wants of consumers.

See MONOPOLY, OLIGOPOLY.

Ricardo, David (1772–1823) an English economist who, in his *Principles of Political Economy and Taxation* (1817), argued that the value of products is determined by the amount of labour needed to produce them, and developed a theory of distribution to explain how this value is shared between major classes in society (see LABOUR THEORY OF VALUE). Ricardo suggested that however prosperous the economy, wages could never rise above subsistence level. As workers became more prosperous they would have more children and, as these children grew up this additional labour supply would force wages down: an 'iron law of wages'.

Ricardo argued that capitalists would not benefit much from economic progress either, since competition would keep their prices down and wage payments would cut into their profits. He regarded landlords as being the only real beneficiaries from economic progress since with a finite amount of arable land and a growing population to feed, the landlords' rental income would grow and the value of their land would rise. Rising rents would raise the cost of food produced and workers would need larger wages to pay for food, eroding capitalists' profits. Ricardo's theories were used by the emerging industrialists to fight for free trade and an end to high tariffs on imported grain so as to lower food prices and keep wages low. See also ECONOMIC RENT.

ridge lines see INDIFFERENCE MAP.

RIE see RECOGNIZED INVESTMENT EXCHANGE.

rights issue the issue by a JOINT-STOCK COMPANY of additional SHARES to existing SHAREHOLDERS at a price which is generally a little below the current market price. Rights are issued to existing shareholders in proportion to their existing shareholdings, and a shareholder can sell his rights if he does not wish to subscribe for extra shares. Compare CAPITALIZATION ISSUE.

risk analysis the systematic analysis of the degree of risk attaching to capital projects. Risk reflects the variability of expected future returns from a capital INVESTMENT and as such the statistical technique of PROBABILITY may be applied to assist a decision.

See also CAPITAL BUDGETING, RISK AND UNCERTAINTY.

risk and uncertainty a situation of potential LOSS of an individual's or firm's ASSETS and INVESTMENT resulting from the fact that they are operating in an uncertain economic environment. Certain risks are insurable (for example, the risk of fire or theft of the firm's stock), but not the firm's ability to survive and prosper. The firm itself must assume the risks of the market place: if it cannot sell its products it will go bankrupt; if it is successful it will make profits. Thus, risk-taking is to be viewed as an integral part of the process of supplying GOODS and SERVICES and in innovating new products. PROFITS, in part, are a reward for successful risk-taking.

Since managers do not know for certain what the future holds, they are forced to formulate EXPECTATIONS or to guess what the most likely outcome of any decision will be, effectively assigning a statistical PROBABILITY to the likelihood of future events occurring. All such estimates of the likelihood of future events occurring must, by their very nature, be subjective, though some estimates are likely to be better than others depending upon the amount of information available. Where large amounts of information are available upon which to base estimates of likelihood, so that accurate statistical probabilities can be formulated, we may talk of risk rather than uncertainty. For example, an insurance company dealing with fire insurance policies and claims for large numbers of manufacturers, will be able to compile detailed statistics about numbers of fires and the amount of damage done by each, and can use this information to predict the likelihood of a business experiencing a fire. This detailed statistical information allows the insurance company to charge manufacturers premiums for indemnifying them against fire losses and to make a profit by so doing. By contrast, a single manufacturer would find it very difficult to predict the likelihood of his premises being damaged by fire and the amount of damage, since such an event would tend to be a unique experience for him.

Faced with a possibility of fire, the manufacturer can either choose to bear the risk of losses resulting from a serious fire or can avoid the risk of fire damage by paying an insurance company a premium to bear the risk. Again, the manufacturer can take the risk that the prices of its main raw materials will be much higher next year, or it can contract now through a commodity FUTURES MARKET to buy raw materials supplies for future delivery at a fixed price.

Uncertainty, unlike risk, arises from changes which are difficult to predict or from events whose likelihood cannot be accurately estimated. Unfortunately, many management decisions fall into this category, since they are rarely repetitive and there is little past data available to act as a guide to the future. Such market uncertainty as to the likelihood and extent of losses which might arise in launching a new product, can only be gauged by managers through combining the limited data which is available with their own judgement and experience.

Managers can improve upon their subjective estimates about the future by collecting information from forecasts, market research, feasibility studies, etc., but they need to balance the cost of collecting such information against its value in improving decisions. Where information costs are prohibitive, managers may turn to various RULES OF THUMB like full-cost pricing which give reasonably good (though not optimum) decisions.

The traditional THEORY OF THE FIRM envisaged a firm armed with perfect knowledge about its future costs and revenues, making pricing and output decisions on the basis of a marginal weighting of costs and revenues. This cognitive assumption of perfect knowledge is open to criticism in the light of what appears above.

See ENTREPRENEUR, HEDGING, RISK PREMIUM, SCHUMPETER.

risk capital any business capital subscribed by an individual ENTREPRENEUR or group of ORDINARY SHAREHOLDERS which entails some risk of loss in the event of the enterprise failing.

See RISK AND UNCERTAINTY, VENTURE CAPITAL.

risk premium the additional return on an INVESTMENT which an individual and business manager requires to compensate them for the RISK of losses if the investment fails. Investors in government BONDS, where there is very little risk of the borrower defaulting, would require a more modest return on such an investment than the return they would require on an investment in, say, a small, newly established company where there is a significant risk that the company will fail and the investors lose some or all of their investment.

Attitudes to risk are partly dependent on the personality of the investor, some investors being very cautious and 'risk adverse' and so requiring a large risk premium to induce them to take the risk. The risk premium demanded by investors is also influenced by the size of the potential gains or losses involved. For example, where an investment project risks making a loss which is so large as to endanger the continued existence of the sponsoring company, then managers would tend to adopt a cautious view about the risks involved.

Robinson, Joan (1903–1983) an English economist from Cambridge University who helped develop the theory of MONOPOLISTIC COMPETITION in her book *The Economics of Imperfect Competition* (1933). Prior to Robinson's work, economists classified markets into two groups: PERFECT COMPETITION, where firms' products are perfect substitutes; and MONOPOLY, where a firm's product has no substitutes. Robinson argued that in real markets, goods are often partial substitutes for other goods, and her theory of monopolistic competition analysed price and output in such markets. She concluded that firms in monopolistic competition would restrict output in order to maintain price resulting in a lower level of plant operation than optimum.

See also CHAMBERLIN, Edward.

Royal Mint see MINT.

royalty an agreed payment made to the owner of an INTELLECTUAL PROPERTY RIGHT, for example a PATENT or COPYRIGHT, for the grant of an exclusive or nonexclusive LICENCE or FRANCHISE to produce and sell for profit the item concerned.

RPB see RECOGNIZED PROFESSIONAL BODY.

RPI see PRICE INDEX.

rule of origin see LOCAL CONTENT RULE.

rule of reason the individual investigation of elements of MARKET CONDUCT (for example, RESTRICTIVE TRADE AGREEMENTS) and MARKET STRUCTURE (MERGERS) under a DISCRETIONARY COMPETITION POLICY to determine whether or not their economic effects are, on balance, beneficial or detrimental.

rule of thumb a rough-and-ready decision-making aid that provides an acceptably accurate, approximate solution to a problem. Where refined decision-making processes are expensive in terms of information gathering and information processing, then rules of thumb may be justified. For example, COST-PLUS PRICING may be used in practice by firms in the absence of sufficient knowledge about future demand and cost conditions to permit marginal weighting of revenues and costs to achieve an optimum decision. See RISK AND UNCERTAINTY.

S

salary a form of pay made to employees of an organization. A salary is similar to a WAGE payment in that it is paid for the use of LABOUR as a factor of production. In economic terms, a salary payment differs from a wage payment in two ways: (a) it is not strictly related to the actual number of hours worked by the employee, whereas wage earners are usually paid on an hourly basis; (b) salaries are usually paid monthly, whereas wages are paid weekly.

sale and leaseback see LEASEBACK.

sales forecasts see FORECASTING.

sales promotion and merchandising the measures used by firms to increase the sales of their GOODS and SERVICES. ADVERTISING is the most visible form of sales promotion, but a wide variety of other techniques can be used to create and boost sales: money-off packs; free trial samples; coupons offering gifts; product competitions offering prizes; trading stamps; in-store demonstrations; point-of-sale displays; etc.

In the economist's models of imperfect competition, all of these items come under the generic heading of PRODUCT DIFFERENTIATION.

sales representative see PERSONAL SELLING.

sales revenue the income generated from the sale of GOODS and SERVICES. Sales revenue depends upon the volume of a product sold and the PRICE of the product.

See TOTAL REVENUE, PRICE-ELASTICITY OF DEMAND.

sales-revenue maximization a company objective in the THEORY OF THE FIRM that is used as an alternative to the traditional assumption of PROFIT MAXIMIZATION. The firm is assumed to seek to maximize sales revenue subject to a minimum profit constraint (determined by the need to pay dividends to shareholders and to finance expansion). In Fig. 159 (overleaf), sales revenue is maximized at output level OQ_s. If the firm's minimum profit constraint is at level A, then the sales-revenue maximizing output level of OQ_s will provide sufficient profits. If the firm's required profit level is B, however, the sales-revenue maximizing output OQ_s is clearly inadequate. The firm's output would then be lowered to level OQ_s*, which is just compatible with the profit constraint. Clearly, the higher the minimum profit figure required, the more important the constraint becomes and the profit-maximizing (OQ_m) and sales-revenue maximizing output levels will be closer together.

See also MANAGERIAL THEORIES OF THE FIRM, FIRM OBJECTIVES, DIVORCE OF OWNERSHIP FROM CONTROL.

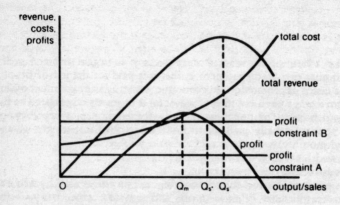

Fig. 159. **Sales revenue maximization**. See entry.

sales tax or **turnover tax** a form of INDIRECT TAX which is incorporated into the selling price of a product and which is borne by the consumer. Sales taxes include VALUE-ADDED TAX and EXCISE DUTY.

satisficing theory a THEORY OF THE FIRM that postulates that firms typically not only seek to secure 'satisfactory' profits rather than maximum profits, as depicted in the traditional theory of the firm, but that other objectives such as increasing sales, market share or the size of the firm may be accorded equal or greater prominence than profits. Organizational theorists suggest that satisficing behaviour is particularly likely to occur in large, hierarchical organizations where consensus decision-making, reconciling the diverse aims of the various subgroups of the organization, tends to be the norm, as opposed to objectives being set by an individual ENTREPRENEUR.

The problem with this approach to firm behaviour is that it is not possible to define unequivocally what is meant by the term 'satisfactory' and hence to construct a *general* theory of the firm. For example, a profit return which is considered to be 'satisfactory' by one firm may be considered too low by some other firm. Thus, the predictive powers of satisficing theory are strictly limited.

See also PROFIT MAXIMIZATION, BEHAVIOURAL THEORY OF THE FIRM, MANAGERIAL THEORIES OF THE FIRM, ORGANIZATIONAL THEORY.

saving the proportion of a person's (personal saving), company's or institution's (retained profits) income that is not spent on current consumption. Savings are typically placed on deposit with a BANK, BUILDING SOCIETY, etc., or used to acquire financial and physical assets such as SHARES or plant. By forgoing immediate spending on consumption, savers seek to augment their future income through dividends, interest and rent receipts and through capital appreciation.

In macroeconomic analysis, saving is the proportion of current NATIONAL INCOME that is not spent on current consumption and as such is a WITHDRAWAL from the CIRCULAR FLOW OF NATIONAL INCOME MODEL. In the simple circular flow model, all saving is undertaken by households; in the extended model, saving is also undertaken by businesses (retained profits) and the government (budget surplus).

In real terms, saving is important in that it 'finances' physical INVESTMENT. Saving (foregoing current consumption) releases resources which can be devoted to increasing the country's CAPITAL STOCK and hence its capacity to produce a greater quantity of goods over time.

See also SAVINGS SCHEDULE, PARADOX OF THRIFT.

savings account see DEPOSIT ACCOUNT.

savings bank a financial institution that accepts deposits from savers, and which specializes in investments in stocks and shares and government securities. Some of the larger savings banks, such as the Trustee Savings Bank (TSB), now offer depositors COMMERCIAL-BANKING facilities (for example, the use of a cheque book).

See also FINANCIAL SYSTEM.

savings ratio the proportion of NATIONAL INCOME which is saved by households (see PERSONAL SAVINGS RATIO); by businesses in the form of RETAINED PROFITS, and by the government in the form of BUDGET SURPLUSES.

savings schedule a schedule that depicts the relationship between SAVINGS and the level of INCOME. In the simple CIRCULAR FLOW OF NATIONAL INCOME MODEL, all consumption and saving is accounted for by households. At low levels of DISPOSABLE INCOME, households consume more than their current income (see DISSAVINGS). At higher levels of disposable income they consume only a part of their current income and save the rest, as in Fig. 160 (overleaf). Thus, the savings schedule is derived by subtracting the CONSUMPTION SCHEDULE from the 45° line, as shown in the lower part of the Fig. The slope of the savings schedule is equal to the MARGINAL PROPENSITY TO SAVE.

See also LIFE-CYCLE HYPOTHESIS, PERMANENT-INCOME HYPOTHESIS.

Say, Jean Baptiste (1767–1832) a French economist who developed Adam SMITH's theory of the market in his *Traité d'économic politique* (1803). Say argued that since every product exchanges for another product, then every product put on the market creates its own demand, and every demand exerted in the market creates its own supply. This statement about interdependence in an exchange economy is often described as SAY'S LAW. The principle has been used to deny the possibility of economic crisis associated with general overproduction of goods and services and to suggest that national economies would automatically function close to full employment.

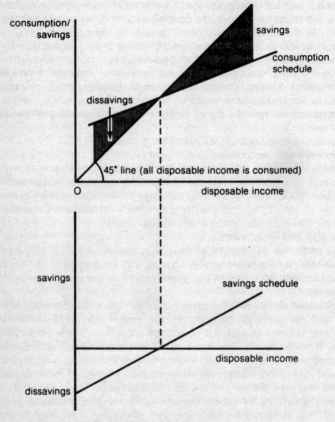

Fig. 160. **Savings schedule**. See entry.

Say's Law the proposition that AGGREGATE SUPPLY creates its own AGGREGATE DEMAND. The very act of producing a given level of national output generates an amount of income (wages, profits, etc.) exactly equal to that output, which if spent is just sufficient to take up the purchases of the whole of the output that has been produced. It follows that, in order to reach the full-employment level at national output, all that needs to be done is to increase aggregate supply.

The key assumptions are that the economic system is 'supply-led' and that all income is spent. In practice, however, some income is 'leaked' into saving, taxation, etc. (see CIRCULAR FLOW OF NATIONAL

INCOME MODEL), and there is no automatic guarantee that all of this income will be subsequently 'injected' back as spending. Thus, in contrast to the above proposition, the economic system is 'demand-led', a fall in aggregate demand leading to a multiple contraction of national income and output.

See EQUILIBRIUM LEVEL OF NATIONAL INCOME.

scale economics see ECONOMIES OF SCALE.

scarcity the limited availability of economic resources (FACTORS OF PRODUCTION) relative to society's unlimited demand for GOODS and SERVICES. See ECONOMICS.

Schumpeter, Joseph A. (1883–1950) an Austrian economist who developed a theory to explain BUSINESS CYCLES in his book *Capitalism, Socialism and Democracy* (1942). According to Schumpeter, the key to ECONOMIC GROWTH is the innovative (see INNOVATION) ENTREPRENEUR who takes RISKS and introduces new technologies to stimulate economic activity, replacing old technologies by a process of 'creative destruction'. However, because such innovative activity takes place irregularly, spurts of such vigorous production are likely to be followed by both collapse and crisis.

See also MONOPOLY, PRIVATE-ENTERPRISE ECONOMY.

science park see INDUSTRIAL ESTATE.

scrip issue see CAPITALIZATION ISSUE.

seasonal index see TIME-SERIES ANALYSIS.

seasonal unemployment UNEMPLOYMENT associated with changes in the demand for particular products at different seasons of the year; for example, strawberry pickers at the end of the summer season; store 'Santa Clauses' at the end of the Christmas period. The incidence of seasonal unemployment will depend on whether people can be easily and rapidly redeployed to other activities, which in turn depends on the availability of alternative jobs and people's own range of skills and willingness to take alternative work.

seasonal variation see TIME-SERIES ANALYSIS.

secondary benefits any additional indirect benefits that stem from the direct primary benefits of an INVESTMENT project. For example, in estimating the benefits of an irrigation project, the increase in grain output resulting from the project would be counted as a primary benefit; while the increased economic activity of grain merchants, millers and bakers handling this extra grain would be counted as a secondary benefit of the project.

See COST-BENEFIT ANALYSIS.

second-best, *adj*. (of an economy) departing from an optimal pattern of resource allocation (see PARETO OPTIMALITY) because, for example, of MONOPOLY distortions and EXTERNALITIES.

If the production of a product such as a chemical leads to environmental POLLUTION then the marginal SOCIAL COST of producing that output will exceed the marginal PRIVATE COST, and the economy will depart from an optimal pattern of resource allocation. In this 'second-best' situation, the government can improve matters by imposing a 'pollution tax' on offending chemical firms. This will, on the one hand, provide an incentive for the firms to adopt less-polluting production processes and, on the other hand, to the extent that the tax is passed on to chemical buyers, will force buyers to pay the full social costs of the products they consume.

See WELFARE ECONOMICS.

sector a part of the economy that has certain common characteristics which enables it to be separated from other parts of the economy for analytical or policy purposes. A broad division may be made, for example, between economic activities undertaken by the state (the PUBLIC SECTOR) and those that are undertaken by private individuals and businesses (the PRIVATE SECTOR). The private sector, in turn, may be subdivided into the PERSONAL SECTOR (private individuals and households), the CORPORATE SECTOR (businesses supplying goods and services) and the FINANCIAL SECTOR (businesses providing financial services).

secular stagnation a situation in which the economy remains trapped in the DEPRESSION phase of the BUSINESS CYCLE for long periods of time with low levels of AGGREGATE DEMAND in relation to productive capacity. This could result from a combination of factors, such as low levels of consumer spending (high savings); a high fixed exchange rate which limits exports and leads to increased IMPORT PENETRATION; reduced investment in the economy reflecting business pessimism.

Typically, governments will seek to counteract a tendency towards secular stagnation by expansionary DEMAND MANAGEMENT policies involving, for example, tax cuts, increased government spending and reduced interest rates to stimulate consumption and investment, and, perhaps, a DEVALUATION of the exchange rate to increase demand for exports and check imports.

See EQUILIBRIUM LEVEL OF NATIONAL INCOME.

secular trend a long-term movement, either upwards or downwards, in some economic variable. For example, Fig. 161 shows that the GROSS DOMESTIC PRODUCT (GDP) of the UK has risen steadily in the period since 1985.

Of course, in some years the increase in GDP has been greater than in other years, and there has been one occasion when GDP has actually fallen, but overall the long-term trend line has been upwards.

See also TIME-SERIES ANALYSIS, CYCLICAL FLUCTUATIONS.

securities see FINANCIAL SECURITY.

Securities and Exchange Commission the US body that regulates the operations of the New York STOCK EXCHANGE.

Index numbers 1990 = 100

1986	89
1987	93
1988	97
1989	99
1990	100
1991	98
1992	98
1993	100
1994	103
1995	106

Fig. 161. **Secular trend**. The movement in the UK's gross domestic product, 1986–95. Source: *Monthly Digest of Statistics*, Central Statistical Office.

Securities and Investments Board a UK body set up in 1986 to oversee the functioning of the STOCK EXCHANGE and FUTURES MARKETS, and the activities of UNIT TRUSTS, INSURANCE broking, and financial advisers.

See FINANCIAL SERVICES ACT, 1986.

self-employed a person who provides his LABOUR (and management) services as a FACTOR INPUT to his own FIRM in the production of a good or service. Self-employed persons act as ENTREPRENEURS, undertaking the risks of running a business, providing some or all of its capital and often hiring EMPLOYEES to perform some of the jobs involved. Self-employed workers constitute a large proportion of workers in such industries as domestic electrical and plumbing services, specialist retailing and hairdressing.

See LABOUR FORCE.

Self-Regulatory Organization (SRO) a body established under the FINANCIAL SERVICES ACT, 1986 to regulate, in part, the UK financial securities and investment industry.

There are currently four SROs:

(a) TSA: The Securities Association, which regulates firms dealing in corporate and government securities who are members of the STOCK EXCHANGE and International Securities Regulatory Organization. In 1991 the TSA merged with the Association of Futures Brokers and Dealers, which covered firms operating in financial and compulsory futures options (originally the fifth SRO under the Act);

(b) IMRO: Investment Management Regulatory Organization, which regulates firms involved in the management and trusteeship of collective investment schemes and PENSION FUNDS;

SELF SERVICE

(c) LAUTRO: Life Assurance and Unit Trust Regulatory Organization. See INSURANCE COMPANY, UNIT TRUST;

(d) FIMBRA: Financial Intermediaries, Managers and Brokers Regulatory Association, which regulates firms dealing direct with the general public in such matters as the taking out of life assurance policies and unit trust investment.

self service a form of retailing whereby customers of a RETAIL OUTLET (shop, filling station, etc.) select for themselves the goods they wish to purchase and pay for them at a 'checkout'. Self service can be applied to both large- and small-scale retailing operations, and by cutting down on VARIABLE COSTS (i.e. eliminating the wages of sales assistants) it can assist a retailer or some other business (restaurant, cafeteria, etc.) to become more price competitive.

See RETAILER.

self-sufficiency the extent to which an individual (or household) restricts his consumption to products produced by himself. Developing countries with a large agricultural sector show a higher degree of self-sufficiency than industrial countries where SPECIALIZATION of labour is the norm.

See NONMARKETED ECONOMIC ACTIVITY.

seller concentration an element of MARKET STRUCTURE that denotes the number and size distribution of suppliers in a given MARKET. Market theory predicts that MARKET PERFORMANCE will differ according to whether there are many suppliers in the market each accounting for only a small fraction to total supply (PERFECT COMPETITION), or only a few suppliers, each accounting for a substantial proportion of total supply (OLIGOPOLY), or a single supplier (MONOPOLY).

See also CONCENTRATION MEASURES, MARKET CONCENTRATION, BUYER CONCENTRATION.

seller's market a SHORT-RUN market situation in which there is EXCESS DEMAND for goods and services at current prices which forces prices up to the advantage of the seller. Compare BUYER'S MARKET.

selling costs the expenditures incurred by suppliers in creating and sustaining a demand for their products. Selling costs include ADVERTISING expenditures; packaging and styling; salaries, commissions and travelling expenses of sales personnel; and the cost of shops and showrooms.

See also PRODUCT DIFFERENTIATION, DISTRIBUTIVE EFFICIENCY.

selling price the PRICE at which a firm offers a product for sale. Selling price is usually set at a level which covers PRODUCTION and SELLING COSTS and an appropriate PROFIT MARGIN.

separation of ownership from control see DIVORCE OF OWNERSHIP FROM CONTROL.

sequestration the holding of part of the ASSETS of parties involved in an INDUSTRIAL DISPUTE or other dispute by a third party (the *seques-*

trator) until the dispute is settled. Sequestrators are often appointed by the courts as a means of enforcing fines against TRADE UNIONS who are in breach of employment legislation.

service contract see EMPLOYMENT CONTRACT.

services any intangible economic activities (hairdressing, catering, insurance, banking, etc.), that contribute directly (see FINAL PRODUCTS) or indirectly (see INTERMEDIATE PRODUCTS) to the satisfaction of human wants. Services are an important component of GROSS NATIONAL PRODUCT.

service sector that part of the economy concerned with the provision of a wide variety of personal and business services: hairdressing and tourism, transportation and retailing, banking and insurance, etc. The service sector, together with the PRIMARY SECTOR and INDUSTRIAL SECTOR form an interlocking chain of economic activities which constitute a modern economy. See STRUCTURE OF INDUSTRY.

shadow price the imputed PRICE or VALUE of a good or service where such a price or value cannot be accurately determined due to the absence of an ordinary price-determined market, or to gross distortions in any markets which exist. To impute a price or value is to make the best estimate possible of what that price or value would be if a normal market existed.

WELFARE ECONOMICS attempts to equate the price of a product to its marginal social cost. The marginal social cost of a product is the summation of all costs associated with it. For instance, the true cost of electricity is not just the capital, labour and inputs of raw material, it is the additional cost of disposing adequately of the waste products such as smoke and dirt, and even the decrease in aesthetic appeal of the area in which the power station is situated. No values are given for these costs because there exists no markets to price them. Shadow prices for such items are frequently estimated in COST-BENEFIT ANALYSIS.

A different use of shadow pricing is when intra-firm trading occurs. The inputs of company division B may be the outputs of company division A. The products in which the two company divisions trade may not have an equivalent market price because no open market for them exists (for example, intermediate components or managerial services). The transactions are given shadow prices, usually based on estimated costs plus a return on the capital involved. Such an estimate of market prices is used frequently in CENTRALLY PLANNED ECONOMIES (see TRANSFER PRICE).

A particular application of shadow-pricing can be found in LINEAR PROGRAMMING where the solution to a problem yields hypothetical prices for scarce factor inputs, showing how much additional profit would result from an extra unit of each fully-used resource.

share a FINANCIAL SECURITY issued by a JOINT-STOCK COMPANY as a means of raising long-term capital. Purchasers of shares pay money to the company and in return receive a SHARE CERTIFICATE signifying their ownership of the shares and have their ownership recorded in the company's SHARE REGISTER. The SHAREHOLDERS of a company are its legal owners and are entitled to a share in its profits, receiving some of these profits in the form of DIVIDENDS. Shares are traded on the STOCK EXCHANGE. There are two broad kinds of shares: PREFERENCE SHARES and ORDINARY SHARES.

See SHARE CAPITAL, SHARE ISSUE, CAPITAL GEARING.

share capital the money employed in a JOINT-STOCK COMPANY that has been subscribed by the SHAREHOLDERS of the company in the form of ORDINARY SHARES (equity) and PREFERENCE SHARES and which will remain as a permanent source of finance as long as the company remains in existence. The providers of share capital share in the (residual) profits of the company in the form of DIVIDEND payments paid out of profits. The dividends paid will tend to vary from year to year with profits earned, though some profits may be retained in the company and added to RESERVES to be used to finance the acquisition of further assets. In this regard shareholders differ from the providers of LOAN CAPITAL who are rewarded by means of regular INTEREST payments. However, shareholders rank after the providers of loan capital both in terms of receiving current income payments and repayment of the capital sums subscribed in the event of company INSOLVENCY.

See CAPITAL-GEARING.

share certificate a document which is issued to a SHAREHOLDER in a company, which serves as proof of ownership of SHARES in the company.

shareholders the individuals and institutions who contribute funds to finance a JOINT-STOCK COMPANY in return for SHARES in that company. There are two main types of shareholder: (a) holders of PREFERENCE SHARES who are entitled to a fixed DIVIDEND from a company's PROFITS (before ordinary shareholders receive anything), and who have first claim on any remaining assets of the business after all debts have been discharged; (b) holders of ORDINARY SHARES who are entitled to a dividend from a company's profits after all other outlays have been met, and who are entitled to any remaining ASSETS of the business in the event of the company being wound up. Generally only ordinary shareholders are entitled to vote at the ANNUAL GENERAL MEETING and elect directors, since they bear most of the risk of losing their money in the event of company INSOLVENCY.

shareholders' capital-employed SHARE CAPITAL originally invested by SHAREHOLDERS in a JOINT-STOCK COMPANY plus any RESERVES which arise, for example, as retained profits are ploughed back into the company.

share issue the process of issuing shares in a JOINT-STOCK COMPANY.

New share capital is most frequently raised through issuing houses or merchant banks which arrange for the sale of shares on behalf of client companies. Shares can be issued in a variety of ways, including: directly to the general public by way of an 'offer for sale' (or an 'introduction') at a prearranged fixed price; an 'offer for sale by TENDER', where the issue price is determined by averaging out the bid prices offered by prospective purchasers of the share subject to a minimum bid price; a RIGHTS ISSUE of shares to existing shareholders at a fixed price; or a *placing* of the shares at an arranged price with selected investors, often INSTITUTIONAL INVESTORS.

Where shares are issued by means of an offer for sale, the company issues a PROSPECTUS inviting members of the public to subscribe for shares, such *applications* for shares being accompanied either by a proportion of the purchase price of the shares or the full purchase price. Then the company arranges for the ALLOTMENT of shares to intending shareholders. If the share issue is oversubscribed with more applications for shares than the number of shares being issued, then the firm must use some formula to allocate shares between applicants. To cover for the possibility that the share issue will be undersubscribed, companies usually contract with a merchant bank to have the issue underwritten, the bank purchasing any unsold shares. Successful applicants then pay any balance of the share price or a second instalment towards the final price in response to a 'call' by the company. At this stage the names of successful applicants are entered on the company's SHARE REGISTER and they become entitled to full shareholders' rights including the right to receive ANNUAL REPORTS AND ACCOUNTS and to vote at the company's ANNUAL GENERAL MEETING.

See STOCK EXCHANGE, CALLED-UP CAPITAL, PAID-UP CAPITAL, ALLOTMENT, SHARE CERTIFICATE, SHARE PREMIUM.

share premium the proceeds from issuing SHARES at a price higher than their NOMINAL VALUE or present market value. Such proceeds are added to a JOINT-STOCK COMPANY'S revenue RESERVES.

See SHARE ISSUE.

share price index an index number of the average prices of a sample of company SHARES which is used as an indicator of general share price movements. In the UK the *Financial Times All-Share Index* records day-to-day movements in the average price of all company shares listed on the London STOCK EXCHANGE, while the *Financial Times' 30 Share Index* and *100 Share Index* show movements in the share prices of the major companies. In the US share price movements are monitored by the *Dow-Jones Index* and in Japan by the *Nikkei Index*.

Share price indices reflect the corporate sector's underlying profit and growth record and also act like a barometer of investor confidence in the state of industry and the economy.

See PRICE INDEX.

share purchase/sale the process of buying and selling SHARES on the STOCK EXCHANGE. This involves a number of steps.

First, the buyer/seller approaches a STOCKBROKER or COMMERCIAL BANK and instructs them to buy or sell a specific number of shares in a particular company. The stockbroker or bank will then undertake this task, being paid for their services by means of a commission.

Second, the stockbroker or bank approaches a MARKET MAKER to buy or sell the shares as instructed. The market maker holds a stock of shares in a limited range of companies determined by the market maker's speciality. The market maker cites two prices to the stockbroker or bank: a lower 'bid' price at which the market maker is prepared to buy shares, and a higher 'offer' price at which he is prepared to sell the shares. The difference or 'spread' between these prices provides the market maker's profit margin. In citing two prices the market maker does not know whether the stockbroker intends to buy or sell shares, and the stockbroker will only disclose whether he wishes to buy or sell and conclude the transaction if he finds the market maker's prices competitive with those being quoted by other market makers. At this stage a 'bargain' is struck and legal title to the shares passes to the buyer.

Finally, the recording of the transfer of ownership of the shares to the buyer can be done either manually through the paper-based *Talisman* system (involving the issue of new share certificates) or electronically through the *Crest* system. See COMPANY REGISTRAR, SHARE RESGISTER.

share register a list of SHAREHOLDERS maintained by a JOINT-STOCK COMPANY that records all company shareholders and the number of SHARES which they hold. As shares are bought and sold on the STOCK EXCHANGE, the register must be constantly amended so as to maintain an up-to-date list of shareholders' DIVIDEND and voting entitlement, new SHARE CERTIFICATES being issued and old ones cancelled as necessary.

See COMPANY REGISTRAR.

share split see STOCK SPLIT.

shark repellants see TAKEOVER BID.

shell company a company that is not actively trading but which is still listed on the STOCK EXCHANGE. Such a company can be purchased in a REVERSE TAKEOVER by a company wishing to obtain a stock-exchange listing.

shift in tax the redirection of the burden of a TAX away from its nominal bearer so that it is ultimately paid for by somebody else.

See INCIDENCE OF TAXATION.

shift system a method of organizing work that enables a production unit (a plant) to be run on a more intensive basis. For many plants the 'standard' working day of the labour force is eight hours, but by using a double- or three-shift system the plant can be worked for up to 24 hours.

This enables a firm to make maximum use of its FIXED FACTOR INPUT and lower its unit costs of production accordingly.

See RETURNS TO THE VARIABLE-FACTOR INPUT.

shop a business premise which is engaged in the retailing of products to customers who visit the shop or store to make purchases. The range of merchandise they stock and sell varies considerably from at one extreme total specialization on the one product (a 'shoe shop', for example) to retail operations involving thousands of different lines (as in a large DEPARTMENT STORE). Shop sizes too vary considerably, ranging upward from small 'corner shop' premises to massive 'hypermarket' complexes (see SUPERMARKET).

See RETAIL OUTLET, RETAILER, DISTRIBUTION CHANNEL.

Shop Act, 1950 a UK Act (but not applicable to Scotland) which contains provisions relating to SHOP opening times and shop workers' hours. The Act allows only shops selling a restricted list of products (newsagents, off-licences) to be open on Sundays. However, in 1994 the Sunday Trading Act was passed, permitting an unrestricted range of products to be sold by, for example, supermarkets and DIY stores. Local courts have the power to fine a trader up to a maximum of £1000 per offence for infringements of the Act.

shop steward a shop-floor employee who is elected by the local members of a TRADE UNION to represent them in work-place negotiations with management.

short position a situation where a dealer or MARKET MAKER in a particular COMMODITY, FINANCIAL SECURITY or FOREIGN CURRENCY is selling more than he is buying so that his working stock of the item becomes depleted (i.e. runs short).

Contrast LONG POSITION.

short run an abstract time period within the THEORY OF SUPPLY in which some FACTOR INPUTS are fixed (FIXED FACTOR INPUTS like plant and machinery), and output can be adjusted only by changing the quantities of VARIABLE FACTOR INPUTS used (for example, raw materials, labour).

In practice, what is defined as the short run can vary greatly from industry to industry. For example, in the petrochemical industry it can take five years or more to commission, build and run-in a new plant so that any expansion of output within this term can only be achieved by increasing the throughput from existing plants. By contrast, in the garment-making industry it may be possible to buy and instal new sewing machines within a few weeks so that in this industry the short-run might be a month or less. Compare LONG RUN. See also RETURNS TO THE VARIABLE-FACTOR INPUT.

shutdown price a market price which is so low that a profit maximizing supplier is unable to recoup the SHORT-RUN unit VARIABLE COST of producing a product. At this price the firm is unable to generate sufficient revenue to make any CONTRIBUTION towards its FIXED COSTS and cannot even cover its variable costs so that losses are incurred, necessitating a decision to close down its production facilities.

See LOSS, LOSS MINIMIZATION.

SIC (Standard Industrial Classification) see INDUSTRIAL CLASSIFICATIONS.

sickness benefit the TRANSFER PAYMENTS in cash or kind made to persons unable to work through illness to provide them with some minimum standard of living until they can return to paid employment. In most countries workers in employment pay NATIONAL-INSURANCE CONTRIBUTIONS to the government in return for sickness benefit rights. See also GOVERNMENT EXPENDITURE, SOCIAL-SECURITY BENEFITS.

sight deposit see CURRENT ACCOUNT, COMMERCIAL BANK.

simple interest the INTEREST on a LOAN that is based only on the original amount of the loan. This means that over time, interest charges grow in a linear fashion. For example, a £100 loan earning simple interest of 10% per annum would accumulate to £110 at the end of the first year and £120 at the end of the second year etc. Compare COMPOUND INTEREST.

Single European Market Act, 1986 (referred to popularly as the '1992' initiative) an Act which extended the principles enshrined in the founding legislation of the EUROPEAN COMMUNITY ('The Treaty of Rome') with the objective of creating a 'single market' (by '1992' if possible) through the removal of various *internal* obstacles to the free movement of goods, services, capital and persons between the member States of the Community. Under the Act, the European Commission has submitted some 400 Directives for eliminating disparities between members in respect of physical, technical and fiscal rules and regulations so as to create a unified Community-wide set of practices: for example, individuals and freight transport will be able to move across national frontiers without undergoing passport and customs checks; common technical specifications are to be introduced relating to product descriptions and design, health and safety standards, etc.; while VAT and other sales taxes are to be applied on a uniform basis.

sinking fund a fund into which periodic payments are made which, with COMPOUND INTEREST, will ultimately be sufficient to meet a known future capital commitment or discharge a LIABILITY. Such a fund may be used to finance the replacement of FIXED ASSETS at the end of their useful life or to purchase back company loan stock or debentures upon maturity.

skill any competence possessed by a person, though in an employment context it often refers to a combination of knowledge and manual dexterity amongst manual workers. JOB or work tasks are often categorized as skilled, semi-skilled or unskilled according to the level of skills apparently required to perform them.

A key factor in upgrading skills is investment in TRAINING, both in terms of the provision of general education facilities by the government and, more specifically, 'on-the-job' or vocational training facilities by firms and by the government.

The general level of skills of a firm's LABOUR FORCE is an important factor in increasing PRODUCTIVITY while, more generally, the skills of the labour force, as embodied in HUMAN CAPITAL, contribute to the achievement of higher rates of ECONOMIC GROWTH.

skimming price a pricing policy that involves charging a comparatively high PRICE for a product to secure large profit margins. This policy will be adopted by a firm where consumers are not expected to be price sensitive, that is, demand is price-inelastic (see PRICE-ELASTICITY OF DEMAND).

See PRODUCT LIFE CYCLE, PENETRATION PRICE.

slump see DEPRESSION.

Smith, Adam (1723–1790) a Scottish economist whose writings formed the basis of CLASSICAL ECONOMICS. Smith's most famous book, *An Inquiry into the Nature and Causes of the Wealth of Nations* (1776), stressed the benefits of division of labour, discussed the need for SPECIALIZATION and exchange, and outlined the workings of the market mechanism (PRICE SYSTEM). Smith argued that if producers were free to seek profits by providing goods and services, then the 'invisible hand' of market forces would ensure that the right goods and services were produced. Provided that markets were free of government regulation then in this LAISSEZ FAIRE environment, competition would organize production in ways which would increase public well-being.

In competitive markets, producers would compete to sell more goods, forcing prices down to the lowest level which covered production costs and allowed normal profit to be made. Furthermore, if certain goods were scarce buyers would offer higher prices, drawing more producers into these industries and swelling supply. In this manner production in the market system would be driven by what consumers wanted.

Smith's outline of the market mechanism described the new economic system which was beginning to emerge in the newly-industrializing Western countries.

However, for the system to work Smith acknowledged that two important conditions needed to be met: (a) markets needed to be free of government intervention without the close government regulation of economic activity as had prevailed prior to Smith's day; (b) the self-seeking behaviour of producers could only be harnessed to the common good where competition prevailed, and Smith was deeply suspicious of MONOPOLIES, considering them to be conspiracies against the consumer.

See PRIVATE-ENTERPRISE SYSTEM.

social capital see INFRASTRUCTURE

social costs the COSTS borne by society resulting from the actions of FIRMS. Consider, for example, a river which is used by both a chemical firm to dispose of its waste and by a town as a source of drinking water. Assume that the continuous dumping of waste causes the river to become polluted. The firm incurs PRIVATE COSTS in producing chemicals but pays out nothing for the use of the river or the POLLUTION caused. The town, by contrast, is forced to instal special water treatment plants to counter the pollution. Thus, the extra cost of cleaning up the river is not borne by the firm but by society.

One way to remedy this divergence of private and social costs is to tax the firm an amount equivalent to the costs of treating the pollution. Making the firm pay the *full* costs of supplying chemicals has the merit of encouraging it to look around for the least-costly way of disposing of its waste; that is, instead of dumping its waste in the river it might be cheaper for the firm to invest in a waste disposal plant.

See also EXTERNALITIES, WELFARE ECONOMICS, COST-BENEFIT ANALYSIS, POLLUTOR PAYS PRINCIPLE.

socialism a political doctrine that emphasizes the collective ownership of the means of production, ascribing a large rôle to the State in the running of the economy with widespread public ownership (NATIONALIZATION) of key industries, though it allows limited scope to market forces. MARX regarded socialism as a transitional stage between the end of a PRIVATE-ENTERPRISE system and the beginnings of COMMUNISM. In practice, the revolutionary, communist form of socialism, which involves abolition of all private property, is limited to only a few countries such as China. Elsewhere the main form of economic system is that of the MIXED ECONOMY which combines elements of democratic socialism and the private enterprise tradition. See CENTRALLY-PLANNED ECONOMY.

social overhead capital see INFRASTRUCTURE.

social products or **merit goods** or **public goods** the GOODS and SERVICES that are provided by the State for the benefit of all or most of the populace (education, health, housing, etc.). Unlike PRIVATE PRODUCTS, there is no direct link between the consumption of a social product and payment for it. Social products are paid for out of general taxation and not by individual consumers buying in the market place. See also COLLECTIVE PRODUCTS.

social security benefits any benefits provided, on social grounds, to low-income members of society such as the unemployed, retired persons, the disabled, single-parent families, etc. Social security benefits can take the form of money payments (for example, unemployment benefit, pensions, etc.) or payments in kind (for example, clothing coupons, food stamps, etc.). Some countries apply a MEANS TEST to determine eligibility for benefits.

In certain cases, where the scale of benefit used to determine benefit entitlement overlaps with the PROGRESSIVE-TAXATION system, this can create disincentive to seek employment.

See POVERTY TRAP, NEGATIVE INCOME TAX, SUPPLY-SIDE ECONOMICS.

social time preference see DISCOUNT RATE.

social welfare function see WELFARE ECONOMICS.

socio-economic group the potential BUYERS of a consumer product grouped together in terms of certain common personal and economic characteristics, for example the nature of their jobs (professional, labourer), level of income (high, low), ages (old, young), etc. Such groups are likely to differ in the level and pattern of their spending and thus can be used as the basis for identifying MARKET SEGMENTS which then can be exploited by targetting 'customized' products to meet the particular customer requirements of those segments.

soft currency a FOREIGN CURRENCY that is in weak demand, but in abundant supply on the FOREIGN-EXCHANGE MARKET. Soft currency status is usually associated with an economically weak country which is running a large deficit in its BALANCE OF PAYMENTS; the supply of the currency is high to finance the purchase of imports, but demand for the currency is relatively weak because the amount of it being required for the purchase of exports is much lower. However, under a FLOATING EXCHANGE-RATE SYSTEM, the demand for, and supply of, the currency should be, in theory, brought into balance by a DEPRECIATION (1) in its EXCHANGE-RATE value. Compare HARD CURRENCY.

soft loan a LOAN that bears an INTEREST RATE charge that is substantially below that of the interest rate which is charged normally on a loan for a similar purpose and risk status. Soft loans are often given as a form of ECONOMIC AID to DEVELOPING COUNTRIES by developed countries and international institutions (see WORLD BANK) and are used as a form of EXPORT SUBSIDY. In addition, soft loans may be used to influence industrial location under a country's REGIONAL POLICY.

sole proprietor see FIRM.

Solow economic-growth model a theoretical construct which focuses on the rôle of technological change in the ECONOMIC GROWTH process.

In the HARROD ECONOMIC-GROWTH MODEL and the DOMAR ECONOMIC GROWTH MODEL, a constant CAPITAL-OUTPUT RATIO is assumed

SPECIAL DEPOSIT

so that there is a linear relationship between increases in the CAPITAL STOCK (through INVESTMENT) and the resulting increase in output. For example, if it requires £3,000 of capital to produce £1,000 of output then the capital-output ratio is one-third, and this is assumed to apply to successive additions to the capital stock. By contrast, the Solow model utilizes a production function in which output is a function of capital *and* labour, with capital being substitutable for labour but with varying degrees of perfection, and which displays DIMINISHING RETURNS. Thus, if capital is increased relative to labour, the resulting increases in output become progressively smaller. On this assumption of a variable capital-output ratio as a country's capital stock increases, diminishing returns set in and produce progressively smaller increments in output. Sustained economic growth thus requires not only CAPITAL-WIDENING but also CAPITAL-DEEPENING investment. Specifically, TECHNOLOGICAL PROGRESSIVENESS (new production techniques, processes and methods, and new products) plays a necessary rôle in offsetting diminishing returns to capital as the capital stock increases.

special deposit an instrument of MONETARY POLICY involving the placement of a specified proportion of the banking sector's liquid assets with the CENTRAL BANK as a means of controlling the MONEY SUPPLY. Special deposits are excluded from the bank's liquidity or RESERVE-ASSET RATIO. Thus, if the monetary authorities wish to reduce the money supply they can call for a special deposit. This will lower the liquidity base of the banking sector. As a result banks will be forced to reduce their lending, leading to a multiple contraction of bank deposits and, hence, a fall in the money supply.

In the UK the Bank of England has occasionally called for special deposits and for 'supplementary special deposits' (referred to as the *corset*) to counteract sudden increases in banking sector liquidity.

See BANK DEPOSIT CREATION.

Special Drawing Right (SDR) a monetary asset held by member countries of the INTERNATIONAL MONETARY FUND (IMF) as part of their INTERNATIONAL RESERVES. Unlike other reserve assets such as GOLD, SDRs have no tangible life of their own. They are 'created' by the IMF itself and take the form of book-keeping entries in a special account managed by the Fund. The SDR is valued in terms of a weighted basket of five currencies: US dollar, German deutschmark, UK sterling, French franc, Japanese yen.

specialization a form of division of labour whereby each individual and firm concentrates their productive efforts on a single or limited number of activities. If a person specializes in a single job or work task, he or she is likely to be much more efficient than if he attempts to be a jack-of-all trades. The specialist can concentrate on the work he or she is best at doing: familiarity and repetition improves work

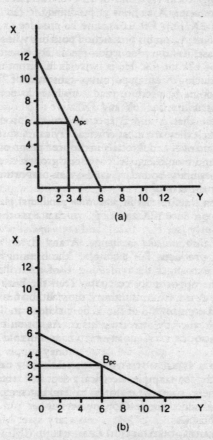

Fig. 162. **Specialization**. (a) A's production/consumption possibility
boundary before specialization. (b) B's production/consumption
possibility boundary before specialization.

skills and time is not lost moving from one job to another. For all
these reasons, a person's output is greater as a result of specialization.

Similarly, specialization enables an economy to use its scarce
resources more efficiently, thereby producing (and consuming) a
larger volume of goods and services than would otherwise be the
case. This fundamental principle can be illustrated assuming, to simplify matters, a two-person, A and B, and two-product, X and Y,
economy. Let us suppose that A has the PRODUCTION-POSSIBILITY

BOUNDARY indicated in Fig. 162a of 12X or 6Y. Thus, A is twice as efficient at producing X as he is at producing Y (an OPPORTUNITY-COST RATIO of 2X/1Y). Let us assume he chooses to produce (and consume) at point A_{pc} on his production possibility line (6X and 3Y).

B, by contrast, has the production-possibility boundary indicated in Fig. 162b of 12Y or 6X. He is twice as efficient at producing Y as he is at producing X (an opportunity-cost ratio of 2Y/1X). Let us assume he chooses to produce (and consume) at point B_{pc} on his production possibility line (6Y and 3X).

Now, assume that A and B specialize in the production of the product in which they are most efficient. Thus, A specializes totally in the production of X and B totally in the production of Y. Transposing Figs 162a and b onto Fig. 162c we see the establishment of a new production-possibility boundary (and a new opportunity cost ratio of 1X/1Y) for the economy).

Specialization thus results in *production gain*, that is, the economy is now able to produce 12X and 12Y, which is 3 more X and 3 more Y than previously (see Fig. 162d), and *consumption gain*, that is, as a result of specialization *and* exchange, A and B can now consume more of both products. For example, A consumes 8 of the X he produces and exchanges the remaining 4X for 4Y from B (i.e. 1X = 1Y from the opportunity cost ratio 1X/1Y). With specialization and exchange, A is now consuming 2 more X and 1 more Y. By the same token, B consumes 8 of the Y he produces and exchanges 4Y for 4X from A, thereby increasing his consumption by 2Y and 1X.

See also PRODUCTIVITY, COMPARATIVE ADVANTAGE, GAINS FROM TRADE.

specialist shop a RETAIL OUTLET that specializes in a narrow range of related products; for example, electrical goods and accessories, sweets and confectionery, sportswear stores, bakers, butchers, etc. Specialist shops may be under single-shop ownership or run as a multiple CHAIN-STORE business.

See also RETAILER, DISTRIBUTION CHANNEL.

specific tax a TAX that is levied at a fixed rate per physical unit of output. See AD VALOREM TAX, VALUE-ADDED TAX.

speculation the purchase or sale of ASSETS, real or financial, to achieve a CAPITAL GAIN. See ARBITRAGE, SPECULATIVE-DEMAND FOR MONEY, SPECULATOR.

speculative demand for money the demand for MONEY balances which are held in highly liquid form in the hope of taking advantage of bargains in the form of low-priced BONDS or real ASSETS.

Speculative balances are associated with the concept of a 'normal' INTEREST RATE. Each holder of speculative balances has their own opinion of what this 'normal' rate is. If the current rate of interest is high, this encourages bond holding but discourages money holding

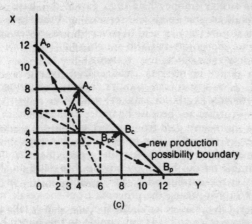

(c)

	Production				Consumption			
	Before		After		Before		After	
	X	Y	X	Y	X	Y	X	Y
A	6	3	12	–	6	3	8(+2)	4(+1)
B	3	6	–	12	3	6	4(+1)	8(+2)
Total	9	9	12	12	9	9	12(+3)	12(+3)

(d)

Fig. 162. **Specialization.**(c) A and B's combined production/consumption possibility boundary after specialization. (d) The production/consumption limits of A and B before and after specialization.

because of: (a) the high OPPORTUNITY COST of holding cash in terms of interest foregone; (b) the negligible risks attached to capital losses, because the interest rate is unlikely to rise even further and so reduce the price of bonds (there being an inverse relationship between the price of bonds and the EFFECTIVE INTEREST RATE).

The speculation arises around the future movement of bond prices and when bonds should be bought and sold. When the interest rate is very low and bond prices are high, then: (c) people will want to hold speculative balances because the opportunity cost in terms of interest foregone is small; (d) there will be a general expectation of a rise in the interest rate, with a consequent fall in bond prices, and thus the preference is for cash holding. The effect of such forces is to create an inverse relationship between interest rates and the demand for speculative balances.

The speculative demand for money together with the TRANSACTION

DEMAND FOR MONEY (money held on a day-to-day basis to finance current expenditures on goods and services) and the PRECAUTIONARY DEMAND FOR MONEY (money held to cover for unforeseen contingencies) constitute the MONEY-DEMAND SCHEDULE.

See LIQUIDITY PREFERENCE, L.M. SCHEDULE.

speculator a dealer in markets characterized by rapidly changing prices (such as a COMMODITY MARKET, STOCK EXCHANGE, FUTURES MARKET or FOREIGN EXCHANGE MARKET) who buys and/or sells commodities or securities not because he trades in them, but in the hope of making a short-term gain from movements in the prices of these commodities or securities. For example, in the stock exchange, a speculator may take a 'bullish' view that a particular share price will rise, and gamble on this hunch by buying that share on short-term credit terms at the current price, and reselling it at a higher price after a week or two, using the proceeds from the resale to pay the original seller. On the other hand, the speculator may take a 'bearish' view that a share price will fall, and gamble on this hunch by arranging to sell these shares at the present price (even though he does not own any), using the proceeds from this sale to buy at a lower price the shares which he has promised to deliver a week or two later.

The activities of speculators within a market may be either stabilizing or destabilizing, depending on whether or not they take a collective view about future price movements. For example, if some stock exchange speculators feel that the price of a share is going to rise while other speculators feel that the price of the same share is going to fall, then the former would seek to buy the share, adding to demand for it; while the latter would seek to sell the share, adding to the supply of it; and their efforts would cancel out, having little net effect on the share price. However, if most speculators take the view that a share price will rise then they will all seek to buy it, and thus artificially add to the demand for it and force up its price; while if most speculators take the view that the share price will fall, they will all seek to sell it, artificially adding to its supply and forcing price down.

Whether speculators reduce or accentuate fluctuations in share prices over time depends on whether their collective view about future prices parallels the underlying price changes or moves in opposition to them. For example, if a share price is rising, and speculators take a collective view that it will continue to rise, then they will seek to buy it in the hope of reselling at a higher price, and this buying will accelerate the upward share price movement. On the other hand, if a share price is rising, and speculators take a collective view that it will begin to fall in the immediate future, then they will seek to sell the share in the hope of buying it back later at a lower price, and this selling will slow down the upward share price movement.

Speculators operate in both SPOT MARKETS and futures markets and often make considerable use of OPTIONS in their dealings. For example, a speculator may purchase a share option which entitles him to buy a certain number of a company's shares at a predetermined price at some future date, if he thinks that the share price will increase to more than the predetermined price plus the cost of the option; for then he can gain by exercising the option and immediately reselling the shares at the higher price.

See also ARBITRAGE, HOT MONEY, STAG.

spot market a market for the purchase and sale of COMMODITIES (tea, rubber, etc.) and financial instruments (FOREIGN EXCHANGE, STOCKS and SHARES) for immediate delivery, as opposed to a FUTURES MARKET which provides for delivery at some future point in time. Spot prices for commodities and financial instruments transacted at different locations are harmonized by ARBITRAGE.

spread see BID PRICE.

stabilization policy see DEMAND MANAGEMENT.

stag a SPECULATOR in fixed-price new SHARE ISSUES who subscribes for large numbers of shares in anticipation of OVERSUBSCRIPTION and a rapid rise in the share price once dealings commence. This enables him to sell his shares for a quick profit.

stagflation a situation of depressed levels of real output combined with increases in prices (INFLATION). Stagflation is caused by the dual forces of (a) a deficiency in AGGREGATE DEMAND relative to POTENTIAL GROSS NATIONAL PRODUCT (see DEFLATIONARY-GAP) and (b) rising FACTOR INPUT costs (see COST-PUSH INFLATION).

Stagflation was a particular problem in many countries during the 1970s and early 1980s as a result of the combined effect of cost-push inflationary pressures emanating from the oil price increases of 1973 and 1979, and the deflationary consequences of reduced real purchasing power in the oil-consuming countries which accompanied these increases. This was exacerbated by the development of higher inflationary expectations.

Orthodox FISCAL POLICY and MONETARY POLICY, accustomed to an apparent trade-off between inflation and employment/output (see the PHILLIPS CURVE) was found wanting in the new situation, and many countries turned to alternative approaches; for example, MONETARISM and SUPPLY-SIDE ECONOMICS.

stagnation see SECULAR STAGNATION.

standard industrial classification see INDUSTRIAL CLASSIFICATION.

standardization the limitation of a firm's product range as a means of achieving low-cost production and marketing. By restricting its product range, a firm may be able to mass-produce each product and secure ECONOMIES OF SCALE through long production runs. However, in reducing its product range the firm may forgo greater sales and profit potential by limiting the number of MARKET SEGMENTS its products are sold in. Thus, as part of their PRODUCT DIFFERENTIATION policies, firms often need to 'trade-off' cost and VARIETY considerations.

standard of deferred payment an attribute of MONEY, enabling people to specify values for future receipts and payments in agreeing contracts.

standard of living the monetary and non-monetary elements which together make up a person's lifestyle. INCOME PER HEAD is used as a proxy for standard of living, though the PERSONAL DISTRIBUTION OF INCOME will mean that many people's income will differ from the average income. Another difficulty lies in assessing those benefits and costs which may improve a person's lifestyle but which have no immediately attributable economic value. For example, two people may have identical salaries but one may live in the country and have splendid scenery, peace and quiet, no traffic jams when driving to work and little pollution. The other person lives in an industrial city which has considerable traffic jams, pollution, noise and crime. Monetary comparisons would suggest a similar standard of living but this may not be the case.

See ECONOMIC DEVELOPMENT.

standard rate of taxation the basic rate of INCOME TAX, for example, 25 pence per £1 of taxable income. In a PROGRESSIVE-TAXATION system the standard rate of taxation applies only to the initial taxable income band; those with taxable income in excess of the initial band paying a higher MARGINAL RATE OF TAXATION on this additional income.

stand-by arrangement an arrangement between the INTERNATIONAL MONETARY FUND and a member country under which the member country is entitled to borrow up to an agreed amount of foreign currency from the Fund to cover a possible deficit on its BALANCE OF PAYMENTS.

standing order see COMMERCIAL BANK.

staple product any product whose consumption does not vary much with changes in INCOME, for example basic foodstuffs like potatoes and bread. Staple products have an INCOME-ELASTICITY OF DEMAND of less than 1. This means that as incomes rise, proportionally less income is spent on such products.

Contrast LUXURY PRODUCTS. See also ENGEL'S LAW, NORMAL PRODUCT, INFERIOR PRODUCT, GIFFEN GOOD.

state enterprise the basic production unit in a CENTRALLY PLANNED ECONOMY which is owned by the State and operates on the basis of production plans and targets laid down in the country's NATIONAL PLAN.

statement of account a periodic statement sent to a customer by a supplier that sets out both the money value of products supplied to the customer over a monthly or other period, and any amounts still owed by the customer for these products. A statement of account is sent by a supplier some time after an INVOICE has been sent. Compare DELIVERY NOTE.

state ownership see NATIONALIZATION.

static analysis see COMPARATIVE STATIC-EQUILIBRIUM ANALYSIS.

statistics 1. a branch of mathematics that studies the theory and methods of collecting, tabulating and analysing numerical data.

  2. a grouping of data. Economic analysis makes extensive use of economic data which are subjected to statistical analysis in order to test ECONOMIC THEORIES.

  See HYPOTHESIS TESTING, ECONOMETRICS.

statute law the law laid down by government legislation (in the UK, an Act of Parliament). Examples include the FAIR TRADING ACT, 1973 and the Companies Act, 1989. Once such legislation is on the statute books, it is then up to the courts to interpret and enforce the provisions of this legislation. Compare COMMON LAW.

sterling the name given to the UK POUND in international dealings to distinguish it from other countries using the pound as the basis of their currencies. Formerly, most countries extensively involved in international trade kept large sterling balances as part of their stock of INTERNATIONAL RESERVES, but nowadays sterling is little used as a reserve asset except by a number of current and former member countries of the British Commonwealth.

sterling area a group of countries (predominantly ex-British colonies) whose own national currencies were formerly linked directly to the value of the British POUND, and who held STERLING as part of their INTERNATIONAL RESERVES.

sterling M₃ (£M₃) see MONEY SUPPLY DEFINITIONS.

stock 1. the part of a firm's ASSETS that are held in the form of raw materials, work-in-progress and finished goods. These are also known as INVENTORIES. Finished goods are held in stock to ensure that goods are available when required by customers. Raw materials and components are held in stock to prevent disruptions to production caused by lack of materials or components and to secure economies from bulk purchasing.

  The rate at which firms accumulate and deplete their stocks influences (see STOCK CONTROL) the oscillations in economic activity (see BUSINESS CYCLE). Although the increase and decrease in stocks operates on the same ACCELERATOR principle as capital investment, the decision as to what *level* of stock to hold may not be entirely in the businessman's hands. Involuntary investment may occur when demand turns out to be less than a producer's expectations so that stock builds up during downturns in the business cycle (see INVENTORY INVESTMENT).

2. a FINANCIAL SECURITY issued by a JOINT-STOCK COMPANY or by the government as a means of raising long-term capital. In some countries (for example, the US) stockholders are the equivalent of shareholders and are the owners of the company. In other countries (for example, the UK) stock is a form of repayable, fixed-interest, DEBT and stockholders are creditors of the company not shareholders. Stocks are traded on the STOCK EXCHANGE. See SHARE CAPITAL.

3. a measurement of quantity at one specific point in time. Unlike a FLOW, a stock is not a function of time. The analogy is frequently made between a tank holding a given stock of water, and water entering and leaving the tank as flows of water per minute.

stock appreciation the increase in the market value of STOCK held during a specific time period, generally because of INFLATION. In a firm the accountant will value stock at the lower of either cost or net realizable value in the BALANCE SHEET, not at replacement cost, and when stock is sold, tax is paid on the profits arising. This gives rise to 'phantom profits' which, when taxed, can result in over-taxing the firm's real profits. Where prices are falling, *stock depreciation* results.

NATIONAL INCOME ACCOUNTS also have to take the problem of stock appreciation into account. The government statisticians have the difficult task of excluding such monetary appreciation from the final calculation so as to include only *real* stock increases.

See also HISTORIC COST, INFLATION ACCOUNTING, STOCK VALUATION.

stockbroker an agent who acts on behalf of clients in buying and selling FINANCIAL SECURITIES such as STOCKS, SHARES and BONDS in return for a commission. Some stockbrokers also act as 'jobbers', that is, they act as principals in 'making a market' in securities.

See MARKET MAKER, STOCK EXCHANGE.

stock control the process of controlling STOCKS of finished products, WORK IN PROGRESS and raw materials, in order to minimize STOCK-HOLDING COSTS, while maintaining an adequate level of service and appropriate safety stocks to meet contingencies like sudden increases in demand. Stock control requires good forecasts of future consumer demand and production requirements, so that purchasing and production can be planned to avoid carrying excessive stocks with their associated stockholding costs.

See JUST-IN-TIME SYSTEM.

stock dividend a DIVIDEND payment whereby a SHAREHOLDER is paid a dividend in the form of additional SHARES or STOCKS in the company rather than in cash.

See also STOCK SPLITS.

stock exchange or **stock market** a MARKET which deals in the buying and selling of company STOCKS and SHARES and government BONDS. The stock exchange, together with the MONEY MARKET (which deals in short-term company and government securities), is the main source of external capital to industry and the government.

Institutions that are involved in the UK stock exchange include MARKET MAKERS (who act as JOBBERS and STOCKBROKERS), specialist stockbrokers, ISSUING HOUSES, MERCHANT BANKS and, as general buyers and sellers of securities, the CENTRAL BANK, COMMERCIAL BANKS, PENSION FUNDS, INSURANCE COMPANIES, UNIT TRUSTS and INVESTMENT TRUST COMPANIES, together with private individuals, industrial companies and overseas investors and institutions.

The stock exchange performs two principal functions. It provides (a) a primary or 'new issue' market where capital for investment and other purposes can be raised by the issue of new stocks, shares and bonds (see SHARE ISSUE), and (b) a 'secondary' market for dealings in existing securities, including forward dealings (see FUTURES MARKET), which facilitates the easy transferability of securities from sellers to buyers.

The stock exchange thus occupies an important position in a country's FINANCIAL SYSTEM by providing a mechanism for channelling savings into physical and portfolio investment.

In the UK, the London Stock Exchange is the country's main centre for dealings in securities, supported by five provincial exchanges (Glasgow, Liverpool, Birmingham, York and Belfast).

In order to obtain a full listing or quotation on the London Stock Exchange for their shares, companies must satisfy various requirements, including proof of their financial standing and previous business history, and be prepared to issue at least 25% of their shares to the investing public. Additionally, more flexible arrangements have been introduced to allow smaller companies to raise capital without obtaining a full listing (see UNLISTED SECURITIES MARKET).

In recent years, stock markets worldwide, such as those based in London, New York, Tokyo, Zurich and Paris, have become increasingly interdependent with the growth of multinational companies, whose securities are traded on a number of exchanges while financial institutions and securities firms themselves have become more internationally based. This has led to an increase in competitive pressures which has brought about a number of important changes, particularly in the case of the UK stock exchange, including (a) the so-called 'big bang' – the termination (under the prodding of the OFFICE OF FAIR TRADING) of the cartel arrangements for fixing minimum commissions on securities transactions and the ending of the traditional division between the stockbroking and jobbing functions; (b) various mergers and joint ventures between UK securities firms and international securities and banking groups so as to provide clients with a more diversified range of financial services and geographical spread; (c) the computerization of dealing systems, using the Stock Exchange

Automatic Quotations System (SEAQ), which provides a mechanism for linking buying and selling transactions on a global basis. This has largely transferred day-to-day business from a physical presence on the stock exchange floor to telephone exchanges and the use of VDU computer terminals in dealing rooms.

In recognition of the growth in international dealings, the London Stock Exchange merged with the International Securities Regulatory Organization (ISRO), which represents the big international securities firms. The London Stock Exchange and ISRO now operate a single market for dealings in domestic and foreign securities: 'The London International Stock Exchange'.

The UK stock market is regulated by The Securities Association (TSA) and the Association of Futures Brokers and Dealers (AFBD) in accordance with various standards of good practice laid down by the FINANCIAL SERVICES ACT, 1986.

See CAPITAL MARKET, CITY CODE, SPECULATOR, SHARE PURCHASE/SALE, SHARE PRICE INDEX, INSIDER TRADING.

stockholding (inventory) costs the cost to firms of holding STOCKS of finished products and raw materials in order to provide immediate customer service or to prevent disruptions to production caused by lack of materials. Stockholding costs include costs of warehouse space, insurance, deterioration and obsolescence of stored items and interest on capital tied up in stocks. Such costs are roughly proportional to the value of the stock held, and to contain such costs, stock levels need to be kept low.

On the other hand, firms also have costs for ordering and delivering goods for stock such as communicating with suppliers, accounting transactions, transport and unloading and inspecting goods. Many of these ordering and delivery costs will remain the same irrespective of the size of the order.

Since many order and delivery costs are fixed costs, in order to reduce these costs the firm should place large orders at infrequent intervals, and such a policy would have the additional benefit of allowing the firm to earn price discounts for bulk purchase. However if orders are placed at infrequent intervals then stocks, and thus stockholding costs, will be high. It is desirable to strike a balance between these two groups of costs by determining the *economic or optimum order quantity* which minimizes total stock cost, and adopting appropriate STOCK CONTROL procedures to maintain stocks at this level.

See JUST-IN-TIME SYSTEM.

stock market a MARKET which deals in the buying and selling of company stocks and shares and government bonds.

See STOCK EXCHANGE for further details.

stockpiling the act of accumulating STOCK over and above normal requirements. National and international trade is dependent upon complex and interrelated supply lines from the raw material to the finished good. If at one point along the supply chain a shortage (or bottleneck) can be perceived in advance by firms beyond that point, then those firms will attempt to purchase much greater stocks than their immediate needs warrant. Stockpiling occurs in many areas of economic life, from the government stockpiling food or weapons, to the individual consumer amassing quantities of food in anticipation of a price rise.

See also BUFFER STOCK.

stock split or **share split** an increase in the number of SHARES in a JOINT-STOCK COMPANY that does not affect the capitalization of the company. For example, Company X has 10,000 authorized, issued and fully-paid up shares each with a par value of £1; and total SHARE-HOLDERS CAPITAL is shown in the BALANCE SHEET at £10,000. The STOCK EXCHANGE values the company at £100,000, making each share worth £10. The company wishes to attract a wider shareholder base by reducing the market PRICE of each share, and so undertakes a two to one stock split, giving existing shareholders two new 50p shares for each share held. The company now has 20,000 authorized, issued and fully paid up shares of 50p nominal value, and capitalization of the company remains unchanged at £10,000. However, now the stock-market price of the shares will be £5, which hopefully will improve the marketability of the shares.

See also SHARE CAPITAL.

stock valuation the placing of an appropriate money value upon a firm's STOCKS of raw materials, work-in-progress and finished goods. Where INFLATION causes the price of several different batches of finished-goods stock bought during a trading period to differ, the firm has the problems of deciding what money value to place upon the units sold in the PROFIT AND LOSS ACCOUNTS since this affects the cost of goods sold and so GROSS PROFIT. This decision simultaneously affects the cost attached to stocks in the BALANCE SHEET.

Various formulas can be used for this purpose. For example, the *first-in, first-out (FIFO)* method assumes that goods are withdrawn from stock in the order in which they are received so that the cost of goods sold is based on the cost of the oldest goods in stock, while the value of stock is based on the prices of the most recent purchases. By contrast, the *last-in, first-out (LIFO)* method assumes that the most recently purchased goods are (theoretically) withdrawn from stock first so that the cost of goods sold is based on the costs of the most recent purchases, while the value of stock is based on the oldest goods available.

See INFLATION ACCOUNTING.

stop-go cycle the application by government of available macroeconomic tools to stimulate and then dampen economic activity. Such tools are used in counter-cyclical DEMAND MANAGEMENT policy to try to offset the fluctuations in economic activity associated with the BUSINESS CYCLE. Stop-go policies are often referred to in a negative sense, in that government policies of this type during the 1960s and early 1970s, especially, were either ill-timed or involved injections or withdrawals of an incorrect magnitude.

See MACROECONOMIC POLICY.

store 1. a secure area for the storage of raw materials or components not required immediately for production; or of finished goods not required immediately for despatch to customers.

2. a SHOP.

store of value an attribute of MONEY, enabling people to hold on to money to finance some *future* purchase of a product or asset without loss of PURCHASING POWER in the interim. More generally, any other ASSET which can be held and converted into money at the same price as its purchase price can serve as a store of value. In a period of INFLATION, however, the PURCHASING POWER of money itself will decline, undermining its function as a store of value and increasing the comparative attractiveness of real property assets whose value rises with inflation.

strategy see BUSINESS STRATEGY, COMPETITIVE STRATEGY, MEDIUM-TERM FINANCIAL STRATEGY.

strike a concerted stoppage of work by a group of workers as part of an INDUSTRIAL DISPUTE. See INDUSTRIAL RELATIONS, LOCKOUT, PICKET.

structural unemployment the long-term UNEMPLOYMENT caused by the decline of certain industries and changes in production processes. It occurs where changing demand-patterns in an economy dislocate existing production-patterns to the extent that labour becomes redundant. This is a long-term phenomenon requiring the work force to seek other jobs outside the declining industries, possibly in a different part of the country. The problem is one which most governments have had to deal with, for example, the decline in the heavy engineering industries, steel and shipbuilding, in the north of England and in Scotland. Technological change and foreign competition forced the reduction in demand for goods associated with those industries, which resulted in mass unemployment of labour. Countering such unemployment requires extensive occupational retraining programmes for the displaced workers, assistance with moving to new areas where jobs are available, and financial inducements to encourage new growth industries to move to regions blighted by concentrations of declining industries.

See REGIONAL POLICY, DEINDUSTRIALIZATION, SUPPLY-SIDE ECONOMICS.

structure of industry the productive activities undertaken in an economy classified according to broad groupings of activities by sector, or more narrowly on an industry-to-industry basis.

The three basic sectors of an economy are: (a) the primary sector (raw materials and farming), (b) the industrial or secondary sector (manufactured goods, construction, gas and electricity, etc.), (c) the service sector (retailing, banking, tourism, etc.).

The relative importance of each of these sectors tends to change as the economy expands over time. For example, DEVELOPING COUNTRIES are characterized by very large primary sectors and small industrial and service sectors, whereas DEVELOPED COUNTRIES are characterized by small primary sectors and large industrial and service sectors. Fig. 163 shows that in the most advanced countries there has been a relative decline in the industrial sector, and a corresponding increase in the importance of the service sector.

See INDUSTRIALIZATION, DEINDUSTRIALIZATION, INDUSTRIAL CLASSIFICATIONS, ECONOMIC DEVELOPMENT.

	Agriculture		Industry		Manufacturing		Services	
	1960	1994	1960	1994	1960	1994	1960	1994
UK	3	2	43	32	32	22	54	66
US	4	2	38	29	29	17	58	69
Japan	13	2	45	40	34	27	42	58
Germany	6	1	53	38	40	27	41	61

Fig. 163. **Structure of industry**. The distribution of gross domestic product in percentages from 1960 to 1993 for the UK, US, Japan and Germany. Manufacturing percentages are also included in those for industry. Source: *World Development Report*, World Bank, 1996.

subsidiary company a company that is owned by another company (see FIRM). A subsidiary company may continue to trade under its own name, but it is subjected to complete or partial centralized control by the 'parent company'. See also HOLDING COMPANY, CONSOLIDATED ACCOUNTS.

subsidy the provision of finance and other resources to support a business activity or person by the government. Subsidies can be direct (cash grants, interest-free LOANS, etc.) or indirect (depreciation write-offs, rent rebates) and can be used for a variety of purposes, including:

(a) PRODUCTION subsidies: the subsidization of suppliers by government to encourage them to increase the output of particular products by partially offsetting their production costs or even financing losses. The objective may be to expand production of some product at a low price which is deemed to be 'essential' (for example, a particular foodstuff, thereby also subsidizing consumers); or, for example, to assist in the start-up of a new firm (see BUSINESS EXPANSION SCHEME) or industry (see INDUSTRIAL POLICY), and encourage firms to locate in particular areas (see REGIONAL POLICY). In the first cases, subsidies are used as an instrument of income redistribution by reducing the price of products such as bread and milk which figure prominently in the budget of lower income groups, or by directly subsidizing incomes.

(b) EXPORT subsidies: the subsidization of a particular product which is exported, or exports in general, by the government as a means of assisting the country's balance of payments.

(c) EMPLOYMENT subsidies: the subsidization of wages by the government as an incentive to businesses to provide more job opportunities, thereby reducing the level of unemployment in the economy.

(d) INCOME subsidies: the subsidization of persons through government transfer payment systems (for example, social security benefits) in order to allow them to enjoy some minimum standard of living.

Subsidies encourage increased output of favoured products, but distort domestic RESOURCE-ALLOCATION processes in general, and can adversely affect international trade.

See REDISTRIBUTION-OF-INCOME PRINCIPLE OF TAXATION, PROTECTIONISM, CROSS-SUBSIDIZATION.

substitute products any GOODS or SERVICES that are considered to be economically interchangeable by buyers. For example, if an increase in the price of coffee causes buyers to switch away from it and buy a greater quantity of tea, these two goods can be regarded as substitutes for one another.

The CROSS-ELASTICITY OF DEMAND between two products serves as a measure of the degree of substitutability between them; products which are close substitutes have a high cross-elasticity, while products which are poor substitutes have a low cross-elasticity.

See COMPLEMENTARY PRODUCTS.

substitution effect the substitution of one PRODUCT for another resulting from a change in their relative prices. A fall in the price of a product normally results in more of it being demanded. A part of this increase is due to the substitution effect. A lower price for good X, with the prices of other goods remaining unchanged, will increase its relative attractiveness, inducing consumers to substitute good X in place of some of the now relatively more expensive items in their budgets. The substitution effect, together with the INCOME EFFECT, provides an explanation of why DEMAND CURVES are downward sloping.

See CONSUMER EQUILIBRIUM, REVEALED PREFERENCE, PRICE EFFECT.

sufficient condition see NECESSARY CONDITION.

sunk costs any expenditure on durable and specific FACTOR INPUTS such as plant and machinery which cannot be used for other purposes or easily be resold. Such sunk costs have no affect on MARGINAL COSTS and do not influence short-term output decisions.

See also OPPORTUNITY COST, BARRIERS TO EXIT.

supermarket a large self-service RETAIL OUTLET. Supermarkets may be under single-shop ownership, or run as a multiple CHAIN-STORE business. The larger supermarket chains are able to effect major economies in distribution both on a group basis by being able to obtain favourable discounts and concessions from manufacturers by BULK BUYING, and at the individual store level by the use of capital-intensive methods of retailing (see EPOS). A significant development has been the introduction of OWN-LABEL BRANDS selling under the supermarket's own name in direct competition with manufacturers' brands.

Hypermarkets are an extended form of supermarket, usually located on the outskirts of towns and cities where space is plentiful.

See RETAILER, DISTRIBUTION CHANNEL.

super-normal profit see ABOVE-NORMAL PROFIT.

supplier see FIRM.

supply the amount of a PRODUCT made available for sale by FIRMS. In economic analysis, the total supply of a product is reflected in the SUPPLY CURVE, Compare DEMAND.

supply and demand see SUPPLY CURVE, DEMAND CURVE.

supply curve a line showing the relationship between the PRICE of a PRODUCT or FACTOR OF PRODUCTION and the quantity supplied per time period. 'Supply' means the total quantity of a product or factor that firms or factor owners are prepared to sell at a given price.

The typical market supply curve for a product slopes upwards from

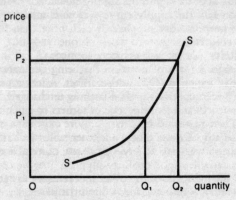

Fig. 164. **Supply curve**. See entry.

left to right, indicating that as price rises more is supplied (that is, a movement along the existing supply curve). Thus, if price rises from OP_1 to OP_2 in Fig. 164, the quantity supplied will increase from OQ_1 to OQ_2.

Fig. 164 shows the supply curve for the market as a whole. This curve is derived by aggregating the individual supply curves of all of the producers of the good which in turn are derived from the producers' cost curves.

Most supply curves slope upwards because, as the price of the product rises, producers will find it more profitable to manufacture, using their existing production facilities, and because any increase in short-run MARGINAL COSTS associated with increasing output will be covered by the higher price obtained.

The slope of the supply curve reflects the degree of responsiveness of quantity supplied to changes in the product's price. For example, if a large rise in price results in only a small increase in quantity supplied (as would be the case where the supply curve has a steep slope), then supply is said to be price-inelastic (see PRICE-ELASTICITY OF SUPPLY).

The supply curve interacts with the DEMAND CURVE to determine the EQUILIBRIUM MARKET PRICE. See SUPPLY CURVE, (SHIFT IN), SUPPLY FUNCTION.

supply curve (shift in) a movement of the SUPPLY CURVE from one position to another (either left or right) as a result of some economic change, other than PRICE.

A given supply curve is always drawn on the CETERIS PARIBUS assumption that all of the other factors affecting supply (costs in particular) are held constant. If any of these change, however, then this will bring about a *shift* in the supply curve. For example, if costs of production fall, the supply curve will shift to the right (see Fig. 165) so that more is now supplied at each price than formerly. See also SUPPLY FUNCTION.

supply elasticity see PRICE-ELASTICITY OF SUPPLY.

supply function a form of notation that links the DEPENDENT VARIABLE, quantity supplied (Q_s), with various INDEPENDENT VARIABLES which determine quantity supplied such as product PRICE (P), prices of factor inputs (P_1 and P_2), the state of technology (T), and business goals (G). The equation states that:

Changes in any of these independent variables will affect quantity supplied, and if we wish to investigate the particular effect of any one of these variables upon quantity supplied then we could (conceptually) hold the influence of the other independent variables constant (CETERIS PARIBUS), whilst we focus upon the particular effect of that independent variable.

See also SUPPLY CURVE, SUPPLY CURVE (SHIFTS IN).

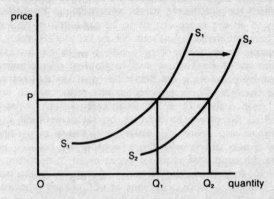

Fig. 165. **Supply curve (shift in).** A fall in production costs shifts the supply curve S_1S_1 to S_2S_2, increasing the quantity supplied at price OP from OQ_1 to OQ_2. The magnitude of this shift depends on the sensitivity of product supply to changes in costs.

$$Q_s = f(P, P_1, P_2, T, G)$$

supply schedule a schedule listing the various PRICES of a PRODUCT and the specific quantities supplied at each of these prices. The information provided by a supply schedule can be used to construct a SUPPLY CURVE showing the price/quantity-supplied relationship in graphical form.

supply-side economics the branch of economic analysis concerned with the productive capability of an economy (POTENTIAL GROSS NATIONAL PRODUCT) and with policies which attempt to expand the stock of factors of production and to improve the flexibility of factor markets so as to generate the largest possible output for a given level of AGGREGATE DEMAND. Supply-side economists have examined institutional rigidities in factor markets and the effect of higher factor prices in 'pricing people out of jobs'. This has led them to condemn the activities of trade unions in labour markets on the grounds that trade unions impose RESTRICTIVE LABOUR PRACTICES (such as overmanning and demarcation boundaries) and push WAGE RATES up to levels which exceed the MARGINAL-REVENUE PRODUCTIVITY of the workers concerned, thereby restricting potential employment and causing COST-PUSH INFLATION. Such ideas have also led supply-side economists to condemn certain SOCIAL-SECURITY BENEFITS systems and PROGRESSIVE-TAXATION systems for creating a POVERTY TRAP which acts as a disincentive for the unemployed to take low-paid jobs.

More broadly, supply-side economics has been concerned with ways in which the AGGREGATE SUPPLY SCHEDULE can be shifted outward so as to enable more output to be produced in response to growing aggregate demand without raising the PRICE LEVEL.

Governments may adopt supply-side policies to increase the stock of factors of production and to improve the efficiency of resource use by promoting the flexibility of markets in responding to demand changes. These policies include reductions in taxation and other disincentives to work to increase labour participation rates; financial incentives to increase capital investment in plant and equipment and promote similar investments in process and product invention and innovation; education and training policies to improve the supply of required skills; more competition in the financial sector to improve the efficiency of capital markets; privatization and reduced government control of industry (deregulation) to encourage industrial efficiency; regional policy assistance, private rented accommodation and portable pensions to encourage labour mobility; lower tax rates and changed social security benefits to provide incentives to work harder and take risks; curbs on the power of trade unions to improve the flexibility of labour markets; wider share ownership and assistance to the self-employed to promote enterprise culture. These measures can help to increase economic growth rates and reduce unemployment.

See also NEGATIVE INCOME TAX, PROFIT-RELATED PAY, LAFFER CURVE.

surplus see CONSUMERS' SURPLUS, PRODUCERS' SURPLUS, BUDGET GOVERNMENT, BALANCE OF PAYMENTS.

swap the exchange of a product, interest rate on a financial debt, or currency for another product, interest rate on a financial debt, or currency respectively:

(a) *product* swaps: individual A offers potatoes to individual B in exchange for a bicycle. See BARTER;

(b) INTEREST RATE swaps on financial debts: a company which has a *variable-rate* debt, for example, may anticipate that interest rates will rise; another company with *fixed-rate* debt may anticipate that interest rates will fall. The second company therefore contracts to make variable interest rate payments to the first company and in exchange is paid interest at a fixed rate. Interest rate swaps may be undertaken simultaneously on a variety of debt instruments thereby enabling corporate treasurers to lower the company's total interest payments;

(c) *currency* swaps: the simultaneous buying and selling of foreign currencies. This can take two main forms: a spot/forward swap (the simultaneous purchase or sale of a currency in the SPOT MARKET coupled with an offsetting sale or purchase of the same currency in the FUTURES MARKET); or a forward/forward swap (a pair of forward currency contracts, involving a forward purchase and sale of a particular currency, which mature at different future dates).

Currency swaps are used by firms which trade internationally to minimize the risk of losses arising from exchange rate changes (see EXCHANGE RATE EXPOSURE).

synergy see DIVERSIFICATION.

T

takeover or **acquisition** the acquisition by one FIRM of some other firm. Unlike a MERGER, which is usually arranged by mutual agreement between the firms involved, takeovers usually involve one firm mounting a 'hostile' TAKEOVER BID without the agreement of the victim firm's management. For publicly-quoted companies this involves one company buying 50% or more of the voting shares of the other so as to exercise effective control over it, though generally the acquiring company would wish to purchase all the shares of the other company.

Three broad categories of takeover may be identified: (a) horizontal takeovers involving firms that are direct competitors in the same market; (b) vertical takeovers involving firms which stand in a supplier-customer relationship; (c) conglomerate takeovers involving firms operating in unrelated markets which are seeking to diversify their activities.

From the firm's point of view a takeover can be advantageous because it may enable the firm to reduce production and distribution costs, acquire BRAND names, expand its existing activities or move into new areas, or remove troublesome competition and increase its market power. In terms of their wider impact on the operation of market processes, takeovers may, on the one hand, promote greater efficiency in resource use, or, on the other hand, by reducing competition, lead to a less efficient allocation of resources. In sum, they may involve, simultaneously, both benefits and detriments (see MERGER for further discussion).

In the UK, takeovers which create or extend a firm's market share of a particular product in excess of 25%, or where the value of assets acquired is over £70 million, can be referred to the MONOPOLIES AND MERGERS COMMISSION to determine whether or not they are in the public interest.

See also ASSET STRIPPER, COMPETITION POLICY, OFFICE OF FAIR TRADING, WILLIAMSON TRADE-OFF MODEL, HORIZONTAL INTEGRATION, VERTICAL INTEGRATION, DIVERSIFICATION, CITY CODE, MARKET ENTRY.

takeover bid an attempt by one FIRM to TAKEOVER another by acquiring the majority of shares in a public JOINT-STOCK COMPANY. The financial terms of the bid may involve a straight cash offer or a mix of cash and shares in the bidder. The price being offered per share in the target company will generally exceed the value of that company's physical assets and the current stock exchange price of its shares. The price premium being offered by the takeover bidder reflects its valuation of the underlying value of that company's physical assets, brands, trade contacts, etc. if they were to be more effectively managed as part of the bidder's overall business. A number of terms are used to describe the various tactics available to the bidding and defending firms, including:

(a) *black knight*: a firm that launches an unwelcome (contested) takeover bid for some other firm.

(b) *golden parachute*: any generous severance terms written into the employment contracts of the directors of a firm that makes it expensive to sack the directors if the firm is taken over.

(c) *greenmail*: a situation in which a firm's shares are being bought up by a (potential) takeover bidder, who is then headed-off from making an actual bid by that firm's directors buying these shares from him at a premium price.

(d) *leveraged bid*: a takeover that is financed primarily by the issue of LOAN CAPITAL (often in the form of *junk bonds*) rather than SHARE CAPITAL which increases the CAPITAL GEARING of the enlarged firm.

(e) *pac-man defence*: a situation in which the firm being bid for itself now makes a bid for the acquiring firm (see REVERSE TAKEOVER).

(f) *poison pill*: a tactic employed in a takeover bid whereby the intended victim firm itself takes over or merges (see MERGER) with some other firm in order to make itself financially or structurally less attractive to the potential acquirer.

(g) *porcupine*: any complex agreements between a firm and its suppliers, customers, or creditors that make it difficult for an acquiring company to integrate this firm with its own business.

(h) *shark repellants*: any measures specifically designed to discourage takeover bidders; for example, altering the company's articles of association to increase the proportion of shareholder votes needed to approve the bid above the usual 50% mark.

(i) *white knight*: the intervention in a takeover bid of a third firm which itself takes over or merges with the intended victim firm to 'rescue' it from its unwelcome suitor.

See CITY CODE.

tangible assets any physical ASSETS such as plant, machinery, equipment, vehicles and STOCK that have a money value.

Compare INTANGIBLE ASSETS.

tap issue the issue of TREASURY BILLS and BONDS by the Bank of England at a predetermined price to government departments which have short-term financial surpluses as a means of covering some of the financial deficits of other government departments.

Contrast TENDER ISSUE.

tariff or **import levy** a duty (a form of TAX) that is levied on IMPORTS. There are two main types of tariff: (a) ad valorem duty which is levied as a fixed percentage of the value of the good; (b) specific duty

TARIFF

which is levied as a fixed sum of money per physical unit of the good.

Tariffs are used to protect domestic industries from foreign competition and to raise revenue for the government.

The economic effects of a tariff are illustrated in Fig. 166. In the Fig., DD and SS are the domestic demand and supply curves of good X. In a closed economy, assuming perfect competition, the domestic price is OP_1. Consider now an open-economy situation with the world price for this particular good being OP_2. Assuming that the country's demand for good X accounts for only a small fraction of total world demand for the good, such that it is unable to affect the terms of trade of the good, then, under conditions of FREE TRADE, the domestic price will also be OP_2. At price OP_2 domestic consumption is O_b, domestic production is O_a, and imports being the difference between the two are equal to ab.

The imposition of a specific tariff, T, will cause the domestic price of imports to rise by the full amount of the duty, to price OP_3 in the Fig. At price OP_3 domestic consumption falls from O_b to O_d, domestic production increases from O_a to O_c and imports are reduced from ab to cd. The area YZLM (import volume cd times tariff per unit OP_2OP_3) represents government revenue from the tariff.

Although producers of the protected good gain by now being able to increase their supply of the good (that is, from O_a to O_c), the overall effect of the tariff is to reduce the productive efficiency of the economy and consumer welfare. The triangle XYZ represents the 'production loss' to the economy. Under conditions of full resource employment production in the tariff-protected industry can only be

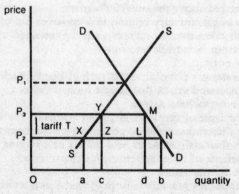

Fig. 166. Tariff. See entry.

increased by diverting resources away from other (nonprotected) industries, which rank higher in the order of productive efficiency. Thus, some resources are allocated less efficiently as a result of the tariff. The triangle LMN represents the 'consumption loss' (loss of CONSUMERS' SURPLUS) to society. As a result of the tariff, some buyers are forced to switch to less desirable substitute products while those consumers continuing to buy the good are now forced to pay a price for it which is in excess of the real economic costs of supplying it.

How effective the tariff is as a means of protecting the domestic industry will depend upon the PRICE-ELASTICITY OF DEMAND for the imported good. If import demand is highly price-inelastic, there will be little reduction in the volume of imports. In these cases a more effective means of protection is a QUOTA which places a physical ceiling on the amount of imports permitted.

See also PROTECTIONISM, NOMINAL RATE OF PROTECTION, EFFECTIVE RATE OF PROTECTION.

tax a levy imposed by the government on the income, wealth and capital gains of persons and businesses (DIRECT TAX), on spending on goods and services (INDIRECT TAX), and on properties. In the UK, taxes on income include personal INCOME TAX and CORPORATION TAX; 'inheritance tax' is used to tax wealth (see WEALTH TAX) and CAPITAL GAINS TAX is used to tax 'windfall' profits; taxes on spending include VALUE-ADDED TAX, EXCISE DUTY and TARIFFS; taxes on properties include the 'council tax' (see LOCAL TAX) and the UNIFORM BUSINESS RATE. Such taxes are used to raise revenue for the government and as a means of controlling the level and distribution of spending in the economy.

See TAXATION, PUBLIC FINANCE.

taxable income the amount of an individual's income that is subject to TAXATION once any tax allowances to which the taxpayer is entitled have been deducted.

taxation government receipts from the imposition of TAXES on persons' and businesses' income, spending, wealth and capital gains, and on properties. Taxes are used by the government for a variety of purposes, including (a) to raise revenue for the government to cover its own expenditure on the provision of social goods such as schools, hospitals, roads, etc. and social security payments made to individuals in respect of unemployment, sickness, etc. (see BUDGET, GOVERNMENT EXPENDITURE); (b) as an instrument of FISCAL POLICY in regulating the level of total spending (AGGREGATE DEMAND) in the economy (see DEMAND MANAGEMENT); (c) to alter the distribution of income and wealth (see PRINCIPLES OF TAXATION, REDISTRIBUTION OF INCOME); (d) to control the volume of imports into the country (see BALANCE OF PAYMENTS EQUILIBRIUM).

TAXATION SCHEDULE

In national income analysis, taxation is a WITHDRAWAL from the CIRCULAR FLOW OF NATIONAL INCOME.

See PUBLIC FINANCE, INLAND REVENUE.

taxation schedule a schedule that depicts the relationship between TAXATION receipts and the level of NATIONAL INCOME. Under PROGRESSIVE TAXATION, the schedule has a positive slope, that is tax receipts rise as the level of income rises (see Fig. 167). Likewise, receipts from expenditure taxes will be greater as the level of spending rises.

See also FISCAL DRAG, PROPENSITY TO TAX.

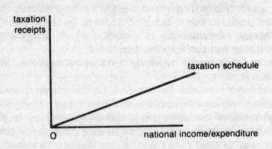

Fig. 167. **Taxation schedule**. See entry.

tax avoidance any efforts by taxpayers to arrange their financial affairs so as to avoid paying TAX by taking maximum advantage of taxation allowances and reliefs. In this way taxpayers can legally minimize their tax burden. Compare TAX EVASION.

tax base the total pool which the tax authorities can tap in levying a TAX. For example, the tax base for INCOME TAX is total taxable income and the tax base for CORPORATION TAX is total taxable profits.

tax burden the total amount of TAXATION paid by the citizens of a country in the form of income tax, corporation tax, value-added tax, etc. The total amount of tax as a proportion of GROSS NATIONAL PRODUCT gives some indication of the overall tax burden. See also INCIDENCE OF TAXATION.

tax credit see NEGATIVE INCOME TAX.

tax evasion any efforts by taxpayers to evade TAX by various illegal means, such as not declaring all of their income to the tax authorities or falsely claiming reliefs to which they are not entitled.

Compare TAX AVOIDANCE. See MOONLIGHTER.

tax haven a country which imposes low rates of personal and corporate TAXES, and which as a consequence tends to attract wealthy individuals and MULTINATIONAL COMPANIES seeking to minimize their taxation liabilities.

See also TRANSFER PRICE.

tax incidence see INCIDENCE OF TAXATION.

tax rate the percentage rate at which a TAX is levied on income or expenditure. Tax rates are varied by government on social grounds (to redistribute income) and as part of FISCAL POLICY to increase or decrease spending.

tax return a form which must be completed by all taxpayers and potential taxpayers for the INLAND REVENUE, giving details of their INCOME and CAPITAL GAINS and any allowances and reliefs to be set against this income.

tax revenue the money raised by government through the imposition of TAXES. Tax revenue from income (INCOME TAX, etc.) depends upon the income TAX RATE and the level of TAXABLE INCOME; while tax revenue from expenditure (VALUE–ADDED TAX, etc.) depends upon the indirect tax rate and the level of taxable expenditure. Government's tax revenue varies with the level of economic activity, increasing during periods of prosperity when more people have jobs and taxable incomes and spend more.

technological efficiency an aspect of PRODUCTION that seeks to identify, in physical terms, the optimal (best possible) combination of FACTOR INPUTS to produce a given level of OUTPUT.

See EFFICIENCY, PRODUCTION FUNCTION.

technological-gap theory a theory that seeks to explain changes in the pattern of INTERNATIONAL TRADE over time, which is based on a dynamic sequence of technological and product INNOVATION and diffusion. Technologically advanced countries with a high propensity to innovate (such as Japan) are able to achieve trade advantages by being able to offer sophisticated new products on world markets, initially unobtainable from other sources. Over time, however, the technology is diffused and adopted by other countries who are then able to supply the products concerned for themselves. Trade thus increases for the duration of the 'imitation lag'.

See PRODUCT LIFE–CYCLE THEORY, THEORY OF INTERNATIONAL TRADE.

technological progressiveness an aspect of MARKET PERFORMANCE that denotes the extent to which firms develop and introduce new and improved products, production and distribution techniques. Radical INVENTIONS and INNOVATIONS may make it possible to reduce manufacturing and distribution costs, thereby permitting a lowering of the supply price to the consumer. See Fig. 168a.

In the theory of costs, firms are assumed to operate within existing technological boundaries in both the SHORT RUN and the LONG RUN, but in the VERY LONG RUN, technological progressiveness serves to change the underlying cost conditions. For example, Fig. 168b shows how the time and cost to undertake a particular data-processing activity has been reduced by improvements in computer technology.

Technological progressiveness in aggregate terms affects a country's rate of ECONOMIC GROWTH.

See also MONOPOLY, PRODUCT PERFORMANCE, RESEARCH AND DEVELOPMENT, SOLOW ECONOMIC–GROWTH MODEL, TECHNOLOGICAL UNEMPLOYMENT, PRODUCTIVITY, AUTOMATION.

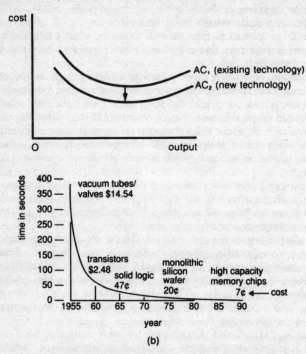

Fig. 168. **Technological progressiveness.** (a) The fall in a firm's long-run average cost curve from AC_1 to AC_2 as a result of technological advance. (b) Advances in computer technology. The time and cost for a computer to process 1700 typical data-processing operations. Source: IBM, cited in *Financial Times*, 15 February 1991.

technological unemployment UNEMPLOYMENT resulting from the AUTOMATION of production activities. Automation serves to improve labour PRODUCTIVITY, reducing the labour needed for making and distributing products, so that some labour may become unemployed. If demand rises as a result of reduced costs and prices of products, labour may not be made unemployed, the same labour force serving to produce a greater output (rather than a reduced labour force producing the same output). In addition, technological change can serve to make particular labour skills obsolete.

Government assistance schemes and retraining of labour can alleviate the problem of technological unemployment to some extent.

See STRUCTURAL UNEMPLOYMENT, TECHNOLOGICAL PROGRESSIVENESS, SUPPLY-SIDE ECONOMICS.

technology the application of scientific and technical knowledge in order to improve products and production processes. See TECHNOLOGICAL PROGRESSIVENESS, PRODUCTIVITY.

tender 1. an invitation from a buyer who requires particular goods or services to prospective suppliers of those products to put in competing price bids. See COMPETITIVE TENDERING.

2. a means of making a SHARE ISSUE by offering shares to the general public who are invited to make a bid for shares, subject to a minimum bid price. The issue price of the shares is determined by averaging out the bid prices offered by prospective purchasers. Anyone making a bid which is below the final issue price will not be offered any shares; whilst those making a bid at or above the issue price will be allotted shares in full at the final price.

Tenders may be similarly used to sell other financial securities such as TREASURY BILLS.

See TENDER ISSUE.

tender issue an issue of TREASURY BILLS by the Bank of England in response to invited TENDERS from DISCOUNT HOUSES and overseas central banks. Each discount house tenders for a given quantity of bills and their combined tender usually exceeds the quantity of bills on offer; the Bank of England then allots the bills to the highest bidders. This permits the Bank of England to borrow money on behalf of the government at a competitive interest rate.

COMMERCIAL BANKS do not tender directly for Treasury Bills but instead purchase their requirements in the DISCOUNT MARKET.

Contrast TAP ISSUE.

term loan a form of BANK LOAN made for a fixed time period at a predetermined rate of interest.

terms of trade a PRICE INDEX that shows a country's EXPORT prices relative to its IMPORT prices. It is constructed by taking an index of prices received for exports, on the one hand, and an index of prices paid for imports, on the other, and then dividing the first by the second (see Fig. 169). An improvement in a country's terms of trade occurs if its export prices rise at a faster rate than import prices over time, as shown for the UK in Fig. 169, and a worsening of the terms of trade if export prices rise more slowly than import prices.

Superficially, an improvement in a country's terms of trade may be considered to be beneficial: in foreign-exchange terms, a given amount of exports will now finance the purchase of a greater amount of imports, or, put another way, a given amount of imports can now be purchased for a smaller amount of exports. A critical factor in this regard, however, is the PRICE-ELASTICITY OF DEMAND for exports and imports. If, for example, export demand is price-elastic, then price rises (which make the country's exports less competitive in world markets) will result in a more than proportionate fall in export volume, thus lowering foreign exchange receipts and adversely affecting domestic output and employment.

See also BALANCE-OF-PAYMENTS EQUILIBRIUM, DEVALUATION, REVALUATION.

1990 = 100

	1988	1995
Index of export prices	92	126
Index of import prices	94	128
terms of trade index	98	99

Fig. 169. **Terms of trade**. See entry.

term structure of interest rates the relationship between the EFFECTIVE INTEREST RATE (yield) on a FINANCIAL SECURITY and the unexpired length of time to its maturity. This relationship is known as *yield to maturity* and can be calculated only for securities which have a fixed rate of interest and specified date of maturity, such as TREASURY BILLS and corporate DEBENTURES. CONSOLS are a notable exception as they do not have a redemption date.

test market a MARKET encompassing a limited geographical area, which firms use to market new products as a means of testing consumer response before engaging in full-scale production and mass national marketing of those products.

See also NEW PRODUCT DEVELOPMENT, PRODUCT LIFE-CYCLE.

test of significance see HYPOTHESIS TESTING.

theory of consumer behaviour the body of theory concerned with how individual consumers allocate their income in buying GOODS and SERVICES. A basic assumption made by the theory is that consumers seek to maximize the UTILITY or satisfaction to be derived from spending a fixed amount of income. The theory provides an explanation of why DEMAND CURVES slope downward.

See CONSUMER EQUILIBRIUM, DIMINISHING MARGINAL UTILITY, PRICE EFFECT, INCOME EFFECT, SUBSTITUTION EFFECT, REVEALED PREFERENCE, ECONOMIC MAN.

theory of demand the body of theory concerned with the determinants of the market DEMAND for GOODS and SERVICES and the effects of market demand (together with market supply) on the prices and quantities transacted of particular goods and services.

See DEMAND FUNCTION, DEMAND CURVE, DEMAND CURVE (SHIFTS IN),

ELASTICITY OF DEMAND, TOTAL REVENUE, MARGINAL REVENUE, MARGINAL REVENUE PRODUCT, EQUILIBRIUM MARKET PRICE, CONSUMER EQUILIBRIUM, THEORY OF MARKETS, PRICE SYSTEM.

theory of international trade the body of theory concerned with the determinants of, and the gains to be obtained from, INTERNATIONAL TRADE and SPECIALIZATION. The theory examines the way in which differences between countries in terms of supply costs and demand structures affect the level, product and area composition of international trade, and the level and distribution of the GAINS FROM TRADE.

See COMPARATIVE ADVANTAGE, HECKSCHER-OHLIN FACTOR PROPORTIONS THEORY, PREFERENCE SIMILARITY THEORY, PRODUCT LIFE-CYCLE THEORY, TECHNOLOGICAL GAP THEORY, EDGEWORTH BOX.

theory of markets the body of theory concerned with how scarce FACTORS OF PRODUCTION are allocated between the multitude of product MARKETS in the economy. More specifically, the theory of markets is concerned with the determination of the prices and outputs of goods and services and the prices and usage of factors of production.

The 'theory of markets' distinguishes between types of markets by reference to differences in their MARKET STRUCTURE. The main structural distinction is made according to the degree of SELLER CONCENTRATION, that is, the number of suppliers and their relative size distribution. Other structural features emphasized include the character of the product supplied, that is, whether it is a HOMOGENEOUS PRODUCT or differentiated (see PRODUCT DIFFERENTIATION), and the CONDITION OF ENTRY to the market. Given these structural distinctions, the theory examines the way in which market structure interacts with MARKET CONDUCT to produce particular patterns of MARKET PERFORMANCE.

See also PERFECT COMPETITION, MONOPOLISTIC COMPETITION, OLIGOPOLY, MONOPOLY, RESOURCE ALLOCATION, MARKET STRUCTURE-CONDUCT-PERFORMANCE SCHEMA, FACTOR MARKETS, PRICE SYSTEM, PARETO OPTIMALITY.

theory of supply the body of theory concerned with the determinants of the market SUPPLY of GOODS and SERVICES, and the effects of market supply (together with market demand) on the prices and quantities transacted of particular goods and services.

See SUPPLY FUNCTION, SUPPLY CURVE, SUPPLY CURVE, (SHIFTS IN), MARGINAL PHYSICAL PRODUCT, COST FUNCTION, MARGINAL REVENUE PRODUCT, DIMINISHING RETURNS, ECONOMIES OF SCALE, ELASTICITY OF SUPPLY, EQUILIBRIUM MARKET PRICE, TOTAL COST, MARGINAL COST, PROFIT MAXIMIZATION, THEORY OF THE FIRM, THEORY OF MARKETS, PRICE SYSTEM.

theory of the firm the body of theory concerned with how individual firms combine quantities of FACTOR INPUTS to produce OUTPUTS of goods and services and their pricing and output decisions. A basic assumption of the theory is that the objective of the firm is PROFIT MAXIMIZATION. The theory provides an explanation of why SUPPLY CURVES slope upwards.

See MARGINAL-PHYSICAL PRODUCT, MARGINAL-REVENUE PRODUCT, COST FUNCTION, MARGINAL COST, MARGINAL REVENUE, FIRM OBJECTIVES, THEORY OF MARKETS, MANAGERIAL THEORIES OF THE FIRM, BEHAVIOURAL THEORIES OF THE FIRM.

The Securities Association (TSA) a body responsible for regulating firms which deal in corporate and government securities on the STOCK EXCHANGE. In 1991, the TSA merged with another regulatory body, the Association of Futures Brokers and Dealers.

See SELF-REGULATORY ORGANIZATION.

third world country see DEVELOPING COUNTRY.

Three i's (formerly Investors in Industry) a holding company owned by the COMMERCIAL BANKS which provides loan and share capital for VENTURE CAPITAL projects.

tie-in sales a type of RESTRICTIVE TRADE PRACTICE whereby a supplier requires that the purchaser of product A (the tying good) must also buy his requirements of one or more other products (the tied goods) from the seller of A. Like an EXCLUSIVE DEALING arrangement this may restrict the freedom of the buyer to obtain these goods from rival suppliers and hence limit effective competition.

See COMPETITION POLICY, OFFICE OF FAIR TRADING.

tight money or **dear money** a government policy whereby the CENTRAL BANK is authorized to sell government BONDS on the open market to facilitate a decrease in the MONEY SUPPLY (see MONETARY POLICY).

The decrease in money supply serves to increase INTEREST RATES which discourages INVESTMENT because previously profitable investments become unprofitable owing to the increased cost of borrowing (see MARGINAL EFFICIENCY OF CAPITAL/INVESTMENT).

Tight money policy, through MONEY SUPPLY/SPENDING LINKAGES, reduces AGGREGATE DEMAND.

Contrast CHEAP MONEY.

till money the CURRENCY (notes and coins) held by the COMMERCIAL BANKS to meet the day-to-day cash requirements of their customers. Till money is included as part of the banks' CASH RESERVE RATIO and RESERVE ASSET RATIO.

time-deposit account see DEPOSIT ACCOUNT.

time lag see LEADS AND LAGS (2).

time-preference an individual's preference for current consumption over future consumption which determines the INTEREST reward which he requires to persuade him to abstain from current consumption. An individual's time preference will determine the DISCOUNT

RATE at which he will discount future money receipts and payments.

Individuals differ in their time preference, some displaying a strong preference for current consumption and being reluctant to save unless very high INTEREST RATES are offered on savings; others displaying a weaker preference for current consumption and being prepared to save if only modest interest rewards are offered. Market interest rates will tend to reflect the aggregate time preferences of members of the community. However, there may be a difference between *private* and *social* time preferences since individuals, given their limited lifespan, will tend to discount long-term receipts and payments heavily, whereas the community continues forever and so may take a longer-term view, discounting long-term receipts and payments less heavily.

See COST-BENEFIT ANALYSIS.

time series any statistical information recorded over successive time periods.

See TIME-SERIES ANALYSIS.

time-series analysis the analysis of past statistical data, recorded at successive time intervals, with a view to projecting this experience of the past to predict what will happen in the (uncertain) future. Thus time-series information can be used for FORECASTING purposes.

Fig. 170 shows a typical time series. The fluctuations in time-series data, which inevitably show up when such series are plotted on a graph, can be classified into four basic types of variation which act simultaneously to influence the time series. These components of a time series are:

(a) SECULAR TREND, which shows the relatively smooth, regular movement of the time series over the long term.

(b) *cyclical variation*, which consists of medium-term, regular repeating patterns, generally associated with BUSINESS CYCLES. The recurring upswings and downswings in economic activity are superimposed upon the secular trend.

(c) *seasonal variation*, which consists of short-term, regular repeating patterns, generally associated with different seasons of the year. These seasonal variations are superimposed upon the secular trend and cyclical variations.

(d) *irregular variations*, which are erratic fluctuations in the time series caused by unpredictable, chance events. These irregular variations are superimposed upon the secular trend, cyclical variations and seasonal variations.

Time-series analysis is concerned with isolating the effect of each of these four influences upon a time series with a view to using them to project this past experience into the future. In order to identify the underlying secular trend in a time series, the statistician may use REGRESSION ANALYSIS, fitting a line to the time-series observations by the method of ordinary least squares. Here time would serve as the

INDEPENDENT VARIABLE in the estimated regression equation and the observed variable as the DEPENDENT VARIABLE. Alternatively, the statistician may use a moving average to smooth the time series and help identify the underlying trend. For example, he could use a five-period moving average, replacing each consecutive observation by the average (MEAN) of that observation and the two preceding and two succeeding observations.

Exponential smoothing provides yet another technique which can be used to smooth time-series data. It is similar to the moving-average method but gives greater weight to more recent observations in calculating the average. In order to identify the effect of seasonal variations the statistician can construct a measure of seasonal variation (called the *seasonal index*) and use this to deseasonalize the time-series data and show how the time series would look if there were no seasonal fluctuations.

Once the trend has been identified it is possible to EXTRAPOLATE that trend and estimate trend values for time periods beyond the present time period. In Fig. 170, for example, the trend for time periods up to and including time t can be extrapolated to time t + 1. Extrapolating thus becomes a method of making predictions or forecasts, though the accuracy of these forecasts will depend critically upon whether underlying forces which affected the time series in the past will continue to operate in the same way in the future.

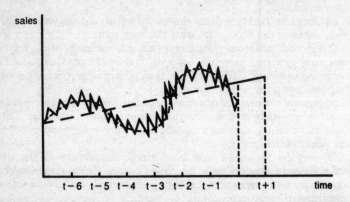

Fig. 170. **Time-series analysis**. See entry.

total cost the COST of all the FACTORS OF PRODUCTION used by a firm in producing a particular level of output. In the SHORT RUN a firm's total cost consists of total FIXED COST and total VARIABLE COST.

The short-run total cost curve in Fig. 171 is the sum of the (constant) total fixed costs and the total variable cost. It has an 's' shape because at low levels of output total variable costs rise slowly (because of the influence of increasing RETURNS TO THE VARIABLE-FACTOR INPUT) while at high levels of output total variable costs rise more rapidly (because of the influence of diminishing returns to the variable-factor input).

Total cost interacts with TOTAL REVENUE in determining the level of output at which the firm achieves its objective of PROFIT MAXIMIZATION and LOSS MINIMIZATION.

In the THEORY OF MARKETS, a firm will leave a market if in the short run it cannot earn sufficient total revenue to cover its total variable costs. If it can generate enough total revenue to cover total variable costs and make some contribution towards total fixed costs then it will continue to produce in the short run even though it is still making a LOSS. In the LONG RUN, the firm must earn enough total revenue to cover total variable and total fixed costs (including NORMAL PROFIT) or it will leave the market.

SEE MARGINAL COST.

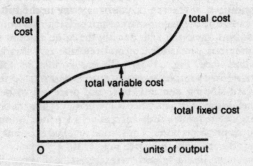

Fig. 171. Total cost. See entry.

total domestic expenditure the total expenditure by residents of a country on FINAL PRODUCTS (excluding expenditure on INTERMEDIATE PRODUCTS). When expenditure on IMPORTS is deducted from this figure and expenditure by nonresidents on domestically produced goods and services is added, the adjusted expenditure provides an estimate of GROSS NATIONAL PRODUCT. See also NATIONAL-INCOME ACCOUNTS.

total physical product the total quantity of OUTPUT produced in the SHORT RUN by utilizing various amounts of the VARIABLE-FACTOR

INPUT (in conjunction with a given amount of FIXED-FACTOR INPUT). The total physical product curve as shown in Fig. 172 rises steeply at first, reflecting increasing RETURNS TO THE VARIABLE FACTOR-INPUT, but then rises more slowly as diminishing returns to the variable input set in.

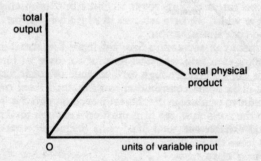

Fig. 172. **Total physical product**. See entry.

total revenue the aggregate revenue obtained by a FIRM from the sale of a particular quantity of output, equal to price times quantity. Under conditions of PERFECT COMPETITION, the firm faces a horizontal DEMAND CURVE at the going market price. Each extra unit of output sold (MARGINAL REVENUE) adds exactly the same amount to total revenue as previous units. Hence total revenue is a straight upward-sloping line (see Fig. 173a). Under conditions of imperfect competition (for example, MONOPOLISTIC COMPETITION) the firm faces a downward-sloping demand curve and price has to be lowered in order to sell more units. As price is lowered, each extra unit of output sold (marginal revenue) adds successively smaller amounts to total revenue than previous units. Thus, total revenue rises but at a decreasing rate, and eventually falls (see Fig. 173b).

Total revenue interacts with TOTAL COST in determining the level of output at which the firm achieves its objective of PROFIT MAXIMIZATION.

total utility the total satisfaction (UTILITY) an individual derives from the CONSUMPTION of a given quantity of a product in a particular time period. An individual's total utility usually increases as he consumes more and more of a product, but generally at a slower rate, each extra unit consumed adding less MARGINAL UTILITY than the previous unit as the individual becomes satiated with the product.

See UTILITY FUNCTION, CARDINAL UTILITY, ORDINAL UTILITY, DIMINISHING MARGINAL UTILITY.

trade association a central body representing the interests of firms

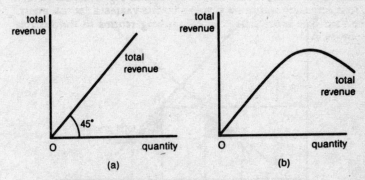

Fig. 173. **Total revenue.** See entry.

operating in the same line of business. Trade associations compile statistics on industry production, sales, exports, etc., for circulation to member firms, provide a forum for the discussion of trade affairs, and liase with other trade organizations and government departments regarding matters of mutual concern.

trade barrier SEE IMPORT RESTRICTIONS.

trade creation an increase in INTERNATIONAL TRADE (and economic welfare) that results from the reduction or elimination of trade barriers such as TARIFFS and QUOTAS. Tariff cuts, etc., may be instigated by a single country, by the formation of a CUSTOMS UNION OT FREE TRADE AREA, or, more generally, by international negotiation (see GENERAL AGREEMENT ON TARIFFS AND TRADE).

The trade-creating effect of a tariff cut is illustrated in Fig. 174 (overleaf), which, to simplify matters, is confined to one country (A) and one product.

DD and SS are the domestic demand and supply curves for the product in country A. W is the world supply price of the product. Initially country A imposes a tariff on imports of the product raising its price in the home market to W_t. At price W_t domestic production is shown by OP, domestic consumption OC, and imports by PC.

The removal of the tariff reduces the price of the product in the home market to W. At price W, imports increase to P_1C_1, domestic production falls to OP_1, and domestic consumption increases to OC_1. The home market obtains an increase in economic welfare from this expansion of trade indicated by the two triangles XYZ and RST. XYZ is the 'production gain' resulting from the reallocation of factor inputs to more efficient uses; RST is the 'consumption gain' resulting from lower prices to consumers.

TRADE CREDIT

See TRADE DIVERSION, GAINS FROM TRADE.

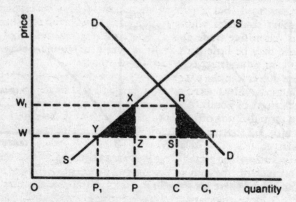

Fig. 174. Trade creation. See entry.

trade credit a deferred payment arrangement whereby a supplier allows a customer a certain period of time (typically two to three months) after receiving the products before paying for them.

See also CREDIT, CREDITORS, WORKING CAPITAL.

trade cycle see BUSINESS CYCLE.

trade debt a deferred payment arrangement whereby a customer is allowed a certain period of time in which to pay for products after receiving them.

See also DEBT, DEBTORS, WORKING CAPITAL.

Trade Descriptions Acts, 1968 and 1972 Two UK Acts that regulate trade descriptions. The 1968 Act makes it an offence to apply a false or misleading description to a GOOD or SERVICE and a false or misleading indication as to the PRICE of a good or service. The term 'trade description' is defined broadly to include, for example, quantity, size or gauge, composition, fitness for purpose, performance, strength, accuracy, method of manufacture, place and date of manufacture, etc. Offenders can be punished by a fine or imprisonment.

The 1972 Act requires that certain imported products should have their country of origin clearly displayed.

See CONSUMER PROTECTION, PRICE MARKING BARGAIN OFFERS ORDER, 1979, COMPETITION POLICY UK.

trade discount see DISCOUNT.

trade diversion a redirection of INTERNATIONAL TRADE resulting from the formation of a CUSTOMS UNION or FREE TRADE AREA. A customs union/free trade area involves the removal of trade obstacles such as TARIFFS and QUOTAS on trade between member countries, but the

536

erection, or continuance, of trade barriers against nonmember countries. This serves to increase trade between member countries (see TRADE CREATION), but a part of this increase is at the expense of nonmember countries whose imports are now displaced from the customs union/free trade area. Thus, unlike across-the-board tariff cuts there may be little net benefit to world economic welfare. See also GENERAL AGREEMENT ON TARIFFS AND TRADE.

trade gap a deficit in the BALANCE OF TRADE that arises when the value of a country's VISIBLE EXPORTS of goods is less than the value of its VISIBLE IMPORTS of goods. A trade gap as such may be of no particular concern provided it is offset by surpluses generated elsewhere on the BALANCE OF PAYMENTS. See TERMS OF TRADE, BALANCE-OF-PAYMENTS EQUILIBRIUM.

trade integration the establishment of FREE TRADE between a number of countries with the aim of securing the benefits of international SPECIALIZATION. There are four main forms of trade integration ranging from a loose association of trade partners to a fully integrated group of nation states:

(a) a FREE TRADE AREA, where members eliminate trade barriers between themselves but each continues to operate its own particular barriers against nonmembers.

(b) a CUSTOMS UNION, where members eliminate trade barriers between themselves and establish uniform barriers against nonmembers, in particular a common external tariff.

(c) a COMMON MARKET, that is, a customs union which also provides for the free movement of labour and capital across national boundaries.

(d) an ECONOMIC UNION, that is, a common market which also provides for the unification of members' general objectives in respect of economic growth, etc., and the harmonization of monetary, fiscal and other policies.

See also GAINS FROM TRADE.

trade mark a symbol (a word or pictorial representation) which is used by a business as a means of identifying a particular good or service so that it may be readily distinguished by purchasers from similar goods and services supplied by other businesses. See BRAND.

In the UK, under the Trade Marks Act, 1938 and the Trade Marks (Amendments) Act, 1984, trade marks can be registered with the PATENT OFFICE, as a means of obtaining exclusive rights to the use of that mark.

Trade marks protect the registered owner from unfair competition from piracy and represent an important means of establishing PRODUCT DIFFERENTIATION advantages over rival suppliers. They also provide consumers with a means of unambiguously identifying the products of their choice.

See INTELLECTUAL PROPERTY RIGHTS.

Trade Marks Acts, 1938 and 1984 see TRADE MARK.

trade union an organization that represents the economic interest of the LABOUR FORCE. Unions come in a variety of forms, for example:

(a) *in-company union*: a union that represents every grade of labour within a single company. This type of union is common in Japan.

(b) *craft union*: a union that represents a particular group of skilled tradesmen (for example, electricians, plumbers) who may work in many different industries. This type of union is common in the UK.

(c) *industrial union*: a union that represents every grade of labour within a single industry. This type of union is common in many European Community countries.

(d) *general union*: a union that represents a broad spread of employees regardless of occupation or industry. These have become more commonplace in the US and Europe, often as the result of mergers between craft and industrial unions.

The prime objective of a union is to protect and advance the interests of its members by negotiating PAY rates and conditions of employment (number of hours worked, grounds for dismissal, etc.). As such, unions have an important influence on the price of labour and supply costs in individual industries, and also, in the broader macroeconomic context, through the impact of wage rate changes on the level of UNEMPLOYMENT and the rate of INFLATION.

Trade unions in the UK are managed by full-time elected officials with assistance from workplace representatives (shop stewards).

See LABOUR MARKET, COLLECTIVE BARGAINING, PHILLIPS CURVE, WORKER PARTICIPATION, INDUSTRIAL RELATIONS, INDUSTRIAL DISPUTE, EMPLOYMENT LAWS.

Trades Union Congress (TUC) a UK organization that represents the collective interests of member TRADE UNIONS in dealings with government and employers' organizations, and formulates general trade union policies.

trade war a situation in which countries engaged in INTERNATIONAL TRADE attempt to reduce competing IMPORTS by the use of TARIFFS, QUOTAS and other import restrictions, and expand their EXPORTS through EXPORT INCENTIVES. Such BEGGAR-MY-NEIGHBOUR POLICIES, bringing with them an escalation of PROTECTIONISM, however, are usually self-defeating, leading to a fall in the total volume of international trade and world income levels.

trade-weighted index a PRICE INDEX that shows the value of one country's CURRENCY measured in terms of a 'basket' of other countries' currencies where each country's currency is given a weight in the basket proportionate to its share of INTERNATIONAL TRADE.

See EXCHANGE RATE.

trading stamps a form of SALES PROMOTION whereby a retailer gives customers stamps with a value related to the value of purchases made, which can then be redeemed for goods or cash.

training the process of extending and improving the SKILLS and KNOW-HOW of people so as to improve the performance of the LABOUR FORCE, and thus enhance PRODUCTIVITY. A broad distinction can be made between 'vocational training', that is training concerned with the acquisition of specific occupational skills, and 'general education', which develops those basic skills such as writing and numeracy which form the basis for the development of more specialized occupational skills.

Vocational training is provided by firms through apprenticeships, in-company short courses, management development programmes, etc. Governments also sponsor and finance vocational training initiatives, as well as undertaking responsibilities for the provision of general education. In the UK the *Training Agency* operates a number of programmes including 'Employment Training', the provision of training for the long-term unemployed, and 'Youth Training Scheme (YTS)', the provision of training for 16–17-year-olds not in education or employment, which comprises work experience, on-the-job training and classroom tuition.

transaction costs the costs incurred in using the MARKET system in buying and selling FACTOR INPUTS and FINAL PRODUCTS. Transaction costs include the costs of locating suppliers or customers and negotiating contracts with them, and the costs associated with imperfect market situations, for example, MONOPOLY surcharges imposed by input suppliers, unreliable sources of supply and restrictions on sales outlets, TARIFFS and QUOTAS.

See also INTERNALIZATION.

transaction demand for money the demand for MONEY balances which are held to finance day-to-day expenditure between the periodic receipt of INCOME (e.g. weekly wages, monthly salaries). The amount of money held for such purposes is dependent on the level of income (and expenditure). The transaction demand for money, together with the PRECAUTIONARY DEMAND FOR MONEY (money held to cover for unforeseen contingencies) and the SPECULATIVE DEMAND FOR MONEY (money held to purchase BONDS in anticipation of a fall in their price) constitute the MONEY-DEMAND SCHEDULE.

See LIQUIDITY PREFERENCE, L.M. SCHEDULE.

transactions in external assets and liabilities the 'capital account' of the BALANCE OF PAYMENTS which records purchases and sales of overseas assets by citizens of one country, say the UK, and purchases and sales by foreigners of assets in the UK. These transactions include inward and outward FOREIGN INVESTMENT in the acquisition of overseas physical ASSETS and FINANCIAL SECURITIES.

transfer earnings the return that a FACTOR OF PRODUCTION must earn to prevent its transfer to its next best alternative use. The earnings that a factor of production receives over and above its transfer earnings is called its ECONOMIC RENT.

transfer payments any expenditure by the government for which it receives no GOODS or SERVICES in return. In the main, such payments involve the 'transfer' of income from one group of individuals (taxpayers) to other groups of individuals in the form of welfare provisions, for example, UNEMPLOYMENT BENEFIT, SOCIAL-SECURITY BENEFIT, old-age PENSIONS, etc.

Because transfer payments are not made in return for products and services, that is, they do not add to total output, they are not included in the NATIONAL INCOME ACCOUNTS which measure the money value of national output.

See also GOVERNMENT EXPENDITURE, WELFARE STATE, BURDEN OF DEPENDENCY.

transfer price the internal PRICE at which FACTOR INPUTS and PRODUCTS are transacted between the branches or subsidiaries of an integrated firm (see VERTICAL INTEGRATION, DIVERSIFICATION). The transfer price may be set by reference to the prices ruling in outside markets for inputs and products (*arms-length pricing*), or it may be administered (see ADMINISTERED PRICE) according to some internal accounting convention (for example, a FULL-COST PRICE).

Transfer pricing gives a firm added discretion in pricing its products, and the danger is that it could well be tempted to employ 'manipulative' transfer pricing to harm competitors (for example, PRICE SQUEEZE a non-integrated rival firm) and, in the case of a MULTINATIONAL COMPANY, to boost its profits (for example, transfer price across national frontiers so that the greater part of the firm's profits are received in a low-taxation economy).

See INTERNALIZATION, TAX HAVEN, SHADOW PRICE.

transformation curve see PRODUCTION-POSSIBILITY BOUNDARY.

transitional unemployment see FRICTIONAL UNEMPLOYMENT.

transmission mechanism see MONEY SUPPLY/SPENDING LINKAGES.

Treasury the UK government department responsible for managing the government's finances, authorizing expenditure plans for various government departments such as Health, Education and Defence, and overseeing the tax-gathering work of the INLAND REVENUE and CUSTOMS AND EXCISE. In addition, the Treasury prepares forecasts of future economic activity levels and advises the Chancellor of the Exchequer on the government's annual Budget.

Treasury Bill a FINANCIAL SECURITY issued by a country's CENTRAL BANK as a means for the government to borrow money for short periods of time. In the UK, three-month Treasury Bills are issued by the Bank of England through the DISCOUNT MARKET. Most Treasury Bills are purchased initially by the DISCOUNT HOUSES and then, in the main, sold (rediscounted) principally to the COMMERCIAL BANKS, who hold them as part of their liquidity base to support their lending operations.

Treasury Bills constitute a significant part of the commercial banks' RESERVE ASSET RATIO. Thus, the monetary authorities use Treasury Bills to regulate the liquidity base of the banking system in order to control the MONEY SUPPLY. For example, if the authorities wish to expand the money supply they can issue more Treasury Bills, which increases the liquidity base of the banking system and induces a multiple expansion of bank deposits.

See also BANK-DEPOSIT CREATION, PUBLIC-SECTOR BORROWING REQUIREMENT.

Treaty of Rome an agreement in 1957 between the six founding countries of the European Economic Community which established the objectives and principles of the EUROPEAN COMMUNITY. The Treaty provided for the removal of trade restrictions between member countries, free labour and capital mobility, harmonization of tax policies and assistance to poorer regions.

trend see TIME-SERIES ANALYSIS, SECULAR TREND.

trough see BUSINESS CYCLE.

trust 1. ASSETS held and managed by *trustees* on behalf of an individual or group. While these assets are held in trust the beneficiaries have no control over the management of them. In the UK trusts have been used extensively to minimize the effects of income-and-wealth taxes.

2. (formerly, in the US) a means of organizing CARTELS, provoking the establishment of antitrust (antimonopoly) legislation.

trustee see TRUST.

TSA see THE SECURITIES ASSOCIATION.

turnover tax see SALES TAX.

two-part tariff a pricing method that involves a charge per unit of GOOD or SERVICE consumed, plus a fixed annual or quarterly charge to cover overhead costs. Two-part tariffs can be used by PUBLIC UTILITIES or firms to achieve the benefits of MARGINAL-COST PRICING whilst raising sufficient revenues to cover all outlays (so avoiding a deficit and problems of financing it). Simple two-part tariffs are presently used to charge customers for gas, electricity, telephones, etc., though more sophisticated multipart tariffs can be adopted to reflect the different marginal costs involved in offering products like electricity and transport services at peak and off-peak periods.

See also AVERAGE-COST PRICING, NATIONALIZATION, PEAK-LOAD PRICING.

two-tier board a structure of the BOARD OF DIRECTORS of a company used in certain European countries such as Germany and Norway which comprises two tiers: (a) a supervisory board on which representatives of workers and managers are represented; (b) a management board which is concerned with the day-to-day running of the business.

The supervisory board is responsible for formulating general policy and the management board with implementing policy. Two-tier boards have gained in popularity in Europe over the past two decades, compared with the UK and US style of unitary boards, and their development has been encouraged by the EUROPEAN COMMUNITY.

See WORKER PARTICIPATION.

type 1 error see HYPOTHESIS TESTING.

type 2 error see HYPOTHESIS TESTING.

U

U-form (unitary form) organization an organizational structure adopted by FIRMS in which the firm is managed centrally as a single unit specialized along functional lines (marketing, production, finance, personnel). Williamson coined this term, and argued that firms organized in this fashion are likely to suffer control-loss and end up pursuing nonprofit management goals (see MANAGEMENT-UTILITY MAXIMIZING), because senior executives responsible for the management functions cannot exert sufficient control over their subordinates selling a wide variety of products in many different markets. By contrast, it is argued that in firms with an M-FORM (MULTIDIVISIONAL-FORM) ORGANIZATION top managers can set clear goals for company divisions and so suffer less control loss.

See also MANAGERIAL THEORIES OF THE FIRM, BEHAVIOURAL THEORY OF THE FIRM.

unanticipated inflation the future INFLATION rate in a country which is not generally expected by business people, trade union officials and consumers, and which thus takes them by surprise. Unanticipated inflation is not incorporated in the current prices set for products, wage rates agreed for workers and asset values, unlike ANTICIPATED INFLATION, and thus is more painful in its effects.

See RISK AND UNCERTAINTY.

uncertainty see RISK AND UNCERTAINTY.

UNCTAD see UNITED NATIONS CONFERENCE ON TRADE AND DEVELOPMENT.

undated security see IRREDEEMABLE FINANCIAL SECURITY.

underdeveloped country see DEVELOPING COUNTRY.

underground economy see BLACK ECONOMY.

undersubscription see OVERSUBSCRIPTION.

underutilized capacity a situation where a plant is operated at output levels below the output level at which short-run AVERAGE COST is at a minimum.

See RETURNS TO THE VARIABLE FACTOR INPUT.

underwriting the acceptance by a financial institution of the financial risks involved in a particular transaction, for an agreed fee. For example, INSURANCE COMPANIES underwrite INSURANCE risks such as damage to property, paying out monies to policy holders wholly or in part to cover bona fide claims for compensation: MERCHANT BANKS underwrite new SHARE ISSUES, guaranteeing to buy up any shares that are not sold in the open market.

undistributed profits see RETAINED PROFITS.

unearned income see EARNED INCOME.

unemployment the non-utilization of LABOUR (and CAPITAL) resources, as a result of which the actual output of the economy (see ACTUAL GROSS NATIONAL PRODUCT) is below its POTENTIAL GROSS NATIONAL PRODUCT. Resources lie idle and output is lost. The elimination of unemployment and the achievement of FULL EMPLOYMENT is one of the main objectives of MACROECONOMIC POLICY.

The rate of unemployment is measured as a percentage of the total LABOUR FORCE currently without a job (see Fig. 175a on page 546).

There are various causes of unemployment which can be broadly divided into three main types: (i) Demand-deficient (cyclical) unemployment; (ii) Unemployment caused by changes in demand patterns; and (iii) Supply-side (or so-called 'natural') unemployment. Demand-deficient or cyclical unemployment occurs whenever AGGREGATE DEMAND is insufficient to purchase full employment AGGREGATE SUPPLY (potential GNP). In the EQUILIBRIUM LEVEL OF NATIONAL INCOME MODEL depicted in Fig. 175b equilibrium national income is Y_1 compared to the full employment national income Y_2, because of a shortfall of spending equal to the DEFLATIONARY GAP (XZ). The traditional remedy for this situation is for the authorities to boost spending by reflationary FISCAL POLICY and MONETARY POLICY measures to shift aggregate demand from AD_1 to AD_2 (see DEMAND MANAGEMENT).

In addition to deficiencies in total demand, changes in demand patterns can cause unemployment. For example, 'structural unemployment' is caused by the secular (long-term) decline in the demand for particular products leading to the contraction of those industries which supply them, such as (in the UK) coal mining, shipbuilding and textiles. These industries are concentrated in particular regions in a country and this may exacerbate 'regional unemployment' as the decline of these industries in turn leads to a lower demand for the outputs of their local suppliers and serves to lower spending in the region as a whole (see MULTIPLIER). Also, short-term 'seasonal' changes in demand can lead to the creation and elimination of jobs (e.g. the loss of jobs in the UK tourist industry during the winter months).

Supply-side unemployment includes several types. First, 'technological unemployment', which is the loss of jobs due to the introduction of new technology which improves productivity, reducing the amount of labour needed to produce a particular quantity of a product and/or making particular labour skills obsolete. Second, 'frictional unemployment', which is unemployment associated with people who are in the process of moving from one job to another. The amount of frictional unemployment and how temporary that unemployment is will depend upon whether workers have the appropriate skills for the jobs which are available and whether these jobs are in the appropriate region of the country. Third, 'involuntary unemployment' amongst workers whose disabilities make it difficult for them to secure jobs. Fourth, 'voluntary unemployment' among those who lack the incentive or commitment to work. Fifth, 'real wage (classical) unemployment' occurs where real WAGE RATES are too high so that workers 'price themselves out of jobs', as shown in Fig. 175c. If wages are set at W_1 rather than W (as a result, say, of MINIMUM WAGE legislation or trade union bargaining power), unemployment equivalent to Q_1Q_2 will be created.

Finally, in an increasingly open and interdependent international economy, countries heavily engaged in international trade may suffer unemployment because of international competition. If a country has concentrated its resources on the production of products for which long-term world demand is declining, or it fails to invest in new products or in modern plant, then its price and non-price competitiveness vis-a-vis overseas suppliers will deteriorate. This can result in the progressive displacement of domestic output by more competitive foreign products (see IMPORT PENETRATION) and a widespread loss of jobs.

Various policy measures may be adopted to remove unemployment caused by changes in demand patterns or supply-side deficiencies. INVESTMENT INCENTIVES (grants, subsidies, tax breaks, etc.) can be used generally to increase the start-up of new businesses and industries and the expansion of existing businesses and industries to assist in the removal of 'structural' and 'technological' unemployment (see INDUSTRIAL POLICY); more particularly, such incentives can be targeted to remove 'regional' unemployment by encouraging new investment in depressed areas (see REGIONAL POLICY). Additionally, assistance with removal expenses and housing can improve the geographic mobility of workers. Likewise, the provision of TRAINING facilities can be used to improve occupational mobility, again helping to offset 'structural' and 'technological' unemployment. Government assistance to organizations to encourage them to employ disabled persons can help alleviate 'involuntary' unemployment, while 'voluntary' unemployment can be tackled by suitable adjustments to the SOCIAL SECURITY BENEFIT system to encourage people to take work. Finally, 'real wage' unemployment can be reduced by improving the flexibility of the LABOUR MARKET by, for example, limiting the power of trade unions to operate 'closed shops' and other restrictive labour practices. Collectively, these measures may serve to increase the general level and efficiency of resource use in the economy, thus improving the output potential and competitiveness of the country vis-a-vis international trade partners.

See DEINDUSTRIALIZATION, INTERNAL-EXTERNAL BALANCE MODEL,

UNEMPLOYMENT

	UK	Germany	Japan	US
1987	10.2	6.2	2.8	6.1
1988	8.3	6.1	2.5	5.4
1989	6.9	5.6	2.2	5.2
1990	6.9	5.1	2.1	5.4
1991	8.0	6.7	2.1	6.8
1992	9.8	7.8	2.1	7.5
1993	10.3	8.9	2.5	6.8
1994	9.3	9.6	2.9	6.1
1995	8.3	9.1	3.1	5.7

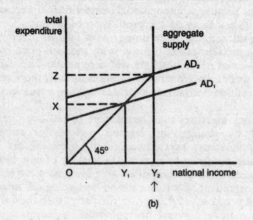

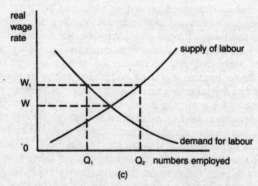

Fig. 175. **Unemployment.** (a) The annual unemployment percentage rates for the UK, Germany, Japan and the US. Sources: OECD, IMF. (b) See entry. (c) See entry.

DISGUISED UNEMPLOYMENT, HIDDEN UNEMPLOYMENT, LUMP OF LABOUR, POVERTY TRAP.

unemployment benefit the TRANSFER PAYMENTS in cash or kind made to unemployed people (see UNEMPLOYMENT) to provide them with some minimum standard of living until they can secure new paid employment. In most countries, workers in employment pay NATIONAL-INSURANCE CONTRIBUTIONS to the government in return for unemployment benefit rights. See also GOVERNMENT EXPENDITURE, SOCIAL-SECURITY BENEFITS.

unemployment rate the number of unemployed workers expressed as a percentage of a country's LABOUR FORCE. Measuring UNEMPLOYMENT rates is, in practice, difficult because of the problems of defining and measuring both numbers of unemployed and the labour force. For example, some workers who are unemployed may not register themselves as unemployed because they are not entitled to UNEMPLOYMENT BENEFIT and thus will not appear in the 'official' unemployment figure.

Unemployment rates can be used to measure changing job opportunities over time and between countries. They also provide a summary measure of the degree of under-employment of FACTORS OF PRODUCTION, that is, the extent to which a country's ACTUAL GNP falls short of POTENTIAL GNP resulting in a DEFLATIONARY GAP.

See ACTIVITY RATE, DISGUISED UNEMPLOYMENT, FULL EMPLOYMENT, VACANCY RATE.

uniform business rate (UBR) the annual charge in England and Wales on business premises. The UBR, along with the 'council tax' (see LOCAL TAX) and central government grants, is used to finance local authority spending. Although the UBR is paid by businesses to the particular local authority in whose area their premises are located, the UBR itself is fixed at one set ('uniform') rate throughout the country by the government.

unitary elasticity see PRICE-ELASTICITY OF DEMAND.

unitary taxation a system of TAXATION operated by a country that taxes a foreign-owned MULTINATIONAL COMPANY on a proportion of its total world-wide income, rather than on the income which the multinational actually earned within that country. Countries might adopt unitary taxation to increase their taxation revenues and to counter manipulative TRANSFER PRICING by multinationals.

See DOUBLE TAXATION.

United Nations (UN) an association of states which have agreed to abide by the principles originally laid down in a charter (the UN Charter). Its main objectives are the maintenance of international peace and security, the upholding of fundamental human rights in all nations and the promotion of social harmonization and progress amongst all nations. The UN Charter was drawn up by 50 nations and officially created on 24 October 1945. The principal departments of the UN are the General Assembly and the Economic and Social Council, a Trusteeship Council and a Secretariat. There are also a number of subsidiaries and affiliated bodies working in accordance with the Charter such as the INTERNATIONAL MONETARY FUND, the FOOD AND AGRICULTURAL ORGANIZATION, the GENERAL AGREEMENT ON TARIFFS AND TRADE, the WORLD BANK, the UNITED NATIONS CONFERENCE ON TRADE AND DEVELOPMENT and the INTERNATIONAL LABOUR OFFICE.

United Nations Conference on Trade and Development (UNCTAD) a multinational institution established in 1965 to represent the economic interests of the DEVELOPING COUNTRIES and to promote the ideals of the NEW INTERNATIONAL ECONOMIC ORDER. Unctad's main work is undertaken at a series of conferences, held every four years, and has centred on three areas of particular concern to the developing countries:

(a) EXPORTS of manufactures, where it has attempted to negotiate TARIFF and QUOTA-free access to the markets of the developed countries. This is in addition to those concessions obtained through the GENERAL AGREEMENT ON TARIFFS AND TRADE.

(b) exports of commodities, where it has promoted the extension of INTERNATIONAL COMMODITY AGREEMENTS aimed at stabilizing the export prices of primary products as a means of stabilizing developing countries' foreign exchange earnings and producers' incomes.

(c) ECONOMIC AID, where it has attempted to secure a greater volume of financial assistance and technology transfer from the developed countries.

So far, Unctad has achieved very little, mainly because developed countries, particularly in the difficult economic conditions prevailing since the oil price increases of 1973, have not been prepared to support Unctad initiatives to the fullest extent.

unit of account an attribute of MONEY that enables people to use money to measure and record the value of GOODS and SERVICES, and financial transactions. A unit of account may take a physical form, for example CURRENCY, or may be an intangible 'book-keeping' asset such as the SPECIAL DRAWING RIGHT and the EUROPEAN CURRENCY UNIT.

unit trust a financial institution which specializes in investment in FINANCIAL SECURITIES on behalf of its 'unit' holders. Some unit trusts offer a single 'fund', but more usually they operate a number of funds catering for different investment requirements (for example, high income, capital growth). Unit trusts pool together the monies of a large number of investors which they use to purchase a varied portfolio of investments, mainly UK and overseas corporate stocks and shares and government fixed-interest securities. They are ideal for smaller investors who wish to secure a wider spread of risk than they could achieve for themselves by direct investment in a limited number of securities, or who require professional management of their investments.

Unit trusts issue 'units' in their funds to buyers, and repurchase units from sellers on the basis of a 'bid' price (lower, for buying) and an 'offer' price (higher, for selling). An initial management charge is required of buyers followed by a smaller annual charge. The value of the individual units in a fund is obtained by dividing the total value of the fund investments plus cash held by the number of units in existence every day.

The unit trust movement in the UK is represented by the Unit Trust Association (UTA), while the investment and management of funds by unit trusts are regulated by IMRO and LAUTRO in accordance with various standards of good practice laid down under the FINANCIAL SERVICES ACT, 1986.

See INSTITUTIONAL INVESTORS, FINANCIAL SYSTEM.

Unit Trust Association see UNIT TRUST.

unlimited liability see LIMITED LIABILITY.

unlisted-securities market a MARKET for dealing in company STOCKS and SHARES that have not obtained a full STOCK-EXCHANGE quotation. The unlisted-securities market enables smaller companies to raise new capital without the formalities and expense of obtaining a full listing on the main exchange. An unlisted-securities market was established in the UK in 1980, currently called the 'Alternative Investment Market'.

upward-sloping demand curve a DEMAND CURVE that shows a *direct* rather than an *inverse* relationship between the price of a product and quantity-demanded per period of time, over part or all of its length.

Most demand curves are based on the assumption that consumers are rational in buying products and have full knowledge of price and product characteristics. Where either of these assumptions are modified then the DEMAND FUNCTION can result, not in a normal product as in Fig. 176a (overleaf), but in an upward-sloping demand curve as in Fig. 176b.

In Fig. 176a, if price increases from OP_1 to OP_2, quantity demanded *falls* from OQ_1 to OQ_2. In Fig. 176b, if price increases from OP_1 to OP_2, quantity demanded *increases* from OQ_3 to OQ_4. This can be due to: (a) conspicuous consumption (see VEBLEN EFFECT); (b) a real or perceived belief that as price increases, quality improves; (c) or because the product is a GIFFEN GOOD.

See also INCOME EFFECT, ENGELS LAW.

util a theoretical measure of UTILITY derived from the CONSUMPTION of a good or service. See CARDINAL UTILITY, MARGINAL UTILITY, ORDINAL UTILITY, TOTAL UTILITY.

utility 1. the satisfaction or pleasure that an individual derives from the CONSUMPTION of a GOOD or SERVICE. See UTIL, CARDINAL UTILITY,

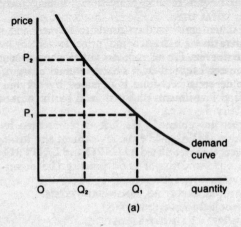

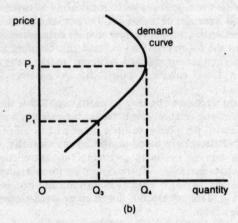

Fig. 176. **Upward-sloping demand curve.** See entry.

ORDINAL UTILITY, MARGINAL UTILITY, TOTAL UTILITY, UTILITY FUNCTION, DIMINISHING MARGINAL UTILITY.

2. See PUBLIC UTILITY.

utility function a function denoting the quantities of goods and services that an individual consumes, of the form:

$$U_t = U(x_1, x_2 \ldots x_n)$$

where U_t = total utility and $x_1, x_2 \ldots x_n$ = products consumed.

In order to achieve CONSUMER EQUILIBRIUM the individual will select a combination of products, in line with his preferences, which maximizes his TOTAL UTILITY from his given income.

See CARDINAL UTILITY, ORDINAL UTILITY, MARGINAL UTILITY.

utility maximization see CONSUMER EQUILIBRIUM.

U-turn a sudden reversal of government ECONOMIC POLICY, often due to some unforeseen event (such as the oil price increases of 1973 and 1979, and the depreciation of the UK pound in 1992); or a rethink of a particular policy initiative which has failed to have its desired effect.

V

vacancy rate the number of available jobs ('officially' notified to local employment exchanges or job centres) which remain unfilled as a percentage of the available LABOUR FORCE. In practice, not all available jobs are notified to the authorities so that the actual vacancy rate is greater than the officially recorded one.

The vacancy rate can be looked at alongside the UNEMPLOYMENT RATE in estimating whether or not the economy is at, or approaching, FULL EMPLOYMENT.

value the money worth of an ASSET or PRODUCT. Early economists such as Adam SMITH and David RICARDO suggested that the value of an asset or product depended upon the amount of LABOUR needed to produce it, while later economists like William JEVONS emphasized that the UTILITY of a product to a consumer determined its value. Nowadays economists accept that both supply and demand factors are important in determining the value of a product, by establishing a MARKET PRICE for it.

See also CONSUMER'S SURPLUS, VALUE ADDED, PARADOX OF VALUE.

value added the difference between the value of a firm's (or industry's) *output* (i.e. the total revenues received from selling that output) and the cost of the *inputs* of raw materials, components or services bought in to produce that output. 'Value added' is the value that a firm adds to its bought-in materials and services through its own production and marketing efforts within the firm.

See VALUE–ADDED TAX.

value-added approach to GDP see NATIONAL INCOME ACCOUNTS.

value-added tax (VAT) an INDIRECT TAX levied by the government on the VALUE ADDED to a good or service. The tax is based on the difference between the value of the output over the value of the inputs used to produce it. The final amount of tax is added on to the selling price of the good and is paid by the buyer. For example, trader B sells output for £100 per unit, the value of his inputs being £80 per unit. Thus, value added is £20 per unit. If VAT is set at 10%, the selling price of the good is £110, with £10 being the amount of tax paid by the final buyer. Trader B would then set off against the £10 VAT output tax collected from the final customer the £8 VAT input tax which he has paid on his £80 of inputs bought, and remit the difference of £2 to the government. In the same way trader A (who supplied trader B with his input for £80 per unit) would have collected £8 VAT-output tax from trader B, against which he will offset any VAT-input tax which he paid on his inputs, and remit the difference to the government. The total of all these sums remitted by traders A, B, etc., to the government will equal the £10 charged on the final sale to the customer.

In the UK, some products are exempted from value-added tax, or zero-rated, while for others VAT is levied at different rates for different groups of product. For example, (currently) children's clothing is exempt from VAT, while cars bear a 17.5% VAT charge.

value for money audit an assessment of whether a public agency or firm is providing 'value for money' in supplying goods or services. This usually involves an independent investigation of the way in which a public agency or firm organizes itself to supply products and the resulting costs of supply, and whether more COST EFFECTIVE means of provision might be employed.

See COST-BENEFIT ANALYSIS.

value judgements see NORMATIVE ECONOMICS.

value of money see PURCHASING POWER.

variable costs any COSTS that tend to vary directly with the level of output. They represent payments made for the use of VARIABLE FACTOR-INPUTS (raw materials, labour, etc.).

The SHORT-RUN total variable cost curve (TC) in Fig. 177a has an 'S' shape because at low levels of output total variable costs rise slowly (because of the influence of increasing RETURNS TO THE VARIABLE FACTOR-INPUT), while at high levels of output total variable costs rise more rapidly (because of the influence of diminishing returns to the variable input). Average variable costs (AVC in Fig. 177b) fall at first (reflecting increasing returns to the variable input), but then rise (reflecting diminishing returns to the variable input).

In the THEORY OF MARKETS, a firm will leave a market if in the short

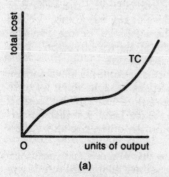
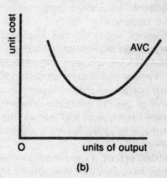

Fig. 177. Variable costs. See entry.

run it cannot earn sufficient TOTAL REVENUE to cover its total variable cost. If it can generate enough total revenue to cover total variable cost and make some CONTRIBUTION towards total FIXED COST then it will continue to produce in the short run even though it is still making a loss.

See also MARKET EXIT, LOSS MINIMIZATION.

variable factor input a FACTOR INPUT to the production process that can be readily varied in the SHORT RUN so as to expand or reduce output within a plant of fixed size. Variable inputs include raw materials, heating and lighting. Variable costs are equal to the quantities of variable inputs used, multiplied by their prices.

See also FIXED FACTOR INPUT, RETURNS TO THE VARIABLE FACTOR INPUT.

variable factor proportions (law of) see RETURNS TO THE VARIABLE FACTOR-INPUT.

variety the number of products sold by a firm as part of its product range. A firm may make many different products and many variants of each product in order to appeal to most MARKET SEGMENTS and maximize its potential sales. However, providing variety can be expensive when short production runs increase unit production costs and the promotion of a large number of brands increases marketing costs. Thus, as part of their PRODUCT DIFFERENTIATION policies, firms often need to 'trade off' variety and STANDARDIZATION considerations.

VAT see VALUE-ADDED TAX.

Veblen, Thorstein Bunde (1857–1929) an American economist whose concern about the consequences of the uncontrolled growth of large companies was first expressed in his book *The Theory of the Leisure Class* (1899). Veblen recognized that companies could be useful instruments for organizing production, but was concerned that large companies could be manipulated by managers so that the prosperity of business enterprises need not coincide with the welfare of the community. In the process of developing this thesis, Veblen attacked some of the materialist characteristics of the PRIVATE-ENTERPRISE ECONOMY, which he labelled 'pecuniary emulation', 'conspicuous leisure' and 'CONSPICUOUS CONSUMPTION.'

Veblen was also interested in the process of economic development and suggested that advances in productivity brought about by technology would increase economic depression, exacerbating conflict between workers and management on the one hand, and shareholders and the broader business community on the other. See also VEBLEN EFFECT.

Veblen effect a theory of CONSUMPTION that suggests that consumers may have an UPWARD-SLOPING DEMAND CURVE as opposed to a downward-sloping DEMAND CURVE, because they practice CONSPICUOUS CONSUMPTION. A downward-sloping demand curve implies that the quantity demanded of a particular good varies inversely with its price (as price increases, quantity demanded falls). The Veblen effect suggests that quantity demanded of a particular good varies directly with a change in price (as price increases, demand increases).

See also VEBLEN, INCOME EFFECT, ENGELS LAW.

velocity of circulation a measure of the average number of times each MONEY unit is used to purchase the year's output of final goods and services (GROSS DOMESTIC PRODUCT). If, for example, the total value of final output is £100 billion and the total MONEY SUPPLY is £10 billion, then, on average, each £1 unit has changed hands 10 times.

There is some controversy between the monetarist proponents of the QUANTITY THEORY OF MONEY and Keynesian economists about the stability of the velocity of circulation of money. Monetarists (see MONETARISM) hold that the velocity of circulation is stable or changes only slowly over time and so argue that there is a direct link between the money supply and the price level, and the rate of growth of money supply and rate of INFLATION. Keynesian economists (see KEYNESIAN ECONOMICS) argue that the velocity of circulation is unstable and that it can change rapidly, offsetting any changes in the money supply.

venture capital any SHARE CAPITAL or LOANS subscribed to a firm by financial specialists (for example, the venture-capital arms of the commercial banks and insurance companies), thus enabling the firm to undertake investment in processes and products which because of their novelty are rated as especially high-risk projects, and as such would not normally attract conventional finance.

See JUNK BOND, THREE I's.

vertical firm see FIRM.

vertical integration an element of MARKET STRUCTURE in which a firm undertakes a number of successive stages in the supply of a product, as opposed to operating at only one stage (HORIZONTAL INTEGRATION). BACKWARD INTEGRATION occurs when a firm begins producing raw materials which were previously supplied to it by other firms (for example, a camera producer making glass lenses); FORWARD INTEGRATION occurs when a firm undertakes further finishing of a product, final assembly or distribution (for example, an oil company which sells petrol through its own petrol stations).

From the firm's point of view, vertical integration may be advantageous because it enables the firm to reduce its production and distribution costs by linking together successive activities, or because it is vital for it to secure reliable supplies of inputs or distribution outlets in order to remain competitive.

In terms of its wider impact on the operation of market processes, vertical integration may, on the one hand, promote greater efficiency

in resource use, or, on the other hand, by limiting competition, lead
to a less efficient allocation of resources.

Various efficiency gains may accrue through vertical integration.
These include technical economies from combining together successive production processes, for example, the savings made in reheating
costs by combining steel furnace operations. Stockholding economies
can also arise from the reduction in intermediate contingency and
buffer stocks. Vertically integrated firms can eliminate some purchasing and selling expenses in negotiating outside supply and advertis-
ing/selling contracts by internalizing these transactions within the
firm (see INTERNALIZATION). Managerial economies may accrue by
having a single administrative system to handle several production
activities, and financial economies may accrue through more advantageous bulk-buying discounts, and by lowering the cost of raising
capital. Where firms achieve such efficiency gains through vertical
integration, their average costs will tend to fall, thus facilitating a
lowering of market prices and an increase in output.

Where a firm *already* dominates one or more vertical stages, vertical
integration may lead to various anticompetitive effects. Forward integration can secure a market but it can also foreclose it to competitors;
similarly, backward integration can guarantee supply sources but it
can also be used to prevent rivals gaining access to those sources.
Moreover, if a firm acquires the supplier of a scarce raw material
which is used by both itself and by its competitors, then it may be
in a position to operate a PRICE SQUEEZE, that is, squeeze the profit
margins of its competitors by raising their costs by charging them a
higher price for the raw material than the price charged for its own
use, while setting a relatively low final product price. Such tactics
serve not only to discipline existing competitors, but also act as a
BARRIER TO ENTRY to potential new competitors. Denied access to
markets or materials or offered access only on disadvantageous terms,
potential competitors would need to set up with the same degree of
integration as existing firms, and the large initial capital requirements
of such large-scale entry can be prohibitive.

Thus, vertical integration may produce, simultaneously, both beneficial or detrimental effects. Under UK COMPETITION POLICY, vertical
integration by an established monopoly firm, or a proposed MERGER
between two vertically-related firms (or a TAKEOVER of one by the
other) involving assets in excess of £70 million, can be referred to
the MONOPOLIES AND MERGERS COMMISSION to determine whether or
not it operates against the public interest.

See also TRANSFER PRICE, OFFICE OF FAIR TRADING, FORECLOSURE.

very long run an abstract time period in the THEORY OF SUPPLY
allowing for the technological framework (known production
methods) under which firms operate to change as a result of new

INVENTIONS and knowledge. See also SHORT RUN, LONG RUN, INNO-
VATION, TECHNOLOGICAL PROGRESSIVENESS, RESEARCH AND DEVEL-
OPMENT.

visible balance see BALANCE OF TRADE.

visible export and import any GOOD such as raw material and
finished manufactures that can be seen and recorded as it crosses the
boundaries between countries. The net exports/imports of these
goods constitute the BALANCE OF TRADE. Visible exports and imports,
together with INVISIBLE EXPORTS AND IMPORTS make up the CURRENT
ACCOUNT of a country's BALANCE OF PAYMENTS.

See EXPORT, IMPORT.

voluntary export restraint see EXPORT RESTRAINT AGREEMENT.

voluntary group a business which operates as a WHOLESALER to a
'group' of small RETAILERS who undertake to place a certain amount
of orders with the voluntary group in return for price concessions
on the purchases they make and various back-up services (pro-
motions, etc.). Voluntary groups such as SPAR in groceries and
Unichem in chemist's goods are able to use their BULK BUYING power
to obtain price discounts from manufacturers, part of which are
passed on to their members.

See DISTRIBUTION CHANNEL.

voluntary unemployment UNEMPLOYMENT which is due to workers
refusing to take paid jobs because they consider that the WAGE RATE
for such jobs is too low, particularly in relation to the unemployment
and/or other social security benefits they are currently receiving.

Contrast INVOLUNTARY UNEMPLOYMENT. See POVERTY TRAP, SUPPLY-
SIDE ECONOMICS.

voting shares the ORDINARY SHARES that allow a SHAREHOLDER to cast
a vote for each share held at a company's ANNUAL GENERAL MEETING.
See also SHARE CAPITAL.

W

wage the PAY made to an employee for the use of his or her LABOUR as a FACTOR OF PRODUCTION. Wages are usually paid on a weekly basis and they will depend on the hourly WAGE RATE and the number of hours which constitute the basic working week. In addition, employees can add to their basic wage by working OVERTIME.

As an alternative to paying workers on the basis of hours worked (a 'payment by time' system) employees may be paid in proportion to their output (a 'payment by results' system).

In aggregate terms, wages are a source of income and are included as a part of NATIONAL INCOME.

See SALARY, NATIONAL INCOME ACCOUNTS.

wage differential the payment of a different WAGE RATE to different groups of workers. Wage differentials arise from three main factors: (a) differences in interoccupational skills, training and responsibilities (surgeons are paid more than nurses, managers are paid more than labourers); (b) differences in inter-industry growth rates and PRODUCTIVITY levels (high-growth, high-productivity industries pay more than declining or low-productivity industries; (c) differences between regions in income per head and local employment levels (prosperous areas in general pay more than depressed areas).

Wage differentials which encourage greater labour MOBILITY between occupations and industries and promote high levels of productivity play an important part in bringing about a more effective use of labour resources. On the other hand, some wage differentials contribute to both economic and social distortions, in particular those that reflect racial or sexual discrimination, and the exploitation of workers by powerful employers ('sweat-shop' labour). By the same token, 'unjustified' wage differentials arising out of the abuse of trade union monopoly power equally mitigate against the best use of labour resources.

wage-price spiral see INFLATIONARY SPIRAL.

wage rate the PRICE OF LABOUR. In a competitive LABOUR MARKET the wage rate is determined by the demand for, and supply of, labour. The demand curve for labour as a factor input is downward-sloping (D in Fig. 178), reflecting a fall in the marginal productivity of labour as more labour is used. The position and slope of the demand curve for a particular type of labour will depend upon the productivity of the workers concerned and the demand for, and PRICE ELASTICITY OF DEMAND for, the product which they make (see MARGINAL-PHYSICAL PRODUCT and MARGINAL-REVENUE PRODUCT). The supply curve (S) for labour is upward-sloping: the higher the wage rate the greater the amount of labour offered. The position and slope of the supply curve for labour will depend upon the skills of the particular workers concerned and their occupational and geographic mobility. The equilibrium wage rate is W_e where the two curves intersect.

In practice, supply and demand forces in the labour market are likely to be influenced by the bargaining power of TRADE UNIONS (see COLLECTIVE BARGAINING) who can affect the supply of labour, and, likewise, powerful employers and employers' associations who can affect the demand for labour; government labour market policies, such as MINIMUM WAGE RATE legislation and the stipulation of maximum hours of work, and government macroeconomic policies, such as PRICES AND INCOMES POLICY. For example, if monopoly trade union suppliers of labour, or government minimum wage rate legislation were to establish a wage rate such as W_m in Fig. 178, then the effect would be to create UNEMPLOYMENT equal to Q_1Q_2.

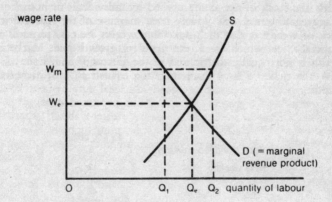

Fig. 178. **Wage rate.** See entry.

wage restraint see PRICES AND INCOMES POLICY.

wages drift see EARNINGS DRIFT.

wages freeze see PRICES AND INCOMES POLICY.

wage stickiness the tendency for WAGES to adjust downward slowly in response to EXCESS SUPPLY in the LABOUR MARKET. To the extent that labour markets are characterized by wage stickiness, a deficiency of AGGREGATE DEMAND will usually lead to INVOLUNTARY UNEMPLOYMENT.

See KEYNESIAN ECONOMICS, ADJUSTMENT SPEED.

Walras's law the proposition that the total value of goods demanded in an economy (prices times quantities demanded) is always identically equal to the total value of goods supplied (prices times quantities supplied).

This situation can occur only in a BARTER economy or an economy which uses some form of MONEY for transactions where all money is immediately used for exchange. In an economy which also uses money as a store of value, it is conceivable that the demand for and supply of money does not equate to the demand for and supply of goods, that is, people may SAVE (or overspend).

See also SAY'S LAW.

wants the desire for GOODS and SERVICES. The attempt to satisfy wants forms the basis of all economic activity. Wants are expressed in the market place not by need or desire but by the willingness and ability to actually purchase the good or service in DEMAND.

See ECONOMICS.

wasting asset any NATURAL RESOURCE such as coal and oil that has a finite but indeterminate life span depending upon the rate of depletion. See ASSET.

wealth the stock of net ASSETS owned by individuals or households. In aggregate terms, one widely used measure of the nations' total stock of wealth is that of 'marketable wealth' that is, physical and financial assets which are in the main relatively liquid. Marketable wealth is not equally distributed in the UK as Fig. 179 shows. In 1994, the richest 5% of the population owned 36% of marketable wealth.

		£2,500 billion
Total marketable wealth		%
Most wealthy	1%	17
"	" 5%	36
"	" 10%	48
"	" 25%	72
"	" 50%	92

Fig. 179. **Wealth**. The distribution of marketable wealth in the UK, 1994. The total includes land and dwellings (net of mortgage debt), consumer durables, stocks and shares, bank and building society deposits and other financial assets. Source: *Social Trends*, 1996.

wealth effect the effect on current CONSUMPTION of changes in a person's WEALTH, in particular changes in the prices of owner-occupied houses. Rapid increases in property values may encourage property owners to spend more on current consumption either out of current DISPOSABLE INCOME or on CREDIT; conversely, falling property prices may serve to reduce property owners' wealth and cause them to curtail their current consumption.

See CONSUMPTION FUNCTION.

wealth tax a TAX levied on a person's private ASSETS when those assets are transferred to the person's beneficiaries. Wealth taxes can be used to redistribute WEALTH within the community as part of government policy on INCOME DISTRIBUTION. The UK's wealth tax has taken various forms over the years, notably *estate duties, capital-transfer tax* and (currently) *inheritance tax.*

wear and tear the gradual deterioration in the efficiency (and value) of a productive ASSET through constant use.

See DEPRECIATION (2), CAPITAL CONSUMPTION.

Weights and Measures Act, 1963 a UK Act which empowers the DEPARTMENT OF TRADE AND INDUSTRY to prescribe permitted weights and measures for the sale of certain products such as food and beverages. The Act established a network of local authority officials to inspect goods sold in shops, public houses and other establishments to see if specified weights and measures are applied correctly and, on finding shortages, instigate proceedings against offenders through the courts. The OFFICE OF FAIR TRADING now acts as a coordinating body, keeping a central register of convictions under the Act.

See CONSUMER PROTECTION.

welfare criteria see WELFARE ECONOMICS.

welfare economics a normative branch of economics that is concerned with the way economic activity ought to be arranged so as to maximize economic welfare. Welfare economics employs value judgements about what *ought* to be produced, how production *should* be organized, the way income and wealth *ought* to be distributed, both now and in the future. Unfortunately each individual in a community has a unique set of value judgements which are dependent upon his attitudes, religion, philosophy and politics, and the economist has difficulty in aggregating these value judgements in advising policy makers about decisions which affect the allocation of resources (which involves making *interpersonal comparisons* of UTILITY).

Economists have tried for many years to develop criteria for judging economic efficiency to use as a guide in evaluating actual resource deployments. The classical economists treated utility (see CLASSICAL ECONOMICS) as if it was a measurable scale of consumer satisfaction, and the early welfare economists such as PIGOU continued in their vein, so that they were able to talk in terms of changes in the pattern of economic activity either increasing or decreasing economic welfare. However, once economists rejected the idea that utility was measurable then they had to accept that economic welfare is immeasurable, and that any statement about welfare is a value judgement influenced by the preferences and priorities of those making the judgement. This led to a search for *welfare criteria* which avoided making interpersonal comparisons of utility by introducing explicit value judgements as to whether or not welfare has increased.

The simplest criterion was developed by Vilfredo PARETO, who argued that any reallocation of resources involving a change in goods produced and/or their distribution amongst consumers, could be considered an improvement if it made some people better off (in their own estimation) without making anyone else worse off. This analysis led to the development of the conditions for PARETO OPTIMALITY which would maximize the economic welfare of the community, for a *given* distribution of income. The Pareto criterion avoids making interpersonal comparisons by dealing only with uncontroversial cases where no one is harmed. However, this makes the criterion inapplicable to the majority of policy proposals which benefit some and harm others, without compensation.

Nicholas Kaldor and John Hicks suggested an alternative criterion (the *compensation principle*), proposing that any economic change or reorganization should be considered beneficial if, after the change, gainers could hypothetically compensate the losers and still be better off. In effect, this criterion subdivides the effects of any change into two parts: (a) efficiency gains/losses, and (b) income-distribution consequences. As long as the gainers evaluate their gains at a higher figure than the value which losers set upon their losses, then this efficiency gain justifies the change, even though (in the absence of actual compensation payments) income redistribution has occurred. Where the gainers from a change fully compensate the losers and still show a net gain this would rate as an improvement under the Pareto criterion. Where compensation is not paid then a SECOND BEST situation may be created where the economy departs from the optimum pattern of RESOURCE ALLOCATION, leaving the government to decide whether it wishes to intervene to tax gainers and compensate losers.

In addition to developing welfare criteria, economists such as Paul Samuelson have attempted to construct a *social-welfare function* which can offer guidance as to whether one economic configuration is better or worse than another. The social-welfare function can be regarded as a function of the welfare of each consumer. However, in order to construct a social-welfare function it is necessary to take the preferences of each consumer and aggregate them into a community-preference ordering, and some economists, such as Kenneth Arrow, have questioned whether consistent and noncontradictory community orderings are possible.

Despite its methodological intricacies, welfare economics is increasingly needed to judge economic changes, in particular rising problems of environmental POLLUTION which adversely affect some people whilst benefiting others. Widespread adoption of the 'pollutor pays principle' reflects a willingness of governments to make interpersonal comparisons of utility and to intervene in markets to force pollutors to bear the costs of any pollution that they cause.

See also NORMATIVE ECONOMICS, RESOURCE ALLOCATION, UTILITY FUNCTION, CARDINAL UTILITY, ORDINAL UTILITY.

welfare state a country that provides comprehensive SOCIAL-SECURITY BENEFITS such as state health services, state retirement pensions, unemployment and sickness benefits, etc.

See TRANSFER PAYMENTS, GOVERNMENT EXPENDITURE.

white knight see TAKEOVER BID.

wholesaler a business which buys products in relatively large quantities from manufacturers which it stocks and on-sells in smaller quantities to RETAILERS. Thus, wholesalers act as 'middlemen' between the PRODUCERS and retailers of a product in the DISTRIBUTION CHANNEL, obviating the need for the producers themselves to stock and distribute their goods to retailers and likewise retailers from undertaking their own warehousing.

Wholesalers typically sell to retailers by adding a mark-up on their buying-in prices from suppliers or by obtaining a commission from the retailer.

Traditionally, wholesalers have provided their retail customers with credit facilities and a delivery service, but in recent years 'CASH AND CARRY' wholesaling has become a prominent feature of distribution systems both in the UK and elsewhere. Moreover, with the emergence of large CHAIN STORE retailers (supermarket, DIY groups) the 'wholesaling function' of stocking and breaking-bulk has itself become increasingly integrated with the retailing operation (see INTERNALIZATION), with retailers taking particular advantage of the price discounts associated with BULK BUYING direct from manufacturers.

Independent wholesalers may operate a single warehouse or a chain of warehouses giving wider regional coverage and in many cases national distribution.

Williamson trade-off model a model for evaluating the possible benefits (lower costs) and detriments (higher prices) of a proposed MERGER which can be used in the application of a DISCRETIONARY COMPETITION POLICY.

Fig. 180 depicts the case of a proposed merger which would introduce market power into a previously competitive market situation. In the premerger market, firms are assumed to produce on identical and constant average-cost curves which are represented in aggregate by AC_1. The competitive price OP_1 is identical with AC_1 (a NORMAL-PROFIT equilibrium) and the competitive output rate is OQ_1. By contrast, the post-merger combine is shown to produce on a lower constant average-cost curve, depicted by AC_2, but to establish a price

WIND-UP

not merely in excess of AC_2 but in excess of AC_1 (i.e., a price higher than in the competitive case *despite* the availability of ECONOMIES OF SCALE). In such circumstances, a welfare trade-off is required between the loss of CONSUMERS' SURPLUS due to the higher price (the shaded area A_1) and the cost savings gain to the producer (the shaded area A_2). In simple terms, if A_1 exceeds A_2, the merger should be disallowed; if A_2 exceeds A_1, the merger should be allowed to proceed. However, even in the latter case there are problems. Any benefits arising from a merger through cost savings accrue initially to producers. For there to be a benefit to consumers these gains must be passed on – but because of the increase in monopoly power there is no guarantee that they will be.

See COMPETITION POLICY, PUBLIC INTEREST.

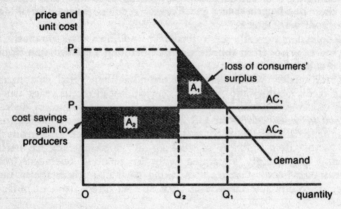

Fig. 180. Williamson trade-off model. See entry.

wind-up see INSOLVENCY ACT, 1986.

withdrawals or **leakages** that part of NATIONAL INCOME not spent by households on the CONSUMPTION of domestically produced goods and services. In the basic CIRCULAR FLOW OF NATIONAL INCOME MODEL all of the income received by households is spent on current consumption. In the extended circular flow of income model, some of the income received by households is saved, some of it is taxed and some of it is spent on imported goods and services. Thus, SAVINGS, TAXATION and IMPORTS constitute withdrawals or 'leakages' from the income-spending flow. Compare INJECTIONS. See also PROPENSITY TO SAVE, PROPENSITY TO TAXATION, PROPENSITY TO IMPORT.

work see JOB.

workable competition the specification of standards of MARKET

STRUCTURE and MARKET CONDUCT that are likely to result in an 'acceptable' MARKET PERFORMANCE. Fig. 181 lists one such classification.

Definitions of workable competition represent an effort to provide more useful guidelines in applying COMPETITION POLICY to real world markets than can be drawn from the theoretical 'ideal' state of PERFECT COMPETITION. There are, however, important operational difficulties involved in stipulating acceptable norms, for example: what is meant by an 'appreciable' number of firms?; what levels of profits are 'fair'?

See also MARKET STRUCTURE–CONDUCT–PERFORMANCE SCHEMA, CONTESTABLE MARKET, PUBLIC INTEREST, THEORY OF MARKETS, MONOPOLY.

Standards of Structure
1. A large or an appreciable number of suppliers, none of whom dominates the market, or at least as many as scale economies permit.
2. No artificial barriers to entry.
3. Moderate and price-sensitive quality differentials.

Standards of Conduct
1. Active competition between rival suppliers, avoiding collusive agreements to fix prices, market shares, etc.
2. No use of exclusionary or coercive tactics (exclusive dealing, refusal to supply, tie-in contracts) aimed at harming rival suppliers.
3. Sensitivity towards consumers' demands for product variety.

Standards of Performance
1. Minimization of supply costs.
2. Prices consistent with supply costs, including a 'fair' profit return to suppliers in relation to efficiency, risks, investment and innovation.
3. Avoidance of excessive promotional expenses.
4. The introduction of new technology and new products.

Fig. 181. **Workable competition**. The standards of structure, conduct and performance.

worker participation the involvement of employees in the decision-making processes of the FIRM that extends beyond those decisions implicit in the specific content of the jobs that they do. Worker participation most commonly refers to those processes or activities which occur at the workplace: in particular the devolution of work planning to work groups or QUALITY CIRCLES.

The term 'industrial democracy' is often used as a synonym for worker participation, but industrial democracy in fact denotes power sharing by the workers with management in corporate decisions decided at higher levels in the organization (that is, up to board of directors level). Whereas worker participation implies the direct involvement of all employees, industrial democracy suggests a system of representation and joint consultation between managers and worker representatives, and worker directors (that is, worker representatives sitting on the board of directors). See TWO-TIER BOARD.

Employee share ownership through EMPLOYEE SHARE OWNERSHIP PLANS (ESOP) can enhance worker participation by providing workers with additional information and commitment as shareholders in the firm.

There is some controversy about the effects of the extension of worker participation upon economic efficiency.

At the operational level, worker participation can improve PRODUCTIVITY (output per man) by instilling a greater commitment to, and sense of achievement in, group activities. At the strategic level, major decisions relating to new investment, etc. may be impaired by the involvement of too many vested interests when what is required is a more detached longer-term view of the issues involved.

working capital a firm's short-term CURRENT ASSETS which are turned over fairly quickly in the course of business. They include raw materials, work-in-progress and finished goods STOCKS, DEBTORS and cash, less short-term CURRENT LIABILITIES. Increases in the volume of company trading generally lead to increases in stocks and amounts owed by debtors, and so to an increase in working capital required. Reductions in delays between paying for materials, converting them to products, selling them and getting cash in from customers, will tend to reduce the working capital needed.

See also OVERTRADING, CASH FLOW, CREDIT CONTROL, STOCK CONTROL, FACTORING.

working population see LABOUR FORCE.

work in progress any goods that are still in the process of being made up into their final form. Work in progress together with raw materials and STOCKS of finished goods constitute INVENTORY INVESTMENT.

World Bank or **International Bank for Reconstruction and Development** a multinational institution set up in 1947 (following the Bretton Woods Conference, 1944) to provide ECONOMIC AID to member countries – mainly DEVELOPING COUNTRIES – to strengthen their economies. The Bank has supported a wide range of long-term investments including infrastructure projects such as roads, telecommunications and electricity supply; agriculture and industrial projects including the establishment of new industries, as well as social, training and educational programmes.

The Bank's funds come largely from the developed countries, but it also raises money on international capital markets. The Bank operates according to 'business principles' lending at commercial rates of interest only to those governments it feels are capable of servicing and repaying their debts. In 1960, however, it established an affiliate agency, the *International Development Association*, to provide low-interest loans to its poorer members.

Another affiliate of the World Bank is the *International Finance Corporation* which can invest directly in companies by acquiring shares.

World Trade Organization (WTO) see GENERAL AGREEMENT ON TARIFFS AND TRADE.

XYZ

X-inefficiency the 'gap' between the actual and minimum attainable supply cost. See Fig. 182. The traditional THEORY OF SUPPLY assumes that firms always operate on their minimum attainable cost-curves. In contrast, X-inefficiency postulates that firms typically operate with higher costs than this. This occurs, for example, because of inefficiencies in work organization (RESTRICTIVE LABOUR PRACTICES such as OVERMANNING, demarcation rules), in the coordination of activities (inefficient deployment and management of resources arising from bureaucratic rigidities); and in motivating workers to achieve maximum output. X-inefficiency is likely to be present in large organizations which lack effective competition 'to keep them on their toes' (especially MONOPOLIES).

See also PRODUCTIVITY, ORGANIZATIONAL SLACK.

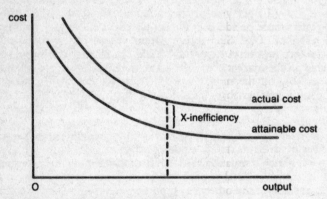

Fig. 182. X-inefficiency. See entry.

yield the return on a FINANCIAL SECURITY, expressed in money terms, related to the current market price of that security, to show the percentage return on the investment.

For example, a financial security (e.g., a BOND) with a face value of £100 and an INTEREST RATE of 5% generates a nominal return of £5 per year. If, however, the bond can be purchased for £50 on the open market, then the yield is 10%, representing 10% return on the £50 invested. The lower the purchase price of a bond or share with a given coupon rate of interest or dividend or profit, the higher its yield will be, and vice versa. There is thus an inverse relationship between the price paid for a bond or share and its yield.

The term *flat yield* or *current yield* is sometimes used to describe a yield calculation which does not take account of the redemption value of a bond. Such a calculation would be appropriate for IRREDEEMABLE FINANCIAL SECURITIES. Yields which take into account not only the annual interest receivable but also any capital profit/loss on redemption of the bond are termed *redemption yields*. Where the current market price of a bond is below its specified redemption price, the potential profit on redemption must be divided by the number of years to the redemption date of the bond, and this annual profit equivalent added to the flat yield on the bond to arrive at its redemption yield. Where the current market price of the bond is above its specified redemption price the annualized potential loss on redemption must be deducted from the flat yield in calculating redemption yield. For example, a bond offering an interest payment of £5 per year and with a current market price of £50 would have a flat yield of 10%. If, in addition, the specified redemption price of the bond is £100 in five years' time, then the bond promises a potential profit of £100 − £50 = £50 which is equivalent to an annualized profit of £50 ÷ 5 = £10 per year or an additional return of £10 ÷ £50 or 20% This would be added to the flat yield of 10% to give a redemption yield of 30%. Such a calculation would be appropriate for REDEEMABLE FINANCIAL SECURITIES. Yield can refer to the interest rate payable on the market price of a bond (INTEREST YIELD); or DIVIDEND rate payable on the market price of a SHARE (DIVIDEND YIELD); or company profit per share (after tax) related to the price of the share (EARNINGS YIELD).

yield curve a line that traces the relationship between the rates of return on BONDS of different maturities. The slope of the line suggests whether INTEREST RATES are tending to rise or fall.

zero-sum game a situation in GAME THEORY where game players compete for the given total payoff, so that gains by one player are at the direct expense of the other player(s). For example, where two firms compete against each other in a mature market where total sales are not expanding then each firm can only increase its sales and market share at the expense of its competitor.